Culture & Sexuality

Fifth Edition

Lois J. McDermott

PEARSON

Custom
Publishing

Cover Art: "Standards: Picasso," Christina Lanzl.

PEARSON CUSTOM PUBLISHING
75 Arlington Street, Suite 300, Boston, MA 02116
A Pearson Education Company

CONTENTS

SEXUAL DIVERSITY

JUVENILE SEXUALITY IN GLOBAL PERSPECTIVE
RICHARD L. CURRIER..3

SAR OF THE SEA
MARY ANN WILLIAMS..10

BONOBO SEX AND SOCIETY
FRANS B. M. DE WAAL 13

SEXUAL ANATOMY AND RESPONSE

RITES OF PURIFICATION AND THEIR EFFECTS: SOME PSYCHOLOGICAL
ASPECTS OF FEMALE GENITAL CIRCUMCISION AND INFIBULATION
(PHARAONIC CIRCUMCISION) IN AN AFRO-ARAB ISLAMIC SOCIETY (SUDAN)
HANNY LIGHTFOOT-KLEIN, MA 25

THE PENIS PIN: AN UNSOLVED PROBLEM IN THE
RELATIONS BETWEEN THE SEXES IN BORNEO
DONALD E. BROWN 32

SEXUAL BEHAVIOR

EXCERPTS FROM TANTRA: THE ART OF CONSCIOUS LOVING
CHARLES AND CAROLINE MUIR..43

INTRODUCTION TO SM: COMMUNICATION AND SAFETY
WILLIAM A. HENKIN, PH.D. AND SYBIL HOLIDAY, CSSE............................57

NONREPRODUCTIVE SEXUAL BEHAVIOR: ETHOLOGICAL
AND CULTURAL CONSIDERATIONS
INA JANE WUNDRAM 67

MENSTRUATION

MALE MENSTRUATION: A RITUAL ALTERNATIVE
TO THE OEDIPAL TRANSITION
RUTH W. LIDZ AND THEODORE LIDZ 75

PREGNANCY AND SEXUALITY

UNDER THE SHADOW OF MATERNITY
J. W. LEAVIT 85

THE POLITICS OF BIRTH PRACTICES: A STRATEGIC ANALYSIS
KAREN E. PAIGE AND JEFFERY M. PAIGE 99

CONTRACEPTION

ORAL CONTRACEPTIVES IN ANCIENT AND MEDIEVAL TIMES
JOHN M. RIDDLE AND J. WORTH ESTES 109

ABORTION

INDUCED ABORTION: AN HISTORICAL OVERVIEW
DEBORAH R. MCFARLANE, DRPH 121

ABORTION PRACTICES AND ATTITUDES IN CROSS-CULTURAL PERSPECTIVE
ROCHELLE N. SHAIN, PH.D. 128

GENDER

THE HIJRAS OF INDIA: CULTURAL AND INDIVIDUAL DIMENSIONS
OF AN INSTITUTIONALIZED THIRD GENDER ROLE
SERENA NANDA..137

FROM SAPPHO TO SAND:
HISTORICAL PERSPECTIVE ON CROSSDRESSING AND CROSS GENDER
BETTY W. STEINER, M.B. 147

NEITHER MAN NOR WOMAN: BERDACHE—
A CASE FOR NON-DICHOTOMOUS GENDER CONSTRUCTION
BRIAN SCHNARCH 154

ORIENTATION

BREAKING THE MIRROR: THE CONSTRUCTION OF LESBIANISM
AND THE ANTHROPOLOGICAL DISCOURSE ON HOMOSEXUALITY
EVELYN BLACKWOOD 167

CHILDHOOD SEXUALITY

EXCERPTS FROM DEFINING NORMAL CHILDHOOD SEXUALITY:
AN ANTHROPOLOGICAL APPROACH
SUZANNE G. FRAYSER 177

MOROCCAN BOYS AND SEX
ANDREAS EPPINK (JANNIE FIGEE—TRANSLATOR)...201

ADOLESCENT SEXUALITY

EXCERPT FROM VARIETIES OF SEXUAL EXPERIENCE:
AN ANTHROPOLOGICAL PERSPECTIVE ON HUMAN SEXUALITY
SUZANNE G. FRAYSER 209

SEXUAL ABUSE OF CHILDREN

LEGAL, SOCIAL, AND BIOLOGICAL DEFINITIONS OF PEDOPHILIA
M. ASHLEY AMES, PH.D. CAND., AND DAVID A. HOUSTON, J.D., PH.D. 217

CULTURAL DIVERSITY AND SEXUAL ABUSE PREVENTION
HELEN NOH AHN AND NEIL GILBERT 225

EXCERPTS FROM THE SEXUAL EXPLOITATION OF CHILDREN
IN DEVELOPING COUNTRIES
OVE NARVESEN AND REDD BARNA 237

SEXUAL ASSAULT OF ADULTS

THE SOCIO-CULTURAL CONTEXT OF RAPE: A CROSS-CULTURAL STUDY
PEGGY REEVES SANDAY 249

ADULT SEXUAL BONDING

HISTORICAL AND CROSS-CULTURAL PERSPECTIVES ON
PASSIONATE LOVE AND SEXUAL DESIRE
ELAINE HATFIELD AND RICHARD L. RAPSON 265

MARRIAGE AND INCEST
EDGAR GREGERSEN..286

AGING AND DYSFUNCTION

SEXUALITY IN AGING: A STUDY OF 106 CULTURES
RHONDA L. WINN, PH.D. AND NILES NEWTON, PH.D....................................299

MAGICAL PENIS LOSS IN NIGERIA:
REPORT OF A RECENT EPIDEMIC OF A KORO-LIKE SYNDROME
SUNNY T. C. ILECHUKWU 307

ENRICHING THE SEXUAL EXPERIENCE OF COUPLES:
THE ASIAN TRADITIONS AND SEXUAL COUNSELING
HARRISON VOIGHT 317

SEXUAL DIVERSITY

JUVENILE SEXUALITY IN GLOBAL PERSPECTIVE

Richard L. Currier

JUVENILE SEXUALITY AMONG THE MURIA

Beautiful Jalaro, 12 years old, slips out of her parents' thatched-roof hut, heading for the *ghotul* compound at the edge of the village. Her bare feet pad softly on the earth of the dusty village street, and her anklets jingle pleasantly in the gathering dusk. She walks with the calm, graceful sensuality for which the women of the Muria tribe are famous, but underneath her placid exterior she is brimming with excitement.

Tonight Jalaro hopes to sleep with Lakmu, her favorite of all the *ghotul* boys. Only last week, she had her first menstrual period, and now all the village boys are eager to sleep with her. She has made love to many of them during her years in the *ghotul*, but now beautiful Jalaro is a real woman at last.

At the edge of the village the other girls are waiting. They talk excitedly among themselves, fussing with their elaborate wooden hair combs, laughing and teasing about the night's activities to come. The boys are already assembled, fires have been lit, and the *ghotul* compound is filled with the scent of wood smoke and marigolds.

With a rush of noise and laughter, the girls swarm though the gate, assembling first in front of their own fire, and then dispersing to mingle with the boys. One group of boys and girls pairs off and begins singing sexual taunting songs. Another group settles down by the fire, talking and joking. From a third group, in a different part of the compound, there is the sudden beat of a drum, and half-naked bodies begin to bob and weave in the darkness.

Here and there, scattered like leaves, still other children lie on the ground with their heads in their arms, too tired to play after a long day of working with their parents in the fields.

Later on, when the singing and dancing have died down and the smaller children have begun to fall asleep, the Belosa (the girls' headmistress) tells each one whom she will massage and with whom she will sleep. These assignments are made arbitrarily by the headmistress, but Jalaro smiles and lowers her eyes when the Belosa, wise and fair for her 17 years, orders her to massage Lakmu and then share his sleeping mat.

Before long, Jalaro is kneeling on the ground a short distance from the fire; Lakmu sits on the ground between her thighs. She takes one of the beautiful hand-carved combs from her head and begins to comb out his long, black tangles, talking softly as she works.

When this is done, she massages his back, chest, arms, and legs—slowly at first, but building up to a violent intensity. Then she runs the teeth of her comb all over his body to stimulate the skin. Finally, she finishes by taking each of his arms in turn and cracking every joint from shoulder to fingertip.

This same scene is repeated in a great many other places throughout the compound. Soon the sleeping mats will be unrolled, and the unmarried young of the Muria, one of the non-Hindu tribal peoples of the Central Indian hill country, in hundreds of *ghotuls* scattered throughout the ancient

Princely State of Bastar, will be engrossed in the lovemaking and sexual play that Verrier Elwin (4) once called "the best of *ghotul* games."

Safe within the protective arms of the enclosing compound walls during the hours of darkness, the children of a Muria village are entirely separated from the adults until sunrise on the next day. The adults like this arrangement because it gives them privacy in their small, crowded huts at night. And to the Muria, the enjoyment of sex—in private and without interference from children—is one of the supreme pleasures of married life.

In this technologically simple society, where privacy is all but impossible to find and where sex—like work, play, food, and sleep—is openly accepted as a normal and natural part of life, children of three or four are already familiar with the basic facts of sexual behavior. And by the time a Muria child is twice that age, sexual innocence is a thing of the past. At this point in the child's life, the parents encourage him or her to begin spending more and more time in the *ghotul*. Muria culture takes a generally positive view of physical and behavioral maturation, welcoming it as the flowering of a long-awaited manhood or womanhood. Muria parents are therefore anxious for their children to achieve the social and sexual sophistication that will make them desirable marriage partners in their young adulthood, and the *ghotul* is an essential training ground in this process.[1]

No Muria child, however, is suddenly or forcibly ejected from the parental household. Instead, the child is encouraged to participate in *ghotul* activities at the end of the day for a while, and later he or she is further encouraged to spend more and more evenings and overnights there. At daybreak, all Muria children return home for breakfast and the beginning of a day of hard work at home and in the gardens, after which the family dines together and the older children go off to the *ghotul* as before.

When they first begin spending their nights in the *ghotul*, Muria children are not immediately expected to have sexual relations, although they are exposed from the start to the extremely sophisticated conversation of the older children. As time passes, however, the neophytes find opportunities to try some of the things they have been hearing about. The less experienced are taught by the more experienced in that natural, almost effortless way children have of teaching each other things. Gradually, as the years pass, the maturing children become more confident, more experienced, and more proficient in their sexuality.

In the more conservative *ghotuls*, children maintain permanent sexual partners, complete with simulated "weddings" and the strict observation of sexual fidelity. But in the majority of *ghotuls* the children are arbitrarily paired off in constantly changing combinations. As a general rule, a boy and girl are not allowed to sleep together for more than three nights in a row before being required to change partners again. The Muria explain that this custom makes it almost impossible for children to form permanent emotional attachments to their sexual partners—attachments that would interfere with the carefully laid marriage plans of the older generation. (Marriage to one's *ghotul* partner was greatly frowned upon and thus quite rare.)

The constant changing of partners had other desirable effects. It insured each child a wide variety of sexual opportunities, discouraged the formation of cliques and other internal divisions, and helped to dampen competitiveness, possessiveness, and jealousy. And like many other preindustrial cultures, the Muria believe that promiscuity itself is a singularly effective contraceptive for adolescent girls. Elwin (4) estimates the rate of premarital pregnancy among the Muria at 4 percent, and the near-infertility of the sexually promiscuous adolescent girls has been reported throughout the Pacific, from the Philippines to Melanesia (4, 1, 10), as well as in Africa and Asia.[2] When a *ghotul* girl did become pregnant, marriage was hastily arranged, either to her *ghotul* lover or to her legally betrothed. In either case, no permanent stigma was applied to the offspring or to the marriage itself.

The Muria regard the *ghotul* as a sacred place. It was created, according to legend, by their most revered deity (Lingo Pen), and therefore nothing that took place within its walls could be a sin. Thus the Muria child's gradual sexual initiation, in a secure, supportive, and culturally legitimized environment, has given the Muria one of the most delightful attitudes toward sex ever recorded in the annals of world ethnography.

The Muria have a simple, innocent, and natural attitude toward sex. . . . They believe that sexual congress is a good thing; it does you good; it is healthy and beautiful; when performed by the right people . . . at the right time . . . and in the right place . . . it is the happiest and the best thing in life (4).

The traditional cultures of the West generally take the attitude that children are not naturally sexual creatures, would not *be* sexual creatures, and should at all costs be kept away from sexual knowledge and ideas lest they somehow *become* sexual creatures before their appointed hour arrives. Yet the members of relatively few cultures studied by anthropologists would have anything but derision for such notions. Indeed, the overwhelming majority of preindustrial cultures consider sex to be an inevitable and harmless aspect of childhood.

HUMAN SEXUALITY IN GLOBAL PERSPECTIVE

Human cultures vary from one extreme to the other in the degree of their acceptance of sex; to highlight the differences among their myriad approaches, it is useful to divide them into four categories: repressive, restrictive, permissive, and supportive.[3] Each represents a characteristic approach to sexuality, and each has a distinctive approach to the emergent sexuality of the young.

Sexually repressive cultures are disposed toward the *denial* of sexuality. They consider sex to be an extremely dangerous area of behavior, and they often accord special virtue to the sexually inactive. These cultures typically prohibit all forms of sex aside from that which is necessary for procreation. This requires premarital chastity and the imposition of sexual ignorance upon the young. Sexual play in childhood is strictly prohibited, generating a pronounced latency period. Adolescent and adult sexuality, such as it exists, is associated with guilt, fear, and anger. Sexual pleasure is valued little, if at all. Sexually repressive cultures are common throughout Europe but are extremely rare on other continents. The traditional rural Irish community of Inis Beag (13) provides one excellent example; the Cheyenne (8), buffalo hunters of the North American plains, is another.

Sexually restrictive cultures are disposed toward the *limitation* of sexuality. Sexual play in childhood is strongly discouraged, and the sexes may be segregated early in life. Premarital chastity is required of at least one of the sexes, although some sexual license is generally granted to the other sex. While juvenile celibacy may be terminated at puberty for one of the sexes by a formal puberty ceremony, the continuing celibacy of the other sex leaves little opportunity for normal heterosexual behavior in adolescence. Sexual pleasure is typically valued more by the sex that was given more sexual freedom in early life. In general, these cultures are ambivalent about sex: they pursue it, but not without reservation. Sex tends to be feared, not as much in itself as for the problems it can cause. Sexually restrictive cultures are common throughout the world. Although they are a minority among primitive cultures, they are the dominant type among civilizations. The Mexican peasant village of Tepoztlán (9) provides one example; the Dani (7), primitive agriculturalists of the New Guinea highlands, provide another.

Sexually permissive cultures are disposed toward the *tolerance* of sexuality. While formal prohibitions exist, they are only loosely enforced and are often more honored in the breach than in the observance. Sexual play in childhood may be technically forbidden, but as long as it is kept out of sight adults who maintain a public pretext that they do not know what is going on. Adolescents of both sexes are usually allowed considerable sexual latitude, and premarital sex is considered normal. Sexual latency in childhood is either weak and short-lived or is missing altogether. Sexually permissive cultures concern themselves far more with the question of whether a given sexual behavior is appropriate than with the question of whether sexual behavior itself is actually taking place. Sexual pleasure is valued by both sexes, and sex is considered a normal, natural, and inevitable part of human life. Sexually permissive cultures are found on every continent; they are rare in Europe, but they are common in the equatorial latitudes of Africa, Asia, and the Americas. The Semai (2), aboriginal inhabitants of the Malay jungles, are an ideal example of this type.

Sexually supportive cultures are disposed toward the *cultivation* of sexuality. Sex is considered indispensable to human happiness, and early sexual experience is seen as a necessary part of proper social and biological maturation. A complex of customs and institutions, validated by traditional beliefs, provides *both sexual information and sexual opportunity* for young people of all ages who are being encouraged, especially by the parental generation, to develop their sexual skills. There is no period of sexual latency in childhood. Special dwellings or meeting places may be designated legitimate social arenas for juvenile and (especially) adolescent sexual activity, and puberty ceremonies may include formal sexual instruction (11). Supportive societies may or may not be tolerant of homosexual relationships, but in either case sexual pleasure is both highly valued and positively demanded by both sexes. The lack of sexual gratification is considered intolerable, and it is sufficient grounds for terminating any sexual relationship, including marriage. Sexually supportive cultures are common in equatorial Africa, Southern Asia, and (especially) Oceania. (Old Polynesia, where this approach predominated, earned a well-deserved reputation among world travellers for the abundance of its sexual gratifications.) The Muria (4) and the Trobrianders (10), inhabitants of a group of coral islands in the South Pacific, furnish classic examples of this type.

As cultures change over time, their approach to sexuality may change as well, and nowhere has this been demonstrated as graphically as in the recent history of western culture. With few exceptions, traditional European cultures were either repressive or restrictive, and Victorian England, the mother of tradition for most of the English-speaking world, had evolved one of the most sexually repressed cultures in the history of civilization. Even so, western society made a successful transition from a repressive to a restrictive sexual culture between 1900 and 1950—a rather short period of time in the history of cultures.

At present, the modern world is in the throes of yet another transition: the old restrictive rules are softening, bending, and in some cases being extinguished by a tide of sexual permission that made its presence felt, and its mass appeal undeniable, in America in the 1960s. The changes wrought by the "sexual revolution" were real enough: the 1970s witnessed an explosive increase in adolescent pregnancies, providing hard evidence that adolescent sexuality had become greatly intensified. Nor does this intensification show any clear sign of abating. Americans born after the early 1960s thus represent the first American generation for whom the psychological release from juvenile celibacy occurred at puberty, rather than several years later, and it seems almost certain that this generation's attitude toward sex will consequently be quite different from that of its parents and grandparents. There is a distinct possibility that this generation will raise its own offspring in an atmosphere of genuine sexual permission. If it does, America's ultimate transition to a sexually permissive society will become all but inevitable.

JUVENILE SEXUALITY AND MARITAL SATISFACTION

The post-Victorian search for marital happiness gave rise to a romantic mythology about the ideal marriage, in which sex would be exciting and freely available. The ethnographic data, however, do not justify this romantic expectation. Sexually restrictive cultures are ambivalent about sex, regard it as a problem area, and do not consider it one of life's most important sources of pleasure and gratification. In fact, the romantic ideal of sexual happiness in marriage probably cannot be achieved by a sexually restrictive society. The mythology, however, flourishes as never before.

Everyone wants a spouse who is sexually proficient, but no one wants a child who is learning *how* to be sexually proficient. Such are the cultural contradictions of which personal tragedies are made. Perhaps the continuing sorrow of the sexually disappointed will fuel a final push toward a sexually supportive modern culture, in which customs and institutions arise to provide the immature members of society with sexual information, opportunity, and permission: these are the essential ingredients for vigorous sexual development. If this ultimate sexual revolution does take place in modern society, will it solve the problem of sexual dissatisfaction in marriage, one of the foremost causes of divorce in America today?[4]

Verrier Elwin spent most of his life among the Muria and other Gond-speaking tribes of Central India, ultimately taking the daughter of a village headman as his wife. He studied scores of villages and thousands of individuals, and he published 17 volumes of ethnographic data. On the basis of this research, Elwin concluded that the Muria had achieved in real life the romantic myth that western society was reaching for but could not seem to grasp: stable, monogamous marriages, in which fidelity was observed and sexual fulfillment was virtually guaranteed. The sexual training every Muria man and woman had received in the *ghotul*, said Elwin, was the single factor responsible for their enviable marriages.

The Muria have a divorce rate of 3 percent. The divorce rate in America was 8 percent in 1900 and had risen to 50 percent by 1975. The extraordinary low Muria divorce rate cannot be explained as the result of social pressure, because in Muria culture divorce is considered neither sinful nor shameful; it is simply regarded as unfortunate. And in other semitribal societies of India, where there are no institutions comparable with the *ghotul*, divorce rates range as high as 46 percent (3). If we were to adopt a modern version of the *ghotul*, would our divorce rate plummet accordingly?

Considerable practice and encouragement is needed if a complex skill is to be mastered, and for this reason the members of sexually supportive cultures have the knowledge, interest, and ability needed to create sexual pleasure in copious amounts with the cooperation of a willing and equally knowledgeable partner. This may be a good recipe for sexual satisfaction in marriage, but it is no guarantee of marital satisfaction in general. The Muria are, unfortunately, a special case: sexually permissive and supportive societies do not always enjoy stable or happy marriages. Indeed, when the expectation of sexual gratification is high, as it inevitably will be in a sexually supportive society, any substantial loss of sexual interest or compatibility will itself be a serious threat to marital stability.

There is little reason to expect that the sexual training of juveniles and adolescents will stop the divorce epidemic. At most, such training would simply remove one of several major factors that produce marital dissatisfaction in our society at this time. The key variable affecting marital satisfaction is the nature of the cultural expectations and the degree to which those expectations are fulfilled in real-life situations. Our society suffers most, I believe, from the contradiction between its romantic expectations of sexual fulfillment in marriage on the one hand and its restrictive approach to sexual development—which makes those expectations almost impossible to fulfill—on the other.

At the same time, it is essential to point out that premarital sex, including juvenile experimentation and adolescent promiscuity, is not at all incompatible with stability, sexual fidelity, and emotional satisfaction in marriage. Muria marriages succeed because *all* the institutions work in concert to support the traditional ideal of marital satisfaction. The same cannot be said of western society at the present time; indeed, it would be unfair to expect sex alone to provide enough bonding power to hold together an institution that is coming apart at the seams *precisely* for lack of social, economic, and religious support from society at large.

SYNTHESIS

The importance of sexual experience in childhood and (especially) adolescence cannot be underestimated, if a vigorous sex life is to be enjoyed in adulthood. This point was stressed 30 years ago by Ford and Beach (5), and it has been made again and again by anthropologists studying the ethnography of sexual behavior.

It is noteworthy that sexual development seems to follow similar patterns throughout a wide range of permissive and supportive societies; when American Indians, equatorial Africans, Asiatic Indians, Malaysians, Melanesians, Polynesians, and many other racial and ethnic groups all display roughly the same pattern of development, one begins to suspect the existence of an underlying biological program governing sexual development in *Homo sapiens sapiens*. The broad outlines of this developmental pattern are as follows:

INFANCY. Sexual stimulation of infants of both sexes is a common form of parental pacification. (For some reason, such stimulation, whether manual or oral, seems much more common between mothers and male infants than in the three other possible parent-child combinations.) Infants are encouraged to stimulate themselves manually.

EARLY CHILDHOOD. Young juveniles become more proficient at autoeroticism, and they may gather in groups for autoerotic happenings. These soon lead to sexual exploration and experimentation of a general kind, both heterosexual and homosexual.

LATE CHILDHOOD. Older juveniles begin losing interest in autoerotic and homosexual gratifications as their sexual identities become more strongly developed. They engage in heterosexual role modeling of all kinds, including repeated attempts at intercourse. Girls of this age may begin having regular intercourse with older boys; boys of this age are still generally unable to perform the full complement of behaviors involved in normal copulation.

PUBERTY. Girls begin a phase of sexual intensification which often involves a period of competitive promiscuity. It is during this period that basic sexual techniques are first mastered; by the end of puberty the transition to adult sexual behavior is complete. Boys also learn basic sexual techniques, but as most of their sexual interactions are with younger girls, the learning process is not nearly so rapid or complete. Both sexes have generally abandoned autoerotic and homosexual behaviors, which they have come to regard as immature.

ADOLESCENCE. Both sexes seek wide sexual experience in adolescence as part of their preparation for adulthood. Adolescent girls may have relationships with adult men of all ages as well as with their male peers, and adolescent boys may similarly range throughout the female age pyramid in their search for sexual variety and excitement. But the passions of promiscuity are, year by year, replaced by the more substantial gratifications of permanent mating, and by late adolescence most females are legally and emotionally ready for marriage. Males may, in some societies, choose marriage partners at this time, but here economic considerations begin to play a major role, and marriage may be deferred while a male devotes his young manhood to the accumulation of sufficient wealth and property to discharge his responsibilities as a husband. Thus he may be slower to give up the pattern of adolescent promiscuity.

Thus, sexual freedom in childhood and adolescence leads, like all other viable cultural pathways, to marriage, procreation, and economic achievement. Those who assert that the relaxation of sexual restrictions on the young will undermine the foundations of society are simply ignorant of the ethnographic facts of life.

Our species exhibits the most powerful sex drive and the most indefatigable sexual capacity of any animal species on earth. Whether it is repressed, restricted, permitted or supported, the existence of important sexual needs in childhood and adolescence cannot reasonably be denied. In the years to come, the biomedical evidence of the linkage between early sexual experience and adult sexual adjustment will accumulate, as surely as the fossils of prehistoric life forms have accumulated in the past 100 years.

In the evolution of cultures, as in the evolution of organisms, a chance combination of factors may lead to an evolutionary blind alley. The quest for the post-Victorian romantic family is just such a cul-de-sac. If it is to be escaped, our culture will have evolved in one of two directions: either backward into the moral certainties of repression and restriction or forward into the uncharted seas of sexual permission.

REFERENCES

1. Barton, R.F. *Philippine Pagans, The Autobiographies of Three Ifugaos.* London: G. Routledge & Sons, 1938.

2. Dentan, R. *The Semai.* New York: Holt, Rinehart & Winston, 1968.

3, Elwin, V. The Duration of Marriage Among the Aboriginals of the Maikal Hills, *Man in India* 22:11 ff., 1942.

4. Elwin, V. *The Kingdom of the Young.* London: Oxford University Press, 1968.

5. Ford, C.S., and Beach, F. *Patterns of Sexual Behavior.* New York: Harper, 1951.

6. Hartman, C.G. On the Relative Sterility of the Adolescent Organism. *Science* 74:226–227, 1931.

7. Heider, K.G. Dani Sexuality: a Low Energy System. *Man* (N.S.) 2:188–201, 1976.

8. Hoebel, E.A., *The Cheyennes: Indians of the Great Plains.* New York: Holt, Rinehart & Winston, 1960.

9. Lewis, O. *Life in a Mexican Village: Tepoztlán Restudied*, Urbana, Ill.: University of Illinois Press, 1951.

10. Malinowski, B. *The Sexual Life of Savages in North-Western Melanesia.* New York: Harcourt, Brace & World, 1929.

11. Marshall, D.S. Sexual Behavior on Mangaia. In Marshall & Suggs, *Human Sexual Behavior*, 1971.

12. Marshall, D.S., and Suggs, R. (Eds.) *Human Sexual Behavior: Variations in the Ethnographic Spectrum.* New York: Basic Books, 1971.

13. Messenger, J.C., Sex and Repression in an Irish Folk Community. In Marshall & Suggs, *Human Sexual Behavior*, 1971.

14. Montagu, A. *The Reproductive Development of the Female, With Special Reference to the Period of Adolescent Sterility.* New York: Julian Press, 1957.

15, Pietropinto, A., and Simenauer, J. *Husbands and Wives: A Nationwide Survey of Marriage.* New York: Quadrangle Press, 1979.

16. Rainwater, L. Marital Sexuality in Four Cultures of Poverty. In Marshall and Suggs, *Human Sexual Behavior*, 1971.

17. Symons, D. *The Evolution of Human Sexuality.* New York: Oxford University Press, 1979.

NOTES

1. The daily affairs of the *ghotul* are administered by the children's government (the office-holders are chosen by the children themselves), which sees that the *ghotul* grounds and buildings are kept clean and orderly, levies fines and punishments on those who fail to perform their allotted work or who violate *ghotul* rules, and settles disputes between *ghotul* members.

2. The phenomenon of adolescent sterility, first delineated by Hartman (6), has been well discussed in the anthropological literature (4, 5, 10, 14). Several factors, including diet, contraceptive techniques, cultural expectations, and hereditary predisposition, seem to be involved. The evidence does not support the theory that promiscuity has any effect on fertility.

3. I have proposed a new set of categories for sexual culture because Ford and Beach's (5) categories do not make clear the essential differences among possible sexual strategies. I would also maintain that my labelling is more appropriate.

4. Pietropinto and Sirnenauer (15) describe a study by the American Association of Marriage Counselors in which sexual problems were the *primary* cause of marital instability for 20 percent of unhappily married women and 40 percent of unhappily married men.

SAR OF THE SEA

Mary Ann Williams

At a time when some members of the far right are advocating heterosexual, married, monogamous intercourse as the only "natural" form of sexual expression, it's interesting to see just what passes for "natural" sex in the animal kingdom. Here's a sampling of courtship and reproductive behaviors in water birds and animals.

Dominatrix dynamics are for the birds. Timid, dull-colored and devoted to the nest, the male red-necked phalarope (*Phalaropus lobatus*) waits for a brash, bright-colored female to woo him. The larger, more colorful female takes the lead in courtship and copulation. Emitting a loud "peet!" she runs off rival females. The pair cement their bond by putting their heads together "cheek to cheek."

It doesn't last. After copulation, the male finds himself building the nest, incubating the eggs and raising the young alone. Once she lays her eggs, the female may leave to mate with other males, if there's still time left in the breeding season.

But can he cook? A male's ability to provide a meal is crucial to a female common tern (*Sterna hirundo*). During courtship, a wooing male brings fish to a female. It's quite possible that she chooses her sexual partner based on his prowess as a fisherman. One thing's for sure—he brings her fish at the exact time when she needs extra food because of the eggs developing inside her. The more fish a female eats, the stronger the shells of the eggs she'll lay. And a courting male brings the same amount of food to his intended that he will later bring to his chicks.

Cichlids stick to oral sex. Mating male and female mouthbreeders (*Pseudotropheus zebra*) swim in circles. The male nibbles at the female's anal fin until she releases an egg into the water. She swoops around and takes the egg in her mouth. Then she nibbles at an egg-like spot near the male's anal fin. He emits sperm, which she inhales to fertilize the egg. After several eggs have been fertilized, the female leaves to mate with other males. The male also goes on to other mates.

The female fasts while the fertilized eggs hatch and develop inside her mouth. Later, she'll let her young fish feed outside, but if danger threatens she will gobble them to safety.

Gulls will be gulls. In colonies of Western gulls (*Larus spp.*), females sometimes pair off and remain together for years, rather than mating with males. In female-female pairs, both partners defend a territory. Sometimes one of the female partners will take on roles usually performed by a male, such as courtship feeding, mounting and attempted copulation.

The females lay eggs in the same nest. Though most are infertile, the small number of eggs that hatch indicates that at least one female also copulates with a male who most likely already has a female mate. Whether or not their eggs are fertile, these females maintain primary bonds with their female partners.

Without their female partners, these gulls couldn't incubate eggs or raise their chicks. At first scientists questioned whether there was a physical or behavioral reason that some females would prefer to mate with another female, rather than with a male. However, research has shown that there's no hormonal or behavioral difference between homosexually and heterosexually paired female gulls.

This Amazon temptress tricks unwitting males. Greek mythology tells of a race of warrior women who scorned the company of men. In fact, there's an all-female species of fish, the Amazon mollie (*Poecilia spp.*). These females lure the males of another species, the sailfin mollie, into having sex with them. But when the sailfin's sperm bumps into the Amazon mollie's egg, the egg starts divid-

"SAR of the Sea," by Mary Ann Williams, reprinted from *Contemporary Sexuality*, Vol. 27, No. 8, August 1993. American Asosciation of Sex Educators, Counselors, and Therapists.

ing on its own. The Amazon gives birth to female offspring, all twins, and all genetically identical to the mother. Though the sailfin may have spent his sperm with the intention of passing on his genetic material, his genes are lost in the transaction.

Some dads get pregnant, too. Just after dawn, courting seahorses (*Hippocampus spp.*) greet each other by blushing to brighter colors. They grasp the same piece of seaweed or coral and circle slowly and gracefully, like carousel horses. After three days of courtship, the seahorses rise through the water, their bellies pressed against each other. Using an egg-transferring organ called an ovipositor, the female places her eggs into an opening in the male's abdominal pouch. Once the pouch has been sealed shut, the male sways to fertilize the eggs and settle them in special pockets in the pouch wall. As embryos develop, they're supplied with oxygen from capillaries in the pouch wall. Meanwhile, the male's prolactin breaks down the egg enzymes to make a "placental" fluid to nourish the embryos.

Neither partner remates while the male is pregnant. In a few weeks, he undergoes a series of strong contractions and gives birth to as many as 1,000 young. In a short time, he'll probably mate again with the same female.

This jelly moons for itself. Why choose? As they pass through different life stages, some jellyfish, like the moon jelly (*Aurelia aurita*), alternate between sexual and asexual reproduction. Sometimes sex takes two; sometimes one is enough.

Adult medusae—the familiar, bell-shaped jellyfish—are either male or female. Males release sperm into the water. As the sperm-laden water passes through the female's body it fertilizes her eggs. They develop into larvae that swim away to anchor themselves to a rock or other hard surface.

Each larvae grows into an anemone-like animal called a polyp. The polyps clone themselves by sending out runners, much like a strawberry plant. In time, each polyp begins to change color and stretch into segments. Like a stack of plates, a pile of minute, juvenile jellyfish appears at one end of the polyp. They pulse and pull until, one by one, they break away. Each juvenile jelly swims off, looking like a tiny contact lens.

When it's hot, it's male. A female dwarf caiman (*Paleosuchus palpebrosus*)—the smallest member of the crocodile family—digs a nest in a shady South American riverbank. She mixes mud, sticks and leaves to cover her eggs. In time, this mixture hardens into an adobe-like egg chamber. On top, she mounds more twigs and leaves. Then she remains nearby.

As the compost heap over the nest rots, it gives off heat that warms the eggs. From time to time, the female will poke a hole in the nest to make sure that the temperature is right. She may add more leaves. As with many reptiles, the sex of the young depends on the temperature of the nest. Eggs develop into females at low temperatures; males at higher temperatures.

Twice the chance of a date on a Saturday night . . . It doesn't matter who a sea hare (*Aplysia california*) meets, these sea slugs are both male and female, though they can't mate with themselves. Sometimes they mate in pairs, transmitting and receiving sperm at the same time. At other times they form lines with the male halves facing front and the female halves facing back. And at still other times, sea hares join in a mating free-for-all known as a "brothel." They look like a pile of slugs playing Twister.

Sea hares lay strings of eggs called cordons; each may consist of a million eggs. Sea hares can't emit sperm while they're laying eggs. However, they still receive sperm during egg laying and store it to fertilize the next batch. Egg-laying sea hares produce pheromones that stimulate the next bout of mass mating.

The only constant. Early in her life, a female rainbow wrasse (*Thalassoma lucasanum*) has two mating options. She can pair off with a large, colorful, powerful male and mate only with him in the privacy of his territory. Or she can become the center of a mating frenzy. A swirling horde of young males will surround her and emit their sperm to fertilize her eggs.

But as the female grows older, things change, and so does she. In fact, if she lives long enough she'll change into a large, colorful, powerful male. And she'll spend the rest of her days mating with a young female in the privacy of her—I mean, his—own territory . . .

If you'd like to talk about this article—or any other article that has appeared or that you think should appear in Contemporary Sexuality—*contact Mary Ann Williams at 1340 West Irving Park Road, Suite 169, Chicago, IL 60613. You can call Mary Ann at 312-275-7931; fax her at 312-878-6857.*

BONOBO SEX AND SOCIETY

*The behavior of a close relative challenges assumptions
about male supremacy in human evolution*

Frans B. M. de Waal

At a juncture in history during which women are seeking equality with men, science arrives with a belated gift to the feminist movement. Male-biased evolutionary scenarios—Man the Hunter, Man the Toolmaker and so on—are being challenged by the discovery that females play a central, perhaps even dominant, role in the social life of one of our nearest relatives. In the past few years many strands of knowledge have come together concerning a relatively unknown ape with an unorthodox repertoire of behavior: the bonobo.

The bonobo is one of the last large mammals to be found by science. The creature was discovered in 1929 in a Belgian colonial museum, far from its lush African habitat. A German anatomist, Ernst Schwarz, was scrutinizing a skull that had been ascribed to a juvenile chimpanzee because of its small size, when he realized that it belonged to an adult. Schwarz declared that he had stumbled on a new subspecies of chimpanzee. But soon the animal was assigned the status of an entirely distinct species within the same genus as the chimpanzee, *Pan*.

The bonobo was officially classified as *Pan paniscus*, or the diminutive *Pan*. But I believe a different label might have been selected had the discoverers known then what we know now. The old taxonomic name of the chimpanzee, *P. satyrus*—which refers to the myth of apes as lustful satyrs—would have been perfect for the bonobo.

The species is best characterized as female-centered and egalitarian and as one that substitutes sex for aggression. Whereas in most other species sexual behavior is a fairly distinct category, in the bonobo it is part and parcel of social relations—and not just between males and females. Bonobos engage in sex in virtually every partner combination (although such contact among close family members may be suppressed). And sexual interactions occur more often among bonobos than among other primates. Despite the frequency of sex, the bonobo's rate of reproduction in the wild is about the same as that of the chimpanzee. A female gives birth to a single infant at intervals of between five and six years. So bonobos share at least one very important characteristic with our own species, namely, a partial separation between sex and reproduction.

A NEAR RELATIVE

This finding commands attention because the bonobo shares more than 98 percent of our genetic profile, making it as close to a human as, say, a fox is to a dog. The split between the human line of ancestry and the line of the chimpanzee and the bonobo is believed to have occurred a mere eight million years ago. The subsequent divergence of the chimpanzee and the bonobo lines came much later, perhaps prompted by the chimpanzee's need to adapt to relatively open, dry habitats [see "East Side Story: The Origin of Humankind," by Yves Coppens; *Scientific American*, May 1994].

In contrast, bonobos probably never left the protection of the trees. Their present range lies in humid forests south of the Zaire River, where perhaps fewer than 10,000 bonobos survive. (Given the

"Bonobo Sex and Society," by Frans B.M. de Waal, reprinted from *Scientific American*, March 1995.

species' slow rate of reproduction, the rapid destruction of its tropical habitat and the political instability of central Africa, there is reason for much concern about its future.)

If this evolutionary scenario of ecological continuity is true, the bonobo may have undergone less transformation than either humans or chimpanzees. It could most closely resemble the common ancestor of all three modern species. Indeed, in the 1930s Harold J. Coolidge—the American anatomist who gave the bonobo its eventual taxonomic status—suggested that the animal might be most similar to the primogenitor, since its anatomy is less specialized than is the chimpanzee's. Bonobo body proportions have been compared with those of the australopithecines, a form of prehuman. When the apes stand or walk upright, they look as if they stepped straight out of an artist's impression of early hominids.

Not too long ago the savanna baboon was regarded as the best living model of the human ancestor. That primate is adapted to the kinds of ecological conditions that prehumans may have faced after descending from the trees. But in the late 1970s, chimpanzees, which are much more closely related to humans, became the model of choice. Traits that are observed in chimpanzees—including cooperative hunting, food sharing, tool use, power politics and primitive warfare—were absent or not as developed in baboons. In the laboratory the apes have been able to learn sign language and to recognize themselves in a mirror, a sign of self-awareness not yet demonstrated in monkeys.

Although selecting the chimpanzee as the touchstone of hominid evolution represented a great improvement, at least one aspect of the former model did not need to be revised: male superiority remained the natural state of affairs. In both baboons and chimpanzees, males are conspicuously dominant over females; they reign supremely and often brutally. It is highly unusual for a fully grown male chimpanzee to be dominated by any female.

Enter the bonobo. Despite their common name—the pygmy chimpanzee—bonobos cannot be distinguished from the chimpanzee by size. Adult males of the smallest subspecies of chimpanzee weigh some 43 kilograms (95 pounds) and females 33 kilograms (73 pounds), about the same as bonobos. Although female bonobos are much smaller than the males, they seem to rule.

GRACEFUL APES

In physique, a bonobo is as different from a chimpanzee as a Concorde is from a Boeing 747. I do not wish to offend any chimpanzees, but bonobos have more style. The bonobo, with its long legs and small head atop narrow shoulders, has a more gracile build than does a chimpanzee. Bonobo lips are reddish in a black face, the ears small and the nostrils almost as wide as a gorilla's. These primates also have a flatter, more open face with a higher forehead than the chimpanzee's and—to top it all off—an attractive coiffure with long, fine, black hair neatly parted in the middle.

Like chimpanzees, female bonobos nurse and carry around their young for up to five years. By the age of seven the offspring reach adolescence. Wild females give birth for the first time at 13 or 14 years of age, becoming full grown by about 15. A bonobo's longevity is unknown, but judging by the chimpanzee it may be older than 40 in the wild and close to 60 in captivity.

Fruit is central to the diets of both wild bonobos and chimpanzees. The former supplement with more pith from herbaceous plants, and the latter add meat. Although bonobos do eat invertebrates and occasionally capture and eat small vertebrates, including mammals, their diet seems to contain relatively little animal protein. Unlike chimpanzees, they have not been observed to hunt monkeys.

Whereas chimpanzees use a rich array of strategies to obtain foods—from cracking nuts with stone tools to fishing for ants and termites with sticks—tool use in wild bonobos seems undeveloped. (Captive bonobos use tools skillfully.) Apparently as intelligent as chimpanzees, bonobos have, however, a far more sensitive temperament. During World War II bombing of Hellabrun, Germany, the bonobos in a nearby zoo all died of fright from the noise; the chimpanzees were unaffected.

Bonobos are also imaginative in play. I have watched captive bonobos engage in "blindman's buff." A bonobo covers her eyes with a banana leaf or an arm or by sticking two fingers in her eyes. Thus handicapped, she stumbles around on a climbing frame, bumping into others or almost falling. She seems to be imposing a rule on herself: "I cannot look until I lose my balance." Other apes and monkeys also indulge in this game, but I have never seen it performed with such dedication and concentration as by bonobos.

Juvenile bonobos are incurably playful and like to make funny faces, sometimes in long solitary pantomimes and at other times while tickling one another. Bonobos are, however, more controlled in expressing their emotions—whether it be joy, sorrow, excitement or anger—than are the extroverted chimpanzees. Male chimpanzees often engage in spectacular charging displays in which they show off their strength: throwing rocks, breaking branches and uprooting small trees in the process. They keep up these noisy performances for many minutes, during which most other members of the group wisely stay out of their way. Male bonobos, on the other hand, usually limit displays to a brief run while dragging a few branches behind them.

Both primates signal emotions and intentions through facial expressions and hand gestures, many of which are also present in the nonverbal communication of humans. For example, bonobos will beg by stretching out an open hand (or, sometimes, a foot) to a possessor of food and will pout their lips and make whimpering sounds if the effort is unsuccessful. But bonobos make different sounds than chimpanzees do. The renowned low-pitched, extended "huuu-huuu" pant-hooting of the latter contrasts with the rather sharp, high-pitched barking sounds of the bonobo.

LOVE, NOT WAR

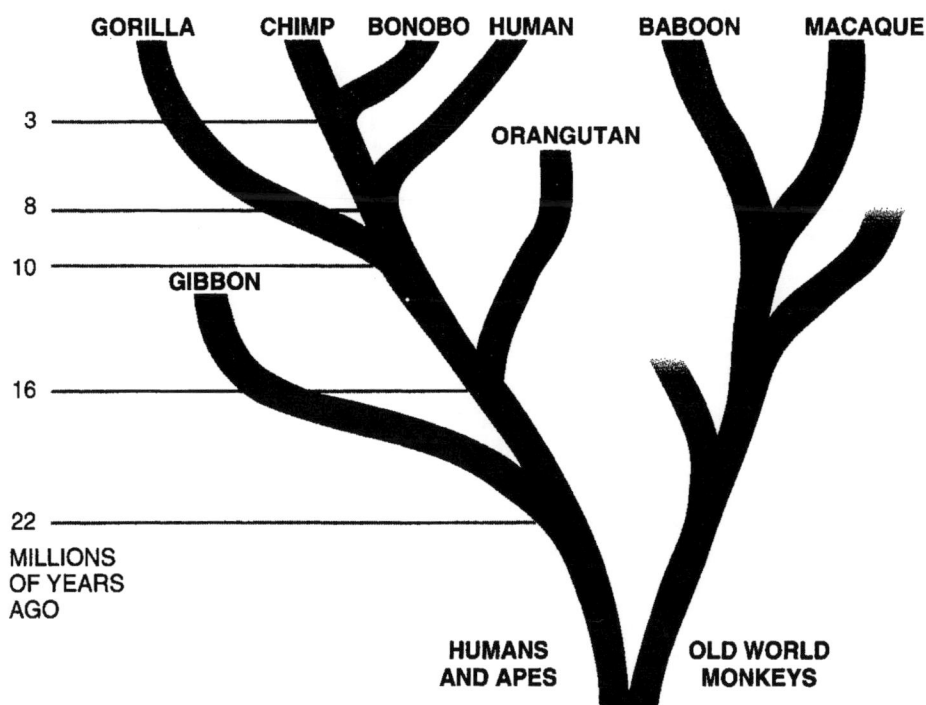

EVOLUTIONARY TREE of primates, based on DNA analysis, shows that humans diverged from bonobos and chimpanzees a mere eight million years ago. The three species share more than 98 percent of their genetic makeup.

My own interest in bonobos came not from an inherent fascination with their charms but from research on aggressive behavior in primates. I was particularly intrigued with the aftermath of conflict. After two chimpanzees have fought, for instance, they may come together for a hug and mouth-to-mouth kiss. Assuming that such reunions serve to restore peace and harmony, I labeled them reconciliations.

Any species that combines close bonds with a potential for conflict needs such conciliatory mechanisms. Thinking how much faster marriages would break up if people had no way of compensating for hurting each other, I set out to investigate such mechanisms in several primates, including bonobos. Although I expected to see peacemaking in these apes, too, I was little prepared for the form it would take.

For my study, which began in 1983, I chose the San Diego Zoo. At the time, it housed the world's largest captive bonobo colony—10 members divided into three groups. I spent entire days in front of the enclosure with a video camera, which was switched on at feeding time. As soon as a caretaker approached the enclosure with food, the males would develop erections. Even before the food was thrown into the area, the bonobos would be inviting each other for sex: males would invite females, and females would invite males and other females.

Sex, it turned out, is the key to the social life of the bonobo. The first suggestion that the sexual behavior of bonobos is different had come from observations at European zoos. Wrapping their findings in Latin, primatologists Eduard Tratz and Heinz Heck reported in 1954 that the chimpanzees at Hellabrun mated *more canum* (like dogs) and bonobos *more hominum* (like people). In those days, face-to-face copulation was considered uniquely human, a cultural innovation that needed to be taught to preliterate people (hence the term "missionary position"). These early studies, written in German, were ignored by the international scientific establishment. The bonobo's humanlike sexuality needed to be rediscovered in the 1970s before it became accepted as characteristic of the species.

Bonobos become sexually aroused remarkably easily, and they express this excitement in a variety of mounting positions and genital contacts. Although chimpanzees virtually never adopt face-to-face positions, bonobos do so in one out of three copulations in the wild. Furthermore, the frontal orientation of the bonobo vulva and clitoris strongly suggest that the female genitalia are adapted for this position.

Another similarity with humans is increased female sexual receptivity. The tumescent phase of the female's genitals, resulting in a pink swelling that signals willingness to mate, covers a much longer part of estrus in bonobos than in chimpanzees. Instead of a few days out of her cycle, the female bonobo is almost continuously sexually attractive and active [*see illustration on page17*].

Perhaps the bonobo's most typical sexual pattern, undocumented in any other primate, is genito-genital rubbing (or GG rubbing) between adult females. One female facing another clings with arms and legs to a partner that, standing on both hands and feet, lifts her off the ground. The two females then rub their genital swellings laterally together, emitting grins and squeals that probably reflect orgasmic experiences. (Laboratory experiments on stump-tailed macaques have demonstrated that women are not the only female primates capable of physiological orgasm.)

Male bonobos, too, may engage in pseudocopulation but generally perform a variation. Standing back to back, one male briefly rubs his scrotum against the buttocks of another. They also practice so-called penis-fencing, in which two males hang face to face from a branch while rubbing their erect penises together.

The diversity of erotic contacts in bonobos includes sporadic oral sex, massage of another individual's genitals and intense tongue-kissing. Lest this leave the impression of a pathologically oversexed species, I must add, based on hundreds of hours of watching bonobos, that their sexual activity is rather casual and relaxed. It appears to be a completely natural part of their group life. Like people, bonobos engage in sex only occasionally, not continuously. Furthermore, with the average copulation lasting 13 seconds, sexual contact in bonobos is rather quick by human standards.

Social Organization among Various Primates

BONOBO

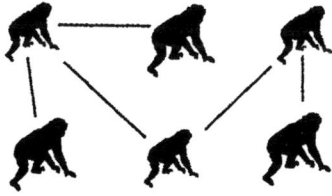

Bonobo communities are peace-loving and generally egalitarian. The strongest social bonds (*blue*) are those among females (*green*), although females also bond with males. The status of a male (*purple*) depends on the position of his mother, to whom he remains closely bonded for her entire life.

CHIMPANZEE

In chimpanzee groups the strongest bonds are established between the males in order to hunt and to protect their shared territory. The females live in overlapping home ranges within this territory but are not strongly bonded to other females or to any one male.

GIBBON

Gibbons establish monogamous, egalitarian relations, and one couple will maintain a territory to the exclusion of other pairs.

HUMAN

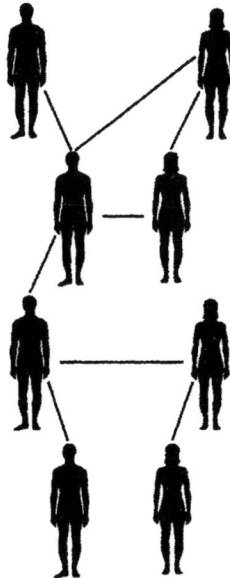

Human society is the most diverse among the primates. Males unite for cooperative ventures, whereas females also bond with those of their own sex. Monogamy, polygamy and polyandry are all in evidence.

GORILLA

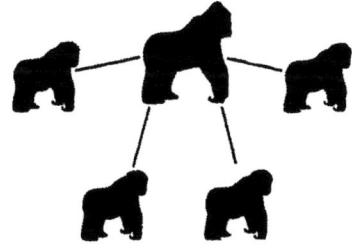

The social organization of gorillas provides a clear example of polygamy. Usually a single male maintains a range for his family unit, which contains several females. The strongest bonds are those between the male and his females.

ORANGUTAN

Orangutans live solitary lives with little bonding in evidence. Male orangutans are intolerant of one another. In his prime, a single male establishes a large territory, within which live several females. Each female has her own, separate home range.

That sex is connected to feeding, and even appears to make food sharing possible, has been observed not only in zoos but also in the wild. Nancy Thompson-Handler, then at the State University of New York at Stony Brook, saw bonobos in Zaire's Lomako Forest engage in sex after they had entered trees loaded with ripe figs or when one among them had captured a prey animal, such as a small forest duiker. The flurry of sexual contacts would last for five to 10 minutes, after which the apes would settle down to consume the food.

One explanation for the sexual activity at feeding time could be that excitement over food translates into sexual arousal. This idea may be partly true. Yet another motivation is probably the real cause: competition. There are two reasons to believe sexual activity is the bonobo's answer to avoiding conflict.

First, anything, not just food, that arouses the interest of more than one bonobo at a time tends to result in sexual contact. If two bonobos approach a cardboard box thrown into their enclosure, they will briefly mount each other before playing with the box. Such situations lead to squabbles in most other species. But bonobos are quite tolerant, perhaps because they use sex to divert attention and to diffuse tension.

Second, bonobo sex often occurs in aggressive contexts totally unrelated to food. A jealous male might chase another away from a female, after which the two males reunite and engage in scrotal rubbing. Or after a female hits a juvenile, the latter's mother may lunge at the aggressor, an action that is immediately followed by genital rubbing between the two adults.

I once observed a young male, Kako, inadvertently blocking an older, female juvenile, Leslie, from moving along a branch. First, Leslie pushed him; Kako, who was not very confident in trees, tightened his grip, grinning nervously. Next Leslie gnawed on one of his hands, presumably to loosen his grasp. Kako uttered a sharp peep and stayed put. Then Leslie rubbed her vulva against his shoulder. This gesture calmed Kako, and he moved along the branch. It seemed that Leslie had been very close to using force but instead had reassured both herself and Kako with sexual contact.

During reconciliations, bonobos use the same sexual repertoire as they do during feeding time. Based on an analysis of many such incidents, my study yielded the first solid evidence for sexual behavior as a mechanism to overcome aggression. Not that this function is absent in other animals— or in humans, for that matter—but the art of sexual reconciliation may well have reached its evolutionary peak in the bonobo. For these animals, sexual behavior is indistinguishable from social behavior. Given its peacemaking and appeasement functions, it is not surprising that sex among bonobos occurs in so many different partner combinations, including between juveniles and adults. The need for peaceful coexistence is obviously not restricted to adult heterosexual pairs.

FEMALE ALLIANCE

Apart from maintaining harmony, sex is also involved in creating the singular social structure of the bonobo. This use of sex becomes clear when studying bonobos in the wild. Field research on bonobos started only in the mid-1970s, more than a decade after the most important studies on wild chimpanzees had been initiated. In terms of continuity and invested (wo)manpower, the chimpanzee

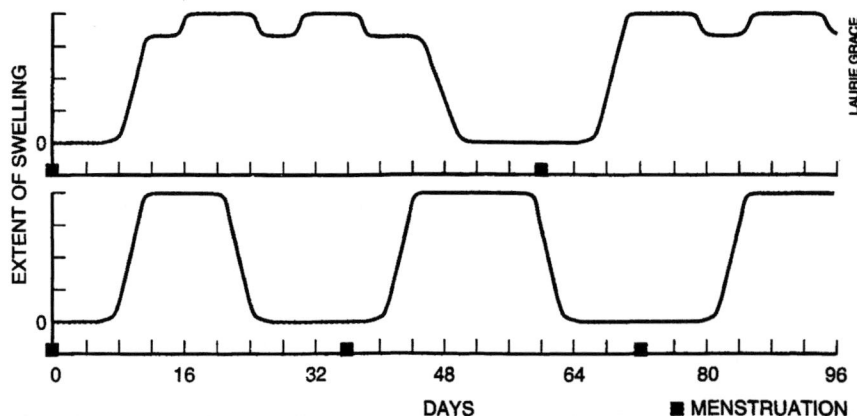

FEMALE RECEPTIVITY for sex, manifested by swollen genitals, occupies a much larger portion of the estrus cycle of bonobos (*top*) than of chimpanzees (*bottom*). The receptivity of bonobos continues through lactation. (In chimpanzees, it disappears.) This circumstance allows sex to play a large part in the social relations of bonobos. The graph was provided by Jeremy Dahl of the Yerkes Primate Center.

projects of Jane Goodall and Toshisada Nishida, both in Tanzania, are unparalleled. But bonobo research by Takayoshi Kano and others of Kyoto University is now two decades under way at Wamba in Zaire and is beginning to show the same payoffs.

Both bonobos and chimpanzees live in so-called fission-fusion societies. The apes move alone or in small parties of a few individuals at a time, the composition of which changes constantly. Several bonobos traveling together in the morning might meet another group in the forest, whereupon one individual from the first group wanders off with others from the second group, while those left behind forage together. All associations, except the one between mother and dependent offspring, are of a temporary character.

Initially this flexibility baffled investigators, making them wonder if these apes formed any social groups with stable membership. After years of documenting the travels of chimpanzees in the Mahale Mountains, Nishida first reported that they form large communities: all members of one community mix freely in ever changing parties, but members of different communities never gather. Later, Goodall added territoriality to this picture. That is, not only do communities not mix, but males of different chimpanzee communities engage in lethal battles.

In both bonobos and chimpanzees, males stay in their natal group, whereas females tend to migrate during adolescence. As a result, the senior males of a chimpanzee or bonobo group have known all junior males since birth, and all junior males have grown up together. Females, on the other hand, transfer to an unfamiliar and often hostile group where they may know no one. A chief difference between chimpanzee and bonobo societies is the way in which young females integrate into their new community.

On arrival in another community, young bonobo females at Wamba single out one or two senior resident females for special attention, using frequent GG rubbing and grooming to establish a relation. If the residents reciprocate, close associations are set up, and the younger female gradually becomes accepted into the group. After producing her first offspring, the young female's position becomes more stable and central. Eventually the cycle repeats with younger immigrants, in turn, seeking a good relation with the now established female. Sex thus smooths the migrant's entrance into the community of females, which is much more close-knit in the bonobo than in the chimpanzee.

Bonobo males remain attached to their mothers all their lives, following them through the forest and being dependent on them for protection in aggressive encounters with other males. As a result, the highest-ranking males of a bonobo community tend to be sons of important females.

What a contrast with chimpanzees! Male chimpanzees fight their own battles, often relying on the support of other males. Furthermore, adult male chimpanzees travel together in same-sex parties, grooming each other frequently. Males form a distinct social hierarchy with high levels of both competition and association. Given the need to stick together against males of neighboring communities, their bonding is not surprising: failure to form a united front might result in the loss of lives and territory. The danger of being male is reflected in the adult sex ratio of chimpanzee populations, with considerably fewer males than females.

Serious conflict between bonobo groups has been witnessed in the field, but it seems quite rare. On the contrary, reports exist of peaceable mingling, including mutual sex and grooming, between what appear to be different communities. If intergroup combat is indeed unusual, it may explain the lower rate of all-male associations. Rather than being male-bonded, bonobo society gives the impression of being female-bonded, with even adult males relying on their mothers instead of on other males. No wonder Kano calls mothers the "core" of bonobo society.

The bonding among female bonobos violates a fairly general rule, outlined by Harvard University anthropologist Richard W. Wrangham, that the sex that stays in the natal group develops the strongest mutual bonds. Bonding among male chimpanzees follows naturally because they remain in the community of their birth. The same is true for female kinship bonding in Old World monkeys, such as macaques and baboons, where males are the migratory sex.

Bonobos are unique in that the migratory sex, females, strongly bond with same-sex strangers later in life. In setting up an artificial sisterhood, bonobos can be said to be secondarily bonded. (Kinship bonds are said to be primary.) Although we now know *how* this happens—through the use of sexual contact and grooming—we do not yet know *why* bonobos and chimpanzees differ in this respect. The answer may lie in the different ecological environments of bonobos and chimpanzees—such as the abundance and quality of food in the forest. But it is uncertain if such explanations will suffice.

Bonobo society is, however, not only female-centered but also appears to be female-dominated. Bonobo specialists, while long suspecting such a reality, have been reluctant to make the controversial claim. But in 1992, at the 14th Congress of the International Primatological Society in Strasbourg, investigators of both captive and wild bonobos presented data that left little doubt about the issue.

Amy R. Parish of the University of California at Davis reported on food competition in identical groups (one adult male and two adult females) of chimpanzees and bonobos at the Stuttgart Zoo. Honey was provided in a "termite hill" from which it could be extracted by dipping sticks into a small hole. As soon as honey was made available, the male chimpanzee would make a charging display through the enclosure and claim everything for himself. Only when his appetite was satisfied would he let the females fish for honey.

BONOBO

CHIMPANZEE

SUZANNE BARNES

DOMINANCE BY BONDING is evinced by female bonobos, who engage in genito-genital (GG) rubbing before eating sugarcane (*a*), while a bigger male displays to no avail. The females then share the food without competition (*b*). Only when they leave can the male get to the sugarcane (*c*). In male-dominated chimpanzee society the male eats first (*d*), while the females wait at a safe distance. After he leaves (*e*), carrying as many bananas as he can, the dominant female gets what is left (*f*). (Small amounts of sugarcane and bananas are provided at some research sites in Zaire.)

In the bonobo group, it was the females that approached the honey first. After having engaged in some GG rubbing, they would feed together, taking turns with virtually no competition between them. The male might make as many charging displays as he wanted; the females were not intimidated and ignored the commotion.

Observers at the Belgian animal park of Planckendael, which currently has the most naturalistic bonobo colony, reported similar findings. If a male bonobo tried to harass a female, all females would band together to chase him off. Because females appeared more successful in dominating males when they were together than on their own, their close association and frequent genital rubbing may represent an alliance. Females may bond so as to outcompete members of the individually stronger sex.

The fact that they manage to do so not only in captivity is evident from zoologist Takeshi Furuichi's summary of the relation between the sexes at Wamba, where bonobos are enticed out of the forest with sugarcane. "Males usually appeared at the feeding site first, but they surrendered preferred positions when the females appeared. It seemed that males appeared first not because they were dominant, but because they had to feed before the arrival of females," Furuichi reported at Strasbourg.

SEX FOR FOOD

Occasionally, the role of sex in relation to food is taken one step further, bringing bonobos very close to humans in their behavior. It has been speculated by anthropologists—including C. Owen Lovejoy of Kent State University and Helen Fisher of Rutgers University—that sex is partially separated from reproduction in our species because it serves to cement mutually profitable relationships between men and women. The human female's capacity to mate throughout her cycle and her strong sex drive allow her to exchange sex for male commitment and paternal care, thus giving rise to the nuclear family.

This arrangement is thought to be favored by natural selection because it allows women to raise more offspring than they could if they were on their own. Although bonobos clearly do not establish the exclusive heterosexual bonds characteristic of our species, their behavior does fit important elements of this model. A female bonobo shows extended receptivity and uses sex to obtain a male's favors when—usually because of youth—she is too low in social status to dominate him.

At the San Diego Zoo, I observed that if Loretta was in a sexually attractive state, she would not hesitate to approach the adult male, Vernon, if he had food. Presenting herself to Vernon, she would mate with him and make high-pitched food calls while taking over his entire bundle of branches and leaves. When Loretta had no genital swelling, she would wait until Vernon was ready to share. Primatologist Suehisa Kuroda reports similar exchanges at Wamba: "A young female approached a male, who was eating sugarcane. They copulated in short order, whereupon she took one of the two canes held by him and left."

Despite such quid pro quo between the sexes, there are no indications that bonobos form human-like nuclear families. The burden of raising offspring appears to rest entirely on the female's shoulders. In fact, nuclear families are probably incompatible with the diverse use of sex found in bonobos. If our ancestors started out with a sex life similar to that of bonobos, the evolution of the family would have required dramatic change.

Human family life implies paternal investment, which is unlikely to develop unless males can be reasonably certain that they are caring for their own, not someone else's, offspring. Bonobo society lacks any such guarantee, but humans protect the integrity of their family units through all kinds of moral restrictions and taboos. Thus, although our species is characterized by an extraordinary interest in sex, there are no societies in which people engage in it at the drop of a hat (or a cardboard box, as the case may be). A sense of shame and a desire for domestic privacy are typical human concepts related to the evolution and cultural bolstering of the family.

Yet no degree of moralizing can make sex disappear from every realm of human life that does not relate to the nuclear family. The bonobo's behavioral peculiarities may help us understand the role of sex and may have serious implications for models of human society.

Just imagine that we had never heard of chimpanzees or baboons and had known bonobos first. We would at present most likely believe that early hominids lived in female-centered societies, in which sex served important social functions and in which warfare was rare or absent. In the end, perhaps the most successful reconstruction of our past will be based not on chimpanzees or even on bonobos but on a three-way comparison of chimpanzees, bonobos and humans.

Frans B. M. deWaal was trained as an ethnologist in the European tradition, receiving his Ph.D. from the University of Utrecht in 1977. After a six-year study of the chimpanzee colony at the Arnhem Zoo, he moved to the U.S. in 1981 to work on other primate species, including bonobos. He is now a research professor at the Yerkes Regional Primate Research Center in Atlanta and professor of psychology at Emory University.

SEXUAL ANATOMY
AND RESPONSE

RITES OF PURIFICATION AND THEIR EFFECTS: SOME PSYCHOLOGICAL ASPECTS OF FEMALE GENITAL CIRCUMCISION AND INFIBULATION (PHARAONIC CIRCUMCISION) IN AN AFRO-ARAB ISLAMIC SOCIETY (SUDAN)

Hanny Lightfoot-Klein, MA

ABSTRACT. In a study conducted over a 5-year period, the author interviewed over 300 Sudanese women and 100 Sudanese men in all walks of life on the physical, emotional and psycho/sexual effects of female genital circumcision and infibulation (Pharaonic circumcision), as it is uniformly practiced in this sexually highly restrictive Afro-Arab Islamic society.

Pharaonic circumcision is a culturally embedded practice which is inextricably interwoven with patrilineage, family honor and social position. It is clung to tenaciously by both sexes, although its long term effects are extremely detrimental to the health of the girls and women, and thereby the well-being of the entire family.

The adverse psychological effects of this practice on women tend to be mitigated by a strong conviction that its performance purifies and ennobles them. Strong marital bonding is common, and Sudanese women are able to come to orgasm (climax) in spite of their genital mutilation.

BACKGROUND AND METHODOLOGY

This report is the result of three periods of six months each, during which the author trekked alone through the Sudan, the second least developed country in the Third World. Only Chad, bordering Sudan to the West is considered to be more poverty stricken, barren, desertized, wind-blighted, disease ridden and impossible to develop. My overland trek took me from the capital, Khartoum, to towns, to villages and into small settlements. I traveled as the natives do, on antiquated colonial trains through the desert, on camelback, on the top of lorry freight and very often on foot. During this time, I interviewed over 400 men and women in all walks of life on all aspects of the female genital mutilation custom practiced in Sudan, a particularly extreme and damaging procedure known as "Pharaonic circumcision." While the information thus obtained would under no circumstances have been accessible to a male researcher, it soon became evident to this female observer that Sudanese society not only prides itself in the severity and "properness" of its extreme practices, but for all intents and purposes defines itself by it. Once I understood this, I was able to obtain information quite readily. I gained access to operating and delivery rooms, to dispensaries and to huts where birth was taking place. I observed over 100 births. Among the people I interviewed were Sudanese psychiatrists, gynecologists, pediatricians, nurses, midwives, pharmacists, paramedics, teachers, college professors and students, high school students, obstetrical patients, mothers of pediatric patients, brides, bridegrooms, homemakers, merchants, historians, religious leaders, grandmothers, village women and men. Some of the interviews were with subjects obtained on a catch as catch can basis, anywhere along the way, carried out within an hour. Others were intensive dialogues with people whom I got to know over a period of years. The scope of the verbal interactions was limited only by what people were or were not willing to discuss. While members of the medical profession were extremely accessible, accommodating and highly critical of the custom, they had the procedure performed on their daughters, along with the rest of the population. The only exceptions I encountered were among the gynecologists and pediatricians, and this appeared to be the case because they had to deal intensively with the tragic consequences of the practice on a day to day basis.

FINDINGS

Pharaonic circumcision of girls as it is practiced in Sudan on small girls involves the excision of the clitoris, the labia minora and the inner, fleshy layers of the labia majora. The remaining outer edges of the labia majora are then brought together so that when the wound has healed they are fused so as to leave only a pinhole sized wound opening, resulting in effect in an artificially created chastity belt of thick fibrous scar tissue, or an infibulation.

To more fully understand the psychological impact of the operation on the girl, it is necessary to view it within its social context. Pharaonic circumcision is a practice that throughout history has distinguished "decent" and respectable women from unprotected prostitutes and slaves, and it carries with it the only honorable, dignified and protected status that is possible for a woman in the society. Without circumcision a girl cannot marry and is thereby unable to produce legitimate sons to carry on the husband's patrilineage. In such a society, an unmarried woman has virtually no rights, and practically does not exist as a social entity (4). As in other Arab Islamic societies throughout the Near East, family honor in Sudanese society is defined in greatest measure by the sexual purity of its women. An indecent behavior on the part of the woman disgraces the whole family, and only the most stringent measures will restore their honor, and this may take the form of divorce, casting the woman out, or putting her to death. It can be seen, therefore, that the creation of an infibulation instills a sense of security not only in the patrilineal family, but in the girl herself.

Pharaonic circumcision has for thousands of years been performed ritually, although it is nowadays often performed routinely in a clinic-like setting in the urban centers. It is performed on small girls, generally between the ages of 4 and 8, regardless of their family's social standing. In the outlying areas, the procedures are conducted in the age-old fashion by medically untrained midwives, without any anesthesia or antiseptic. The struggling child is held immobile throughout the 15 to 20 minute long operation, and it is obvious that under such conditions the likelihood of hemorrhage, infection, trauma to adjacent structures, shock from pain, urinary retention due to sepsis, edema or scarring is extremely high. It is almost impossible to imagine that tremendous psychic trauma should not occur.

The "purifying" functions of the procedures are multiple. Circumcision serves as purification by removing the clitoris and inner labia, which are believed to be the source of irresistible temptation to unbridled and totally promiscuous sexuality in girls. It is also believed that if these structures are not removed, they will grow to enormous size, rivaling the male penis by dangling between the legs of the woman, a concept that is regarded with great revulsion and anxiety by the men of the culture. Growing out of these beliefs is the conviction on the part of women that these structures are the source of foul discharges and odors. Their removal is considered necessary as this is believed to reduce the sex drive as well as sexual sensitivity, both of which are undesirable and dangerous attributes in a "decent" woman. The infibulation is seen as serving as a deterrent to rape, while effectively guarding the girl against her own errant sexual impulses. The intact infibulation assures the bridegroom and his family that the purity, chastity and honor of the girl and thereby of her family are unsoiled.

One would expect to see some profound personality changes commonly occurring in young girls subjected to circumcision, that is, a lively and outgoing child becoming timid and withdrawn. Verzin (13) reports that he discussed this aspect of circumcision on many occasions with teachers, psychiatrists and other gynecologists, and all agree that this change, if it occurs at all, is not noticeable in Sudanese girls. Some other observers, however, categorically state that there is evidence that a child becomes withdrawn in the first year or two following circumcision. This, however, gives place to contentment and an observable pride when girls are a few years older.

The physical consequences of Pharaonic circumcision are far reaching and life long. I will deal with them only briefly here. After a girl has been infibulated to a pinhole sized opening, urination is generally difficult, and often takes many minutes to accomplish. Urinary debris may accumulate behind the infibulation, causing urinary tract infections. When the girl reaches puberty, menstruation is almost invariably agonizingly painful, greatly prolonged and embarrassingly malodorous due to retention of menstrual blood. Blood clots form and remain behind the infibulation, once more creating a fertile breeding ground for infection. When a girl marries, her infibulation has to be opened by her bridegroom, who does so generally with the help of "the little knife," creating a tear, which he then gradually enlarges with his penis over a period of days, weeks, or even months, until it is large enough to permit intercourse. When the woman gives birth, her infibulation prevents her from dilating normally, and the vulva therefore has to be extensively incised anteriorly to allow expulsion of the newborn. After giving birth, she is once more infibulated to pinhole size, and the process of reopening is repeated after each birth. Persistent or recurrent infections are quite naturally an integral part of this picture, considering the overwhelmingly septic conditions under which all of this takes place. Hemorrhage is equally common (5).

Like so many things concerning women in an Afro-Arab Islamic culture, emotional pathology among them is not highly visible there. Although I did see occasional evidence of it among women and girls on a day to day basis in Sudan, it was rare. Major psychiatric breakdown as a result of circumcision and its consequences is rarely observed among the Sudanese, and this was verified by all the health professionals that were interviewed in this study.

Quite possibly this is related to the fact that among the Sudanese, female circumcision is regarded as an entirely normal event, necessary not only to the welfare of the entire family, but health promoting and necessary to the well-being of the girl herself, and this is an attitude that is strongly communicated to the little girl also. (Both women and men interviewed expressed surprise, shock, and often genuine concern when I revealed that I myself was not circumcised, fearing for me in my thereby unprotected state and expressing anxiety that all manner of evil was about to befall me.)

Sudanese psychiatrists who were interviewed also cited the cohesive and warmly supportive influence of the Sudanese extended family as a powerful force in creating emotional stability and adaptability in girls. My own experiences in Sudan verify that the emotional life of children there is characteristically rich, secure and joyful, and that they develop in an atmosphere of enviable emotional security relative to the experience of the average child in the Western world. This early emotional security tends to further a strong marital bonding for both sexes in later life.

Uncircumcised girls are often subjected to great peer pressure, and have been known to press for their own circumcisions when parents do not do this promptly enough. They are ridiculed by those who have already undergone the rite for still having "that dirty thing dangling between their legs," and they are told that they smell bad. Although there is some small tendency among the educated classes to perform less drastic or "modified" circumcisions, the girls are indoctrinated that if they are not "properly" circumcised, that is pharaonically, no one will want to marry them, or that their husbands will reject them, patronize prostitutes or take a second wife. In a country where women have absolutely no economic power, these are potent threats.

A "proper" circumcision, the girl is assured on the other hand, will make her sweet smelling and pure, pleasing to Allah and to the man she is to marry. It will bring honor to her family, place high value on her in the eyes of the community, and will be a source of pride to her.

How fully all of this is accepted by a girl is evidenced most clearly by the fact that when a woman is asked at what age her circumcision occurred, she is likely to answer: "This was done for me by my family when I was such and such an age." *For* me, not *to* me.

As McLean observes in her Minority Rights Group Report (7):

> Clearly, if in a community sufficient pressure is put on a child to believe that her genitals are dirty, and dangerous, or a source of irresistible temptation, she will feel relieved to be made like everyone else. To be different produces anxiety and mental conflict. An unexcised, noninfibulated girl is despised and made the target of ridicule, and no one in the community will marry her. Thus what is clearly understood to be her life's work, namely marriage and childbearing, is denied her. In a tightly-knit society where mutilation is the rule, it will be the . . . [uncircumcised woman] . . . who suffers psychologically, unless she has another very strong identity to substitute for the community identity which she has lost.

In interviewing a small handful of uncircumcised girls in Sudan, the daughters of educated families that had been exposed to non-circumcising cultures such as the Western world or Saudi Arabia, I found this to be a very accurate observation.

The rites themselves are couched in mystery, and although the girl generally realizes that something fearsome will happen to her, that there will be pain as something is cut from her, she is helped not to focus on this aspect of the event. When girls request of their families that they be circumcised, they are totally ignorant of the consequences of this act on their future health and welfare. In the interviews women often voiced their feelings about this: "I had no idea. I was so young, hardly more than a baby, and they never tell you about that part of it. You don't realize what it is really all about until they do it to you, and by then it is too late."

Girls tend to look forward to their circumcision with a mixture of dread and eagerness. It is not uncommon for them to manifest severe anxiety and a generalized phobic reaction as the time approaches. They become afraid of being touched, of knives, of social gatherings, of going to sleep. This is occasioned by the fact that by the time their turn comes, they have experienced at a distance, if not actually seen, the circumcision of other girls, have heard the frantic screams, quite possibly seen the blood of their predecessors.

The day of circumcision is considered the most important day in a girl's life, far more important than her wedding day. The principal effects of the operation is to create in young girls an intense awareness of their sexuality and anxiety concerning its meaning, its social significance. In general, the practice emphasizes punishment and social control, clearly indicating to the small child a sense of the mystery and importance of sex, at the same time creating an all-consuming terror of the evils of unchaste behavior in her (1).

Uneducated Sudanese women are aware of no alternatives to circumcision, and 98% of them still never see the inside of a school. Education for females is not a positive value in an Afro-Arab Islamic society. Everything is clearly defined for the Sudanese girl. There are no complicated choices for her to make. Circumcision is a fact of her life, just as tremendous hardship, poverty, scarce water and little food, back breaking labor, overwhelming heat, dust storms, crippling disease, unalleviated pain and early death are facts of her life. Circumcision happens to everyone. This is the only reality, and she accepts it as everyone else accepts it. She adapts, and while nearly every town has its isolated madman or madwoman, flight into unreality makes its appearance only rarely.

Koso-Thomas (3) in a study of clitoridectomy in Sierra Leone points out that women in some African societies actually oppose any attempts to abolish circumcision practices:

Because traditional patrilineal communities assign women a subordinate role, women feel unable to oppose community dictates, even when these affect them adversely. Many women even go to great lengths to support these dictates by organizing groups which mete out punishment to non-conforming women, and conduct hostile campaigns against passive observers. Women championing many of the cultural practices adopted by their communities do not realize that some of the practices they promote were designed to subjugate them, and more importantly, to control their sexuality and to maintain male chauvinistic attitudes in respect to marital and sexual relations. Most African women have still not developed the sensitivity to feel deprived or to see in many cultural practices a violation of their human rights. The consequence of this is that, in the mid-1980s when most women in Africa have voting rights and can influence political decisions against practices harmful to their health, they continue to uphold the dictates and mores of the communities in which they live; they seem, in fact, to regard traditional beliefs as inviolable.

It is only among a small group of educated women in the capital that an awareness is growing, fed by outside sources, that other options exist, and it is among these women that a sense of outrage is beginning to make its appearance. It is among this group that the interviewer found evidence of surfacing rage, rejection of the assigned feminine role, rejection of sexuality in marriage, rejection of the parental family. Here the woman grapples with the realization that she has been, if not an unconsenting victim, at least an uninformed and unconsulted one. It is here that one encounters the determination in a woman not to subject her children to what she herself has suffered. This determination is, however, in nearly every case thwarted by the older, tradition dominated women of the family, who frustrate and override the desires of the educated parents, by abducting and circumcising their daughters while the parents are away from home. Nonetheless, this tiny group of women bears watching for the effects that it may have on the practice of circumcision in the next generation, when the decision concerning their own granddaughters will be up to them.

Pharaonically circumcised women are only rarely able to receive medical care, since most Sudanese physicians are male, and most Sudanese men will not allow their wives to be examined by a male doctor. Moen (8) comments that obviously only rare cases obtain psychiatric evaluation or care, but among those females who have received attention, diagnoses have included loss of self esteem, feelings of victimization, severe anxiety prior to the operations, depression associated with complications such as infection, hemorrhage, shock, septicemia and retention of urine, chronic irritability and sexual frustration.

Maher (6) in a study done in Cairo, where Pharaonic circumcision as well as the less severe practice of clitoridectomy are common, compared circumcised with uncircumcised women. He found that about 10% of the former had feelings of inferiority physically and psychosexually. The difficulties they experienced in their marital and sexual life resulted in depression in about 5%. This was ten times the frequency reported for the uncircumcised group. Divorce occurred in 6% of the circumcised group, as opposed to less than 1% in the non-circumcised.

Upon questioning circumcised women about their orgasmic ability in what they often professed to be very happy and strongly bonded marriages, the interviewer found that the larger number of them claimed to have regular and often frequent and intense orgasmic experiences (climax). Although the object of Pharaonic and other forms of circumcision is to reduce or cancel out the sex drive in women by attenuating sexual sensitivity, it fails to do so in the majority of cases. Obviously, the sex drive resides not in the structures that are excised, but in the brain, and whatever else constitutes the sexual nervous system. This being the case, it is not surprising that when the clitoris and labia are removed from this sexual nervous system in a small child, she will compensate by developing a greater sensitivity in other parts of the system when it reaches maturation. The interviewer found no reason to doubt the veracity of the claims of sexual satisfaction made by the circumcised women she interviewed, given particularly the animated and joyous demeanor that often accompanied the telling, and the vivid and credible descriptions of the experiences that were elicited.

Orgasm that is elicited in women without clitoral or even vaginal stimulation has been discussed by other researchers, and is definitely known to exist (9, 10, 11, 12).

A considerable number of women, however, are able to overcome neither the physical nor the psychological damage that circumcision and the adult series of trauma that follow it has left them with. Among doctors interviewed, several reported cases, especially among Pharaonically circumcised educated women, where these expressed the fear that they might not be adequate to their husbands' sexual needs, and many, paradoxically suffer from feelings of guilt because they are not able to function better sexually, due to physically or psychologically disabling circumstances.

Interviews with gynecologists reveal that the women suffer acutely from anxiety and depression particularly during the stressful periods occasioned by an impending marriage or birth. They are tormented by the knowledge that there will be tremendous pain, that it is inescapable, and that they are totally powerless to avoid or stop it.

Adolescent girls are tortured by the pressure of damned up menstrual fluid, which a tight infibulation prevents them from discharging, and depression is common among them. Doctors report that when the infibulation is surgically eased, in the few cases where the family allows this to be done, the depression recedes.

Such evidence of psychosexual and emotional distress comes as no surprise, in view of the cumulative sexual trauma experienced by Sudanese females in the course of a lifetime. So far only a handful of studies discussing the emotional repercussions of Pharaonic circumcision and other, less drastic forms of female circumcision have come to light. While familial and social factors tend to mitigate the emotional effects of these practices on women, and most of them by necessity develop a truly remarkable degree of adaptation, there is evidence that there are many who experience not only repeated intense physical suffering, but who periodically suffer intense emotional pain as well.

DISCUSSION

Pharaonic circumcision as it is practiced in the Sudan is a stunning illustration of the impact of cultural beliefs and values in shaping personal/psychological experiences. A practice which to the Western mind appears both abusive and degrading, is interpreted in the Sudanese mind as purifying and ennobling. Its staunchest defenders are its survivors, self-assured, respected old women, who choose to inflict the most extreme mutilations on their granddaughters, in order to optimally enhance their value as a family commodity and to insure a favorable marriage for them.

While the consequences of such extreme circumcision and infibulation are often ruinous to the physical health of the girls and young women involved, it is perceived by them as a totally normal phenomenon, a manifestation of family concern and love, a purification, and it thereby constitutes a source of pride and self-esteem to them. It strengthens their sense of security in the family and of social worth in the society at large.

It is these positive values that basically differentiate what we as Westerners might describe as physical mutilation and abuse from the various types of emotional mutilations and physical abuse inflicted so frequently on children in our own culture, which are so characteristically destructive to their self-esteem, their ego strength and their sense of security.

Darcer (2), a Sudanese researcher, shows that among a cross section of 3,210 Sudanese women interviewed by her, 82.6% favor a continuation of the practice, in spite of the fact that many aspects of the quality of their lives are obviously blighted and reduced by it. This number only barely differs from the 87% of men favoring its continuation. Even among the remainder, who give voice to doubts about the desirability of or even outspoken opposition to the custom, an actual refusal to continue its practice on their own daughters is practically unheard of.

A recent news item reported Ugandan adolescents of both sexes, about to be circumcised in their villages, attempting to escape *en masse* into non-circumcising territories, and being hunted down by the village elders. In Sudan, where circumcision is performed on very small girls, not even this remote possibility of escape exists for those who wish to avoid circumcision. The rite is performed before the child is capable of choice, and it is likely that this is a major factor in making the entire concept of choice so inconceivable at a later stage in life, when decisions are made about their own children.

Sudanese gynecologists, who are at the forefront of the truly minute group of educated individuals that actively opposes the practice of Pharaonic circumcision, have adopted the policy of advising conflicted mothers to delay the circumcision of their daughters until they themselves can make an informed decision. To reinforce their argument they tend to say that times may be changing, and that with more upper class Sudanese men being influenced by Western ideas and education, they will want modern and uncircumcised wives, who will be healthier marital partners. They argue that the most advantageous marriages may soon be made by uncircumcised girls.

One would like to believe that there is some sort of solution to be found there. But in view of the powerful culturally embedded forces and the rule of ancient custom that lock these practices into place, it does not appear likely that there will be a meaningful change of any sort in the foreseeable future.

(Note: A more exhaustive treatment of this topic may be found in the author's forthcoming book, *Prisoners of Ritual: An Odyssey into Female Genital Circumcision in Africa*, The Haworth Press, New York, in press.)

REFERENCES

1. Abdalla, R. M. D. (1982). *Sisters in Affliction—Circumcision and Infibulation of Women in Africa*. London: Zed Press.

2. Darcer, A. el. (1982). *Women Why Do You Weep?* London: Zed Press.

3. Koso-Thomas, O. (1987). *The Circumcision of Women: A Strategy for Eradication*. London: Zed Books Ltd.

4. Lerner, G. (1986). *The Creation of Patriarchy*. New York: Oxford University Press.

5. Lightfoot-Klein, H. (in press) *Prisoners of Ritual: An Odyssey into Female Genital Circumcision in Africa*. New York: The Haworth Press.

6. Maher, M. (1981). Medical Dangers of Female Circumcision. *Int. Planned Parenthood Fed.*, 2, 1–2.

7. McLean, S. (Ed.). (1980). *Female Circumcision, Excision and Infibulation, Report No. 47*. London: Minority Rights Group.

8. Moen, E. W. (1983). Genital Mutilation: Everywoman's Problem, Working Paper #22. In *Working Papers on Women in International Development*. East Lansing, MI: Michigan State Univ.

9. Money, J. et al. (1955). Hermaphroditism: Recommendations Concerning Assignment of Sex, and Psychologic Management. *Bull. of Johns Hopkins Hospital 97(4)*, 284–300.

10. Ogden, G. (November 10–13, 1988). Women and Sexual Ecstasy. Paper presented at the *31st Annual Meeting of the Society for the Scientific Study of Sex*, San Francisco.

11. Otto, H. A. (November 10–13, 1988). The Extended Orgasm: New Perspectives. Paper presented at the *31st Annual Meeting of the Society for the Scientific Study of Sex*, San Francisco.

12. Verkauf, B. S. (1975). Acquired Clitoral Enlargement. *Medical Aspects of Human Sexuality, 9(4)*, 134.

13. Verzin, J. A. (1975). Sequelae of Female Circumcision. *Tropical Doctor, 5*, 163–169.

THE PENIS PIN: AN UNSOLVED PROBLEM IN THE RELATIONS BETWEEN THE SEXES IN BORNEO

Donald E. Brown

Although little is known about human sexuality in Borneo, one aspect of Bornean sexuality has been the subject of scholarly writing in every decade since the 1830s: the use of the penis pin. In spite of this long period of scholarly attention, we still don't really know what the penis pin is all about; that is, we don't know what motivates the practice. Let us begin with a summary of what *is* known about Bornean penis pins.

The penis pin is a part of the Southeast Asian cultural complex that in its commonest form involves surgery to the penis to install a device that allegedly enhances female sexual pleasure. This complex may have had its origin in India, and portions of the complex have diffused to peoples far outside Southeast Asia (6,52).

In Borneo the surgery involves piercing the penis—much as one might pierce an earlobe—so that a pin can be worn in it.[1] Sometimes the pins are simply straight rods with rounded ends. More typically, the pins have protuberances at each end, at least in part to keep the pins from falling out. In the simplest of these forms, the pins look like little barbells; in more complex variants, the protuberances have a considerable variety of shapes and textures. Sometimes a tube is inserted into the pierced hole in the penis to serve as a sleeve within which the pin can rotate (14, 29). One recent account (34) says that the Berawan of Long Terawan use the various sizes of shear pins of outboard motor propellers as penis pins. (1, 2, 14, 23, 24, 29, 38, 40, 41).

Palang, which in Malay or Iban means cross or crossbar, is probably the commonest name for the penis pin in the literature. But the Kayan term, *uttang*, is also widely reported. Less frequent are the Kenyah term, *aja*, and a term used in southeast Borneo, *kaleng* or *kaling*. (For discussions of these terms and many of the terms for parts of the penis pin and the devices used to install them, see especially 3, 11, 15, 37.)

The shafts of the penis pins are made from a variety of materials, including bone, bamboo, wood, and metal; brass is particularly common. The materials employed to construct the protuberances show even greater variation—including, for example, gemstone, glass, seeds, feathers, and pig's bristles (4, 10, 17, 20, 22, 23, 25, 37, 38, 42, 46, 49, 53). The diameters of the pins vary from about 2 to 4 mm; lengths vary from 21 mm to more than 5 cm (1, 8, 11, 15, 27, 34, 46). One source (46) says that the pin should be as long as the middle phalange of one's finger, while another source (11) says as long as the distance between the teeth (assuming that distance between the teeth means between the upper and lower incisors when the mouth is held wide open, these two measures are both about the same).

The pins always or nearly always pierce the glans penis, and probably most commonly are placed in a horizontal position above the urethra (4, 8, 10, 11, 17, 25, 29, 30, 41, 42, 46, 51). But sometimes the piercing deliberately transects the urethra (17, 30, 46), and sometimes the piercing is vertical or at an angle (2, 11, 42). As many as five pins may be worn at once (46), but a single pin is probably commonest. Most pins appear to be easily removable (1, 14, 17, 30, 37, 42, 43, 53).

The Penis Pin: An Unsolved Problem in the Relations Between the Sexes in Borneo," by Donald E. Brown, reprinted from *Female and Male in Borneo: Contributions of Challenges to Gender Studies*, Borneo Research Council, 1990.

A clamp made of wood or bamboo is usually placed on the penis prior to the piercing operation in order to drive blood from the penis at the point where it will be pierced. This desensitizes the penis and reduces bleeding. The man who is about to be pierced may achieve further desensitizing by standing in water. A pointed shaft is then driven through the penis, guided by holes in the clamp. After the penis is pierced and the clamp has been removed, a temporary pin or wire may be employed to keep the piercing open during healing (1, 22, 24, 27, 29, 30, 33, 39, 42, 43, 46).

There is little consensus on the extent of pain and risk of medical complications that the penis pins entail for either men or woman (4, 10, 15, 17, 33, 37, 42, 49). Kuhlewein (30) looked into the matter most carefully—examining the genitals of 2500 Bornean men—and reports only that he found no evidence of lesser fertility among those native groups with the higher percentages of men who had penis pins. Friesen and Schuman (14) give the only specific evidence of a medical problem: a penis pin that had been left inserted for a lengthy period acquired calcium deposits and thus had to be removed surgically.

Penis pins are normally installed at puberty or later (8, 10, 14, 30, 42, 43, 53). Sometimes specialists perform the operation (10, 19, 21, 46). There appears to be little ritual or supernatural belief associated with the practice, though the piercing operation is conducted in secret among the Iban (46). For some peoples there are reports of certain qualifications that must be met before one can wear the pin (11, 37, 42). For example, a man may have to have been on a headhunt or have taken a head before he can wear the pin. Sometimes rank is indicated by the quality of the material of the man's penis pin or by such ornamentation as accompanies it (10, 33, 42, 53).

There is considerable variation in the proportion of men who wear penis pins. For example, among some groups in south central Borneo virtually all men had pins; among Iban in recent times about one third of the men wore them (10, 30, 46).

Although penis pins are either absent or rare among the coastal Malays of Borneo, the pins are widely reported among the pagans in all areas (4, 8, 11, 14, 15, 17, 18, 20, 22, 25, 27, 29, 30, 31, 33, 34, 41, 42, 46, 47, 51, 54) except north-central and northwest Borneo (1, 54). The most frequent reports seem to be from the south or southeast. The Kayan are the only group credited with the invention and dissemination of the practice within Borneo—allegedly having introduced it to the Iban, Kenyah, and some Punan groups (8, 21, 33, 53, 54).

Among some peoples penis pins are very much a part of public culture. The Iban, for example, commonly depicted penis pins on fabrics (18), and an Iban or Berawan man may tattoo himself in a way that advertises that he is equipped with a penis pin (34, 46). Derek and Monica Freeman found the penis pin in a sketch by a young Iban boy, which implies that the use of the pins was common knowledge from an early age (D. Freeman, personal communication). In central Borneo, statues designed to ward off spirits are equipped with ostentatious penis pins (43).

Finally, we know that one explanation for the use of penis pins is very widely reported, but that other explanations are given too. By far the commonest explanation is that the penis pin enhances sexual pleasure for women (2, 10, 11, 14, 15, 17, 21, 29, 33, 37, 38, 46). The point is embroidered in a number of ways. For example, it is said that women may request their husbands to get pierced, or that women will divorce husbands who won't be pierced (15), or that once habituated to it women cannot go without the pin (38). Women are alleged to say that the penis pin is to sex what salt is to rice (15,37). On the other had, it is also said that it is older women in particular (and so presumably not just women in general) who want their husbands to have the penis pin (11, 29, 37).

Among the alternative explanations, two that appear in the primary sources referring to Borneo require only brief comment. First, Miller (40) says that the purpose of the penis pin is to infibulate, i.e., to ensure celibacy. But there is little reason to trust his testimony—which runs counter to all other evidence—for he was merely a traveller in Borneo and he did not speak the local languages. Second, it is sometimes alleged—and the allegation may be indigenous to Borneo—that penis pins have been inspired by the *palang*-like protuberances on the penis of the Bornean rhinoceros (21, 34, 46). However, even if this allegation is correct, it is not an alternative explanation of the purpose of the penis pin, of *why* the rhinoceros was imitated.

Three other explanations are found in the secondary or non-Bornean literature. One is that the penis pin is a precautionary measure against folk illness, called *koro*, that is found in China and parts of Southeast Asia (56). It is believed that the penis of a man afflicted with this disease shrinks into his body; when it shrinks all the way in, the man dies. The penis pin, according to this explanation, prevents the penis from shrinking all the way, or gives one something to hold on to should this fate seem imminent. There is no indication, however, that this explanation is known in Borneo. Another explanation from secondary sources is that the penis pin is an antidote or weapon against the vagina *dentata*, the vagina with teeth (32). A belief that the vagina has teeth is widespread, and the penis pin might conceivably be a response to this male fear. Again, however, there is no evidence that this is a Bornean explanation. Yet another explanation is that penis piercing, like other forms of body piercing, results from the idea that such practices magically strengthen the body, or at least the part of the body that is pierced, (29). Judging by published materials on penis inserts somewhere in Southeast Asia (6), this explanation may have merit, but it is an idea that has not been pursued in literature on Bornean penis pins. Since none of these three explanations has so far been put to the test by persons with experience in Borneo, their relevance to Bornean peoples is uncertain.

The only explanation of the penis pin that is found in the literature and that commands attention as a serious alternative to the woman-pleaser explanation is that the penis pin is a product of male machismo (bravado). This explanation is discussed in later sections of this paper.

The claim that the penis pin is a woman pleaser, even though it appears to be a widespread indigenous explanation, poses some real and very interesting problems—problems that lead away from what is known into areas of uncertainty. A few considerations about the woman-pleaser explanation are particularly important:

First, there is all too little evidence that it is *women* who say the penis pin gives them pleasure. Only a single published source gives unequivocal evidence that a woman was interviewed to obtain this explanation in Borneo, but what she is reported as actually saying is not a ringing endorsement of penis pins. When asked "how she enjoyed" her husband's three penis pins, she replied that "she preferred to make love when he only had one" (2). Moreover, this woman was interviewed by a man, in a bantering manner, in mixed company, and through two interpreters—so the result carries little weight anyway. While two anthropologists and a linguist (James Peter Brosius, B.J.L. Sellato, and Patricia Wittier, personal communications) report that at least one woman told each of them that the penis pin gave them pleasure, the questioning was not private and was not pursued in depth.

Second, the neurology, physiology, and anatomy of the female genitalia provide little or no clear evidence that the penis pin could bring pleasure to women. According to Kinsey and his associates (28), the inner walls of the vagina are generally insensitive (a partial exception will be discussed below). This suggests that once intromission is achieved, the penis pin should give the woman neither pleasure nor pain (unless the pressure of the penis pin were transmitted through the insensitive vaginal walls to sensitive tissue that lies beyond).

Third, the subjective reports of women in the West provide little support for the woman-pleasing explanation of penis pins. Comfort (9) reports that women in the West show little interest in "French ticklers," which are the nonsurgically-attached functional equivalents of penis pins. In the literature on piercers in the West, which is strongly oriented to a male—and particularly a male homosexual—audience, there are only a few statements by women who report enjoying sex with pierced men, along with a few who report not enjoying it, and a few noticing no difference (5, 7, 52).

Fourth, the shapes and sizes of some of the penis pins seem more likely to do damage in sexual intercourse than to give pleasure. Kuhlewein (30) describes some of the penis pins as "monstrous" and "sharp"; Harrisson (22) says some are elaborated with broken glass. Women that I have spoken to in the U.S. not only express skepticism that penis pins would enhance their sexual pleasure, they sometimes indicate that the very thought of some of the penis pins is painful and repugnant.

Thus there is no solid evidence from Bornean women that penis pins enhance their sexual pleasure, and there is little in the way of non-Bornean evidence to suggest that the pins really should or normally do give pleasure. What other evidence bears on the matter, and what are we to make of these reports that Bornean women find pleasure in the penis pin?

A potentially relevant piece of evidence is that traditional pagan Bornean societies were among the most sexually egalitarian societies known to ethnography (see, e.g.,13, 55). Given the high level of female autonomy that this entails, perhaps it makes sense that Bornean men should go to unusual lengths to try to please Bornean women.

Another consideration is that under certain circumstances perhaps penis pins *could* give pleasure, or at least cause no harm. For example, if the pin had smooth ends and did not protrude too far it might cause no harm. If the pin caused no physical harm, the psychological effect of a man wearing a penis pin might be beneficial for a number of reasons (for example, Jerome Rousseau has suggested to me that a woman might derive an indirect pleasure from knowing how much her man was willing to endure in order to try to please her—the "thought" counting more than the actual "give" to her). Or, since recent literature on what is called the "Grafenberg spot" (see, e.g., 26) suggests that there may be a region in the vaginal wall that *is* pleasurably sensitive, perhaps the penis pin rubs this post. In most cases, however, this does not seem likely: the Grafenberg spot—if indeed it exists—is on the upper surface of the vagina, while most penis pins protrude on the sides. Another possibility, mentioned above, is that the penis pin is felt through the vaginal walls, causing pleasurable sensations elsewhere (e.g., in the perineum, which, according to Kinsey *et al.* [28, 36], probably is pleasurably stimulated in some forms of deep vaginal penetration). Finally, since some individuals in the West find pleasure in pain, perhaps what is rare here might be commoner elsewhere (assuming that the penis pin could be felt at all).

But in contradistinction to these conditions that might make the woman-pleaser explanation plausible, consider the following questions:

If the idea is to give women greater sexual pleasure, why attach the device surgically? Why not just wrap something around the penis? Non-surgically attached penis augmentations for sexual intercourse (like the "French ticklers" mentioned above) are widely reported in Southeast Asia: among Bornean people they were already known in the nineteenth century, at least to the Iban (33). Surgical attachment must have some rationale that has no obvious connection with pleasing women (unless there are the indirect psychological benefits mentioned above).

If the penis pin is a woman-pleaser, why is it often associated with rank, prestige, or achievement? The association between rank and surgically installed penis augmentations of one sort or another is widespread in Southeast Asia (6)—probably in part because rank-consciousness spills over into many facets of Southeast Asian societies (3). Whatever the reason may be for this association, it suggests some factor or factors with no clear connection to providing sexual pleasure for women.

If the penis pin is a woman-pleaser, why is it associated with weapons? There are at least three indications in the literature that Bornean peoples saw the penis pin as a sort of sexual weapon:

One is that in an upland Kenyah account of the introduction of the penis pin the first woman on whom it was used died as a consequence: this would have ended the practice, according to Harrisson, "had counterbalancing impulses not been so strong" (22). I take this to mean that although the Kenyah were willing to risk the danger of the penis pin for the pleasure that it allegedly afforded, they knew that the penis pin was lethally dangerous—and thus like a weapon.

Another indication is that the Mendalam Kayans erected large warrior-like figures to ward off disease-causing spirits. The figures had exposed and outsized genitals with penis pins (43). Since neither the Kayans nor other Borneans normally expose their genitals, and since such phallic displays are widely regarded as threats (12), there is reason to think that the inclusion of the penis pin is part of the figures' threatening aspect. Surely it makes little sense to prominently place an object designed to give pleasure on a figure that is designed to frighten.

Yet another indication of the equation of the penis pin with weapons is found in the taunts from women that an Iban man is reported to endure if he does not wear a penis pin: that he is "unarmed" or is "with spear unsharpened" (46). The latter taunt implies that the penis itself is seen as a weapon—as it sometimes is elsewhere.

In addition to the troubling questions I have just posed, there are a few indications of a skeptical attitude toward the woman-pleaser explanation from scholars well informed about Borneo. One of the most important is found in the report of an extensive medical study of men who wore penis pins (30). As noted above, the medical personnel who conducted this study in 1929 examined the genitals of 2500 adult males, representing several ethnic groups dwelling in the upper Mahakam region of Kalimantan. Kuhlewein thought that the "one sex will rather inculpate the other" for the perpetuation of the practice (30). If I understand him correctly, Kuhlewein was suggesting that although men gave him the usual reason for wearing penis pins—that "the wives will it so" (30)—he somehow formed the impression that women told a different story, i.e., that men wore the pins for their own (unstated) reasons.

Even Harrisson, who clearly accepts the woman-pleaser explanation (22), notes that masculine ideals—the ability and willingness to endure the pain and danger of piercing—is part of the story (24). Derek and Monica Freeman, who studied the Iban, concluded that male bravado was even more important than Harrisson thought (D. Freeman, personal communication).

The Freemans were able to discuss the penis pin with a few Iban women, who denied that it gave them pleasure and who viewed the penis pin as a "potentially, if not actually, injurious and injury-inflicting device." The women saw the use of penis pins as "a peculiar male conceit." The Freemans concluded that among the Iban the penis pin is an ornament that men wear for essentially male reasons: wearing the penis pin is a male "conceit or affectation," and the claim that it pleases women is "a male rationalization and projection" (D. Freemen, personal correspondence). If the Freemans are correct, the sexual pleasure of women may be a very small part of the explanation of penis pins.

What the evidence suggests, then, is a wide-spread Bornean folk conception that men wear penis pins in order to enhance the sexual pleasure of women—but with no clear evidence that this conception adequately captures the real reason(s) why Bornean men wear penis pins. The most glaring problem is that the validity of this conception is not supported by the most relevant kind of evidence: reliable female testimony to the effect that they do enjoy penis pins—or even that they allow their men to have intercourse with them while wearing the pins. Clearly we need a Bornean women's perspective on this matter, and those who are presently in a position to throw light on it—women's health care professionals, for example—could be of real assistance in providing this obviously important evidence (use of the "monstrous" and "sharp" penis pins would presumably leave telltale signs for the gynecologist or obstetrician, and surely even women from the more backward populations in Borneo occasionally see these specialists). If it should turn out that Bornean women do find pleasure in penis pins, it would then be of some interest to know why and how (in the anatomical and physiological sense).

But if it should turn out that Bornean women are not so pleased by penis pins as the reported folk belief would have it, the next question is: why is the practice nonetheless perpetuated? Two answers can be suggested, both having more to do with the male psyche than with female sexuality. One, already mentioned, is male machismo. Since machismo manifests itself in painful and dangerous mutilations of the male body among many peoples throughout the world, it is entirely reasonable to assume that penis piercing is a Bornean variant of the phenomenon, i.e., that machismo is at least a substantial component in the explanation of penis pins. Another component, I will argue, is the possibility of some Bornean cultural *mis*conceptions.

One of the striking ways in which cultural conceptions and reality can and often do diverge is each sex's conceptions of the other sex's sexuality (50). Male conceptions of female sexuality in the West are heavily influenced not merely by ignorance but by wishful thinking and the projection of male attitudes onto females. Marcus (35) coined the term "pornotopia" to refer to certain aspects of the fantasy world of pornography. The penis pin is perhaps an element in a Bornean pornotopia, a reflection less of Bornean female sexuality than of the Bornean male's image of female sexuality. Now, given the autonomy of Bornean women, as noted earlier, it is understandable that Bornean men might be particularly preoccupied with how to win and keep their women—and so long as men imagined that penis pins would give them greater sexual access to women, the incentive to wear the pin might be substantial.

One of the few Bornean accounts of the origin of the penis pin clearly expresses this concern for men to please women *and*, in all probability, provides a glimpse of pornotopia. In a Kayan version of the invention of the penis pin, a woman who masturbates with a rolled up leaf tells her lover that he is no better than the leaf. So he invents and installs the penis pin, which she does find better (23). There are some clear messages in this story—that the man wanted to please a woman, that he didn't think he could do it with nature's equipment alone, that the penis pin seemed like a reasonable solution to his problem, and that it worked.

But in spite of the concern for womanhood that this story expresses, there is reason to think that it isn't a woman's story: it assumes that vaginal penetration is a normal or even necessary part of female masturbation. This assumption, according to the findings of Kinsey *et al.* among American women, is another male "conceit" (28, 36). Few women in the West masturbate in a manner that involves anything more than superficial penetration of the vagina (since that is all that is required to stimulate the clitoris). Like so many origin stories, then, this one may be, as Freeman suggests, a rationalization rather than an explanation.

In sum, the most widely reported explanation of the penis pin in Borneo—an explanation that focuses on female sexuality and that derives from or is compatible with Bornean cultural conceptions—may have little or no validity. The true explanation may lie more with males than with females, most with male machismo and male fantasies than with female sexuality. At present we simply do not know which motives—conscious or unconscious—are the principal ones that lie behind the use of the penis pin.

The state of our ignorance is of course partly the result of the privacy or secrecy that surrounds the sexual act itself and often much else that relates to sexuality, in Borneo as everywhere else. But part of the problem is that many of those who have written about the penis pin probably did not realize that there even was a problem: the thought that Bornean women crave the stimulation of an augmented penis, even a dangerously augmented one, is a thought as much at home in Western pornotopia as it appears to be in Bornean. Until the pioneering research of Kinsey and his associates, and of Masters and Johnson—all of whom *did* get female perspectives on sexuality—most men simply lacked a reason for thinking that female sexuality might be other than what they imagined it to be. In readily accepting the woman-pleaser explanation of the penis pin, as many Western observers did, they may have been content to perpetuate a myth rather than identify it as such.

A careful attempt to find out what the penis pin *is* all about would not only give us a much better understanding of the traditional peculiarities of sexuality, of images of sexuality, and of the relations between the sexes in Borneo, but might well throw light on these topics nearly everywhere. For what may be fundamental components of the Bornean penis pin complex—male and female sexualities, machismo, and pornotopia—may also be fundamental components in the relations between the sexes among many if not all peoples, differing only in the local ways in which they are combined and expressed.

NOTE

1. There is a single report of an alternative form of surgery to the penis in Borneo: after presenting a conventional account of Bornean penis pins, Hansen (1988) also states that "Bahau River villagers" scarify the upper surface of the glans penis by making incisions into which ash is rubbed. As a modern variant, men go to a government dispensary, where the operation is performed with an anesthetic and the incisions are sutured so as to leave 3 to 5 parallel ridges.

REFERENCES

1. Appell, G. N. (1968). The Penis Pin at Peabody Museum, Harvard University, Journal of Malaysian Branch, Royal Asiatic Society 41:203–205.

2. Barclay, James (1980). A Stroll Through Borneo. London: Hodder and Stoughton. (See pp. 90, 94, 96, and photo.)

3. Barth, J. P. J. (1910). Boesagsch-Nederlandsch Woordenbock. Batavia: Lansdrukkerij. (See p. 174.)

4. Bock, Carl Alfred (1887). Reise in Oost-en Zuid-Borneo van Koetei naar Banjarmassim . . . in 1879 en 1880. 's-Gravenhage: Martinus Nijhoff. (See p. 98).

5. Brown, Donald E. (1976). Principles of Social Structure: Southeast Asia. London: Duckworth.

    _____. n.d. Piercers in America. Unpublished typescript.

6. Brown, Donald E., James W. Edwards, and Ruth Moore (1988). The Penis Inserts of Southeast Asia: An Annotated Bibliography with an Overview and Comparative Perspectives. Occasional Paper No. 15. Center for South and Southeast Asian Studies, University of California, Berkeley.

7. Buhrich, Neil (1983). The Association of Erotic Piercing with Homosexuality, Sadomasochism, Bondage, Fetishism, and Tattoos. Archives of Sexual Behavior 12:167–71.

8. Burns, Robert (1849). The Kayans of the North-West of Borneo. Journal of the Indian Archipelago and Eastern Asia 3:140–52. (Reprinted in the Sarawak Museum Journal 3:477–489; see p. 486.)

9. Comfort, Alex ed. (1972). The Joy of Sex: A Gourmet Guide to Love Making. New York: Simon and Schuster.

10. Dalton, John (1837). [1831] Mr. Dalton's Essay on the Diaks of Borneo, In Notices of the Indian Archipelago and Adjacent Countries. Ed. by J.H. Moor. Singapore. Pp. 41–54. (See p. 53.)

11. DeWall, H. von (1855). Aanteekeningen omtrent de Nordoostkust van Borneo. Tijdschrift voor Indische Taal-, Land- en Vokenkunde 4:423–458. (See pp. 457–58.)

12. Eibl-Eibesfeldt, Iranaus (1979). Human Ethology: Concepts and Implications for the Sciences of Man. The Behavioral and Brain Sciences 2:1–57.

13. Freeman, Derek (1981). Some Reflections on the Nature of Iban Society. An Occasional Paper of the Department of Anthropology, Research School of Pacific Studies. The Australian National University, Canberra.

14. Friesen, Stanley R. and Norvid D. Schuman (1964). Medicine in Sarawak: The Medical Missionary Program at Work. The Journal of the Kansas Medical Society 65:125–131. (See pp. 128, 129.)

15. Gaffron, von (1859). Over Menschen met Staarten op Borneo. Natuurkundig Tijdschrift voor Nederlansch-Indi 20:227–232. (See pp. 231–32.)

16. Galvin, A. D. [1967] [Kenyah Vocabulary]. Ms. [Miri, Sarawak]. (See p. 2.)

17. Griffith, G. T. (1955). Health and Disease in Young Sea Dayak Men. Sarawak Museum Journal 6:322–327. (See p. 327.)

18. Haddon, Alfred C. and Laura Start (1936). Iban or Sea Dayak Fabrics and Their Patterns. Cambridge: The University Press. (See pp. 42, 44.)

19. Hansen, Eric (1988). Stranger in the Forest: On Foot Across Borneo. London: Century (See pp. 224–29.)

20. Hardeland, August (1859). Dajacksch-Deutsches Worterbuch. Amsterdam: Frederik Muller. (This source anomalously describes the *palang* as a ring worn on the male genitals. See p. 400.)

21. Harrisson, Tom (1956). Rhinoceros in Borneo: and Traded to China. Sarawak Museum Journal 7:263–74.

22. _____. (1959). World Within: A Borneo Story. London: The Cresset Press (See pp. 58, 61–62.)

23. _____. (1964). The "Palang," Its History and Proto-History in West Borneo and the Philippines. Journal of the Malaysian Branch, Royal Asiatic Society 37:162–174. (Note that the Povedano MS 1578, which is quoted, has been shown to be a forgery by William Henry Scott.)

24. _____. (1966). The "Palang": II. Three Further Notes. Journal of the Malaysian Branch, Royal Asiatic Society 39:172–74.

25. Hose, Charles and William McDougal (1912). The Pagan Tribes of Borneo: A Description of their Physical, Moral and Intellectual Condition with Some Discussion of their Ethnic Relations. Vol II. London: Macmillan. (Reprinted 1966 by Barnes and Noble.) (See p. 170.)

26. Jayne, Cynthia (1984). Freud, Grafenberg, and the Neglected Vagina: Thoughts Concerning an Historical Omission in Sexology. Journal of Sex Research 20:212–15.

27. Juynboll, H.H. (1909). Katalog des Ethnographischen Reichsmuseums. Band I: Borneo. Leiden: E.J. Brill. (See p. 60.)

28. Kinsey, Alfred C. et al. (1953). Sexual Behavior in the Human Female. Philadelphia: W.B. Saunders Company.

29. Kleiweg de Zwaan, J.P. (1920). Over de Penis-staafjes der Inlanders van den Indischen Archipel. Nederlandsch Tijdschrift voor Geneeskunde II (A):289–293.

30. Kuhlewein, M. von (1930). Report of a Journey to Upper Mahakam (Borneo), February-May 1929. Mededeelingen van den Dienst der Volksgezondheid in Nederlansche-Indie. Foreign-Edition 19:66–152. (See pp. 83, 92, 94–95, 112. This article appeared simultaneously in a Dutch-language version of the same journal.)

31. Le Bar, Frank M., ed. (1972). Ethnic Groups of Insular Southeast Asia. Vol. I. New Haven: HRAF Press (See p. 188.)

32. Legman, G. (1975). No Laughing Matter: An Analysis of Sexual Humor. Bloomington: Indiana University Press. (See p. 431.)

33. Low, Brooke (1892). The Natives of Borneo. Ed. from the Papers of the Late Brooke Low, Esq., by H. Ling Roth. Journal of the Anthropological Institute 22:22–64. (see p. 45.)

34. Macdonald, David (1982). Expedition to Borneo: The Search for Proboscis Monkeys and Other Creatures. London: J.M. Dent & Sons. (See pp. 166–67.)

35. Marcus, Steven (1966). The Other Victorians: A Study of Sexuality and Pornography in Mid-Nineteenth-Century England. New York: Basic Books.

36. Masters, W.H. and V.E. Johnson (1966). Human Sexual Response. Boston: Little, Brown and Company.

37. Mayer, A.B. (1877). Ueber die Perforation des Penis bei den Malayan. Mittheilungen der Anthropologischen Gesellschaft in Wien 7:242–244.

38. Miklucho-Maclay, N. V. (1876a). Ueber die kunstlich Perforatio Penis bei den Dayaks auf Borneo. Verhandelingen der Berliner Gesellschaft fur Anthropologie, Ethnologie und Urgeschichte 22–24.

39. _____. (1876b). Perforatio gandis penis bei den Dajaks auf Bornew und analoge sitten auf Celebes und auf Java. Verhandlelungen der Berliner Gesellschaft fur Anthropologie, Ethnologie und Urgeschichte 24–26 (and addendum).

40. Miller, Charles C. (1942). Black Borneo. New York: Modern Age Books. (See photo opp. p. 199.)

41. Moll, Albert (1912). Handbuch der Sexualwissenschaften, vol. I. Leipzig: F.C.W. Vogel. (See p. 240.)

42. Nieuwenhuis, A.W. (1900). In Centraal Borneo: Reis van Pontianak naar Samarinda. Leiden: E.J. Brill. (See pp. 68–69, 118.)

43. _____. (1904–07). Quer durch Borneo: Ergebnisse Seiner Reisen in den Jahren 1894, 1896–97, und 1898–1900. Leiden: E.J. Brill. (See Vol. I, pp. 78–79, 223; Vol. II, p. 369 and plate opp. p. 390.)

44, O'Hanlon, Redmond (1984). Into the Heart of Borneo. New York: Random House. (See pp. 8–9, 17, 82–83.)

45. Perelaer, M. T. H. (1870). Ethnographische Beschrijving der Dajaks. Zalt-Bommel: Joh. Noman & Zoon. (See pp. 60–61 for the only doubts in a primary source that penis pins even exist.)

46. Richards, Anthony (1981). An Iban-English Dictionary. Oxford: Clarendon Press. (See pp. 245–56.)

47. Schneebaum, Tobias (1979). Wild Man. New York: The Viking Press. (See p. 124.)

48. Schwaner, C. A. L. M. (1853). Borneo, Beschrijving van het Stroomgebied van den Barito, Vol. I. Amsterdam: P.N. van Kampen. (See p. 127.)

49. St. John, Spenser (1863). Life in the Forests of the Far East: or Travels in Northern Borneo, Second ed., revised, Vol. I. London: Smith, Elder and Company. (See pp. 122–23.)

50. Symons, Donald (1979). The Evolution of Human Sexuality. New York: Oxford University Press.

51. Tillema, H. F. (1934–35). Poenans (Apo-Kajan en Tidoengsche landen). Tropisch Nederland 7:2–11, 18–24, 43–48. (See p. 24.)

52. Vale, V. and Andrea Juno (1989). Modern Primitives: And Investigation of Contemporary Adornment and Ritual. Re/Search #12. San Francisco: Re/Search Publications.

53. Veth, P. J. (1854). Borneo's West-afdelling, geographisch, statistisch, historisch, voorafgegaan door eene algemeene schets des ganschen eilands, Vol. I. Zaltbommel: Norman. (See p. 177–78.)

54. Walchren, E. W. F. van (1907). Eene reis naar de bovenstreken van Boeloengan (Midden-Borneo), 12 Nov. 1905–11 April 1906. Tijdschrift van het Nederlandsch Aadrijkundig Genootschap 24:755–844. (See pp. 822, 823.)

55. Ward, Barbara (1963). Men, Women and Change: An Essay in Understanding Social Roles in South and South-East Asia. In Women in the New Asia: The Changing Social Roles of Men and Women in South and South-East Asia. Ed. by B.E. Ward. UNESCO. Pp. 25–99.

56. Wulfften Palthe, P. M. von (1936). Psychiatry and Neurology in the Tropics. In A Clinical Textbook of Tropical Medicine, ed. by C.D. de Langen and A. Lichtenstein. Batavia: G. Kolff & Co. Pp. 525–47. (See pp. 536–38.)

SEXUAL BEHAVIOR

EXCERPTS FROM TANTRA:
THE ART OF CONSCIOUS LOVING

Charles and Caroline Muir

INTRODUCTION

The word *Tantra* refers specifically to a series of esoteric Hindu books that describe certain sexual rituals, disciplines, and meditations. These ancient Indian books, over two thousand years old, were written in the form of a dialogue between the Hindu god Shiva, who is "the penetrating power of forced energy," and his consort, Shakti, who represents the female creative force and is sometimes called "the Power of Tantra." Ancient Tantra is a spiritual system in which sexual love is a sacrament. We are not teachers of ancient tantric traditions and rituals, but we have developed a system based on tantric philosophical concepts and techniques that we have found applicable in our life and in the lives of our students. It is a system that can elevate a couple's relationship to the level of art. We refer to it as the Art of Conscious Loving.

Unfortunately, and contrary to what we would like to believe, we are not born naturally good at sex or at relationships. Few of us have benefited from a formal education in sexuality or sexual love. Even though we are children of the sexual revolution, we are still largely conditioned by belief systems that may have instilled in us guilt or fear or insecurity or shame. Such negative imprints, although they may reside quietly in the subconscious and cause only minor or occasional disturbances, rarely allow us to journey into the spiritual potential of sexual love. Tantra can help us do just that because a spiritual goal is as important to the tantric couple as their love.

Tantra is a school of many courses in which there are many levels of study and an unlimited degree of potential for spiritual gain, for sexual delight, and for worldly success. In our workshops and seminars we use techniques that we have developed from some of the ancient tantric lessons. These techniques are designed for the uninitiated, for the beginner. We share them with love and with deep respect for the potential for pleasure, for healing, and for spiritual growth they can provide.

It is one of the tenets of tantric philosophy that the discipline—the tantric lessons—is reborn age to age. We hope you will share our excitement over how extraordinarily well suited to our modern age and culture these ancient eastern lessons are. They are important tools for today's couples who are searching for a significantly different way of relating to each other, couples who want to sustain love and sexual passion for a lifetime together. We have seen men and women leave our seminars and workshops in a heightened state of awareness of themselves and of their love, and we have been gratified to learn from the many cards and letters we receive that this heightened awareness between them was not just an anomaly, not just a fleeting occurrence, but has become a permanent part of their relationship. Tantric sex does not promise instant results; it is not a "one-minute" technique for achieving sexual prowess. But for couples who want to enrich their relationship, it can release a particular kind of energy that can bring about harmony between them and increase their sexual pleasure and intimacy. In sum, tantric sex can create an extraordinary partnership.

Excerpts from *Tantra: The Art of Conscious Loving*, by Charles and Caroline Muir, Mercury House, 1989.

We've arranged this book in two parts. The first is an initiation into Tantra, its goals, its philosophy of life, and the science on which its practice is based—how it works, in other words, and specifically how it works for the couple. The second part addresses sexual rituals, the yoga or "union" couples practice to achieve an ecstatic connection in loving.

Charles and Caroline Muir
Kahului, Hawaii

TWO
THE TANTRIC WAY

The six regions of the body
The five states
They all have left and gone
Totally erased
And in the open
Void
I am left
Amazed . . .
The Unobtainable Bliss
Has engulfed me . . .

Pattinattar, A Tamil Tantrica
in The Poets of the Powers, edited by Kamil V. Zvelebil

Although relics of tantric rituals date back nearly five millennia, the tantric texts began to appear within a few centuries of the beginning of the Christian era. There are said to be 108 original volumes in which the tantric system is defined and its practices enumerated, but there are numerous commentaries and essays, or "expansions," upon the first books, which are also known as Tantras (the word *Tantra* means expansion).

These ancient books offer their practitioners a complete way of living; they encompass physical and material realms, mental and psychological aspects, and spirituality. Although it has gained a reputation for being the "yoga of sex," Tantra's sexual element is only a part of its focus, a part of a means to an end. Tantra's goals are more exalted and broader in scope than simply accomplishing proficiency in love. The ultimate goal is Unity. Tantricas aspire to a spiritual connection or union, to experience the individual self as part of the Indivisible All. To help them attain Unity, they employ techniques of visualization and meditation and they practice ritual sexual union and a highly developed form of communication with a partner.

Although we interpret some of the ancient tantric teachings from an end-of-the-twentieth-century point of view, it is not our intention to replace tantric goals or methods with our own. Tantra was our inspiration as we developed a system to help provide contemporary partnerships with a great reservoir of regenerative energy that expresses itself sexually, physically, and creatively. Before we get into a "how to" discussion of this system, we will briefly introduce you to the paradigm, or larger-than-world-view on which tantric theory is based, and then to the science of it.

TANTRIC VIEW OF REALITY

To help us understand the tantric philosophy, we need to make a distinction between a higher plane of reality, a state of cosmic consciousness, which we will refer to as Reality with a capital R, and our microcosmic or worldly reality, which we will call reality with a lowercase r. In our lowercase reality, there exists a fundamental condition of duality that expresses itself as *masculine* and *feminine*. This is not an exclusively eastern concept; many cultures demonstrate a similar perception in their languages. The Romance languages, for example, designate objects and subject by gender. Tantra, too, sees that everything in this reality contains masculine and feminine energies. But in the uppercase Reality, this duality does not exist. In the higher Reality one finds Unity. There is no masculine or feminine; there is only the One. Tantra's word for the One is *Shive-Shakti*, the union of cosmic consciousness with creative energy, the force that moves creation, the perfect combination of masculine and feminine that produces the undifferentiated One.

Remember, the tantric goal is that condition of Unity or Oneness. In more contemporary terms, we might say that the goal is to achieve self-actualization, or personal integration, or simply wholeness. For Tantricas, the couple is the vehicle in which one crosses from reality to Reality.

TANTRIC SCIENCE

Early tantric sciences included mathematics, medicine, astronomy, and surprisingly sophisticated atomic, space-time, and sound wave theories, as well as alchemy, palmistry, and astrology. Tantra is credited with inventing the decimal, discovering zero in ancient India, and introducing the concept of *chakras*, or psychic energy centers, as part of human biology. (The word means "wheels" or "disks" of energy.)

Among the most beautiful of tantric artifacts and relics are the paintings and scrolled charts that illustrate these chakras in men and women. Chakras are organs of the energetic or *subtle body*, which is considered to be distinct and independent from the outward physical or *gross body*. Tantra recognizes five layers of the body, which are called *sheaths*. The outermost layer is the skin and the bones. Next is the more subtle system of respiration; beyond that is the even more subtle system of cognition. Then comes discretion, and finally, the most subtle of all, the chakra system, the body's intuitive or psychic energy system through which one may achieve physical ecstasy and spiritual unity.

There are seven major chakras in the subtle chakra system, each of which is both a generator and a reservoir of energy and psychic consciousness. The chakras are connected to one or more of the five sheaths by means of "subtle channels" called *nadis*. In this way the energy from each of the chakras nourishes the whole body. These channels are not unlike the meridians on which acupuncture is based, and they are also similar to our understanding of the body's neural connectors and circuitry.

THE SYSTEM OF THE SEVEN CHAKRAS

In tantric art, each of the seven major chakras is symbolized by a different lotus blossom to signify its particular nature. Each blossom is composed of its own combination of colors, petals, and symbolic designs. Each is understood to contain a positive or a negative charge, a numerical and an alphabetic value, a particular affinity with an element of nature (air, earth, water, etc.), with one of the several senses (taste, touch, smell, etc.), and with a particular tonal quality. This latter aspect suggest an analogy: Consider the chakras as the strings of a guitar. Each string vibrates at a different frequency and gives off a different note. Over time the strings may resonate sharp or flat, and they require tuning. When they are in tune, the sound the guitar produces is harmonious. Similarly, when the chakras are in tune, one achieves harmony.

Each chakra corresponds to a specific area of the body, and each is believed to generate a particular form of what we call "drive." The seven chakras align through the center of the body, with the spine as their axis. They begin at the base of the spine with the first or base chakra. According to the tantric books, the first chakra's drive is toward the material; its desire is to acquire and possess. Ironically, its bodily function deals with elimination. The second chakra is located in the region of the genitals, out of which is generated the sex drive. The third chakra, behind the navel, relates to power issues and influences the digestive system. The fourth chakra, which governs respiration, is near the

SEVENTH CHAKRA
Crown of head
Formless supreme
    light
Yantra: lotus flower
    with 1000 radiant
    petals
Mantra: OM (ends as
    …MMM in the
    seventh chakra)

SIXTH CHAKRA
Between the eyebrows
Yantra: full moon color and shape
Mantra: OM (begins as OOO…
    in the sixth chakra)

FIFTH CHAKRA
Throat
Ether element
Yantra: white circle
    inside inverted
    triangle
Mantra: HAM

FOURTH CHAKRA
Heart
Air element
Yantra: six-pointed star
    inside circle
Mantra: YAM

THIRD CHAKRA
Behind the navel
Fire element
Yantra: inverted red
    triangle inside
    circle
Mantra: RAM

SECOND CHAKRA
Genital area
Water element
Yantra: moon-
    colored crescent
    inside circle
Mantra: VAM

FIRST CHAKRA
Base of spine
Earth element
Yantra: inverted red
    triangle inside
    yellow square
Mantra: LAM

Note: Each mantra is pronounced to rhyme with "mom" except OM, which
rhymes with "home." The OM mantra begins as "OOO…" in the sixth chakra
and ends as "…MMM" in the seventh chakra.

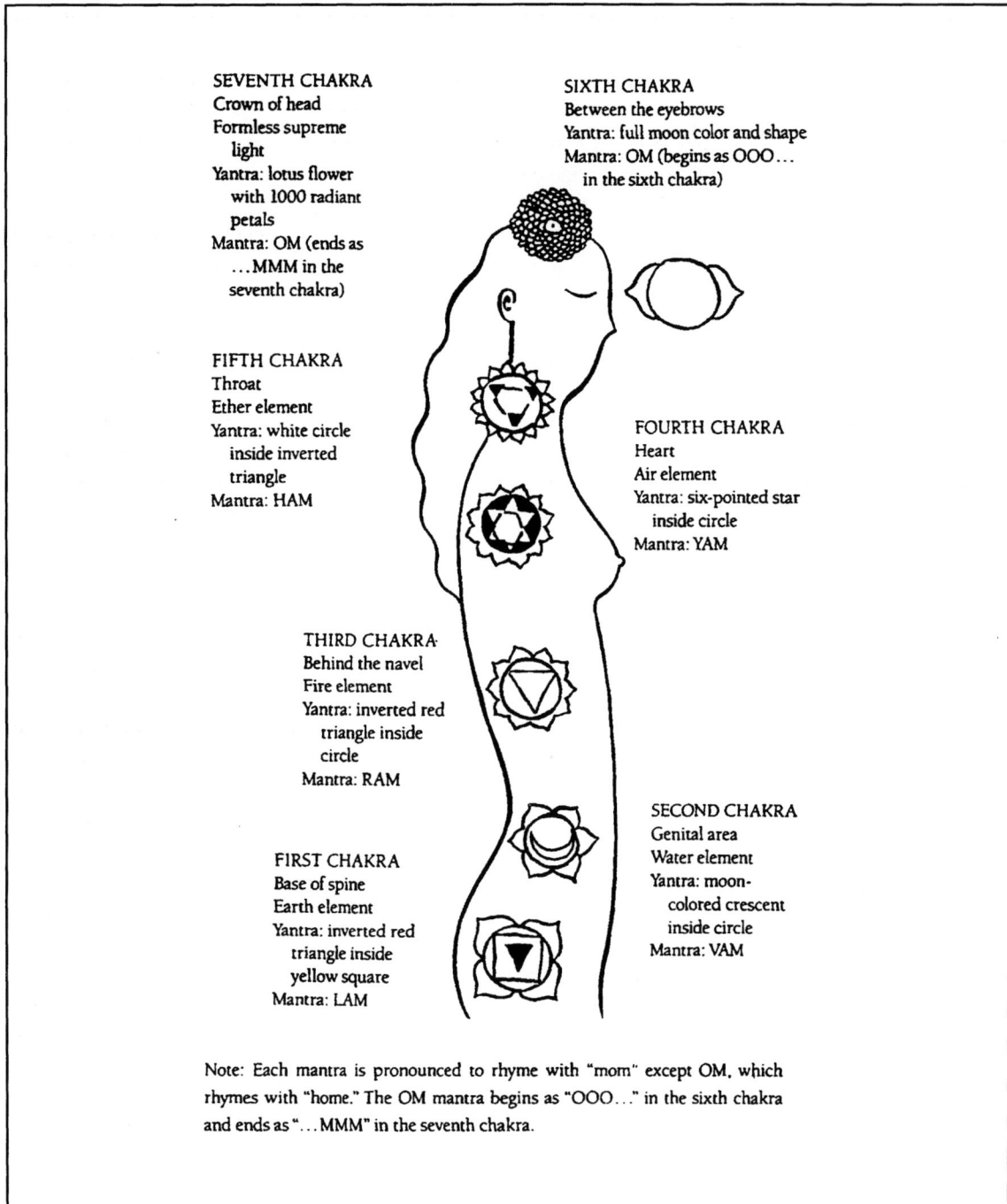

heart, and is considered the energy source of intimate connection. The fifth chakra, at the throat, influences the glandular system and contains the drive to communicate as well as the spiritual drive. The sixth chakra exists between the eyebrows, where it generates intellect, and in the back part of the brain (the reticular formation), where it affects consciousness as well as the potential for inner vision. A "thousand-petaled lotus" represents the seventh chakra, which is located at the crown of the head inside the cranium and also in the area just above the head, in the realm we seek outside of ourselves. When this exterior portion of the seventh or crown chakra is emanating energy, we refer to it as a halo.

Although a western skeptic might raise an eyebrow over much of the system we've just outlined, similar metaphorical values apply in our own perception of the human body. For example, we make an obvious association with the first chakra, located just above the anus, when we refer to "anal retentiveness," or when we say that a person who seems extremely possessive or obsessive is "tight-assed." And few would deny the powerful charge that occurs in the region of the second chakra when one is sexually aroused. This is the reproductive center—a *generator* of the most creative sort.

The third chakra controls digestion and affects the drive for power. We know it as the solar plexus, and we are certainly familiar with its energetic expression on the physical level. We call someone "gutsy" who demonstrates drive and forcefulness; we know that a "gut-level" feeling about something should be respected. This area is the site of ulcers in many modern-day westerners who are simply "driving" themselves too hard.

The fourth chakra, too, is easy to envision in contemporary terms. Eastern tradition ascribes to the heart rulership of compassionate instincts, of love and sympathy and intimate association; and western language echoes this ascription. We say "Have a heart!" when we ask for mercy or compassion; we talk about heartbreaks and heartthrobs and heartaches. We know what a heartwarming situation is, and that it is not measured by Fahrenheit or centigrade. We are often "led by our heart," when we think we should be directed by our head. And although we don't literally mean that our heart has us on a leash, we do mean that we are moved, directed, affected by some power or influence the heart has over us.

It's easy enough to accept that the fifth chakra, located in the throat, holds the equipment for communication and that the voice, a function of vibration, is an energetic expression. The fifth chakra's symbolic relationship to spirituality may be harder to fathom, but we do know that emotion expresses itself in this region. We get a "catch in the throat" when we are moved, for example, and we feel our "heart in our throat" in extreme situations. We can appreciate the throat's symbolic position as the connector of the body to the mind—the mind being the gateway to a spiritual union—if we remember that at the end of life, in the ultimate spiritual journey, a "death rattle" may occur in the throat. This is considered to be the sound of the soul departing the body on its way into the cosmic arena.

The sixth chakra, source of intellectual energy, cognition, and concentration, can be viewed as a metaphor for the brain and the brain's power or energy. Some people call the sixth chakra the "third eye," and ascribe to it powers of inner vision or insight.

Each chakra, then, represents a natural human desire—to possess, to copulate, to achieve, to love, to communicate, to understand, and finally to ascend, to exceed ourselves by touching God or the cosmic consciousness or a higher level of being, or whatever your words are for it. The tantric way uses these natural urges in men and women as the basis for establishing a continuously passionate loving relationship.

THE SEXUAL/SPIRITUAL CONNECTION

It is traditional in many cultures, even western cultures, to practice celibacy in the pursuit of spiritual life. This is true as well for the hundreds of schools of yoga that recognize sexual energy as a spiritual force, and aim to conserve the energy for the spiritual path. But celibacy as a spiritual motivator pretty much limits the quest for a raised form of consciousness to a cloistered community; and of course, if everyone followed this path, the number of people making a spiritual journey would quickly diminish and disappear.

Today many of us common folk aspire to spiritual growth. But we also desire to grow with a partner. Tantric yoga was the path couples chose thousands of years ago to satisfy this dilemma, since the tantric discipline allows men and women to have a mate, to enjoy sex, *and* to experience spiritual fulfillment, often simultaneously. How can this be? How can sexuality coexist with spirituality—

the one base, the other sublime? For an answer we look inside, to the Tantra's subtle body, and to its ascending energy centers beginning with the most "base" and ending in the cosmic zone.

At the first chakra, coiled tightly like a spring at the base of the spine, resides what Tantra calls kundalini shakti. Its literal meaning is "coiled feminine energy," but it exists in men and women to the same degree, and could as well be called "creative energy," or "life energy," or "motivating energy," or the "energy of pure consciousness." This energy exists inside us as well as outside of us, which means that we contain within us that which we seek; spiritual connection, that higher Reality we strive for, need only be awakened from inside ourselves to be realized.

When the kundalini is aroused it begins to unwind, releasing its energy up through the body. It follows the spinal column to the second chakra, the third, the fourth, and higher. As it goes, its near-electric charge imparts energy to and receives energy from the seven body centers, awakening dormant consciousness as it ascends, until it unites with the topmost chakra, and in so doing achieves its goal: Unity, spiritual ecstasy, called *ananda in* Sanskrit. Ananda is also know as *nirvana*, as *satori*, as enlightenment, as sainthood. The tantric texts assure us that it is within the grasp of each of us. In fact, the books call it our birthright.

Achieving the tantric goal of Unity, however, can take a lifetime of study and devotion, and it is not our purpose here, although envisioning the possibility of attaining such a goal and working toward it can enhance all aspects of life. In our seminars we encourage couples to remain aware of this ultimate tantric goal as they strive for Unity in their relationship. If your practice of the art of conscious loving leads you to desire more information about Tantra, we suggest you consult the bibliography at the back of the book as a starting point.

Before leaving this very brief discussion of the kundalini, we need to point out that this energy is released in varying degrees in each person. It may be stirred but not uncoiled; it may be aroused but not propelled with enough force to make its way all the way up through the body. Often it becomes stuck very close to home, in the second chakra, where it expresses itself sexually and then retracts to its original position and goes back to sleep. The forced and premature awakening of kundalini energy can be dangerous. The techniques for creating a releasing energy that we use in our seminars and share with you here are safe and very gentle. If at any time, however, you feel uncomfortable with any of them, we urge you not to do them. Wait for a time when you may be more receptive, or simply pass over them.

FOCUSING THE MIND

Tantric yoga is practiced in a serene, calm frame of mind, a condition that is often difficult to achieve in our high-tech, high-stake, fast-paced world. Tantra urges meditation, the conscious turning of the mind away from things of this world, in order to experience a deep inner space.

To help us to get that state, Tantra offers several techniques. Concentration is one, and while it seems simple enough, it is not easily achieved. To aid us in our efforts to concentrate, Tantra suggests a variety of meditations that directly affect the brain, quieting the intellectual, analytical left hemisphere and activating the experiential, intuitive right hemisphere. It is in the right hemisphere of the brain that "mystical" experiences transpire. (As a general rule, to the extent that a person is operating in the left side of the brain during lovemaking, he or she misses much of the ecstatic potential tantric sexual love offers.)

Another method to still the mind is a breathing technique called "cosmic intercourse." To practice this exercise, focus awareness on your spine beginning at the base chakra, and then bring that awareness up in a slow, deep-drawn inhalation, conscious of each energy center from the spinal axis, from base to the crown. At the end of the inhalation, hold your breath for three to ten seconds, during which time you should try to actually feel the energetic air that fills the cranium at the crown of the head, the "Seat of Shiva." Now begin the exhalation, also a slow, deep breath, as you accompany that rarefied air back down through your body, visiting the same energy reservoirs in the opposite direction, maintaining awareness all the while. At the base chakra, hold your breath out for several seconds, and focus your mind on this reservoir or seat of kundalini energy. Then begin again. The rhythm is one of waves washing up a sandy shore and back, up and back, smoothing the beach, like a caress. Try it now; it will refresh and relax you. As you inhale, picture the air freshening each spinning wheel of energy inside you; as you exhale let your breath carry away all the day's exhaustion.

A Yogic Breath Consists of 4 Parts:
1. Slow inhalation.
2. Several seconds of held breath.
3. Slow exhalation.
4. A moment's holding of the breath out or pause before beginning the next inhalation.

Breath control as a technique for establishing a meditative state is common to all yogic disciplines. In eastern traditions it is the breath that keeps the vital life-force circulating throughout the body. To control the breath is to increase life's essence. For tantric couples, breath control is one of the most important techniques for achieving the interpersonal harmony required to sustain and nurture the relationship.

Intermediate and advanced students of Tantra use two other powerful techniques to deepen their meditations and their physical and energetic connections. These are yantra and mantra techniques. *Yantras*, literally "tools," are symbolic or archetypal diagrams. There are 960 of them in total, all symbolic of various aspects of cosmology. Like a *mandala*, also a graphic representation of the cosmos, the yantra is considered a "power image"; its geometry, its spatial characteristics, its elements of dynamism are designed to appeal to the psyche and to cause a specific mental response—in this case, a focusing of the mind. Yantras send a geometric thought wave to the chakras that says, "Awaken! Purify! Activate!" In our workshops we use the seven yantras that correspond to the seven chakras described earlier (see page 46). Initiates begin by staring at the yantra diagrams, in ascending order. Once the designs have been learned their visualization, combined with a deep, palpable awareness of the corresponding chakra centers, is a very effective method of focusing the mind in meditation.

Bija mantra is another advanced technique for awakening, purifying, and activating the chakras. These mantras are the tonal equivalents of yantras, vibrational syllables that stimulate and resonate with the seven chakras to create a harmonic inner chord. Repeating these syllables as a chant acts like a tuning fork to bring the mind to peace and awaken the chakras' dormant energies. Most of us are familiar with the syllable *OM*, considered to be the "sound of the universe." Its associated chakras are the sixth and seventh. The mantras (all pronounced to rhyme with "mom" except the final "OM," which rhymes with "home") and their corresponding chakras are shown in the chart on page 46.

Mudras are also used by advanced students of Tantra in the ritualistic focusing of the mind. These are forms of nonverbal communication that use various hand and finger gestures and body postures to symbolize aspects of the higher Reality and to influence and redirect energy to parts of the body not usually empowered in this way, including the regions of the higher chakras.

Tantricas also practice *White Tantra* techniques as a form of meditation and to focus the mind. White Tantra is the grandfather of what we know as Hatha Yoga; it uses beneficial stretching techniques combined with breathing, concentration, and "feeling," to direct awareness and emotion to the physical body, which activates the chakra system. It is the breathing, concentration, and feeling aspects of White Tantra that separate it from most forms of Hatha Yoga.

We mention some of these more advanced techniques so that you will be aware of them and can learn more about them when you desire. They are not essential practices for *elementary* students of Tantra, but they grow in importance as you advance, and they will add variety and depth to your mind-focusing techniques.

There is another aspect to concentration and mind focusing in tantric yoga that is very important to the successful practice of the art of conscious loving because it allows us to shift the focus from the individual to the couple. In this way, couples can sustain concentration on their relationship as much as on one another. This is not as easy as it may sound. It takes effort to remain continually conscious, or focused, or attuned to one another and to the relationship. But this is a large part of tantric discipline, and it plays a very important role in our programs. To be considerate, in the most literal sense, of the other *and* the we *and* the I, to stay awake, is in fact the key to the passionate and evolutionary, perhaps *revolutionary*, relationship that Tantra offers.

SIX
AWAKENING THE GODDESS

The valley spirit never dies;
It is the woman, primal mother.
Her gateway is the root of heaven and earth . . .

Lao Tsu, *Tao Te Ching,* number 6

In the last chapter we noted that tantric books describe our age as the end of the Kali Yuga, or Age of Darkness, a period that began more than two thousand years ago. The Kali Yuga has been marked by corruption and difficulty, and, according to the tantric texts, it has been an era during which female power has been suppressed. Metaphorically, the Hindu Goddess Shakti, who represents the female principle, has lain sleeping for over two millennia. There are various theories about the Goddess's slumber. One explanation is that man became frightened by the intensity of woman's shakti, or energetic power, and by what she was capable of—creation, for one thing—so he maneuvered her into a subordinate position in order to suppress that power.

While historians differ as to the exact date when the Kali Yuga began, many authorities believe it was in the third and fourth centuries B.C., at about the same time that Taoism reached its apogee in China and Confucianism was gaining new popularity. What had been a fairly egalitarian political and social system in China began to change. Whereas previously emperor and empress had ruled as equals, now the emperor alone was sovereign. Similarly, in Taoist tantric lovemaking the man began to assume a new role. Where the original tantric techniques required an equal exchange between man and woman of positive and negative energies, of yang and yin, the beginning of the Age of Darkness found the man using his consort's energies for his own resources and longevity, without regard to her replenishment. No wonder the Goddess preferred to sleep.

Even earlier, in India, a similar male domination prevailed after the country was defeated by warrior tribes whose influence overwhelmed the predominantly matriarchal society. And so that force we call the *shakti*, which is personified by the Goddess, fell out of power and into the realm of dreams.

DAWN OF A NEW AGE

Now, as we stand on the cusp of a New Age, which Tantra calls Satya Yuga, the Age of Truth, we see the female fires beginning to glow again. We believe that the Goddess began her reawakening in the 1960s, during the period we know as the Sexual Revolution, and that she is still in the early stretching stages of waking up. Women's interest in physical fitness, in exercise and health, in self-improvement can be viewed as a literal manifestation of this stretching. Their expansion into business, politics, and spiritual pursuits is also a demonstration of their emergence as a new force in the modern world.

In fact, what we call the Women's Movement can be perceived as a dramatic play, an acting out of the Goddess awakening. It is movement up out of the subconscious. It is movement into the world. She opens her eyes. She shakes the Age of Darkness from her as she shakes off the dreams of centuries. Soon she will step out into the light, and her radiance will illuminate all humankind. When this happens, when women awake from their slumber and their enormous orgasmic energy is released to the world, we will have attained the New Age, the Age of Truth. For women themselves the difference will be as profound as the difference between night and day.

Of course it's one thing to talk metaphorically, and quite another to speak in terms of reality. In reality this business of the Goddess awakening isn't such a simple thing. During two thousand and more years of suppression, women's fire has grown cold. Now suddenly it's the "New Age" and women are supposed to be more evolved on many levels, particularly on the sexual level. Not only are women expected to be having fabulous orgasms, they are also supposed to be experiencing multiple ones. It's enough to make anyone a little nervous, especially women who don't feel orgasms easily. "That's all well and good for the Goddess," a modern woman might say, "but what about me?"

The fact is, both men and women have to be taught how to rekindle the woman's dormant sexual energy. In the old days, Tantricas were tutored by teachers in the art of love, as well as the sixty-four other arts and sciences a disciple of Tantra was expected to know. Today, men and women can learn to teach each other, and Tantra can help them. They might consider Tantra as a kind of extension course—a master class in love and relationship. In this continuing education they guide each other, and the experience can be extremely powerful. For when a woman's fire is rekindled after such a long time, and tended, and fed by her most intimate partner, the benefits to both can be manifold. But for women, especially, the rekindling of dormant sexual fires can lead to startling, unexpected sensations. A woman's sexual awakening can, unlike a man's, propel her on a spiritual path. Men can practice celibacy and achieve spiritual enlightenment, but according to the tantric texts women's enlightenment is facilitated by the electric charge of her orgasmic nature. Through sexual sharing a woman activates a powerful sexual/spiritual energy, her shakti, which then releases itself into her physical body and into her psyche, creating the atmosphere for her awakening and spiritual enlightenment. Tantra recognizes spirituality as a kind of rearrangement of the same energy as sexuality, so when a woman increases her sexual power she adds, on an almost cellular level, to the strength of her spiritual aspect as well.

Once a woman is awakened, both partners benefit. The woman's pleasure and her desire for lovemaking increase and can even be *greater* than the pleasure potential and sexual desire in the man. Tantric lovemaking promotes health and vitality, and both the man and the woman benefit physically. Psychologically, too, Tantra is a healing art. We've discussed the various negative charges that can be associated with the second chakra, the energy center for the genitals—negative associations that can come from information our parents may have passed along, from our own hurtful past experiences, or from embarrassments we learned somewhere along our own particular path. Tantric practices can discharge the negative power infusing the second chakra, and in so doing make enormous resources of positive energy available to all areas of life, not just the sexual. You will discover an energy you never knew you had, a creative energy that will refresh your mind, replenish your stamina, and restore your enthusiasm.

FIVE LEVELS OF ORGASMIC EXPERIENCE

When her sexual resources have been awakened and her passion fired, a woman can come to an orgasm in a minute or two if she so desires. Multiple orgasms are no longer a mere myth to her, and she discovers that her sexual energy (not the Goddess's sexual energy, but her own) is limitless.

We can identify five levels of orgasmic activity in women, beginning with the zero or *preorgasmic* level, which includes women who have never experienced an orgasm at all, as well as those who aren't sure. Women on this level may not have had the experience of making love, or perhaps then have never masturbated or have not been able to masturbate to climax. Perhaps they are sexually active but suffer a psychological block due to negative associations or previous incompatibilities. Or they may have been indoctrinated with the belief that nice girls shouldn't enjoy sex; or perhaps they are simply afraid of "losing control."

The second level, which we call *sometimes orgasmic*, can be much more frustrating than the pre-orgasmic level. To have experienced the feeling of an orgasm and not to be able to call it up, not to have access to one's own power, can be intensely upsetting.

Next there is the *orgasmic* level. These women do have access to that potent energy. They have experienced orgasms and they know which positions and which combination of kisses and touches will induce it. And that's where women on this level are content to stop. "I've had my orgasm, dearest, and you've had yours. I love you. Good night."

Then there is the fourth level, *multiple orgasms*, like fireworks on the Fourth of July—there is that much color and intensity—a chain of pleasure possibility beyond the orgasmic stratosphere.

Beyond this is the fifth level, which sexologists call *extended orgasm* and Tantricas know as the Wave of Bliss. This is a level of arousal that grows in intensity and can last ten or twenty minutes or even longer. The tantric writings describe Shakti's achieving seven peaks of ecstasy, each peak higher, stronger, more powerful then the one preceding, until at the topmost place she releases her nectar, her *amrita*, the female ejaculate.

This is not a fairy tale. Every woman has such potential, but she must desire to awaken it, and she must desire it for *herself* first, not for her partner or for his satisfaction.

ANATOMY OF A GODDESS:
A WOMAN'S TWO PLEASURE POLES

There has been a highly publicized debate recently about the existence of the Grafenberg Spot or g spot. Freud started it, even before Mr. G, with his assertion that a clitoral orgasm is an immature orgasm, which suggests that there must be such a thing as a "mature" orgasm, achieved otherwise than through the clitoris. Psychologists went along with this theory for a while, defining two separate areas for the female orgasm, the clitoris and the vagina. Then in the 1960s, William Masters and Virginia Johnson, considered gurus in the field of sexology, superseded Freud's unfortunate phrase, maintaining that in fact the vaginal orgasm was a myth. Female orgasm is achieved by stimulating the clitoris, they said, and that's all. There are stronger orgasms and weaker ones, but they all come from the same source. Today, many researchers dispute the Masters and Johnson theory. John Perry and Beverly Whipple, for example, agree that the clitoris is one point that may be stimulated to trigger a woman's orgasm, but they assert that it is not the only point.

Tantricas do not engage in this debate. They have known since Shiva pronounced it in the sacred books that inside a woman lie two sensitive poles, or charged spots, the northern or forward pole, which is the clitoris, and the deeper southern pole, called the *sacred spot*, which is the same as the g spot.

As we have noted, the tantric texts were written as a dialogue between the Hindu God Shiva and his beloved Shakti. Perhaps because they are deities in the Hindu tradition, not bound by human inhibitions, Shiva and Shakti are able to speak openly to one another about very intimate things—things that we poor mortals find difficult to discuss. Things, in fact, that we may believe we should *not* discuss.

We are a little embarrassed by sex. Some of us are a lot embarrassed. We blush about it. We lower our eyes. Even the vocabulary we have for sex and for our sexual organs is embarrassing—too clinical, too slangy, or too crude. Compare, for example, such eastern designations for the male organ as Jade Stalk and Scepter of Light, to our western monikers "pecker," "prick," and "wang"; compare Precious Gateway, Golden Doorway, and Flower Heart to "hole."

Obviously we cannot communicate without words, particularly in a book. And if the only words we have to communicate with are charged with negative, infantile, or derogatory innuendo, and *what* we have to communicate is a positive, enriching, and laudatory message, it seems we have a problem. We have attempted to solve this problem by adding a few new words to the language of love.

Actually, they are old words, Sanskrit words, the same ones Shiva and Shakti used in their "pillow talk." We used the word *lingam* for the male sexual organ; it literally means a wand of light, or God's organ. We use the word *yoni* to describe the female genitalia; it translates as "sacred space." Because these are new words to most of us in the West, they don't have the history, and they don't automatically touch off a conditioned response. We haven't heard them used in nasty jokes, for instance, and mother never said, "Girl, don't touch your yoni!" They are softer words, too, on the tongue and to the ear. They need some getting used to, but it doesn't take long. In a very short time, most of the couples who attend our seminars find they are more comfortable using these words than those they may have used in the past. Many couples adopt these new words and take them home; the words become another intimate connection between them, their own private "twilight" language. We hope that you, too, will become familiar with these words as we continue to use them in describing the sexual nature of Tantra.

THE JEWEL IN THE CROWN

The clitoris sits like a bell or a jewel in the topmost part of the yoni. It is the only organ in the body whose sole function is to generate pleasure. Although the tip of the clitoris is tiny in most women, it has a shaft that may extend an inch deep into the crown wall of the yoni. If the mood is right, stimulating the tip and the shaft (which becomes palpably erect when excited) with fingers or mouth or lingam can usually arouse a woman to an orgasm. During intercourse, either the man or the woman herself can stimulate this area while he is inside her. Or one of them can use the lingam as a wand, holding it around the shaft and manipulating it over and around the clitoris, but not penetrating any deeper than one inch. (These techniques are described in detail in Chapter Ten.)

Learning the right touch is important. Overstimulation can short-circuit a woman's building energy. The right touch is something a woman can learn by herself, however, and pass on to her lover, by stroking or pressing or rubbing the jewellike tip and shaft of her own clitoris. Remember that it is not just the clitoris, but the whole first inch of the yoni that is extremely sensitive. Great love and attention are given to this electrical first inch by Tantricas when they perform the rituals known as "Honoring the Yoni," for Tantricas respect the clitoris as the gateway to the chamber that is the source of all life. (See Chapter Nine for a description of the tantric rituals for honoring the yoni and the lingam.)

THE SACRED SPOT

This energetic access spot is the other pole for sexual fulfillment in women. Deep inside, protected as the clitoris is not, it is a place that can produce the most profound pleasure, both physically and on a psychic level. But because it is so deep inside and so well hidden, it is often a receptacle for storing all manner of hurtful things associated with sexuality. If that is the case, the spot's negative charge can be shocking—and it is important to know this when you begin the process of arousing it. If a woman has had painful experiences with sex, physical or emotional, her first contact with the spot may be unpleasant, even painful, in the way a bruise hurts when you put pressure on it. If she perseveres, however, if she and her loved one go slowly and love tenderly, the sore spot inside her will heal, and with it her past wounds; and in healing herself in this way a woman can awaken a power she has never known. This power can illuminate life in all areas, and can provide access to the tantric Wave of Bliss. It is the power of the Goddess Shakti, the power of Tantra, and it can be yours.

HOW TO FIND THE SACRED SPOT

Finding the sacred spot requires a touch that often is difficult for a woman to accomplish alone. She may find a position in which she can just about reach her own sacred spot, but it will be awkward, and she probably won't be able to do much more than locate it, if that. It will be very difficult for her to stimulate or massage it, which one must do to access its healing power and its sexual and spiritual potential. A few women who've attended our seminars tell us they've been able to locate the spot themselves by squatting and pressing up toward the navel with two fingers from the inside, while pressing down just about the pubic bone with the other hand. If a woman can manage to stimulate or massage the area the spot will swell, which may make it palpable between the two sets of fingers. For most women, though, this part of their awakening process requires the loving touch of a partner. And he should be prepared to respect the vulnerable nature of the spot, both physically and psychologically. It is most important that couples approach this moment together in harmony. For initiates, both men and women, it's a little scary; it's an intimate connection of a new kind. Use the tools we've described for creating harmony between you and your lover, for example, the nurturing meditation and the breathing and mind-focusing techniques, so that the two of you become physically at ease and in sync with one another.

At this point in our seminars we divide the men and women into separate groups, and in this somewhat safer-feeling environment we talk about the process of finding the sacred spot: where it is located, how to approach it, how it may feel. We use this time, too, to talk about our personal experiences and to share our difficulties and to learn from one another. The separate-by-sex congregation is a kind of tribal gathering of initiates before a ritual. We speak openly. We aren't there to impress one another. The conversation is anything but locker room. Charles leads the men in a discussion of their role in the discovery of the sacred spot. He explains that they will be assuming the role of the healer, and that for the moment this will take precedence over their role as lover. He stresses that psychic hurts often reside inside a woman's vagina, and that she may respond emotionally, even violently, when they are awakened and remembered, which may well happen when the spot is touched. As the healing partner in this case, the man must be there for the woman one hundred percent. He must accept her emotions, even her anger, understanding that they are the expressions of ghosts; that the past is spinning out of her; that the room full of her preconceptions is emptying.

Caroline discusses with the women some of the emotions they may expect to feel when the sacred spot is touched for the first time, but she emphasizes that it can be a profound, moving, and intimate experience. She explains that it can be an extraordinary psychological breakthrough for some women, as well as an experience of pure pleasure, a phenomenal new kind of orgasmic ecstasy.

Before beginning, the woman should empty her bladder. The sacred spot lies close to the bladder, and its stimulation may feel at first like the need to urinate. She can lie on her back, with her legs raised so that the back of one or both of her thighs rest against her lover's chest, or with her feet on the mattress while her lover kneels beside her. She can place a pillow under her buttocks for support and comfort. The vagina should be well lubricated.

The first few times you experiment with this, the man should begin by using only one finger to make contact—specifically, the ring finger, which is said to have a harmonic affinity with the second chakra, and which is smaller than the index or middle finger. Slip the finger in gently, and then curl it so the pad of the fingertip touches the ceiling of the yoni. Using the crooked-finger "come here" gesture, slowly pull the finger forward along the ceiling toward the front of the yoni, as if you were returning to the clitoris. Somewhere in this forward stroke—usually about halfway between the back of the pubic bone and the clitoris, is the area of the front wall toward the opening—both lovers will distinguish the spot.

The heart of the sacred spot does not actually lie *on* the wall, but can be felt through it. Its texture is different from the smooth silky tissue around it; it is tougher, and ridged or bumpy, like the areola of the nipple when it is aroused, or the palate of the mouth. The size of the sacred spot varies from a pea to a half dollar, and it swells when it's stimulated, rising slightly in the middle.

The lover's ring finger or the ring and middle finger provide the easiest and most comfortable access to the sacred spot, with the other fingers resting lightly against the labia minora and the heel of the hand in a position to exert light pressure against the clitoris, stimulating it slightly. Or the thumb can rest against the clitoris, if the lover is using his index and/or middle finger to touch the sacred spot.

AWAKENING THE SACRED SPOT

As mentioned earlier, the first few times the sacred spot is touched can be a little frightening for some women; some may even experience pain. Many women also feel as if they need to urinate, even though they have just emptied the bladder. This feeling lasts only a short while, however, from ten to forty seconds or so, after which the sensation usually changes to one of powerful sexual pleasure. But this may not happen right away; it can take weeks or even months of healing before this great pleasure is experienced. Sometimes a woman will feel a pleasant sensation the first few times the sacred spot is touched, but it will suddenly disappear; the spot can become too sensitive, so that any pressure at all is too much. The man must maintain close contact with his beloved on a conscious, emotional level, so that he can be immediately responsive to her feelings. He must lighten his touch or withdraw if need be, until she can tolerate more. Each time a couple engages in this very intimate touching, the woman's tolerance will extend and her potential for pleasure will increase. The sacred spot can usually take more intense stimulation for longer periods than the clitoris can. In the beginning, though, the man must be extremely gentle. His goal should be to charge the sacred spot with positive power, to heal any negative residue; his only aim should be to afford her a pleasurable and healing touch. He should not think about orgasm now, but about healing. The woman should try not to think at all; she should concentrate on *feeling*, her mind receptive and quiet. For her this is a sensory rather than a cerebral pursuit.

Once the man has found the spot he should stop, the fingers of one hand quiet in their position inside the yoni, while the other hand exerts light pressure on the clitoris, or rests between the woman's breasts, over the heart chakra, or presses just above the pubic bone, which can cause a pleasurable pressure on the sacred spot from above. In this quiet moment, the lovers should maintain eye contact and breathe together.

After a moment or two the man should gently stroke the sacred spot for about two minutes; then he should stop again and be still. He can apply more stimulation to the clitoris at this point, but he must remember that stimulation of both power poles at once is almost always too much for the beginner. Alternating one with the other, maintaining a balance of stillness with movement, and focusing attention on his partner's pleasure will produce deep sensations. This cycle should be repeated for several rounds. The number of rounds can be gradually increased over time.

The exotic mundras can also be used to great advantage during the massage of the sacred spot. The combination of these elements—concentration, focusing the mind on the partner's pleasure, and balancing stillness with movement—is one way of practicing love as meditation.

The sacred spot may also be accessed anally; with lots of lubrication some women find this most pleasurable. The lover must be sure to use a separate hand or separate finger for this kind of lovemaking, as it is important not to introduce bacteria from the anus into the yoni.

For the woman, the reviving of the sacred spot is an exercise in expanding her feelings. She will be able to tell just how much feeling she is ready to experience or accept, and she will be able to watch that quantity grow as she and her partner continue the technique over a period of months. The man must be careful not to get carried away. Seeing his beloved beginning to respond pleasurably to his arousal, he may go too far, become too yang (too active, or fast, or hard), and may inadvertently short-circuit her growing energy. During this period of awakening, treat this loveplay as an intimate meditation rather than an orgasmic opportunity. When the sacred spot has become fully alive its tenderness will turn to passion, and then its potential for pleasure will be easily accessed and easily fulfilled.

NECTAR OF THE GODDESS

When the sacred spot is fully awakened, when it is free of negative influences, then the Goddess and her mortal sisters are able to experience an extraordinary elevation in orgasmic potential, enjoying multiple as well as extended orgasms. Women with this kind of sexual facility may also experience the release of a light liquid, which modern sexologists have likened to a man's ejaculation, and Tantra calls the *amrita*, or divine nectar. A woman may perceive a kind of joyful explosion of energy when it occurs, but this experience is quite different from male ejaculation. The nectar is produced once the sacred spot has been activated, but it need not rely on stimulation of the spot to occur. In fact, the release may occur to a powerfully orgasmic woman without her even having an orgasm, and it may happen in situations other than sexual ones.

In our seminars we have met women who produce the amrita during episodes of profound laughter. You have heard the expression "losing it," applied to uncontrolled laughter. And you have probably seen someone actually "cry" with laughter. In such situations, the nectar can flow. Aerobic exercise can also produce the kind of energy that triggers the release. The experience is similar to a physical surrender. We say a woman loses control—to laughter, to energy, to love, to joy—when the amrita is released, but really she is becoming one with the laughter, she is *becoming* the energy, the love, the joy. And in this she is *gaining* the essence of these ecstatic feelings, not losing it at all.

Biologically, the fluid appears to originate in one of the Bartholin's glands, which lie on either side of the lower part of the vagina. It is a very light, clear or slightly milky liquid, which can be almost astringent in nature, and evaporates quickly. It may have a very pale flavor, from nearly sweet to slightly bitter, or no taste at all. Since it is expelled from the urethra, the first several drops may have the slightly salty taste of urine.

The amrita is considered highly nutritious, according to tantric texts, and seems to impart its nutrition both physically and psychically. A tiny taste will almost immediately cause a genuine power surge. And both lovers will experience a resonating energy in its presence.

What's most amazing about the amrita is the quantity of it; a woman may produce as much as a cupful at a time, and she may "ejaculate" several times in the course of one loving meditation with her partner. Tantra describes the female power or shakti as limitless; this liquid demonstration of it appears to affirm this. The release of the nectar often produces a dramatic effect. If the woman releases her fluid while her lover is outside of her, it may burst from her in a fine mist, or explode like a fountain, high into the air—up to six feet high! If her lover is inside of her, the nectar will drench his lingam in an incredible energetic bath.

Every woman has the potential for experiencing the outpouring of her amrita, but it is not possible to *try* to experience it or to practice proficiency at it. The only "exercise" that can be used to encourage or activate it, beyond learning to surrender oneself to a deep happiness that may or may not be sexual, is regular loving massage of the sacred spot. Even women for whom the amrita occurs occasionally cannot consciously influence it. When it happens it is a gift, inspirational and divine.

INTRODUCTION TO SM:
COMMUNICATION AND SAFETY

William A. Henkin, Ph.D. and Sybil Holiday, CSSE

INTRODUCTION TO THE BOOK

Welcome to the wonderful world of consensual sadomasochism. As our personal introductions may suggest, this is not a world populated by mass murdering serial ogres, but rather by people much like you, your neighbors, and your friends. We are computer programmers and sociologists, physicians and attorneys, police and sales personnel, professors and prostitutes, housewives, plumbers, artists, CEOs, union organizers, and the unemployed. A variety of research studies have shown that unless we're in costume or have specifically identified ourselves ahead of time in some other way, you probably won't be able to pick us out on the street, in your workplace, or at the PTA meeting. Not only are we a great deal *like* you: since you're reading this book, to some extent we *are* you.

But unique as each of us may be, we are not *just* individuals. This book emerges out of the SM community, which is sometimes called the leather community because in its early days it was organized in and around the image of bikers: outlaw—especially gay outlaw—motorcycle gangs, whose members wore leather pants, jackets, and boots both for physical protection against the spills they occasionally took from their bikes, and for the psychological protection a commanding uniform affords members of many warrior and outcast groups, from the Hell's Angels to your local constabulary.

The *Oxford English Dictionary* defines *community* as a religious fellowship, a sharing or holding in common with others, a mutual spiritual intercourse. Although the organized SM community began in gay biker clubs in the late 1960s and early 1970s, it spread to gay biker bars, to gay bars that did not specifically cater to bikers, and finally out into the lesbian, heterosexual, bisexual, and transsexual worlds, often without motorcycles, bars, alcohol, or even leather clothing. It is not uncommon by now in some parts of the leather community for gay men and gay women to play together, even though they would never want their SM partners to be their lovers or spouses. Homosexual, heterosexual, and bisexual people may also play with one another without jeopardizing their orientations, or their standings as members of one group or another. The mutual spiritual intercourse of the SM world is the exchange of erotic energy, not necessarily, for example, the exchange of body fluids; and since the exchange of energy that underlies SM is highly erotic even though it is not necessarily genitally sexual, it has been said that leather transcends gender.

Though the SM community began in the gay male subculture, where restricted enclaves flourish even today, by now it also clearly includes people of all genders, all inclinations, and all sexual orientations. As the authors of the book in your hands, we do not hold that gays are better than straights, that women are better than men, that Tops are better than Bottoms, or vice-versa—although you will find people both in and out of the community who do believe those things.

In this book you get the perspectives of Sybil and Bill very specifically. SM as we do it and describe it is an evolving activity within an evolving subculture in an evolving society; its language, too, is evolving. We've come to what we know by experience, by practice, by examination, by thought, and by our own life processes. Other people may have very different positions about some issues than we have, and we urge you to find out what they have to say. That way you can make your own informed decisions about what these activities and this community have to offer you, what they mean to you, what you have to offer them, and where you fit in or if you do at all.

As we have written it, this book is *not* a justification for SM, a scholarly examination of SM, a tool to recruit or proselytize for SM, or a pop-psychology self-help tome. It *is* an examination of the language and processes that surround and infuse SM, sometimes known as *erotic power exchange.* The *Oxford English Dictionary*—once again—interprets *erotic* as whatever is sexual, sensual, and amatory; *power* means the ability to do or act, authority, influence, or force; *exchange* means to give or receive in trade. *Erotic power exchange* means, therefore, to give and/or receive sexual, sensual, amatory force or authority to, from, or with someone else.

Because some form of give-and-take is involved, the practice of SM, or erotic power exchange, implies parity among players. By parity we do not quite mean equality. If *A* gives *B* a candy bar, *B* should give *A* an identical candy bar in a strictly equal exchange. But when *A* gives *B* a candy bar, *B* may give *A* a dollar instead. While *A* cannot eat the dollar, and *B* cannot spend the candy bar, if they have agreed that the *worth* of the two objects is equal then their exchange is one of parity. In exactly the same way two people may achieve parity in an exchange of erotic energy when one person who likes to spank, spanks another who likes to serve and serves the first person.

In order to encourage the greatest pleasure and safety for people who enjoy these activities, we propose our own Six Commandments of Healthy SM:

1. *Tell the truth,* first to yourself and then to the people with whom you play, at least as far as you know it at the time;
2. *Keep your agreements* with the people with whom you play, to the best of your ability; and if you cannot keep them for any reason, don't change your agreements unilaterally: negotiate with the other parties to those agreements, let them know alterations are in the works, and let them participate in the changes;
3. *Play safely:* SM is a sophisticated form of sexuality, and sometimes it does entail physical and psychological risks; learn enough to know what you and your play partners are doing, to know the difference between what is safe and what is not, and to know what to do if something gets out of hand;
4. *Play consensually:* don't involve people with your sexuality who have not agreed to become involved; play only with people who have agreed to play with you;
5. *Play sanely:* physically, psychologically, emotionally, and spiritually, SM can be very intense; like any intense activity it has the short-term potential to draw people farther into it than they might on other occasions regard as wise; learn your limits, learn the limits your partners want to adhere to, and play within the limits you and your partners have agreed upon;
6. *Play non-exploitively:* not everybody is ready, willing, or able to be involved in SM, but not everyone who is *un*ready, *un*willing, or *un*able knows it; honor people where they are: don't take advantage of someone else's ignorance or vulnerability to satisfy your own ego or desires.

These Commandments, like the underpinnings of all satisfying, safe play, include a bow to the Delphic Oracle: Know Thyself.

WHAT IS SM? WHAT IS IT NOT?

Myths, Fears, and Stereotypes

When you think about SM what images come to mind? What words? What feelings or sensations? What myths do you believe about its practices? What stereotypes do you adhere to as if they were fact? What fears or excitements do you have about exploring your interest in this form of erotic expression? And what do you imagine other people important to you—relatives, friends, colleagues, neighbors—might think if they knew you were reading this book? It might be worth your while to set the book aside for a few minutes now to consider those questions for yourself; you might even write your answers down, because the myths, fears, and stereotypes about SM that are alive in you are likely to color the way you learn and the way you play.

Once you've answered the questions, either on paper or in your mind, see if you have these same concerns about sex in general. Probably you do, to some extent. It's become a platitude to say that we live in a sex-negative society where titillation is fine while reality is not, but the evidence is all around. Each year while beer and soda companies sell their products with images of leggy women and chesty men, scarce municipal funds are spent to roust prostitutes in cities teeming with violence; prominent members of Congress try to proscribe the very mention of homosexuality in our schools, while many history, psychology, and sociology textbooks make little or no mention of sexual behavior at all; and major public health officials risk their jobs if they advocate protections against pregnancy and STDs, or say that masturbation is a normal human activity.

If our society holds such a pejorative view of common sexual practice, those of us who live in the society must carry those prejudices somewhere within us, even if we know they are wrong. We will improve our odds for having a truly healthy sex life—whether it includes SM or not—if we first know which of our beliefs are based in myth and which in fact. Where knowledge is power of a psychological sort, the power comes from facing our fears and prejudices and learning the truths beneath them. Truth may have the capacity to set us free, but first we have to know what the truth is.

For centuries people in Europe believed the sun, moon, and stars circled the Earth, and Galileo was nearly burned at the stake for suggesting otherwise. For centuries people in Europe believed the Earth was flat, and few explorers were so intrepid they would risk falling over its edge. For centuries western physicians believed that trepanning the skull and letting blood with leeches cured all sorts of disease, and for most of the 19th century they preached that women did not enjoy sex and that male masturbation depleted male vitality.

All these beliefs, which we now know to be false, were "known" to be true to their adherents. They were all based on fear and secured in place by fear, and they crippled people's freedom to think as well as to act. As each prejudice was examined, however, the fears that underlay it were demystified and the truth, revealed, was clearly defined.

In order to define and demystify SM we must first examine the prejudices that underlie fears and apprehensions about it. It would be a monumental task to tackle all the false beliefs that people commonly hold about any form of sexuality, and so we've asked you to think a bit about the Topic for yourself. Since our names are on this book, we'll start you off by debunking a few of the most common myths, fears, and stereotypes about SM.

Sexual Theatre

SM does not necessarily replicate reality. Erotic fantasy enactment can, instead, be a form of participatory entertainment for adults. As in any other form of theatre, a successful scene requires certain kinds of consistency. Dressing in futuristic space-age garb would create dissonance in a Victorian Ladies' School caning session, just as playing military music would impose a jarring backdrop on a nurturing baby scene. Seen in this light, the activities of SM can be understood as sexual theatre.

As we will discuss at greater length later in this book, it is the Top's job to orchestrate the elements of an SM scene, which is why the Top is often compared to the director, and the Bottom to an actor, in what amounts to an improvisational play. Costumes, lighting, location, music, atmosphere, and equipment are the physical components that contribute to the creation of an SM session, which we call—not by accident—a "scene" where people "play" in "roles."

Attitude and intent are the psychological components that illuminate any of the several purposes behind even a simple spanking scene. Where intent is concerned, for example, a Top might spank a Bottom as part of a *training* scene designed to teach the Bottom about the limits of pain that he can tolerate or the extent to which the Top likes to spank; a Top might spank a Bottom who likes intense sensation as a *reward;* a Top might spank a Bottom as a demonstration of *power,* as an experiential statement that he has the right to spank her; or a Top might spank a Bottom as *punishment.*

Attitude, too, informs a scene's purpose and direction. The punishment in a punishment scene may be *real,* to take just one example, if the Bottom has genuinely displeased the Top, or it may be *fantasy* if the Bottom enjoys being "naughty" and the Top enjoys finding "reasons" to punish.

In a real punishment spanking the Top is likely to be very formal and strict, and to take a firm, no-nonsense approach, providing little in the way of warm-up or cool-down. In a reward or sensual spanking, on the other hand, the Top is likely to be kind and even affectionate, taking the Bottom on a pleasurable physical journey. This kind of spanking may be fully as intense as any other sort, but it is generally delivered with affection, and includes a warm-up of milder sensations at the beginning and a cool-down at the end.

Although it is also consensual, a spanking designed to demonstrate the Top's power—"I spank you because I have the *right* to spank you, even if you're not pleased about being spanked right now"—can bring about a Bottom's deep submission since it demands that she honor her agreement to place the Top's desires above her own: an agreement that goes to the very heart of consensual power exchange.

There is always danger in a Top's playing when she is really angry, since the powerful emotion can wrest control from her. If she is not in control of her feelings she may do damage: she may strike too hard or swing wildly and hit some place that should never be hit, such as her bottom's tailbone. Besides, if she is out of control emotionally, her bottom cannot safely be out of control as well: someone must remain in charge, and that is really the Top's responsibility and privilege. For all these reasons real punishment scenes are best executed after the Top has had a chance to calm down and can proceed with a level head. That way she can enjoy the scene, and the bottom can take the opportunity to learn not to do whatever created the need for punishment in the first place.

Certainly, if the bottom *likes* intense sensation, spanking will be an ineffective punishment that may leave the Top with a bottom who deliberately makes mistakes. But in any case brutality and excessive force never have a place in consensual SM. Quite often successful punishment can be effected through such mild means as the Top's emotional withdrawal, or standing the bottom in the corner of the room holding a penny to the wall with his nose, or having the bottom write 100 times, "I will not . . ." or "I will always. . . ." Often it can be accomplished through denial of some favorite activity for a specific length of time, such as having no orgasms for a week.

Though all this talk of punishment may sound like pretty strict behavior modification, there is another component to it: we are all adults in the world of consensual SM, and we assume one another to be responsible. Therefore, we can understand and discuss among ourselves what we are seeking to learn and to do. Punishment, we know, doesn't work very well with children, prisoners, or other people who are forced to accept it against their wills, or who are bullied into taking it without their consent. But punishment may work very well indeed when the person being punished has the capacity to know its purposes, supports those ends, and has consented to its practice to further them

Fantasy punishment is an altogether different scene. There is no *real* error to correct: punishment just happens to be a scenario both Top and bottom like to play with, so the Top finds fault with the bottom's posture, phrasing, or failure to follow some impossible command, such as an order to kneel while tied standing to the wall. A fantasy punishment scene may *look* just like a real punishment scene, but it is accompanied by the good-natured irony that underscores SM's theatricality. The bottom may protest like a lamb at the slaughter, but she would be truly unhappy only if the Top did not follow through.

Pain and Violence, Abuse and Consent

There's a scene in David Lean's *Lawrence of Arabia* in which T.E. Lawrence, portrayed by Peter O'Toole, holds his hand in a candle flame before pinching out the wick. "Doesn't it hurt?" asks his companion. "Of course it hurts," Lawrence replies; "the trick is not *minding* that it hurts."

The sensations we recognize as pain are designed by our bodies to be taken as warning signals by our brains so that we can fight, flee, or otherwise save ourselves from danger. But we do not have to live as slaves to our biological programming. Once we know that some particular pain does not really represent a danger to us, we no longer *have* to counter or avoid the sensation if, for some reason, we do not choose to do so: we begin to have some freedom of choice regarding our responses to what really is just an intense sensation. But while we may exercise to build our bodies, repeating with every set of reps, "No pain, no gain," we still react with the instincts of self-preservation when we stub our toes or catch our fingers against the jamb of a closing door.

Pretend for a moment that you're a doctor, and a man comes to your office to have you treat his broken leg.

"How'd you break the leg, Charlie?" you ask.

"Football game," he answers, wincing as you examine the break. "I went out long and my buddy Steve just tagged me."

You set the bone and it heals, and Charlie is fine.

But six months later Charlie is back again, this time with a smashed finger.

"What happened, Charlie?" you inquire.

"Football again," he replies. "I was holding the snap and I didn't get my hand out of the way fast enough when Tom kicked the ball."

You put his finger in a splint and in a few weeks Charlie is fine again.

But three months later Charlie is brought in on a stretcher with what turns out to be a concussion.

"What happened this time, Charlie?" you ask.

"Football," he says in a blurry voice. "That new guy, Frank, has a really mean block, and I just got hit."

As a responsible physician you'll probably advise Charlie to be a bit more careful in his game, but you're not likely to suggest that he's emotionally disturbed, or that he should stop playing football—and if you did, Charlie might well think you were overstepping your bounds: he *likes* to play ball, it's good exercise, it's a chance to unwind with his friends, and, well, you take a few risks to have a good time in life.

Now imagine the same set of scenarios, but each time Charlie comes to your office the reason he gives for his bruises and scrapes is that he likes to be whipped, or he likes rough sex. Now do you think he's in need of psychotherapy to cure what ails him? Now would you suggest he stop doing what he enjoys?

In our society we have some peculiar attitudes toward sex, and particularly toward sexual behaviors and activities someone else told us were bad and wrong. Since, until the mid-1980s, nearly the entire range of literature available about SM was made up of misinformed pornography and equally misinformed psychological theory, the range of our prejudice about it should come as no surprise.

Uneducated pornographers, misinformed psychologists, and ignorant legislators have contributed to a popular notion that SM is or is tantamount to abuse. But abuse occurs when at least one party to an action doesn't want to participate in some activity and is compelled or coerced into it anyway, or when a person such as a young child gives consent he is really incapable of giving because he does not understand what he is consenting to.

One of the fundamental principles of SM as we understand it is that it *is* consensual. For an activity to be consensual all participants must have agreed to it; consensuality implies not only that they are conscious of what they are going to do, but also that they are competent to give their consent.

Although some people dislike having their erotic pleasures associated with the activities the Marquis de Sade and Gustave von Sacher-Masoch wrote about, consensual sadomasochism still is the generally accepted term for a complex group of erotic behaviors that involve intense sensation and/or intense mental discipline. Since the behaviors are erotic, people who engage in them usually find them sexually stimulating; since the activities are consensual, everyone involved must have agreed to engage in them, and to be capable of making such an agreement. Children do not engage in consensual sadomasochism because they are not capable—legally if not psychologically—of giving consent; adults who are coerced into these or other activities have also not consented.

Whether consent is construed as a psychological or a legal matter, it underlies everything we've written in this book. As a psychotherapist and a sex educator, as a man and a woman, and simply as human beings, we are deeply opposed to non-consensual behavior: to any activity in which people participate against their wills, or in which they are persuaded to engage—or to refrain from engaging—without having access to information that might alter their desires to participate, whether that activity concerns war, sex, religion, or eating. When one person is abused we are all abused.

In part it is precisely consensuality that enables us to distinguish between activities we regard as abusive and those we regard as traumatic. When soldiers kill each other in war we understand that at least they knew what they were getting into when they put on their uniforms and picked up their guns. Whether we like it or not, and whether we approve of war or not, the soldiers consented to the dangers of their profession. When civilians are killed on our city streets we rightly call it murder: they did not consent to this sort of danger.

We make the same distinction with commonplace sexual intercourse, which we call sex when it is consensual, and rape when it is not. And for the purposes of this book we make the same distinction between forms of SM that may look to outsiders like physical, sexual, or emotional abuse, and abuse that is the real thing.

Many dictionaries define violence in terms of an event's or an action's intensity—a violent hurricane is identified by winds that are unusually strong even for that sort of storm, a violent headache by how much it hurts rather than by the nature of the pain or by how long it continues. But violence in the human realm may be better understood by the effects of a behavior or the intention behind it.

In general, the purpose of violence is to cause non-consensual physical or psychological harm or damage to someone or something. Someone may be violent regardless of sex, gender, size, age, political agenda, social status, profession, or SM role. People who become violent with sex, play, or domestic partners frequently do so as a means of forcing or intimidating the partners to accept behaviors to which the partner has not consented. Violence is usually motivated by a desire to avenge real or imagined slights or offenses, and fueled by feelings of anger, hostility, or fear, whether those feelings are acknowledged consciously or not. Once begun, violence often recurs in cycles, and escalates in severity.

As we said a few pages ago, we are all adults in the world of consensual SM, and we assume one another to be responsible. Nonetheless, violence occurs in the SM community as it occurs every place else, and abuse does sometimes masquerade as SM.

If someone is involved in a great many real punishment scenes; if a Top often plays when angry; if a bottom can never please a Top and is frequently in some sort of unhappy trouble; if a Top wants to be in complete control all the time and a bottom, displeased with this situation, goes along with it anyway; if a bottom often manipulates a Top in order to get attention of some sort: all these are signs of the kind of trouble that can provoke the anger that can lead to violence. Then what looks like consensual SM may become something very different. It may become something that happens, as the recovery movement reminds us, in the dark, in isolation: without witnesses or the possibility of intervention. Human violence, we reiterate, is nonconsensual and *intends* to harm: that is part of what makes it true abuse.

The first hallmark of abuse is that something is happening between or among people that is not negotiated, nonconsensual, and unpleasant for at least one party. Apart from the SM-specific behaviors we mentioned in the paragraph above, certain types of behavior are signs that abuse is probably taking place in SM, as they are elsewhere. For instance,

- if one partner physically hurts or restrains another against her will outside a consensually negotiated scene;
- if a partner intentionally, consistently, or repeatedly violates negotiated limits in *or* outside a scene;
- if one partner forces or coerces another to do things the second partner has not clearly agreed to do, including but not limited to sexual acts;
- if one partner feels trapped in a role or relationship and cannot extricate himself because of another partner's behavior;
- if one partner isolates another from family, friends, community, or free associations with other people;
- if one partner belittles, demeans, or ridicules another outside a scene specifically negotiated to involve humiliation or consensual nonconsent, or attempts to undermine her self-esteem, especially regarding limits she has set for herself;
- if one partner steals from another, or withholds food, money, or other goods outside a negotiated scene;
- if one partner damages, destroys, or threatens the property of another, including pets; or harms or threatens friends or family of another;
- if one partner becomes afraid of another with cause.

Top, bottom, or switch, no one has the right to abuse another. People do sometimes elect to remain in abusive relationships or situations, but even when it is disguised as love or altruism, or acknowledged as a form of co-dependency, their motive is usually fear, such as the fear that the abuse will only get worse when the abuser learns of the abused partner's wish to leave, or fear of real or imagined financial, material, or emotional hardship that may follow a separation.

Abuse is never pleasant, and it can be emotionally crippling and physically dangerous—even fatal. If you believe you are in an abusive situation and feel you cannot leave, seek help from any abuse survivor's network in your area. If you don't know of such a network, start with any hospital, clinic, crisis or self-help hotline you can reach, including Suicide Prevention, and follow their suggestions until you get the help you need. If you are in an actively violent situation, call 991 for emergency assistance.

SELF-ESTEEM

One reason some people subject themselves to abuse is that they believe they deserve it, or don't believe they deserve better. This belief is not always conscious, and it is not always what the people would say they believe about themselves, but sometimes what people *do*—the patterns in the ways we live our lives—speaks more eloquently than what we say.

It's easy to become acquainted with the SM stereotypes of low self-esteem, since they're what much bad SM porn (and bad SM press) is based on: the groveling bottom who regards himself as a lowly worm and believes he deserves nothing more than to be hurt and used as someone's doormat; the sneering Top who lives behind a stoic, aloof, or cynical mask, unable to acknowledge the fear, tenderness, and other vulnerable sides to his human nature.

Real people fully embody these sorts of stereotypes only rarely, if for no other reason than that they're difficult to sustain in daily life. But many people, SM players and vanilla folk alike, have some small facet of these sides to our personalities. Just as there is real abuse in the SM world, as well as in mainstream society, so also there are real self-esteem issues among SM players as well as among the populace at large.

It isn't a sin, a crime, or a disease to have low self-esteem: it's a problem in living that most people experience from time to time, at least as bouts of self-doubt during periods of severe stress or emotional upheaval. For some people low self-esteem is chronic: a nearly constant fear or belief that they are just not good enough—either for some particular task, role, or partner, or as a general state of being. Whether chronic or transient, however, low self-esteem is never enjoyable; it limits a person's freedom and joy in life whether she finds her pleasures in SM, horse racing, child rearing, or all three. Most therapists and other people in the helping professions know various techniques and strategies by which even chronic low self-esteem can be raised to some extent, and people whose value goes up in their own eyes usually feel better about themselves, and frequently live more satisfying and productive lives as well.

Sometimes a person who is coming out in SM experiences low self-esteem for reasons that are specific to her situation. After all, it is not uncommon to feel confused when we find that our wants and needs differ from the expressed values of the society in which we live. One cause of such confusion is that someone neglects to distinguish between what she wants in the uniquely focused erotic theatre of SM and what she wants in the more broadly-based world that includes her job, her friends, her family, and the evening news, because what's awkward or dangerous to want in our usual lives may well be pleasing and even highly desirable in the dungeon. We've all grown up in a society that tells us we are not supposed to hit people we love, for example, nor are we supposed to allow ourselves to be hit by the ones we love: isn't that what domestic abuse is frequently about? Yet, in a negotiated, consensual SM scene we may hit or be hit most intensely by the person we love best in all the world—and say Thank you for the opportunity afterwards.

Whatever this implies about us and our self-esteem, it does *not* mean that we think poorly of ourselves, or can't find love in any other way, or are collections of rabid psychopaths champing to be released from our little private hells. The person who finds delight in being treated as a lapdog now and then may simply like to be petted and coddled without having to do anything except loll his tongue: the experience of being cherished can be hard to find in much of modern life. Alternatively, the person may have discovered some rare strength or value in his psychological makeup that being treated as a pet brings out in him. Many pre-Industrial societies understood that people share characteristics with other animals, that there is no such thing as an inherently bad animal, and that every animal has its own special traits. A chief called Sitting Bull may have been known for his grounded, stolid, earthy nature; a warrior may have been called Crazy Horse to honor his powerful intuition in battle. What strengths, powers, and values might inhere in being known as Lap Dog?

Because submission can be a charged issue in our relatively aggressive social order, women sometimes wonder how they can reconcile being submissive with being feminists, as men sometimes wonder how they can reconcile themselves to being submissive in a world that seems to demand dominance from males. (Other women may fear that being dominant will conflict with their desires to appear feminine, and other men may wonder how to be dominant without seeming arrogant, but these questions more rarely have to do with self-esteem.)

In order to answer those questions it is important to know, first, what a person means by "submissive." Does he mean that he does what his Top says in a scene, or does he mean he likes to get done? Is he a submissive Top ("Which crop should I should hit you with? That one? Okay")? If a bottom, does he submit willingly, or is he a rebel? In any case, is he submissive 24 hours a day, or does he occupy a subordinate role only for the duration of a scene? Does he submit to a special someone, to any or many people who negotiate with him, or to the universe at large?

Clearly, there is a difficulty inherent in defining actions by labels; that difficulty becomes more obvious when we seek to define "feminist." Andrea Dworkin claims that title, and she has lobbied actively to ban SM, pornography, and most male-female erotic activity you have ever imagined, let alone enjoyed. Pat Califia has also been referred to as a feminist, but her books, such as *Macho Sluts* and *Doc and Fluff,* include female Tops, female bottoms, male Tops, male bottoms, variously dominant and submissive, all playing with one another and many switching roles and partners in remarkable and often unexpected combinations. Cynthia Slater, the founder of the Society of Janus, certainly thought of herself as a feminist, and she was a bisexual switch: she was interested in the energy exchange, not the label. In one perhaps apocryphal story either Pat or Cynthia, depending on who tells the tale, was dressed in a high-necked white lace Victorian gown while in Top mode for a party. A horrified guest, expecting her to be in heavy black leather, objected, "Tops don't wear white lace!" To which Pat or Cynthia is supposed to have replied, "Tops wear anything they want to wear."

The same position is useful for SM feminists. As we see it, feminists do what they want to do in their sex lives. the key is that *they* want to. Feminism is not defined by what someone does in bed: feminism is defined by what a person does in her head—and in the voting booth, the planning committee meeting, the workplace, and sometimes in the streets.

People can be bound to some extent by their assumptions about definitions, and so they may be freed somewhat by thinking about their behavior instead. For example, engaging in submissive behavior for erotic pleasure is not the same as being *a* submissive. It is, instead, a way to enjoy oneself, or to meet one's erotic needs or desires—just as engaging in dominant behavior is a way for someone else to get what she wants, or for the same person to get what she wants at some other time, with some other person, or in some other set of circumstances.

Nor does engaging in submissive behavior for erotic pleasure imply that one is submissive or engages in submissive behavior for any other reason: professional dominatrice have frequently said that their clients include many high-powered people who are extremely dominant in their professional and social lives, and who simply need a break from being in charge.

Questions about submission are very closely tied to questions about self-esteem because they frequently imply that being submissive means a person has no power. But this is a notion we dispute. No one can give up power he doesn't already have, so the more power a person has, the more he can give up, and, consequently, the more empowering his submission can be. Speaking only for ourselves, when we Top we don't want to play with people who think badly of themselves: we want someone's bottoming to be a worthy gift. Similarly, when we bottom we give a great deal: a Top who can't recognize that gift is not likely to be able to receive all we have to offer, nor is she likely to be able to give much back to us.

This is also why submission can actually *build* an individual's personal power: through genuine submission a person can realize how much he has to give and how valuable it is; can realize that he is able to control himself enough to give it away when and how he chooses to and not at other times; can realize that he is able to master his own will to give that power up the way his Top wants it instead of the way he thinks his Top *should* want it; and can realize whole new levels of pride in who and what he is—not the false pride of an inflated ego, but the true pride that, like humility, comes from knowing the depths of one's self.

The world in which dominance is demanded from a male is not a world that recognizes the value of females or feminine components in males; nor does it value the traditionally receptive qualities inherent in submission, service, or surrender. As a result, we who live in this world are always, to some extent, cut off from others, and from essential parts of ourselves as well. When we discover the strength that can come from gracefully turning our power over to another, we can also discover the limits stereotypes impose on us, and the freedom that lies in living for our experience rather than our labels.

We're not taught in or society to be gracious about serving: we're taught that it's menial and even demeaning. But submissive service is the ideal that underlies chivalry: being and doing your very best for the pleasure and honor of someone you esteem. Neither are we taught to be gracious and humble when served, so to cover our awkward embarrassment we become haughty and distant when offered respect; we are mean to our servants, thereby robbing ourselves as well as them of the intimacy devotion entails.

When politics is as anti-sexual as it is throughout the power blocs of the modern world, very few sexual activities—let alone sexual fantasies—are politically correct. So we don't mean that someone's fantasy to be a useless worm trod upon by some contemptuous bitch or brute should not be valued as highly as any other, nor that such a scene cannot be hot. We do mean that sex is not politics (however politicized sexuality may become), that fantasy and reality are different realities (yes, we said that), and that it behooves us all to distinguish between them.

Juicy Lucy had a very useful observation about the process of consensual SM that was published in the indisputably feminist lesbian SM manifesto, "If I Ask You to Tie Me Up, Will You Still Want to Love Me?" in the Samois anthology *Coming to Power* listed in our Bibliography. She wrote,

> Sadist and masochist are terms I have a schizophrenic reaction to. When and how I use these terms changes depending on the context and on who I'm with. In a sexual context sadist and masochist are roles that define erotic poles of power and have meanings of passion trust and intensity that flow from a fully consensual situation. . . . I also use the terms top and bottom to describe the two basic power positions in S/M. . . . The exchange is: sadist/top/dominant/sender flowing into masochist/bottom/passive/receiver. However, it is an oversimplification to talk about the erotic exchange as though it only flowed one way. Each side has many levels of apparent and actual power. In sexual S/M the exchange is mutual, with both sides giving and receiving erotic intensity. For example, the trust/openness of the bottom is a constant turn-on to the top, even though it's the bottom who's being had. The power and erotic exchange always flows full circle. If it doesn't then it's not satisfying and the satisfaction of all concerned is a prime goal in S/M. . . . Heal and be healed. Spirit surround you.

WHAT IS SM?

So what is SM if it is not abuse or violence and it is not coercive, even though with its grand flourishes it may look like or even present itself as any or all of these? It is a highly dramatic and sophisticated form of sexual theatre, requiring the consent of all participants and expressing its drama through physical and psychological intensity that is consensual, erotic, and fun. On with the show.

Nonreproductive Sexual Behavior: Ethological and Cultural Considerations

Ina Jane Wundram

Sexual behavior in humans and other animals has traditionally been associated with reproduction and continuity of the species. Many of us take that association for granted, for it is an old idea in Western thinking although not necessarily obvious to all human minds. For example, the Trobriand Islanders believe that sexual intercourse is not responsible for the baby that results; instead, the male is merely opening the door for the baby, making a little less difficult its way into the world (14). In our own tradition, however, it has been known for centuries that the production of offspring is necessarily preceded by copulation.

This association of sexuality and reproduction has been further reinforced by the Judeo-Christian ethic and the ancient need for males to secure possession of females and to establish paternity. The influence of Christian morality on Western thinking perhaps reached a peak during the Victorian era, when it was believed that intercourse should occur for procreation only and that all other forms of sexuality were perversions. Even in this decade of the 20th century, many educated persons, although better informed about such matters than their Victorian forebears, assume that sexuality exists primarily for reproduction.

It is entirely possible, however, that the assumption is ill-founded. Not only is considerable sexual behavior unrelated to reproduction, but this nonreproductive behavior makes up a major portion of human sexuality in Western society.

What is meant by nonreproductive sexual behavior? It can be defined as all sexual behavior wherein the probability of a sperm reaching an egg approaches zero. Contrast that with the definition of reproductive sexual behavior, wherein the probability that some sperm will reach an egg approaches one, or 100%. One can immediately see a difficulty in determining the meaning of 'sexual' when it is taken out of a reproductive context. Even so, most of us would agree to include as sexual such forms of behavior as masturbation, homosexuality, voyeurism, pedophilia, various fetishisms, necrophilia, and so on. In none of the above is there any possibility that a sperm will reach an egg. Even in heterosexual couplings, many of the positions employed do not allow access of sperm to egg, such as anal intercourse or oral sex. Moreover, since the maximum length of time a woman is fertile is about four days per month, the majority of standard, missionary-position couplings cannot result in the production of offspring.

There is a temptation to dismiss these phenomena as being unique to humans, for surely sexual behavior in other animals is closely tied to reproduction. Yet, here again, we are on shaky ground, for nonreproductive sexual behavior is not restricted to the human species.

For fuller understanding of the scope of the problem, we should begin at the beginning, phylogenetically speaking, with the protozoa. It is with those simple, single-celled animals that we first find the distinction between reproduction and sexuality. The protozoa were presumably early inventors of sexual reproduction, having somehow learned to come together in pairs for the purpose of exchanging bits of genetic information before separating to divide into daughter cells. All the same, protozoa are quite content to reproduce asexually as well, through simple cell division, so sexual behavior is not a prerequisite for reproduction in this animal group. Whether there is any nonreproductive sexual behavior in protozoa is uncertain because of our poor understanding of the meaning of 'sexual' here, but there is a mysterious process, called 'autogamy' (10), that is difficult to classify in any other way. In that process the protozoan encysts (builds a protective cyst or wall around itself), as protozoa do occasionally, and undergoes changes as if it is preparing for sexual union with another protozoan. That is, it splits its nuclear material into a macronucleus and a micronucleus, but, instead of exchanging micronuclei with another of its kind, it "autogamizes"—allows the two subnuclei to reunite. The cyst then opens, and this same protozoan swims forth invigorated, as if somehow revitalized by the process. The point is that, although protozoa are able to reproduce either with or without sex, the process of autogamy includes a sexual-like behavior that is not followed by reproduction.

Moving up the phylogenetic scale to multi-cellular animals, one finds very little information in the literature on nonreproductive sexual behavior in those forms. The reason for the lack may partly be that scientists, like most people, have been taught to equate sexual behavior with reproduction, so they do not look for nonreproductive sexual behavior. In addition, as we have seen, when sexual behavior is removed from a reproductive context, it becomes difficult to define, especially as it might occur in life forms so alien to our own.

The behavior patterns of mammals, however, have been studied more thoroughly, and nonreproductive sexual behavior has been reported for virtually every eutherian mammalian species, with the most dominant forms being masturbation and homosexuality. Female dogs that are not in heat will rub their clitorises on any suitable object until some sort of seemingly pleasurable resolution is achieved. At least one female spayed cat has been famous for shoe fetishism: when guests would remove their shoes to relax and be comfortable, the cat would dash out of hiding and attack the shoe in a matter most embarrassing to guest and host alike. Sheep, prairie dogs, horses, rats—all provide innumerable examples of behavior in the mammalian class that can be described only as sexual but cannot result in the production of offspring (8). Even in the dolphin there are many reports of masturbation and homosexuality in both sexes. In one recorded case of necrophilia in this group a male dolphin carried a dead female about for five hours, copulating with her several times (5).

The mammalian order of most direct concern to anthropologists is that of the primates. It is no surprise that nonreproductive sexual behavior has been observed in every major primate group: prosimians (4), new-world monkeys (1), old-world monkeys (2), and apes (17). Traditionally, primatologists have tended to dismiss such behavior in captive primates as an expression of frustration, confinement, or stress: "zoo-behavior," as it is sometimes called. Recently, however, field studies of primate groups in the world have revealed that nonreproductive sexual behavior is not restricted to captive primates. Reports of masturbation, male and female homosexuality, and heterosexual mountings out-of-season are becoming more frequent as observation and data-gathering techniques improve (16, 18).

At this point an important distinction should be made. In virtually all primate groups where dominance hierarchies are important in the social structure, sexual gestures are used for communicative purposes. For example, subordinate males present themselves to dominant males, who often respond by briefly mounting the subordinate male. While it is difficult to know the subjective impressions of the primates involved, this behavior probably has no sexual meaning but is merely a way of reaffirming the social status of the two individuals. Yet, here again, the uneasy feeling arises that when sexual behavior is removed from a reproductive context it becomes elusive and difficult to define.

Even if we ignore all forms of social behavior that use sexual gestures, we find numerous reports of behavior that serves no reproductive function but can be classified only as sexual. For example, Itani (9), from study of the Japanese macaque, describes males masturbating while holding in a paternal manner infants that they have adopted. Blurton-Jones and Trollope (3) have observed that stump-tailed macaque mothers often comfort their infants, male or female, by rhythmically stroking the infants' genitalia. Tokuda et al. (19) observed in the pigtail macaque that an estrous female would sometimes mount other females. Among orangutans there have been numerous reports of rape, both homosexual and heterosexual, when the female was not in estrus (18).

It is the human primate, though, who has perhaps the highest frequency of nonreproductive sexual behavior. Sexually speaking, humans are quite different from the other primates. Not only does the human male have a proportionally larger penis than any other primate, but the human clitoris is one of the smallest relative to the size of the individual. Most primate females have rather long clitorises, and in some species, such as the gibbon, it is longer than the penis.

The clitoris is a unique organ in the animal kingdom. All mammalian females have clitorises, although their evolutionary significance is unknown. While the penis serves three physiological functions—excretion, reproduction, and pleasure—the clitoris has evolved purely as an organ of pleasure. It has no other function. Its pleasure function, moreover, is not related to reproduction, or is so only incidentally. This fact is especially striking in humans, for it is not at all uncommon for a woman never to have experienced orgasm (indeed, be unaware of the existence of the clitoris) and give birth to many children. The opposite situation also exists: some women capable of multiple orgasms may be sterile. The clitoris, then, is a sexual organ with no reproductive function. It could be argued that in many cases the reproductive act brings pleasure to the female via the clitoris, but that is an incidental pleasure. It is not reproductively necessary. Masters and Johnson (15), Kinsey et al. (12), and others have repeatedly shown that most positions for intercourse do not stimulate the clitoris enough to produce orgasm in most females, and yet it is the clitoris, not the vagina, that is the major transducer of sexual stimuli.

Although various speculations have been offered about why the human clitoris is so small (6), none is completely satisfactory, and no one has explained why such an organ has evolved, if it has no reproductive significance, and how it is adaptive.

Humans are sexually different from other primates in another way. Instead of having periods of estrus occurring at certain times of the year, humans are in constant sexual readiness. Sexual activity can and does occur at any time of any month. Nonhuman primates often show prolonged estrus periods during captivity, and indulge in much more nonreproductive sex than they do in the wild. Allison Jolly (11) has pointed out that in this regard humans are somewhat like captive primates. Is culture our jail?

There is no doubt that humans are strongly influenced by culture, and sexual behavior patterns are no exception. Not only does culture prescribe how, when, and with whom we shall engage in reproductive sex, but every culture has some way of dealing with nonreproductive sexual behavior as well. Cultural attitudes toward this aspect of human sexuality range from outright prohibition to formalized sanction (7, 20). Some cultures encourage this behavior, others ignore it, still others ritualize it (8). Now that anthropologists are beginning to shake off their own Victorian heritage, more and more information becomes available about the varieties of human sexual behavior. And much of the behavior has no reproductive significance.

Distinguishing between reproduction and nonreproductive sexual behavior is thus an essential task for ethnographers, but, even with the definition provided herein, the task is not an easy one. Just as the colors of the visible spectrum are categorized differently by different cultures, so are the patterns of behavior that accompany sexual arousal. Physiological arousal, which may or may not result in orgasm, is a natural result of sexual stimulation (15). There is a strong cultural determinant to this stimulation, as there is to the behavior associated with it. Theoretically, sexual arousal can be measured and recorded in a clinical or laboratory setting by techniques pioneered by Masters and Johnson (15), but those techniques may be difficult to employ in the field. Still, ethnologists have an advantage over ethologists in that they can ask their informants about their subjective feelings. At present there is no way of obtaining this information from nonhuman animals, although preliminary studies on physiological sexual arousal are being conducted on primates in captivity (13).

If we are to accept the existence of nonreproductive sexual behavior in humans and other animals we find ourselves in an intellectual predicament. How has such behavior evolved if it indeed serves no immediate reproductive function? What other functions does it serve, and how is it adaptive? We are a long way from answering those questions, although we can find some correlations between this type of behavior and other social parameters.

The association between sexual gestures and primate dominance hierarchies has already been mentioned. The major portion of nonreproductive sexual behavior, however, seems unrelated to dominance or social status, especially in humans.

This form of sexual behavior appears closely correlated with aggression in some instances, but aggression is also associated with reproduction sex, especially in nonhuman species (20).

It has been suggested that nonreproductive sexual behavior has some relationship to population density. Studies of caged rats have shown an increase in male homosexual activity with crowding, and numerous other investigations indicate an increase in nonreproductive sex under crowded conditions (8). Sociobiologists would say that this behavior is adaptive because it helps curb population growth, and that it always exists at a low frequency in populations of any size. The problem with this interpretation is that this behavior is common in populations that have not reached their maximum limit, and does not always come to the rescue when a limit *is* reached.

Perhaps there is some correlation between nonreproductive sexual behavior and length of childhood dependency. As we go up the phylogenetic scale in primates we find an increase in the length of time that an individual spends in growing up. The period is longest in humans. During childhood many behavioral patterns are learned, among them forms of sexual behavior, and in all higher primates sexual behavior is more learned than innate. So, during a prolonged childhood an individual perhaps has time to learn many ways of achieving sexual pleasure that have little or nothing to do with reproduction.

There also seems to be a strong correlation between nonreproductive sexual behavior and relative size of the cerebral cortex. The more important that cortically determined behavior is to the species, the greater frequency of nonreproductive sexual behavior. For example, we find more homosexuality and autosexuality among apes than we do among prosimians.

Obviously, the answers to these questions are not simple at our present level of knowledge. More observations are needed on nonhuman primates and other animals, as well as on humans from many different cultures. This paper seeks to bring to general awareness the existence of an important but neglected category of behavior: behavior that seems to be sexual but serves no reproductive function. Up to now, such behavior has been ignored or relegated to insignificance by scientists and laypersons alike, but in the near future we may be faced with the problem of redefining the meaning of the word 'sexual.' Only when this situation has been clarified can we hope for a better understanding of many aspects of animal and human behavior.

REFERENCES CITED

1. Altman, S.A. 1959. Field Observations on a Howling Monkey Society. Journal of Mammalogy 40:317–330.

2. Bernstein, I. S. 1967. A Field Study on the Pigtail Monkey (Macaca nemestrina). Primates 8:217–228.

3. Blurton-Jones, N. G., and J. Trollope. 1968. Social Behavior of Stump-Tailed Macaques in Captivity. Primates 9:365–394.

4. Bourne, G. H. 1974. Primate Odyssey. New York: G.P. Putnam's Sons.

5. Caldwell, M. C., and D. K. Caldwell. 1966. Epimeletic (Care-Giving) Behavior in Cetacea. *In* Whales, Dolphins, and Porpoises. K.S. Norris, ed. Pp. 755–789. Berkeley: University of California Press.

6. Campbell, B. G. 1966. Human Evolution. Chicago: Aldine.

7. Churchill, W. 1967. Homosexual Behavior Among Males. Englewood Cliffs, N.J.: Prentice-Hall.

8. Ford, C. S., and F. A. Beach. 1951. Patterns of Sexual Behavior. New York: Harper and Bros.

9. Itani, J. 1959. Paternal Care in the Wild Japanese Monkey, Macaca fuscata fuscata. Primates 2:61–93.

10. Jahn, T. L. and F. F. Jahn. 1949. How to Know the Protozoa. Dubuque, Iowa: Wm. C. Brown.

11. Jolly, A. 1972. The Evolution of Primate Behavior. New York: Macmillan.

12. Kinsey, A. C., et al. 1953. Sexual Behavior in the Human Female. Philadelphia: W. B. Saunders.

13. Lemmon, W. B. 1978. Folia Primatologica. In press.

14. Malinowski, B. 1929. The Sexual Lives of Savages in Northwestern Melanesia. New York: Halcyon House.

15. Masters, W. H., and V. E. Johnson. 1966. Human Sexual Response. Boston: Little, Brown.

16. Morris, D., ed. 1969. Primate Ethology: Essays on the Sociosexual Behavior of Apes and Monkeys. Chicago: Aldine.

17. Nishida, T. 1970. Social Behavior and Relationships Among Wild Chimpanzees of the Mahali Mountains. Primates 11:47–87.

18. Rijksen, H. D. 1978. A Field Study on Sumatran Orangutans (Pongo pygmaeus abelii Lesson 1827). Wageningen, Netherlands: Mededelingen Landbouwhogeschool.

19. Tiduka, K., R. C. Simons, and G. D. Jensen. 1968. Sexual Behavior in a Captive Group of Pigtailed Monkeys (Macaca nemestrina). Primates 9:283–294.

20. Tripp, C. A. 1975. The Homosexual Matrix. New York: McGraw-Hill.

MENSTRUATION

MALE MENSTRUATION: A RITUAL ALTERNATIVE TO THE OEDIPAL TRANSITION

Ruth W. Lidz and Theodore Lidz

The term 'male menstruation' often seems to elicit a reaction of disbelief bordering on shock, or a sense of having misunderstood. It does not refer to a phenomenon resembling hysterical stigmata but to a usage among at least three peoples—the Australian Aborigine, the Indigene of Papua/New Guinea, and the Mohave Indians. Here we shall examine its widespread practice in Australian New Guinea. We do not turn to the study of an esoteric ritual in a remote corner of the globe because of its curiosity, but because we believe it leads to some important insights into problems of sexual identity in the male and the relationship between masculine envy of women and the young boy's initial identification with his mother. These topics have aroused considerable attention in recent years both because of the psychoanalytically oriented studies of transsexuals by Stoller (1966), Greenson (1968), Socarides (1973) and others, and because of various challenges to the psychoanalytic emphasis on women's penis envy without a counterbalancing interest in men's envy of women's generative capacities (Bettelheim, 1971; Greenson, 1966). It is evident from Jaffe's (1968) review of the psychoanalytic literature pertaining to masculine envy of women that the topic needs clarification. The examination of a way of life that differs profoundly from that of Western civilizations enables us to set aside some of our basic preconceptions and take a fresh look at some cardinal problems of human development. The material would seem to require a re-examination of the functions of the oedipal transition, the incest taboo and men's feelings of superiority to women.

We became interested in the topic of male menstruation while working with psychiatric patients in New Guinea several years ago. We were struck by the severe sexual anxieties of male patients. One believed that a girl to whom he was attracted was a witch who was seeking to seduce him in order to drain and kill him, and another feared his wife possessed a dentate vagina. Healthy men as well as patients had an inordinate fear of menstrual blood; a fear we came to realize seemed to be an important factor in determining the social structure of the villages. Then when we started studying these matters, we were surprised to learn that the practice of male menstruation was widespread and important, if not essential, to fostering a firm male identity in youths who had been raised primarily by their mothers for the first eight to fifteen years of their lives.

Before we consider the implications of male menstruation to psychoanalytic developmental theory, we shall examine the practice in two different localities in Papua/New Guinea in which, even though the means of promoting menstruation are very different, we can find underlying similarities in the rituals and in the functions they serve. The anthropologist Kenneth Read (1965, pp. 158–177) has provided us with a vivid and dramatic account of the male initiation ritual of the Gahuka-Gama people in the Asaro Valley in the Eastern Highlands, a high plateau country divided by 13,000 foot mountain ranges; and Philip Newman (1965) has described the similar practices of the Gururumba in the same valley. These Highlands were undiscovered and the people unknown until 1937 and, aside from occasional government patrols and a few widely scattered administrative centres and missions, had scarcely been penetrated by Europeans until after World War II. The Gahuka-Gama were still an almost pure Stone-age people when first studied by Read in 1950.

"Male Menstruation: A Ritual Alternative to the Oedipal Transition," by Ruth W. Lidz and Theodore Lidz, reprinted from *International Journal of Psychoanalysis,* Vol. 58, 1977.

We shall then examine the initiation rituals and the practice of male menstruation of the Island of Wogeo, in the Schouten group off the north coast of Papua/New Guinea not far from the mouth of the Sepik River. The island is just some 350 miles from the Asaro Valley as the crow flies, but the peoples have been separated for thousands of years—so long that the people in the Asaro Valley did not even know that an ocean existed but rather believed that the shells they highly prize, and which are traded up to them, came from a land in which shells grow on trees, and no mention of the sea or coast occurs in their myths. When Ian Hogbin studied the people of Wogeo in 1934, he believed that he was the first white person to remain on the island for more than a few hours.

In the Asaro Valley, male menstruation forms a central part of the adolescent initiation ritual of males. The boys live with their mothers until some time between the ages of ten and fifteen and are raised primarily by their mothers as the fathers sleep in the special men's hut most of the time. The boys, ages five to seven, are subjected to a mild preliminary ritual experience when they are taken to the river to the accompaniment of the shrill sounds of the sacred flutes which they believe are the voices of the ancestor spirits. There they find themselves surrounded by a throng of armed and decorated warriors whose continual chanting is accompanied by the shrilling of the flutes. The experience is probably quite terrifying to the children but they then return home to continue living with their mothers.

The actual initiation ceremony is carried out only once every five or six years because it must be accompanied by an elaborate and expensive pig killing festival, which drains the community's resources, and therefore the initiates vary in age rather notably, but most are still prepubertal. After many weeks during which the tunes of the sacred flutes resound through the hills each night and preparations for the pig killing festival are made, the boys are assembled one morning in the various villages together with all of the men who are in full warrior regalia. The mothers of the initiates wear mourning, their bodies smeared with clay 'in recognition of their separation from their sons, who are formally crossing over into the male division of the society' (Read, 1965, p. 158). Then the men, with the initiates bunched in their centre, rush down the mountainsides, shunning the paths but crashing through the bush, shouting and chanting, and with the shrill sound of the flutes beating at the eardrums, until they reach the river towards which warriors with initiates from other villages are descending in all directions in a symbolic show of strength. There the boys, placed in the front ranks of a vast crowd, see a score of naked men standing in the river exhibiting their erect penises and masturbating. Then several of the men stride into the river in front of the initiates and one, soon to be followed by the others, takes two cigarette-shaped objects fashioned from razor-sharp leaves and thrusts them up and down in his nostrils until blood gushes profusely into the water. He is rewarded by a chorus of approving shouts from the multitude. When the bleeding stops, he staggers to the river bank, knees buckling from the self-inflicted pain. A half dozen men simultaneously follow his example; and then each initiate with his mind 'numb with apprehension of pain, the urge to struggle and escape constrained only by the greater force of shame' (Read, 1965, p. 167) is held firmly by his sponsor, and a man thrusts the leaves back and forth in his nostrils until he bleeds profusely into the river.

When the bleeding phase of the ritual has been completed, the men who had bled themselves again move into the river and each takes a length of cane, doubles it up into and V, and thrusts it like a sword-swallower down his esophagus into his stomach and draws it back and forth until he vomits into the water[1]. The procedure is then repeated on the initiates now weakened and slack from the earlier bleeding.

When, after some hours, the procedures are completed, some of the stronger men take the initiates on their shoulders and make their way uphill along the paths to the villages. Then, as they approach a village, they are suddenly attacked by the massed women of the village who hurl rocks and heavy clubs at them and threaten with bows and arrows, seriously hurting some of those struck until the men, abandoning their reserve, turn to counterattack and scatter the women. The attack is not symbolic but a venting of pent-up hostility by the women who are markedly subjugated among these people and are enraged at having their sons taken from them and forced through the painful ritual.

The initiates are then carried back to the men's hut where the secret of the magic flutes is disclosed to them; namely that the sounds are made by flutes rather than by ancestor spirits in the form of mystical birds. They are told that they must keep the secret from the women and children on pain of death. During six weeks of seclusion in the hut they are taught to play the flutes and are then paraded about the village in their new ceremonial outfits to be greeted by their women kinfolk who pretend to have difficulty in recognizing them now that they have become men. The youths then remain some years in the men's hut and are permitted only minimal contact with women. They rove about in small bands, practice nose bleeding and vomiting, learn how to play the flutes properly and how to participate in the affairs of men. Some years later, when they are between the ages of 15 and 19, and have been betrothed, they go through the ceremony again; and after a period of stringent dietary restriction and intense practice of playing the flutes during which they have their duties and rights as men fully explained, they emerge at the start of the pig festival with full male status.

To grasp the meaning and importance of the initiatory ritual, it is necessary to understand something of the structure of the society and the polarity between men and women who live in a state of uneasy collaboration, a balance between independence and a reluctant realization of the interdependence forced upon them by economic and sexual needs.

The people live in small villages, or in huts proximate to their gardens scattered around their village. Each village has at least one men's hut in which the men usually sleep and in which they keep the sacred objects—while a man's wife, or his wives, lives in a separate hut with her children. There is a criss-crossing of permanent enmity and alliances between the villages of a tribe or subtribe with, until very recently, constant warfare between enemy villages. The need for constant defence of the community and the protection of the women and children from murder, rape and cannibalism, made it imperative that boys were reared to become strong warriors. There is a strict practice of exogamy in that the men marry women from other villages, and in some localities almost 70 per cent of the wives came from enemy villages so that the man's mother and wife may both come from enemy villages. In these patrilocal villages, the mothers of the boys have been raised in a tradition that differs to some extent from the one that must be handed on to their sons. The separation of the sexes is heightened by the men's marked fear of menstrual blood, a fear probably more intense in New Guinea than any place in the world. Indeed, the malignant qualities of menstrual blood to men seem to be one of the major determinants of the societal structure. Because contact with a menstruating woman will sicken, and ingestion of a drop of menstrual blood will kill a man, the men fear sleeping with their wives or even living in close proximity to them. The danger from menstrual blood, however, provides a source of protection to women living among alien men. A husband who mistreats his wife does so at the risk of his life, for she can kill him by putting menstrual blood in his food. The danger from women, however, extends beyond contamination by her menses, for there is something about the vital essence of women that is antipathetic to men's vitality and men will be weakened and their health undermined by prolonged proximity to a woman. Loss of semen is also considered weakening, and adolescents and young men are stringently warned against overindulgence as they are not yet strong enough to withstand the powers of women and the loss of semen. A man runs the additional danger that his wife might give his semen to a sorcerer, for it is a certain way of procuring his death. We believe it is apparent, even without elaborating further, that any pleasure derived from sex is greatly diminished if not offset by the multiplicity of dangers it provokes and that many barriers exist to comfortable relationships between men and women.

The men's secret cult everywhere forms the core structure of the society and the secret of the sacred flutes, objects central to most ritual, is kept from the women and children. However, it seems clear enough that many if not all women know that the sounds are made by flutes, as well as many other secrets of the initiation rituals, but women take the attitude that as they have everything of importance—the babies, the pigs, the gardens—they will let the men have their flutes and their ceremonies if it makes them feel satisfied and if they are willing to accept this crucial responsibility. However, the women believe, as much as do the men, that the group's well-being and the fertility of the women, pigs and soil, as well as the growth and maturation of the children, depend on the mediation of the ancestor spirits who must be summoned and placated, if not controlled and satisfied, by the rituals the men carry out.[2] It is of interest that everywhere myth, in one form or another, tells that the flutes originally belonged to the women or, at least, to a woman who gave it to a man, or to a boy who turned into a man after learning to play the flute.

Now, although it is essential that the villages raise strong warriors, we have noted that the boys are raised primarily by their mothers for the first ten, or even fifteen, years of their lives; and by mothers who come from different villages and often from enemy villages. The children's attachment to their mothers is fostered by the way of life. They are breast fed for three to five years and sleep alongside of their mother for many years, while the father usually sleeps in the men's hut. A strict postpartum sexual taboo keeps the parents from having sexual intercourse for at least a year and thus enhances the mother's erogenous investment of her child. Further, the mother is the principal authority figure for the first decade of the child's life.

With this very sketchy background of the way of life of these people, let us consider what the initiation ritual and, in particular, the nose bleeding, the vomiting, and the playing of the sacred flutes are all about. What do the Indigenes consider the purpose of the rituals and what has seemed rather obvious to the ethnologists who have observed them?

It is apparent to all that the initiation ritual serves to separate the boys from their mothers and establish a new solidarity relationship to the men's group, and particularly to their male age-mates with whom they go through the many years as novitiates. They are, in a sense, reborn as men who are not only independent of women but markedly superior to them. The ritual also provides the boy with an artificial marker of his entrance into puberty that parallels the natural and obvious dividing line in the girl's life brought about by breast development and menstruation.

The vomiting is said to rid the boy of any of the mother's womb blood swallowed while he was in her womb and of any dangerous menstrual blood he had inadvertently ingested with the food his mother prepared for him. Further, according to Newman (1965), the use of the vomiting cane performs a function analogous to the artificial breaking of the hymen in the girl at the time of her first menstruation. It is believed to break a membrane inside the body which permits the boy to develop secondary sexual characteristics and become a man.

The nose bleeding is referred to as male menstruation. There is a belief, similar to that concerning the vomiting cane, that menstruation permits the girl to develop into a woman and that unless the boy is taught to menstruate he will not mature into a man. It not only permits or assures his development but, like the vomiting, is carried out to rid the boy's body of his mother's contaminating menstrual blood and, according to some, also of her womb blood that entered into his composition. These people have the genial belief that the foetus is composed of womb blood and semen and that the baby must be built up by repeated and frequent acts of copulation. However, beyond ridding the boy of his mother's womb blood and menstrual contamination, it is a means of purification from contamination in general, but particularly from the dangerous vital essence of women. Men envy women's natural means of self-purification by menstruation that preserves their health, and men who are properly concerned with their health and the attainment and maintenance of strength and attractiveness will periodically purify themselves both by vomiting and nose bleeding.

Male menstruation is also deemed an essential precursor of learning to play the sacred flutes. The sacred flutes seem to represent male creativity and provide a counterpart to women's natural creativity. As they represent the ancestor spirits who control the fertility of the people, the pigs and the land, the possession of the flutes and the ritual that influences the ancestor spirits bestows upon the man a control of fertility which, like creativity, comes more naturally to women.[3] Because of the flutes, the women have become spiritually dependent on the men who have control over the ritual contact with the ancestor spirits without whom the people could not survive.

Newman (1965, p. 80), in describing the Gururumba rituals, points out that whereas female initiation celebrates the fact of growth and the onset of reproductive power, and teaches control of this power insofar as it may affect others deleteriously, the male initiation has the purpose of inducing growth and reproductive power rather than simply celebrating its existence. It is held for the good of the initiates, not for the welfare of others. The newly initiated boys, according to the Gururumba, are not yet the equivalent of mature girls, they are not strong enough to cope with the vital sexuality of the girls, and contact with them would impair the boy's growth and development of his own vital essence. Even after they are fully developed, the males must continue to strengthen themselves through ritual and protect themselves by avoidance. Thus, by means of the initiation, the male assumes a ritual control over the same vital powers as the female acquires naturally after she begins to menstruate. The disparity between men and women is overcome 'in the rituals of the secret cult aimed at generating and maintaining a similar vital essence in men. The men reproduce symbolically all the important elements that women have naturally: the flutes are reproductive power, nose bleeding is menstruation, and breaking the tissue during the first vomiting is breaking the hymen' (Newman, 1965, p. 80). Newman points out (p. 81) the rather apparent identification of the vital essence with sexual energy; or, as we might wish to say, with 'libido'.

Although we may seem to have presented a multiplicity of purposes for the male initiation ritual including the artificial menstruation, they all relate to a single theme—providing men with powers and attributes which they believe women possess naturally.

Let us now transfer our attention to the island of Wogeo where the way of life differs considerably and the rituals are very different and yet serve the same functions. Wogeo society is much freer sexually than those in the Asaro Valley. On the small island, though marriage is exogamous, the several villages on the island are not at warfare with one another and marriage may be with a person from the opposite moiety in the same village. Premarital promiscuity is the rule; and although marriages are arranged, a girl is unlikely to marry a man she dislikes and elopement is common. Whatever danger from enemies exists comes from other islands and apparently is not great. However, according to Hogbin (1970, p. 86), the social separateness of the sexes 'is constantly underlined, and generally when working or at leisure they remain apart'. The sexes are in more or less balanced opposition. Men blame women for undermining male solidarity; and women make fun of men's assumed self-importance. Here, rather than only women being dangerous to men, each sex is dangerous to the other. 'The established doctrine is that members of each sex group would be safe and invulnerable, healthy and prosperous if only they would keep to themselves and refrain from mixing with the other sex group' (Hogbin, 1970, p. 86). However, small children would die without mothers, couples are dependent upon one another economically and sexual drives force them together, with the result that everyone is 'perpetually weakened, liable to disease and misadventure' (p. 88). The females are considered more fortunate than males because menstruation regularly frees them from contamination whereas the men must take positive measures to purify themselves.

As in the Asaro Valley, there is a preliminary to the initiation, here held between the ages of three and five; and the initiation is not fully completed until the youth is 19 or 20 years old. The relatively simple preliminary ritual consists of an ear piercing ceremony. The mythical Nibek monsters who represent the ancestor spirits are summoned from the sea by the sound of the sacred flutes. After a ceremonial or ritual fight among the men of the village, the man who has undertaken the task enters the hut where the boy is hiding with his mother, blindfolds him and pushes him outside to join other boys who are having their ears pierced and are yelling and crying from fright. They are told that 'the Nibek monsters have bitten you; they have made their first mark and will come back later and eat you up'. Like the preliminary ceremony among the Gahuku-Gama, it would seem to mark the child's first major movement towards separation from his mother when he can wander about with his peers.

The actual initiation takes place when the boy is about ten years old. After being fed a variety of nuts eaten by women and children but not by men—a symbolic farewell to childhood—the Nibek monsters are summoned from the sea. The terrified boys are taken to the men's hut to be eaten by the monsters, but they are soon quieted by the men who seek to reassure them that if they remain quiet, being eaten will not hurt them. Outside, the boys' mothers weep and sing mournful songs. Various taboos and restrictions are placed on the initiates and on the following day they are taken to the beach where they are stretched to make them grow. The men demonstrate how the sacred flutes are played and explain that these are the Nibek monsters; and that this is all that being 'swallowed' means. The boys are then taken into the sea where they are scrubbed with sand and water to remove all traces of the monsters' digestive juices and excrement. Each boy is then dragged ashore by a spear blade twisted into his hair which is supposed to help him grow. Back in the men's hut, the men explain to the initiates that the ceremony was invented by culture heroes long ago to turn boys into men—'to separate them from their mothers, to make them grow, and to prepare them for handling the instruments' (Hogbin, 1970, p. 110). The tradition must be continued and they are warned that the women must never learn the truth or they would laugh at the men and make fun of them. They are told the myth of a boy who revealed the secrets to the women and children, made fun of these secrets, and then had to flee to the mainland to save his life, and could never return home.[4] The next day the initiates are dressed in finery and are paraded around the village. Finally pairs of boys from opposite moieties drink together from a brook to become blood brothers and thereafter are considered closer than siblings. There are further rituals, and the boys henceforth live in the men's hut and have only minimal contact with women.

The important menstruation ceremony is reserved until the boys begin to develop pubic hair several years later and are more responsible, for if a single drop of blood should fall upon the boy, he would be certain to sicken and die. The bleeding ritual is carried out only once every three to five years because the taboos placed upon the men who perform the rite are so extremely restrictive that men are reluctant to undertake the task. On Wogeo, too, it is believed that a boy cannot grow into a man unless he learns to play the flutes and he cannot do so until he has been purified by the elimination of injurious elements absorbed from women during his childhood. The tongue is chosen as the site of the initial bleeding because the boy has absorbed the pollution through nursing and the inadvertent ingestion of menstrual blood; but it is also thought that the abrading and cleansing of the tongue makes it more pliable and suitable for playing the flutes. It does not seem necessary to present the details of the ceremony. Each initiate sits with his head protruded over a small fire with his tongue thrust out and is warned repeatedly not to swallow or to let a drop of blood fall upon him rather than into the fire. The specialist who performs the ritual then carefully scrapes the boy's tongue with an abrasive leaf until blood drops steadily into the fire. After the bleeding stops, the tongue is sponged with leaves but the boy continues to keep his tongue out and spit into the fire for another hour or so until he washes his mouth with a magical potion. Strong taboos are maintained for several days by the boys and still more elaborate precautions are taken by the specialist and his assistants. Among other measures, the specialist rubs his hands with a sap that causes the skin to slough and both the specialist and his assistants induce menstruation on two successive days in the adult manner that will be described in order to purify themselves. In the following weeks the boys are given a series of magical potions to restore their strength and improve their health and growth; and they remain secluded in the men's hut and practise playing the flutes for several months.

At the time of the tongue scarification, the boy is warned of the grave risk in indulging in sexual relations before he learns how to purify himself by inducing menstruation by cutting his glans penis. He is taught to do this around the age of 18 or 19 by a man of the opposite moiety who is not a close relative. He must wade knee-deep into the ocean where he cuts the head of his penis with a sharp crab claw deeply enough to produce a gush of blood. After the practice he must seclude himself in the men's hut for several days and not have sexual relations until after the next new moon. Men are not required to menstruate every month but ought to do so at regular intervals; but actually most wait until they are ill which they blame on female pollution. Men are also obliged to menstruate as part of certain rituals, e.g., when they participate in the tongue abrasion ceremony. The benefits of the procedure are immediate—the man's muscles harden, his hair and skin become more lustrous and he feels stronger and more self-confident, and therefore men will be certain to menstruate before setting out on a raid or trading expedition.

As in the Asaro Valley, the youth does not attain the status of manhood until he goes through one more rite. Here, the ritual has to do with secretly growing his hair long enough to wear in the traditional manner through a wicker cone. He is then considered capable of marrying and having children.

On Wogeo the girl's menarche is also marked by a significant but brief ritual that is more of a celebration than an ordeal. Various minor rites are conducted and potions are given in order to assure the girl's growth and health, and to enhance her grace and good looks. A celebration is held for each individual girl at the time of her menarche on a mountain top where old rags, representing the girl's childhood, are buried and the women collectively mourn her lost childhood. The girl is then decorated, a feast is held and games are played. Apparently the women enjoy themselves and aggravate the men by rudely mocking the male ceremonials and rituals. It becomes clear that women know much about the men's secrets and use the opportunity to make fun of the men's sexual capacities.

In other localities still different means of menstruating are utilized (Berndt, 1951, p. 90; Salisbury, 1965, p. 62). In some places, slivers of bamboo or small wads of sharp leaves are inserted into the penile urethra to scarify it. Still, whatever the method and the precise nature of the ritual, an examination of the rites makes it clear that they are not simply painful initiation rites imposed upon the youth to torment or terrify him but they are believed to be an essential for the boy's welfare and to permit his physical and sexual development as well as to protect him from the malignant emanations of women. The men are not threatening the boy with damage to his penis to keep him in his place but are, rather, trying to make it possible for him to mature and to have sexual relationships without endangering himself.

NOTES

1. The vomiting, bleeding and ejaculation into the flowing water, as the bleeding into a fire in the Wogeo ritual that will be described, assures that the vital substances eliminated from the body will not fall into the possession of a sorcerer.

2. The importance and significance of the ancestor spirits in mediating between man and nature has been described and discussed by the authors in their paper on Cargo Cultism (Lidz, R., Lidz, T. & Burton-Bradley, 1973).

3. The flutes have a sexual as well as a religious connotation. According to Read (1952, p. 16) when properly played, they have a sexually exciting effect on both men and women.

4. As the peoples on the mainland were taught the rituals by this brash, partially initiated youth, it is no wonder that they carry them out aberrantly.

PREGNANCY
AND
SEXUALITY

UNDER THE SHADOW OF MATERNITY

CHILDBIRTH AND WOMEN'S LIVES IN AMERICA

J. W. Leavit

In 1846 a young woman in Warren, Pennsylvania, gave birth to a son and soon after was taken with "sinking spells." Her female friends and relatives were there to help her; they took encouragement when she appeared better and consoled each other when she fell into a stupor. A woman who was with her during these days wrote to a mutual friend describing the scene around Mary Ann Ditmar's bed:

> Oh my beloved Girl—You may imagine our sorrow, for you too must weep with us—How can I tell you: I cannot realize myself—Mary Ann will soon cease to be among the living—and numbered with the dead . . . Elizabeth, it was such a scene that is hard to be described—L and I remained until the afternoon. Mrs. Mersel came and relieved us, also Mrs. Whalen came. We took a few hours sleep and returned—She had requested us to remain as long as she lived—there was every indication of a speedy termination of her suffering—Mary had come over—Mrs. N remained to watch . . . all thought she was dying—She was very desirous of living till day light—She thought she might have some hope if she could stand it until morning—She retained her sense perfectly—She begged us to be active and not be discouraged that she might live yet—that life was so sweet—how she clung to it—Elizabeth I would wish you might be spared such a sight—we surrounded her dying bed—Each one diligent to keep life and animation in the form of one they so much loved and who at that very time was kept alive with stimulating medicines and wine—I cannot describe it for o my God the horrors of that night will ever remain in the minds of those who witnessed it—our hearts swelled at the sight.

Mary Ann lingered a few days, during which time she bestowed rings and locks of hair upon her friends so they might remember her; she made her peace with God and provided for her child. Then she died.

Mary Ann's story represents a reality visited upon countless American women in the eighteenth and nineteenth centuries, and it is a reality with supreme significance for understanding women's lives. During most of American history, an important part of women's experience of childbirth was their anticipation of dying or of being permanently injured during the event. This chapter will examine how potential dangers of childbirth influenced women's life expectations and experiences; and it will set the stage for understanding why and how women worked so hard to overcome these risks.

The physical dangers associated with childbearing—the "shadow of maternity"—helped provide the justification of limiting women's lives to the domestic duties of homemaking and child-rearing. Most married women, and some unmarried women, had to face the physical and psychological effects of recurring pregnancies, confinements, and postpartum recoveries, which all took their toll on their time, their energy, their dreams, and on their bodies. The biological act of maternity, with all its risks, thus significantly marked women's lives as they made their way from birth to death.

Maternity's shadow had many dimensions. Most significantly were high fertility rates. At the beginning of the nineteenth century, white American women bore an average of more than seven live children. This implies considerably more than seven pregnancies, because many terminated in

"Under the Shadow of Maternity: Childbirth and Women's Lives in America," by J.W. Leavit, reprinted from *Brought to Bed: Childbearing in America 1750–1950*, Oxford University Press, 1986.

miscarriage or stillbirths. For many groups in the expanding American population, fertility rates remained close to this high level throughout the nineteenth century. Pregnancy, birth, and postpartum recovery occupied a significant portion of most women's adult lives, and motherhood defined a major part of their identity.

The life of Mary Vial Holyoke, who married into a prominent New England family in 1759, illustrates the strong grip that frequent pregnancies could hold over women's lives. In 1760, after ten months of marriage, Mary gave birth to her first baby. Two years later, her second was born. In 1765 she was again "brought to bed" of a child. Pregnant immediately again, she bore another child in 1766. The following year she delivered her fifth, and in one more year her sixth. Free from pregnancy and childbirth in 1769, she gave birth again in 1770. During the next twelve years, she bore five more children. Mary Vial Holyoke spent the majority of the first 23 years of her married life, the years of her youth and vigor, pregnant, nursing her infants, and recovering from childbirth. (See Figure 1.) Because only three of her twelve children lived to adulthood, she also withstood frequent tragedies. She devoted her body and her life to procreation throughout her reproductive years. Mary Holyoke had more pregnancies and suffered more child deaths than her average contemporary, but her story presents a poignant example of the extreme physical trials some women endured. Her life reveals how the biological capacity of women to bear children has translated historically into life's destiny for individual women.

Mary Vial Holyoke and two of her daughters kept diaries, portions of which have since been published, and these journals meticulously record the family's birth and death experiences. Entered frequently amidst the notations of family occasions, visiting schedules, and daily housework were citations of confinements in the family and friendship circle. In 1765, for example, one third of the entries in Mary Vial Holyoke's diary contained references either to her own confinement or to those of her close friends. Eleven of her friends were "brought to bed" that year, and three others in the months of December and January immediately surrounding the calendar year. Historian Mary Beth Norton concluded from such accounts that married fertile colonial women accepted a child every two or three years as a "rhythmic part of . . . everyday existence." Women chose to document childbirth frequently in their diaries and letters in part because it happened so often, but they found it a worthy topic also because of the significant physical risks it held for almost all women. Both the frequency of the event and its physical dangers created the burdens that women of the past carried with them through life.

MARY VIAL HOLYOKE

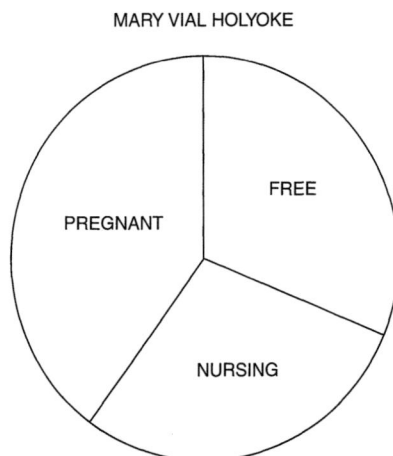

Figure 1. Chart dividing the first 23 years of Mary Vial Holyoke's married life into three parts. She had 12 pregnancies, nursed her infants an estimated 12 months if they lived, otherwise calculated by months of life, and was free from bodily reproductive duties the remainder.

A closer look at the obstetrical histories of the women in the Holyoke family reveals how commonly childbirth affected the course of women's adult lives. Before marrying Mary Vial in 1759, Edward Augustus Holyoke had been married to Judith Pickman. Judith became pregnant within the first six months of her marriage. She carried to term an infant daughter, but both mother and daughter died within months. This woman's life was snuffed out from childbirth-related causes eighteen months after her wedding. Edward and Mary Vial's daughter Susanna Holyoke Ward bore six live children and endured one still birth (thus putting her closer to the average white American woman of the period, who bore seven live babies). Susanna's obstetrical history, shown in Figure 2, illustrates that even if a woman produced below the average number of children, childbirth and the ensuing lactation could dominate her adult life. Judith Holyoke Turner, Susanna's sister, bore eight children during the first 18 years of her married life; four of her children died in infancy.

Of the other women in the Holyoke family whose obstetrical histories can be reconstructed through the family diaries, Mary Elliot Holyoke bore ten children between 1677 and 1697; Elizabeth Holyoke bore two infants in 1718 and 1719 and died herself before her second wedding anniversary; (another) Elizabeth Holyoke bore nine children between 1725 and 1739; Margaret Holyoke bore eight children between 1726 and 1739; Susannah Holyoke bore eight children in the years 1731 to 1746; Mary Holyoke bore five children with her first husband and one with her second between the years 1724 and 1742; Hannah Holyoke bore eight children in the twenty years between 1761 and 1781; Anna Holyoke Cults gave birth to eight children between 1763 and 1777; and Sarah Holyoke bore ten children during her first twenty years of marriage from 1775 and 1795. For all of these women childbearing and childrearing consumed a major portion of their adult lives.

The obstetrical history of Sarah Everett Hale, wife of Nathan Hale and mother of Edward Everett Hale, provides an early nineteenth-century example of childbirth's domination over women's time and energy. She experienced eleven confinements during the first twenty years of her marriage. (See Figure 3.) Sarah Everett married Nathan Hale on the morning of her twentieth birthday on September 5, 1816. One month later she was pregnant, and nine months later she delivered her first child. In another eight months Sarah again conceived, bearing her second child after a little more than two years of marriage; her next nine children followed in rapid succession. Sarah's diary reveals the

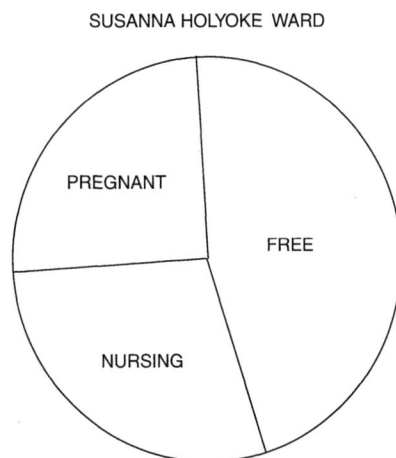

SUSANNA HOLYOKE WARD

Figure 2. Chart dividing the first 20 years of Susanna Holyoke Ward's married life into three parts. She had seven pregnancies, nursed six live children, and was free from bodily reproductive duties the remainder.

centrality of childbearing and rearing to her life, and it illustrates the dimensions of the experience that women could share with one another. Looking back on her married life on her twenty-fifth wedding anniversary, in 1841, Sarah Hale wrote:

> I have borne eleven children, and have been permitted to keep until this day seven—One blossom of hope, just dawned upon this world, lived but a brief hour, and was transplanted by the all knowing Creator to his garden of joy.—Another remained with us for seven months, learned to return smile for smile, and was just beginning to show the germs of intelligence when a short space of suffering and anxiety was closed by our laying him away in the dark chamber, which then was but a few paces from the nursery where we had cherished and nourished him—Then came another bright cherub—our darling "other Susie"—bright and hopeful and promising with her earnest and deep glance, and her thoughtful spirit, and in her seventh year, it pleased God to take her from us. . . . Three weeks had past away after her death, when another little girl was given us—She has been spared to this time—Is like, very like her sister,—God grant she may be long spared to us, and be so trained here that she may be joined to the "other Susie"—in heaven—Since then another little girl has been given and taken, and now there are seven here, and four awaiting us on the other side of Jordan.

Sarah Hale's memories offer a poignant example of another part of the shadow that women carried throughout their married lives, the frequency and the tragedy of infant and child mortality. The woman who did not lose any children either at birth or in the early years of their lives was rare in the eighteenth and nineteenth century. Far more common to women's experience was the necessity of accepting the deaths of numerous offspring. To the thirteen women in the Holyoke family mentioned above, ninety-seven children were born, and thirty-eight of them died as infants or small children. Statistics of course do not tell the whole story; a woman might lose just one child and carry the grief forever. But coming to terms with the deaths of numerous small children added a particular burden to women, especially during the time they were pregnant and had to anticipate the possibilities of disaster. For women, birth and death, life and loss, were intimately entwined in their daily existence.

Experiences with frequent pregnancies like Sarah Hale's and Mary Holyoke's became less common in nineteenth-century America as fertility rates declined. By 1900, white women, showing the

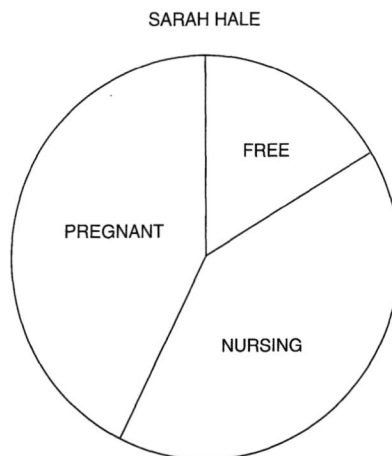

Figure 3. Chart dividing the first 22 years of Sarah Hale's married life into three parts. She had eleven pregnancies—ten live births, and one infant died at six months—and was free from bodily reproductive duties the remainder.

ability to cut their fertility in half over the century, averaged 3.56 children. Historians and demographers trying to understand this decline have suggested that as much as 75 percent of the dropping fertility can be explained by active fertility control, including abortion and birth-control techniques. Some people seem to have succeeded in beginning to assert control over the size of their families, but it is important to keep in mind, also, that the fertility decline that demographers have identified in nineteenth-century America applies mostly to white native-born women; immigrant and black women continued to have babies in large numbers. Significant differences even among white native-born women suggest that fertility control was exceedingly variable. Southern white farm women, for example, continued to bear an average of almost six children at the end of the nineteenth century. Black women bore an average of more than five children. Demographers have noted significant variations in fertility according to ethnic group. Foreign-born white women averaged 4.54 children at the end of the nineteenth century; but Michael R. Haines, who studied fertility among Philadelphia's German and Irish residents during the second half of the nineteenth century, showed that German immigrants averaged 7.22 and Irish 7.34.

Among all groups in the population, the popular perception that large families were common continued throughout the nineteenth century. One woman wrote to her sister in 1872: "Mother said that she did not know whether she had mentioned the fact that we have another son. Such a common occurrence that it is no novelty." Ellen Whitehead wrote in 1877 to her pregnant sister confidentially that she was pregnant and that five of her friends found themselves in the same condition.

Fertility rates illustrate only part of the impact of childbirth on women's lives. Maternity cast a shadow greater than its frequent repetition alone could have caused. Maternity, the creation of new life, carried with it the ever-present possibility of death. The shadow that followed women through their childbearing years was the fear of the physical risks of bearing children. Young women perceived that their bodies, even when healthy and vigorous, could yield up a dead infant or could carry the seeds of their own destruction. As Cotton Mather had warned at the beginning of the eighteenth century, and as many American women continued to believe, conception meant "your *Death* has Entered into you." Nine months of gestation could mean nine months to prepare for death. A possible death sentence came with every pregnancy.

Women spent considerable time worrying and preparing for the probability of not surviving their confinements. During Nannie Stillwell Jackson's pregnancy in 1890, she wrote in her diary: "I have not felt well today am afraid I am going to be sick I went up to Fannies a little while late this evening & was talking to her, & I told her to see after Lizzie & Sue [other children] if I was to die & not to let me be buried here . . . & I want Lizzie & Sue to have *everything that is mine*, for no one has as good a rite [sic] to have what I have as they have." A pregnant Clara Clough Lenroot confided in her diary in 1891, "It occurs to me that *possibly* I may not live. . . . I wonder if I should die, and leave a little daughter *behind* me, they would name her 'Clara.' I should like to have them." Three days later she again was worrying: "If I shouldn't live I wonder what they will do with the baby! I should want Mamma and Bertha [sister] to have the bringing up of it, but I should want Irvine [husband] to see it every day and love it so much, and I should want it taught to love him better than anyone else in the world." With the successful termination of the birth, Clara's husband wrote in his wife's diary, "Dear Clara, 'mamma and Bertha' won't have to take care of your baby, thank God." He continued, "Everything is all right, but at what a cost. My poor wife, how you have suffered, and you have been so brave. . . . I have seen the greatest suffering this day that I have ever known or ever imagined."

When her sister Emma experienced a difficult pregnancy in 1872, Ellen Regal went to be with her and found her "so patient and resigned." Ellen wrote to her brother, "it is not strange that she should tremble and shrink at the thought of that Valley of the Shadow of Death which she must so soon enter." Another woman wrote to her parents late in her pregnancy, "If I live and regain my health I will surely write to [all the people to whom she owed letters]." Lizzie Cabot in the middle of the nineteenth century wrote to her sister when she was pregnant with her first child, "I have made my will and divided off all my little things and don't mean to leave undone what I ought to do if I can help it." Sarah Ripley Stearns, returning from church near her time of confinement, wrote in her diary: "perhaps this is the last time I shall be permitted to join with my earthly friends." Writing to her friend in 1821, another pregnant woman confided, "Could I have you . . . with me I should enjoy it much . . . for this life may soon be closed. I feel my dear friend that there may be but a step between me and eternity." Young Nettie Fowler McCormick confided in her diary, "I am feeling quite well but the time is *near at hand*—O God preserve my life to my husband & children." Young, vigorous, healthy women who should have been anticipating a long life instead faced the very real possibility that in creating life they would pay with their own.

Death fears remained central to women's perceptions of their birth experiences throughout the nineteenth and early twentieth centuries. Georgiana Kirby began to keep a journal when she learned she was pregnant in 1852 because, she wrote, "I think perhaps I may die and my babe live." She was afraid she might not survive "this great trial of my physical powers" and wanted the child to have a remembrance of its mother. Bessie Rudd, whose tuberculosis compounded her worries just a few years later, wrote to her husband that preparatory to her confinement she was arranging her household accounts so that he could understand them. "I have everything in order & fixed to my mind, should any unforeseen Sorrow come to me. You know we think of all things, Edward must have everything in readiness . . . I sometimes think I am ready to [die] . . . though Life was never dearer to me than now, with *you to live for* & help along life's *pathway*." Another day she wrote, "What record have I left for you, dear Edward, should I be taken away?" Even more melancholic, she wrote again, "if a Separation comes you *will* believe the I *loved you devotedly* dear Edward and I shall wait for you in the better home to which I know you will have an entrance and be blessed."

Women like Bessie Rudd, whose illnesses portended especially dangerous labors and deliveries, had particular reason to fear death as their pregnancies advanced. Similarly, women whose mothers or other relatives had died during childbirth carried strong fears for their own possible demise. Sarah Jane Stevens, for example, whose mother had died in confinement, became acutely apprehensive during her own first pregnancy in 1880. She confided her fears to her doctor, who wrote to assure her that her labor "probably will be slow and tedious, as first labors almost always are, but with a strong will and resolution, such as I know you have, no such abnormal conditions as you apprehend, will mar the normality of your confinement." Despite a successful first delivery, Sarah's fears did not diminish during her second pregnancy in 1885. Her brother, a physician, wrote to her that she should "look forward to confinement with less apprehension than to the last. The circumstances of our mother's unfortunate death were altogether abnormal," he concluded. "The immediate cause of her death was nervous shock at the *brutal* and *brutally ignorant* preparations for a surgical operation. . . . The lack of a skilful physician with good sense and humane instincts. . . . You have nothing of that sort to fear." Despite constant reassurances from her family, friends, and medical adviser, Sarah Stevens continued to feel anxious throughout both of her pregnancies.

The extent to which these fears of death spread beyond the parturients to other family members is evident in the diary of Albina Wight, whose sister was pregnant and near confinement in another state. In 1870 Albina wrote, "I am so afraid [sic] she won't live through it." Three days later, she continued to think of her sister: "I could not keep Tilda out of my thoughts [.] It has seemed like a funeral all day . . . I fear she is not living." With relief Mary E. Cooley wrote her daughter-in-law: "I am very thankful that you are safely and comfortably through your trial."

Women and family members were not the only ones who anticipated maternal death. Physicians who attended parturients through the fearful hours of labor and delivery also brooded over mortality. Dr. James S. Bailey of Albany, New York, in the 1870s, pondered the sometimes sudden and unexplained deaths of women following childbirth. He wrote, "To see a female, apparently in vigorous health until the period of accouchement, suddenly expire from some unforeseen accident, which is beyond the control of the attending physician, is well calculated to fill the mind with alarm and gloomy forebodings" and make it impossible "while attending a case of confinement, to banish the feeling of uncertainty and dread as to the result of cases which seemingly are terminating favorably." Similarly, Dr. William Lusk, after relating the tragic story of a 23-year-old "very beautiful young woman" who died after delivery, warned his fellow physicians, "the exhausted condition in which the woman is left after childbirth render[s] her an easy prey to the perils of the puerperal state." Fort Wayne, Indiana, physician H. V. Sweringen agreed that "Parturition under the most favorable circumstances is attended with great risk." Physicians and families were well aware of the possibility of death: fears of the dangers of childbirth permeated society.

The extent to which society's fears reflected a reality of high death rates is almost impossible for historians to determine with any degree of confidence. The graphs that can be constructed from the available evidence illustrate that deaths from causes associated with maternity seem to have been declining toward the last part of the nineteenth century. But the statistics also show that the death rate leveled out toward the end of the century and continued at a high (and even increasing) level in the twentieth century. The statistics show that deaths from maternity-related causes at the turn of the twentieth century were approximately 65 times greater than they are in the 1980s, a comparison that helps us to understand the dangers women faced.

The best available evidence of the maternal mortality calculation comes from the statistics from New York City. Although New York is not necessarily representative of the rest of the country, health officials there collected information about maternal deaths for a longer time and in a more reliable way than elsewhere. Graph 2, based on health officer Haven Emerson's relatively complete recording of births and deaths in New York City, illustrates these trends in maternal mortality.

These data are of limited value in determining the actual dangers women faced from childbirth-related causes before the middle of the twentieth century. The graph illustrates maternal death rates—that is, the number of maternal deaths per number of live births, which is calculated by dividing the number of deaths by the number of births. But the number of live births represents only part of the total pregnancy and delivery experiences. The figure omits from the denominator stillbirths, abortions, miscarriages, and other accidents that terminate pregnancy prematurely or unsuccessfully. If we are interested in determining the actual dangers a woman faced when she became pregnant, we need to base our calculations on the total number of pregnancies women experienced, not just the ones that resulted in live births. But this tabulation is unavailable: we simply do not know how often women in the past found themselves pregnant or even how frequently women labored to give birth. It is only in the twentieth century that the recording of births (living and still) began to be noted reliably by local and state health departments, and even today we cannot calculate precisely the risks women face each time they become pregnant. Because we can not be sure about the number of labors or pregnancies, our statistical conclusions have limited meaning.

Even more frustrating for the historian trying to reconstruct the actual degree of danger associated with maternity is the fact that the recording of puerperal deaths itself (the numerator in our equation) is frequently incomplete and may bear little relationship to actual causes of death. Officials might have recorded that women who died while pregnant or within a month of childbirth died from other than puerperal causes. They might instead have implicated tuberculosis or any number of other diseases. Attributing the death to tuberculosis masked a large percentage of deaths that were actually childbirth-related. Physicians knew that an active case of tuberculosis could be exacerbated by pregnancy and especially by a difficult labor and delivery, but they attributed the death the woman suffered to the disease of tuberculosis rather than to the "disease" of childbirth. Their assumption that the women in fact died from tuberculosis may have been technically correct; but the result of their labeling hampers our ability to determine the actual risks parturient women faced. Tuberculosis in the nineteenth century disproportionately attacked young women between the ages of 15 to 45, and frequent pregnancies in these same women put them at a greater risk of early death. Because women suffered extensively from tuberculosis, their often repeated pregnancies were more dangerous to them.

Further complicating our reading of the mortality data is the practice of some physicians of knowingly reporting a childbirth-related death as due to another cause to cover their reputations in the community. One doctor wrote of this tendency in fellow physicians who wanted to pretend that they never had a case of puerperal infection: "he may have avoided signing a death certificate for a patient recently delivered, the certificate bearing the words, 'peritonitis,' 'blood-poisoning,' 'inflammation of the bowels,' or 'puerperal fever'; but cases occasionally perish some weeks after labor, with 'jaundice,' 'pneumonia,' 'congestion of the liver,' or 'malaria,' that, on closer study will be found to be the results of puerperal septic infection."

The further frustration historians face with historical mortality statistics is that even the imperfectly reported maternal deaths and live births are available in the nineteenth century only for certain parts of the country for certain years. Much of women's experience, therefore, is unavailable through the statistical records. Those numbers we do have must be used with extreme caution.

Despite the inability of the statistics to speak adequately to our question of just how dangerous childbirth was, we can interpret the data that do exist to underscore society's perceptions of the dangers of childbirth for young women. Early in the twentieth century, by which time statistics had improved considerably over nineteenth century standards, approximately one mother died for each 154 living births (compared to 1980 standards of one maternal death for each 10,000 live births.) If women delivered, let us estimate, five live babies during their childbearing years (the fertility rate for white women was 3.56, but an estimate that includes black and immigrant women would increase the rate to around five), then one of every thirty women might have expected to die in childbirth over the course of her fertile years. That is, her risk during each pregnancy may have been one in 150, but her risk over her five pregnancies compounds to one in 30. Put this way, it is possible to understand women's fears for themselves in a more dramatic and realistic way.

One of every 17 men who applied for life insurance in an early twentieth-century study said they had a mother or sister who had died as the immediate result of childbirth. This figure included the women whose deaths might have been medically attributable to tuberculosis or other diseases, but which family members attributed to childbirth because of its proximity to the woman's confinement.

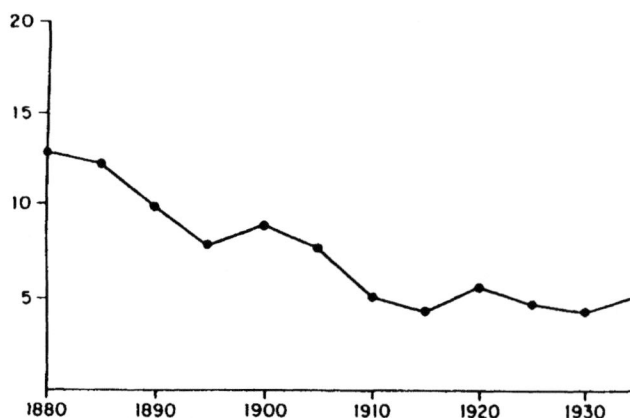

Graph 2. Maternal deaths per 1,000 live births in New York City, 1880–1935.
Source: Haven Emerson and Harriet Hughes, *Populations, Notifiable Diseases and Deaths Assembled for New York City, New York* (New York: Dehamar Institute of Public Health/College of Physicians and Surgeons, 1941). My thanks to Eve Fine for constructing this graph.

If the figure one in seventeen represents family experiences, as this particular tabulation indicates was the case for many families in the early twentieth century, women's and family's fears of maternal death were based in reality.

Certainly the perception of childbirth's dangers, as we have already noted, was a constant in the minds of pregnant women and their families. Ellen Regal wrote to her brother in 1872 that their sister had survived her confinement: "It was a hard day for her in every respect; but she has escaped the fever we feared and is, apparently, doing well in every respect." A.G. Chatfield wrote to his brother in 1837 expressing relief that his brother's wife "got over the worst of all human Perils, that of giving birth to a child," and he reported that his own wife had just "had a fearful time" delivering a baby.

Over and over again, the fears of death in childbirth were confirmed. A daughter wrote: "My mother died suddenly, giving premature birth, when I was seventeen in (1879). She herself was only thirty-eight." A husband wrote: "In June [1875] my wife gave birth to my youngest daughter. From this sickness she never recovered. She suffered terribly . . . and finally died . . . leaving three boys and two girls to mourn her loss." A neighbor wrote of a mission wife in Oregon who, while her husband was away, "went down into the valley of the shadow of death" after delivering her first baby. A New England woman wrote: "My friend, Mrs. John Howard, of Springfield, has died as she has expected to,—under the most aggravated circumstances that a woman can leave the world. She never gave birth to her child; but died in the effort. In this dreadful manner have six of my youthful contemporaries departed this life." A desolate husband turned from his wife's death in childbirth in 1830: "I am undone forever." Another husband wrote to his mother-in-law in the 1860s:

> My dear wife is no more, your dear daughter is gone, Melissa is dead. In our deep and mutual affliction let us weep scalding tears of sorrow and anguish, my pen will not describe the depth of my woe. The world that so lately seemed so bright and lovely before me with happiness, is suddenly but a dark and dreary wilderness before me. . . . She was confined on the 28th of Nov. and after extreme suffering brought us a little girl . . . a fever set in, with inflammation, known as child bed Fever . . . She has suffered on until this morning at 10 minutes past 4 Oclock death came to her relief . . . our dear little baby . . . will never know a mothers love.

These were not isolated incidents. The U. S. Children's Bureau studies in the early twentieth century catalogued the intimate knowledge of death that pregnant women, especially in isolated rural areas, carried with them along with their swollen bellies. Childbed deaths were so familiar to Americans, from the eighteenth to the twentieth century, that fearful anticipation characterized the common and realistic attitudes toward pregnancy.

Despite the decline in number of births women endured, and somewhat of a decline in the rate of maternal deaths, women remained fearful of maternity. Women might have been at risk of puerperal death fewer times during their lifetimes, but for them the fear of dying during childbirth continued to define the shape of their lives. In the early twentieth century part of this fear was related to the fact that maternal deaths continued at higher than expected levels. Women and physicians saw that deaths from various infectious diseases were dropping rapidly at the turn of the twentieth century, but that deaths from childbirth-related causes remained high. Since many of those deaths could be attributed to infection, and since physicians supposedly understood how to prevent infection after the 1880s, both the medical and lay communities agreed that much of maternal mortality should be preventable. Furthermore, maternal mortality statistics from other countries showed that women in several nations fared better than they did in the United States. In 1910, when the United States recorded that one mother died for every 154 babies born alive, Sweden's record showed that one mother was lost to every 430 live births.

Another reason birth anxieties continued, despite declining fertility and mortality, was that first births contained the largest actual risk (i.e., maternal deaths were higher for primiparas than for multiparas), and women continued to have first babies at the same rate throughout the nineteenth century. That is, between 1800 and 1900 when the size of families declined, the percentage of families in the population remained the same; women had smaller families, but they still had families. Married women continued to bear first children as their grandmothers had, but the total size of their families diminished. Their fears continued to be related to the experiences of their first pregnancies, when, young and vulnerable, they faced the possibility of their own death. Dr. Beatrice Tucker, Director of the Chicago Maternity Center, realized as late as 1948, "There are all kinds of women who come into a doctor's office to seek care during pregnancy. Some are educated and well-bred; some ignorant; some well adjusted; some phlegmatic, and some neurotic and high-strung. But most of them have this in common—fear."

Death fears were promoted, too, in the culture at large. Religion taught that childbirth was God's punishment to women, and this perspective of women's fate was strong in women's private writings. Countless women, either explicitly or implicitly, related their fears and their pregnancy-related trials to God's will and accepted it as such. Nineteenth-century fiction writing also shaped women's perceptions of what to expect during their confinements and led them to anticipate suffering.

Women today continue to think about mortality for themselves or their offspring, even when their own experience and the experiences of their friends and relations contradict the probability of death. Whether dangers are reported as one in every 150 births or one in 10,000, women find themselves thinking about death as soon as they discover they are pregnant. Part of this represents a lag time in perceptions catching up with improving statistics. But, in addition, the few cases of women dying in childbirth reported in the United States today are enough to force pregnant women to face their own mortality. Because they are young and because the possibility of death, even though remote, occurs to them perhaps for the first time in their lives, its emotional impact is beyond its actual danger. The centrality of childbearing to women's lives emphasizes the seriousness of the dangers it holds.

In the past, the shadow of maternity extended beyond the possibility and fear of death. Women knew that if procreation did not kill them, it could maim them for life. Postpartum gynecological problems, some great enough to force women to bed for the rest of their lives, others causing milder disabilities, hounded many of the women who survived childbirth. For some women, the fears of future debility were more disturbing than fears of death. The worse problems were the vesicovaginal and rectovaginal fistula (holes between the vagina and either the bladder or the rectum caused by the violence of childbirth or by instrument damage), which brought incontinence and constant irritation to sufferers. Women knew also that unsutured perineal tears were likely to cause slow postpartum recovery and significant daily discomfort. Postpartum infections similarly threatened young women's health and life during their prime. Newly married women looking forward to life found themselves almost immediately faced with the prospect of permanent physical limitations that could follow their early and repeated confinements.

Chicago physician Henry Newman believed that the "normal process of reproduction [is] a formidable menace to the after-health of the parous woman." Lacerations—tears in the perineal tissues or in the walls of the vagina, bladder, or rectum—probably caused the greatest postpartum trouble for women. The worse of these, the fistulas, which led to either urine or feces constantly leaking through the vaginal opening without the possibility of control was, in the words of one sympathetic doctor, "the saddest of calamities, entailing . . . endless suffering upon the poor patient . . . death would be a welcome visitor." Women who had to live with this condition sat alone and invalided as long as they lived unless they were one of the beneficiaries of Dr. J. Marion Sims' repair operation after the middle of the century. Their incontinence made them unpleasant companions, and even their friends and relatives found it hard to keep them constant company.

More frequent and less debilitating, but still causing major problems for many women, were tears in the vaginal wall, cervix, and perineal tissues that might have led to prolapsed uterus, uncomfortable sexual intercourse, or difficulties with future deliveries. One physician noted, "the widespread mutilation . . . is so common, indeed, that we scarcely find a normal perineum after childbirth." Most perineal lacerations were probably minor and harmless; but if severe ones were not adequately repaired, women might suffer from significant postpartum discomfort. Women complained most frequently of prolapsed uteri. This displacement of the womb downwards, sometimes even through the vaginal opening, usually resulted from childbirth-related perineal lacerations and relaxation of the ligaments. The practice of keeping women in bed for ten days to two weeks postpartum and the corset women donned soon after childbirth exacerbated this problem. One doctor noted that fallen womb was often a temporary condition; but he also found it recurrent: "Any woman subject to ill turns, lassitude, and general debility, will tell you that not infrequently upon these occasions she is sensible of a falling of the womb."

The condition caused misery for women. Albina Wight's sister Eliza, to give just one example from the 1870s, had a difficult delivery that was followed by prolapsus. Six weeks after one of her sister's confinements, Albina recorded, "Eliza is sick yet can only walk across the room and that overdoes her. She has falling of the Womb. poor girl." Eliza's medical treatment by "a calomel doctor" who gave her "blue pills" did not help. Five months following the delivery she could only walk a few steps at a time and cannot sit up all day." A second doctor predicted, "it will be a long time before she will get around again."

The typical treatment for this common female ailment was the use of a pessary, a mechanical support for the uterus inserted into the vagina and left there for as long as necessary. (See illustration.) Pessaries, of which there were literally hundreds of types, themselves often led to pelvic inflammations and pain for the women whose conditions they were meant to alleviate. In the opinion of one doctor, "I think it is indisputable that a pessary allowed to remain for a very short period will invariably produce irritation, and if continued longer, will produce almost as certainly, ulceration. I have removed many pessaries that have produced ulceration; one in particular, hollow and of silver gilt, was completely honey-combed by corrosion, its interior filled with exuviae of the most horrible offensiveness, the vagina ulcerated through into the bladder, producing a vesico-vaginal fistula, and into the rectum, producing a recto-vaginal fistula; the vagina in some portion obliterated by adhesive inflammation and numerous fistulae made through the labia and around the mons veneris for the exit of the various discharges."

Uterine displacements puzzled doctors and pained women throughout the nineteenth century. A midcentury physician noted that uterus-related problems were "the dread of almost every physician, and the constant, painful perplexity of many a patient." He told of his recent case:

> In the winter of 1863, I was consulted by a young lady from a distant part of the State, on account of a disease from which she had suffered for nearly four years. She had received the advice of many a physician of high and low degree—had worn the ring pessary—the globe pessary—the horseshoe pessary—the double S pessary and the intra-uterine stem pessary— and the common sponge. . . .
> The patient gave a history of frequent inflammation of the uterus and ovaries, and there appeared to be quite strong adhesions binding the womb in its assumed place. She had had too frequent menstruation—profuse and intolerably painful—frequent and painful micturition [urination].

The physician inserted his "modified" ring pessary and happily reported that "the patient went to her home after a few weeks entirely relieved from all bad symptoms."

In the last half of the nineteenth century physicians reported increased numbers of perineal and cervical lacerations and their accompanying gynecological problems, attributed by many observers to increased use of forceps in physician-directed deliveries. If it is true that physicians' interventions caused increasing problems for women in this period (a question explored in Chapters 2 and 6), it is also the case that physicians became increasingly adept at repairing the problems. The medical journals were filled with case studies of women whose badly managed delivery had caused them problems, which could then be resolved by superior medical care. For example, an Iowa physician,

Dr. Nicholas Hard, reported in 1850 a case he salvaged: a 35-year-old woman "with her first child, having had the forceps applied at an improper time during her labor suffered from inflammation of the vulva, vagina, and contiguous soft parts, and had a tardy convalescence. . . . The vaginal orifice was perfectly closed . . . she suffered exceedingly from retained catamenial [menstrual] fluid." The doctor instrumentally reopened the vagina and reported that his patient now "walks to church, visits, and does housework."

Women who had already had children were more likely than first-time mothers to worry about the possible aftereffects of labor and delivery. Remembering how long it took them the first time to recover from the birth and how they had suffered, they were particularly loath to repeat the ordeal. "As the time draws near I fear & tremble," wrote Persis Sibley Andrews in her diary in 1847, "I have suffered much in the last four weeks & often find myself indulging in forbodings of evil—of years of ill health as was the case before & all & the worst ills to be feared in the case. God help me." Andrews feared childbirth the more because of the invalidism that followed her first birth, and her fears were shared by many other women who had survived their first births only to find themselves soon again pregnant. Agnes Reid's second pregnancy evoked this letter: "I confess I had dreaded it with a dread that every mother must feel in repeating the experience of child-bearing. I could only think that another birth would mean another pitiful struggle of days' duration, followed by months of weakness, as it had been before." Another mid-nineteenth-century woman found herself again "walking under the shadow of maternity. . . . Then came the week when there seemed no hope from day to day that even one life could be given for the other, but that both would perish together." Mary Kincaid resigned herself to her coming trials when she found herself again pregnant in 1896. She wrote this poignant message to her cousin:

Mamie I got two hard months before me yet that if I count right, I just dread the time coming. . . . O Mamie I wish there was no such thing as having babies. I wish I took George Willard's receit [for abortion?] and left the nasty thing alone. I will next time you bet I will not have any more if I live through this time what I hope I will. Well, Mamie it is there and it has to come out where it sent in. Sumner [husband] says that I could cough all I am [she had a cold] and I couldn't cough it up. Well might as well laugh as cry it be just the same.

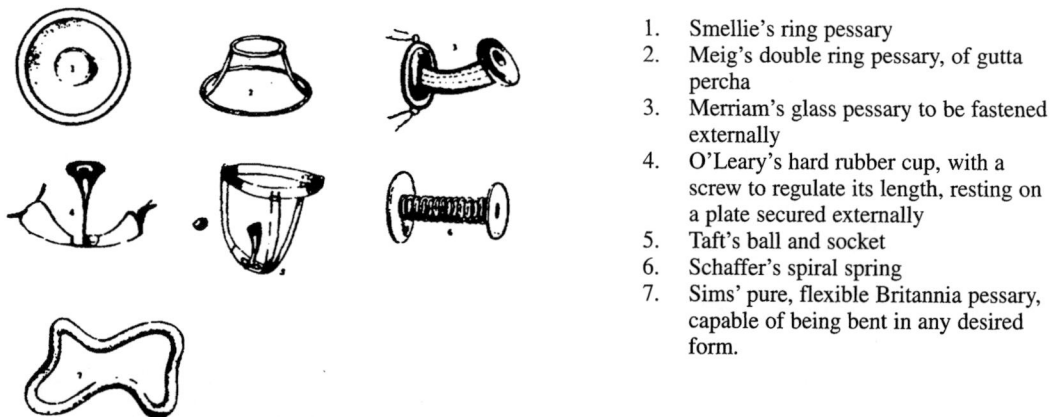

1. Smellie's ring pessary
2. Meig's double ring pessary, of gutta percha
3. Merriam's glass pessary to be fastened externally
4. O'Leary's hard rubber cup, with a screw to regulate its length, resting on a plate secured externally
5. Taft's ball and socket
6. Schaffer's spiral spring
7. Sims' pure, flexible Britannia pessary, capable of being bent in any desired form.

A selection of nineteenth-century pessaries, used internally to support a prolapsed uterus. Hundreds of varieties existed.
Source: Augustus K. Gardner, "On the Use of Pessaries," *Transactions of the American Medical Association* 15 (1865): 109–22.

Apart from their fears of resulting death or debility, women feared pain and agony and "suffering beyond bearing" during the confinement itself. They worried about how they would bear up under the pain and stress, how long the confinement might last, and whether trusted people would accompany them through the ordeal. The short hours between being a pregnant woman and becoming a mother seemed, in anticipation, to be interminably long, and they occupied the thoughts and defined the worries of multitudes of women. Women's descriptions of their confinement experiences foretold the horrors of the ordeal.

"Between the oceans of pain," wrote one woman of her third birth in 1885, "there stretched continents of fear; fear of death and dread of suffering beyond bearing." Surviving a childbirth did not allow women to forget its horrors. Lillie M. Jackson, recalling her 1905 confinement, wrote "While carrying my baby, I was so miserable. . . . I went down to death's door to bring my son into the world, and I've never forgotten. Some folks say one forgets, and can have them right over again, but today I've not forgotten, and that baby is 36 years old." Too many women shared Hallie Nelson's feelings upon her first delivery: "I began to look forward to the event with dread—if not actual horror." Even after Nelson's successful birth, she "did not forget those awful hours spent in labor."

Women recounted their trials with wrenching repetitiveness. One wrote that her child "nearly killed me as he tore his way into life." Another: "My body and spirits were so extremely weak, I could only just bear to look at those I loved." Another: "The two of us were close to death. . . . The strain of having him exhausted me." Another: "The angels of life and death wrestled over my baby's life and over mine in that little pioneer fort." Another: "I lay at the point of death. And out of that hour in which I touched the hand of death, two months before her time, came my daughter." Women suffered in the anticipation and in the reality of childbirth.

Most women managed to find joy or purpose in the experience despite their hard times. Mary Foote recounted her 1877 childbirth as a "long dreadful day and night . . . a dim bewildering Hell of pain all day—growing worse & worse and then came Heaven at last. . . . I am weak and happy." In another letter to her friend she admitted that motherhood was "a sort of pendulum . . . between joy & dread." Josephine Preston Peabody wrote in her diary of the "most terrible day of [her] life" when she delivered her firstborn, the "almost inconceivable agony" she lived through during her "day-long battle with a thousand tortures and thunders and ruins." Her second confinement brought "great bodily suffering," and her third, "the nethermost hell of bodily pain and mental blankness. . . . the *will-to-live* had been massacred out of me, and I couldn't see why I *had* to." But, she concluded in her diary, "Now that it is over—I would not for anything—give up the awfulness of it. For I am wiser in the height and the depth, for this knowledge of the almost inconceivable agony . . . I can never forget—or explain—that apocalyptic hugeness of the thing. . . . I have crossed the abyss now . . . That anything so wonder-small and wonder-soft and helpless and exquisite should come of anything so cruel and unimaginable as Birth," she marveled. And yet another new mother rejoiced that out of her "time of great difficulty and distress" she had emerged "the living mother of a living and perfect child."

Regardless of the particular fear that women carried along with their swelling uterus, the prospect of often repeated motherhood promised hardship and anxiety, even at the same time as it might have promised wonderment and hope. Hannah Whitall Smith understood this and wrote in her diary in 1852:

I am very unhappy now. That trial of my womanhood which to me is so very bitter has come upon me again. When my little Ellie is 2 years old she will have a little sister or brother. And this is the end of all my hopes, my pleasing anticipations, my returning youthful joyousness. Well, it is a woman's lot and I must try to become resigned and bear it in patience and *silence* and not make my home unhappy because I am so. But oh, how hard it is.

Hannah Smith wrote in this short diary passage, which has strong religious overtones, how unhappy she was when she found herself pregnant, because pregnancy meant that she had to give up the parts of her life that she enjoyed—the youthful happiness and the hopeful days. But she accepted what was coming with her pregnancy, she determined not to complain about it, and she knew it was what her position demanded. The diary entry is all the more poignant because it voiced meaning for two generations in this family. Hannah Whiteall Smith's niece, . . . M. Carey Thomas, found her aunt's journal and was so moved by this notation that she copied it into her own diary in 1878. For Hannah Smith, as well as for Carey Thomas, marriage meant having children. Unable to prevent conception, Hannah Smith accepted its demands even while expressing to her diary how much against her wishes it was. Her lot—woman's lot—was to be Mother.

Many women walked with Hannah Smith under the shadow of maternity, experiencing repeated and agonizing births in unrelenting succession with no relief throughout their fertile years. Many women suffered physical complications through their confinements that stayed with them the rest of their lives. For many women the physical hardships of childbearing determined the parameters of their lives and defined their social destiny. Mithilde Shillock, a German immigrant who settled on the Minnesota frontier in the 1850s, wrote to her sister how childbearing compounded her already difficult settler life:

> God has entrusted us with a son, a blooming healthy child. He was born on the 1st of December. It seems that his father is happy over it; I myself do not wish for any more children, as I look upon life as a heavy burden. The three years of western life have so thoroughly exhausted me that I am no longer capable of joy or hope or love. I am speaking the naked truth so that I may in a measure at least write quietly without exertion of dissumalation [sic]. What a cleft there is between the outpourings of my heart over our first children and this little stranger! pity is all that I can offer him. Pitty [sic] and a feeling of duty towards him to lighten his blameless fate.

Although childbearing and the ensuing motherhood held many rewarding times for women, the hardships and the dangers created the boundaries within which most women had to construct their lives. The childbirth experience was, of course, heavily influenced by cultural and economic conditions, the particular time and place in which women lived, and their socioeconomic class or ethnic group. But much of the meaning of childbirth for women was determined not by the particulars of the event but by what women shared with each other by virtue of their common biological experience.

The biological capacity to bear children itself was not what determined the course of women's lives, but rather the cultural use to which that capacity was put during most of American history. Because women found themselves repeatedly pregnant and because this condition involved certain physical risks, women found themselves bound by what appeared to be their biology. In fact, they were bound equally by ideology, an ideology of domesticity and nurturance, which the women as well as the men in society accepted as the proper order of things. The ideology affected all women, although the difficulty of raising large families under conditions of poverty meant that it became particularly burdensome for poor women.

In the following chapters I shall examine how women coped with their lives led under the shadow of maternity. The analysis centers on the event of childbirth itself, and looks at how birthing women participated in changing the event, particularly after the middle of the eighteenth century when physicians first began attending normal labors and deliveries. The next chapter examines the initial impact of physician obstetrics by focusing on the introduction of the forceps, the instrument that worked particularly to the advantage of doctors as they began to participate in the traditional women's event of childbirth.

THE POLITICS OF BIRTH PRACTICES: A STRATEGIC ANALYSIS*

Karen E. Paige and Jeffery M. Paige

A theory is proposed to account for cross-cultural variation in the customary birth practices of women and men. We suggest that the restriction of women during childbirth and the husband's ritual involvement in birth are both strategies for asserting or defending paternity rights. When paternity rights are established by agreements based on property transfers and enforced by organized kin groups, women will be restricted to insure that nothing upsets the agreements. When such agreements cannot be made and enforced, paternity claims will be asserted by the husband's ritual involvement in the birth. These hypotheses were tested in a sample of 114 societies based on Murdock and White's Standard Cross-Cultural Sample. The data confirm the hypotheses for the birth practices of both sexes. We suggest that birth practices represent a special case of bargaining mechanisms in societies without centralized authority.

INTRODUCTION

The customary practices and beliefs associated with childbearing have been the subject of much detailed ethnographic description and speculative analysis (cf. 4, 8, 10, 27, 31). Description and theory have both focused on two widespread birth customs—the restriction and segregation of women during pregnancy and childbirth and the observance of couvade by men during their wife's post-delivery confinement. Some customary restrictions on women such as sexual abstinence for specified periods during the pregnancy or the avoidance or prohibition of particular foods or articles of clothing are almost universally observed. However, some societies restrict a woman's normal social contacts by instituting special rules of avoidance, particularly the avoidance of men, ostensibly to protect the society against the contamination and uncleanness associated with feminine reproductive activities. In some cases women are strictly segregated during the birth process and may be confined in special huts, restricted to their own residence, or removed to another community. The most widely discussed birth custom involving men is the couvade which usually includes customary dietary and occupational observances and postpartum seclusion of the husband. In some societies the husband observes all the restrictions observed by his pregnant wife; and when she goes into delivery, he may seclude himself in his residence and fast for a week or more. While in some cases the restrictions for the husband are even more extensive than the wife's, in most societies he performs such minimal ceremonial duties as cutting the umbilical cord after delivery, preparing a birth feast for relatives, performing sacrifices, or helping his wife with her daily chores. While these minor practices are generally not classified as couvade, they are similar in form if not in intensity.

Birth practices have been examined from several theoretical perspectives including sociological functionalism (20, 29), psychoanalytic personality theory (2, 6), and the social psychological theory of ritual (24). While these theories have been the focus of much cross-cultural study and theoretical debate (1, 3, 12, 33), relatively less attention has been paid to the earliest theory of birth practices first proposed by Tylor in 1889. Tylor claimed that couvade was most often practiced in societies in which paternity rights were customarily held by the mother's kinsmen rather than by her husband and concluded that the couvade represented a pre-legal method by which husbands attempted to establish paternity rights over their biological offspring. Tylor's theory has been handicapped by his inadequate sample of societies and by its association with discredited 19th century theories of the evolution of descent systems. Malinowski (15), however, suggested a similar explanation of couvade in a discussion of social paternity. He argued that paternity rights must be socially legitimated and that performance of rituals during the birth process served that purpose. "The function of couvade," he argued, "is the establishment of social paternity by the symbolic assimilation of the father to the mother . . . and is an integral part of the institution of the family." (15). Neither of these theories is described in sufficient detail to permit prediction of cross-cultural variation in birth practices; and neither, of course, is connected with the birth practices of women. Nevertheless the idea of social paternity is central to understanding the determinants of birth practices. This paper extends the argument of Tylor and Malinowski to account for both cross-cultural variations in birth practices and for the practices of women as well as men.

THEORY

Were social paternity an automatic consequence of biological parenthood, there would be no need to engage in birth practices to assert claims to offspring. But as Malinowski (14) demonstrated, paternity rights are established through social consensus or contractual agreement and not through the biological process of conception, pregnancy, and childbirth. The birth of a child not only affirms biological parenthood but also allows an opportunity for interested parties to lay claim to the child's allegiance. These claimants are not limited to the biological parents. In fact the individual with the greatest biological involvement in the birth—the mother—is rarely given authority over her own children. Jural rights to control a child's political allegiance, economic activities, property, or inheritance usually rest with males, though not necessarily with the child's biological father. These rights define the role of sociological father, or *pater*, who is customarily distinguished from the biological father or *genitor*. It is not uncommon for the two roles to be played by different individuals. Paternity rights may be claimed by an individual or group of individuals who provided property used as brideprice regardless of their gender or kinship relation to the genitor. The role of sociological father may be played by the maternal brother, a lineage head, ceremonial kinsmen, state agencies, women, or even decedents. In most societies, of course, the biological father has jural as well as personal authority over his offspring. Even in this case, however, paternity rights are established by the marriage contract; and the competing claims of the wife's kinsmen may be relinquished only in exchange for property or personal service on the part of the husband.

Since paternity rights depend on social consensus or contractual agreements, individuals or groups can attempt to influence the consensus or renegotiate the agreement to their advantage. Paternity rights are subject to dispute in all societies, but the problem is acute in simpler societies where kinship is the major determinant of social position, economic resources, and political power. The greater the importance of such ties in determining social structure, the greater the significance of paternity rights in controlling the political and economic activities of others. Gaining paternity rights means gaining a contributor to the communal economy, a new supporter of a political faction, and an additional ally in a feud. With such important issues at stake, it is not surprising that the birth of a child is the focus of paternity conflict in many societies.

While legitimate rights to offspring may have been theoretically established at marriage, the birth of a child gives them practical significance. It requires that nominal rights be recognized, that ambiguities in customary rights be clarified and that conflicting claims be resolved. Childbirth represents an opportunity for all potential claimants to reopen negotiations, accuse other claimants of bad faith, to demand compensation for real or imagined malfeasance. No matter who is recognized as the sociological father or how his rights have been established, claims can always be challenged and rights ignored.

In societies in which the wife's kinsmen hold jural authority over her children, the husband may try to use his personal authority to claim his children's allegiance for his own kin group. In societies where the husband's and wife's kinsmen share jural authority or where authority is shared by members of a corporate lineage, there may be continual competition for children's primary allegiance. Even in societies where the wife's kinsmen relinquish paternity rights at marriage, they may try to reclaim these rights after a child is born.

Competition over paternity is most apparent in divorce proceedings when the husband may have to relinquish his paternity rights or choose between yielding parental authority or forfeiting wealth or property transferred to the wife's family at marriage. In some cases, the husband may retain authority over male children but yield it over the female children. Whatever the social arrangements concerning paternity, a claimant can always find some grounds for questioning the rights of the sociological father.

In complex societies paternity disputes are the subject of litigation, and a formal judicial apparatus is available to settle them and enforce claims. But those societies in which kinship is most important in determining social structure are the least likely to have such formal mechanisms. This does not mean, of course, that agreements cannot be reached or claims successfully defended; but it does suggest that the tactics of paternity disputes should take a different form in simple societies. Paternity rights are often the subject of bargains negotiated between groups of kinsmen. These bargains may involve substantial amounts of property and can be enforced by the organized military power of the respective kin groups. While such agreements are not legally enforceable, their terms cannot be violated without serious financial or political consequences. In such a situation the main interest of both parties is to insure that nothing upsets their agreement. Ceremonial attempts by males of either faction to assert additional paternity rights would only threaten the agreement. Where explicit, enforceable bargains exist, male birth rituals are neither necessary nor desirable. Both parties to the bargain have an interest in making sure that the contract is fulfilled by the birth of a healthy offspring with unambiguous paternity. Their main focus during pregnancy and birth should be to insure that nothing happens to the biological mother that could threaten either the health of the child or their claims to its allegiance. Given the biological uncertainties of childbearing and the benefits of claiming paternity rights, this may be a formidable task. The restriction or segregation of women during pregnancy and birth can be interpreted as a method of protecting the established rights of claimants against these dangers.

Their interpretation suggests that maternal restrictions during pregnancy and birth and the couvade are alternate strategies to establish or defend paternity rights. The birth practices of both men and women depend on the nature of the bargains over paternity rights in a given society. Since the nature of the bargains which lead to restrictions on women should differ from those which lead to ritual involvement by men, each will be considered separately.

Maternal Restrictions

If the restriction of women during the birth process represents an attempt to insure the fulfillment of a previously negotiated contract, then a potential claimants' interest in the proceedings should vary with the importance of the bargain. When breach of contract leads to a great financial loss or to the threat of violent retaliation from other interested factions, concern with a successful birth and efforts to monitor the birth process should increase. The importance of the bargain and the subsequent interest in the birth process should depend on two major factors: 1) the amount of property involved in the negotiations and 2) the claimants' power to enforce the agreement. These considerations, of course, are not limited to disputes over paternity and stated more generally simply indicate that the significance of a bargain depends on the size of the payoff and the finality of the terms.

Payoffs.—The payoffs in a paternity bargain always involve the relative wealth and power of individuals and kin groups, but the payoffs may be increased by direct property exchanges either at marriage or after a successful birth. While paternity rights do not always depend on the exchange of wealth and may be established by the marriage itself, substantial payments usually confer rights to the woman's offspring. The institution of brideprice in particular in usually interpreted as a direct payment for the reproductive capacity of the wife (cf. 9, 13, 23, 25). The close association between brideprice and paternity rights is indicated by the fact that payments may be made in installments contingent on the wife's continued fertility. The brideprice represents compensation to the wife's kinsmen for the loss of potential offspring to their lineage. As Mair has observed the sum paid in brideprice may be equivalent to the sum paid in compensation for homicide, an indication of the close association between the loss of living and potential kinsmen.

The payment of brideprice or any other exchange of wealth does not assure that paternity rights will be realized. Accidents of reproduction may make the contract meaningless. Given the high rate of fetal and infant mortality in most pre-industrial societies, the possibility is strong that the terms of the paternity agreement will not be fulfilled. Failure to produce an offspring may result from such purely medical problems as barrenness, fetal death or infant disease; but it may also result from infanticide or abortion. Whatever the cause, the potential claimant may demand compensation from the wife's kinsmen. If the wife is barren, her husband may demand that her father give him an additional wife, a child of his own, or some of his property or animals. If a wife is guilty of abortion, her kinsmen may be compelled to pay for the fetus. Any irregularity in the birth process may also occasion additional demands for compensation. The potential claimant can use a breach birth, a birth mark, or even suspected witchcraft to reopen negotiations. However the wife's kinsmen may be in a poor position to meet demands for compensation. Property received for paternity rights is not saved but dispersed among kinsmen, used to buy wives, or pay blood debts and other outstanding obligations. Failure to produce offspring may therefore disrupt an elaborate pattern of financial and kinship obligations. It will certainly lead to renewed haggling and mutual recrimination and may prompt sorcery or outright violence. Clearly, both sets of kinsmen have a vested interest in fulfilling the original contract. The husband's kinsmen must assure that offspring are born in return for wealth already expended and the wife's kinsmen are interested in avoiding the return of wealth they have already spent. The main interest of both parties during pregnancy and birth should be in insuring that nothing happens to upset the contract.

There are a number of ways maternal birth practices might function to protect a bargain. Rules requiring social isolation, avoidance of men, confinement in birth huts or removal to another community all facilitate the surveillance and control of both the mother and potential claimants. Restricting and confining the mother limits the possibility of disrupting the birth through abortion, infanticide, or kidnapping. Segregation from men limits the possibility that other male claimants, such as an unsuccessful suitor or an adulterer, can present their claims. Confinement and isolation also mean that contact with the mother can be limited to the agents of the kin groups with a legitimate interest in the birth. Often, agents of both interested parties will be present at delivery which enables them not only to monitor the mother but also one another. Often it is only after some indication that delivery is successful and the infant's sex determined that additional negotiations and transfer of brideprice occur. If some biological accident disrupts the birth, the limited contacts of the mother and the presence of kin group agents insure that conflict over compensation can be limited and that blame will not be unjustly assigned. In a society with no recourse to police or judiciary, kin groups must monitor other claimants and their own members to insure that contracts will be respected.

Enforcement Power.—The importance of a paternity bargain depends not only on the amount of property exchanged but also on the enforcement power of the interested parties. There would be little point in carefully monitoring the birth process were there no way to apply sanctions to those who disrupted it. Similarly there would be little point in investing substantial amounts of property in rights to future offspring were there no way to defend these rights or demand compensation for default. In simple societies, enforcement power depends on the organized military and political power of groups of kinsmen. A man without kin backing has only his own strength and personality to defend his rights. Enforcing paternity bargains requires that the males of the kin group act together and use force if necessary to defend their interests. Such groups have been termed *fraternal interest groups* by Van Velzen and Van Wettering (30). They demonstrate that fraternal interest groups are indeed associated with the use of force to defend kin group interests. Societies with such groups were significantly more likely to engage in violent retaliation over adultery, personal injury, and murder. Otterbein (21), Otterbein and Otterbein (21), and Ember and Ember (7) have similarly demonstrated that internal warfare and blood feuds are more likely in societies containing fraternal interest groups. Paige (in press) has demonstrated that factional conflicts between fraternal interest groups are reflected in the form of the sovereign decision-making structure in the society. The political power of a fraternal interest group gives kinsmen the ability to enforce the restrictions on maternal behavior and maintain the mother's isolation from other claimants.

The existence of fraternal interest groups depends on a society's dominant residence pattern. Their formation is facilitated by patrilocal and avunculocal residence and inhibited by matrilocal, bilocal and neolocal residence. In both patrilocal and avunculocal residence consanguinally related males live together in the same community. In patrilocal residence sons live with their fathers after marriage, and in avunculocal residence nephews live with their maternal uncles. In matrilocal, bilocal and neolocal residence kin are dispersed rather than localized. In matrilocal residence sons live with their wives' families, in neolocal residence sons live separately, and when residence is bilocal sons may or may not live with their father. Patrilocal and avunculocal residence has therefore been generally used to indicate the presence of fraternal interest groups. While patrilocal and avunculocal residence produces communities in which residence and kinship reinforce one another, other forms of residence produce conflicting patterns of allegiance. An individual owes allegiance both to his own kinsmen, many of whom live elsewhere, and to the members of his local community. In patrilocal and avunculocal societies, groups of related males with similar interest in a paternity dispute will be able to act as a unit. In societies with other residence patterns, communities will likely contain individuals whose loyalties lie with competing claimants, and concerted action will be difficult.

Residence patterns which facilitate the formation of fraternal interest groups should make both contractual agreements over paternity and restrictions on women more likely. Clearly, however, the effect of fraternal interest groups on maternal restrictions are not independent of the effects of wealth exchange and demands for compensation. Compensation cannot be successfully demanded if sanctions are not available to enforce the demand, and wealth will not be risked when no agreement can be enforced. Wealth exchange and demands for compensation should, therefore, both be associated with the presence of fraternal interest groups. Since wealth exchange, demands for compensation, and the presence of fraternal interest groups can each be considered a measure of the presence of explicit paternity bargains, each should be positively associated with the presence of maternal restrictions. While these zero-order relationships are clearly implied by the argument associating maternal restrictions with paternity bargains, the effect of each variable controlling for the others is less clear. Specifying the complete causal model associating the characteristics of paternity bargains with maternal restrictions requires empirically investigating the indicators' interrelationships. If our theory is incorrect, however, even the zero-order relationships will not hold, so that is seems advisable to examine these predictions empirically before examining the entire causal model in more detail.

Husband Ritual Involvement

The ritual involvement of husbands in the birth process through dietary observances or post-delivery seclusion can be viewed as an attempt to assert paternity rights in the absence of more potent sources of influence. While such observances can be used to influence public opinion in any society they are most effective in societies where enforceable paternity agreements do not exist. No amount of ritual activity is likely to alter paternity agreements based on the expenditure of several years' earnings or the power of an important lineage. In fact when paternity agreements are carefully monitored unwarranted ritual claims could be viewed as a threat to the agreement and lead to attempts at retaliation. When the backing of the courts or organized kinsmen is available, ritual is a poor substitute for legal or political action. A potential claimant would be ill advised to spend two weeks in a hammock or avoid turtle meat if he could claim his child by hiring a lawyer or organizing a war party. If such enforcement power is unavailable, however, a husband loses little by making ritual claims since none of the other claimants are in any position to stop him except by engaging in ritual themselves. In particular, the husband's ritual involvement helps offset the implicit claims of his wife's kinsmen dramatized by the wife's undeniable role in the birth. The husband's involvement in the birth can then be viewed as a form of psychological warfare useful when opportunities for more direct forms of conflict are restricted.

Ritual conflict is not limited to paternity disputes and, as Service (26) and Gluckman (11) have pointed out, is a common method of adjudicating quarrels in societies which lack organized enforcement power. Such ritual conflicts as the Eskimo song duel or the Tiwi spear throwing contest provide alternatives to litigation or private vengeance. As Service suggests, these contests allow each party to state his grievances publicly and attempt to influence community opinion in his favor. They also allow other community members to decide which side they favor. Eventually the contests make clear where the majority opinion lies, and the losing party will usually not press his claims further. Ritual conflict is particularly likely when disputes involve kinsmen or members of the same community or when societies lack the organization necessary for military activity. Gluckman suggests that ritual may also be used if individual and group interests are in conflict or if cross-cutting allegiance patterns inhibit more direct forms of conflict.

If the husband's ritual involvement in the birth occurs in the absence of enforcement power, then husband involvement and maternal restriction represent alternate strategies in paternity disputes. Maternal restrictions depend on the presence of enforceable bargains, while husband involvement depends on their absence. The inverse relationship between husband involvement and maternal restrictions depends fundamentally on the unequal role of men and women in the birth process. While women bear children, paternity rights are almost invariably controlled by men. Thus women are objects not actors in most paternity negotiations. Both the ritual involvement of husbands in the birth and the restriction of women are primarily tactics used by male claimants to protect their rights over offspring being produced by women. When males are effectively organized they can use this power to control the birth process to their own advantage. When they lack such power, they must find alternative strategies to assert their claims.

REFERENCES

1. Ayres, Barbara. 1954. A Cross-Cultural Study of Factors Relating to Pregnancy Taboos. Unpublished Ph.D. Dissertation, Harvard University.

2. Bettelheim, Bruno. 1954. Symbolic Wounds. Glenco, Ill: Free Press.

3. Burton, R. and J. Whiting. 1961. "The absent father and cross-sex identity." Merrill-Palmer Quarterly 7 (Winter): 85–95.

4. Crawley, Ernest. 1902. The Mystic Rose. London: Macmillan.

5. Duncan, Otis. 1966. "Path analysis: sociological examples." American Journal of Sociology 72 (July): 1–16.

6. Deveraux, George. 1950. "The psychology of feminine genital bleeding." International Journal of Psychoanalysis 31 (Winter): 237–57.

7. Ember, Melvin and Carol Ember. 1971. "The conditions favoring matrilocal versus patrilocal residence." American Anthropologist 73 (June): 571–94.

8. Ford, Clellan. 1964. A Comparative Study of Human Reproduction. Yale University Publication in Anthropology Number 32. New Haven: Human Relations Area File Press.

9. Fortes, Meyer. 1962. "Introduction," In Meyer Fortes (ed.), Marriage in Tribal Societies. Cambridge: Cambridge University Press.

10. Frazier, J.G. 1922. The Golden Bough. London: Macmillian.

11, Gluckman, Max. 1965. Politics, Law, and Ritual in Tribal Society. Chicago: Aldine.

12. Homans, George. 1941. "Anxiety and ritual: the theories of Malinowski and Radcliffe-Brown." American Anthropologist 43 (April): 164–72.

13. Mair, Lucy. 1971. Marriage. London: Penguin.

14. Malinowski, Bronislaw. 1927. Sex and Regression in Savage Society. New York: Harcourt, Brace.

15. _____. 1931. "Culture." In Seligman, E. (ed.) Encyclopedia of the Social Sciences. London: Macmillan.

16. Murdock, George. 1967. "Ethnographic atlas: a summary." Ethnology 6 (April): 109–236.

17, _____. 1968. "World sampling provinces." Ethnology 7 (July): 305–26.

18. Murdock, George and Douglas White. 1969. "Standard cross-cultural sample." Ethnology 8 (October): 329–69.

19. Murdock, George and Susanne Wilson. 1972. "Settlement patterns and community organization: cross-cultural codes 3." Ethnology 11 (July): 254–95.

20. Norbeck, Edward. 1961. Religion in Primitive Society. New York: Harper Brothers.

21. Otterbein, Keith. 1968. "Internal War: a cross-cultural study." American Anthropologist 70 (April): 277–89.

22. Paige, Jeffery. Forthcoming. "Kinship and polity in stateless societies." American Journal of Sociology.

23. Radcliffe-Brown, A. 1950. "Introduction." Pp. 1–85 in A. Radcliffe-Brown and D. Forde (eds.), African Systems of Kinship and Marriage. London: Oxford University Press.

24. _____. 1952a. "Taboo." Pp. 133–52 in A. Radcliffe-Brown, Structure and Function in Primitive Society. London: Oxford University Press.

25. _____. 1952b. "Patrilineal and matrilineal succession." Pp. 32–48 in A. Radcliffe-Brown, Structure and Function in Primitive Society. London: Oxford University Press.

26. Service, Elman. 1966. The Hunters. Englewood Cliffs, N.J.: Prentice-Hall.

27. Sumner, William. 1934. Folkways. Boston: Ginn.

28. Tylor, Edward. 1889. "On the method of investigating the development of institutions; applied to laws of marriage and descent." Journal of the Royal Anthropological Institute 18: 245–69.

29. Van Gennep, Arnold. 1961. The Rites of Passage. Chicago: University of Chicago Press.

30. Van Velzen, H. and W. Van Wettering. 1960. "Residence, power groups and intra-societal aggression . . ." International Archives of Ethnography 49: 169–200.

31. Webster, H. 1942. Taboo: A Sociological Study. Stanford: Stanford University Press.

32. White, B. and E. Saltz. 1967. "The measurement of reproducibility." Pp. 241–57 in D. Jackson and S. Messick, Problems in Human Assessment. New York: McGraw Hill.

33. Young, Frank. 1965. Initiation Rites. New York: Bobbs-Merrill.

NOTE

*This study was supported by funds granted to Karen Paige by the Dept. of Psychology, University of California, Davis. We are particularly indebted to Linda Fuller, who supervised data collection, and to the coders—Kathy Barchak, Christi Bengard, Hart Guenther, and Setha Low. We also wish to thank the Survey Research Center, University of California, Berkeley, for providing services and facilities.

Appendix 1. Sample Societies and Sampling Provinces (SP), Husband Involvement Scores (H), and Maternal Restrictions Scores (M).

SP	Society	H	M	SP	Society	H	M	SP	Society	H	M
AFRICA				**EAST EURASIA (con'd)**				**NORTH AMERICA (con'd)**			
1	Nama	2	5	78	Ainu	5	3	140	Twana	4	4
2	Kung	1	4	80	Korea	1	5	141	Hupa	4	2
3	Thonga	3	4	81	Tungus	1	4	142	Klamath	2	5
6	Suku	1	1	85	Lepcha	4	2	144	Yokut	4	2
7	Lamba	1	1	87	Garo	4	1	146	Paiute	3	2
9	Nyakyusa	3	4	88	Lakher	2	1	149	Sanpoil	3	5
11	Luguru	1	2	90	Lamet	4	2	150	Gros Ventre	2	4
13	Ganda	3	5	91	Thai	1	1	152	Micmac	2	4
14	Mongo	1	5	92	Andaman	3	2	153	Ojibwa	2	4
15	Mbuti	3	2	96	Rhade	•	•	154	Hidatsa	1	3
19	Dahomey	2	4	8	Tanala	1	3	157	Creek	4	3
20	Ashanti	2	5					159	Pawnee	4	1
24	Bambara	2	5	**INSULAR PACIFIC**				161	Apache	1	3
26	Tallensi	3	4	101	Iban	4	2	162	Navaho	3	2
29	Tiv	2	5	104	Bali	2	4	163	Papago	4	5
33	Azande	3	2	107	Alor	4	3	165	Tarasco	2	3
37	Shilluk	1	5	108	Murngin	2	3	166	Zapotec	1	1
38	Masai	2	5	109	Arunta	1	5				
				112	Kiwai	5	4	**SOUTH AMERICA**			
CIRCUM MEDITARRANEAN				113	Wogeo	5	5	168	Miskito	4	5
28	Hausa	1	5	114	Kapauku	2	2	169	Bribri	3	4
32	Fur	5	5	115	Palauan	1	5	170	Cuna	5	2
41	Somali	1	4	116	Yap	3	5	172	Goajiro	2	4
42	Amhara	1	5	117	Ifaluk	3	3	173	Callinago	5	3
46	Tuareg	1	5	118	Marshall	2	4	175	Warrau	5	1
47	Rif	1	2	120	Manu	1	5	178	Carib	5	3
51	Hebrew	1	4	121	Lesu	1	4	179	Saramacca	1	2
52	Rwala	1	4	122	Trobriand	2	5	180	Mundurucu	5	1
55	Cheg	1	2	123	Kurtatchi	5	2	182	Witoto	5	3
56	Basque	1	•	124	Ontong Java	1	1	183	Jivaro	5	3
58	Lapp	1	4	125	Tikopia	2	4	184	Amahuaca	1	•
62	Kurd	1	1	128	Fiji	3	5	186	Aymara	1	1
				129	Samoa	1	2	187	Siriono	5	2
EAST EURASIA				130	Maori	2	4	188	Nambicuara	5	2
63	Basseri	1	1	131	Marquesa	5	5	190	Timbira	5	3
66	Vedda	1	1					191	Tupinamba	5	1
67	Chenchu	2	1	**NORTH AMERICA**				194	Aweikoma	•	1
68	Baiga	1	3	132	Aleut	1	4	196	Lengua	3	2
70	Burusho	2	5	133	Copper Eskimo	4	2	198	Mapuche	1	5
72	Kazak	1	1	136	Eyak	4	5	200	Yahgan	5	4
73	Yurak Samoyed	1	4	138	Kaska	3	3				
76	Chukchee	1	4	139	Kwakiutl	3	4				

CONTRACEPTION

ORAL CONTRACEPTIVES IN ANCIENT AND MEDIEVAL TIMES

John M. Riddle and J. Worth Estes

In the hills near Cyrene, an ancient Greek city-state in North Africa, there once grew a plant of such economic importance that its image was carried on Cyrenian coins. Bundles of the plant, which was called silphion by the Greeks and silphium by the Romans, were shipped throughout the Mediterranean trading area, where they commanded a price that was said to exceed the plant's weight in silver. Farmers in Greece and Syria tried in vain to cultivate it, but silphion would grow only in Cyrene, where it was finally harvested to extinction.

The loss of silphion was a blow not only to the economy of Cyrene, but quite possibly to medicine. Its great value apparently derived from a singular use of the plant: Silphion's sap may have been the ancient world's most effective antifertility drug.

Could the Greeks have had an effective oral contraceptive? Modern historians are skeptical. During certain periods many ancient and medieval societies experienced declines in numbers, even in times that were peaceful, prosperous and plague-free. The common wisdom holds that they limited their population by non-medicinal means, from abstinence to infanticide. Their antifertility drugs are usually relegated to the realm of magic and superstition. Yet the archaeological and written record is sprinkled with evidence that drugs were a trusted way to prevent conception or induce early-term abortions. These claims, tested against recent studies of plant-based contraceptives, offer one plausible explanation for the fact that ancient and medieval people were able to control their numbers.

Silphion, for example, probably worked. Recent experiments with rodents have shown that extracts taken from some of silphion's surviving relatives can inhibit conception or prevent the implantation of a fertilized egg. Since ancient writers described silphion as far more effective than the other species in its family, perhaps it is not surprising that it was driven to extinction.

Unfortunately, knowledge about agents such as silphion has become nearly extinct as well. The faint trail of historical information about plant-based oral conception begins in ancient Greece but disappears during the Middle Ages, centuries before the pioneering endocrinological studies of John Rock and Gregory Pincus in the 1950s led to the development of "the pill." Premodern people probably had knowledge about birth control methods that we do not.

Some of the reasons for the disappearance of such knowledge have to do with the hidden nature of female culture. Although many graphic discussions of sexual practices can be found in ancient literature, the writers had only secondhand knowledge of the birth-control practices of women. All surviving medical works in the West, at least until the 12th century, were written by males. But women were the practitioners of medicinal contraception: Only women knew the secrets of what plants to gather and when to gather them, the part of the plant to use, the method of extracting and preparing the drug, the optimum dose and the best time to take it within the menstrual cycle.

Never an important part of professional medical knowledge, antifertility lore came to belong almost exclusively to midwives as professional medicine developed during the Middle Ages. In time, much of the midwives' knowledge was lost, especially as male physicians forced them out of business and gynecology became part of professional medical practice. By the 19th century abortion was a criminal act in many Western countries, and the use of antifertility drugs was excluded from professional

"Oral Contraceptives in Ancient and Medieval Times," by John M. Riddle and J. Worth Estes, reprinted from *American Scientist*, Vol. 80, No. 3, May/June 1992, reprinted by permission of Sigma Xi.

medicine. By the time society began to look for medicinal means of birth control again in the 20th century, the historical trail had gone cold.

Traces of the ancient legacy of antifertility drugs are found in folk practices today—in the herbal medicine of China and India, and even in the mountain regions of the United States where midwives still use herbs in their practice. These bits of folklore, combined with the archaeological and written record hinted at what was probably a thriving oral culture of contraception. They offer a trail worth picking up once again, both to re-examine our assumptions about the civilizations that preceded ours and to expand the range of solutions available to a world in need of broader choices.

Population control sometimes seems a modern quandary. Ancient Greeks and Romans did not have to worry about the limits of planetary resources, but they did turn their thoughts to population issues from time to time. "If too many children are being born," said Plato, writing of the ideal city, "there are measures to check propagation."

The Roman Senate of Caesar Augustus's day was alarmed not by population growth but by the economic consequences of a declining birth rate. Abortions were outlawed, and the use of contraceptives forbidden, according to one Roman historian. During the Roman Empire and the early Middle Ages, demographic records show that there were absolute declines in the populations of the Western European continent and the Mediterranean area. There are various theories about why populations declined, but it is possible that neither Augustus's subjects nor the Romans of the Empire's waning days paid much heed to the Senate's dictates. The gap between public policy and private behavior is the subject of much speculation.

Changes in sexual activities in and out of wedlock do not provide an adequate explanation. Although many ancient sexual practices are well documented, especially in the Roman literature, the record supplies little evidence that coitus interruptus was widely practiced in the ancient world. In antiquity neither religion nor ethical restrictions regulated sexual activity for males. One French writer, Philippe Ariès, has postulated that both ancient and medieval people limited family size by engaging in other sexual activities (behavior he called *perversitè sexuelle*) that could not lead to childbirth. The documentary evidence reveals that sexual practices were indeed varied during classical antiquity, but this variety does not provide a sufficient explanation for population declines. The rhythm method is unlikely to have had a major impact, since the ancients' understanding of the menstrual cycle would have led those trying this approach to have intercourse during fertile periods.

The condom and the diaphragm are relatively modern inventions, although experiments with barrier devices and vaginal suppositories began deep in antiquity; these are varied and their impact hard to evaluate. Abortions were always available, but it is difficult to find evidence that they were routinely employed for birth control. Both ancient and medieval medical texts recognize surgical or manipulative abortions as dangerous, an agreement that leads modern historians to believe that they were used primarily in desperate situations. Drug-induced abortions are an area of greater debate, and will be discussed in more detail below.

In the Middle Ages all conduct including that of married couples, was closely regulated in Europe by the church. Procreative intercourse within the bounds of marriage was the only sexual activity condoned, and women of the late Middle Ages and Renaissance tended to marry somewhat later than their classical counterparts. Yet it is interesting that the sexual restraint imposed by Christianity had no obvious impact on population; the demographic ups and downs of medieval times are remarkably similar to the patterns of antiquity. Given the hard-to-explain population declines found throughout the record, it is hard to resist the conclusion that some effective form of family limitation may have been practiced during both periods.

The explanation that has satisfied most historians has been infanticide. The strongest evidence supporting this theory comes from data that appear to show the persistence of a higher ratio of males to females than would be expected in a biologically neutral environment free from interference. Contraception and abortion would have taken place before the sex of a child was known, so they should not have produced the alleged lopsided sex ratio. An interesting body of evidence in this debate comes from the field of paleopathology: Close examination of adult female skeletons—which bear marks that can be used to estimate the number of full-term pregnancies—suggests that there were periods in antiquity during which births declined, a contradiction of the infanticide theory. The precision of the method, however, may not be sufficient to support a comparison between population and birth rate.

Since the hard documentary evidence for widespread infanticide is scant (consisting of occasional references to the abandonment of unwanted babies, who might have died from exposure), the case for this hypothesis rests largely on circumstantial evidence and remains controversial. Some scholars argue that a larger male population is natural in certain conditions. While the debate continues, it is worthwhile to examine an alternative explanation—the use of oral contraceptives.

Ancient medical experts, in both Eastern and Western cultures, regularly prescribe antifertility preparations made from the secretions of plants. But until the 1960s, when studies of such botanical agents began to be reported in Indian and Chinese medical and pharmaceutical journals, Western scientists maintained great skepticism about the possibility that any of these ancient prescriptions worked. A re-examination of these beliefs has been slow to come.

The development of modern oral contraceptives has its roots not in the historical experience of women but in the science of endocrinology, which has supplied an understanding of the human ovulatory cycle that is good enough to point the way to effective birth control. In order to be fertilized, an ovum must first mature while still within its ovarian follicle. Its maturation is prompted by the release of follicle-stimulating hormone from the anterior pituitary gland. The release of this hormone is inhibited when the concentration of estrogenic hormones, which control other parts of the menstrual cycle, rises in the blood. Thus modern oral contraceptive pills inhibit the maturation of follicles and their ova, so that fertilization cannot occur, by keeping estrogen concentrations in the blood at a relatively high level.

Estrogens were long thought to be produced only by animals; it was assumed that plants do not synthesize compounds with estrogenic properties. But this assumption was challenged in the 1930s and 1940s as improved techniques of chemical analysis became available. Two studies published in 1933 offered the first clues. Boleslaw Skarzynski reported to the Polish Science Academy that he had obtained from the willow a substance, trihydrooxyoestrin, that resembled a human female sex hormone in its physico-chemical properties. The same year, Adolf Butenandt and H. Jacobi reported that the date palm and pomegranate produced female sex hormones. Although the latter report could not be duplicated experimentally, the principle that plants can produce substances with estrogenic properties had been established by 1966.

Evidence of how substances in plants might affect animal fertility came, meanwhile, from the observations of Australian sheep breeders who noticed that fertility was sharply reduced in animals that grazed on one species of clover, *Trifolium subterraneum.* A study in the 1940s traced the clover's antifertility effect to isoflavonoids, which stimulate estrogen production when they are metabolized by mammals.

Sheep are not human, and so skepticism about the contraceptive effect of plant extracts in humans persisted following these studies. The question was reopened, however, in 1960, when chemists D. B. Bounds and G. S. Pope followed up on a report by anthropologists that Thai women took an extract of the root of *Pueraria mirifica,* a close relative of kudzu, to induce abortion. They isolated from the plant an estrogenic compound called miroestrol.

The Indian and Chinese scientific literature produced at that time has reported many studies of crude traditional drugs made from indigenous plants; interestingly, the plants used in the East are often related to species described in the ancient Western literature. Combined with evidence from animal science, anthropology, pharmacy and medicine—and the historical record itself—these studies provide grounds for new investigations of the historical use of plant-based antifertility drugs. The possibilities are many and varied; here we will be able to offer only a few examples. Before we look into the ancient pharmacy, however, it is useful to consider the state of knowledge and belief that guided ancient and medieval approaches to contraception.

The story of ancient oral contraceptives must be woven from threads supplied not only by writers on medicine but also by legend, art and writings of ancient poets, philosophers, playwrights and satirists. Fortunately, there is a large body of such work in the West, and so we shall focus our attention there; although botanical contraceptives may have been used in China as early as they were in Greece, the nature of Chinese archival evidence makes that record far more obscure. We can press onward from antiquity into the Middle Ages in Western Europe, but it is here that the trail becomes obscured because much of the written record is the record of the church. Eventually church opposition helped to smother birth control in taboo and secrecy.

The ancients did not understand the hormonal basis of the menstrual cycle, but they had some ideas about how conception occurred. Because these ideas sometimes blurred what is now considered the boundary between contraception and early-term abortion, it is not always easy to determine how ancient antifertility drugs acted. Soranus, antiquity's foremost authority on gynecology, did make a distinction in his writings during the second century C.E., explaining: "A contraceptive differs from an abortifacient, for the first does not let conception take place while the latter destroys what has been conceived." Soranus recommended contraception as preferable for safety reasons.

But ancient writers did not, in general, understand conception as we do. They thought that it occurred after sexual union at a time when the male seed began to grow. Indeed, many of the ancients did not believe that the female possessed a "seed." Employing an agricultural analogy, they asserted that the female supplied only nourishment, and that the male seed could live within the female for several days before conception took place. This period corresponds roughly with what we now recognize as the time required for implantation of the fertilized ovum in the uterus. The definition of contraceptives (*atokioi,* as the Greeks called them) therefore encompassed drugs taken shortly after intercourse. A further confusion arises from the fact that it was not always possible to know whether menstruation had ceased because of pregnancy or for another reason, perhaps fever, chronic disease, malnutrition or depression. Women took a variety of drugs during ancient and medieval times to provoke menstruation. In modern terms, these drugs could be called early-term abortifacients, but a woman of earlier times who took an emmenagogue (as such drugs have been called since the 17th century) to regulate her menses could not know whether she had caused an abortion.

It is important to note that the ancient ideas about the beginning of life provided a woman a period of time in which she was free to stop a pregnancy without considering the act an abortion. The Stoics believed in the potentiality of life at conception, but maintained that the soul originated at birth. Most ancient cultures provided a legal and moral zone for action during the period between conception and "animation" or quickening. Under ancient Hebrew law, a woman was regarded as pregnant 40 days after conception. Western society's tacit acceptance of the "morning-after pill" persisted for many centuries; it was not until the 19th century that the taking of a drug to regulate menstruation became widely outlawed as abortion.

There is some evidence of contraception in ancient Egypt, but the first well-documented example of an oral contraceptive is the mysterious silphion. The historian Theophrastus, who wrote about 310 B.C.E., traced the Cyrenians' discovery of silphion to a date 300 years earlier. Botanical descriptions indicate that it was a species of *Ferula,* or giant fennel. A Greek vase of the sixth century B.C.E. shows workers aboard a ship weighing and storing packages under the eye of Arkesilas, king of Cyrene. Although we cannot be sure, the packages have long been believed to contain silphion.

We know that silphion was a valued contraceptive from both objects and writings of the day. On the face of a Cyrenian four-drachma coin, the leaves of the silphion plant just touch the right hand of a woman, who is seated with her left hand pointing to her genital area. The iconography suggests a connection between the plant and reproduction. Both the Greek comedy writer Aristophanes and the naturalist Pliny the Elder mention silphion's high cost, and Hippocrates recorded the failed efforts to cultivate it in Syria and Greece. The reason for the plant's high value was best explained by Soranus, who said that the sap of silphion, taken by mouth, prevented conception. Soranus provided several prescriptions for "Cyrenaic juice," which he said would either prevent or halt a pregnancy.

The related species still growing in North Africa include *Ferula assa-foetida* L., commonly called asafoetida and used today as an aromatic ingredient in Worcestershire sauce. *F. assa-foetida* was reported to act as a human contraceptive in 1963, and crude alcohol extracts of *F. assa-foetida* and another relative, *F. orientalis,* inhibited implantation of fertilized ova in rats at rates of 40 percent and 50 percent, respectively (16). Other *Ferula* species have produced even more impressive effects: In 1985, organic and aqueous extracts of *F. jaechkaena* were reported to be nearly 100 percent effective in preventing pregnancy when administered to adult female rats within three days of coitus (21). (The effect was not seen in hamsters, which are far less sensitive than rats to conventional estrogenic inhibitors of fetal implantation.)

The idea of a chemical means of birth control is as old as the oldest surviving medical records. The earliest medical writing from Egypt, the Kahun Medical Papyrus, dating from around 1850 B.C.E., contains fragments of three contraceptive recipes. They call for using crocodile feces, honey and saltpeter to make vaginal suppositories. The Egyptian record is sketchy and full of such questionable (and indecipherable) remedies, but by the time of the Greeks and Romans women had gained more sophistication about contraception. It is no coincidence that two plants used as oral contraceptives in ancient times, and for many centuries since, carry the names of famous women of ancient legend.

Artemis, the goddess of women and the woodland and the protector of childbirth, gave her name to a group of shrublike plants that can grow to about four feet. Whereas silphion was a rare, exotic plant, Artemisia is the name of a common genus whose members can now be found over much of North America. Their featherlike leaves are gray-green and highly indented. Artemisia is also the name given the drug that can be produced from some of these plants.

In ancient times, artemisia was said to protect against the pangs of childbirth, although no one stated whether it did so by preventing or terminating a pregnancy or by some other means. During the Roman Empire, both Soranus and Dioscorides, a first-century herbalist and writer on pharmacology, reported that physicians prescribed an *Artemisia* species, wormwood or *A. absinthium,* as an antifertility drug. Other ancient medical authorities classified wormwood as an abortifacient, a reputation that survived many centuries. Macer, the author of the most popular herbal of the central Middle Ages (1000–1300) and probably a bishop in the 11th century, discussed artemisia. At that time the Christian church opposed abortion, to a limited degree, after the fetus had "formed." Macer related that the plant was given its name by the goddess Artemis herself because she had discovered that it "mainly cures female ailments and, when drunk . . . , it produces an abortion." (Despite the church's position in favor of procreation, medieval writers—many of whom were churchmen—related practical information about contraceptives and early-term abortifacients. Indeed, one of the prolific writers on birth-control techniques was Peter of Spain, author of the *Treasury of the Poor,* who became Pope John XXII.)

Artemisia had not been forgotten. One of the most popular herbals in print today, the 1986 *Reader's Digest* book *Magic and Medicine of Plants,* says that artemisia provokes menstruation. There is modest scientific support for the abortion-inducing effects of the drug (3), and animal studies over the past 20 years have reported that wormwood has delayed the production of estrus and ovulation and interfered with implantation. One study indicates that wormwood has an effect on males as well—interfering with spermatogenesis. (It is important to note that artemisia, taken internally, has several toxic side effects; it is perhaps because of its toxicity that ancient physicians such as Soranus and Dioscorides recommended that it be taken along with two other drugs, myrrh and rue.)

Another legendary figure gave her name to a less widely used substance—the precious resin myrrh, the sap of shrubs of the genus *Commiphora,* which grows in East Africa. Although myrrh is most famous for its uses as a fragrant ointment in the Bible, the Roman poet Ovid recounted its origin in legend. Myrrha was the daughter of Theias, also called Cinyras, a legendary king of Assyria. A great misfortune befell the innocent girl because of her father's impiety. When he angered Aphrodite, the goddess of love, Aphrodite caused him to lust after his daughter. As a result of their incest, Myrrha bore a son, Adonis. But Theias continued to assault her, until at length she fled. When Myrrha called upon the gods to help her escape from her father, they transformed her into the plant known by her name. Her tears, the plant's sap, became the rescuer of daughters victimized by a father's lust. "Even the tears have fame," Ovid wrote in his *Metamorphoses,* "and that which distills from the tree trunk keeps the name of its mistress and will be remembered through all the ages."

Myrrh's effectiveness is uncertain; it is listed among the antifertility drugs used in the traditional medicine of India, but does not seem to have been tested experimentally. Records indicate that it was often a component of antifertility prescriptions in ancient and medieval Western medicine; its exotic nature and high cost may have limited its use.

Artemisia and myrrh are not the only birth-control agents that turn up in ancient legend. Pennyroyal, the aromatic mint plant *Mentha pulegium* L., plays a role in Aristophanes' play *Peace,* first produced in Athens in 421 B.C.E. Trigaius is in need of a female consort. The god Hermes provides him with Harvesthome. Trigaius says to her: "Come here and let me kiss you—but, Hermes, won't it hurt me if I make too free with fruits of Harvesthome at first?" Hermes replies: "Not if you add a dose of pennyroyal."

Pennyroyal was known as an antifertility agent throughout classical antiquity and the Middle Ages. Ancient experts and modern science appear to agree that an ingredient of pennyroyal, pulegone, is an abortifacient—and a potentially dangerous one. Quintus Serenus, writing on medicine in the second century C.E., said that, when a pregnancy was less than a month old and the "fetus" (Latin did not provide a meaningful distinction between fetus and embryo) was weak, one should "rush into the bedroom" to administer pennyroyal in tepid water to the woman.

The ingestion of pulegone has been shown in recent studies to induce abortions in women and in animals (5, 7, 25, 26). A young woman died in Colorado in 1978 when she took pennyroyal oil to induce an abortion—an incident that may serve to demonstrate both the hazards of herbal abortifacients and the fact that ancient knowledge may have been passed on, but imperfectly. Pulegone is more concentrated in the oil than in the tea taken by premodern women. The oil would be expected to damage the liver of both mice and human beings, if taken in a sufficient dose (6, 24).

Pennyroyal and *Artemisia* grow wild in many parts of the world. They are two of dozens of plants that women have gathered over the centuries in hopes of preparing a tea, potion, powder or seed preparation to prevent or stop pregnancy. Finding a potent plant, it turns out, is easier than you think.

Queen Anne's lace grows profusely in many areas of North America. Its reddish, slender, strongly aromatic root gave the plant, *Daucus carota* L., the ancient name of wild carrot. Its stems, two or three feet high and covered with coarse hair, carry the white flowers that are recalled by the plant's modern name. The flowers produce the many small seeds that generate the next growth, and that contain substances with estrogenic activity.

A small number of women in Watauga County, North Carolina, in the Appalachian mountains, gather the seeds of Queen Anne's lace and save them. Each time they have sexual intercourse, those who wish not to be with child drink a glass of water containing a teaspoonful of seeds saved from the autumn harvest. Rural populations in Rajasthan, India, chew dry seeds of Queen Anne's lace to reduce fertility. Both are practices that were known to women 2,000 years ago.

Dioscorides said that the seeds of the wild carrot brought forth the menses and aborted an embryo. Hippocrates had prescribed the plant in the fifth century B.C.E. for preventing or aborting pregnancy, as did the ancient physicians Scribonius Largus, Galen and Paul of Aegina in the first through the sixth centuries.

Extracts of Queen Anne's lace seeds have been tested on rats, mice, guinea pigs and rabbits. When mice were given the seeds by mouth (in doses of 80 to 120 milligrams) on the fourth to sixth days of pregnancy, the seeds totally prevented implantation (20). In other experiments with rodents, the seeds were found to inhibit implantation and ovarian growth and to disrupt the estrous cycle (8, 9). The seeds' antifertility effect is antagonized by progesterone, and recent evidence suggests that terpenoids in the seed block crucial progesterone synthesis in pregnant animals (12). A crude boiled preparation of *D. carota* seeds, on the other hand, was found not to block fertilization in two rat experiments; neither did it stimulate rat uterine contractions in vitro (14, 15). Despite such conflicting evidence, the seeds (or their active ingredient, which has not been isolated) have been viewed as a promising postcoital antifertility agent.

Like Queen Anne's lace, the strong-smelling woody herb rue *(Ruta graveclens* L.) seems to turn up in many regions and, as an antifertility agent, in many times and cultures. The ancients used rue both as a contraceptive and as an abortifacient. Rather than recommending it, Pliny the Elder—who opposed abortion—wrote: "Pregnant women must take care to exclude rue from their diet for I find that the fetus/embryo is killed by it." Today rue is employed as an abortifacient throughout Latin America and among the Hispanic population of New Mexico as an abortifacient (in the form of a tea), and in the traditional medicine of India.

Chinese investigators have explored the antifertility effects of rue by administering chloroform extracts of the whole rue plant in daily oral doses of 0.8 to 1.2 grams per kilogram of body weight to female rats over the first eight to 10 days of pregnancy. The extracts reduced the number of pregnancies in the experimental group by 20 percent to 75 percent (depending on the potency of the extract administered). As was the case with the *Ferula* extracts, the same effect was not observed in hamsters. Because the active substance in rue, chalepensin, is highly toxic, its effect on fertility may be simply the result of nonselective toxicity (13).

Rue belongs to a botanical family, Rutaceae, that includes several plants that produce antifertility agents. Chinese scientists have studied the active substance in another Rutacea species. The substance, called *yuehchukene* and extracted from the plant *Murraya paniculata* var. *M. sapientum* L., has been reported to be 100 percent effective in preventing pregnancies in rats when administered orally at doses of 2 milligrams per kilogram during the first six days of pregnancy, or as a single dose of 3 milligrams per kilogram on the first day after coitus (12). It is interesting that another Rutaceae species, *Pilocarpus jaborandi* Homes, produces a cholinergic agent called pilocarpine that has been given to horses to induce abortion. Pilocarpine is not known, however, to have the same effect in women.

The botanist and physician Carolus Linnaeus named a third common plant for its abortion-inducing effect. Squirting cucumber, so called because its fruit squirts its seed out when it dries, carries the Linnaean name *Ecballium elaterium,* from the Greek word *ekballion,* which means "abortion." Linnaeus was hardly the first to notice its effect; Hippocrates is alleged to be the author of a treatise on women's diseases and problems in which squirting cucumber is recommended for abortion. In fact, the author indicated that *sikos agrios,* as the Greeks called it, was the abortifacient of choice.

Recent animal tests support the notion that squirting cucumber has a contraceptive effect. When mice were given daily doses of 20 to 100 milligrams per kilogram of extracts from the whole plant or from the flower alone, they failed to ovulate (4). The abortifacient effect has not been confirmed, and it is possible that the drug's other known effects—catharsis, emesis and diuresis—may have led physicians to connect it with abortion.

It is possible to conclude that women of any ancient and medieval times were fooled by physicians, witch doctors, herbalists, witches, midwives, village wise persons and charlatan medicine-show salesmen into taking birth-control potions that did not work. Placebo and psychological effects are bound to be common in experiments with herbal medicines, but in the prevention of pregnancy they work only one way. A woman who takes a potion to prevent conception cannot be sure that it did the trick, but a full-term pregnancy is a sure sign that it doesn't work. Thus any drug that simply does not work should, over time, be discredited.

If the plants we have discussed survived as birth-control drugs on the strength of false reputations, they did so for a very long time. "We've too many sure-fire drugs for inducing sterility!" remarked the Roman satirist Juvenal in the second century C.E., as the emperors continued to struggle with population declines. St. Jerome three centuries later condemned those who "drink sterility and murder those not yet conceived," as well as people who use poison to destroy those yet to be born. And in the eighth century priests asked in confession: "Have you drunk any *maleficium*, that is, herbs, or other agents so that you could not have children?"

If, as we suggest, modern scientists and historians decide to consider the efficacy of ancient oral contraceptives an open and useful question, a number of interesting avenues of inquiry lie ahead. Do some herbs prevent or disrupt pregnancy simply because they are toxic? Probably. The unintended effects of plant substances are many; no one should try the ancient Greeks' recipes at home. But other plant substances may have clearly defined actions and controllable toxicity; there is much that is yet unknown about them, and in some circles skepticism still seems to inhibit research. We too quickly draw a hard line that separates us from the premodern period, dismissing the ancients' solutions to problems.

Historians are likely to be intrigued by another question raised by the record: Why do so few now know what so many once did? The disappearance of knowledge—the severing of a trail of learning that extended over many centuries—ought to be of concern to all scholars. In a world in which population control promises to be a growing concern, a closer look at what once was known about contraception might broaden the options that science can offer.

BIBLIOGRAPHY

1. Ariès, Philippe, 1953. Sur les origines de la contraception en France. *Population* 8: 465–72.

2. Dioscorides. *De Materia Medica.* 3 vols. Berlin: Weidmann. 1907.

3. Dake, J. A. 1985. *CRC Handbook of Medicinal Herbs.* Boca Raton, Louisiana: CRC Press.

4. Farnsworth, N. A., A. S. Bingel, G. A. Cordell, F. A. Crane and H. H. S. Fong, 1975. Potential value of plants as a source of new antifertility agents. Part 1, *Journal of Pharmaceutical Sciences* 64 (April): 535–98. Part 2, 64 (May): 717–754.

5. Froehlich, O., and T. Shibamato. 1990. Stability of pulegone and thujone in ethanolic solution. *Journal of Agricultural and Food Chemistry* 38. 2057–2060.

6. Gordon, W. P., A. J. Forte, R. J. McMurry, J. Gal and S. D. Nelson. 1982. Hepatotoxicity and pulmonary toxicity of pennyroyal oil and its constituent terpenes in the mouse. *Toxicology and Applied Pharmacology* 65: 413–424

7. Gordon, W. P., A. C. Huitric, C. L. Seth, R. H. McClanahan and S. D. Nelson. 1987. The metabolism of the abortifacient termene, (R)-(+)-pulegone, to a proximate toxin, menthofuran. *Drug Metabolism and Disposition* 15:589–594.

8. Kaliwal, B. B., and R. N. Ahamed.1987. Maintenance of implantation by progesterone in carrot seed *Daucus carota* extracted treated by albino rats. *Indian Journal of Physical and Natural Sciences* Section A7:10–14.

9. Kaliwal, B. B., R. Nazeer Ahamed and M. Appaswomy Rao. 1984. Abortifacient effect of carrot seed (*Daucus carota*) extract and its reversal by progesterone in albino rats. *Comparative Physiology and Ecology* 9:70–74.

10. Kant, A., and N. K. Lohiya. 1986. The estrogen efficacy of carrot *Daucus carota* seeds. *Journal of Advanced Zoology* 7:36–41.

11. Kong, Yun Cheung, C. P. Lau, K. H. Wat. K. H. Ng. P.P.H. But, K. F. Cheng and P. G. Waerman. 1989. Antifertility principle of *Ruta graveolens. Planta Medica* 55:176–178.

12. Kong, Yun Cheung, J.-X. Xie and P. P.-H But. 1986. Fertility regulating agents from traditional Chinese medicines. *Journal of Ethnopharmacology* 15:1–44.

13. Kong, Yun Cheung, K. H. Ng. K. H. Wat, A. Wong, I. F. Saxenza, K. F. Cheng, P. H. But and H. T. Chang. 1985. Yuehchukene, a novel anti-implantation indole alkaloid from *Murraya paniculata. Planta Medica* 51:304–307.

14. Lal, R. M. Gandhi, A. Anakaranarayanan, V. S. Mathur and P. L. Pharm. 1986. Antifertility effect of *Daucus carota* seeds in female albino rats. *Fitoterapia* 57:243–246.

15. Lal, R. A. Sankaranarayanan and V. S. Mathur. 1984. Antifertility and uterine activity of *Daucus carota*. A preliminary report. *Bulletin of Postgraduate Institute of Medical Education and Research Chandigarh* 18: 28–31.

16. Prakash, Anad O., V. Saxena, S. Shukla, R. K. Tewari, S. Mathur, A. Gupta and S. Sharma. 1986. Anti-implantation activity of some indigenous plants in rats. *Acta Europaea Fertilitatis* 24: 19–24.

17. Riddle, John. 1992 (in press). *Contraception and Abortion from the Ancient World to the Renaissance.* Boston: Harvard University Press.

18. Russell, Josiah. 1985. *The Control of Late Ancient and Medieval Population.* Philadelphia: American Philosophical Society.

19. Scarborough, John. 1989. Contraception in antiquity: the case of pennyroyal. *Wisconsin Academic Review* 35: 19–25.

20. Sharma, M. M., G. Lel and D. Jacob. 1976. Estrogenic and pregnancy interceptory effects of carrot *Daucus carota* seeds. *Indian Journal of Experimental Biology* 14:506–508.

21. Singh, M. M., D. N. Gupta, V. Wadhwa, G. K. Jain, M. M. Khanna and V. P. Kamboj. 1985. Contraceptive efficacy and hormonal profile of ferujol: a new coumarin from *Ferula jaeschkeana. Planta Medica* 51:268–270.

22. Singh, M. M., A. Agnihotri, S. N. Garg, D. N. Gupta, G. Keshri and V. P. Kamboj. 1988. Antifertility and hormonal properties of certain carotane sesquiterpenes of *Ferula jaeschkeana. Planta Medica* 54:492–494.

23. Soranus. *Gynaeciorum.* J. Ilberg, ed. Leipzig: Teubner. 1927.

24. Sullivan, John B., Barry H. Rumack, Harold Thomas Jr., Robert G. Peterson and Peter Bryson. 1979. Pennyroyal oil poisoning and hepatotoxicity. *Journal of the American Medical Association* 242:2873–2874.

25. Thomassen, D., P. G. Pearson, J. T. Slattery and S. D. Nelson, 1991. Partial characterization of biliary metabolites of pulegone by tandem mass spectrometry detection of glucuronide glutathione and glutathionyl-glucurionide conjugates. *Drug Metabolism and Disposition* 19:997–1003.

26. Thomassen, D., J. T. Slattery as S. D. Nelson. 1990. *Journal of Pharmacology and Experimental Therapy* 253:567–572.

John M. Riddle is the recipient of the Urdang International Medal for his writings on the history of pharmacology and professor of history at North Carolina State University. He is the author of five books, including *Contraception and Abortion from the Ancient World to the Renaissance*, scheduled for publication in June by Harvard University Press. J. Worth Estes is professor of pharmacology (history of pharmacology) at the Boston University School of Medicine and secretary-treasurer of the American Association for the History of Medicine. His books include *The Medical Skills of Ancient Egypt*, published in 1990. Address for Riddle: Department of History, Box 8103, NCSU, Raleigh, NC 27695-8108.

ABORTION

INDUCED ABORTION:
AN HISTORICAL OVERVIEW

Deborah R. McFarlane, DrPH

Abortion is one of the most controversial issues of late twentieth century American society: yet the practice and regulation of abortion are not new. Abortion has been practiced in "every known culture, whether literate or preliterate, primitive or modern."[1] Indeed, anthropologists have concluded that abortion is an absolutely universal phenomenon.[2] This article provides a brief history of abortion worldwide, as well as a discussion of the historical practice and prevalence of abortion in the United States, including the development of American public policy toward abortion until 1973 when *Roe v Wade* was decided.

HISTORY OF ABORTION

Throughout the ages, induced abortion has revolved around three principal questions. The first is, "When does the fetus become a person?" From ancient times through the present, people have speculated and debated about when a fetus should be considered human. The second question is, "Under what circumstances should abortion be permitted?" The second question "involves the collision of competing sets of values" and often, the discrepancy between beliefs and practice. The third question is, "Who should decide?" This question addresses whether the choice belongs to the individual or to society: it clearly encompasses the issue of women's rights in society.[3]

JUDAISM

Like their contemporaries in the ancient world, Jewish scholars debated the issue of ensoulment. By about AD 500, "the Talmud concluded that this question was unanswerable and irrelevant to abortion."[4] Moreover, the Talmud maintained that the fetus was part of the woman and did not become fully human until birth. On this point, the Talmud was quite specific, requiring that a fetus be destroyed should it pose a threat to the mother's life during delivery. However, if the greater part of the body or the head were exposed, the fetus was not to be harmed, "for one may not set aside one person's life for the sake of another."[5-7]

According to Jewish tradition, the only situation in which abortion was justified was to save a pregnant woman's life: that is, abortion was to be used for maternal rather than fetal indications. However, abortion outside of the aforementioned circumstances was not considered to be murder. Traditional Jewish law did prescribe penalties for deliberate abortion, "but these penalties were not as harsh as those prescribed for killing a human being."[8]

Apparently, the penalties associated with induced abortion were related to gestational age. Prior to 40 days after conception, the fertilized egg was considered "mere fluid." After 40 days' gestation, the fashioning or *formation* of the fetus was believed to have occurred. A woman who aborted after the 40th day following conception was required to bring an offering "just as if she had given birth to a live child."[9]

"Induced Abortion: An Historical Overview," by Dr. Deborah R. McFarlane, reprinted from *American Journal of Gynecological Health*, Vol. 142, No. 3, Macor Publishing, 1993.

Compared to early Christian writings, Jewish sources have very few references to abortion. Most scholars agree that induced abortion for reasons other than to save the life of the mother was rare in ancient Jewish society.[10–11]

THE ANCIENT GREEKS

Within ancient Greek society, abortion was viewed "with a variety of conflicting attitudes."[12] Both Plato and Aristotle considered abortion to be a method of population control.[13] Aristotle believed that a woman who became pregnant after bearing her allotted number of children should be compelled to terminate her pregnancy "before she felt the life."[14]

The Greek philosophers were very concerned with the time of *animation,* that is, when the fetus became human. Based on their respective theories, abortion was not considered to be murder, at least under certain circumstances.[15] Aristotle hypothesized that the fetus had a succession of souls: vegetable, animal, and rational. The final development, the rational soul, was the most important. According to Aristotle, animation and formation occurred at the same time, although he believed that these processes occurred later in female fetuses than in male fetuses. He postulated that animation occurred 40 days after conception in male fetuses and 80 days after conception in females. He developed this theory from observations of aborted fetuses.[16]

Although abortion was common in ancient Greek society, it was not nearly as widespread as infanticide. Hippocrates, the most famous Greek physician of ancient times, rejected abortifacients. However, in his book, *On the Nature of the Child,* he advised a method to procure abortion by jumping so that the buttocks are touched with the feet.[17] Greek religion did not profess any strong concern for the unborn, "although Greek inscriptions on temples describe birth, miscarriage, and abortion as occasions of ritual impurity. A woman was to abstain from worship and follow purification rituals after any of these events."[18]

THE ROMAN EMPIRE

The views of Roman society were similar to those found in Jewish law.[19] The fetus became a person at birth. Until birth, the fetus was merely a part of the pregnant woman's body.[20] It did not have a soul until it was born and had begun to breathe. Under Roman law, the fetus had no rights, except the right to inherit.[21]

Abortion was widely practiced throughout the Roman Empire, though infanticide was more common. Roman law and custom did require the father's consent for an abortion. Indeed, abortion was considered a crime only when it was performed against the father's will.[22, 23]

CHRISTIANITY

In the early days of Christianity, it was generally accepted that the fetus was not alive until sometime after conception. From AD 1 to 400, there was considerable debate about the precise time of animation of ensoulment. Early Christian scholars were certainly aware of Aristotle's theories on the subject. At this time, the relatively few Christians were widely scattered geographically, so the actual practice of abortion among Christians probably varied considerably, influenced by regional customs and practices.[24]

Between AD 300 and 600, the abortion debate among Christian scholars extended to whether or not there was a distinction between a formed and an unformed fetus. St. Augustine (AD 354–430) contributed a description of fetal development: the first six days in milky form. 9 more days for it to turn to blood. 12 days more for the mass of blood to solidify, and 18 more days for the mass to become fully formed with all of its members. St. Augustine accepted Aristotle's theory of delayed animation for the female fetus, as well as delayed development or formation.[25]

From AD 600 to 1100, the distinction between the formed and the unformed fetus became widely accepted. A woman was considered to have had an abortion only if a formed fetus were extracted. In practice, abortion among early Christians remained a local issue, and penances imposed for procuring abortions varied among localities.[26]

In the early thirteenth century, St. Thomas Aquinas (1225–1274) expanded upon the ideas of his predecessors. He recognized St. Augustine's description of fetal development and "followed Aristotle in ascribing to male semen the power of creation. . . . In fact, according to Aquinas, since beings tend to produce their own kind, ordinarily the products of conception should be male. Females resulted because of flaws in the semen or some act of God, such as the south wind."[27]

The ideas of Aquinas influenced Pope Innocent IV, who declared in 1257 that abortion before the infusion of the soul was not homicide. However, the Pope did not specify when animation occurred.

In 1588, Pope Sixtus V, legislating for the first time for the "universal church" on the issue of abortion, attached excommunication to the sin of abortion.

In 1591, Pope Gregory XIV withdrew the penalty of excommunication for the sin of abortion. The penalty was believed to be too severe in light of the debate on animation. This declaration in 1591 continued to be the abortion policy of the Catholic Church until 1869, when Pope Pius IX restored the policy of Pope Sixtus V and "eliminated the distinction between the animated and unanimated fetus."[28]

Pope Pius IX's position on animation reflected the thinking of some prominent European physicians who had begun to espouse a theory of immediate, rather than delayed, animation. Indeed, nineteenth century physicians in the United States and Europe had much more influence on abortion policies than theologians or philosophers had ever had.[29]

ABORTION IN THE UNITED STATES

The Nineteenth Century

"In 1800, no jurisdiction in the United States had enacted any statutes whatsoever on the subject of abortion. Most forms of abortion were not illegal, and women who wished to practice abortion did so."[30] Abortions were sought primarily by single women. Abortion itself was not perceived as a great moral issue, only the illicit sexual behavior that led to it.[31]

Abortions were readily available. Many of the home health manuals prescribed methods and techniques. Common law permitted abortion until "quickening," when the woman felt the first movement of the fetus.[32] For some, quickening, a notion developed in the 13th century, also signified that the fetus had a soul.[33]

Given the scientific limitations of the time quickening was also the method used for diagnosing a pregnancy. After all, one could not be absolutely certain that a woman was pregnant until quickening. Under common law, abortion was not punished before quickening and thereafter was not treated as homicide. Regardless of whether the fetus had "quickened," the patient herself was immune from prosecution.[34]

The first wave of anti-abortion legislation in the United States occurred between 1821 and 1841. Ten states and one territory enacted legislation that made some abortions illegal.[35] Women's health was the primary motive for these laws. Connecticut passed the first statute in 1821, prohibiting the administration of poisons to produce post-quickening abortions. In 1828, New York banned post-quickening abortions by all methods.[36] However, "there was no popular support for these laws, except from politicians and physicians."[37] Moreover, these abortion laws "were little noticed and rarely enforced."[38]

In 1846, Massachusetts launched the second wave of anti-abortion legislation by enacting the most restrictive law in the nation. Noteworthy is the fact that physicians supported this legislation, and that the general public did not even testify. This law ignored the notion of quickening and included jail sentences and fines for attempted abortions. New York followed suit in the same year with the passage of an abortion law that disregarded quickening and prescribed punishments for abortionists and abortion patients.[39]

Throughout the nineteenth century, the demographics of U.S. fertility in general and abortion in particular were changing. From 1800 to 1900, the completed fertility rate (the number of children born per woman) dropped from 7.04 to 3.56 for whites, the only group for whom reliable data are available. From 1820 to 1830, an estimated one in every 25 to 30 pregnancies ended in induced abortion. Estimates for 1850–1860 vary from one in four to one in six U.S. pregnancies that ended in abortion. In the forty years between 1840 and 1880, "the majority category of abortion seekers changed from single women to rich, married, white women."[40]

Although widely advertised, induced abortion was very risky in the nineteenth century. For example, it was popular to administer poisons to pregnant women to induce abortion, based on the "dubious theory that a dosage sufficient to kill the fetus might spare the woman." Available statistics from the period also support the fact that mortality from surgical abortion must have been extremely high. "Statistics from New York in the early nineteenth century demonstrate a *30% death rate* from infections after abdominal surgery even when performed in hospitals." During the same period, the mortality rate from childbirth *was under 3%.* [41] Obviously, many women were willing to assume tremendous risks in order to terminate their unwanted pregnancies.

Beginning in 1860, the American Medical Association (AMA) became a major advocate for anti-abortion legislation. The leader in this effort was Dr. Horatio Robinson Storer, who believed that abortion was professionally and personally wrong. His efforts coincided with trends in Europe to disprove the old theory of delayed animation and replace it with the theory of immediate animation.[42]

The Catholic Church was not active in the anti-abortion campaign prior to the Civil War. Even after the war, Catholic support for the AMA's strategy was tentative. Some conservative Protestant clergy eventually got on the bandwagon, but nineteenth century clergy on the whole were reluctant to deal with sexual matters.[43]

Between 1860 and 1880, 40 anti-abortion state laws were passed (30 from 1866 to 1877). The most important common element was that interruption of gestation at any time during pregnancy was considered a crime by the state. For the most part, this legal situation persisted until the 1960s.[44]

The Twentieth Century

By 1900, induced abortion was a criminal offense in virtually every jurisdiction in the United States.[45] The only exception was therapeutic abortion to save the life of the woman.[46] Nevertheless, during the first half of the twentieth century, women continued to have abortions in roughly the same proportions as they had prior to its criminalization. Indeed, at least one researcher estimates that one in three pregnancies was terminated by abortion during this period.[47]

The rationale for therapeutic abortions expanded over time. Poverty was a widely accepted reason for performing therapeutic abortions in the 1930s during the Great Depression. In the 1940s and 1950s, doctors increasingly performed abortions for psychiatric reasons. Most abortions, however, were illegal and not "therapeutic." Consequently, poor and rural women suffered especially high morbidity and mortality. Nevertheless, there were few indictments, and even fewer convictions, during the first half of the twentieth century.[48]

During the 1950s, therapeutic abortions became increasingly subject to hospital review boards. Heretofore, physicians had made the decision "to save the life of the mother," privately. In response to the increasing scrutiny of the practices of individual physicians, the American Law Institute (ALI) revised its Model Penal Code to include three defenses against the charge of criminal abortion. The first was that continuation of the pregnancy would gravely impair the physical or mental health of the mother. The second was that the child was likely to be born with grave physical or mental defects. The third defense was that the pregnancy was the result of rape or incest. This widely copied Model Penal Code also required certification by two physicians describing the circumstances that justified an abortion.[49]

In the 1960s, two events attracted even more public attention to the abortion issue than had the ALI Model Penal Code. In 1962, Sherii Finkbine, an Arizona mother of four, was unable to obtain a legal abortion in the United States even though she had taken thalidomide during her pregnancy. The second focusing event was the rubella outbreak of 1962–1965. Like thalidomide, rubella causes severe birth defects. This epidemic produced some 15,000 infants with birth defects.[50]

Ironically, the medical profession, which had lobbied for criminalizing abortion in the nineteenth century, became a principal advocate for changing those laws. In 1967, the AMA issued a statement favoring the liberalization of these laws. By this time, abortion had become a relatively safe procedure. In 1955, 100 of every 100,000 abortions resulted in the woman's death. By 1972, it was 3 in 100,000.[51] (In 1985, the risk of death was 0.4 per legal 100,000 abortions compared to 6.6 per 100,000 births.[52])

Between 1967 and 1972, most state legislatures considered changes in their abortion laws. Nineteen states passed new and more liberal abortion laws, although most of these were based upon the modest ALI Model Penal Code. In 1970, Hawaii became the first state to repeal its criminal abortion law and to legalize abortion performed before the twentieth week of pregnancy. In the same year, New York enacted the most liberal of the new laws, allowing abortion to be performed up to 24 weeks' gestation. As a result of these changes, women from more restrictive states flocked to less restrictive states to obtain abortions.[53]

No state repealed any criminal abortion law during 1971 and 1972. However, on January 22, 1973, in a 7 to 2 decision, the U.S. Supreme Court struck down all abortion laws in the land, including those in states with recently liberalized laws. In handing down *Roe v Wade,* the Court found that a woman's right to decide whether or not to terminate her pregnancy was a *fundamental right.*[54]

Given the history of abortion, it is not surprising that *Roe v Wade* did not settle the abortion issue. Indeed, history shows that there have always been disagreements about abortion, but nothing like the controversy that followed the Supreme Court's decision in 1973. For the next twenty years, the abortion debate in the United States greatly intensified.

Dr. McFarlane is Associate Professor, School of Public Administration, University of New Mexico, Albuquerque, NM.

REFERENCES

1. Sheeran, P. J.: Women, Society, the State and Abortion: A Structuralist Analysis. Praeger, New York. 1984. p. 49.

2. Devereux, G.: A typological study of abortion in 350 primitive, ancient, and pre-industrial societies. In: Abortion in America. Edited by H. Rosen, 1967 (Cited in Tribe, L. H.: Abortion: The Clash of Absolutes. W. W. Norton & Company, New York, 1990. p. 52.)

3. Rosenblatt, R.: Life Itself: Abortion in the American Mind. Random House, New York. 1992. pp. 50–51.

4. Rosenblatt, R.: Life Itself: Abortion in the American Mind. Random House, New York. 1992. pp. 60–61.

5. Jakobovits, I.: Jewish views on abortion. In: Abortion and the Law. Edited by DT Smith. The press of Western Reserve University, Cleveland. p. 129.

6. Rosenblatt, R.: Life Itself: Abortion in the American Mind. Random House, New York. 1992. pp. 50–51.

7. Sheeran, P. J.: Women, Society, the State, and Abortion: A Structuralist Analysis. Praeger, New York. 1987. pp. 50. 78–79.

8. Sheeran, P. J.: Women, Society, the State, and Abortion: A Structuralist Analysis. Praeger, New York. 1987. p. 5.

9. Rosner, F.: Medical and Jewish Law. Yeshiva University Press. 1972. pp 66–67. (Cited in Sheeran, P. J.: Women, Society, the State, and Abortion. A Structuralist Analysis. Praeger, New York. 1987. p. 79.)

10. Jakobovits, I.: Jewish views on abortion. In: Abortion and The Law. Edited by DT Smith. The Press of Western Reserve University, Cleveland. p. 130.

11. Rosenblatt, R.: Life Itself: Abortion in the American Mind. Random House, New York. 1992. p. 63.

12. Rosenblatt, R.: Life Itself: Abortion in the American Mind. Random House, New York. 1992. p. 58.

13. Sheeran, P. J.: Women, Society, the State, and Abortion. A Structuralist Analysis. Praeger, New York. 1987. p. 50.

14. Tribe, L. H.: Abortion: The Clash on Absolutes. W. W. Norton & Company, New York. 1990. p. 55.

15. Sheeran, P. J.: Women, Society, the State, and Abortion: A Structuralist Analysis. Praeger, New York. 1987. p. 50.

16. Sheeran, P. J.: Women, Society, the State, and Abortion: A Structuralist Analysis. Praeger, New York. 1987. pp. 79–80.

17. Himes, N. E.: Medical History of Contraception. Schocken Books, New York. 1936, 1970. p. 89.

18. Rosenblatt, R.: Life Itself: Abortion in the American Mind. Random House, New York. 1992. p. 60.

19. Sheeran, P. J.: Women, Society, the State and Abortion. A Structuralist Analysis. Praeger, New York. 1987 p. 50.

20. Rosenblatt, R.: Life Itself: Abortion in the American Mind. Random House, New York. 1992. p. 63.

21. Sheeran, P. J.: Women, Society, the State, and Abortion: A Structuralist Analysis. Praeger, New York. 1987. p. 50.

22. Rosenblatt, R.: Life Itself: Abortion in the American Mind. Random House, New York. 1992. pp. 63–64.

23. Tribe, L. H.: Abortion: The Clash of Absolutes. W. W. Norton & Company, New York. 1990. p. 55.

24. Sheeran, P. J.: Women, Society, the State, and Abortion: A Structuralist Analysis. Praeger, New York. 1987. p. 51, 79.

25. Sheeran, P. J.: Women, Society, the State, and Abortion: A Structuralist Analysis. Praeger, New York. 1987. p. 52. 80–81.

26. Sheeran, P. J.: Women, Society, the State, and Abortion: A Structuralist Analysis. Praeger, New York. 1987. p. 52.

27. Sheeran, P. J.: Women, Society, the State, and Abortion: A Structuralist Analysis. Praeger, New York. 1987. p. 81.

28. Sheeran, P. J.: Women, Society, the State, and Abortion: A Structuralist Analysis. Praeger, New York. 1987. p. 53, 81.

29. Sheeran, P. J.: Women, Society, the State, and Abortion: A Structuralist Analysis. Praeger, New York. 1987. p. 53.

30. Mohr, J. C.: Abortion in America: The Origins of and Evolution of National Policy. 1800–1900. Oxford University Press. New York. 1978. p vii. (Cited in Sheeran P. J.: Women, Society, the State, and Abortion: A Structuralist Analysis. Praeger, New York. 1987. p. 53.)

31. Tribe, L. H.: Abortion: The Clash of Absolutes. W. W. Norton & Company, New York. 1990. p. 29.

32. Sheeran, P. J.: Women, Society, the State, and Abortion: A Structuralist Analysis. Praeger, New York. 1987. p. 54.

33. Tribe, L. H.: Abortion: The Clash of Absolutes. W. W. Norton & Company, New York. 1990. p. 28.

34. Tribe, L. H.: Abortion: The Clash of Absolutes. W. W. Norton & Company, New York. 1990. p. 28.

35. Sheeran, P. J.: Women, Society, the State, and Abortion: A Structuralist Analysis. Praeger, New York. 1987. p. 54.

36. Tribe, L. H.: Abortion: The Clash of Absolutes. W. W. Norton & Company, New York. 1990. p. 29.

37. Sheeran, P. J.: Women, Society, the State, and Abortion: A Structuralist Analysis. Praeger, New York. 1987. p. 55.

38. Rosenblatt, R.: Life Itself: Abortion in the American Mind. Random House, New York. 1992. p. 86.

39. Sheeran, P. J.: Women, Society, the State, and Abortion: A Structuralist Analysis. Praeger, New York. 1987. p. 54–55.

40. Sheeran, P. J.: Women, Society, the State, and Abortion: A Structuralist Analysis. Praeger, New York. 1987. p. 55.

41. Tribe, L. H.: Abortion: The Clash of Absolutes. W. W. Norton & Company, New York. 1990. p. 29.

42. Sheeran, P. J.: Women, Society, the State, and Abortion: A Structuralist Analysis. Praeger, New York. 1987. p. 56.

43. Sheeran, P. J.: Women, Society, the State, and Abortion: A Structuralist Analysis. Praeger, New York. 1987. p. 56.

44. Sheeran, P. J.: Women, Society, the State, and Abortion: A Structuralist Analysis. Praeger, New York. 1987. p. 56–57.

45. Mohr, J. C.: Abortion in America: The Origins of and Evolution of National Policy. 1800–1900. Oxford University Press, New York. 1978. p. vii (Cited in Sheeran, P. J.: Women, Society, the State, and Abortion: A Structuralist Analysis. Praeger, New York. 1987. p. 53.)

46. Rosenblatt, R.: Life Itself: Abortion in the American Mind. Random House, New York. 1992. p. 88.

47. Luker, K.: Abortion and the Politics of Motherhood. The University of California Press, Berkeley. p. 32. (Cited in Tribe, L. H.: Abortion: The Clash of Absolutes. W. W. Norton & Company, New York. 1990. p. 32.)

48. Tribe, L. H.: Abortion: The Clash of Absolutes. W. W. Norton & Company, New York. 1990. p. 35.

49. Tribe, L. H.: Abortion: The Clash of Absolutes. W. W. Norton & Company, New York. 1990. p. 35–36.

50. Tribe, L. H.: Abortion: The Clash of Absolutes. W. W. Norton & Company, New York. 1990. p. 37.

51. Tribe, L. H.: Abortion: The Clash of Absolutes. W. W. Norton & Company, New York. 1990. p. 36, 38.

52. Gold, R. B.: Abortion and Women's Health: A Turning Point for America! The Alan Guttmacher Institute, New York. 1990. p. 28.

53. Sheeran, P. J.: Women, Society, the State, and Abortion: A Structuralist Analysis. Praeger, New York. 1987. p. 57.

54. Tribe, L. H.: Abortion: The Clash of Absolutes. W. W. Norton & Company, New York. 1990. pp. 10–13, 48–51.

ABORTION PRACTICES AND ATTITUDES IN CROSS-CULTURAL PERSPECTIVE

Rochelle N. Shain, Ph.D.

Fertility control is as old as mankind, and has been utilized throughout recorded history and in societies representing all levels of socioeconomic development, from hunting and gathering groups to agricultural peasant societies to, of course, modern technologic cultures. Abortion has been one of the most prevalent methods of effective fertility regulation.[1] Devereux,[2] in his study of abortion, found that "there is every indication that abortion is an absolutely universal phenomenon."

ABORTION CROSS-CULTURALLY

Throughout history, women have either performed their own abortions or have sought help from others. Techniques are extremely varied, including strenuous physical effort; jolts to the body; heat applied externally; skin irritants; bleeding; starvation; and the use of abortifacients, magic, and mechanical methods such as construction, instrumentation, and insertion of foreign bodies into the uterus.[1, 2]

Preindustrial societies. The following examples attest to how strongly women have desired to control their fertility, in the absence of effective contraception. In Alor, Melanesia, and Papua, women jump from high objects such as rocks and trees. Among the Kroe of Sumatra, hot ashes are placed on the woman's abdomen. Pima women of North America strain themselves, whereas Kgatla of Africa and Bukaua women of Dutch New Guinea bleed themselves, either by incision or by the use of leeches.[1, 2]

Abortifacients range from the seemingly innocuous to the toxic. Substances such as writing ink, potassium permanganate, purgatives, turpentine, castor oil, quinine, horseradish, ginger, Epsom salts, ammonia, mustard, and opium have been reported. The more toxic are indirectly effective—that is, they either poison or irritate the woman's body, with expulsion of the fetus as a side effect. The more innocuous are often accompanied by magic ritual. For example, some Algerian Arab women, while simultaneously reciting a magic formula, drink water from a cup in which sacred words were written and their ink dissolved.[1, 2]

Various herbal abortifacients are a part of folk culture and are transmitted from generation to generation. For example, marjoram, thyme, parsley, and lavender, used in tea form, are part of old German folk medicine, both as abortifacients and as contraceptives. Some of these appear to be mild emmenagogues that stimulate menustration.[1]

Some of the more "exotic" folk abortifacients used in preindustrial societies have also been found to be potentially effective. For example, German peasant women and Baholoholo women from Africa who drink the water from the smithy's fire buckets are consuming iron sulfate, an emmenagogue.[1]

The range of societal attitudes toward abortion is almost as varied as the techniques employed. Although abortion is extensively and rather openly practiced in many primitive societies, few groups give it unqualified approval. Cross-culturally, the most prevalent condition for approving abortion occurs when the father is not married to the mother. Other circumstances in which abortion is permitted include lactation of the mother, death of the father, consent of the father, rape, and many varieties

"Abortion Practices and Attitudes in Cross-Cultural Perspective," by Rochelle N. Shain, Ph.D., reprinted from *American Journal of Obstetrics and Gynecology*, Vol. 142, No. 3, 1982. Reprinted by permission of Mosby-Year Book, Inc.

of illegal union.[2] Since unwanted children are conceived under many other circumstances, clandestine abortion is resorted to. Consequently, anthropologists often learn about abortion when women describe "what happens to others" as opposed to themselves.

Changes in abortion attitudes through time. Attitudes in western civilization are also variable and have in most cases been changing.

The Old Testament briefly refers to accidental miscarriage, but does not touch on induced abortion. The Talmud, however, which historically follows the Old Testament, mentions that the fetus can be sacrificed to save the life of the mother. Most of the Greek philosophers, especially Plato and Aristotle, approved and even encouraged abortion primarily for eugenic reasons. Both believed that a woman should abort her pregnancy if she conceived after her fortieth year.[3]

The early Christian era was a difficult and demanding time. Survival, after persistent martyrdom, was at stake; consequently, the early Christians believed that anything that interrupted human life, whether it was a contraceptive agent or an abortion, was equivalent to murder.[3] Although the New Testament itself does not specifically refer to abortion, many of the early sources of Christian law treated it as a grievous sin.[4]

Between the fifth and twelfth centuries, a number of church councils unequivocally condemned abortion. Nonetheless, the distinction between the "formed" (ensouled) and "uninformed" fetus, Aristotelian in origin and advocated by the Eastern Church, gradually became established in Catholic doctrine. By 1140, when the first fully systematic compilation of ecclesiastic legislation was published, the distinction was operative. In 1234, Pope Gregory IX sustained this distinction. The existence of canonical texts legitimatizing the distinction between the formed and unformed fetus provided the basis for theoretical debate between the fifteenth and the eighteenth centuries as to when human life began and whether abortion was justified to save the mother's life. During this latter period, theologians attempted to strike a balance between the life of the early conceptus and that of the mother. It was argued, particularly by Jesuit Leonard Lessius and Saint Alphonsus, that abortion was justified to save the woman's life when the fetus was not fully formed.[4] However, in 1869, Pope Pius IX effected sharp changes in church law: the distinction between a formed and an unformed fetus was eliminated and abortion was prohibited even to save the mother's life. [4-6.]

Whereas other religions have changed their views according to the needs of the time, Catholicism has not. Moreover, Catholic views have strongly influenced laws within European Catholic countries. For example, in France, a 1939 law stipulated the guillotine as a punishment for abortion, and in 1942, a female abortionist was put to death in this way. One of the highest incidences of illegal abortion and accompanying morbidity and mortality is found in such Catholic countries as Portugal, where the laws do not allow abortion even to save the mother's life.[3]

Until the second quarter of the twentieth century, all Protestant denominations opposed contraception and abortion. In 1930, contraception was conditionally approved, and in 1958, it was more widely approved. Abortion was also considered and approved on conditions of undeniable medical necessity, covering health as well as life.[3]

Moslem attitudes have also changed somewhat according to people's needs. In 1355, The Grand Mufti issued a dictum allowing contraception. Abortion was considered only for reasons such as interruption of a lactating mother's milk which would endanger the existing child. However, after quickening took place, abortion was prohibited under all circumstances. In 1964, the Grand Mufti of Jordan allowed abortion, provided that the embryo had not achieved human shape, interpreted as 120 days. However, whereas abortion is legal in Tunisia, and Jordan and Syria allow for broadly defined reasons of health, the remainder of the Moslem countries permit termination of pregnancy only to save the life of the mother, or not at all.[3, 7]

Status of abortion in the "modern" world. In the last 15 years, abortion laws have been liberalized in many countries, primarily to combat high rates of illegal abortion with its associated complications, and in recognition of the woman's right to control her reproductive destiny. At present, approximately two thirds of the world's population live in countries which allow abortion on request of the pregnant woman, either without a specific reason or on the basis of broadly interpreted economic, social, and personal reasons.[7]

The Soviet Union was the first nation to legalize abortion. In 1920, the right of Russian women to terminate an unwanted pregnancy on the grounds of health and for other reasons was recognized in keeping with the 1917 revolution and its cry for complete feminine equality and freedom. Abortion was unrestricted until 1936, when it was permitted only for medical and eugenic reasons. In 1955, this law was repealed, and abortion was again made available virtually on demand.[3] This liberal attitude also prevails in most of the Society bloc countries. Although Rumania and Hungary have restricted termination of pregnancy in order to combat very low birth rates, their laws still allow abortion for broad reasons of health and on demand to certain categories of women, for example, those over 40 years.[7]

Following the Soviet Union, the Scandinavian countries began liberalizing their abortion laws in the 1930s. Iceland began in 1935, followed by Sweden in 1938, Denmark in 1939, and, finally, Finland and Norway in 1950 and 1960. Liberalized abortion legislation was passed in the British parliament in 1968. Until 1975, the remainder of the countries in Western Europe had restrictive laws. At that time, Austria passed a law allowing elective abortion during the first trimester, and France authorized abortion on request during the first 10 weeks of pregnancy, subject to a number of provisions. West Germany followed in 1976, Italy in 1978, and the Netherlands in 1981. Switzerland has a restrictive law, permitting abortion only on medical grounds; however, in some cantons the law is more liberally interpreted than in others. In Spain, the Republic of Ireland, Malta, and Portugal, abortion is prohibited under all circumstances.[3, 7, 8]

Abortion laws in Latin America are generally restrictive: three of the 22 Latin American countries forbid it under all circumstances, and another 12 permit it only to avert the threat to the pregnant woman's life.[7] With respect to other countries, a rather liberal abortion law was adopted by India in 1971. In Africa south of the Sahara, restrictive policies introduced during colonial rule still exist in the newly independent countries, except Zambia; in 1972, the latter passed a law similar to the British Abortion Act. South Africa allows broad indications for termination of pregnancy. Since 1948, abortion has been available virtually on demand in Japan and is a major method of fertility control in that country.[7]

Although the existence of restrictions against abortion is common knowledge, societal control takes many forms, and the full range of societal reaction to abortion includes its active promotion, as illustrated by current conditions in the People's Republic of China.[9] Since passage in 1957 of an unrestricted abortion law, abortion has become very popular and is becoming even more important because of the Chinese government's present insistence on the one-child family. In addition to significant economic and social sanctions placed upon families to have only one child, family planning is no longer a personal matter, but is supervised by the state. The regulation of fertility is presently controlled by the State Council's Planned Reproduction Group. Tens of thousands of branches at the provincial and local levels report to this national department. In turn, they receive their information from paid or unpaid volunteers on production teams in the rural communes and work teams in factories, shops, and offices. Specifically, individual menstrual charts are maintained, which facilitate the detection of missed periods and the avoidance of "childbearing that does not conform to the national plan."[9] Additionally, there are planned reproduction cards for each married woman that contain such information as the number of previous births by sex, date of last birth, current contraceptive methods, etc. These data form the basis of reports to higher units. Thus, women whose reproductive behavior or goals fall outside national plans can be quickly detected and supervised. Although China places emphasis on contraception and sterilization, induced abortion appears to have played a key role in reducing fertility.[9]

Incidence of abortion. To date, it is still impossible to estimate correctly the number of abortions, legal and illegal, performed each year throughout the world. The most recent estimates have ranged to 55 million, which corresponds to abortion rates of 70 per 1,000 women of reproductive age and to an abortion ratio of 300 per 1,000 known pregnancies (live births plus abortions). These data are highly speculative.[7] However, if they are at all representative of what is happening in the world, and if, as suspected, many of these abortions are illegal, this would mean that, every day, approximately 100,000 women seek abortion in un-hygenic surroundings and face possible complications and even death in preference to carrying their pregnancies to term.[3]

Illegal abortion has reached almost epidemic proportions in Latin America. In 1974, close to 5 million illegal abortions were performed, which corresponds to an abortion rate of at least 65 per 1,000 among women of reproductive age and abortion ratio of 300 per 1,000 known pregnancies. Rates of hospitalization for resulting morbidity have been approximately 40 per 1,000 women of reproductive age in Mexico City and Santiago, Chile.[7] Abortion rates in China have also increased. In 1979, 58% of *all* pregnancies in Chengdu (one municipality for which we have data) were terminated by abortion. This incidence of legal abortion is second only to that in the Soviet Union.[9]

Thus, it seems obvious that throughout the "modern world" abortion is employed as a major method of controlling fertility. In some cases, legal apparatus coincides with women's needs; in others, it does not, thus forcing women to seek abortion under less than appropriate conditions. In still others, what is one person's freedom becomes another's burden, as in China, where abortion is apparently used to eradicate individual freedom.

THE UNITED STATES

History of the status of abortion. Before the American Medical Association was founded in 1847, abortion *before quickening* was commonly practiced in the United States. Moral concerns were not commonly expressed, nor was there a single piece of legislation restricting abortion at this gestational stage. As the century progressed, vendors of abortifacients and abortion practitioners became increasingly bold. Newspapers and even religious journals were utilized to advertise these products and services. However, with its intent to professionalize medical training and to improve physicians' status, the American Medical Association launched an antiabortion drive. Stress was placed on fighting the morbidity associated with carelessly performed terminations of pregnancy and the advertisements of lay practitioners. The American Medical Association was joined in these efforts by upper-class, white Anglo-Saxon Protestants, by antiobscenity crusaders, and by feminists who associated abortion with suppression of women. The religious sectors did not support this campaign until the 1860s. By 1865, the religious press was speaking against abortion, and, as noted earlier, in 1869, Pope Pius IX prohibited it under all circumstances. Protestant clergy joined forces with the Catholics and with organized medicine by the mid-1870s, and by 1900 abortion was illegal throughout the United States.[6, 10] "With the medical establishment condemning the practice of abortion and disdaining contraception, terminations of unwanted pregnancy were driven underground for nearly another century until human rights activists, some leading physicians, lawyers, feminists and organized family planning groups, led the struggle that eventually resulted in the January, 1973 Supreme Court abortion decisions."[10]

It is estimated that before the present liberal abortion laws the incidence of induced abortion ranged from 700,000 to 2 million a year, and that one out of every five pregnancies in the United States terminated in an illegal abortion.[3] Polgar and Fried[11] state that, in New York City alone, 500,000 clandestine abortions were obtained annually in the preliberalization years. The Allan Guttmacher Institute estimates that 30% of pregnant women in 1979 chose to terminate their pregnancies, with 1.4 million abortions resulting. Approximately one third of these were obtained by teenagers. Nonetheless, an estimated 641,000 women who wanted an abortion were unable to obtain one because of inaccessibility or unavailability of the service.[12]

Current attitudes toward abortion. Now that liberalized laws have been institutionalized in the United States for 8 years, how do people feel about abortion? Specifically, what is the attitude of the United States consumer?

The National Fertility Study. Recent data on attitudes toward abortion are provided by the National Fertility Study[13] and by Planned Parenthood.[14] The National Fertility Studies are a series of probability sample surveys of married women of reproductive age taken at 5-year intervals, starting in 1965. The first study contained six items on abortion, and a seventh was added in 1970 and repeated in 1975. The wording and order of the questions remained the same, and the majority of respondents interviewed in 1970 were reinterviewed in 1975; this technique allowed researchers to determine response change over time, both for specific individuals and the public at large.

Subjects were asked to approve or disapprove abortion according to a list of reasons that might impel a woman to terminate her pregnancy. "Hard" reasons involved physical welfare, specifically, health of the mother, rape, and deformity; "soft" reasons involved social welfare, such as marital and economic status, just not wanting additional children. Resultant data indicate a continued trend toward liberalization of attitudes. This trend is particularly obvious for the soft reasons. Since 87% of the women in 1965 already approved of abortion for health reasons, there was not much room for additional liberalization; in 1975, 93% approved. The most liberal positions showed the greatest gains: 15.5% of the sample approved of abortion for any reason in 1970, compared to 30.4% in 1975; 6.9% of the sample approved of abortion on the grounds of wanting no more children in 1965, compared to 20.4% in 1970, and 36% in 1975. Approval of abortion for rape and for deformity increased from 50% of the sample in 1965 to approximately 75% in 1975.

In order to more closely examine attitudinal change through time, Jones and Westoff[13] totaled the number of favorable responses to the six reasons included in the three surveys and obtained an index score ranging from zero to six. A score of zero meant that the subject rejected all six reasons as grounds for abortion, and a score of six meant that she accepted them all. Resultant data indicated that, in 1965, women, on the average, approved of 2.2 reasons for abortion; this number increased to 3.7 by 1975.

Attitudes toward abortion were found to be closely associated with religious affiliation. Although people of all religious preferences have liberalized their attitudes, Jewish women, along with those who report no religion, are the most accepting, and Catholics and Mormons, the least. Liberal attitudes are positively correlated with level of educational attainment, low parity, and modern conceptualization of the female role. For example, people who completed college scored 4.4, compared to 2.5 those who completed only elementary school. Interestingly, the degree of association has increased in time; that is, in 1965, the differences between educational groups were not so significant as they are today. Moreover, the greatest gains since 1965 have occurred in the higher educational categories.

Not every respondent became more liberal. Change occurred in both directions. However, clearly, more women accepted a more liberal position than those shifting to a more conservative one: 37% of the sample became more liberal, whereas 19% became more conservative. Moreover, those women who became more conservative did not shift to total rejection of abortion; their disapproval focused on the soft reasons for abortion.

Planned parenthood poll. The second survey discussed in this article was conducted in August, 1979,[14] and involved a national probability sample of 1,500 adults age 18 years and over, male and female, who were interviewed over the telephone. They were asked to describe their feelings toward termination of pregnancy, with use of the following options: favor strongly, favor somewhat, oppose somewhat, or oppose strongly.

Resultant data indicate that attitudes toward abortion are closely associated with education, age, religious preference, and regularity of church attendance. The more highly educated, those between ages 18 and 39, non-Catholics, and those who attend church only occasionally tend to be more supportive of abortion than are their counterparts. Interestingly, differences between Catholics and Protestants are not so great as those between frequent churchgoers of either faith and those who attend only occasionally.

The greater influence of degree of religiosity, as opposed to religious preference per se, is corroborated by a poll conducted by NBC News in conjunction with the Associated Press. In October, 1975, researchers found, on the one hand, that 46% of non-Catholics compared to 50% of Catholics either disapproved of the *wide availability* (italics mine) of abortion or were unsure of their attitudes. On the other hand, the corresponding percentage among the more religious members of all faiths (defined as those who agreed that, in order "to be good Christians or Jews, people should attend church religious services") was 60%, compared to 35% among less religious persons.[13]

Examining reasons for approval and opposition, the Planned Parenthood poll determined that people who oppose abortion generally cite moral objections to killing, whereas those who favor it generally cite another moral value, freedom of choice.[14]

It was further shown that individuals who either favor abortion or have mixed feelings are more likely to support sex education in the schools. Whereas people who have mixed feelings about abortion are not against issues of human sexuality per se, or against sex education, 40% of those who strongly oppose abortion also oppose sex education in schools. The authors believe that this group may be opposed to dealing realistically with problems of human sexuality in general. Sociodemographic analysis indicates that they tend to be older women living in rural or small town areas, who attend church regularly and are slightly less educated than the rest of the sample.

People who oppose abortion are also more fearful that sex education will lead to increased teenage sexual activity and are less likely to believe that sex education should include facts of reproduction, anatomy, and contraception, and principles of ethics and responsible sexual behavior. They are also more likely to oppose ever giving girls the legal right to buy contraceptives or to obtain birth control pills without parental permission

How well do individuals who favor and those who oppose abortion communicate and mobilize support for their feelings? These data indicate that people who oppose and have mixed feelings toward abortion are slightly and more likely to own their own homes. The researchers think that this implies higher levels of voter registration, stronger stability and commitment to statewide issues, and greater familiarity with the names of legislative representatives. Although these differences are not great, the authors note that small differences in the past have resulted in electoral wins for antiabortion forces.

Finally, data on membership in or contribution to organizations in the past 2 years indicate that, although only 9% of those who strongly oppose abortion have belonged or contributed to any special interest group, one third of this involvement related to antiabortion concerns. On the other hand, whereas 24% of the people who strongly favor abortion have belonged or contributed to a special-interest organization, only one twelfth of this activity involved proabortion concerns. Moreover, approximately one third of those who strongly oppose abortion have either written position letters or signed appropriate petitions, compared to only one fifth of those who feel strong support. The researchers initially posed the question of why, despite majority support for legal abortion, antiabortion forces have continued to win major political concessions throughout the country. They conclude, on the basis of the above data, that the proabortion respondents have done less well than those in the antiabortion group in mobilizing their favorable attitudes into either money or tangible support.[14]

Future prospects. As of this writing, antiabortion forces have concluded that they lack the votes necessary to pass a constitutional amendment prohibiting abortion; consequently, they have launched efforts to achieve the same end through the less burdensome procedure of passing a law. To pass legislation, only a simple majority vote in each House of Congress is needed, as opposed to the two-thirds majority required to propose an amendment to the states for ratification. Since the "Human Life Bill" (Helms, Hyde, and Mazzolie) proposes that human life exists from conception, its passage would severely limit the 1973 Supreme Court decision that voided some state laws against abortion. The justices, refusing to deal with the question of when life begins, acted on the belief that the law does not treat the unborn as persons; thus, their primary concern was the woman's privacy. Since the new bill decrees that a fetus is a person from conception, abortion would then legally constitute the taking of human life and, thus, effectively nullify the 1973 Supreme Court decision.[16] With the strong conservative bias expressed in the last presidential election, the antiabortion forces may exert more power than they ever have before. Unless proponents of abortion reverse the trend indicated in the Planned Parenthood poll, and more actively support their attitudes, this country may face another era of illegal abortion. Since some proposed legislation would prohibit termination of a pregnancy, even to save a woman's life, the prohibition of abortion may be even more strictly defined than it was before the 1973 Supreme Court decision.

REFERENCES

1. Shain, R. N., and Lane, R.: Population Growth and Regulation from a Cross-Cultural Perspective, *in* Shain, R. N., and Pauerstein, C. J., editors: Fertility Control: Biologic and Behavioral Aspects, New York, 1980, Harper and Row, p. 235.

2. Devereux, G.: A typological study of abortion in 350 primitive, ancient and preindustrial societies, *in* Rosen, H., editor: Abortion in America, Boston, 1967, Beacon Press, p. 97.

3. Chandrasekhar, S.: Abortion in a Crowded World, Seattle, 1974, University of Washington Press.

4. Callahan, D.: Abortion: Law, Choice and Morality, New York, 1970, Macmillan Publishing Co., Inc.

5. David, H. P.: The abortion decision: National and international perspectives, *in* Burtchaell, J. P., editor: Abortion Parley, Kansas City, 1980, Andrew and McMeel, p. 57.

6. Mohr, J.: Abortion in America: The Origins and Evolution of National Policy, 1800–1900, New York, 1978, Oxford University Pres.

7. Tietze, C.: Induced Abortion: A World Review 1981, ed. 4, New York, 1981, The Population Council.

8. Lincoln, R., editor: Netherlands liberalizes abortion law after ten years of wide availability, low abortion rates, Fam. Plann. Perspect. 13:151, 1981.

9. Tien, H. Y.: Wan, Xi, Shao: How China meets its population problem, Inter. Fam. Plann. Perspect. 6:65, 1980.

10. David, H.: Abortion: A continuing debate, Fam. Plann. Perspect. 10:313, 1978.

11. Polgar, S., and Fried, E.: The bad old days: Clandestine abortions among the poor in New York City before liberalization of the abortion law, Fam. Plann. Perspect. 8:125, 1976.

12. Henshaw, S., Forrest, J. D., Sullivan, E., and Tietze, C.: Abortion in the United States, 1978–1979, Fam. Plann. Perspect. 13:6, 1981.

13. Jones, E. and Westoff, C.: How attitudes toward abortion are changing, J. Popul. 1:5, 1978.

14. R. L. Associates (Princeton, New Jersey): Public Attitudes Toward Birth Control, Sex Education, and Abortion. Commissioned by Planned Parenthood Federation of America, Inc., New York, 1979.

15. Lincoln, R., editor: Catholics agree with Protestants that abortion and contraception should be widely available, Fam. Plann. Perspect. 12:53, 1980.

16. Reid, T. R.: Hill abortion opponents seek new law to nullify '73 Supreme Court decision, The Washington Post, February 7, 1981, p. A2.

From the Department of Obstetrics and Gynecology, The University of Texas Health Science Center at San Antonio.

Reprint requests: Dr. Rochelle N. Shain, Department of Obstetrics and Gynecology, The University of Texas, Health Science Center at San Antonio, 7703 Floyd Curl Drive, San Antonio, Texas 78284.

GENDER

The Hijras of India: Cultural and Individual Dimensions of an Institutionalized Third Gender Role

Serena Nanda

The hijra (eunuch/transvestite) is an institutionalized third gender role in India. Hijra are neither male nor female, but contain elements of both. As devotees of the Mother Goddess Bahuchara Mata, their sacred powers are contingent upon their asexuality. In reality, however, many hijras are prostitutes. This sexual activity undermines their culturally valued sacred role. This paper discusses religious meanings of the hijra role, as well as the ways in which individuals and the community deal with the conflicts engendered by their sexual activity.

The hijra, an institutionalized third gender role in India, is "neither male nor female," containing elements of both. The hijra are commonly believed by the larger society to be intersexed, impotent men, who undergo emasculation in which all or part of the genitals are removed. They adopt female dress and some other aspects of female behavior. Hijras traditionally earn their living by collecting alms and receiving payment for performances at weddings, births and festivals. The central feature of their culture is their devotion to Bahuchara Mata, one of the many Mother Goddesses worshipped all over India, for whom emasculation is carried out. This identification with the Mother Goddess is the source both of the hijras' claim for their special place in Indian society and the traditional belief in their power to curse or confer blessings on male infants.

The census of India does not enumerate hijras separately so their exact numbers are unknown. Estimates quoted in the press range from 50,000 (10) to 500,000 (28). Hijras live predominantly in the cities of North India, where they find the greatest opportunity to perform their traditional roles, but small groups of hijras are found all over India, in the south as well as the north. Seven "houses," or subgroups, comprise the hijra community; each of these has a guru or leader, all of whom live in Bombay. The houses have equal status, but one, Laskarwallah, has the special function of mediating disputes which arise among the others. Each house has its own history, as well as rules particular to it. For example, members of a particular house are not allowed to wear certain colors. Hijra houses appear to be patterned after the *gharanas* (literally, houses), or family lineages among classical musicians, each of which is identified with its own particular musical style. Though the culturally distinct features of the hijra houses have almost vanished, the structural feature remains.[1]

The most significant relationship in the hijra community is that of the guru (master, teacher) and *chela* (disciple). When an individual decides to (formally) join the hijra community, he is taken to

For their assistance is developing the ideas in this paper, grateful acknowledgement is made to Joseph Carrier, David Greenberg, A.M. Shah, Rajni Chopra, Evelyn Blackwood, John Money, the participants of the Columbia University Seminar on the Indian Self, and most especially, Owen Lynch and Alan Roland. I am also grateful to Mrs. Banu Vasudevan, Bharati Gowda, and Shiv Ram Apte, as well as my friends among the hijras, without whom this paper could not have been written.

Serena Nanda, is Professor of Anthropology at John Jay College of Criminal Justice (CUNY).

Bombay to visit one of the seven major gurus, usually the guru of the person who has brought him there. At the initiation ritual, the guru gives the novice a new, female name. The novice vows to obey the guru and the rules of the community. The guru then presents the new chela with some gifts.

The chela, or more likely, someone on her behalf, pays an initiation fee and the guru writes the chela's name in her record book. This guru-chela relationship is a lifelong bond of reciprocity in which the guru is obligated to help the chela and the chela is obligated to be loyal and obedient to the guru.[2] Hijras live together in communes generally of about 5 to 15 members, and the heads of these local groups are also called guru. Hijras make no distinctions within their community based on caste origin or religion, although in some parts of India, Gujerat, for example, Muslim and Hindu hijras reportedly live apart (25). In Bombay, Delhi, Chandigarh and Bangalore, hijras of Muslim, Christian, and Hindu origin live in the same houses.

In addition to the hierarchical guru-chela relationship, there is fictive kinship by which hijras relate to each other. Rituals exist for "taking a daughter" and the "daughters" of one "mother" consider themselves "sisters" and relate on a reciprocal, affectionate basis. Other fictive kinship relations, such as "grandmother" or "mother's sister" (aunt) are the basis of warm and reciprocal regard. Fictive kin exchange small amounts of money, clothing, jewelry and sweets to formalize their relationship. Such relationships connect hijras all over India, and there is a constant movement of individuals who visit their gurus and fictive kin in different cities. Various annual gatherings, both religious and secular, attract thousands of hijras from all over India.[3]···

CULTURAL DIMENSIONS OF THE HIJRA ROLE

Hijras as Neither Man Nor Woman

. . . Individual hijras also speak of themselves as being "separate," being "neither man nor woman," being "born as men, but not men," or being "not perfect men." Hijras are most clearly "not men" in relation to their claimed inability and lack of desire to engage in the sexual act as men with women, a consequence of their claimed biological intersexuality and their subsequent castration. Thus, hijras are unable to reproduce children, especially sons, an essential element in the Hindu concept of the normal, masculine role for males.

But if hijras are "not men," neither are they women, in spite of several aspects of feminine behavior associated with the role. These behaviors include dressing as women, wearing their hair long, plucking (rather than shaving) their facial hair, adopting feminine mannerisms, taking on women's names, and using female kinship terms and a special, feminized vocabulary. Hijras also identify with a female goddess or as wives of certain male deities in ritual contexts. They claim seating reserved for "ladies only" in public conveyances. On one occasion, they demanded to be counted as women in the census.[4]

Although their role requires hijras to dress like women, few make any real attempt to imitate or to "pass" as women. Their female dress and mannerisms are exaggerated to the point of caricature, expressing sexual overtones that would be considered inappropriate for ordinary women in their roles as daughters, wives, and mothers. Hijra performances are burlesques of female behavior. Much of the comedy of their behavior derives from the incongruities between their behavior and that of traditional women. They use coarse and abusive speech and gestures in opposition to the Hindu ideal of demure and restrained femininity. Further, it is not at all uncommon to see hijras in female clothing sporting several days growth of beard, or exposing hairy, muscular arms. The ultimate sanction of hijras to an abusive or unresponsive public is to lift their skirts and expose the mutilated genitals. The implicit threat of this shameless, and thoroughly unfeminine, behavior is enough to make most people give them a few cents so they will go away. Most centrally, as hijras themselves acknowledge, they are not born as women, and cannot reproduce. Their impotence and barrenness, due to a deficient or absent male organ, ultimately precludes their being considered fully male; yet their lack of female reproductive organs or female sexual organs precludes their being considered fully female . . .

Hijra Impotence and Creative Asceticism

. . . The link between the Hindu theme of creative asceticism and the role and power of the hijras is explicitly articulated in the myths connecting them to their major point of religious identification—their worship of Bahuchara Mata, and her requirement that they undergo emasculation. Bahuchara was a pretty, young maiden in a party of travelers passing through the forest in Gujerat. The party was attacked by thieves, and, fearing they would outrage her modesty, Bahuchara drew her dagger and cut off her breast, offering it to the outlaws in place of her body. This act, and her ensuing death, led to Bahuchara's deification and the practice of self-mutilation and sexual abstinence by her devotees to secure her favor.

Bahuchara has a special connection to the hijras because they are impotent men who undergo emasculation. This connection derives special significance from the story of King Baria of Gujerat. Baria was a devout follower of Bahucharaji, but was unhappy because he had no son. Through the goddess' favor a son, Jetho, was born to him. The son, however, was impotent. The King, out of respect to the goddess, set him apart for her service. Bahucharaji appeared to Jetho in a dream and told him to cut off his genitalia and dress himself as a woman, which he did. This practice has been followed by all who join the hijra cult (15).

Emasculation is the *dharm* (caste duty) of the hijras, and the chief source of their uniqueness. The hijras carry it out in a ritual context, in which the client sits in front of a picture of the goddess Bahuchara and repeats her name while the operation is being performed. A person who survives the operation becomes one of Bahuchara Mata's favorites, serving as a vehicle of her power through their symbolic rebirth. While the most popular image of Bahuchara is that of the goddess riding on a cock, (26) her original form of worship was the *yantra,* a conventional symbol for the vulva. A relation between this representation of the goddess and emasculation may exist: emasculation certainly brings the hijra devotee into a closer identification with the female object of devotion.

Identification of the hijras with Bahuchara specifically and through her, with the creative powers of the Mother Goddess worshipped in many different forms in India, is clearly related to their major cultural function, that of performing at homes where a male child has been born. During these performances the hijras, using sexual innuendos, inspect the genitals of the infant whom they hold in their arms as they dance. The hijras confer fertility, prosperity, and health on the infant and family.

At both weddings and births, hijras hold the power to bless and to curse, and families regard them ambivalently. They have both auspicious functions and inauspicious potential. In regard to the latter, charms are used during pregnancy against eunuchs, both to protect against stillbirth, and a transformation of the embryo from male to female. Hiltebeitel (9) suggests that the presence of eunuchs at birth and weddings:

> marks the ambiguity of those moments when the nondifferentiation of male and female is most filled
> with uncertainty and promise—in the mystery that surrounds the sexual identity of the still unborn
> child and on that [occasion] which anticipates the re-union of male and female in marital sex.
> (p. 168)

Thus, it is fitting that the eunuch-transvestites, themselves characterized by sexual ambiguity, have ritual functions at moments that involve sexual ambiguity. . . .

The evidence suggests that intersexuality, impotence, emasculation and transvestism are all variously believed to be part of the hijra role, accounting for their inability to reproduce and the lack of desire (or the renunciation of the desire) to do so. In any event, sexual abstinence, which Hindu mythology associates with the powers of the ascetic, is in fact, the very source of the hijras' powers. The hijras themselves recognize this connection: They frequently refer to themselves as *sannyasin,* the person who renounces his role in society for the life of a holy wanderer and begger. This vocation requires renunciation of material possessions, the duties of caste, the life of the householder and family man, and, most particularly, the renunciation of sexual desire *(kama)*. In claiming this vocation, hijras point out how they have abandoned their families, live in material poverty, live off the charity of others, and "do not have sexual desires as other men do."

Hijras understand that their "other-worldliness" brings them respect in society, and that if they do not live up to these ideals, they will damage that respect. But just as Hindu mythology contains many stories of ascetics who renounce desire but nevertheless are moved by desire to engage in sexual acts, so, too, the hijra community experiences tension between their religious, ascetic ideal and the reality of the individual human's desire and sensuality.

INDIVIDUAL DIMENSIONS OF THE HIJRA ROLE

Hijras as Homosexuals

... A widespread belief in India is that hijras are intersexed persons claimed or kidnapped by the hijra community as infants. No investigator has found evidence to support this belief. Given the large and complex society of India, the hijra community attracts different kinds of persons, most of whom join voluntarily as teenagers or adults. It appears to be a magnet for persons with a wide range of cross-gender characteristics arising from either a psychological or organic condition (16). The hijra role accommodates different personalities, sexual needs, and gender identities without completely losing its cultural meaning.

While the core of the positive meaning attached to the hijra role is linked to the negation of sexual desire, the reality is that many hijras do, in fact, engage in sexual activities. Because sexual behavior is contrary to the definition of the role such activity causes conflict for both the individuals and the community. Individual hijras deal with the conflict in different ways, while the community as a whole resorts to various mechanisms of social control. ...

My own data (17), gathered through fieldwork in Bangalore and Bombay, and in several North Indian cities, confirm beyond doubt that, however deviant it may be regarded within the hijra community, hijras in contemporary India extensively engage in sexual relations with men. This phenomenon is not entirely modern: 19th-century accounts (2, 7) claim that hijras were known to kidnap small boys for the purposes of sodomy or prostitution. Such allegations still find their way into the contemporary popular press (10).

Although hijras attribute their increased prostitution to declining opportunities to earn a living in their traditional manner, eunuch-transvestites in Hindu classical literature also had the reputation of engaging in homosexual activity. The classic Hindu manual of love, the *Kamasutra,* specifically outlines sexual practices that were considered appropriate for eunuch transvestites to perform with male partners.[6] Classical Hinduism taught that there was a "third sex," divided into various categories, two of which were castrated men, eunuchs, and hermaphrodites, who wore false breasts, and imitated the voice, gestures, dress and temperaments of women. These types shared the major function of providing alternative techniques of sexual gratification (4). In contemporary India, concepts of eunuch, transvestite and male homosexual are not distinct, and the hijras are considered all of these at once (20).

The term hijra, however, which is of Urdu origin and the masculine gender, has the primary meaning of hermaphrodite. It is usually translated as eunuch, never as homosexual. Even Carstairs' informants, among whom the homosexuality of the hijras was well known, defined them as either drum players at the birth of male children, or eunuchs, whose duty was to undergo castration. In parts of North India, the term for effeminate males who play the passive role in homosexual relations is *zenanas* (women); by becoming a hijra, one removes oneself from this category (see also 13).

Furthermore, a covert homosexual subculture exists in some of the larger cities in North India (1), but persons who participate in it are not called hijras. In fact, as in other cultures (5, 30) men who play the insertor role in sexual activities between men have no linguistically or sociologically distinguished role. Unlike western cultures, in India sexual object choice alone does not define gender. In some South Indian regional languages, the names by which hijras are called, such as kojja in Telegu (5) or potee in Tamil, are, unlike the term hijra, epithets used derogatorily to mean a cowardly or feminine male or homosexual. This linguistic difference, however, is consistent with the fact that in South India the hijras do not have the cultural role which they do in North India.

According to my research, homosexual activity is widespread among hijras, and teenage homosexual activity figures significantly in the lives of many individuals who join the community. As Sinha's interviews also indicate (27), those hijras who engage in homosexual activity share particular life patterns before joining the community. Typically such individuals liked during childhood to dress in feminine clothes, play with girls, do traditionally female work, and avoid the company of boys in rough play. In lower class families, the boy's effeminancy is both ridiculed and encouraged by his peers, who may persuade him to play the insertee role for them, possibly with some slight monetary consideration. At this stage the boy lives with his family, though in an increasingly tense atmosphere. He thinks of himself as a male and wears male clothing, at least in public. As his interest in homosexual activity increases, and his relations with his family become more strained, he may leave home. In most cases their families make serious attempts to inhibit their feminine activity with scoldings, surveillance, restrictions, and beatings, so that the boy finally has no choice but to leave.[7]

There are two modes of sexual relations among hijras. One is casual prostitution, the exchange of sexual favors with different men for a fixed sum of money, and the other is "having a husband." Hijras do not characterize their male sexual partners as homosexuals; they quite explicitly distinguish them as being different than homosexuals. One hijra, Shakuntala, characterizes the customers in the following way:

> these men . . . are married or unmarried, they may be the father of many children. Those who come to us, they have no desire to go to a man . . . they come to us for the sake of going to a girl. They prefer us to their wives . . . each one's tastes differ among people. . . . It is God's way; because we have to make a living, he made people like this so we can earn. (Field notes, 1981–2)

. . . Having a husband is the preferred alternative for those hijras who engage in sexual relations. Many of my informants have, or recently had, a relatively permanent attachment to one man whom they referred to as their husband. They maintain warm and affectionate, as well as sexually satisfying and economically reciprocal, relationships with these men, with whom they live, sometimes alone, or sometimes with several other hijras. Lalitha, a very feminine looking hijra in her middle thirties, has had the same husband for nine years. He used to come for prostitution to the hijra commune in which Lalitha lived and then they lived together in a small house until he got married. Now Lalitha has moved back with the hijras, where she cooks their meals in return for free food and lodging, but she still maintains her relationship with her "husband":

> My husband is a Christian. He works in a cigarette factory and earns 1000 rupees a month. He is married to [another] woman and has got four children. I encouraged him to get married and even his wife and children are nice to me. His children call me chitti [mother's sister] and even his wife's parents know about me and don't say anything. He gives me saris and flowers and whenever I ask for money he never says no. When he needs money, I would give him also. (Field notes, 1981–2).

Hijras who have husbands do not break their ties with the hijra community, although sometimes their husbands urge them to do so. Sushila, an attractive, assertive, and ambitious hijra in her early thirties has a husband who is a driver for a national corporation headquarters and earns 600 rupees a month. She continues to be very active in the local hijra community, however, and even refuses to give up practicing prostitution in spite of her husband's objections:

> My husband tells me, "I earn enough money. Why do you go for prostitution?" I tell him, "You are here with me today. What surety is there you will be with me forever? I came to you from prostitution, and if you leave me, I'll have to go back to it. Then all those other hijras will say, 'Oh, she lived as a wife and now look at her fate, she has come back to prostitution.' "So I tell him, "don't put any restrictions on me; now they all think of me as someone nice, but when I go back to prostitution, they will put me to shame." If he gives me too much back talk, I give him good whacks. (Field notes, 1981–2)

Sushila is saving the money she makes from prostitution and from that her husband gives her so that she can buy a business, probably a bathhouse for working class men. In Bangalore, bathhouses are commonly run by hijras.

Although many hijras complain that it is hard for them to save money, some have a good business sense and have invested in jewelry and property so that they can be relatively independent financially in their old age. For hijras who are not particularly talented singers and dancers, or who live in cities where their ritual performances are not in demand, prostitution provides an adequate way of earning a living. It is a demanding and even occasionally dangerous profession, however, because some customers turn out to be "rowdies." Although a hijra living in a commune has to pay 50% of her fees from prostitution to her household head, few of the younger hijra prostitutes can afford their own place; and living with others provides a certain amount of protection from rough customers and the police. In spite of the resentment and constant complaints by younger hijra prostitutes that they are exploited by their elders, they are extremely reluctant to live on their own.

Hijra Sexuality as a Source of Conflict

The attraction that the hijra role holds for some individuals is the opportunity to engage in sexual relations with men, while enjoying the sociability and relative security of an organized community; these advantages are apparent in contrast to the insecurity and harassment experienced by the effeminate homosexual living on his own. But, whether with husbands or customers, sexual relations run counter to the cultural definitions of the hijra role, and are a source of conflict within the community. Hijra elders attempt to maintain control over those who would "spoil" the hijras' reputation by engaging in sexual activity.

Hijras are well aware that they have only a tenuous hold on respectability in Indian society, and that this respectability is compromised by even covertly engaging in sexual relations. Ascetics have always been regarded with skepticism and ambivalence in Indian society. While paying lip service to the ascetic, conventional Hinduism maintained a very real hostility to it. It classed the non-Vedic ascetic with the dregs of society, "such as incendiaries, poisoners, pimps, spies, adulterers, abortionists, atheists and drunkards"; these fringe members of society found their most respectable status among the Siva sects (26). This ambivalence toward ascetics accurately describes the response of Indian society to the hijra as well, who are also, not coincidentally, worshippers of Siva. In addition, the notion of the false ascetic (those who pretend to be ascetics in order to satisfy their lust) abounds in Hindu mythology. This contradictory attitude, a high regard for asceticism coupled with disdain for those who practice it, characterizes contemporary as well as classical India. Even those families who allow the hijras to perform at births and weddings ridicule the notion that they have any real power.

Indian audiences express their ambivalence toward the hijras by challenging the authenticity of hijra performers. The hijras' emasculation distinguishes them from *zenanas,* or practicing effeminate homosexuals, who do not have the religious powers ascribed to the hijras, but who sometimes impersonate them in order to earn a living. Thus, hijras state that emasculation is necessary because, when they are performing or asking for alms, people may challenge them. If their genitals have not been removed, they will be reviled and driven away as imposters. Hijra elders themselves constantly deride those "men who are men and can have children" and join their community only to make a living from it, or to enjoy sexual relations with men. The parallel between such "fake" hijras and the false ascetics is clear.

Hijras consider sexual activity offensive to the hijra goddess, Bahuchara Mata. Upon initiation into the community, the novice vows to abstain from sexual relations or to marry. Hijra elders claim that all hijra houses lock their doors by nine o'clock at night, implying that no sexual activities occur there. In the cities where hijra culture is strongest, hijras who practice prostitution are not permitted to live with hijras who earn their living by traditional ritual performances. Those who live in these respectable or "family" houses are carefully watched to see that they do not have contact with men. In areas more peripheral to the core of hijra culture, including most of South India, prostitutes do live in houses with traditional hijra performers, and may, in fact, engage in such performances themselves whenever they have an opportunity to do so.

Sexually active hijras usually assert that all hijras join the community so that they can engage in sexual relations with men. As Sita, a particularly candid informant, said:

> Why else would we wear saris? Those who you see who are aged now, when they were young they were just like me. Now they say they haven't got the sexual feeling and they talk only of God and all, but I tell you, that is all nonsense. In their younger days, they also did this prostitution and it is only for the sexual feeling that we join. (Field notes, 1981–2)

The hijras who most vehemently denied having sexual relations with men were almost always over 40. It appears that as they get older, hijras give up sexual activity. Such change over the life cycle parallels that in India generally; in the Hindu cultural ideal, women whose sons are married are expected to give up sexual activity. In fact, not all women do so, but there is social pressure to do so. People ridicule and gossip about middle aged women who act in ways that suggest active sexual interest (Vatuk, 1985). The presentation of self as a non-sexual person that occurs with age also appears among the hijras. The elderly ones may wear male clothing in public, dress more conservatively, wearing white rather than boldly colored saris, act in a less sexually suggestive manner, and take on household domestic roles that keep them indoors.

Although hijra elders are most vocal in expressing disapproval of hijra sexual relations, even younger hirjas who have husbands or practice prostitution admit that such behavior runs counter to hijra norms and lowers their status in the larger society. Hijra prostitutes say that prostitution is a necessary evil for them, the only way for them to earn a living. They attribute the frequency of hijra prostitution to the declining economic status of the hijras in India since the time of Independence. At that time the rajas and nawobs in the princely states, who are important patrons of hijra ritual performances, lost their offices. Hijras also argue that in modern India, declining family size and the spread of Western values, which undermine belief in their powers, also contributes to their lowered economic position, making prostitution necessary.

INDIA AS AN ACCOMMODATING SOCIETY

India is characteristically described as a sexually tolerant society (4, 5). Indeed, the hijra role appears to be elastic enough to accommodate a wide variety of individual temperaments, identities, behaviors, and levels of commitment, and still function in a culturally accepted manner. This elasticity derives from the genius of Hinduism: although not every hijra lives up to the role at the highest level, the role nonetheless gives religious meaning to cross-gender behavior, that is despised, punished and pushed beyond the pale of the cultural system, in other societies.

Several different aspects of Hindu thought explain both the ability of Indian society to absorb an institutionalized third gender role, as well as to provide several contexts within which to handle the tension between the ideal and real aspects of the role. Indian mythology contains numerous examples of androgynes (see 20), impersonators of the opposite sex, and among both deities and humans individuals with sex changes. Myths are an important part of popular culture. Sivabhaktis (worshippers of Siva) give hijras special respect because one of the forms of Siva is Ardhanarisvara, ("the lord who is half woman"). Hijras also associate themselves with Vishnu, who transforms himself into Mohini, the most beautiful woman in the world, in order to take back the sacred nectar from the demons who have stolen it. Further, in the worship of Krishna, male devotees may imagine themselves to be female, and even dress in female clothing; direct identification with Krishna is forbidden, but the devotee may identify with him indirectly by identifying with Radha, that is, by taking a female form. Thousands of hijras identify themselves as Krishna's wives in a ritual performed in South India. These are only a few of the contexts within which the hijras link themselves to the Great Tradition of Hinduism and develop a positive definition for their feminine behavior.

In handling the conflict between the real and the ideal, hijras and other groups in the Indian population are confronted with the seemingly conflicting value which Hinduism places on both eroticism and procreation, on the one hand, and non-attachment and asceticism, on the other. Both Hinduism and Islam are what Bullough calls "sex-positive" religions (4). Both allow for the tolerance of a wider range of sexual expression than exists in western culture with its restrictive Judeo-Christian, religious heritage. Hinduism explicitly recognizes that humans achieve their ultimate goals—salvation, bliss, knowledge and (sexual) pleasure—by following many different paths because humans differ in their special abilities and competencies. Thus, Hinduism allows a different ethic according to one's own nature and affords the individual temperament the widest latitude, from highly idealistic morality, through genial toleration, and, finally, to compulsive extremes (12).

Hindu thought attempts to reconcile the value conflict between sexuality and chastity through the concept of a life cycle with four stages. Each stage has its appropriate sexual behavior: In the first stage one should be a chaste student, in the second a married householder, in the third a forest dweller preparing for withdrawal from society, and in the final stage, a sannyasin, the ascetic who has renounced everything. Thus, the Hindu ideal is a fully integrated life in which each aspect of human nature, including sexuality, has its time. Hijras implicitly recognize these stages in their social organization through a hierarchy in which one begins as a chela and moves into the position of guru as one gets older, taking on chelas and becoming less sexually active.

Hindu mythology also provides some contexts within which the contradictions between the ascetic ideal and the sexual activity are legitimate: Siva himself is both the great erotic and the great ascetic. In myths he alternates between the two forms. In some mythic episodes Siva is unable to reconcile his two roles as ascetic and householder, and in others he is a hypocritical ascetic because of his sexual involvement with Parvati, his consort (19). Indian goddesses as sexual figures also exist in abundance and in some stories a god will take on a female form specifically to have sexual relations with a male deity.

Where Western culture feels uncomfortable with contradictions and makes strenuous attempts to resolve them, Hinduism allows opposites to confront each other without a resolution, "celebrating the idea that the universe is boundlessly various, and . . . that all possibilities may exist without excluding each other" (19). It is this characteristically Indian ability to tolerate, and even embrace, contradictions at social, cultural and personality levels, that provides a context for hijras. Hijras express in their very bodies the confrontation of femaleness and maleness as polar opposites. In Indian society they are not only tolerated but also valued.

NOTES

1. I would like to thank Veena Oldenburg for calling this to my attention. A similar pattern exists among the courtesans in North India (Oldenburg, 1984).

2. Alan Roland (1982) has insightfully examined some of the emotional and psychological aspects of

hierarchy within the Hindu joint family, and many of his conclusions could well be applied to the hijra hierarchy.

3. Some of these religious occasions are participated in by non-hijras as well, while others celebrate events specific to the hijra community, such as the anniversary of the deaths of important gurus.

4. More recently, hijras have been issued ration cards for food in New Delhi, but must apply only under the male names.

5. A more detailed description of this literature is found in Nanda (1984) and Nanda (in press).

6. "Mouth Congress" is considered the appropriate sexual activity for eunuchs disguised as women, in the Kama Sutra. An Editor's note (Burton, 1962, p. 124) suggests that this practice is no longer common in India, and is perhaps being replaced by sodomy, which has been introduced since the Muslim period.

7. Social class factors are relevant here. Boys who are born with indeterminate sex organs (I came across three such cases by hearsay) to upper middle class families would not be likely to join the hijras. In two of these cases the men in question were adults; one had been sent abroad to develop his career in science with the expectation that he would not marry, but at least would have the satisfaction of a successful and prestigious career. The other was married by his parents to a girl who, it was known, could not have children. The third is still a toddler and is being brought up as a boy. I also had the opportunity to interview a middle-aged, middle-class man who was desperately trying to find a doctor to perform the transsexual operation on him in a hospital. He chose not to join the hijras because of their "reputation" but envied them their group life and their ability to live openly as women.

REFERENCES

1. Anderson, C. (1977). *Gay men in India.* Unpublished manuscript, University of Wisconsin.

2. Bhimbhai, K. Pavayas. (1901). Gujarat population, Hindus. In J. M. Campbell (Compiler), *Gazetteer of the Bombay Presidency, 4*, part 1. Bombay: Government Central Press.

3. Bradford, N. J. (1983). Transgenderism and the cult of Yellamma: Heat, sex, and sickness in South Indian ritual. *Journal of Anthropological Research, 39,* 307–322.

4. Bullough, V. L. (1976). *Sexual variance in society and history,* Chicago: University of Chicago Press.

5. Carrier, J. (1980). Homosexual behavior in cross cultural perspective. In J. Marmor (Ed.), *Homosexual behavior: A modern reappraisal* (pp. 100–122). New York: Basic Books.

6. Carstairs, G. M. (1957). *The twice born.* London: Hogarth Press.

7. Faridi, F. L. (1899). Hijras. In J. M. Campbell (Compiler), *Gazetteer of the Bombay Presidency, 9,* part 2. Bombay: Government Central Press.

8. Freeman, J. M. (1979). *Untouchable: An Indian life history.* Stanford, CA: Stanford University Press.

9. Hiltebeitel, A. (1980). Siva, the goddess, and the disguises of the Pandavas and Draupadi. *History of Religions,* 20(1/2), 147–174.

10. *India Today.* Fear is the key. (1982, September 15), pp. 84–85.

11. *The Kama Sutra of Vatsyayana.* (1964). (R. F. Burton, Trans.). New York: E. P. Dutton.

12. Lannoy, R. (1975). *The speaking tree.* New York: Oxford University Press.

13. Lynton, H. S., & Rajan, M. (1974). *Days of the beloved.* Berkeley: University of California Press.

14. Mark, M. E. (1981). *Falkland Road: Prostitutes of Bombay.* New York: Knopf.

15. Mehta, S. (1945–1946). Eunuchs, pavaiyas and hijadas. *Gufarat ahitya Sabha,* Amdavad, Karyavahi, Part 2. Ahmedabad.

16. Money, J., & Wiedeking, C. (1980). *Handbook* of *human sexuality* (pp. 270–284). B. B. Wolman & J. Money (Eds.), Englewood Cliffs, N.J.: Prentice-Hall.

17. Nanda, S. (1984). The hijras of India: A preliminary report. *Medicine and Law, 3,* 59–75.

18. Nanda, S. (in press). Dancers only? In Murray (Ed.), *Cultural diversity and homosexualities.* New York: Longman.

19. O'Flaherty, W. (1973). *Asceticism and eroticism in the mythology of Siva.* London: Oxford University Press.

20. O'Flaherty, W. (1980). *Women, androgynes, and other mythical beasts.* Chicago: University of Chicago Press.

21. Oldenburg, V. (1984). *The making* of *colonial Lucknow.* Princeton, N. J.: Princeton University Press.

22. Opler, M. (1960). The hijara (hermaphrodites) of India and Indian national character: A rejoinder, *American Anthropologist, 62,* 505–511.

23. Rajagopalachary, C. (1980). *Mahabharala.* Bombay: Bharatiya Vidya Bhavan.

24. Roland, A. (1982). Toward a psychoanalytical psychology of hierarchical relationships in Hindu India. *Ethos, 10*(3), 232–253.

25. Salunkhe, G. (1976, August 8). The cult of the hijaras. *Illustrated Weekly,* pp. 16–21.

26. Shah, A. M. (196 1). A note on the hijaras of Gujerat. *American Anthropologist, 61,* 1325–1330.

27. Sinha, A. P. (1967). Procreation among the eunuchs. *Eastern Anthropologist, 20,* 168–176.

28. *The Tribune,* (1983, August 26). Five eunuchs in India, Pak. p. 2.

29. Vatuk S. (1985). South Asian cultural conceptions of sexuality. In J. K. Brown & V. Kerns (Eds.), *In her prime: A new view of middle-aged women* (pp. 137–152).

30. Wikan, U. (1977). Man becomes woman: Transsexualism in Oman as a key to gender roles. *Man, 12,* 304–319.

FROM SAPPHO TO SAND: HISTORICAL PERSPECTIVE ON CROSSDRESSING AND CROSS GENDER

Betty W. Steiner, M.B.

A search through literature shows that crossdressing and cross gender wishes in both men and women have existed throughout time and throughout history. Buhrich (1) in a brief communication discusses transvestism in history and suggests this may help to broaden the present day reports on transsexualism and homosexuality. Bullough (2) has written two papers. In the first he discusses the sociological aspects of transvestism in the middle ages and in the second paper (3), he reviews transsexualism over the last 200 years in Europe and America. He suggests that crossdressing may be viewed in terms of gain and/or loss in social status. He notes that all the transvestite saints were female, and thus they could only gain by crossdressing in men's clothes as men were considered superior to women. On the other hand, he argues that males lost status by dressing in women's garments and the only way this loss of status in men could be justified was by attaching an erotic connotation to transvestism.

Other publications include Pauley's (4) survey of 100 cases of crossdressing published in the medical literature since 1916, and Green (5) has reported briefly on mythological and historical characters who crossdressed. In a later publication he elaborates on the historical and cross-cultural aspects of cross gender (6).

This paper attempts to glance further back in time through the pages of history and literature, in order to illustrate how numerous are the examples of crossdressing and cross gender desires. It is in no way intended to be a definitive article, but the writer attempts to paint a larger canvas, against which today's gender disorders may be viewed in a more illuminating perspective.

IN THE BEGINNING: THE GREAT MOTHER CULT

Before the Greco-Roman civilization, man is said to have worshipped the Great Mother, all-giving and all-encompassing, symbol of love, nourishment and fecundity (7). To the Egyptians she was Isis, to the Corinthians, Aphrodite, and to the Phoenicians, she was Astarte. But by whatever name she was called, she was served by the temple maidens and the priests. Herodotus, writing of the Babylonians, tells of their custom where every woman born in Babylon had to go once in her lifetime to the temple of Venus and submit to sexual intercourse with a stranger. The sex of the stranger is not clear, but indications are this could be either a man or a woman. The priests or heiroduli, (meaning literally servants of the goddess) were said to be eunuchs, transvestites, or both, and were in addition, male temple prostitutes. The women or girls of the temple also acted as prostitutes and were subjects of ritual intercourse, by which an individual was united with the gods through the medium of a third person. It appears that both heterosexual and homosexual intercourse was practised.

Whether the Great Mother cult ever existed is open to question, but some writers have postulated that the Mother Cult was superseded by the patriarchal society of the Hebrews, which displaced woman from her position of power as the source of life, and saw her merely as an instrument for man's use and pleasure. Gordon Rattray-Taylor (8) wrote that "in societies which conceive of their deities as mother figures, incest is regarded as the overwhelming danger and is hedged with taboos, whereas homosexuality has little importance. Conversely, in societies which conceive of their deities as father figures, homosexuality is regarded as the overwhelming danger and is surrounded with taboos and condemnation."

THE GRECO-ROMAN ERA

The facts and myths of the past are filtered down to posterity so that their interpretation is coloured by man's need today. Yet ancient Greece still stands unchanged in man's imagination, a strange mixture of aesthetic and intellectual greatness mixed with erotic abandonment. The island of Lesbos is rich in legends and from here in the sixth century before Christ, the voice of Sappho (9) spoke of her love for other women. Little of her poetry remains, as much was destroyed by subsequent zealous Christians including most of her erotic writings. There are writers today who insist that Sappho was a practising homosexual, just as nineteenth century writers assertively stated she was an innocent teacher and writer, incapable of "impure" love. Wherever the truth lies, the island of Lesbos is immortalized forever in the concept of lesbianism.

Greek art and literature indicates that women, neglected by their husbands and with little freedom to commit adultery, constructed an artificial phallus or olisbo, which they used in their sexual practices with other women, imitating heterosexual intercourse. The women in Aristophanes' "Lysistrata" weep, because they have no more of the special leather out of which the olisbos were made. The Greek historian Lucian (10) who lived in the second century A.D., describes an incident in "Dialogues of the Courtesans."

A group of women give a party and at the end many of them are intoxicated. Two of them, Megilla and Demonassa invite Leaena, a woman from Lesbos, to sleep with them. Later Leaena tells the tale as follows:

At first they kissed me like men, not simply bringing their lips to mine, but opening their mouths a little, embracing me, and squeezing my breasts. Demonassa even bit me as she kissed, and I didn't know what to make of it. Eventually Megilla being now rather heated, pulled off her wig, which was very realistic and fitted very closely, and revealed the skin of her head, which was shaved close, just as on the most energetic of athletes. This sight gave me a shock, but she said, "Leaena, have you ever seen a good-looking fellow?" "I don't see one here, Megilla," said I. "Don't make a woman out of me," said she. "My name is Megillus, and I've been married to Demonassa here for ever so long; she's my wife." I laughed at that, Clonarium, and said, "Then . . . you have everything that a man has, and can play the part of a man to Demonassa?" "I haven't got what you mean" said she, "I don't need it at all. You'll find I've a much pleasanter method of my own." "You're surely not a hermaphrodite," said I, "equipped both as a man and a woman, as many people are said to be?" But she said, "I was born a woman like the rest of you, but I have the mind and the desires and everything else of a man . . . just give me a chance . . . I have a substitute of my own. Only give me a chance, and you'll see."

Greek literature (11) is replete with references to male homosexuality but it was Anacreon of Teos, who was the first poet to write of the love of man for man, in the fifth century before Christ. In Homer's tales, Ganymede, a beautiful youth, was abducted by the god Zeus, who fell in love with him and made him cupbearer to the Olympian gods. Subsequently the task of cupbearer in a Greco-Roman household was given symbolically to a homosexual slave. Another legend has Ganymede cross-dressed as a woman, forever spinning wool at the feet of Queen Omphale, whom he was said to serve.

With the decline of the Great Mother cult, and the growth of the patriarchal society, woman lost her privileged position and was relegated to an inferior and secondary role to man. She was portrayed as a harridan, shrew, virago, witch or hag, and all things pertaining to femininity were degrading. Greek youths, admired for their grace and beauty, were the lovers of older, married men, marriage being a way of denying their homosexuality, and enabling their relationship with young men to become merely "educational pederasty." Many Greek males alternated intercourse with youths and women, falling in and out of love, in an unending attempt to find a lasting, meaningful relationship. Today, this indiscriminate sexual behaviour possibly could lead to an impaired sense of masculinity, but to the ancient Greek, bisexuality was resolved by the simple expediency of classifying both women and boys as passive, submissive "non-males." Thus, a man could possess women and boys openly without any threat to his masculinity, providing he played the active, dominant role and "feminized" his partners of both sexes. Plato incorporated the love of men into his philosophy, by stating simply that "beautiful is good; love is love of the good-and-beautiful; men are better and more beautiful than women; therefore one should love men"!

History records the worship of bisexual gods, where men castrated themselves and dressed in female robes (12). The ancient Cypriots worshipped a bearded Aphrodite, a figure depicting a woman's body, but with a beard and large, external male genitalia. Those who served the masculinized goddess, crossdressed, men as women and women as men. The offspring of Hermes, god of Science and Commerce, the patron of love, who sprang from the foam of the sea (aphros=foam) was named Hermaphrodite, and was depicted as an exaggeratedly masculine male with breasts, or alternatively as a statuesque, maternal being with large, male genitalia. In Ovid's "Metamorphoses," the nymph, Salmacis, falls in love with Hermaphrodite and prays that she is united with him, so that "the twain might become one with the flesh" (13). Her prayer is answered and immortalized in the rare genetic abnormality, hermaphroditism, where the nymph and the boy become, in reality, one being. By this union, Hermaphrodite becomes half-woman (semivir) or half-man, similar to a virago, a woman with a man's soul.

Plutarch in his "Parallel Lives" writes of the custom of the bridegrooms of the island of Cos who wore women's robes at their wedding, similar to the brides of Argos who wore beards on their wedding night. The reason for such customs has been lost with time but they may have symbolized a prayer to the gods for fertility in the marriage, or a fantasized omniscience and denial of the need for the marriage partner, in order to procreate. Perhaps, even this may have been one of man's earliest acknowledgments to transsexualism. With the passage of time, these bisexual deities lost most of their aggressive, sexual characteristics and by the age of Ovid and Seneca, Dionysus, the God of Wine was no longer a virile, masculine figure with breasts, but a beautiful youth, with dark eyes and flowing golden curls, "a girl-faced" boy (12).

The Roman sexual life was very different from the Greeks, being strongly influenced by their Etruscan ancestors. Seneca, and Cato, wrote of civic corruption, adultery and effeminacy as a result of the growth in wealth and power of the Roman empire and deplored the influence of Greek mores on the Roman culture. Scholars predicted the fall of Rome as an indication of its growth of prosperity, wealth and sexual freedom which they interpreted as a sign of decadence, perhaps a lesson for our twentieth century.

Horace, Ovid, Catullus and others wrote love poems to women and youths, just as readily as they had sexual intercourse with them. Every type of sexual perversion was practised, from anal intercourse to sadomasochistic orgies, the most terrible atrocities being performed by the emperors. Caligula, the mad, epileptic, incestuous youth who reigned in A.D. 37 frequently appeared in public, dressed as a female, and Nero, incestuous with his mother whom he later had assassinated married his male lover and subsequently imitated a virgin's screams on his wedding night.

THE JUDEO-CHRISTIAN RELIGION

The numerous pagan religions, which flourished before Christ, promised to save mankind by denaturing him and curing him of all his evil passions, including his sexual desires. In contrast, the monotheistic religion of Hebrews believed that God had created the world, and much of the poetry in the Old Testament is in praise of the material world, including celebration of love and the flesh, rather than a prayer for the soul's immortal salvation (12). It contains no paeans to celibacy or virginity, although it does condemn adultery, and also proscribes homosexuality and bestiality.

Perhaps one of the earliest references in the Bible to transvestism or even transsexualism is in the Book of Deuteronomy, Chapter XXII, 5: "The woman shall not wear that which pertained unto a man, neither shall a man put on woman's garment; for all that do so are an abomination unto the Lord thy God."

"The state of the world shows that the fullness of time has come." (Galatians, Chapter IV, 4) and with the coming of Jesus and the birth of Christianity peace appeared to encompass civilization. Yet in spite of this outward appearance of prosperity and unity, moral death, corruption and sexual debauchery were still very prevalent. Man's feeling of aloneness was never felt more strongly, philosophers regarded all religions as false and man's faith in his fellow man was at its lowest ebb. It was at this moment in history that Christianity was seen as the life-giving faith, with its promise of immortal life, which a disillusioned populace was ready and eager to espouse.

With the decline and ultimate fall of the Roman Empire, sexual promiscuity was curtailed. The ancient laws were revised and both homosexuality and the wearing of the clothes of the opposite sex became a crime, punishable by death. One tale which may be apocryphal is worth recounting. On the death of Pope Leo IV in A.D. 855, Pope John VIII, nominated to be his successor, was found in fact to be a woman, and who is said to have been delivered of a child before a number of witnesses. Both mother and infant died shortly thereafter.

Early in the second millennium, Scandinavian countries made transvestism for either men or women grounds for divorce. It is interesting to note that, at that time, women must have crossdressed and functioned publicly in the male role (1). During this same period the great witch hunts began and were to continue into the nineteenth century. In 1484, Pope Innocent III issued the "Summa Desiderantes" by which decree he acknowledged demonology (12). Three years later in 1487, two Dominican monks, Sprenger and Kramer published the infamous "Malleus Malleficarum" which was accepted by both Church and State. Six of the seven chapters of this infamous document dealt with sexual matters and, indeed, it reads today like a textbook of sexual anomalous preferences. Among the many evils that witches were said to perform, was the ability to turn men into women, and women into men by the use of special drugs. On the basis of trivial, frequently anonymous information, thousands of people, mainly women, were tortured and burned at the stake. It culminated in the Spanish Inquisition where Torquemada dispatched more than ten thousand people to their death. The Malleus Malleficarum also contains an eye-witness description of a girl being turned into a man by the devil. And in 1429 Joan of Arc, the Maid of Orleans, was burned at the stake, accused of heresy which included a belief that she was a witch and for her refusal to wear women's clothing, which was one of the main indictments against her (14).

THE RENAISSANCE

The Renaissance is often looked upon as one of the most glorious periods in man's history with its exuberant expansion in the arts, philosophy and literature. Many of the famous people who lived during this era have been accused of homosexuality, but Karlen (12) attributes this fact to the invention of apologists of the late nineteenth and early twentieth centuries. Certainly bisexuality was common and pornography widespread with frequent reports of cross gender behaviour (15). In France, King Henri III was a notorious womanizer until his mid-twenties, when he began to go about publicly dressed as a woman and had numerous male lovers. He frequently appeared at court wearing elaborate ball gowns and flamboyant jewelry, with heavy makeup on his face. His effeminate behaviour became the theme for many poets, writers, and satirists. The Huguenot poet, Agrippa d'Aubigne, accuses Catherine de Medici of feminizing all three of her sons, of whom Henri III was her favourite; and Catherine herself was said to be sexually and morally corrupt (16).

In England, James I (also James VI of Scotland, the son of the ill-fated Mary, Queen of Scots) was known for his love affairs with his page, Robert Carr, and later with George Villiers, whom he subsequently created Duke of Buckingham and made him cupbearer to His Majesty's household, in true Greek tradition (17). Bisexual behaviour has also been imputed to such eminent individuals as Sir Francis Bacon, philosopher and statesman, Richard Barnefield (18), the poet, and two of the greatest Elizabethan dramatists, Christopher Marlowe (19) and William Shakespeare (20). However, the evidence is very controversial as to whether any of these men were bisexual, since rumor flourished in their age at the flimsiest provocation, mainly for political or religious reasons.

In the Renaissance, for the first time since the pre-Christian era, lesbianism appears openly in literature. In "Huon of Bordeaux" (21), a medieval romance, a girl disguised as a boy is forced to marry another woman. Two English plays written in the sixteenth century are based on the real-life figure of Mary Frith, alias Moll Cutpurse (22), who dressed and lived as a man all her life and was known to be a robber and forger, her only personal allegiance being to her pet mastiff. In Spain, the play, "La Monja Alferez" was based on the life of a Basque female transvestite who was similarly romanticized by the playwright. In two of Shakespeare's plays, "Twelfth Night" and "As You Like It," the heroine crossdresses as a youth, and it appears that women wore clothes similar to, or the same as, men, on occasions as a form of disguise and also for erotic stimulation. Montaigne's "Journal of a Voyage in Italy," (23) written in 1581, tells the tale of seven or eight women who crossdressed as men and sought work as weavers. One passed as a male so successfully that she married another woman. She was betrayed, however, and sentenced to be hanged. On the scaffold she is purported to have said that she "would even prefer this to living again as a girl," and was hanged for using "illicit inventions to supply the defect of the sex."

THE SEVENTEENTH TO NINETEENTH CENTURY

The Sun King, Louis XIV of France was described as the greatest autocratic monarch to rule France. His brother the Duc d'Orleans, ("Monsieur") although a brave and courageous soldier, rode into battle wearing jewelry and heavy make-up but without a hat on his head for fear that he might flatten his peruke! According to the Abbé de Choisy, himself a transvestite, when "Monsieur" was a child he had been raised as a girl, wore women's clothes and had his hair styled like a girl's; but whether this was a conspiracy of the French Court to feminize him is not clear. Certainly, Francis Timoleon also known as the Abbé de Choisy, was himself raised as a girl by his mother and his memoirs reveal the extent of his cross gender identification.

The Abbé's mother wanted a daughter at the time of his birth and so encouraged all feminine behaviour even to the extent of having his ears pierced and negating all signs of masculinity. He entered the Church but ran away on several occasions. Once he went to Bordeaux where he lived as a woman for five months, working as an actress. Before his death in 1724 at the age of 83, he still loved to dress in the elegant gowns and elaborate jewelry which his mother had left him. He was a distinguished scholar and a member of L'Academie Francaise (12).

Masculine behaviour in women, with or without any sexual relationship with members of the same sex, appears to have been quite common among the upper classes throughout Europe in the seventeenth century. Pierre de Brantôme's "Lives of Gallant Ladies" published in 1655 states: "For a woman to be masculine and a very Amazon and lewd after this fashion (is better) than for a man to be feminine, for the more manlike she is, the braver she is."

The eighteenth century was renowned for its sexual debauchery and the rake and the lecher became common figures in society. Private clubs sprang up to cater to a variety of deviant sexual tastes. Edward Ward (24) describes one such club known as "The Mollies" where the men met to crossdress as females and to drink and cavort. Transvestism in both sexes seems to have been more frequent, or at last more public. The "Annual Register" shows a record of fifteen cases of women passing as men between the years 1761 and 1815. The most famous character was the Burgundian aristocrat, the Chevalier d'Eon, who lived forty-nine years of his life as a man and the remainder as a woman until his death at the age of eighty-three. History states that when he made his debut at the Court of Louis XV he rivalled the beauty of Madame la Pompadour, the King's new mistress. He was said to be small, beautiful and delicate as a child. His parents treated him as a girl but subsequently he became an expert swordsman, distinguished diplomat and spy in the service of Louis XV. Following the death of the King, the Chevalier d'Eon retired to England where he lived out the remainder of his life as a woman. He passed so successfully in his chosen gender that at his death in 1810 an autopsy was performed to determine his true sex. History records that he was a virgin, having had sexual relations with neither man nor woman during his long lifetime.

In 1858, a woman who had lived in the Palace of Versailles in France as a King's pensioner was found at the time of death to be a biological male. The first colonial governor of New York, Lord Cornbury, appointed by the English Crown, frequently crossdressed in public as a woman. Dr. Mary Edward Walker (1832–1919) wore an officer's uniform and was the first woman to be commissioned into the Army. She dressed as a man for fifty of her eighty-seven years. She was also the first vociferous champion of women's rights.

Victorianism ushered in the age of piety and hypocrisy towards sex reinforced by the religious morality of John Wesley at the end of the eighteenth century. With the evolution of a strong Methodist middle-class in Europe, women became "desexualised" and the era of romantic love was born. At the same time the new feminist movement began to grow, the foundation stone being Mary Wollstonecraft's "Vindication of the Rights of Women." During the first few decades of the nineteenth century feminism was typified by a group of flamboyant artists and writers, the most famous of whom was George Sand, the pseudonym of the French novelist, Aurore Dupin (25). She wore men's suits, smoked cigars and was celebrated for her many love affairs, the most notorious being with Chopin, the composer and de Musset, the dramatist. In England, Marian Evans published her novel *Adam Bede* under the pen name of George Eliot. She wore men's suits and is said to have emulated George Sand in her manners and behaviour. The Brontë sisters, Charlotte, Emily and Anne used the pseudonym "Bell" when submitting their manuscripts as they feared that books written by women would never be accepted for publication.

CONCLUSION

It has been said that when an age writes history, it paints its self-portrait. Yet today's extreme preoccupation with sexuality is not new, and is perhaps more apparent than real. This paper has attempted to illustrate that cross gender behaviour and crossdressing are not new phenomena, but have been present since the beginning of time.

REFERENCES

1. Buhrich N. Transvestism in history. J Nerv Ment Dis 1977; 165(1).
2. Bullough VL. Transsexualism in history. Arch Sex Behav 1975; 4(5).

3. Bullough VL. Transvestites in the middle ages. Am J Soc 1974; 79(6).

4. Pauly IB. Female transsexualism. Part I and II. Arch Sex Behav 1974; 3(6).

5. Green R. Mythological, historical and cross-cultural aspects of transsexualism. In: Green R. Money J, eds. Transsexualism and sex reassignment. Baltimore: Johns Hopkins Univ. Press. 1969: 13–22.

6. Green R. Historical and crosscultural survey. In: Sexual identity conflict in children and adults. New York: Basic Books, 1974: 3–15.

7. Bachofen JJ. Myth, religion, and mother right. Princeton: Princeton Univ. Press. 1967.

8. Rattray-Taylor G. Sex in history. New York: Vanguard, 1954.

9. Sappho. In: Lyrics, translated by Willis Barnstone. Garden City, N.Y.: Doubleday Anchor, 1965.

10. Lucian. In: Collected works. Translated by AM Harman and MD MacLeod. 8 Vols. Vols. 1–2. New York: MacMillan, 1913–15. Vols. 3–4 New York: GP Putnam & Sons, 1921–25. Vols. 5–7 Cambridge, Mass: Harvard Univ. Press, 1936–61. Vol. 8 New York: MacMillan, 1967.

11. Herodotus. In: The Greek historians, Vol. 1. Francis R. Bed. Transl by George Rawlinson, New York: Random House, 1942.

12. Karlen A. Sexuality and homosexuality. New York: W. W. Norton, 1971.

13. Masters R. Eros and evil. New York: Julian Press, 1962.

14. D'Aubigne Agrippa. Les tragiques. Livre 2, les princes. Baltimore: Johns Hopkins Press, 1953.

15. Brinton C. A history of western morals. New York: Harcourt, Brace & World, 1959.

16. L'Estoile, Pierre de. Journal de choses memorables advenues durant le regne de Henri III. . .1621. Paris: Gallimard, 1943.

17. Wilson DH. King James VI and I. New York: Oxford Univ. Press, 1967.

18. Barnfield R. The complete poems. Grosart AB. ed. London: JB Nichols & Sons, 1876.

19. Wraight AD. In search of Christopher Marlowe. New York: Vanguard Press, 1965.

20. Pearson H. A life of Shakespeare. London: Carroll and Nicholson, 1949.

21. Huon of Bordeaux. In: The book of Duke Huon of Bordeaux. Translated by Lord Berners. London: Truber & Co. 1884.

22. Middleton Dekker. The roaring girl. Works, Vol. 4 Bullen AH ed. Boston & N.Y.: Houghton Mifflin, 1885–86.

23. Montaigne, Michel de. Journal of Montaigne's travels in Italy. London: John Murray, 1903.

24. Ward Edward (Ned). The London spy. Hayward A. ed. New York: George H. Doran, 1927.

25. Sand George. Histoire de ma vie. Adaptation de Noelle Roubaud. Pairs: Stock (Delamain et Boutelleau).

RÉSUMÉ

Cette histoire du travestissement, depuis le grand culte de la fécondité jusqu'au dix-neuvième siècle, en passant par l'ère gréco-romaine, l'èpoque judéo-chrétienne et la Renaissance. s'accompagne de références passablement complètes.

Address reprint requests to: Dr. B. W. Steiner, Gender Identity Clinic, Clarke Institute of Psychiatry, 250 College Street, Toronto, Ontario, M5T IR8.

NEITHER MAN NOR WOMAN:
BERDACHE—A CASE FOR NON-DICHOTOMOUS
GENDER CONSTRUCTION[1]

Brian Schnarch[2]

The existence of two sexes and of two genders is largely taken for granted as "irreducible facts" within our Euro-Western cultural tradition (18). Like our other basic and often related dichotomies, this pair of dichotomies is pervasive. In our mythology (e.g., Adam and Eve) and in our everyday social interactions, from the first question we ask about a newborn to the ways in which we conceptualize the universe, a (gender) dichotomizing framework is discernible.[3]

Sex: From an essentialist perspective, sex is viewed as a determinant of the biological, social and psychological make-up of a male or female. From a more recent feminist perspective, sex is distinguished from gender as the biological dimension in defining and constructing what it is to be male or female.[4] In both versions, sex consists of what one is born with. But, at this point, distinguishing that which is biological from that which is not remains contentious and therefore sex should be understood as a folk classification system which divides humanity into two or more categories (e.g., male and female) on the basis of both biological *and* cultural criteria *in the belief that the criteria being used are biologically determined or "natural."*[5-8]

Gender: By contrast, gender has typically been used to refer to the psychological, social and cultural elements in the constructions of males and females (32). Herein gender classifications will be viewed as folk classifications dividing humanity into two or more types based on what *are believed to be non-"natural," i.e., cultural elements.* One might note that at this point androgyny exists only in theory and fiction.

Sex/Gender System:[9] This is the folk classification of both gender and sex categories. The system varies in its construction from culture to culture but invariably (i.e., cross-culturally) contains a minimum of two sexes and two genders.

Gender Attribution and Sex Attribution: According to Kessler and McKenna (18), gender attribution, or "assigning" a gender, is the act of deciding whether someone is a man or a woman. In keeping with the preceding definitions, I must expand the definition to include other genders that are neither men nor women (as defined by folk classifications). Gender attribution is made on the basis of numerous and redundant morphological (e.g., breasts and beards) and cultural (e.g., hairstyle, clothing, posture) elements. In this way Western gender assignments tend to coincide with Western sex assignments. As such is not necessarily the case in all societies, sex and gender attribution are analytically distinguished. Following Kessler and McKenna, *gender attribution* precedes and defines *gender role* and *gender identity,* although there is dynamic interplay between the three. It should be clear from this, that neither a person's sex nor gender are simply innate.

Gender Role and Gender Identity/Sex Role and Sex Identity: One's gender role is the sum of all behaviours that a person engages in to indicate to others or to the self that one is a man, a woman or some other gender. Gender role is the outward (public) manifestation of one's gender identity, and gender identity is the personal experience of one's gender role (18). The concepts of sex role and sex identity should be distinguished here from gender role and gender identity as sex and gender do not necessarily have a one-to-one relationship. The study of gender (and sex) identity is primarily the focus of psychologists. My focus here is socio-cultural and is thus more closely related to gender (and sex) roles and gender (and sex) attribution.

Female/Male—Woman/Man: The terms female and male are used to designate two most common varieties of *sex* assignments. The terms man and woman represent the two most common *gender* assignments. All are folk classifications and are not necessarily universal or paired.

Intersex: This is a person with genitalia that are neither typically male nor female. The term itself implies a "middle" position which should not be assumed. The folk classifications hermaphrodite and Nadle (14) fall into this category.

Transsexual: A person is transsexual when the individual's gender identity and gender assignment conflict. The term only has meaning because we make gender attributions for everyone.

Transvestite: A transvestite is a person whose gender assignment and gender identity are in correspondence with each other but are both in contrast to the gender association of the clothes that this person wears. This category is highly contextual and, therefore, relatively ambiguous and difficult to apply.

Heterosexuality, Homosexuality and Bisexuality: These categories relate to one's (choice of)[10] sexual partners. The choice lies, respectively, between different gender partners, same gender partners and "either" gender partners. These terms traditionally imply two genders, as well as one-on-one sexuality.

The term bisexual most explicitly implies two dichotomous gender categories and is, therefore, culture-specific. An appropriate alternative term, which would incorporate the possible variations, would be "multisexual." Sexuality, it should be noted, is an element of variable importance in different sex/gender systems. Gender attribution of each partner must logically precede the labels of sexual practices (or preferences).

The critical or sensitive reader might think that the preceding presentation of "analytical distinctions" sounds itself very much like a folk classification model. Inasmuch as the notions are shared by some, it is. The framework outlined is intended to facilitate comparisons of different sex/gender systems and is itself subject to revision as "evidence" and "anomalies" dictate. The berdache will now be considered in the context of the preceding framework.

THE BERDACHE STATUS

The berdache has been characterized in many different ways by different authors. This multiplex depiction is doubtless a reflection, in part, of the great variation that characterizes the role. I will briefly sketch a basic consensus regarding this role as interpreted by several authors, before discussing the more controversial and interesting theoretical views.

The berdache is a person who is usually male but sometimes female or intersexed.[11] This person assumes at least some of the occupations, dress, and other behaviours associated with the "other" (or different) sex, at least some of the time. This type of person is labeled by Native American societies with a title distinct from "man" or "woman," and the berdache has a recognized and accepted social status which is frequently rooted in mythology. They often serve a mediating role between men and woman; a position afforded by their distinctness and special spirit. This distinct and even unusual status also affords the berdache special spiritual power as the mediator between the spiritual and physical worlds. Sexuality is variable (4, 6, 18, 35).

State of Research and Documentation
Williams discusses the state of research on the berdache (35). The documentation on the berdache has been, until recently, largely hidden away as a peripheral topic in ethnographies or in early explorers'

and missionaries' accounts of what was presented as the base immorality of the savages. There are a number of reasons for the lack of information. Historians have typically shown a basic lack of interest in the internal organization of Native societies. Furthermore, historians and more recently ethnohistorians have tended to consider men killing each other to be of far more importance in understanding the past than the history of sexuality and sex/gender systems. Homophobic Western attitudes have led to voluntary, and even mandatory censorship, such as the 1975 decision of the Executive Board of the American Anthropological Association which voted "not to endorse research on homosexuality across national borders" (cited in Williams 1986:13). According to Read this "is indicative of the persistence of [homophobic] Western attitudes . . . though it [homosexuality] is probably as prevalent as witchcraft [it] is morally distasteful" (ibid.).

Additional reasons for the lack of knowledge available on the berdache status include: missed references; "extinct" societies; inhibitions of anthropologists about discussing sex and sexuality and native inhibitions about discussing such matters for reasons of secrecy or, amongst some Christian natives, out of fear of embarrassment and the self-conscious desire to suppress the "shameful" traditions of the past.

Range and Distribution

Collander and Kochems find the berdache institution to be present in 113 societies in North America, north of Mexico, as recorded by anthropologists and others since the time of contact. In many societies the evidence for the status is either missing altogether or ambiguous. A complete absence of the institution is only explicitly reported for nine groups. But even these instances are on shaky ground because numerous cases of explicit denials of the berdache status have been reported for societies in which the status is known to have existed (1983:444–445). Furthermore, the presence of the very similar "soft man" status amongst the Chuckchee of Northern Siberia (3) points to the possibility that the berdache status was brought to America by the first people to come across the Bering Strait. If this is correct, the implications for antiquity and distribution are enormous. Combined with the reasons delineated above, it seems likely that berdache status was even more widespread than currently acknowledged: "We cannot assume that berdaches were completely absent from any Native American culture, and we need to question statements that suggest its nonexistence" (35).[12]

Sexuality

Berdaches, without recorded exception, had sexual relations only with non-berdaches. Otherwise, they were not restricted. Non-berdache women and men could have sex with men, women and berdaches. Sexuality, in general, was highly variable.

Sexuality was not considered as important an element in definitions of gender within North American Native societies as it is in Euro-Western societies. Williams (35) argues that a person's spiritual essence was of primary importance, while Whitehead explains that North American Native gender attributions, in contrast to Euro-Western ones, foregrounded occupation and social behaviour. Choice of sexual partners, she says, was the secondary interest (1981:97) in assigning gender. Unlike Euro-American society heterosexuality was not rigidly mandatory (10). This is not to suggest, though, that man-woman "marriage" unions were not also the norm.

Clothing

Although, generally speaking, berdaches "cross dressed" (i.e., wore the clothing of the "other" sex), there is great variability in the literature about this. Male berdaches often wore the clothes and hairstyles of women and often imitated their voices. Female berdaches often dressed as men. Most frequently clothing choice would be contextual. Often elements of men's wardrobes and women's wardrobes were combined. Sometimes the berdache would make and wear clothing that was completely distinct from women or men.

Clothing, like many aspects of the berdache status, was variable across cultures. For example, the Pima's male berdaches took the speech and postures of women but not their dress (14), while in other societies there were female berdaches who did not wear men's clothing. There were instances of individual choice in dress but most commonly the choice of clothing depended on the gender association of the task at hand (e.g., cooking, hunting) or the "marital status" of the berdache (6).

According to Landes and Lurie, becoming a male berdache is a transformation which occurred in several stages. The status was adopted gradually with the adoption of women's clothing as the final stage and the end of the process (19, 22). The label of transvestite as applied to berdaches will be discussed below.

Occupations

Berdaches usually adopted the occupations of the gender whose clothing they assumed. This was particularly significant characteristic of their status. It is one of the most often noted traits and, like cross dressing, it is one of the most significant (6).

Another feature of the status was the very frequently cited proficiency that the berdache had in performance of the tasks specified to the gender whose clothing s/he assumed. For example, there are many accounts of very successful female berdache hunters (8).

The berdaches tended to be very successful in their ventures and very productive. This success and wealth is attributed to a number of factors including: the productive capacities of a male berdache-to-man marriage which did not need to raise offspring (8, 14); the claim that they had superior strength; their supernatural powers and, perhaps most significantly, their ability to combine men's and women's economic activities. Without the restrictions of the sexual division of labour, the berdache had great economic opportunities (6).

In some societies the berdache performed special services, often at birth or death. One of the most significant roles played by the berdache was that of mediator and intermediary between men and women in cases of disputes. This follows a tenet widespread in native American religions: Where there are polarities, there are mediators. These mediators hold the polarities together "to keep the world from disintegrating" (35).

Warfare

Berdache status has occasionally been associated with men who did not want to be warriors out of fear (i.e., the berdache as coward). The male berdache was frequently, but not always, excluded from warfare, which was, on the whole, a male-only activity. On the other hand, in many societies, male berdaches did fight, but wore men's clothing at this time. Sometimes they even had particularly significant roles in the "war complex," as they had special powers (amongst the Cheyenne Indians, for instance 15]). Female berdaches, it seems, took part in warfare to an even greater extent than non-berdache woman warriors.

Regardless of the extent to which berdaches took part in warfare, or of their specific relation to it, like their relation to other aspects of culture they were, in this respect, notably distinct from men or women.

Spiritual Aspects and Ceremonial

The spiritual power and position is the most difficult aspect of the berdache's role to understand because it requires understanding of, and contextualization within, Native American religious belief and ceremonialism. A rigorous description of this spirituality is beyond the scope of this paper and beyond the scope of my knowledge. Nonetheless, it is important to note the great significance of this aspect of life, and the spirituality of berdaches in particular, to traditional Native Americans. Williams (35), throughout his work, strongly emphasizes that the berdache's spirit, or spiritual essence, is considered to be the most salient aspect of their existence. Referring to Native American spirituality:

They have the greatest faith in dreams, by which they imagine that the deity informs them of future events, [and] enjoins them certain penances . . . I have known several instances of some of their men, who by virtue of an extraordinary dream, have been affected to such a degree as to abandon every custom characteristic of their sex and adopt the dress and manners of the women. They are never ridiculed or despised by the men on account of their new costumes, but are, on the contrary, respected as saints or beings in some degree inspired. (Early 19th century, Peter Grant, as cited in Williams 35)

These dreams or visions which "instruct" the person to become a berdache are very widely known and reported. For example, such vision experiences are described amongst the Winnebago and Iowa (22) and amongst the Santee Dakota and Potawatomi (19). The other primary, though less widespread, factor which is widely reported as preceding the assumption of berdache status is an unusual interest on the part of a child in the work and member of the "other sex." These two factors are neither contradictory nor mutually exclusive. In fact, they are often found in combination with each other, as well as with other forms of "recruitment."

Certain mythological figures could be considered to validate and, by association, valorize the role of berdache. Normally, though, the mythological figure was not a berdache, but an intersex or intersex twins born to first man and first woman (14). Real and mythological intersexes were strongly associated with berdaches. Consider for example, the Navajo distinction, as reported by Hill (14), between "real Nadle" (intersex) and "those who pretend they are Nadle." While this real vs. pretend Nadle represents an example of an application of the sex/gender distinction (perhaps third sex and third gender), it also draws attention to the difficulty of distinguishing sex (real) from gender (fake).

The ceremonial-religious role of the berdache overlaps with that of Shaman. Their responsibilities include mediation between the worlds of spirit and flesh (i.e., the physical and spiritual), healing and general responsibility for the welfare of the whole society. Shamans are not necessarily berdaches, but berdaches are usually considered to be powerful sorts of shamans. The Mohaves believed that women shamans were more powerful than men shamans and berdache shamans were more powerful yet. The berdache's ceremonial and spiritual roles involved them in very significant ways with almost every aspect of Native life (35).

CHARACTERIZING THE BERDACHE

The berdache institution has been variously described as, and confused with, intersex, institutionalized homosexuality, transvestism, gender crossdressing or transsexuals and gender-mixing. I suggest that all of these characterizations are a result of misunderstandings of the nature of the status resulting from an ethnocentric perspective that is unable or unwilling to conceptualize more than two sexes or genders. The writers come from a culture in which the gender and sex system is rigid and dichotomous. Gender attribution into one of two categories is taken for granted. When a puzzling gender role is presented, the Western writers have tried to fit it into their own sex/gender system and conceptualizations. They search for somewhat analogous categories in Western society and call it a match. The basic errors can be simply understood as ethnocentrism and can be avoided by understanding folk classification systems and the nature of the specific sex and gender construction in the societies in question. In doing so, I will hopefully arrive at a more appropriate gender attribution for the berdache.

Berdache as an Institutionalized Homosexuality
Devereux (8) and more recently Katz (16) are two of the people who conceptualize berdaches as an example of the institutional sanctioning of homoerotic behaviour. Devereux's belief in rigidly dichotomized gender role categories kept him from understanding that the berdache role is not synonymous with either the man or the woman gender role (18). Katz's political agenda of reclaiming and writing Gay American history may have been the motivation for his characterization of the berdache as homosexual.

There are two reasons to reject the homosexual characterization. First of all, as outlined earlier, a berdache's sexuality was highly variable. Neither same sex sexuality nor same gender sexuality is necessary correlate of berdachehood.

Secondly, if we accept that berdaches are neither men nor women but rather third and forth genders, the only berdache-berdache sexuality could be construed as homosexual and as noted, this did not occur. From this perspective, male berdache-man sexuality or female-berdache-woman sexuality are by definition heterosexual.

Berdache as Transvestite

Devereux (8) uses the terms "berdache" and "transvestite" inter-changeably. A great deal of the anthropological literature refers to berdaches as transvestites. There are several reasons that this is not an accurate characterization. Firstly, there are instances in which men dressed as women but were not berdaches. These cases were related to disgrace for cowardice in battle and have no relation to berdachehood (6, 22). Secondly, berdaches, as stated earlier, did not always wear the clothing of the "opposite sex." Furthermore, they frequently wore a combination of both men and women's clothing or even altogether unique clothing.

In the terminology outlined, a berdache's gender assignment and gender identity are consistent with each other but are *not* in contradiction with her/his choice of clothing. The berdaches choice of clothing matches her/his gender role or is an example of the great license (freedom of choice) that s/he (. . .) has and therefore berdache and transvestite cannot be considered synonymous.

Berdache as Intersex

Non-Natives, including anthropologists, have been so confused by the strange berdache role that they have sometimes mistaken berdaches with hermaphrodites. This term implies genitalia that are neither "properly" male or female. Berdaches have "normal" genitalia, as has been confirmed by curious and invasive whites. One possible reason for the confusion is linguistic. Natives sometimes characterize berdaches as "half-man/half-woman" or "half and half people." Combine this with Western gender construction's emphasis on physical traits—hair and body hair, breasts, genitalia—and we can understand the mistake. By contrast, the North American natives place far more emphasis on a person's spirit or spiritual essence, the physical body is secondary (35).

Another simple distinction between the berdache and the intersex is the physical/cultural distinction. Intersex status is permanent, berdachehood is not. Even amongst the Navajo, who explicitly recognize an intersex category as well as a berdache category, there is a distinction made. Intersexes are Nadle and berdaches are "those who pretend to be Nadle" (14, 23).

Berdachism and Transsexualism

Angelino and Shedd successfully steered away from the terms hermaphroditism and transvestism to arrive at the notion of gender crossing or transsexualism. They write that a berdache is a person who "assumes the role and status of the opposite sex" (1). Whitehead, more recently characterized berdaches as "gender-crossers . . . becoming a member of the opposite sex." She considers the transsexual in our society to be an appropriate analog (34).

While male berdaches sometimes do women's work and wear women's clothing, they do not bear children. They act as mediators between men and women, have special responsibilities and a distinct "spirit." It seems, therefore, inappropriate to assign them the status of transsexual, which essentially entails fulfilling all of the roles of the "other" sex.

At the root of this transsexual designation is the Western dichotomous view of sex and gender. There are two genders and they are "opposites." You must be one or the other. In our society, transsexuals (i.e., people whose gender assignments and gender identities do not match) often opt for surgery to establish this match. A berdache's gender assignment and identity do not conflict. The berdache's gender identity, though, *does* conflict with Euro-Western gender assignments.

Berdachism as Gender Mixing

Collander and Kochems refer to berdache as a kind of gender mixing or "movement toward a somewhat intermediate status" (6). This is a much more subtle definition than those discussed above. There is certainly some validity to this notion if we understand that berdaches take on some of the behaviour and roles of men and some of those of women. But if we alternatively view this not as "taking on" behaviours of men and women, but as "sharing" behaviours with men and women, then the term "mixing" becomes invalid.

Furthermore, the distinct behaviours and roles of the berdache (for example, their special spirituality and the very ability to "combine" activities) are all elements of the berdache status which are not "mixed in" from women or men.

The concept of gender mixing is another appropriate response from a gender dichotomizing perspective which is unable to perceive this institution outside the basic Euro-Western framework. On the other hand, the notion of mixing does entail the recognition of individuals who are not precisely equal to women or men.

CONCLUSION

As I have elaborated, the berdache has a combination of dressing patterns and sex assignment that is shared neither by men nor women. The combination of their sex assignment and their occupational roles are also distinct. Their position in the "war complex" is often distinct from the warfare role played by people with the gender assignment of man or woman. In their sexuality, berdaches, unlike men or women, never have sexual relationships with other berdaches. Their spiritual role, although overlapping with shamanism to some extent, is distinct in that berdaches act as mediators between women and men and sometimes perform specialized services that no one else could. Their spiritual powers are impressive and unparalleled. Linguistically, natives used different referents for berdaches than they did for ordinary men and women. Finally, living traditionalist natives and berdaches consider the spiritual essence of the berdache to be distinct from men's and women's, and unique. Therefore, they should be understood neither as women nor as men. Female berdaches are a third gender and male berdaches are a fourth. But if we follow some of the mythology, the berdache was the first gender. In fact a berdache was the first human, preceding not only European arrival in this land, but men and women as well.

Kessler and McKenna question the premise that gender is an inevitable dichotomy and argue that it is continuous. They conclude that "biological, psychological and social differences do not lead to our seeing two genders. Our seeing two genders leads to the "discovery" of biological, psychological, and social differences (18). This radical perspective asserts the primacy of gender attribution and has far reaching implications for all aspects of gender or sex research.

From the evidence of the berdache, there emerges the conclusion that gender as a bipolar classification system is a cultural construct. Berdaches should be understood as third and fourth genders and the sex/gender system should be understood as a way to divide up humanity. The full implications of this sort of argument for sex/gender studies and for Euro-Western (at least) feminism and feminist theorizing remain to be seen, but I would argue that the existence of the berdache, as well as other non-dichotomous gender systems cross-culturally,[13] strongly support certain feminist models for a sexually egalitarian society. The existence of third and fourth genders serve as strong buttresses in the construction of new models of sex and gender which eschew the basic dichotomies.

Amongst the fluorescence of new feminist ideas, particularly since the 1970s, is a stream of thought which I have referred to as "Gender Proliferation" (31). An ideal society within a gender proliferation model would not propose a "unisex" world (like that of some liberal feminist models), instead, a diversity of (gender) roles would be possible. An individual could hold "masculine" traits (e.g., objectivity, aggressiveness, rationality) and "feminine" traits (e.g., nurturing, responsibility, sensitivity) in any combination, including "pure" masculine or feminine. Given time, these traits would lose their gender associations and simply become gender-neutral traits to be adopted (or not) by individuals hodge-podge, mix-and-match or don't match if you prefer.

Gender proliferation is *not,* as the label might imply, specifically about adding third and fourth genders. It is about diversity. It proposes the abolition of a formula for both gender and genders, as well as the lack of a formula by which sex and gender are linked. Knowledge about radically different sex/gender systems in other societies can help inform and support such feminist models and goals for social change. This knowledge can serve to take us beyond the rigid dichotomous conceptions of sex and gender that are central to the organization of the Euro-Western patriarchal system.

NOTES

1. This paper was the winning entry of the 1991 Northeastern Anthropological Association Student Essay Competition, undergraduate category.

2. I would like to thank those who helped me in various ways while working on this paper: H. Bristol, R. Keesing and especially my insightful undergraduate friends.

3. Feminist analyses and discussions of gender-related dichotomies can be found, amongst others, in de Beauvoir (1940), Hein (1984), Ortner (1974) and Whitbeck (1984).

4. The cultural construction of "woman" and "man" has been fairly well explored in feminist writings and has been developed in cross-cultural perspective in Rosaldo and Lamphere (1974) and in Ortner and Whitehead (1981).

5. The number of distinctions, though, has been occasionally exaggerated due to the linguistic error of failing to distinguish prefixes and adjectives from nouns.

6. Brown (1984) and Atran (1990) each discuss "regularities" and "uniformities" in cross-cultural folk classification.

7. Keesing (1987) addresses the question of how cultural (i.e., folk) models can be portrayed as monolithic, idealized and normative.

8. Keesing (1987) discusses the questionable distinction of "folk" vs. "expert" models. A discussion of the concept of folk classification and its specific applications with respect to sex and gender can be found in Martin and Voorhies (1975).

9. My usage of this term differs from that of Rubin (1975) who coined it originally.

10. In "Compulsory Heterosexuality and Lesbian Existence," Rich (1980) argues that (within a Euro-Western framework at least) there is not much "choice" involved.

11. It should be noted here that the "female" and "male" labels used here, whether they were berdaches or not, are Native American (folk) sex categories. Amongst the Navajo, the Nadle, an intersex, was also recognized (Hill 1935:273). Geertz (1983) discusses the Nadle as a third sex.

12. The berdache status continues to exist in the late 20th century. In fact, Williams' *The Spirit and the Flesh* (1986) is, in part, based on the field research he carried out in 1980 interviewing and living with "real live" berdaches.

13. These include the "soft man" of the Chuckchee in Siberia (Bogoras 1907), the Mahu role in Polynesia (Levy 1971, 1973), the Hijras of India (Nanda 1990) and the Xanith of Oman (Wikan 1977), amongst others. See Williams (1986), Nanda (1990) and Schnarch (n.d. a and b) for comparative outlines and discussions.

REFERENCES CITED

1. Angelino, Henry, and Charles L. Shedd. 1955. A Note on Berdache. American Anthropologist 57:121–126.

2. Atran, Scott. 1990. Cognitive Foundations of Natural History. Cambridge: Cambridge University Press.

3. Bogoras, W. 1907. The Chuckchee Religion, Vol. 2. Leiden: C.S. Brill.

4. Bolin, Anne. 1987. Transsexualism and the Limits of Traditional Analysis. The American Behavioral Scientist 31:41–65.

5. Brown, Cecil H. 1984. Language and Living Things: Uniformities in Folk Classification and Naming. New Brunswick, NJ: Rutgers University Press.

6. Collander, Charles, and Kochems, Lee M. 1983. The North American Berdache. Current Anthropology 24(4):443–470.

7. de Beauvoir, S. 1940. The Second Sex. New York: Bantam.

8. Devereux, G. 1937. Institutionalized Homosexuality of the Mohave Indians. General Biology 9:498–527.

9. Donchin, A. 1984. Concepts of Women in Psychoanalytic Theory: The Nature-Nurture Controversy Revisited. In Beyond Domination, edited by Carol C. Gould. New Jersey: Rowman and Allanheld.

10. Firestone, Shulamith. 1970. The Dialectic of Sex: The Case for Feminist Revolution. New York: Bantam Books.

11. Frye, M. 1975. Male Chauvinism: A Conceptual Analysis." In Philosophy and Sex edited by Robert Baker and Fred Elliston, pp. 65–82. Buffalo: Promethus Books.

12. Geertz, Clifford. 1983. Common Sense as a Cultural System. In Local Knowledge. New York: Basic Books.

13. Hein, H. 1984. Liberating Philosophy: An End to the Dichotomy of Spirit and Matter. In Beyond Domination, edited by Carol C. Gould. New Jersey: Rowman and Allanheld.

14. Hill, W. W. 1935. The Status of the Hermaphrodite and the Transvestite in Navajo Culture. American Anthropologist 37:273–279.

15. Hoebel, E. A. 1960. The Cheyennes: Indians of the Great Plains. New York: Holt, Rinehart and Winston.

16. Katz, J. 1976. Gay American History: Lesbians and Gay Men in the USA. New York: Crowell.

17. Keesing, Roger. 1987. Models, "Folk" and "Cultural": Paradigms Regained? In Cultural Models in Language and Thought, edited by D. Holland and N. Quinn, pp. 369–393. Cambridge: Cambridge University Press.

18. Kessler, S. S., and W. McKenna. 1978. Gender: An Ethnomethodological Approach. New York: John Wiley and Sons.

19. Landes, R. 1970. The Mystic Lake Sioux. Madison: University of Wisconsin Press.

20. Levy, Robert. 1970. The Community Function of Tahitian Male Transvestism: A Hypothesis. Anthropological Quarterly. 44:12–21.

21. _____. 1973. Tahitians: Mind and Experience in the Society Islands. Chicago: University of Chicago Press.

22. Lurie, N. O. 1953. Winnebago Berdache. American Anthropologist 55:708–712.

23. Martin, M. K., and Barbara Voorhies. 1975. The Female of the Species. New York: Columbia University Press.

24. Nanda, Serena. 1990. Neither Man nor Woman: The Hijras of India. Belmont, CA: Wadsworth.

25. Ortner, S. 1974. Is Female to Male as Nature is to Culture? In Women, Culture and Society, edited by Michelle Rosaldo and Louise Lamphere, pp. 68–88. Stanford: Stanford University Press.

26. Ortner, S., and H. Whitehead. 1981. Sexual Meanings: The Culture Construction of Gender and Sexuality, edited by Shelley Ortner and Harriet Whitehead. New York: Cambridge University Press.

27. Rich, Adrienne. 1980. Compulsory Heterosexuality and Lesbian Existence. Signs 5(4):631–660.

28. Rosaldo, Michelle Z., and Louise Lamphere, eds. 1974. Woman, Culture and Society. Stanford: Stanford University Press.

29. Rubin, G. The Traffic in Women: Notes on the "Political Economy" of Sex. In Toward an Anthropology of Women, edited by R. R. Reiter, pp. 56–74. New York: Monthly Review Press.

30. Schnarch, Brian. n.d. a Gender Reduction and Gender Proliferation: Two Feminist Models Compared. MS.

31. n.d. b "Strange" Gender: The Mahu of Tahiti, the Hijras of India, the Berdaches of Native America and the

Xaniths of Oman. Western Sex/Gender Construction in Cross-Cultural Perspective. MS.

32. Stoller, R. J. 1968. Sex and Gender, Vol. 1. New York: J. Aronson.

33. Whitbeck, C. 1984. A Different Reality: Feminist Ontology. *In* Beyond Domination, edited by Carol C. Gould. New Jersey: Rowman and Allanheld.

34. Whitehead, H. 1981. The Bow and the Burden Strap: a New Look at Institutionalized Homosexuality in Native North America. *In* Sexual Meanings: The Culture Construction of Gender and Sexuality, edited by Sherry Ortner and Harriet Whitehead, pp. 80–115. New York: Cambridge University Press.

35. Williams, Walter. 1986. The Spirit and the Flesh. New York: Beacon Press.

ORIENTATION

Breaking the Mirror: The Construction of Lesbianism and the Anthropological Discourse on Homosexuality

Evelyn Blackwood

THE CONSTRUCTION OF LESBIANISM

Systems of gender, kinship and economy (as suggested by Adam, in this issue) affect the construction of both female and male homosexuality. Yet, the differential experiences of gender provide the basis for divergent lesbian and male homosexual patterns. In order to understand the cultural factors significant to the construction of lesbian behavior, the focus in this section will be on the female role and the contexts within which lesbian behavior appears. In particular it will outline the influence of differing gender systems and different levels of social stratification on the development of patterns of lesbian behavior.[1]

Putting aside cross-gender behavior for the moment, the construction of lesbianism, where it occurs, takes place within the sphere of female activities and networks. Women in all cultures are expected to marry and bear children: in many they are betrothed and wed before or soon after puberty. Consequently, for the most part lesbian behavior locates within the structure of marriage relations, but within that system a variety of sexual relations are possible.

The range of lesbian behavior that appears cross-culturally varies from formal to informal relations. These patterns may be described as follows. Informal relations among women are those which do not extend beyond the immediate social context. Examples of such would be adolescent sex play and affairs among women in harems or polygynous households. Formal lesbian relations are part of a network or social structure extending beyond the pair or immediate love relationship, and occur within such social relationships as bond friendship, sisterhoods, initiation schools, the cross-gender role, or woman-marriage. An examination of social stratification suggests that, in societies where women have control over their productive activities and status, both formal and informal relations may occur. Where women lack power, particularly in class societies, they maintain only informal lesbian ties or build institutions outside the dominant culture.

Non-Class Societies

In non-class societies, depending on the degree of economic autonomy of women, several patterns of formal and informal lesbian relations occur. These patterns can be found in both highly stratified states, such as those of the Azande and Dahomey in Africa, and the more egalitarian !Kung of southern Africa and the Australian aborigines. The patterns in each group result from cultural factors such as kinship regulations, the marriage system, trade rights, and sexual customs. Among the Azande the husband's kin arranged marriage by paying a brideprice to the wife's kin. The brideprice gave them the right to claim the offspring of the wife for their lineage. Wealthier men married several wives and built a dwelling in the compound for each wife. Wives were given a plot of land to cultivate, and they controlled the profits made from the produce through trade. Women married shortly after puberty, but as they fulfilled their duties as a wife, certain rights accrued to them. Consequently, despite the demands of the marriage system, some Azande women established formal lesbian relationships, often with their co-wives. According to Evans-Pritchard (20), "All Azande I have known well enough to discuss this matter have asserted . . . that female homosexuality . . . was practiced in polygamous homes in the past and still [19] is sometimes."

Azande women usually kept the sexual nature of their friendships secret from their husbands, who felt threatened by such activities, yet could not forbid them. Such relationships may have been fairly common for adult women in certain other African groups where marriage was polygynous, as among the Nupe (47), the Haussa (33), and the Nyakyusa (73). A relationship between two Azande women could be formalized through a ritual that created a permanent bond (20). This bond secured the emotional and economic support of the partner, and may have served to widen the trade network of the woman and possibly enhance her position in the community. Thus, both formal and informal relationships occurred within the context of marriage among women who were in daily contact through their domestic and trade activities. It indicated that male control of female activities did not extend to interactions and concerns between females.

In other non-class societies lesbian relations occurred in sex-segregated childhood and adolescent groups. Among the highly stratified Dahomeyans, adolescent girls prepared for marriage responsibilities by attending initiation schools, where, among other activities, they performed exercises in each other's presence to thicken their genitalia. It has been noted that they engaged in sexual activities on these occasions (30). Such activity was congruent with their school training and served to heighten awareness of their erotic responses. Among the egalitarian !Kung, girls engaged in sexual play with other girls before they did so with boys (63). In another egalitarian group, the Australian aborigines, adolescent sex play was an acknowledged and integral part of the social system. It conformed to the kinship regulations for marriage partners (56), occurring among girls who were cross-cousins. Thus, an Australian girl formed lesbian relations with her female cross-cousin, whose family would later give her to their son to marry, the girlfriends thereby becoming sisters-in-law.

In comparing the highly stratified social structure of Dahomey or the Azande to the more egalitarian Australian aborigines, the different constraints on lesbian behavior stand out. Herskovits (29) stated that the adolescent period for Dahomeyan women was an acceptable time for lesbian activity. Some adult women also engaged in it, probably in the context of polygynous marriages, but this was secretly done. Azande women also maintained clandestine relationships. Roheim (57) reported that married Australian women engaged in lesbian activities, one form of which was called *kityili-kityili*, ticking the clitoris with the finger. Although a woman's first marriage was controlled by her kin, she had the choice, following the death of her first husband, to engage in various marital and extra-marital relations (3, 4). While Dahomeyan women were forced to conceal their lesbian activities, the lesbian relationships of the Australian women were an acknowledged part of their sexual behavior and were included in ritual activities (32). Thus, different levels of social stratification and marriage systems shape different patterns of lesbian behavior in non-class societies.

Class Societies

The contrast in patterns of lesbian behavior is sharper between non-class and class societies. In those with rigid hierarchical gender systems women's sexual activities are strictly confined. Formal lesbian patterns do not exist unless they maintain a status marginal to the dominant culture. In such societies, with control of women's productive and reproductive rights vested in male kin, not only were women confined to heterosexual marriage, but also their sexual activities were restricted by law or custom to their marital partner. Islamic law called for imprisonment for homosexuality and death or divorce for a wife caught in adultery (45). In this context, lesbian behavior, if it occurred at all, was informal and private. Clandestine relationships developed among Near Eastern women in harems and within the Muslim institution of purdah. Wives of ruling class men rarely saw their husbands and therefore sought alternative sources of relationships. Some wealthy, educated Near Eastern women could choose to remain unmarried and found great satisfaction in lesbian relationships (1, 11, 67). Ultimately, the strict segregation of the sexes provided the only context for lesbian relations.

Conditions were similarly restrictive for Chinese women. The sisterhoods of Kwangtung province provide the only available evidence of lesbian relationships in China (62). This institution of bond friendship necessarily arose outside the traditional marriage and kin structure. Although still guided by the cultural values of the dominant society, these women rejected the traditional gender role to form sisterhoods based on the traditions of girls' houses and celibacy vows. The availability of silk work in Kwangtung province gave them the economic independence to refuse marriage. Some women did engage in heterosexual relationships because of cultural sanctions imposed on those who took non-marriage vows. Others formed lover relationships with a "sister" (61). Thus, in the class societies of the Near East and China the construction of lesbian relations showed two opposing trends: First, an informal pattern resulting from the restrictions of male-dominant institutions and, second, a sisterhood existing outside the social relations of the dominant culture and dependent on the success of female bonding and the tolerance of the larger society. This second type applies as well to the lesbian subculture of Western society in the last 80 years.

A formal pattern of age-graded lesbian relations appears in cultures with a dual economic system, such as black South Africa and Carriacou in the Caribbean. In both areas males participate in a capitalist wage-labor system through migration to industrial areas, while women work the land and direct the affairs of the household. On Carriacou husbands are separated from their wives for most of the year and at home are unable to command the exclusive attention of their wives. Older married women secure the affections and assistance of younger, often single women whom they support with income from the absentee husband (64). This relationship provides both economic and emotional support and is a viable alternative to the domestic isolation of the women. A similar pattern exists in South Africa, the mummy-baby game. It maintains the same functions of emotional and economic support as in Carriacou but the age range between women is smaller (8, 25, 46). Despite the imposition of a capitalist wage-labor system on these groups, its effects are mitigated through female bonding in mutually beneficial relationships. In South Africa these relationships may have derived from a traditional pattern of affective relations between older and younger women (25).

Cross-Gender Role

The cross-gender role for women constitutes another formal pattern of lesbian relations, which appears in certain classless societies and, in particular, in egalitarian societies. This role was institutionalized mainly among western Native American tribes and integrated into the social structure of the larger society. Five western tribes in which the cross-gender role has been observed at some length include the Mohave, Maricop, Cocopa, Kaska, and Klamath (10). Depending on their interest and ability, some women in these tribes took on the male gender role, usually at puberty, and performed duties associated with men, such as hunting, trapping, and, for Cocopa *warrhameh*, fighting in battle. These women were not denied the right to marry and frequently took wives with whom they established a household and raised children. The significance of the female cross-gender role lay in the ability of women to take on a male role regardless of their biology. Further, it was possible for them to cross roles without threatening the definition of the male role because men and women had equal status and occupied complementary rather than antagonistic gender roles (10).

In contrast to the flexibility of gender roles in egalitarian societies, class societies that have hierarchical gender systems define gender more rigidly. In such cultures the gender system is structured in a dichotomous fashion: neither sex participates in behaviors nor activities of the other. In male-dominant cultures such as western Europe or the Near East, it is impossible for women to assume a cross-gender role because such behavior poses a threat to the gender system and the very definitions of maleness and femaleness. Those who did, such as the passing women of western Europe, risked grave repercussions: if discovered, they faced serious punishment or even death (15, 21).

CONCLUSION

The construction of lesbianism shatters some basic assumptions about women which have been propounded in the discourse on homosexuality. The perception that men maintain universal hegemony over women's sexuality is contradicted by the data on alternative sexual relationships for women. Rubin (59) theorized that women were forced, through marriage, to be heterosexual and that this condition prevailed in all cultures. Others have subscribed to the concept of "enforced heterosexuality"; for example, Adrienne Rich has suggested lesbianism "comprises both the breaking of a taboo and the rejection of a compulsory way of life . . . a direct or indirect attack on male right of access to women" (54). In contrast to this analysis, the history of sexual relations is not one of total heterosexual dominance. The construction of sexuality in many non-class societies validated variant sexual behavior for women. Women's lives were not wholly constrained by the dictates of marriage and child-bearing, nor did they live in total submission to men. Other types of sexual relations existed both before and after marriage. As the Azande example shows, various formal and informal lesbian relations co-existed with marriage, giving women several options and avenues for control of their lives and sexual activities. In many tribal societies lesbian relations were not considered deviant nor were the women "breaking taboos": on the contrary, lesbian bonds were institutionalized and integrated into kinship and other social structures.

Social stratification and gender ideology may place serious restrictions on women's sexuality. The constraints of marriage and lack of property rights imposed on women in many societies apparently limits the development of non-marital homosexual behavior and institutions. These constraints, however, should not be construed to be the result of the "limitations" of the female's biological sex. Enforced heterosexuality is tied to women's lack of economic power and restriction of female activity to the domestic sphere. Further, the embeddedness of sexuality with gender roles in Western societies proscribes homosexual activity and defines women as male sex objects.

The barriers to female power and sexuality in modern society reside in the male-dominant ideologies of gender and sexuality. Nevertheless, as the Chinese sisterhoods exemplify, even within strongly patriarchal societies women are capable of forming alternative institutions that circumvent male control. Similarly, lesbians in the United States are now building their own institutions and kin structures as well as creating sexual ideologies in opposition to the dominant society (Lockard, this issue).

Patterns of lesbian behavior develop from the particular conditions of the female gender role and the types of constraints which arise from the subordinate status women occupy in many societies. These constraints establish patterns which in many cases diverge from those for male homosexual behavior and yet are not less critical to a general understanding of homosexuality. Hopefully, future research will provide a more balanced approach to the study of the construction of both female and male homosexual behavior.

NOTE

1. Gender systems can be drawn to roughly parallel levels of social stratification, i.e., increased stratification, increased inequality of the sexes, though any particular society will need much greater analysis than can be provided here. The analysis here is suggestive rather than definitive.

REFERENCES

1. Abbott, N. (1946). *Two Queens of Bagdad.* Chicago: University of Chicago Press.
2. Adam, B. D. (1985). Age, structure, and sexuality: Reflections on the anthropological evidence on homosexual relations. *Journal of Homosexuality.* II (3/4), 19–33.

3. Bell, D. (1980). Desert politics: Choices in the "marriage market." In M. Etienne & E. Leacock (Eds.), *Women and colonization* (pp. 239–269). New York: J. J. Bergin.

4. Bell, D. (1981). Women's business is hard work: Central Australian aboriginal women's love rituals. *Signs: Journal of Women in Culture and Society, 7,* 314–337.

5. Benedict, R. (1934). *Patterns of culture.* New York: Houghton Mifflin.

6. Benedict, R. (1939). Sex in primitive society. *American Journal of Orthopsychiatry, 9,* 57–573.

7. Berndt, R. M. & Berndt, C. H. (1963). *Sexual behavior in western Arnhem Land.* New York: Johnson Reprint.

8. Blacking, J. (1978). Uses of kinship idiom in friendships at some Venda and Zulu schools. In J. Argyle & E. Preston-Whyte (Eds.), *Social system and tradition in southern Africa* (pp. 101–117). Cape Town: Oxford University Press.

9. Blackwood, E. (1984a). *Cross-cultural dimensions of lesbian relations.* Unpublished master's thesis. Department of Anthropology. San Francisco State University.

10. Blackwood, E. (1984b). Sexuality and gender in certain Native American tribes: The case of cross-gender females. *Signs: Journal of Women in Culture and Society, 10.* 27–42.

11. Bullough, V. L. (1976). *Sexual variance in society and history.* New York: John Wiley and Sons.

12. Burton, R. F. (1956). Terminal essay. In D. W. Cory (Ed.), *Homosexuality, a cross-cultural approach* (pp. 207–224). New York: Julian Press (originally published 1886).

13. Callender, C. & Kochems, L. (1985). Men and not-men: Male gender mixing statuses and homosexuality. *Journal of Homosexuality, II* (3/4), 165–178.

14. Carrier, J. N. (1980). Homosexual behavior in cross-cultural perspective. In J. Marmor (Ed.), *Homosexual behavior: A modern reappraisal* (pp 100–122). New York: Basic Books.

14. Crompton, L. (1981). The myth of lesbian impunity: Capital laws from 1270 to 1791. *Journal of Homosexuality, 6* (1/2), 11–25.

16. De Cecco, J. P. & Shively, M. G. (1984). From sexual identities to sexual relationships: A contextual shift. *Journal of Homosexuality 9* (2/3), 1–26.

17. D'Emilio, J. (1983). *Sexual politics, sexual communities: The making of a homosexual minority in the U.S., 1940–1970.* Chicago: University of Chicago Press.

18. Ellis, H. & Symonds, J. A. (1975). *Sexual inversion.* New York: Arno Press (reprint of Studies in the Psychology of Sex, Vol. I. 1897).

19. Evans-Pritchard, E. E. (1933). Zande blood-brotherhood. *Africa, 6.* 369–401.

20. Evans-Pritchard, E. E. (1970). Sexual inversion amongst the Azande. *American Anthropologist, 72,* 1428–1434.

21. Faderman, L. (1981). *Surpassing the love of men: Romantic friendship and love between women from the Renaissance to the present.* New York: William Morrow.

22. Firth, R. (1936). *We, the Tikopia.* New York: American Books.

23. Fitzgerald, T. K. (1977). A critique of anthropological research on homosexuality. *Journal of Homosexuality, 2,* 385–397.

24. Ford, C. S. & Beach, F. A. (1951). *Patterns of sexual behavior.* New York: Harper and Brothers.

25. Gay, J. (1985). "Mummies and babies" and friends and lovers in Lesotho. *Journal of Homosexuality: II* (3/4), 97–116.

26. Gray, J. P. (1985). Growing yams and men: An interpretation of Kiman male ritualized homosexual behavior. *Journal of Homosexuality, II* (3/4), 55–68.

27. Herdt, G. H. (1981). *Guardians of the flutes: Idioms of masculinity.* New York: McGraw-Hill.

28. Herdt, G. H. (1984). *Ritualized homosexuality in Melanesia.* Berkeley: University of California Press.

29. Hershkovits, M. J. (1932). Some aspects of Dahomeyan ethnology. *Africa, 5.* 266–296.

30. Hershkovits, M. J. (1967). *Dahomey: An ancient West African kingdom* (2 vols.). Evanston: Northwestern University Press.

31. Hill, W. W. (1935). The status of the hermaphrodite and transvestite in Navaho culture. *American Anthropologist, 37,* 273–279.

32. Kaberry, P. M. (1939). *Aboriginal woman, sacred and profane.* London: George Routledge and Sons.

33. Karsch-Haack, F. (1975). *Das gleichgeschlechtliche leben der naturvolker.* [The homosexual life of primitive peoples.] New York: Arno Press (1st ed. Reinhardt 1911).

34. Katz, J. (1976) *Gay American history: Lesbians and gay men in the U.S.A.* New York: Thomas Y. Crowell.

35. Kroeber, A. L. (1925). *Handbook of the Indians of California.* United States Bureau of American Ethnology. (Bulletin 78).

36. Kroeber, A. L. (1940). Psychosis or social sanction. *Character and Personality, 8.* 204–215.

37. Layard, J. (1959). Homo-eroticism in a primitive society as a function of the self. *Journal of Analytical Psychology, 4.* 101–115.

38. Levy, R. I. (1971). The community function of Tahitian male transvestitism: A hypothesis. *Anthropological Quarterly, 44.* 12–21.

39. Lindenbaum, S. (1984). Variations on a sociosexual theme in Melanesia. In G. H. Herdt (Ed.), *Ritualized homosexuality in Melanesia* (pp. 337–361). Berkeley: University of California Press.

40. Lockard, D. (1985). The lesbian community: An anthropological approach. *Journal of Homosexuality, II* (3/4), 83–95.

41. McIntosh, M. (1981). The homosexual role, with postscript: The homosexual role revisited. In K. Plummer (Ed.), *The making of the modern homosexual* (pp. 30–49). Totowa, N.J.: Barnes and Noble.

42. Mead, M. (1935). *Sex and temperament in three primitive societies* (3rd ed.). New York: William Morrow and Co.

43. Mead, M. (1961). Cultural determinants of sexual behavior. In W. C. Young (Ed.), *Sex and internal secretions* (2 vols.) (pp. 1433–1479). Baltimore: Williams and Williams.

44. Metraux, A. (1940). *Ethnology of Easter Island.* Honolulu: Bernice P. Bishop Museum.

45. Minai, N. (1981). *Women in Islam.* New York: Saview Books.

46. Mueller, M. B. (1977). *Women and men in rural Lesotho: The periphery of the periphery.* Unpublished doctoral dissertation. Brandeis University.

47. Nadel, S. F. (1942). *A black Byzantium: The kingdom of Nupe in Nigeria.* London: Oxford University press.

48. Newton, E. (1972). *Mother camp: Female impersonators in America.* Englewood Cliffs, NJ: Prentice-Hall.

49. Opler, M. (1965). Anthropological and cross-cultural aspects of homosexuality. In J. Marmor (Ed.), *Sexual inversion: The multiple roots of homosexuality* (pp. 108–123). New York: Basic Books.

50. Padgug, R. A. (1979). Sexual matters: On conceptualizing sexuality in history. *Radical History Review, 20,* 3–23.

51. Plummer, K. (1981). *The making of the modern homosexual.* Totowa, NJ: Barnes and Noble.

52. Read, K. E. (1980). *Other voices: The style of a male homosexual tavern.* Novato, CA: Chandler and Sharp.

53. Reiter, R. R. (1975). *Towards an anthropology of women.* New York: Monthly Review Press.

54. Rich, A. (1980). Compulsory heterosexuality and lesbian existence. *Signs: Journal of Women in Culture and Society, 5.* 631–660.

55. Richardson, D. (1984). The dilemma of essentiality in homosexual theory. *Journal of Homosexuality, 9* (2/3), 79–90.

56. Roheim, G. (1933). Women and their life in central Australia. *Journal of the Royal Anthropological Institute of Great Britain and Ireland, 63.* 207–265.

57. Roheim, G. (1950). *Psychoanalysis and anthropology.* New York: International Universities Press.

58. Ross, E. & Rapp, R. (1981). Sex and society: A research note from social history and anthropology. *Comparative Studies in Society and History, 23,* 51–72.

59. Rubin, G. (1975). The traffic in women: Notes on the "political economy" of sex. In R. R. Reiter (Ed.), *Towards an anthropology of women* (pp. 157–210). New York: Monthly Review Press.

60. Rubin, G. (1984). Thinking sex: Notes for a radical theory of the politics of sexuality. In C. Vance (Ed.), *Pleasure and danger: Exploring female sexuality* (pp. 267–319). Boston: Routledge and Kegan Paul.

61. Sankar, A. P. (1978). *The evolution of the spinsterhood in traditional Chinese society: From village girls' houses to chai t'angs in Hong Kong.* Unpublished doctoral dissertation. University of Michigan.

62. Sankar, A. P. (1985). Sisters and brothers, lovers and enemies: Marriage resistance in southern Kwangtung. *Journal of Homosexuality. II* (3/4), 69–81.

63. Shostak, M. (1981). *Nisa, the life and words of a !Kung Woman.* Cambridge: Harvard University Press.

64. Smith, M. G. (1962). *Kinship and community in Carriacou.* New Haven: Yale University Press.

65. Sonenschein, D. (1966). Homosexuality as a subject of anthropological inquiry. *Anthropological Quarterly, 39* (2), 73–82.

66. Spencer, B. Sir & Gillen, E. J. (1927). *The Arunta* (2 vols.) London: Macmillan and Co.

67. Walther, W. (1981). *Women in Islam.* C. S. V. Salt, transl. Montclair, NJ: Abner Schram.

68. Weeks, J. (1981). *Sex, politics and society: The regulation of sexuality since 1800.* London: Longman.

69. West, D. J. (1977). *Homosexuality re-examined.* Minneapolis: University of Minnesota Press.

70. Westermarck, E. (1956). Homosexual love. In D. W. Cory (Ed.), *Homosexuality, a cross-cultural approach* (pp. 101–136). New York: Julian Press.

71. Whitehead, H. (1981). The bow and the burden strap: A new look at institutionalized homosexuality in native North America. In S. B. Ortner & H. Whitehead (Eds.), *Sexual meanings: The cultural construction of gender and sexuality* (pp. 80–115). Cambridge: Cambridge University Press.

72. Whitehead, H. (1984). *Discussion of gender-crossing.* Paper presented at the 83rd Annual Meetings of the American Anthropological Association, Denver.

73. Wilson, M. (1963). *Good company: A study of Nyakyusa age-villages.* Boston: Beacon Press.

74. Wolf, D. G. (1979). *The lesbian community.* Berkeley: University of California Press.

CHILDHOOD SEXUALITY

Excerpts from Defining Normal Childhood Sexuality: An Anthropological Approach

Suzanne G. Frayser

From the outset, the concept "normal childhood sexuality" raises questions of meaning: What is normal? What is childhood? and What is sexuality? Beyond questions of conceptual precision and theory are those about empirical research on the topic: What is the nature of available data on normal childhood sexuality? How reliable and valid are the empirical findings? To what populations do these data apply? To what extent can the array of findings be generalized? In addition, the very notion of normal childhood sexuality may arouse strong emotions in professionals and laypeople alike, based on their personal experiences of sexuality during childhood within the social and cultural context within which they were raised. (Ryan et al., 151, found that among 87 professionals who worked with abused children and their abusers, 43% reported instances of childhood sexual abuse, almost twice the 22% rate reported for the general population.)

However, relative to other research on child development and human sexuality, there is a paucity of *systematic* data on normal childhood sexuality. The available theory and research are scattered over a wide range of fields (e.g., biology, history, anthropology, psychology, psychiatry, sociology, social work, ethnology, and law), and much of it is dated. The paucity of data alone raises questions of why so little recent research is available on this topic, particularly in light of the current proliferation of claims about the deleterious long-term effects of child sexual abuse. Because definitions of abnormality and abuse usually relate to baselines of what is normal, data on normal childhood sexuality are conspicuous because of their scarcity.

Regardless of their discipline, investigators who have focused on sexual normality in childhood comment on this gap in empirical research. In his recent overview of childhood sexuality, Martinson concluded that "rational discussions of age-appropriate sexual behavior and research on human sexual development have scarcely begun" (104). Goldman and Goldman, in their review of the theoretical background for their cross-cultural study of children's sexual thinking remarked, "Sexuality in children is comparatively unresearched largely due to the cult of childhood innocence, usually defined as meaning sexual innocence, and a reluctance to admit sexuality as part of child development before the pubertal phase" (62). In Rutter's (148) review of the literature on normal sexual development, reference was made to studies that were anecdotal or based on small samples. Often, potentially useful information is ignored, perhaps because it is scattered in so many fields. Gadpaille (57) attempted to synthesize a wide range of information relevant to normal psychosexual development in *The Cycles of Sex*. In his preface to that book he commented, "There is not a single book for the professional or lay reader that attempts to correlate the vast interdisciplinary knowledge on psychosexual development" (p. xii). Few works approach the scale of Gadpaille's interdisciplinary effort, published almost 20 years ago.

Like other primates, humans rely on social life as a way to adapt to their environment. The long dependency period of children has brought with it new social forms—sharing of food, greater

Excerpts from "Defining Normal Childhood Sexuality: An Anthropological Approach," by Suzanne G. Frayser, reprinted from *Annual Review of Sex Research*, Vol. 5, 1994.

participation of males in ensuring the survival of their offspring, a sexual division of labor, and male/female pair bonding, at least long enough for children to survive (40). Because human infants cannot walk on their own or cling to their mothers as they move around, they need to be carried, intensifying the need for caretaking. As Harlow demonstrated in his research with nonhuman primates (68), mothers have to learn how to care for their infants, and touch plays a significant role in that process (122). Learning becomes even more important as a way for infants to adapt. Nonverbal communication with the mother and other caretakers, and then play (exploring and trying out new behaviors in a safe context), particularly with peers, are major ways that infants and children become acquainted with their social context and learn the skills to survive.

Just as the link between parents and children intensified in humans, so too did the ties between males and females (16). The nature of sexual interaction changed and with it emerged the distinctive aspects of human sexuality. The ovarian cycle was no longer marked by obvious alterations in female anatomy (e.g., a swollen sex skin around the genitals) during ovulation. Upright posture meant that the genitals shifted forward, assuming an anterior rather than posterior position. Males' genitals were more exposed and vulnerable, but females' genitals were less exposed and less easily observed. Consequently, males had to rely more on females' behavioral cues of readiness for sexual interaction than on visual inspection of genitals. There is some evidence to support the idea that females have a higher level of proceptivity (i.e., body movements, visual signs, nonverbal communication with gestures to elicit sexual behavior) than males (131, 141). Hrdy hypothesized that a female who is passive and uninterested in sex is *The Woman That Never Evolved* (74).

Learning began to play a larger role in sexual interaction, both in terms of partner recognition and variety of sources of sexual stimulation. Placement of the genitals on the anterior part of the body made face-to-face copulation easier than rear entry and facilitated the recognition of sexual partners. Partners could explore each other's body and stimulate skin and genitals with the sensitive tips of their fingers. Apocrine glands, sweat glands that occur only around hairy parts of the body (arm pits, groin, navel, behind the ears), produce odors that can be stimulating during sexual excitement and may have been an added inducement to body exploration (30). Human males rely on physical or psychological stimulation to obtain a penile erection, which can be facilitated by females who know how to enhance this stimulation. Females are able to have orgasms, providing a means for reinforcing the link to a partner. (Rancour-Laferriere [136] argued for the adaptive role of female orgasm; Symons [160] suggested that female orgasm has no real adaptive value, but only exists because of its adaptive role in males). During the process of human evolution, nonreproductive sexual activity increased to the extent that humans are sometimes called "the sexiest of the primates" (42). The disjunction between sex and reproduction is a particularly notable aspect of the human species. Unlike other primates, that go through a period of anestrus after offspring are born, human females retain an interest in sex after the birth of a child and are able to conceive again. This allows infants to be born in closer succession and increases the need for a male to participate in contributing to the survival of his children.

Two other characteristics complete the picture of the development of human childhood and human sexuality: culture and psychology. Cultural development went hand in hand with changes in anatomy and physiology—like the intertwined strands of a rope. Culture is a pattern of ideas and beliefs that give meaning to behavior; is shared; is learned; is passed down from one generation to the next (i.e., is traditional); is transmitted through symbols, particularly language; and can be explicit or implicit (92). Traditional ideas and beliefs, shared and communicated between individuals, provided another source of nonphysical adaptation for humans, one that could be learned by large-brained infants and children. Because culture itself has been so advantageous in the survival of humans, its transmission to children is a potential advantage to them. In addition, symbolic communication expanded the range of meanings that could be applied to behavior. This means that cultural ideas and beliefs can shape the meaning of sexual behavior and define the participants in and limits to that behavior. Finally, because humans are able to think about and reflect about their own experiences, individuals have the capacity to learn from themselves, not just from others. As Rancour-Laferriere (137) put it, "somehow in the course of hominid evolution enormously complex systems of signs . . . have managed to make the space between genes and behavior much larger than in any other creature on the planet" (p. 62).

All of these broad trends in human evolution have shaped what we can expect to happen during normal childhood sexual development. Based on the foregoing evidence, we can define childhood as a relatively long period of dependency on caretakers, characterized by an initial period of helplessness followed by an intensive period of learning in a social group. Normal learning includes how to interact with others in a group, how to love, how to be sexual, how to be a caretaker, how to follow social rules, and how to interpret behavior through cultural beliefs. The definition of sexuality includes biological, social, cultural, and psychological aspects, all of which are developing in a social context. An interpretation of a behavior as sexual does not depend upon its contributing to reproduction, since humans engage in a wide range of nonreproductive sexual activity.

THE DEVELOPMENTAL CONTEXT

Given the evolution of human sexuality, it would be surprising if children did *not* have an interest in or express sexual behavior, particularly because humans rely on learning to such a great extent and engage in as much nonreproductive sexual behavior. In this section, I review some of the available theory and empirical evidence about sexual development in prenatal development, infancy, and childhood based primarily upon research in western society. There are a number of major theories of child development that contain concepts that could be applied to sexuality in infancy and childhood (34, 84, 133). They are not, however, specific to sexual development per se but rather involve considerations of sociality (Erikson), cognition, intellect, and reasoning (Piaget), or moral development (Kohlberg). In contrast to what she regards as male-oriented views of child development, Gilligan offered the view that there are differences in male and female gender development that involve different world views and forms of decision-making (60).

Freud and many adherents of the psychoanalytic school of psychiatry (56, 144, 146, 175) offered more direct considerations of the role of sexuality in development, confronting the roles of emotion (e.g., desire) and body (e.g., oral, anal, and genital aspects) in shaping psychological attributes. In *The Cycles of Sex,* Gadpaille (56) presented one of the few attempts to integrate evolutionary, psychoanalytic, and cognitive theory as they apply to sexual development.

Money's (118) most recent synthesis of the current state of knowledge regarding the developmental sequence and differentiation of gender identity/role provides a rich reservoir of concepts and hypotheses to guide and to foster an integrated approach to normal childhood sexuality. The power of this approach lies in the use of concepts and data from psychology, biology, sociology, and anthropology to explain variations in gender and eroticism. Money's impressive body of research, much of it conducted while he was the director of the Office of Psychohormonal Research at Johns Hopkins Hospital and School of Medicine, is based on longitudinal and group studies of individuals assembled since 1951 and takes into account the complex intersection of variables that affect human sexual development from conception to puberty.

Martinson (103) gathered evidence that points to the emergence of the embryo's and fetus's "sensory capacity for erotic experience" (p. 58). He notes that one of the first sensory systems to function in the system is the skin, which is the main way that the embryo, as early as 6 weeks, experiences its life; it is responsive to pressure and touch and is stimulated by massage from the mother's movements. In addition to sucking and grasping reflexes, the fetus may engage in "purposeful autostimulation before birth" (p. 59) and is capable of genital erection and genital play.

Newborns and Infants (0–12/18 Months)

All of these prenatal developmental processes prime the fetus for sexual development after birth. External genitalia provide distinct insignia to label the bodies of males and females as different. Newborn females, perhaps still reacting to maternal estrogen, have prominent labia and a dull-pink vaginal lining, which change in size and color as the influence of the mother's estrogen subsides. Their labia become smaller, and the vaginal lining becomes bright red during the prepubertal periods of childhood (11). An imperforate hymen may be evident at birth as a "thin, bulging membrane" (11). Furthermore, the external genitalia are functional: Male erections and female vaginal lubrication are present from birth and may continue as spontaneous activities every 80 to 90 minutes during sleep throughout life (103).

Newborns are prosocial, not passive, even though they are dependent on their caretakers. They may even take the initiative in forming attachments with others (1, 103), a behavior that may be adaptive in ensuring that someone will protect them from danger and harm (12). The interface between sensuality, sexual potential, and social interaction is aptly illustrated by what is likely to be the child's first experience of social reciprocity—between the child and his/her mother during breastfeeding.

During breastfeeding, there is a pattern of interaction between the infant and the mother that facilitates nursing. The infant's sucking on the mother's nipple stimulates the pituitary to release oxytocin, which triggers the release of milk. The intense bodily involvement of the infant seems to be very sensual. At the very least, it includes auditory, tactile, visual, and olfactory senses. The infant relaxes after an ardent period of nursing. The bodily contact as well as the giving and receiving of milk can be sensual and possibly sexual experience for both mother and child (103). Penile erections as well as "oral orgasmic convulsions" (5) are seen in response to sucking, although it is not clear whether the sucking causes these responses. Conservatively speaking, the experience seems to be a pleasurable one for the infant. However, mothers are not likely to attribute the genital responses of the infant to eroticism, nor are they likely to interpret them as sexual (142).

It is tempting to speculate that the mother may derive sexual pleasure from breastfeeding because the neural pathways of sexual response to breast stimulation are the same whether the stimulation derives from a sexual partner or a breastfeeding infant. The release of oxytocin during breastfeeding also stimulates the uterus to contract, an attribute of sexual response. The refusal to acknowledge or frame the mother's experience of nursing in sexual terms may derive from the cultural distinction between the breast as an erotic organ and the breast as a nutritive organ for an infant. A scan of the medical literature indicates that the information about the breast during breastfeeding is focused on the nutritive properties of the milk for the infant, not on its potential as a source of erotic stimulation during breastfeeding (44). This separation between sexual and reproductive functions of the breast may also derive from the incest taboo, which prohibits sexual interaction between mother and child.

During the period of infancy, from 0–18 months, termed by Freud the "oral-phase," by Erikson, a period of "trust/mistrust," and by Piaget, "sensori-motor," infants become acquainted with their bodies, add to their sensual and erotic capacities, acquire a sense of others' responses to them, and learn to love (67). In addition to the mother-infant bond, reinforced by breastfeeding, there are other attachments that relate to the child's "need for protection and nurturance, as it is centered around the feeding experience and other bodily care situations" (23). Infants engage in attributes of adult sensory/erotic intimacy by hugging, kissing, clutching, gazing, vocalizing, stroking, sucking, and biting (103). Colonna and Solnit (23) commented on the meaning of infant sexuality in analytic terms:

> Conceptually, infant sexuality refers to the psychological role that the child's erotic experiences play in organizing the infant's dawning awareness of his/her body and certain of its functions. This takes place in the context of the infant's being helpless and dependent upon the life-sustaining care of the parent. Thus, sensuous gratifications are associated with the organization of personal rela-

tionships that are developed as the affectionate parent feeds, bathes, cleans, comforts, and plays with the child. (p. 1)

This context also becomes the basis for the infant to acquire a sense of others' attitudes toward his or her body, primarily through bodily rather than verbal communication. This may be the first step toward bodily acceptance or rejection, which affects body image.

In *Sexual Images of the Self,* Fisher (1989) discussed the "slow, zigzag process" of constructing a body map, which begins when children try to make sense of their body and give it meaning. Parents, reluctant to provide information about the genitals, unwittingly initiate a process of body distortion in their infants, who are "usually elaborately deceived and put off as they seek to define their genitality; . . . most children find it a formidable and puzzling task to decode what their genitals are about." (41)—a conclusion supported by ample research (8, 21, 24, 62, 89, 123, 142). Gadpaille asserted, "Sexual development does not occur separately from all other aspects of human growth and maturation. To treat it separately is to some degree a distortion" (56). Yet many caretakers in the United States have done just that—obfuscated the significance of sexual development by ignoring or denying genitalia as important parts of the body.

Infants experience a variety of sensations from their body (58). This is a continuation of the process begun prenatally, when the fetus experiences changes in pressure, movement, sound, and touch, much of it through the skin. Martinson (104) suggested that "the cutaneous stage" might appropriately capture the significance of this period. In exploring the body, the infant casually touches his/her body parts, including the genitals. Boys begin genital play (i.e., fingering or touching the genitals) at 6–7 months, girls at 10–11 months (103). The rhythmic manipulation of the genitals characteristic of masturbation does not occur until 2 1/2 to 3 years when small muscle control is more well developed (104). Rocking behavior at 6 months is an indirect source of genital sensation that precedes that child's ability to masturbate (94). Kinsey, Pomeroy, and Martin (82) reported that infants less than 1 year are able to experience orgasms; an infant female at 4 months and 7 males from 5 to 11 months of age were observed to have orgasms (82). They commented:

> The orgasm in an infant or other young male is, except for the lack of an ejaculation, a striking duplicate of orgasm in an older adult. . . . The behavior involves a series of gradual physiologic changes, the development of rhythmic body movements with distinct penis throbs and pelvic thrusts, an obvious change in sensory capacities, a final tension of muscles, especially of the abdomen, hips, and back, a sudden release with convulsions, including rhythmic anal contractions—followed by the disappearance of all symptoms. (p. 177)

Rutter also reported orgasm in infant boys as young as 5 months (148). Other researchers (66), however, have suggested that such responses are reflexive, resulting from mechanical stimulation; they may also result from a full bladder or bowel, strong sucking during breastfeeding, or frustration in not receiving adequate nourishment (155).

During the first 18 months, when the infant is exploring his/her own body and developing social relationships and attachments, the brain continues to grow to over 60% of its size, a 35% increase since birth (168). This underscores the significance of learning for the sexual development of human infants and the impact of caretaking during these early months of life outside of the womb. Martinson commented, "The highly emotional and physiologically charged interaction of parents and infants is an important phase in a child's sexual development" (104). The connection between the infant's awareness of his/her body and how adults respond to him/her and his/her body lays the foundation for the symbolic significance of the body in a social context and its psychological importance to the individual. Social anthropologist Turner suggested that much of the power of symbols stems from multiple layers of meaning, which derive from sensory and ideological poles of interpretation, which, in turn, have their sources in the body and the mind (161). The nonverbal communication of these early months may become a critical component of a child's attitude toward his/her body, his/her gender, and his/her sexuality.

Toddlers (12/18 Months–3 Years)

Identified by Freud as the "anal phase"; by Erikson, "a period of autonomy" and "doubt/shame"; and by Piaget as a "symbolic" period, when language and labeling occur, toddlerhood is a significant period of bodily exploration, developing relationships, and psychological awareness. Gadpaille said that the most significant experience of this period is the development of body autonomy—to be and to explore (56). Toddlers are curious about their own bodies and those of others (103). Roiphe and Galenson described an endogenously rooted "genital phase" that emerges early in the second year of life. It is characterized by psychological awareness of the genitals and reflects deliberate attempts to masturbate which are accompanied by signs of pleasure (e.g., giggling, smiling, affectionate gestures toward others) (144). In addition to manual manipulation of their penis, boys may lie on their stomachs or rub their genitals on an object to stimulate their penis; girls may place a soft toy or blanket between their legs, wiggle their pelvis, or place an object in the vagina (94). Progressive nerve myelinization in the sphincters of the bowel and bladder that occurs from 15–18 months significantly demarcates toddlers from infants and may result in pleasurable sensations from the enervation of the mucosa. All the while, specific reproductive development is proceeding slowly; secretions of FSH, LH, and sex steroids are low (140). The low level of activity in the pituitary allows the ovaries of girls to develop slowly and gradually through childhood (11).

Toddlers are interested in interacting with both peers and adults. There may be no major gender differences in playing with peers (75), although there may be sporadic sexual interactions. Spiro found that when children up to 3 years old played with each other, heterosexual behavior ranged from a simple embrace, to stroking, caressing, kissing, and touching the genitals—in that order (158). Toddlers like to look at and touch adults, particularly mothers and babies (103), and continue to engage in prosocial activities like helping or comforting peers, siblings, and parents (79).

Despite their rapid acquisition of language, children learn early that they should not talk about sex (2, 134); parents often sidestep accurate identification of genitals (41). Therefore, the nature of children's fantasy life about sex is difficult to ascertain, because they do not have nor are they encouraged to have the language to describe such experiences. Because children do not have as much experience to draw from as adults, their fantasy life may not be very rich (103). However, it is possible that enculturation may limit rather than expand the thoughts of children; if this is so, then children may have more creative and expansive fantasies than adults. At the very least, there is curiosity and thought about the body in conjunction with perceptions about adults' responses to it (62); both of these factors are integral to the development of gender identity (120).

Early Childhood/Preschool/Kindergarten (3–5)

Labeled "genital/Oedipal" by Freud, "initiative/guilt" by Erikson, "intuition/representational" by Piaget, and the beginning of "preconventional morality" by Kohlberg, early childhood is a time when children articulate their interest in sex by asking about physical differences between the sexes (e.g., the origin and function of body parts), reproduction (e.g., the role of the father, the origin of babies, the process of birth, pregnancy and the growth of the baby), and relationships (e.g., marriage) (69). Concomitantly, they are learning limits to touching their bodies and those of others. Lewis reports that 3- and 4-year-old children are socialized away from contact with their own bodies and those of others (95), particularly the bodies of their parents (9). Therefore, this time of intense interest about bodies is also a time when parents define and limit body parts that can or cannot be touched in interaction—verbally and nonverbally communicating a body map with acceptable and unacceptable areas of touch. In addition, children are learning more than rules about touch. They are learning about the symbolic limits on intimacy and affectionate relationships as expressed by touch. Parents may experience discomfort from too much touching and therefore curb it in their children (142). Yet the "absence of infantile and childhood sex activity, principally masturbation, disrupts . . . aspects of essential ego formation" (56). Parents may also continue to restrict conversation about sex even though both boys and girls are asking about sex by age 5 (148). This accentuates the discomfort communicated nonverbally during infancy and the verbal reticence about sex acquired as a toddler. Negative labeling (e.g., the parent labels his/her perception of sexual parts or behaviors as bad), nonlabeling (e.g., the parent gives the child no vocabulary for sexuality that allows him/her to develop concepts and values), and mislabeling (e.g., the parent warns the child of a harmful effect of sexuality that is unrelated to sex) can deprive the child of a way to evaluate his/her own development because he/she is not able to accurately label and discuss it (56).

Nevertheless, young children continue to engage in sexual activity and express an interest in it. Money and Ehrhardt (120) said that between ages 3 and 6 is the "developmental stage when children can be outrageously flirtatious and seductive, impersonating mannerisms of parents, older siblings, television actors, or whoever" (p. 192). Rutter (148) reported that female preschoolers are involved in thigh rubbing and that boys and girls engage in undressing or sexual exploration games by age 4. Genital interest and play continue to be common in the 2–4-year-old group. Parental attitudes and children's experience of sex may be in conflict, adding to the child's confusion about how to deal with body parts and what attitude to have about them and him/herself for having them. Money and Lamacz (121) have pointed to the potential damage that can result from a caretaker's denial, inhibition, or punishment of sexual behavior: vandalized lovemaps. Like other primates, children engage in sex play as a safe rehearsal for adult activities. Experiences between the ages of 5 to 7 may be critical periods of learning that are incorporated into one's lovemap. If the learning is distorted, then paraphilias may develop, which are resistant to change later in life.

Middle Childhood (6–12)

Termed "latency" by Freud, "industry/inferiority" by Erikson, "concrete operational" by Piaget, and "conventional morality" (from 10–13) by Kohlberg, this is a period of physical and mental growth. There are increases in the secretion of FSH and LH, in the responsiveness of the gonads to FSH and LH, and in the secretion of gonadal hormones (140). These hormonal changes may result in menarche in girls and the capacity for boys to ejaculate (103). The timing of these events, however, may vary according to the individual. Most girls do not menstruate until they are 12 or 13, and boys are not usually capable of ejaculation until 13 or 14 (62).

The sexual repertoire increases for these children. Boys are able to have erections quickly and in response to a variety of erotic (e.g., talk about sex, pictures of nude females, films, nude art) or nonerotic (e.g., fear, excitement) stimuli (136). Masturbation is more common among boys as their age increases: Ramsey reported that 14% of the 8-year-olds he studied masturbated, and 73% of the 12-year-olds. However, this seems to be less common among girls.

Children experiment with partnered sex. They prefer sex play with peers rather than people older than they (25). Rutter said that 25–30% of 13-year-old boys reported at least one instance of same-sex play in the few years before then (148). Kinsey et al. (82) reported that by 12, one boy in every four or five had at least tried to have intercourse with a female, and that only one girl for every seven boys was having heterosexual sex play as they neared adolescence (83). Broderick and Fowler (13) reported that preadolescent boys engage in more sex play of every kind than girls.

In addition to more physical changes and experimentation with partners, children may become aware of themselves as sexual beings and of their peers as potential partners—erotic or affectional (103). As Martinson pointed out, "sexual-erotic responses and encounters occur more commonly than previously thought," and the "sexual, psychological, and social changes that begin during these years and mature later are essential to the transition to full adult sexual functioning" (p. 74). The capacity for abstract thought, however, does not develop until age 11 or 12 (57). Thought may be more focused on concretely experienced objects (57).

Emotional involvement with peers may develop in the form of crushes and attachments outside of the family. It is interesting that this coincides with the development of reproductive maturity and complete brain growth. Yet children learn to conceal their interest in their bodies and in sex according to cultural standards (54). Even though they have many names for the genitals, children may not use them because they regard them as dirty (24).

Conclusion

Martinson pointed out in his important 1991 article, "Normal Sexual Development in Infancy and Early Childhood," that infants and small children have the physiological capacity for sexual response, that they are curious about their bodies and the bodies of others, and that they are attracted to intimate interaction with others have been established. With modeling, encouragement, and education there appears to be no need for a cessation of sensory/sexual activity from first discovery through childhood. The capacity for sexual response is very much shaped by experience" (p. 79). Friedrich et al.'s (34) study of the relative frequency of a variety of sexual behaviors among a sample of apparently healthy 2- to 12-year-old North American children with no history of sexual abuse confirmed the variety of sexual behaviors in which children are engaged.

The preceding data uphold the conclusion that human sexuality includes a process of development that begins with prenatal development and continues through infancy and childhood. As Moll pointed out decades ago, sexuality does not begin with reproduction (113), but in childhood, shortly after birth. Martinson's research, as well as Money's, bolsters this early finding by documenting the ways in which sexual development occurs before birth. The question remains as to whether the preceding developmental findings apply across cultures. Cross-cultural evidence is needed to compose an answer.

THE CROSS-CULTURAL CONTEXT

Developmental theories, like other scientific theories, are generated by scientists who are influenced by the cultural context in which they operate. Likewise, the selection of research issues, definition of concepts, and collection of data relevant to research topics is filtered through a cultural lens. Consequently, theory and research that purport to be universal in their applications may relate to a specific cultural context rather than generalize to *human* development—despite the best intentions and "objective" measures of the researchers.

Cross-cultural research provides checks and balances to culture-bound research and conclusions. It presses us to define and to optionalize concepts so that they can be identified in a variety of social and cultural contexts, to consider the range of variation in behavior and its meaning, to examine the effect of the investigator's point of view on the conceptualization of an issue and relevant data, and to question whether current theories are really applicable to all humans. These considerations are crucial in investigations of normal childhood sexuality.

Cross-Cultural Findings on Childhood Sexuality

Infancy and early childhood. Prominent sex researchers have pointed out the importance of an individual's body image to his/her developing sense of gender identity (118, 120) and adequate sexual functioning during adulthood (41). Developmental theories emphasize the significance of early social contacts and nonverbal communication, particularly touch, to later psychological development. Rohner (143) highlighted the active role of the infant and child in perceiving events around him/her—the phenomenological experience—and assessing whether another is being accepting or rejecting toward him/her. Therefore, the "objective" behavioral indications of warmth may not be construed as affection by all children. Like Herdt and Stoller, Rohner suggested that scientists include subjective aspects of human behavior in their accounts. Noting that humans engage in "near universal" behaviors, which always have exceptions, he postulates that "children everywhere have a phylogentically acquired tendency to respond in specific ways when warmth, affection, love, or other forms of positive response are withdrawn from them by the people most important to them" (143). Harlow's research reinforced the assertion that humans learn to love, beginning at a very early age (67).

Systematic cross-cultural data on infancy and early childhood (6), traits inculcated in childhood (7), agents and techniques for child training (1), and sociocultural aspects of the sexual and reproductive cycles (45) provide information pointing to some general trends in behavior that can affect a child's experience of his/her body. (All of the studies by Barry apply to a worldwide, standard cross-cultural sample [SCCS] of 186 cultural groups. Frayser's study applies to a subsample of 62 cultural groups from the SCCS.)

Among mammals in general and humans in particular, the first social interaction of an infant is usually with the mother—shortly after birth and during breastfeeding. Most societies (77% of 47) provide a special place where the woman will give birth, often in a partitioned area of the dwelling where she usually lives (23% of 47); other arrangements include going to a place near where she lives or to a place removed from most social activity (13% of 47), to a special structure for giving birth (23% of 47), or to the home of a kinsperson (17% of 47), usually a consanguineal relative (45). It is not unusual for other relatives to be present, including the husband and/or maternal kin. For example, female attendants accompany a Nicobarese woman to a birth house outside of the village area and help provide for her. Her husband also shares responsibility for caring for her (45). When a Palauan woman gives birth, one of her close relatives—a mother, sister, mother's sister—attends her in their home. Her 5 to 10 day confinement includes daily bathing and rubs with tumeric and coconut oil by a midwife, as well as a steambath on her final day of seclusion. (See Jordan, (81) for a cross-cultural investigation of birth in Yucatan, Holland, Sweden, and the United States.) Raphael (138) claimed that "mothering" the mother facilitates breastfeeding by lowering anxiety about how to proceed. Psychological stress can inhibit the release of prolactin and oxytocin from the pituitary gland, thus hampering the production and release of milk. Social support also allows the mother to devote more relaxed attention to her infant.

Several other practices demonstrate the priority given to the mother/infant relationship. An analysis of Barry and Paxson's data (6) shows that weaning occurs between 24 and 36 months in most societies (45% of 166 societies). In many (35%), it occurs after 3 years of nursing but only in some (20%) does it take place before 24 months (55). In addition to the body contact entailed by several years of breastfeeding is the contact between the infant and the mother while they sleep. Of 126 societies surveyed by Barry and Paxson (6), none separated the sleeping area of the infant from that of the caretakers. Infants always slept in the same room with their mothers, often in the same bed (65% of 126 societies) (45). Fathers often slept in the same room as their infants (67% of 119), but not usually in the same bed (19% of 119) (45). Sleeping with the infant not only provides further body contact with him/her but also makes it easier to breastfeed during the night without the mother losing much sleep. Finally, an analysis of Barry and Paxson's data (6) on body contact (a measure of the proportion of the day when the baby is held or carried by any caretakers) shows that few societies limit body contact with the child to routine and precautionary care or to only occasional contact, either during the first few months (15% of 129) or during the period when the infant can crawl, at about nine months (14% of 124) (Frayser, 1994b). More typical is for caretakers to hold or carry the infant up to half of the time (28% of 129 in early infancy; 36% of 124 in later infancy) or more (39% of 129 in early infancy, 36% of 124 in later infancy) (47). In some societies (18% of 129 in early infancy; 14% of 124 in later infancy), caretakers hold or carry the child almost constantly.

Attitudes toward the infant's body may be reflected in practices of covering the genitals. An analysis of Barry and Paxson's data (6) shows that caretakers in most societies do not cover the child's genitals until very late in the transition from infancy to childhood (59% of 155). Some do it late (e.g., after the child can walk well [10% of 155]), but some do not do it at all, in instances where adults are naked or uncovered (7% of 155) (48). Most of these societies are in the insular Pacific, sub-Saharan Africa, and South America. Nevertheless, almost a quarter of the societies (23% of 155) cover the genitals at or shortly after birth. Most of these groups are in the Circum-Mediterranean, Asia, and the northwest coast of North America (48).

There is little systematic documented evidence about the attention given to the sexual behavior of infants and young children. This may indicate an absence of the behavior or an investigator's omission in reporting it. The latter possibility is more likely, given Western biases about childhood sexuality. However, such information may be found scattered in ethnographies or in sections of edited volumes dealing with broader topics. For example, in his overview of adult and nonadult sexual behavior in traditional Hawaii, Diamond (29) described social attention to the sexuality of infants and small children. Nudity of children was common, and genitals were covered only when pubic hair began to show. Rather than a gesture of modesty, this was regarded as a sign of respect for the genitals and protection for the organs that would produce children. Entire families would bathe or swim together nude, often several times a day. Diamond commented that nudity did not have sexual significance. Rather, it was a convenient adaptation to the warm climate.

The genitals and sexuality were held in high regard by the traditional Hawaiians. Stone carvings or formations resembling genitals were thought to enhance fertility or sexual ability. An infant's genitals were named, and respectful, affectionate songs and stories were composed about them to highlight social pride in their role in life. To prepare for subincision of the penis when he was 6 or 7, a boy's aunt or grandmother blew into the foreskin of his penis every day from the day he was born. This practice was thought to ensure good health, satisfactory intercourse, and facilitate subincision by making the foreskin easier to slit. Female relatives of girls (e.g., a mother, grandmother, or aunt) began to prepare them at birth for sexual relations later in life. The mother squirted her breast milk into her infant's vagina and pressed the labia together, a practice that continued through infancy. The infant's female relatives would also try to flatten the vulva with the palm of their hand and mold it so that the labia did not separate. Suggs reported a variation of this practice in the Marquesas, where female caretakers stretch the labia minora of a young female to make them longer (159). Buttocks of infant males and females, which were regarded as related to sexuality, and the genitals were molded so that they were rounded, not flat. Diamond commented that "all of the practices discussed in relation to the preparation of the genitals exemplified adult/nonadult behavior that was not seen as being erotic, sexual, or abusive. It was seen as being an appropriate aspect of adult care of nonadults, a necessary chore" (29).

Restrictions on other activities channel more attention to the interaction between the mother, the infant, and sometimes the father. Postpartum restrictions, which variably apply to the mother, the child, and the father, structure the period after birth and may aid in psychological adjustments of the parents to the baby and the baby to the parents. Usually postpartum restrictions emphasize the welfare of the child (35% of 37 societies) or the child and the mother (38% of 37) rather than the mother alone (8% of 37) (45). Extension of the restrictions to include the father occurs in many societies (59% of 47) (45). Restrictions may include spatial separation from others, cessation of domestic duties, and rules about food intake and other behavior. Usually these postpartum restrictions do not last long. In most societies (41% of 50 societies), a woman resumes her domestic and economic duties within a week after birth, but many societies extend the postpartum restrictions longer (2 to 4 weeks in 12% of 50; 1 to 2 months in 12% of 50; more than 2 months in 6% of 50) (45).

Of major significance may be the postpartum sex taboos prohibiting the new mother from engaging in sexual relations for a specified period after the birth of a child. This can have the effect of focusing attention on the child rather than the husband. It may also serve to structure the potential conflict between sexual and reproductive behavior, and it may function as a form of birth control to space births. Analysis of Barry and Paxson's data (6) shows that most societies (93% of 41) have post-partum sex taboos, and the period of abstinence lasts less than a year (68% of 41). Usually the taboo is in force for 1 to 5 months (34% of 41) (48). However, many societies (32% of 41) extend the taboo beyond a year, and some extend it beyond 2 years (15% of 41).

The overall theme that emerges from these data is that caretakers are concerned with nurturing infants. Body contact with the mother is likely to be frequent—during sleep, during breastfeeding, and during the daily routine. The baby's genitals are not likely to be covered up. Analysis of Barry and Paxson's 1971 data on general indulgence (a measure of all relevant aspects of treatment and care, in particular, expressions of affection and permissiveness, and the consistency and effectiveness of nurturance and care) supports this conclusion (48). Caretakers in most societies (92% of 120 societies) treat infants with gentle, affectionate concern, although this theme persists to a lesser degree into early childhood (up to the ages of 4 or 5), when caretakers in quite a few societies (20% of 136) display harsh treatment toward their children.

Korbin (87), however, suggested caution in interpreting cross-cultural information on child maltreatment or neglect because most cross-cultural researchers have not focused their research on these topics. Like information on childhood sexuality, data on parental mistreatment or neglect are sparse and are derived from descriptions of other topics. Concentration of researchers, particularly anthropologists, on acceptable, normative behavior rather than deviations from norms may account for the paucity of information (88). Korbin's *Child Abuse and Neglect: Cross-Cultural Perspectives* (87) demonstrates the importance of articulating useful definitions of child abuse and neglect and of identifying social and cultural factors that increase or decrease the likelihood that maltreatment of children will occur. These factors include the cultural value of children, beliefs about specific categories of children, beliefs about age capabilities and developmental stages of children, and embeddedness of child rearing in kin and community networks (87, 88).

The importance of structuring the treatment of children according to cultural beliefs is highlighted by the existence of incest taboos in every human society about which we have information, although the strength and extent of their application to specific people varies. Since the 19th century, many social and behavioral scientists (e.g., 4, 28, 31, 32, 37, 43, 49, 50, 98, 110, 124, 130, 147, 152, 162, 166, 172, 173) have turned their attention to an explanation of the origin and persistence of incest taboos in human societies. Until recently, few investigators have concentrated on descriptions of the incestuous behavior itself. Furthermore, current information about incest in the United States is skewed toward its harmful effects, because inferences about its consequences are inferred primarily from clinical populations rather than representative samples of the population at large. Cross-cultural data about the existence of incest taboos and social responses to incest demonstrate that incest is not regarded as normal childhood sexual behavior in most societies (22, 45, 126). Therefore, its relevance to this discussion is confined to understanding the significance of specifically avoiding certain types of sexual behavior and relationships with relatives.

Definitions of incest vary and have expanded over the last 100 years in the United States to include a wide range of sexual activities between relatives, regardless of whether intercourse has occurred. It is important to keep in mind that the incest taboo is a prohibition on *sexual relations* between kin of a specified category; it is a *sexual taboo, not a reproductive one,* although it can have reproductive consequences if violated during the reproductive life of one of the participants. Concentration on its biological effects draws attention away from its cultural power and psychological impact. For example, rarely do investigators mention the possibility of same-gender incest, concentrating instead on heterosexual relations that conform more readily to a reproductive model of sexual relations. Such a conceptual framework ignores the consequences of sexual relations between same-gender kin. Incest taboos are the earliest cultural edicts about appropriate sexual partnerships and behavior that apply to a child, and they are unique in their lifetime application to the specified kin, including nonreproductive phases of life such as childhood.

The social significance of incest taboos is indicated by the types of punishments that different societies mete out for violation of the taboo. In most societies (62% of 29), punishments are severe (e.g., death, mutilation, expulsion from the community) or are thought to extend beyond the individuals involved and affect the well-being of their kin, children, or community as a whole (45). Yet some groups only confer mild (e.g., temporary disapproval, mild ostracism in 28% of 29) or moderate (e.g., whipping, extended ostracism in 10% of 29) punishments when taboos are violated (45). In general, the punishments are either very mild or very severe, demonstrating the great variability of social involvement in these behaviors.

Cohen (22) distinguished two aspects of incest taboos—the core taboo, which applies to all individuals in the nuclear family (mother, father, their children) with the exception of husband and wife, and the extended taboo, which includes any relatives beyond the nuclear family. Not all core taboos are applied with equal force to all individuals within the family 45), and all societies extend core taboos to include other relatives. The patterning of extended taboos indicates the significance of having incest taboos.

The cross-cultural studies of Murdock (126), Cohen (22) and Frayser (45) confirm an extremely high association between the type of extended incest taboo and the form of kinship organization (i.e., the way in which the group organizes the definition of people as relatives). Only rarely (1 of 41 societies studied by Frayser) are nonkinship extensions (e.g., household members, communities) a basis for extensions of the incest taboo. Matrilateral extensions (i.e., those on the mother's side) occur most often (7 of 9 societies or 39%) in matrilineal societies. Patrilateral extensions (i.e., those on the father's side) occur most often (6 of 7 societies or 86%) in patrilineal societies. Nonlineal extensions are present most often in societies with bilateral, ambilineal, or double descent (19 or 25 societies or 76%) (45). Because the definition of kinship is a purely cultural matter, biological explanations do not suffice to explain extended incest taboos. More likely is an explanation relating to the social, cultural, and psychological anchoring of the individual within a group, regardless of his/her gender orientation or reproductive capabilities.

Cohen's (22) cross-cultural research on the prevalence and patterning of incest taboos led him to generate hypotheses centering on the social and psychological implications of incest taboos, all of which are relevant to understanding cross-cultural variations in childhood sexuality. His interpretations focus on two main themes: (a) the individual need for privacy and (b) the nature of boundary-maintaining groups. Individuals establish their social and psychological identity within social networks, the earliest and most immediate of which are their family and kinship groups. These boundary-maintaining groups foster close social ties between individuals, regardless of how they feel about each other. Societies depend upon these groups for a variety of social functions, particularly socialization of children into the rules of the society and culture. Because the social ties are so close, these bonds could threaten an individual's privacy, which is needed to maintain a psychological boundary from others and buffer the individual from extreme emotional and physical stimulation. Incest taboos apply directly to members of the boundary-maintaining group and prohibit the added intimacy of specific kinds of sexual relations to the ties already in existence. Therefore, they serve to maintain psychological boundaries of the individual and social boundaries within the group. Overall, Cohen's conclusions point to the significance of incest taboos in maintaining the child's bodily integrity, free from intrusion by adults. This allows the child to differentiate himself/herself from others and to develop a sense of gender identity, apart from caretakers who already occupy a major role in his/her life.

What is defined as acceptable sexual behavior between relatives and what is not, however, varies a great deal across societies. Likewise, what is defined as incestuous is likely to vary as well. The previously described cross-cultural findings on infancy and early childhood show that infants are likely to receive nurturance, close and extended body contact with relatives, and acceptance of their bodies. In the section on evolution, I noted the importance of play as a significant aspect of child development (i.e., the ability of the child to explore the environment, whether physical or social, in a context of safety). Cohen's (22) hypotheses suggest that incest taboos define a context of social and psychological safety for the child, within which he/she can explore social roles and psychological identity. This cultural safety net probably also includes the option to safely explore a variety of sexual behaviors during childhood, depending upon the overall degree of sexual and reproductive restraint in the society.

Middle and late childhood. There are few monographs that focus on normal sexual practices during childhood. (See 65, 73, 96, 99, 106, 107, 108, 109, 111, 159 for some extensive descriptions of sex during childhood within a single social context.) Herdt commented that "ethnographic studies suggest, above all, an urgent need for new research on sexual development in children and adolescents across cultures" (73). However, there are systematic descriptions of different sexual practices during childhood drawn from a wide range of ethnographic sources. They are usually included in monographs focused on cross-cultural aspects of sexuality (42, 45, 64, 99, 165); in books dealing with broader topics, such as child training (169, 170), adolescence (153), masculinity (61), homosexuality (10, 71, 171), sex roles (125), or gender (127, 145), or in works related to sexuality with individual chapters on childhood sexuality in different cultures (26, 35, 56, 132, 174, 175). It is from these sources that the following specific examples of sexuality in middle and later childhood are derived.

As discussed in the section on the evolution of human sexuality, sex is not reproduction, and the identification of the two as one kind of behavior is a matter of cultural definition, not biological fact. Humans engage in a wide range of nonreproductive sexual activities, and many of these occur during childhood. Ford and Beach (42) generalized, "Where permitted to do so, children gradually increase their sexual activities both as they approach puberty and during adolescence" (p. 190). They concluded from their review of the cross-species and cross-cultural evidence that

> tendencies toward sexual behavior before maturity and even before puberty are genetically determined in many primates, including human beings. The degree to which such tendencies find overt expression is in part a function of the rules of the society in which the individual grows up, but some expression is very likely to occur under any circumstances. (p. 198)

The developmental information in the last section confirms this assertion, as does the cross-cultural evidence pertaining to middle and later childhood, when groups pay more overt attention to sex differences and rules regarding specific sexual behaviors in which children may engage.

According to an analysis of data from Barry et al. (7) on traits inculcated in childhood, it is more usual (67% of 157 for boys, 58% of 157 for girls) for societies to establish sexual restraint mildly (measure of taboo or restrictions on heterosexual play, masturbation, or other erotic activity) during early childhood than to impose strong restrictions then (48). The emphasis shifts, however, during later childhood to moderately strong (50% of 164 for boys; 47% of 166 for girls) or very strong (4 % of 164 for boys; 22% of 166 for girls) training in sexual restraint (48). Overall, girls are more subject to this training than boys. Differences in ratings on sexual restraint are either the same for boys and girls or showed that girls were trained more strongly in sexual restraint, whether during early or late childhood. These findings are consistent with restrictions placed on men and women after puberty. Generally, sexual restrictions apply with equal force to men and women, but when there is a double standard, women's sexuality is restricted whereas a man's is not (45). Preparation for restrictions later in life may be related to the pattern of restraint found in childhood. If we assume that there is some coherence in human social organization and that human development dovetails with its social organization and culture, this makes sense. Ford and Beach (42) noted that

> a double standard during late childhood and adolescence is characteristic of many societies, but not of human beings in general . . . most other societies that discourage infantile and childhood sex play also attempt to control premarital experimentation in sexual matters on the part of adolescents or young adults. (p.185)

There is wide variation in parents' attitudes toward children expressing sexual interest or engaging in sexual behavior. In some societies, parents encourage children's sexual activities. Hopi men masturbate boys while singing them to sleep as a way of giving the boys pleasure (164). Children among the Aymara in Bolivia and Peru have prepubertal sexual experiences that adults regard with "amused tolerance" (Werner, 1986). Among the Polynesian Pukapukans, boys and girls freely engage in masturbation in public, without adult censure (42). Young Trobriand boys and girls may participate in a variety of sexual activities—from oral stimulation of the genitals to simulations of intercourse—if adults don't control their behavior (42). And on Easter Island, children from 6 years on imitate adult sexual behavior with impunity (42). In Mangaia, daughters may engage in intercourse with their suitors in the hut where they reside with other family members (159).

Parents may actively encourage their children to engage in sexual behavior. The Chewa of Africa believe that their children will never have progeny later in life if they do not involve themselves in sexual activities early (42). Therefore, older boys and girls, with their parents' approval, play at being husband and wife in little huts built away from the village. Playing husband and wife is also allowed among the Maori and the Ila-speaking people of Africa (42). The Lepcha of India do not believe that girls will mature without having intercourse (42). Therefore, they allow early sex play among boys and girls, which may result in attempts at intercourse. By the time they are 11 or 12, most girls have engaged in intercourse. Explicit instruction about sexual activity begins between 6 and 8 for Trobriand girls and boys; their older companions inform them about types of sex play in which they can engage—masturbation, oral stimulation of the genitals of same- or opposite-gendered persons, and heterosexual intercourse (42). Parents fully approve of their youngsters going to a convenient place (e.g., the bush, a bachelor's hut, or a yam house) to participate in extended sex play. They believe that testing sexual compatibility and depth of affection are important preliminaries to marriage.

Children in many cultures not only talk with adults about sex but also have opportunities for observing adults engage in it. Alorese and Ponapean adults describe the details of sexual intercourse to children by the time they are 5, and Trukese children learn about sexual matters by watching adults at night or by asking adults (42). Because many adults and children may reside together in one dwelling in many societies, children have the opportunity to hear and observe sexual activities among adults. For example, Gregor (65) said that Mehinaku children in central Brazil grow up in an "erotically charged atmosphere" (p. 29) and experience "a 'lush' period of physically intimate contact with the mother" (pp. 177–178), who breastfeeds and sleeps with them during their first years. Later, the hammocks of adults and children hang together in the communal dwelling, where children can hear and observe the sexual activity of adults. In traditional Hawaii, children could observe their parents having intercourse in the family house, where all members slept in the same room. Likewise, there was little privacy in the homes of rural Europeans before the 18th century. Separate rooms for special purposes gradually developed in the 18th century, but even then privacy was not easy to attain (15). Children, adults, and sometimes animals would share the same living space; children heard bawdy talk and learned about sex and reproduction from an early age (15).

Sexual activities may take the form of games with other children. For example, lower class Goajiro children as well as Amhara children in Ethiopia play games in which they imitate the sexual activities of various animals (165). In other societies, children seem to imitate adult activities in their games. Among the Toba of Argentina, boys and girls as young as 5 years may spend hours every day engaging in "violent sexual games" that include snatching the genitals of each other, thrusting their fingers up another's anus, or rubbing penises together. Boys chase and throw girls down in attempts to touch their vaginas, and 5-year-old girls may attempt intercourse with little boys whom they take to bed with them (164). In their cross-cultural research on male homosexuality in four societies (Brazil, Guatemala, the Philippines, and the United States), Whitam and Mathy (167) suggested that a preference for same-gender sex play during early childhood may indicate same-gender sexual orientation in later development.

However, rather than imitating adult sexual activity, children may engage in sexual activities with them. Xokleng children of southern Brazil often sleep with adults who engage in sexual activities with them; such relations are regarded as amusing and playful (165). Siriono women in Bolivia often had sex with the prepubescent brothers of their husbands, and older Tupinamba women in Brazil who did not have the favor of older men might constantly accompany young boys, to whom they gave presents and instruction in sexual matters (165). Unmarried adult Aranda men in Australia might take young boys of 10 or so to engage in sexual activities with them until the adult men married (165).

Sometimes the reason given for sexual relations with adults is to hasten the advent of maturity. The Etoro of New Guinea require boys to ingest the semen of older men so that they will physically mature into men (165). A similar practice occurs among the Sambia (72). The Azande of Zaire, the Lepcha of the Himalayas, and the Bororo of Brazil think that intercourse with a mature man causes menstruation to occur (165) Another reason for sexual relations with adults is to receive training in sexual relations from the adults. In Polynesia, older Marquesan women initiated and served as sexual partners for young boys, and older Mangaian women gave boys their first training in sex (165).

Sexual relations with adults might also occur in the context of marriage. In some societies, girls might be married and have intercourse before they reached puberty. In Mongo, Zaire, it is legal for men to have intercourse with their child-brides; husbands try not to hurt their brides and insert progressively larger plant shoots in the vagina to prepare it for intercourse (165). However, it is not likely that this practice was widespread in traditional societies. Although most women married when they were 17 or younger, they were usually past puberty, often between the ages of 12 and 15 (45). Bullough (15) commented on the extent of adult/child sexual behavior in Western societies:

> The evidence, scanty as it is, would indicate that it was not very widespread and that probably most such behavior took place within the family, although the answer has to be dependent upon how sexual behavior is defined . . . there are very few historically documented incidents [of adult sexual behavior with children under 9-years old] that this author has found. (p. 77)

In general, cultures have looked with disfavor upon adult/child sexual behavior, although adult/adolescent sexual behavior "has been accepted as the norm throughout much of humankind's documented past" (15).

Most of the foregoing descriptions relate to societies in which there is adult acceptance of a range of sexual behavior in children—whether during play, daily activities, rituals, or training for adult life. The sources indicate that acceptance rather than censure of childhood sexual behavior from adults has been much more common in traditional societies. Ford and Beach (42) concluded that only a minority of societies are very restrictive about sexual expression during childhood, subjecting boys and girls to severe restrictions and punishments and allowing them few, if any, sexual options.

Attempts at denying children sexual expression include explicit verbal prohibitions, physical punishment when sexual behavior is observed, avoidance of conversations about sex with children or when children are nearby, surveillance of children's behavior, and prevention of young children from observing sexual behavior (42). Cuna adults prohibit children from engaging in heterosexual or homosexual play, and Ashanti fathers warn their young children not to engage in any form of sex play or to masturbate (42). The prohibition on touching the genitals is so strong among the Kwoma of New Guinea that a woman will beat a boy's penis with a stick if she sees him with an erect penis, and boys learn how to urinate without touching their penis at all (42). The Chiricahua and the Apinaye whip children for engaging in activities such as masturbation or sex play (42). Among the Cuna, children are not permitted to watch animals giving birth and receive no instruction about sex from adults until the last stages of the marriage ceremony (Ford & Beach, 1951). Murngin adults in Australia cluster boys of 4 or 5 years of age in a bachelor's hut to prevent them from observing sexual behavior in the family dwelling (42). At the end of their discussion of societies highly restrictive of children's sexual expression, Ford and Beach concluded, "Such adult attitudes toward children's sexuality may prevent youngsters from engaging in sexual practices in the presence of their elders, but whether they successfully suppress sexual activity in secret is another matter. There is some evidence that in some of these societies children do engage in a certain amount of sexual behavior despite strong adult disapproval" (p. 181).

Overall, Ford and Beach (42) categorized societies as restrictive, semi-restrictive, and permissive in their attitudes and responses to childhood sexual expression. This categorization is consistent with adult patterns of sexual expression in traditional societies worldwide (45). Frayser's cross-cultural research demonstrates that sexual attitudes and behavior are systematically patterned into clusters of components ranging from more restriction to more acceptance of varieties of adult sexual behaviors. The factors underlying these patterns relate to the degree to which sexual behavior is confined to a reproductive context (i.e., marriage). Societies that stress the importance of confining sexual behavior to a reproductive context are more restrictive about sexual behavior, particularly women's sexual behavior. Those that do not emphasize the importance of confining sexual behavior to a reproductive context are more accepting of a range of sexual expression. Restrictive cultural beliefs about sexuality center on ideas that sexual behavior is and should be reproductive behavior. Therefore, nonreproductive sexual activities (e.g., sexual behavior in childhood, oral sex, masturbation, homosexuality, premarital sex, and extramarital sex) are prohibited and punished. The most sexually restrictive societies are in the Circum-Mediterranean area, and the most sexually accepting societies are in the insular Pacific (45). Broude's (14) overview of the cultural management of sexuality, combined with other large-scale cross-cultural surveys of sexual behavior (42, 45, 64, 139, 165), and intensive studies of child development in specific social groups (169, 170) should provide rich resources for developing sound hypotheses about *human* childhood sexuality. It would not be surprising if further research shows that societies restrictive of children's sexuality are also those that are restrictive of adult sexual expression.

Whether or not sexual behavior is expressed in childhood, the results of a recent cross-cultural study of boys and girls from 5 to 15 years demonstrate that children think about sex long before puberty. Goldman and Goldman's (62) research on children's sexual thinking in four societies—the United States, England, Sweden, and Australia—led to the conclusion that there is no latency period in sexual development, as Freud hypothesized, and that children construct theories about such issues as marriage, parents' sex roles, pregnancy, birth, abortion, sexual vocabulary, nakedness; and sexual identity.

CONCLUSION:
THE CONTEMPORARY CONTEXT IN THE UNITED STATES

Several researchers (15, 42, 44, 45, 46, 77) have concluded that sexual attitudes in the United States are relatively restrictive, particularly in regard to children's sexual behavior. Not only does the paucity of substantive research on normal sexuality support this conclusion, but also the breadth of historical developments that have shaped cultural beliefs about sexuality in the West.

"Historical research shows that interest in and speculation about childhood sexuality is historically specific" (46). Different historical periods can be interpreted as different cultural periods, because beliefs and attitudes change over time. Jackson's historical research on children and sexuality in the West (76, 77, 78) is particularly enlightening about the social basis for cultural changes in attitudes about childhood and sexuality. Jackson pointed out that the concept of childhood sexuality is relatively recent, as the idea of children as a special group of people did not emerge until the 16th and 17th centuries and the interpretation of sexuality as a distinctive aspect of life did not develop until the 19th century. The development of a market economy led to changes in family and community structure, leading to the importance of privacy, family households without nonkin residents, and children. By the end of the 19th century, childhood was regarded as a period of innocence, particularly sexual innocence. Bullough (15) pointed out that "children as a group are much more naive about sex than they once were" (p. 90), because they don't grow up in rural areas, have fewer siblings with whom they can explore, engage in more structured play, have parents who fear genital exploration, and are constrained by diapers from exploring their bodies during infancy and early childhood as they once did. He concluded that "it is necessary to find ways of giving developmentally appropriate sex education to children and adolescents to make up for the lack of the knowledge that their counterparts gained in the past as part of the process of growing up" (p. 86).

During the last 100 years, however, in the United States sex education materials for young people have emphasized fearful and dangerous aspects of sexuality (e.g., disease, pregnancy, behavioral aberrations) (19). Krivacska (91) suggested that current child sexual abuse prevention programs are educating children to prevent childhood sexuality altogether. The current emphasis on allegations of child sexual abuse leads to questions about the basis for the increase in such reports (33, 47, 125, 153) and whether harm to the child is more likely to stem from the sexual behavior itself or from intervention by the courts, social services, and "helping" professionals (85). As stated in the introduction to SIECUS's *Guidelines for Comprehensive Sexuality Education,* fewer than 10% of children in the United States receive comprehensive sex education that includes a discussion of sexual behaviors, "although two-thirds of the curricula [for sex education programs] affirm that sexuality is a natural part of life" (128). I agree with Bullough that "the priorities in the value system in Western society are changing, and the job of empirical researchers is to look at this change, pointing out the benefits as well as the disadvantages" (15). It is clear that the current cultural emphasis on child sexual abuse and the paucity of balanced, comprehensive programs of sex education for children reveal a culture at odds with the bulk of evolutionary, developmental, and cross-cultural evidence demonstrating that children are sexual beings, whose exploration of sexual knowledge and play, is an integral part of their development as fully functioning human beings.

REFERENCES

1. Ainsworth, M. D. (1964). Patterns of attachment behavior shown by the infant in interaction with his mother. *Merrill-Palmer Quarterly, 10,* 51–58.

2. Ames, L. B. (1966). Children's stories. *Genetic Psychology Monographs, 73,* 337–396.

3. Anderson, C. M., & Bielert, C. (1990) Adolescent/adult copulatory behavior in nonhuman primates. In J. Feierman (Ed.), *Pedophilia: Biosocial dimensions* (pp. 176–200). New York: Springer-Verlag.

4. Arens, W. (1986). *The original sin: Incest and its meaning.* New York: Oxford University Press.

5. Baker, E. F. (1969). A further study of genital anxiety in nursing mothers. *The Journal of Orgonomy, 3,* 46–55.

6. Barry, H., & Paxson, L. M. (1971). Infancy and early childhood: Cross-cultural codes 2. *Ethnology, 10,* 466–508.

7. Barry, H., Josephson, L. Lauer, E., & Marshall, C. (1977). Agents and techniques for child training: Cross-cultural codes 6. *Ethnology, 16,* 191–230.

8. Bernstein, A. C., & Cowan, P. A. (1975). Children's concepts of how people get babies. *Child Development, 46,* 77–91.

9. Blackman, N. (1980). Pleasure and touching: Their significance in the development of the preschool child—An exploratory study. In J. M. Samson (Ed.), *Childhood and sexuality: Proceedings of the International Symposium 1980* (pp. 175–202). Montreal: Editions Etudes Vivantes.

10. Blackwood, E. (Ed.). (1986). *The many faces of homosexuality: Anthropological approaches to homosexual behavior.* New York: Harrington Park.

11. Blake, J. (1994). Pediatric and adolescent gynecology. In L. J. Copeland (Ed.), *Textbook of gynecology* (pp. 592–618). Philadelphia: W. B. Saunders.

12. Bowlby, J. (1969) *Attachment and loss I: Attachment.* New York: Basic Books.

13. Broderick, C. B., & Fowler, S. E. (1961). New patterns of relationships between the sexes among preadolescents. *Marriage and Family Living, 23,* 27–30.

14. Broude, G. J. (1981). The cultural management of sexuality. In R. H. Munroe, R. L. Munroe, & B. B. Whiting (Eds.), *Handbook of cross-cultural human development* (pp. 633–674). New York: Garland.

15. Bullough, V. L. (1990). History in adult human sexual behavior with children and adolescents in western societies. In J. Feierman (Ed.), *Pedophilia: Biosocial dimensions* (pp. 69–90). New York: Springer-Verlag.

16. Buss, D. M. (1994). *The evolution of desire: Strategies of human mating.* New York: Basic Books.

17. Calderone, M. S., & Johnson, E. W. (1981). *The family book about sexuality.* New York: Harper and Row.

18. Calderone, M. S., & Ramey, J. W. (1982). *Talking with your child about sex: Questions and answers for children from birth to puberty.* New York: Random House.

19. Campbell, P. J. (1986) *Sex guides: Books and films about sexuality for young adults.* New York: Garland.

20. Cassell, C., & Wilson, P. M. (1989). *Sexuality education: A resource book.* New York: Garland.

21. Cohen, B., & Parker, S. (1977). Sex information among nursery-school children. In E. K. Oremland & J. D. Oremland (Eds.), *The sexual and gender development of young children: The role of educator* (pp. 181–190). Cambridge, MA: Ballinger.

22. Cohen, Y. A. (1964). The transition from childhood to cross-cultural studies of initiation ceremonies, legal systems and incest taboos. Chicago: Aldine.

23. Colonna, A. B., & Solnit, A. J. (1981). Infant sexuality. *SIECUS Report, 9* (4), 1,2 6.

24. Conn, J., & Kanner, L. (1947). Children's awareness of sex differences. *Journal of Child Psychiatry, 1,* 3–57.

25. Constantine, L. L. (1981). The effects of early sexual experience: A review and synthesis of research. In L. L. Constantine & F. M. Martinson (Eds.), *Children and sex: New findings and perspectives* (pp. 217–244). Boston: Little, Brown.

26. Constantine, L. L., & Martinson, F. M. (Eds.). (1981). *Children and sex: New findings and perspectives.* Boston: Little, Brown.

27. Daily, M., & Wilson, M. (1978) *Sex, evolution, and behavior: Adaptations for reproduction.* North Scituate, MA: Duxbury.

28. Darwin, C. (1981). *The descent of man and selection in relation to sex.* Princeton: Princeton University Press. (Original work published 1871)

29. Diamond, M. (1990). Selected cross-generational sexual behavior in traditional Hawaii: A sexological ethnography. In J. Feierman (Ed.), *Pedophilia: Biosocial dimensions* (pp. 422–444). New York: Springer-Verlag.

30. Doty, R. L. (1981). Olfactory communication in humans. *Chemical Senses, 6*(4), 351–376.

31. Durkheim, E. (1963). *Incest: The nature and origin of the taboo.* New York: Lyle Stuart. (Original work published 1898)

32. Engels, F (1942). *The origin of the family, private property, and the state.* New York: International Publishers. (Original work published 1884)

33. Ennew, J. (1986). *The sexual exploitation of children.* Cambridge: Cambridge University Press.

34. Erikson, E. H. (1968). *Childhood and society* (Rev. ed.). New York: Norton.

35. Feierman J. (Ed.). (1990). *Pedophilia: Biosocial dimensions.* New York: Springer-Verlag.

36. Finkelhor, D. (1979). *Sexually victimized children.* New York: Free Press.

37. Finkelhor, D. (1984). *Child sexual abuse.* New York: Free Press.

38. Finkelhor, D. (1986). *A sourcebook on child sexual abuse.* Beverly Hills, CA: Sage.

39. Fisher, H. E. (1983). *The sex contract: The evolution of human behavior.* New York: Quill.

40. Fisher, H. E. (1992). *Anatomy of love: The natural history of monogamy, adultery, and divorce.* New York:

Norton.

41. Fisher, S. (1989). *Sexual images of the self: The psychology of erotic sensations and illusions.* Hillside, NJ: Lawrence Erlbaum.

42. Ford, C. S., & Beach, F. A. (1951). *Patterns of sexual behavior.* New York: Harper.

43. Fox, R. (1980). *The red lamp of incest.* New York: E. P. Dutton.

44. Frayser, S. G. (1984). *Breast feeding and sex.* Unpublished manuscript.

45. Frayser, S. G. (1985). *Varieties of sexual experience: An anthropological perspective on human sexuality.* New Haven: HRAF Press.

46. Frayser, S. G. (1993) Anthropologic perspective. In A. Yates (Ed.), *Child and adolescent psychiatric clinics of North America: Sexual and gender identity disorders* (Vol 2, No. 3, pp. 369–384). Philadelphia: W. B. Saunders.

47. Frayser, S. G. (1994a, August). A cultural examination of child sexual abuse, part I: The cultural framework of child sexual abuse. *Defense,* 10–12.

48. Frayser, S. G. (1994b). [Analyses of the cross-cultural data in Barry & Paxson (1971), Barry, Josephson, Lauer, & Marshall (1976, 1977)]. Unpublished analyses.

49. Frazer, J. (1910). *Totemism and exogamy* (Vol. 4). London: Macmillan.

50. Freud, S. (1950). *Totem and taboo: Some points of agreement between the mental lives of savages and neurotics.* New York: W. W. Norton. (Original work published 1913).

51. Freud, S. (1963). *On the sexual theories of children.* New York: Macmillan. (Original work published 1908).

52. Freud, S. (1963). *The sexual enlightenment of children.* New York: Macmillan. (Original work published 1907)

53. Freud, S. (1975). *Three essays on the theory of sexuality* (J. Strachey, Trans.) New York: Basic Books. (Original work published 1905)

54. Friedrich, W. N., Grambsh, P., Broughton, D., Kuiper, J., & Beilke, R. L. (1991). Normative sexual behavior in children. *Pediatrics, 88*(3), 456–464.

55. Friedrich, W. N., Grambsch, P., Damon, L., Hewitt, S. K., Koverola, C., Lang, R. A. Wolfe, V., & Broughton, V. (1992). Child sexual behavior inventory: Normative and clinical comparisons. *Psychological Assessment, 4*(3), 303–311.

56. Gadpaille, W. J. (1975). *The cycles of sex.* New York: Charles Scribner's Sons.

57. Gadpaille, W. J. (1978). Psychosexual developmental tasks imposed by pathologically delayed childhood: A cultural dilemma. In S. Feinstein & P. Giovacchini (Eds.), *Annals of Adolescent Psychiatry, 6,* 136–155.

58. Galenson, E., & Roiphe, H. (1974). The emergence of genital awareness during the second year of life. In R. C. Friedman, R. M. Richart, & R. L. Van de Wiele (Eds.), *Sex differences in behavior* (pp. 223–231). New York: Wiley.

59. Gil, E., & Johnson, T. C. (1993). *Sexualized children: Assessment and treatment of sexualized children and children who molest.* Rockville, MD: Launch Press.

60. Gilligan, C. (1982). *In a different voice: Psychological theory and women's development.* Cambridge, MA: Harvard University Press.

61. Gilmore, D. D. (1990). *Manhood in the making: Cultural concepts of masculinity.* New Haven: Yale University Press.

62. Goldman, R., & Goldman, J. (1982). *Children's sexual thinking: A comparative study of children aged 5 to 15 years in Australia, North America, Britain and Sweden.* London: Routledge and Kegan Paul.

63. Gordon, S., & Gordon, J. (1983). *Raising a child conservatively in a sexually permissive world.* New York: Simon & Schuster.

64. Gregersen, E. (1983). *Sexual practices: The story of human sexuality.* New York: Franklin Watts.

65. Gregor, T. (1985). *Anxious pleasures: The sexual lives of an Amazonian people.* Chicago: University of Chicago.

66. Halverson, H. M. (1938). Genital and sphincter behavior of the male infant. *Journal of Genetic Psychology, 56,* 383–388.

67. Harlow, H. F. (1973). *Learning to love.* New York: Ballantine.

68. Harlow, H. F., & Harlow, M. (1962) Social deprivation in monkeys. *Scientific American, 207*(5), 136–146.

69. Hattendorf, K. W. (1932). A study of the questions of young children concerning sex: A phase of an experimental approach to parent education. *Journal of Social Psychology, 3,* 37–65.

70. Herdt, G. (1981). *Guardians of the flutes: Idioms of masculinity.* New York: McGraw Hill.

71. Herdt, G. (Ed.). (1982). *Rituals of manhood: Male initiation in Papua, New Guinea.* Berkeley, CA: University of California.

72. Herdt, G. (1987). *The Sambia: Ritual and gender in New Guinea.* New York: Holt, Rinehart and Winston.

73. Herdt, G. (1990). Cross-cultural issues in the development of bisexuality and homosexuality. In M. Perry (Ed.), *Handbook of sexology: Vol. 7. Childhood and adolescent sexology* (pp. 52–63). Amsterdam: Elsevier.

74. Hrdy, S. B. (1981). *The woman that never evolved.* Cambridge, MA: Harvard University Press.

75. Ilg, F. L., & Ames, L. B. (1955). *Child behavior.* New York: Dell.

76. Jackson, S. (1982). *Childhood and sexuality.* Oxford: Basil Blackwell.

77. Jackson, S. (1990). Demons and innocents. Western ideas on children's sexuality in historical perspective. In M. Perry (Ed.), *Handbook of sexology: Vol. 7. Childhood and adolescent sexology* (pp 23–49). Amsterdam: Elsevier.

78. Jackson, S. (1993). Childhood and sexuality in historical perspective. In A. Yates (Ed.), *Child and adolescent psychiatric clinics of North America: Sexual and gender disorders* (Vol. 2, No. 3, pp. 355–368). Philadelphia: W. B. Saunders.

79. Johnson, D. B. (1982). Altruistic behavior and the development of the self in infants. *Merrill-Palmer Quarterly, 28,* 379–388.

80. Jolly, A. (1972). *The evolution of primate behavior.* New York: Macmillan.

81. Jordan, B. (1993). *Birth in four cultures: A crosscultural investigation of childbirth in Yucatan, Holland, Sweden, and the United States* (4th ed.) (R. Davis-Floyd, Rev. Ed.). Prospect Heights, IL: Waveland Press.

82. Kinsey, A. C., Pomeroy, W., & Martin, C. (1948). *Sexual behavior in the human male.* Philadelphia: W. B. Saunders.

83. Kinsey, A. C., Pomeroy, W., Martin, C., & Gebhard, P. (1953). *Sexual behavior in the human female.* Philadelphia: W. B. Saunders.

84. Kohlberg, L. (1981). *Essays on moral development.* San Francisco: Harper & Row.

85. Konker, C. S. (1994, August). A cultural examination of child sexual abuse, part II: The construction of child sexual abuse edifices. *Defense,* 12–15.

86. Konner, M. (1982). *The tangled wing: Biological constraints on the human spirit.* New York: Holt, Rinehart and Winston.

87. Korbin, J. E. (1981). *Child abuse and neglect: Cross-cultural perspectives.* Berkeley, CA: University of California Press.

88. Korbin, J. E. (1981). Child sexual abuse: Implications from the cross-cultural record. In N. Scheper-Hughes (Ed.), *Child survival* (pp. 247–265). Dordrecht, Holland: D. Reidel.

89. Krietler, H., & Krietler, S. (1966). Children's concepts of sexuality and birth. *Child Development, 37,* 363–378.

90. Krivacska, J. J. (1990). *Designing child sexual abuse prevention programs: Current approaches and a proposal for the prevention, reduction and identification of sexual misuse.* Springfield, IL: C C Thomas.

91. Krivacska, J. J. (1991). Child sexual abuse prevention programs: The need for childhood sexuality edu-

cation. *SIECUS Report, 19*(6), 1–7.

92. Kroeber, A. L., & Kluckhohn, C. (1963). *Culture: A critical review of concepts and definitions.* New York: Vintage Books, Random House.

93. Lancaster, J. B. (1979). Sex and gender in evolutionary perspective. In M. Katchadouian (Ed.), *Human sexuality.* Berkeley: University of California Press.

94. Levine, M. I. (1957). Pediatric observations on masturbation in children. *Psychoanalytic Study of the Child, 6,* 117–124.

95. Lewis, W. C. (1965). Coital movements in the first year of life: Earliest anlage of genital love? *International Journal of Psychoanalysis, 46,* 372–374.

96. Malinowski, B. (1955). *Sex and repression in savage society.* New York: Meridian. (Original work published 1927)

97. Marcus, S. (1975). Introduction. In S. Freud, *Three essays on the theory of sexuality* (pp. xix–xli). New York: Basic Books.

98. Malinowski, B. (1955). (1929). *The sexual life of savages in the north-western Melanesia: An ethnographic account of courtship, marriage, and family life among the natives of the Trobriand Islands, British New Guinea.* London: Routledge and Sons.

99. Marshall, D. S., & Suggs, R. C. (Eds.). (1971). *Human sexual behavior: Variations in the ethnographic spectrum.* Englewood Cliffs, NJ: Prentice-Hall.

100. Martinson, F. M. (1973). *Infant and child sexuality: A sociological perspective.* St. Peter, Minnesota: The Book Mark.

101. Martinson, F. M. (1980). Childhood sexuality. In B. B. Wolman & J. Money (Eds.), *Handbook of human sexuality* (pp. 29–59). Englewood Cliffs, NJ: Prentice-Hall.

102. Martinson, F. M. (1981). Eroticism in infancy and childhood. In L. L. Constantine & F. M. Martinson (Eds.), *Children and sex: New findings, new perspectives* (pp. 23–44). Boston: Little, Brown.

103. Martinson, F. M. (1991). Normal sexual development in infancy and early childhood. In G. Ryan & S. Lane (Eds.), *Juvenile sex offending: Causes, consequences, and correction* (pp. 57–82). Boston: Lexington Books.

104. Martinson, F. M. (1994a). Children and sex, Part II: Childhood sexuality. In V. L. Bullough & B. Bullough (Eds.), *Human Sexuality: An encyclopedia* (pp. 111–116). Garland: New York.

105. Martinson, F. M. (1994b). *The sexual life of children.* Westport, CT: Bergin & Garvey.

106. Mead, M. (1928). *Coming of age in Samoa.* New York: Morrow.

107. Mead, M. (1930). *Growing up in New Guinea: A comparative study of primitive education.* New York: Morrow.

108. Mead, M. (1935). *Sex and temperament in three primitive societies.* New York: Morrow.

109. Mead, M. (1949). *Male and female: A study of the sexes in a changing world.* New York: Morrow.

110. Meiselman, K. C. (1978). *Incest: A psychological study of causes and effects with treatment recommendations.* San Francisco: Jossey-Bass.

111. Messenger, J. C. (1969). *Inis Beag: Isle of Ireland.* New York: Holt, Rinehart and Winston.

112. Moll, A. (1897). *Libido sexualis: Studies in the psychosexual laws of love verified by clinical case histories.* New York: American Ethnological Press.

113. Moll, A. (1912). *The sexual life of the child* (E. Paul, Trans.). New York: Macmillan.

114. Money, J. (1968). *Sex errors of the body: Dilemmas, education, counseling.* Baltimore: Johns Hopkins University Press.

115. Money, J. (1980). *Love and love sickness: The science of sex, gender difference and pair bonding.* Baltimore: Johns Hopkins University Press.

116. Money, J. (1986a) *Lovemaps: Clinical concepts of sexual/erotic health and pathology, paraphilia, and gender transposition in childhood, adolescence, and maturity.* New York: Irvington.

117. Money, J. (1986b). *Venuses penuses: Sexology, sexosophy, and exigency theory.* Buffalo, NY: Prometheus.

118. Money, J. (1988). *Gay, straight, and in-between: The sexology of erotic orientation.* New York: Oxford University.

119. Money, J. (1990). Historical and current concepts of pediatric and ephebiatric sexology. In M. E. Perry (Ed.), *Handbook of sexology: Vol. 7. Childhood and adolescent sexology* (pp. 3–21). Amsterdam: Elsevier.

120. Money, J., & Ehrhardt, A. A. (1972). *Man and woman, boy and girl: The differentiation and dimorphism of gender identity from conception to maturity.* Baltimore: Johns Hopkins University Press.

121. Money, J., & Lamacz, M. (1990). *Vandalized lovemaps.* Buffalo, NY: Prometheus.

122. Montagu, A. (1986). *Touching: The human significance of the skin* (3rd ed.). New York: Harper & Row.

123. Moore, J. E., & Kendall, D. C. (1971). Children's concepts of reproduction. *The Journal of Sex Research, 7,* 42–61.

124. Morgan, L. H. (1964). *Ancient society.* Cambridge, MA: Belknap. (Original work published 1877.)

125. Munroe, R. L., & Munroe, R. H. (1975). *Cross-cultural human development.* Monterey, CA: Brooks/Cole.

126. Murdock, G. P. (1965). *Social structure.* New York: Free Press. (Original work published 1949)

127. Nanda, S. (1990). *Neither man or woman: The Hijras of India.* Belmont, CA: Wadsworth.

128. Nnational Guidelines Task Force. (1991). *Guidelines for comprehensive sex education, grades kindergarten – 12th Grade.* New York: SIECUS.

129. Okami, P. 91990). Sociopolitical biases in the contemporary scientific literature on adult human sexual behavior with children and adolescents. In J. R. Feierman (Ed.), *Pedophilia: Biosocial dimensions* (pp. 91–121). New York: Springer-Verlag.

130. Parker, S. (1976). The precultural basis of the incest taboo. *American Anthropologist, 78,* 285–305.

131. Perper, T. (1985). *Sex signals: The biology of love.* Philadelphia: iSi Press.

132. Perry, M. (Ed.). 1990. *Handbook of sexology: Vol. 7. Child and adolescent sexology.* Amsterdam: Elsevier.

133. Piaget, J. (1932). *The moral judgment of the child.* New York: Harcourt Brace.

134. Pitcher, E. G., & Prelinger, E. (1963). *Children tell stories: An analysis of fantasy.* New York: International Universities.

135. Pusey, A. (1990). Mechanisms of inbreeding avoidance in nonhuman primates. In J. Feierman (Ed.), *Pedophilia: Biosocial dimensions* (pp. 201–220). New York: Springer-Verlag.

136. Ramsey, G. V. (1943). The sexual development of boys. *American Journal of Psychology, 56,* 217.

137. Rancour-Laferriere, D. (1985). *Signs of the flesh: An essay on the evolution of hominid sexuality.* Berlin: Mouton de Gruyter.

138. Raphael, D. (1976). *The tender gift: Breastfeeding.* New York: Schocken Books.

139. Reiss, I. L. (1986). *Journey into sexuality: An exploratory voyage.* Englewood Cliffs, NJ: Prentice-Hall.

140. Reiter, E. O. (1986). The neuroendocrine regulation of pubertal onset. In J. B. Lancaster & B. A. Hamburg (Eds.), *School-age pregnancy and parenthood: Biosocial dimensions* (pp. 53–76). New York: Aldine de Gruyter.

141. Remoff, H. T. (1984). *Sexual choice: A woman's decision.* New York: Dutton/Lewis.

142. Roberts, E. J., Kline, D., & Gagnon, J. (1978). *Family life and sexual learning: A study of the role of parents in the sexual learning of children.* Cambridge, MA: Population Education.

143. Rohner, R. R. (1986). *The warmth dimension: Foundations of parental acceptance-rejection theory.* Beverly Hills, CA: Sage.

144. Roiphe, H., & Galenson, E. (1981). *Infantile origins of sexual identity.* International Universities Press.

145. Roscoe, W. (1991). *The Zuni man-woman.* Albuquerque: University of New Mexico Press.

146. Rosenfeld, A. A., & Wasserman, S. (1993). Sexual development in the early school-aged child. In A. Yates (Ed.), *Child and adolescent psychiatric clinics of North America: Sexual and gender identity disorders*

(Vol. 2, No. 3, pp. 393–406). Philadelphia: W. B. Saunders.

147. Russell, D. E. H. (1986). *The secret trauma: Incest in the lives of girls and women.* New York: Basic Books.

148. Rutter, M. (1971). Normal psychosexual development. *Journal of Child Psychology and Psychiatry, 11,* 259–283.

149. Ryan, G. (1990). Sexual behavior in childhood: Normal and deviant. In J. McNamara & B. McNamara (Eds.), *Adoption and childhood sexual abuse.* Portland, ME: University of Southern Maine.

150. Ryan, G., & S. Lane (Eds.). (1991). *Juvenile sex offending: Causes, consequences, and correction.* Boston: Lexington Books.

151. Ryan, G., Miyoshi, T., & Krugman, R. (1988). *The early childhood experiences of professionals working in child abuse.* Paper presented at the National Symposium on Child Abuse and Neglect, Keystone, CO.

152. Scheper, J. (1983). *Incest: A biosocial view.* New York: Academic Press.

153. Scheper-Hughes (Ed.). (1987). *Child survival.* Dordrecht, Holland: D. Reidel.

154. Schlegel, A., & Barry, H. (1991). *Adolescence: An anthropological inquiry.* New York: Free Press.

155. Sears, R. R., Maccoby, E. E., & Levine, E. H. (1957). *Patterns of child rearing.* Evanston, IL: Row, Peterson.

156. Smuts, B. B. (985). *Sex and friendship in baboons.* New York: Aldine de Gruyter.

157. Snyder, S. U., & Gordon, S. (Eds.). (1984). *Parents are sexuality educators: An annotated print and audiovisual bibliography for professionals and parents (1970–1984).* Phoenix, AZ: Oryx Press.

158. Spiro, M. E. (1958). *Children of the kibbutz: A study of child training and personality.* Cambridge, MA: Harvard University Press.

159. Suggs, R. C. (1966). *Marquesan sexual behavior.* New York: Harcourt, Brace and World.

160. Symons, D. (1979). *The evolution of human sexuality.* New York: Oxford University Press.

161. Turner, V. (1969). *The ritual process: Structure and anti-structure.* Chicago: Aldine.

162. Twutchell, J. (1987). *Forbidden partners: The incest taboo in modern culture.* New York: Columbia University Press.

163. Vance, C. (1991). Anthropology rediscovers sexuality: A theoretical comment. *Social Science and Medicine, 33,* 875–884.

164. Waal, F. B. M. DE (1990). Sociosexual behavior used for tension regulation in all age and sex combinations among bonobos. In J. Feierman (Ed.), *Pedophilia: Biosocial dimensions* (pp. 378–393). New York: Springer-Verlag.

165. Werner, D. (1986). *Human sexuality around the world.* Unpublished manuscript, University of Santa Caterina, Florianopolis, Brazil.

166. Westermarck, E. (1925). *The history of human marriage* (5th ed., Vols. 1–3). London: Macmillan.

167. Whitman, F. L., & Mathy, R. M. (1986). *Male homosexuality in four societies: Brazil, Guatemala, the Philippines, and the United States.* New York: Praeger.

168. White, E., & Brown, D. M. (1973). *The first men.* New York: Time-Life Books.

169. Whiting, B. B. (Ed.). (1963). *Six cultures.* New York: Wiley.

170. Whiting, B. B., & Whiting, J. W. M. (1975). *Children of six cultures: A psychocultural analysis.* Cambridge, MA: Harvard University Press.

171. Williams, W. (1986). *The spirit and the flesh: Sexual diversity in American Indian culture.* Boston: Beacon.

172. Wolf, A. P. (1966). Childhood association, sexual attraction, and the incest taboo: A Chinese case. *American Anthropologist, 68,* 883–898.

173. Wolf, A. P. (1993). Westermarck redivivus. In W. H. Durham, E. V. Daniel, & B. Schieffelin (Eds.), *Annual Review of Anthropology 22,* 157–175.

174. Yates, A. (1978). *Sex without shame: Encouraging the child's healthy sexual development.* New York: William Morrow and Company.

175. Yates, A. (Ed.). (1993). *Child and adolescent psychiatric clinics of North America: Sexual and gender identity disorders* (Vol. 2, No. 3). Philadelphia: W. B. Saunders.

MOROCCAN BOYS AND SEX

Andreas Eppink (Jannie Figee—translator)

"The" Moroccan boy is brought up in a stern family with strict rules of pride, family honor, and consideration. At first there is for him nothing but the family, later boys of his quarter become important, and finally the world, i.e., the world of men.

At home sexuality is taboo (*harãm*, holy, forbidden, protected). Bourdieu[1] and Demeerseman[2] say that discussing intimate matters would embarrass both parties, because they are seen as their respective personal 'insides.' Not hearing his parents discussing this subject, the boy has to get his sex education from the 'peer group.' So sexuality is seen as something not belonging to the family, something 'outside,' consequently suspect, shameful. The outside ('the street') is considered a source of bad influence, which could affect the family honor. The street and the danger of forbidden sex are also connected.

Here it has to be noted that particular acts are not so much judged according to an inner, 'absolute' standard as according to the situation in which the act takes place.[3] Sexuality itself is neither good nor bad: it depends on the situation.[4] There are, for example, situations that "make coition praiseworthy."[5] On the other hand, any coition outside marriage and concubinage is forbidden.

But there is less emphasis on what people do than on what becomes known. The stress is on 'good behavior' and 'consideration' (li^etbãr) not 'sin.'[6]

In order to regulate his sexual feelings and needs a Moroccan boy can either masturbate, accept passive anal contact (homosexual), or try to have active anal contact (homo-, heterosexual, or with animals) or heterosexual genital contact. Moroccans attach the highest value to the last, and the lowest to the first possibility mentioned. Never did the respondents mention oral-genital contact (kissing will be discussed later on).

SEX WITH FEMALES

In general the sexually mature boy will feel shame about approaching a girl or prostitute.[7] Because of the separation of the sexes and the seclusion of 'decent women,' any girl in the street is 'indecent,' is 'a whore.' The boy has little experience with girls of his age or unrelated women. He does not know how to behave in their presence. He feels a distance, if not fear.

Apart from family and fellow students a boy may only have contact with lower status women. Moreover every woman is considered to be unclean;[8] sexual intercourse with a woman during her period is forbidden.

On the one hand a boy running into a girl will want to have sex with her: he is expected to show his virility by instant sex with any woman on her own: but on the other hand he will be afraid—certainly the first time.

In North Africa everyone is taught to do things with others: a child is not encouraged to do things on its own or to develop self reliance. In the peer group one feels safe and strong.

A boy scarcely dares to do something of which he is not sure that his friends approve. It hardly happens that a boy 'sees' a girl alone. Normally the most courageous one tries to pick up a 'prostitute' with whom they all have intercourse one by one. When everything is shared, so are the girls: what is good for my friends is good for me, and vice versa. (But this changes after marriage when sexual intercourse will be an exclusive prerogative of the husband.)

What a Westerner might take as lack of privacy is seen by Moroccans as security: as long as one sees that others do the same as you do, there is no need to be afraid or to feel shame.

MASTURBATION

Masturbation as a possibility for sexual fulfilment is strongly repudiated and least valued, because it lacks an object.[9] This has to do with the value attached to intromission and ejaculation.[10, 11]

In the Western middle-class frame of reference, sexuality is highly related to eroticism and love. This is by no means the case in all cultures and in all times. Vanggaard describes types of aggressive sexuality in cultures of pre-Christian Europe: The sexual act of the active man is intended to make the object passive, to submit him.[12] This seems to be true for North Africa as well. Masturbating—not submitting some other person—is not manly; therefore 'kafat/masturbator' is a term of abuse.

Nevertheless (fitting the pattern of group security) boys often masturbate together, outside. or in a room, or at the movies where it is quite common. This is done touching each other, but it is not normal to look at each other's penis and to talk about it.

Masturbation is one of the most delicate topics to talk about. Often it is claimed that it is not necessary, "because there are so many other possibilities."

MALE-MALE SEX

In fact it is more likely that in a country where women tend to be segregated, masturbation is necessary because there are not so many other possibilities . . . unless one gets up the courage to do it with younger boys. Peers and friends are your equals and therefore difficult to submit: and women are kept away from you; and if you were to chance upon a girl, the lack of experience in contact with them remains a great hindrance.

With younger boys these barriers do not exist: they are younger, therefore they can be submitted; going with them does not cause shame. Therefore boys look for younger boys (7–13 years old) who are 'fit for this.'[13] Persuasion is effected by nice words, money or force. From my conversations it is clear that tips are exchanged about boys/young men/men who could be/are 'fit.' Usually one cannot claim somebody for oneself. A 'personal' relation between an 'active' and a 'passive' boy is exceptional, not to mention a love relation. (Anyhow that is the opinion stated by the interviewees.) But it may happen that one feels a strong sexual attraction toward a particular boy.

This 'informing' has as a consequence that some boys get the reputation of zāmel (somebody submitting to anal intercourse). If a boy has this image it will be most difficult for him to submit another from his own circle; he will be forced to fulfill the passive role until he goes outside his circle or gets married.

The striking aspect of this pattern is the distinction between 'active' and 'passive,'[14] thus creating two categories: men (in hetero-or homosexual intercourse) and non-men—males known to be both agens and patiens being exceedingly rare.

SEX—AFFECTION—LOVE

As we already saw the emphasis in sexual contacts between boys is not on friendship or romantic love, but on penetration and ejaculation. This is true for relations between male and female as well. Friendship, being possible only between equals, can exist between men of the same status/age group and between women of equal status. The relation with a sexual object—boy, woman or 'buggered one'—is a relation with an inferior; penetration is felt to be a manifestation of male power. Sex is, essentially penetration.

A boy told me: "We are so quickly excited and therefore we want the 'act' at once, otherwise we would lose our semen early." No emphasis is given to sexual excitement by caressing, foreplay and petting. A 'real man' prefers intromission and quick ejaculation.

This does not mean that affection is never felt; but romantic love does not predominate in a sexual relationship (nor in marriage).

Kissing[16] and oral-genital contact are not customary. Foreplay and petting—like masturbation are held to be inferior; such behavior is often labeled as 'weak' or 'strange.'

MARRIED MEN—CELIBATES

Marriage both offers the possibility of lawful, unproblematic intromission and confirms the status of adult man (women's status only improves with the birth of the first boy). Without marriage one is not 'a real man,' not a full member of society.

Some married men will continue to have anal intercourse with boys or their wives or both. This was repeatedly indicated in conversations, but contradicted by others. Some said that while the man might like to have anal intercourse with his wife, she would repudiate this, as boys were the more suitable object for it. Premarital sex, however, could often be anal in order to preserve the girl's virginity.[17]

For whatever reason, quite a number of married men go on looking for (young) boys.[18] This is all right provided the man does not neglect his wife sexually.

Somebody old enough to and capable of supporting a wife, yet who does not marry, is abused as *zúfri* (celibate). When he is still looking for boys, it is called childlike. Here it is interesting to note that a distinction is made: to wit, whether somebody is having intercourse with boys as well, or exclusively. The first can boast of his exploits; he is sometimes admiringly called *how*ãi(big fuck) or *sah-sãh* (good seducer). The latter is regarded with scorn.

Even worse is the man who lets others use him as patiens; he is called 'no-real-man' or '*has-sãs*'. The penetratee is strongly condemned and scorned.

CONCLUSION

In the Moroccan cultural pattern genital (heterosexual) penetration is the most highly valued form of sexuality, since it is considered to be the most active. But for youth, sex with other boys is a more likely sexual outlet and is accepted as an initial experience. The attitude toward the 'active' is positive, toward the 'passive' boy one of tolerant pity, and toward the adult who gets penetrated, one of scorn. Alternating between penetrating and being penetrated is rare. The only escape for a patiens is marriage.

In Morocco—as among working class Americans of the Fifties[19]—sexuality is seen as neutral in itself, but it has to be regulated, ideally in marriage. If sex is not confined therein, people can excuse it by saying that man is weak and Allãh forgiving. But not only is the frame important; so is the form: active/on top/above/*fauq*/male, or passive/laid/at the bottom/below/*taht*!/female.

Comparing our results with Kinsey's data (North America 1949) we found many points in common with his 'lower level,' such as:

- taking intromission as the essential activity in 'normal' sexual behavior (Kinsey p. 369).
- rejection of masturbation (Kinsey p. 375) and petting, kissing (Kinsey p. 369).
- acceptance of hetero- and homosexual sex from childhood (Kinsey p. 383).

- no conflicting loyalties with regard to hetero- and homosexual activities during the same period (Kinsey p. 361).
- acceptance of the 'active' role in homosexual anal contact (Kinsey p. 616) and sometimes continuation of these contacts, even after marriage (Kinsey p. 384).

In Morocco the main distinction is not between hetero- and homosexuality (i.e.. the choice of the sex of the partner), but between 'activity' and 'passivity' (penetration), i.e., the choice of the form of sexual behavior, regardless of the sex of the partner. Friendship, romantic love, and sexual intercourse are thought of as distinct and hardly 'combinable.'

NOTES

1. P. Bourdieu: *The Sentiment of Honour in Kabyle: Society in Honour and Shame* (ed. J. G. Peristany), London. 1965.

2. A. Demeerseman: *La famille Tunisienne et les temps nouveaus,* Tunis, 1972.

3. L. Gardet: *L'lslam,* 1959, and P. Shustery: *Outlines of Islamic Culture*, Galore,1954

4. Charnay: *Pluralisme normatif et ambiguit dans le Fiqh,* Paris, 1967, p. 183: «. . . l'acte sexuel . . . est (si les interdictions légales sont respectées) neutre en lui même».

5. Charnay, 1967: «peuvent rendre louable l'acte sexuel».

6. Charnay, 1967.

7. Prostitution is common in towns; the prices are so low that even young boys can afford them.

8. Cf. E. Westermarck: *Ritual and Belief in Morocco,* London, 1928, vol. II p. 3; uncleanness is seen "as loaded with magic influence" and therefore one tries to have to do with it as little as possible.

9. Kinsey, 1949, p. 375: "At lower levels, and particularly among the older generations of the lowest level, masturbation may be looked down upon as abnormal, a perversion, an infantile substitute for socio-sexual contacts."

10. Since all of my informants have attended primary school during the French protectorate, and thus mastered French, the discussions were held in that language; they spoke of "the act/l'acte."

11. Kinsey. 1949, p. 369: "Many persons at the lower level consider that intromission is the essential activity and the only justifiable activity in a 'normal' sexual relation."

12. Vanggaard: *Phallos*, 1971, p. 95:,,. . .daß gewisse Beziehungen, die für uns lediglich eine sexuelle Bedeutung haben, von den Alten im Lichte der Herrschaft oder Unterwerfung geschen wurden, d.h. in der Sphäre der Aggression fielen." (certain relation being for us only sexual were seen by the Ancients in the light of dominance or submission) and p. 103/4: „Ich habe betont, daß die Manner. . .vom Verlangen nach einem gewaltsame analen Koitus erfült waren, dem als treibende Kraft Aggression und nicht Erotik zugrunde lag. Das soll natürlich nicht besagen, daß mit dem Orgasmus, der sich aus solchem gewaltsame Tun ergib, kein Lustenpfinden verbunde ist. Aber zunächst hat ein solcher Akt nicht mit erotischen Gefühlen zu tun. Er ist nicht der Ausdruck warmer Zuneigung, des Verlangens nach Vereinigung sowie eines Wunsches, zugeben und zu nehmen, zu besitzen und sich besitzen zu lassen. Vielmehr handelt es sich hier in erster Linie um eine Befreiung von aggressiver Spannung, eine Äbßerung des Verlangens, Macht auszuüben, zu unterwerfen, zu demütigen und dem Opfer die Manneskraft zu nehmen." (I stressed that men were driven by an aggressive—not erotic—desire for anal coition. That is not to say that orgasm resulting from rape is without lust. Yet primarily it is not an expression of warm affection, of an erotic desire for union, of the wish to give and to take, to possess and to be possessed. It is rather release of aggressive tension, an expression of the desire to dominate, to subjugate, to humilitate and to rob the victim of his virility).

13. Duvert: *Journal d'un innocent,* Paris, 1976, p. 77: «Je ne crois évidemment pas le chiffre, mais la chose est balane: un cul percé attire les jeunes célibataires de la populace comme un pot de miel fait venir les mouches. On se nomme le coupable, on en parle, on va à lui quand on a besoin à soulager, et quelquefois on Ie contraint: ce serait révoltant qu'il refuse, puisqu'il est déjà troué.» (. . . from the moment an arse-hole is pierced it attracts the bachelors like a pot of honey attracts the bees. One gives the name of the fallen one

to the other, one speaks about it, one goes to him whenever the need arises. Sometimes he is raped; it is out of the question for him to refuse once the entrance is made.) p. 78: «un garçon sera l'homosexuel [le pénétré] du groupe parce qu'il a regardé, désiré, sollicité avant qu'un autre s'y décide. On ne voit pas le désir (on est train d'apprendre à le chasser), on repére le trou et on l'utilise. Un enfant obéissant se ferme l'anus: celui qui garde le sien ouvert devient Ie putain des autres garçons et donc les aide à sauver Ieur propre trou. C'est comme un jeu éducatif: on serre les fesses ensemble, le premier qui relâche est pédé.» (one boy will be fucked by the rest of the group, because he gazed, he seemed to desire it, to beg for it more than anybody else. The desire of the fucker is ignored, he just fills a hole, uses an arse. A good boy keeps his arse tight. The one, who does not seal it, becomes the whore of the other boys, thus helping them to keep theirs intact. . . .)

14. Some speak of 'positive' and 'negative.'

15. C. von Balen (Erotik des Ostens, 1955) remarks that ejaculation is the centre of Arab eroticism (p. 160). The concentration on vaginal and anal intromission can become understandable. An informer told me: «Pour se satisfaire, on peut prendre tout: la femme, l'âne ou la vache.» ("To satisfy oneself one can take everything: woman, donkey or cow.")

16. Duvert, op. cit. p. 163: «Puis j'ai appris que le baiser à la français était peu répandu dans les flirts: on bisote, on picore le visage, on se prend pas les langues. Les baisers vus au cinéma n'y changent rien.» (I noticed that French kisses are quite uncommon in spite of what is shown in the pictures.) Kinsey, op. cit. p. 369: "Many a college male will have kissed dozens of girls, although he has had intercourse with none of them. On the other hand, the lower level male is likely to have had intercourse with hundreds of girls, but he may have kissed a few of them . . . for he is likely to have considerable distaste for the deep kiss which is fairly common in upper level histories."

17. The concept 'virginity' is a question of shame—not of 'guilt.' A man takes possession of a wife and does not want a second-hand item; the father wants to give his daughter intact to her husband, otherwise she is 'worth' nothing. The virginal membrane is proof of her value, as it shows that she was well guarded and is 'virtuous.'

18. Kinsey. op. cit. p. 384: ". . . it is not surprising to find a fair number of the males at (the lower) level continuing both types of activity through the major portion of their lives. It is notable, however, that there are few individuals in this group who become exclusively homosexual. There are some who definitely conform of sex" Ibid. p. 631.: "(In very remote rural areas) homosexual activity rarely conflicts with heterosexual relations, and is quite without argot, physical manifestations, and other affections so often found in urban groups. There is a minimum of personal disturbance or social conflict over such activity."

19. Kinsey, op. cit. p. 383: "At the lowest level, sex, whether it be heterosexual or homosexual, is more or less accepted as inevitable. The children here are the least restrained sexually and usually become involved in both heterosexual and homosexual activities at an early Age."

In my study I tried as much as possible not to impose a theory on data, neither to start from my frame of reference (European middle class sociological), nor from one found in the ethnological literature on the Arabs. Ordering the information I obtained in conversations with boys and girls from a medium sized Moroccan town—mainly middle class: clerks, small shopkeepers, craftsmen—I tried to see things in their (culture's) frame of reference, in their value system.

After elaborate discussions with a boy aged 22 and a girl aged 23 I wrote my questionnaire with 51 points for girls and 68 points for boys, which were filled in by about twenty boys and twenty girls. The questions were in French and if necessary explained in Arabic by the two Moroccan interviewers.

Of special interest were the questions not fully understood by the respondents—thus revealing that these questions presupposed a European middle class frame of reference not applicable to Moroccans.

Most of my observations are confirmed by the French writer Duvert *Journal d'un innocent* (see note 13) and by studies among students of the American University of Beirut: Levon H. Melikian and E. Terry Prothro: *Sexual Behavior of University Students in the Arab Near East* in *The Journal of Abnormal and Social Psychology* 49, 1954 and Melikian: *Social Change and Sexual Behavior of Arab University Students* in *The Journal of Social Psychology* 73, 1967.

ADOLESCENT SEXUALITY

Excerpt from Varieties of Sexual Experience: An Anthropological Perspective on Human Sexuality

Suzanne G. Frayser

SOCIOCULTURAL DIMENSIONS OF PUBERTY AND ADOLESCENCE

Puberty involves a variety of physical changes over a period of years. How does the social group mark this time in a person's life? Does the group draw attention to it at all? If it does, which physical characteristics are emphasized? The biological changes provide ample possibilities for sociocultural elaboration. Do the changes mean the same thing in all societies? If not, what sorts of variations are there?

Social attention and cultural interpretations at the onset of puberty. A Goajiro (159) girl in North Columbia or Venezuela is not likely to forget the onset of puberty, especially if she is a member of the upper class. Upper-class people in that part of the world have more extended and elaborate versions of the same ceremonies that are conducted by people in the lower class. Despite differences in the scale of the ceremonies, the underlying theme remains the same for all of them: first menstruation is a signal to prepare a girl for womanhood. The period that she undergoes after first menstruation emphasizes the importance of the transition. I will focus on the upper-class ritual, since it is richer in its symbolic elements.

Constraint marks the life of a child approaching puberty. Treatment of the young girl's body symbolizes the restrictions to which she is subject. Many of her ordinary activities are curtailed. She is wrapped in a robe, and she must lie down in her house for five days. She should not move, scratch herself, spit, or eat. As if to emphasize the necessity for her to empty herself of her previous stage in life, she must drink an herbal mixture which makes her vomit. Her spatial seclusion and departure from her usual routine mark her withdrawal from childhood and her approach to womanhood. After her first phase of seclusion, her friends and consanguineal relatives join together in a feast and dancing. They express their feeling for the special nature of the occasion by dressing up, engaging in group activities—e.g., races—contributing food for the feast, and prolonging their participation over a period of days.

When the next phase of seclusion begins, the girl becomes even more separated from social life than she was in the first phase. She is lowered into a room separate from the main household, or she retreats to a room from which she can communicate to the household only through a small opening. Separation from men is a particularly important aspect of her segregation. Not only should she not be visited by men; she should not even see them. Needless to say, sexual relations are out of the question. Her seclusion lasts for a significant period of time. Poor people can manage social withdrawal of the woman for one month or less, while middle- to high-income people can extend her segregation from six months to a year.

Why does a young woman participate in such practices? In terms of Goajiro beliefs, the answer is permeated with some of the most significant aspects of a woman's life in Goajiro society. The point of the ritual is to ensure a successful marital life for the woman who takes part. The ceremonial elements are supposed to aid a girl in avoiding bad pregnancies, hard or abnormal deliveries, exhaustion from frequent childbearing, and ill children. In other words, the focus of the ritual is to prepare a girl for the Goajiro's version of womanhood, i.e., marriage and children.

An elaborate ceremony marks the conclusion of the ritual. Unlike the first feast, the young woman may participate in the festivities; she is now considered a marriageable young woman. Friends, family members, and important people from the surrounding region attend the celebration. The young woman's appearance expresses her new status. Her haircut, facial painting, and garment are now those of an adult woman. Her jewelry and ornaments supplement other physical indicators of adulthood by indicating her family rank. The lengthy ritual is now complete.

The social group has helped the girl to effect a transition from girlhood to womanhood. The girl has shown her commitment to the transition by observing the rules of her seclusion. The group has shown its recognition of her commitment and her new responsibilities by their affirmations of her new status; feasts, dances, and acceptance of her new appearance reinforce her new station in life.

Like the Goajiro, most societies regard first menstruation as an important event (39 of 42 societies, or 93%). However, the significance attributed to it varies considerably. Although some societies (9 of 42 societies, or 21%) interpret first menstruation solely in physical terms, i.e., as a cue that the girl is mature enough to engage in intercourse (6 of 42 societies, or 14%) or a sign that she can now reproduce (3 of 42 societies, or 7%), most do not. Such physical capabilities are usually combined with or overshadowed by social translations of the biological facts. Menstruation may mean that a woman is eligible for marriage (12 of 42 societies, or 28.6%) or that she is an adult (7 of 42 societies, or 16.7%). However, the significance of first menstruation need not be confined to one meaning. The power of the symbolic elements attached to it may derive from the layers of meaning that enfold it. Quite a few societies (11 of 42 societies, or 26%) attach multiple meanings to first menstruation. For example, the Goajiro believe that first menstruation signifies adulthood, eligibility to marry, and ability to reproduce. When the onset of menstruation has multiple meanings attached to it, eligibility to marry is always among them. Overall, eligibility to marry emerges as one of the most consistently important meanings attached to first menstruation (23 of 42 societies, or 55%).

The social definition of the onset of menstruation has implications for the type of attention given to the girl at this time. The severity of the ordeal that a girl undergoes is significantly associated with the meaning that is attached to initial menstruation. When adulthood and/or marriage are the primary emphases, the ordeal is likely to be moderate to severe; when sex and/or children are emphasized, it is unlikely that much of an ordeal will follow ($X^2 = 4.9$, 1 df, $p = < .05$, $N = 35$).

A sizable proportion of the world's societies (19 of 46 societies or 41%) require a woman to undergo moderate to severe restrictions. Seclusion and rules that prohibit movement, touch, sight, sound, or physical alterations of the woman's body are frequent elements in such ordeals. For example, a young Hadza (9) girl of Tanzania submits to a painful clitoridectomy and removal of part of her labia (Woodburn 1964: 312). The Kaska (129) of British Columbia sequester the young girl for a few months; only women can visit her (Teit 1956: 121-129) She dresses in a robe and hood to hide her already blackened face. She is not allowed to comb her hair or scratch her head. She has to exclude fresh meat from her diet and sip water through a straw.

The significance of first menstruation, the ordeal that the girl undergoes, and the celebration that follows the girl's ordeal are linked together. When the group invests menstruation with the meaning of adulthood or marriageability, then a moderate to severe ordeal is likely to mark the transition. In addition, a moderate to elaborate celebration is likely to follow a relatively severe ordeal. The girl who has exhibited restraint and discipline during seclusion emerges into an arena of social celebration. Her transition to her new status and role is now complete. Friends, relatives, and community members may gather around her to acknowledge her difficult experience and to accept her as a new addition to her social context.

Although first menstruation is often the trigger for social elaboration of puberty, it is not the only physical change at puberty to which groups pay attention. The budding of a woman's breasts may become the focus for a shift in social attitudes toward her. After an Otoro (30) girls breasts begin to fill out, she can go to the "girls' house" and receive lovers (Nadel 1947: 133). The Fon (18) call a girl a "woman-small" when her breasts begin to appear (Herskovits 1938: 1,277); while the Wolof (21) think that a girl should not marry or have intercourse before her breasts develop (Ames 1953: 53). Marriage transforms her into her adult status. Therefore, breast development becomes one step toward adulthood but does not signify adulthood. The Siuai (99) of the Solomon Islands think that a girl can have intercourse when her breasts fill out, but it is only when a girl actively does have intercourse that she becomes a young woman; first menstruation is incidental, and a woman reaches full adult status only after marriage (Oliver 1955: 141, 143). These examples are sufficient to show that the definition of adulthood is quite variable for girls and not necessarily attached to any one physical aspect of puberty. Biology provides the baseline for social and cultural elaboration.

Schlegel and Barry's recent study of adolescent initiation ceremonies shows how variable the social recognition of adolescence can be (Schlegel and Barry 1979). They define an adolescent initiation ceremony as "some social recognition, in ceremonial form, of the transition from childhood into the next stage" (Schlegel and Barry 1979: 199). The ceremonies are absent more often than they are present. Since male initiations have been emphasized so much in the literature. Schlegel and Barry were surprised to find that initiations are held more frequently for girls than for boys; 21 of the 182 societies they studied held them only for girls, while 9 had them only for boys: 25% held them for both girls and boys (Schlegel and Barry 1979: 201). One reason for this discrepancy may be that ceremonies for girls tend to include the immediate family or the local group, while those for boys tend to include a larger group, such as the total community. The elaborate scale of male initiations, as well as the preponderance of male ethnographers, may have led to more interest in male initiations.

Changes in physical functioning or appearance usually provide the impetus for the timing of the ceremony for both sexes. Ceremonies generally occur close to the time that boys first ejaculate and girls first menstruate (Schlegel and Barry 1979: 203). The initial signs of physical maturation, i.e., pubic hair, breast development, and masculine/feminine body contours, are the sparks for social attention to the developing child; most societies conduct ceremonies that parallel specific physical changes at puberty.

Although there are a number of similarities between male and female initiation ceremonies, there are also some striking differences. The Arunta of Australia provide a memorable contrast to the Goajiro's ceremony for girls. Although Freud referred to these Australian aborigines as "the most backward and miserable of savages" (Freud 1950: 1), the rich symbolic matrix that marks the transition of Arunta males into manhood belies his characterization. It is misleading to mistake the quantity of material culture for the quality of a person's mental life.

While both boys and girls have initiation rites around the time of puberty, boys' rites last longer and are more elaborate. Service divides the series of ceremonies into four parts: (1) painting the boy and tossing him into the air, (2) circumcision, (3) subincision, and (4) fire ordeals and bloodletting (Service 1978: 29). The intensity of the individual ordeal, as well as the degree of social participation in the initiation, escalate with each phase of the ritual. The young, ten- to twelve-year-old boys may find some comfort in the Arunta practice of initiating a group of boys, together rather than individually. Many of the rites are quite painful and require discipline and courage. The boys know they are not alone in their pain and in their fears. A bond can develop between them in the face of their ordeal.

The first rite is relatively small and tame compared with those that follow. Until this time, the boys have associated primarily with other noninitiated children and the women. When they have passed through the initial rite, they can participate in some of the economic activities performed by adult men. Their status begins to change. To qualify for the change, the boys must submit to the actions of the men who initiate them. As the women dance in a circle around them, shouting and waving their arms, the men throw the boys in the air several times (Service 1978: 28). Prospective brothers-in-law paint the backs of their young, potential relatives. The men begin to modify the bodies of the boys by piercing their nasal septums: they can now lodge a nasal bone in the newly created opening.

Seclusion and secrecy mark the second phase of the initiation ceremony. The men snatch the boys from their ordinary setting and carry them to a secret place which has been stocked with food and firewood. Their ritual singing and dancing transmit some of the tribal myths to the young boys. Once again, the boys submit to alterations in appearance. The men wrap their heads with fur strings and girdle their waists with bands of human hair. After this, they sequester the boys in an even more hidden spot, where the men reveal the tribe's sacred knowledge to them. Their instruction lasts almost a week and is followed by another painful rite: circumcision. While they recover from the removal of the foreskins of their penises, they must submit to further physical manipulation by their elders. The men intermittently bite the scalps of the boys until they bleed; they say that biting stimulates hair growth. The boys come out of seclusion after they have completely recovered from their wounds.

The third phase of initiation begins a few weeks after the second. The men return the boys to their last place of seclusion and transmit sacred knowledge to them again. The completion of this phase is marked by a physical modification in the boys bodies: subincision: the men cut the underside of the penis to the urethra.

Physical modifications of the initiates' bodies continue into the last and most elaborate phase of the ceremony, the "*engwura*." The boys undergo bloodletting and fire ordeals as a final testimony to their stamina and value as adult men. They learn more details about the privileged reservoirs of secret information pertinent to the tribe and their group. At last they have become men and are accorded fully adult status by their group. The extensive dancing and feasting of the group express their evaluation of the importance of the occasion. Masses of people from miles around congregate to participate in the celebration. The festivities may continue for months.

Each boy's puberty provides an occasion for a peak in social activity. His initiation shows the gradual imprint of his group on him. He is physically and socially sequestered from the life he had led before. He withdraws from women's activities and begins to accept the tasks of men He shares his transition with other boys and with the men who initiate him. He is filled with knowledge of the society he is about to enter as an adult. As if to symbolize the social importance of the transition, the group imposes its own physical transformation on the boy during puberty. His penis is altered by circumcision and subincision, according to social rules; these physical modifications remain permanent symbols of the boy's transformation to manhood. The group affirms his new status and their own solidarity by the communal ceremonies, which finalize the ritual.

The scale of participation in the Arunta boys' initiation ritual contrasts with that of the more subdued, individualistic initiation of the Goajiro girl. According to Schlegel and Barry, this is a common distinction between male and female initiations. Girls are usually initiated alone (87%, or 73 of 84 societies) within the context of their immediate families or the local group (Schlegel and Barry 1979: 201). Boys' initiations are more likely to include groups of young men and to draw the participation of groups of people beyond the local community (48%, or 29 of 61 societies) (Schlegel and Barry 1979: 201). Perhaps one reason that boys' ceremonies can be held in groups is that their initiations are less tied to the physical aspects of puberty than are those of the girls. Therefore, the group has more flexibility to decide when to plan its rituals. Schlegel and Barry find that 82% (68 of 83 societies) of the societies for which they have information initiate girls at the first signs of genital maturation or at genital maturation. On the other hand, only 39% (24 of 62 societies) of the societies use genital maturation as a cue for performing initiation ceremonies for boys; they may occur before genital maturation (21%), a year after maturation (27%), or later, (13%) (Schlegel and Barry 1979: 202).

It is notable that boys' initiations are more likely to include pain and genital operations (40 of

63 societies, or 64 %) than are those of girls (28 of 84 societies, or 33%) (Schlegel and Barry 1979: 202). Physical manifestations of masculinity at puberty are more subtle than those of femininity; no change in boys is as dramatic as the uncontrolled bleeding of girls at first menstruation. Does the group compensate for this difference by engraving the boy with its own assessment of his manhood? The focus of male initiation ceremonies is oriented more toward social than biological concerns. In other words, the male ceremonies seem to enhance the identification of men with areas of social concern, while those of women dramatize the classification of women with the physical, "natural" elements of life. I have discussed this theme as a major social belief about the foundation for assigning responsibility for child care. Since women bear children, the group reinforces the view that it is "natural" for women to care for their offspring. The evidence provided by Schlegel and Barry supports these inferences (Schlegel and Barry 1979: 203). They find that fertility and sexuality are the principal foci of female initiation ceremonies (62%, or 52 of 84 societies) while valor, wisdom, and, particularly, responsibility (65%, or 40 of 62 societies) dominate the emphases of male initiations. Both sexes share the importance of initiation as a status marker and as recognition of physical change or behavior change (males—65%: females—89%). Men's initiations are more likely to be interpreted in terms of spiritual changes or in terms of death and rebirth (29%, or 18 of 63 societies) than are those of girls (5%,or 4 of 84 societies). Once again we see that the group invests much of its creative, symbolic load onto the physical changes that signal the beginning of puberty.

However, the secrecy that characterizes the Arunta male initiation ceremony is not a common component of male or female initiations; only 5 % of the male initiation ceremonies and 4 % of the female rituals concentrate on learning skills and sharing secrets (Schlegel and Barry 1979: 202). More common is the importance of seclusion and observing taboos (males—53%; females—76%); males are more likely than females to have to deal with fear (males—11%; females—2%) and absorbing symbolic meanings (males—32%; females—18%) (Schlegel and Barry 1979: 202). Overall, the ceremonies seem to prepare men for participation in a wider social matrix than that of the women. The primary social consequences of female initiations are negligible, or else they merely revolve around their relationships to a small group of people, e.g., their families and their mates. In contrast, the main social consequences of male initiations are more likely to include the importance of same-sex bonding (males—37%; females—8%) and relationships to a larger group of people.

SEXUAL ABUSE
OF CHILDREN

LEGAL, SOCIAL, AND BIOLOGICAL DEFINITIONS OF PEDOPHILIA

M. Ashley Ames, Ph.D. Cand., and David A. Houston, J.D., Ph.D.[1]

Although there is substantial evidence in the historical and anthropological record of the sexual use of children by adults, surprisingly little is known about the etiology of pedophilia or its relation to other forms of sexual aggression. After briefly reviewing the research on pedophilia, we argue that one major difficulty in conducting or interpreting such research lies in the different definitions "pedophilia" has received. Most important, much of the research has accepted a legal definition of pedophilia, treating all offenders convicted of "child molestation" as pedophiles, regardless of the age or appearance of the victim. We argue that a distinction should be made between biological children and sociolegal children. Laws governing child molestation reflect sociolegal childhood, regardless of its discrepancy with biological childhood. "True" pedophiles should be identified by their preference of biological children. By using legal classifications, researchers may well be confusing two distinct types of offenders, child molesters and rapists, and confounding attempts to understand pedophilia.

Key Words: pedophile; sex offender; cross-generational sexuality.

INTRODUCTION

The paper (i) briefly reviews some of the historical attitudes toward the sexual use of chidren, (ii) examines on an atomistic level what is known about those individuals who act on their arousal to children, and (iii) examines how societal values have influenced the concept of adult/child sex and how this influence has impacted on the quest for scientific knowledge. Behavior that constitutes the sexual use of children in a sociolegal sense is not identical to what constitutes the sexual use of children in a biological sense. Accordingly, "sociolegal pedophilia" has different dimensions than "biological pedophilia." The confusion surrounding the differences between these two conceptualizations has hindered research into pedophilia, hampering our efforts to understand this problem. We must distinguish between violations of sociolegal norms and the more biologically dysfunctional problem of true pedophilia (i.e., sexually attracted by biologically prepubescent children).

HISTORICAL OVERVIEW

The historical record reveals no universal consensus on the appropriateness of adult/child sex outside the nuclear family. Nonetheless, while little recorded history exists pertaining to children, the evidence that does exist indicates that the sexual use of children has a long history.

The sexual use of pubescent boys was practiced in Ancient Greece where young males, barely past puberty and as yet "unbearded," were solicited by warriors as proteges and lovers (43). These boys always took the passive role, since men who allowed themselves to be sodomized were held in the lowest contempt (42).

"Legal, Social and Biological Definitions of Pedophilia," by David A. Houston, J.D., Ph.D., and M. Ashley Ames, Ph.D. candidate, from *Archives of Sexual Behavior*, Vol. 19, No. 4, Plenum Publishing, 1990. Reprinted by permission.

The growth of Christianity led to the condemnation of these practices, though apparently not to protect the young males as much as to prevent onanism (21). These condemnations served to protect male children somewhat, but no such protection was afforded female children. Medieval Canon law officially forbade the marriage of girls less than 12 years old, but it was not uncommon to find girls of 10 married to very old men (31). The streets of 14th century Florence were alive with children of both sexes acting as prostitutes (21).

Historical accounts from the 18th century indicate that adult/child sex (particularly same-sex pairings) were an accepted practice in China, Japan, Africa, Turkey, Arabia, Egypt, and the Islamic areas of India (41). In 19th century London the going price for a virginal, 12-year-old girl, of good background, was reported to be 400 pounds (10).

Two recent "travel guides for gentlemen" show that the desire for sexual interactions with children is still apparent in the Western world. The *Discreet Gentlemen's Guide to the Pleasures of Europe* (1975) reported on where one can find "Lolita-eyed nymphettes who make pocket money with every orifice but the natural one." Along the same lines, *Mankoff's Lusty Europe* (30) revealed where one can find prostitutes as young as 10 years old. The full scope of such sexual practices is indicated in a report on child pornography given to the Congress of the United States. This report stated that at least 250 publications exist in the U.S. devoted to the graphic depiction of erotica using children from 3 to 5 years of age. The U.S. Humane Society estimated that 1.2 million children annually are involved in illegal commercial enterprises revolving around sexual exploitation. Another 100,000 children are estimated to be sexually abused annually by individuals (25).

Adult sexual interest in children is not confined to the Western world. Ritualized homosexuality involving young boys is practiced in 10 to 20% of Melanesian societies (23). Variations of the manner in which sex is allowed are found from one tribe to another with some using fellatio, others anal intercourse, and still others masturbation. In these societies, girls as young as 8 years old are also used for special ceremonies that involve making medicine from seminal fluids gathered from the child after intercourse. Young brides of the Kiman Papuan tribe are "tested" by many men prior to the wedding ceremony to insure their fitness for marriage (39).

The historical and cross-cultural record clearly reflects the long-standing existence of the use of children in sexual practices. The accounts given thus far have all centered on extrafamilial liaisons. Evidence indicates that intrafamilial adult/child sex has an equally pervasive history.

HISTORICAL AND CROSS-CULTURAL PERSPECTIVES ON INCEST

The factor of relatedness has resulted in a different conceptualization of adult/child sex when the act occurs between a child and a relative. The ubiquity of the incest taboo has been debated by sociologists and anthropologists. Sociologists have generally contended that the prohibition against incest is societally determined and is not universal (40), while anthropologists have generally contended that the incest taboo is one of the most universal of all rules (17). Whether universal or just extremely widespread, the prevalence of the incest taboo indicates a common cross-cultural process that has led to its adoption in varying degrees in divergent cultures.

In spite of the debate over how and why the incest taboo came about, empirical evidence is convincing that intrafamily mating lead to a selective disadvantage (27). In Middle Eastern societies, where relatives frequently married, increased rates of genetic disease have been found (15). Also in Japan, where as many as 5% of all marriages were between first cousins, Schull and Neel (38) found that inbred offspring were not as healthy as outbred offspring. Evidence from the United States is similar; children of incestuous matings display inordinately high rates of mental retardation and physical anomalies (2).

Some form of the incest taboo appears to be in place not only cross-culturally but also across species. Among primates, where paternity is often in question, either the males or the females of the species leave the home troop at sexual maturity, thus rendering incestuous matings unlikely. Female chimpanzees in estrus have been observed to display violent behavior to ward off the sexual advances of a brother (20).

Due to the widespread cross-species and cross-cultural nature of the incest taboo, sociobiologists contend that avoidance of incest has evolved as an adaptive pattern. Bischof (8) contends that natural selection seems to favor behavior patterns that render incest very improbable. Breuer (9) stated that "in the light of today's ethological knowledge it must be assumed that the notion of incest was not 'invented' at all, but rather that men inherited from their ancestors unconscious behavior patterns of inborn incest avoidance that later were woven into their culture."

Whether the avoidance of incest is a biological or a sociological imperative, intrafamilial adult/child sex involves a second dimension of deviance over and above the societal prohibitions against the sexual use of children. If we assume that the practice of incest involves the breaking of two norms, we can expect to find lower rates of incest than rates of extrafamilial adult/child sex within the population. Evidence on the prevalence of sexual abuse reviewed below generally supports this statement.

This hypothesis of double deviance serves to confound research into the etiology of incest. Natural questions that have arisen but are as yet unanswered concern the specificity of the incestuous father's arousal. Certainly, some pedophiles marry and have children (1). Instances of inappropriate sexual age preferences are found less frequently among incestuous fathers than among nonincestuous child molesters (35). If this finding remains constant under replication, somewhat different processes are involved in the etiology of incest and in the etiology of pedophilia.

PREVALENCE OF ADULT/CHILD SEX

Ascertaining a definitive estimate of the prevalence of adult/child sex is understandably difficult. Estimates derived from crime statistics involve only reported cases and are likely to be an underrepresentation. Retrospective reports carry their own inherent problems but are perhaps our best source of knowledge. Finkelhour (16) questioned 530 female and 266 male college students about their sexual experiences in childhood. Results revealed that 11% of the females and 4% of the males reported having had an unwanted sexual experience with an adult before the age of 12. Females reported that 46% of such encounters involved a relative, 33% an acquaintance, and 24% a stranger. Males were less often abused by a relative (17%) and more often by acquaintances (53%) and strangers (30%).

Apparently, a large percentage of the population has experienced some form of unwanted sexual abuse. Data on the differential incidence of offending across perpetrators indicates that a relatively small number of men are responsible for a large number of offenses. Self-report data gathered from nonincarcerated pedophiles indicate that some pedophiles are responsible for a very large number of victims. Reports obtained from 232 child molesters, who were guaranteed confidentiality, revealed that on average they had victimized 76 children (1). Incarcerated pedophiles also report a high incidence of encounters and, on average, report having 11 more victims than those for which they were prosecuted (22). An accurate estimate of the number of pedophiles is probably impossible to obtain with the current data. What can be said is that pedophiles commit many offenses across a lifetime of offending and are never prosecuted for many of the offenses that they commit.

NATURE OF THE OFFENDER

A great deal of the existing literature on pedophiles is of an atheoretical nature. Many of the studies that have attempted to find causal variables in pedophiles have either not used control groups or have attempted such controls based solely on the type of offense (26). Furthermore, the existing data are almost exclusively obtained from incarcerated pedophiles, thus limiting the generalizability of findings. Nonetheless, some valuable information has been found and should help to illuminate the nature of the men who seek out children as sexual partners.

In a sample of 34 child molesters incarcerated in Canada, only 26% had committed their crimes under the influence of drugs or alcohol. Consistent with current beliefs about the intergenerational effect of abuse, 53% of this sample claimed to have been victims of sexual abuse themselves (14). These findings have been replicated in a U.S. sample of 68 pedophiles, incarcerated in Massachusetts for sexual abuse of children. Of these men, 57% reported having been victims of sexual abuse in childhood. This finding compared to 23% of 107 rapists in the same institution. Significantly more child molesters than rapists had siblings with psychiatric histories. Pedophiles also had more chronic medical problems and lower IQs than rapists (7).

Attempts to make comparisons of the psychological functioning of sexual offenders based on the age of the victim have revealed some interesting findings, although the utility of using control groups based upon such comparisons has been questioned (34). Men whose offenses were committed against children have higher frequencies of avoidant and dependent personalities and lower frequencies of antisocial and borderline personalities than men who agress against adult women (5). This finding supports the stereotype of the weak, passive, socially isolated, and inept man who turns to children for sexual fulfillment. This stereotype is further supported by the findings of Wilson and Cox (45) who interviewed 77 members of a self-help club for pedophiles in London. Using the Eysenck Personality Questionnaire these men presented themselves as introverted, shy, sensitive, lonely, depressed, and humorless.

Men who are involved in incestuous relationships do not present the same picture of pathology as do men who are involved with nonrelated children. In constrast to the findings cited above, incest very frequently involves alcohol abuse (29, 44). Gebhard *et al.* (19) reported that incestuous fathers seldom display diagnosable mental problems but usually fall at the ends of the spectrum of dominance; some incestuous fathers are very dominant, others, very passive, with few at intermediate levels. Even though little agreement exists in the literature about the nature of the men who practice incest, agreement is found about the nature of the family where incest is found. De Francis (12) reported that the greater the family disorganization, the higher the proportion of relatedness in cases of sexual abuse. Along these same lines, Avery-Clark *et al.*, (6) and Patterson (32) have reported that extreme chaos and frequent crisis situations are often found in incestuous families. They also reported that incestuous families frequently have high rates of general disorganization and disturbed marital relationships.

What then can be said about the nature of pedophiles? Given the existing research, about half of incarcerated pedophiles have themselves experienced sexual abuse as children. As a group, they are less prone than other offenders to abuse drugs or alcohol. They often report being sickly as children and having chronic illnesses. They describe themselves in terms of being shy and introverted, and they are often given a DSM-III (4) diagnosis that supports this view they hold of themselves.

THE NATURE OF THE SOCIETY

Societies have dealt with adult/child sex with a great deal of variance. Even the presumed universal taboo of father/daughter incest has been inconsistently enforced throughout European and American history (29). This legal ambivalence is perhaps a reflection of a social ambivalence about the appropriateness of adult/child sex.

Societies that practice a form of ritualized homosexuality between men and boys are usually societies in which women have very low status (3). In addition to holding low status, women in these societies are often looked upon as a toxic force to be avoided except for procreative purposes (23). These beliefs leave men little choice but to turn to younger males for recreational sexual liaisons. These societies also tend to be warrior societies that highly value virility. Age-appropriate homosexual acts would not be tolerated since one of the partners (whoever was the recipient of the other's penis) would be viewed as submissive and thus unworthy of his place with other men. After observing several of these cultures as they exist today, Herdt (23) has said that the belief that the semen given to the child during these practices will facilitate his growth is merely a rationalization for homoerotic play.

Children of high social status frequently escaped being subjected to these practices. This observation is evidenced by the practice in Ancient Rome of having young boys of high status wear a gold ball around their necks so that any potential abusers would know that they were not to be used (13).

The use of female children also seems to have been primarily restricted to girls of low social status. When outrage was expressed about an adult/child liaison, the liaison frequently involved a man of low status and a child of high status. When cases involved parties from the same social status, concern was more for the father's loss of a commodity (his daughter's virginity) than for any loss incurred by the child (37).

During the 17th, 18th, and 19th centuries, childhood was much briefer, and children worked in factories or were apprenticed at very young ages. Children no less than women were the property of the father (36). The line between childhood was not clear, and biological rather than chronological dictates were used to determine the end of childhood. This situation was true not only in our own preindustrial society but in all primitive cultures yet studied. The end of childhood for the female was marked by the commencement of menstruation and for the male by his ability to physically assume a man's role (13).

The trend in Western society has been to arbitrarily set dates as milestones along the way to adulthood, instead of observing the more natural biological markers. This prolongation of childhood has led to a limbo period wherein young people are physiologically, but not sociologically, prepared for reproduction. At this point in our history, a very real conundrum exists for the researchers of adult/child sex. This problem is reflected in the question of what truly marks the point beyond which sexual interaction with a child is pathological and not just criminal. The remainder of this paper is devoted to exploring that question.

WHERE DOES PEDOPHILIA BEGIN?

We turn to the discipline that rests at the intersection of sociology and biology, sociobiology. A basic tenet of sociobiology is that traits producing behaviors resulting in a higher rate of reproductive success become more highly represented in the population over time. The selection of fecund sexual partners can be viewed as such a behavior.

Men who consistently prefer prepubescent children as sexual partners are practicing a very unsound reproductive strategy. In contrast, men who prefer postpubescent girls are practicing a sound reproductive strategy. Sociobiological research has consistently found a distinct preference among males of all primates for young females (28, 32). In an interesting study with males between age 7 and adulthood, Cross and Cross (11) found that all males, regardless of age, rated the faces of 17-year-olds as more appealing than the faces of any other age group. These findings are suggestive of a pervasive male preference for youthful females. From the standpoint of sound reproductive strategy and increased reproductive success, this preference makes intuitive sense.

The biological line of demarcation between childhood and adulthood seems to be a more natural discriminator in efforts to classify men as pedophiles or nonpedophiles. As in all classification systems, those individuals who fall at or near the intersection are hardest to classify. If, however, one is using the secondary sex characteristics of the victim as the crucial discriminator, whether the man is aroused by children or by postpubescent girls should be fairly apparent. If the offender's victims are consistently without secondary sexual characteristics, the man is a pedophile.

The importance of body-shape in the construct of pedophilia is demonstrated in research by Freund (18). Using a group of homosexually oriented and heterosexually oriented pedophiles, Freund found that erectile responses were more dependent on their explicit preference for an immature or mature body-type than upon their preference as to gender of sexual partner. In a series of similar experiments involving the elicitation of erectile responses via visual stimuli, Quinsey *et al.* (35) found that incest offenders were not as aroused by models of an inappropriate age as were pedophiles. This finding supports the hypothesis that incest follows a different etiological course than does pedophilia. In a third set of experiments, Howell (24) found that pedophiles demonstrated a marked preference for slimness and a small body build when compared to other offenders. All these findings suggest that for the pedophile the lack of secondary sex characteristics is the arousing criterion, whereas for nonpedophiles, the presence of secondary sex characteristics is the arousing criterion. If this line of thinking proves to be correct, age is an irrelevant factor in the diagnosis of pedophilia. Instead of age, body-type should become the crucial discriminant.

The desire among men to have sexual interactions with children is not uncommon. We suggest that a distinction should be made between biological children and sociolegal children. The end of biological childhood is clearly marked in females by the onset of menarche. While the age of the onset of menarche can vary from one culture to another, it is marked by discernible signs. The redefinition of body-type from flat and slim to mature is a universal determinant of the end of biological childhood. The end of sociolegal childhood is not so apparent and is extremely variable across cultures and times. Laws governing child molestation reflect this sociolegal childhood, regardless of its discrepancy with biological childhood. This discrepancy has served to cloud what should be a natural distinction between offender types, between child molestation and rape. By making this distinction, important differences between these populations will perhaps be found and the eitology of pedophilia will become more apparent.

David A. Houston was supported during the preparation of this article by a National Science Foundation Graduate Fellowship.

NOTES

1. Indiana University, Bloomington, Indiana 47401.

REFERENCES

1. Abel G., Mittleman, M., and Becker, J. (1987). Sexual offenders: Results of assessment and recommendations for treatment. In Ben-Aron, M. H., Hucker, S.J., and Webster, C.D. (eds.), *Clinical Criminology: The Assessment and Treatment of Criminal Behavior,* Butterworth, Toronto, Canada.

2. Adams, M., and Neel, J. (1967). Children of incest. *Pediatrics* 40:55.

3. Allen, M. (1984). Homosexuality, male power, and political organization in North Vanuatu: A comparative analysis. In Herdt, G. H. (ed.), *Ritualized Homosexuality in Melanesia*, University of California Press, Berkeley, pp. 83–126.

4. American Psychiatric Association. (1980). *Diagnostic and Statistical Manual of Mental Disorders*, 3rd. ed., APA, Washington, DC.

5. Ames, A., Fleming, D., Knight, R., and Straus, H. (1987). The incident of antisocial personality disorder among rapists and child molesters. Unpublished manuscript.

6. Avery-Clark, C., O'Neil, J., and Laws, D. (1981). A comparison of intrafamilial sexual and physical child abuse. In Cook, M., and Howells, K. (eds.), *Adult Sexual Interest in Children*, Academic Press, Toronto, Canada, pp. 3–39.

7. Bard, L., Caster, D., Cerce, D., Knight, R., Rosenberg, R., and Schneider, B. (1987). A descriptive study of rapist and child molesters: Developmental, clinical and criminal characteristics. *Behav. Sci. Law* 5:

203–220.

8. Bischof, N. (1975). Comparative ethology in incest avoidance. In Fox, R. (ed.), *Biosocial Anthropology*, Malaby, London, England.

9. Bruer, G. (1984). *Sociobiology and the Human Dimension*, Cambridge University Press, Cambridge, England.

10. Bullough, V. (1964). *The History of Prostitution*, University Books, New Hyde Park, NY.

11. Cross, J., and Cross, J. (1971). Age, sex, race, and the perception of facial beauty. *Dev. Psychol.* 5: 433–439.

12. De Francis, V. (1969). *Protecting the Child Victim of Sex Crimes Committed by Adults*, American Humane Society, Children's Divisions, Denver, CO.

13. De Mause, L. (1974). *The History of Childhood,* Psychohistory Press, New York. *The Discreet Gentlemen's Guide to the Pleasures of Europe.* (1975). Bantam Books, New York.

14. Earls, C., Bouchard, L., and Laberge, J. (1984). *Etude Descriptive des Delinquents Sexual Incarceres Dans les Penitencier Quebicios*, Cashier de Recherce No. 7, Institute Philippe Pinel de Montreal, Montreal, Canada.

15. Feldman, M. (1980). Genetics and social behavior. In Markl, H. (ed.), *Evolution of Social Behavior: Hypothesis and Empirical Tests*, Dahlem Konferenzea, Berlin, Germany.

16. Finkelhour, D. (1979). Psychological, cultural and family factors in incest and family sexual abuse. *J. Marr. Fam. Counsel.* 4: 41–49.

17. Fox, R. (1972). Alliance and constraint: Sexual selection and the evolution of human kinship systems. In Campbell, B. (ed.), *Sexual Selection and the Descent of Man 1871–1971*, Heineman, London.

18. Freund, K. (1965). Erotic preference in pedophilia. *Behav. Res. Ther.* 3: 229–234.

19. Gebhard, P., Gagnan, J., and Pomeroy, W. (1965). *Sex Offenders: An Analysis of Type*, Harper & Row, New York.

20. Goodall, J. (1971). The behavior of free-living chimpanzees in the Bombe stream area. *Anim. Behav. Monogr.* 1: 161–311.

21. Goodrich, M. (1976). Sodomy in medieval secular law. *J. Homosex.* 1: 295–302.

22. Groth, A., Longo, R., and McFadin, J. (1982). Undetected recidivism among rapists and child molesters. *Crime Delinquency* 28: 450–458.

23. Herdt, G. (1984). *Ritualized Homosexuality in Melanesia*, University of California Press, Berkeley, pp. 1–81.

24. Howell, K. (1979). Some meanings of children for pedophiles. In Cook, M., and Wilson, G. (eds.), *Love and Attraction*, Pergamon, New York, pp. 519–526.

25. Kemp, C. (1980). *The Battered Child*, University of Chicago Press, Chicago.

26. Kopp, S. (1962). The character structure of sex offenders. *Am. J. Psychother.* 16: 64–70.

27. Lindzey, G. (1967). Some remarks concerning incest, the ancient taboo and psychoanalytic theory. *Am. Psychol.* 22: 1051.

28. Mackey, W. (1980). A sociobiological perspective on divorce patterns of men in the United States. *J. Anthropol. Res.* 36: 419–430.

29. Maisch, H. (1972). *Incest*, Stein & Day, New York.

30. Mankoff, A. (1973). *Mankoff's Lusty Europe*, Viking Press, New York.

31. Nobile, P. (1976). Introduction. In Kramer, W. (ed.), *The Normal and Abnormal Love of Children*, Sheed, Andrews & McMeel, Kansas City, MO.

32. Paterson, C., and Pettijohn, T. (1982). Age and human mate selection. *Psychol. Rep.* 51: 70.

33. Patterson, G. (1982). *Coercive Family Process*, Castalia, Eugene, OR.

34. Quinsey, V. (1986). Men who have sex with children. In Weisstub, O.N. (ed.), *Law and Mental Health: International Perspectives*, Vol. 2, Pergamon, New York.

35. Quinsey, V., Chaplin, T., and Carrigan, W. (1979). Sexual preferences among incestuous and nonincestuous child molesters. *Behav. Ther.* 10: 562–565.

36. Radbill, S. (1980). Children in a world of violence: A history of child abuse. In Kempe, C.H., and Helfer, R. E. (eds.), *The Battered Child*, University of Chicago Press, Chicago.

37. Rush, F. (1980). *The Best Kept Secret*, Prentice-Hall, Englewood Cliffs.

38. Schull, W., and Neel, J. (1965). *The Effects of Inbreeding in Japanese Children*, Harper & Row, New York.

39. Serpenti, L. (1984). The ritual meaning of homosexuality and pedophilia among the Kimam-Papuans of South Irian Jaya. In Herdt, G. H. (ed.), *Ritualized Homosexuality in Melanesia*, University of California Press, Berkeley, pp. 318–335.

40. Solomon, R. (1978). Sociobiology, morality, and culture. In Stent, G.S. (ed.), *Morality as a Biological Phenomenon*, Dahlem Konferenzen, Berlin, Germany, pp. 283–387.

41. Trumbach, R. (1977). London's sodomites: Homosexual behavior and Western culture in the eighteenth century. *J. Soc. Hist.* 11: 1–33.

42. Ungaretti, J. (1978). Pederasty, heroism and the family in classical Greece. *J. Homosex.* 3: 291–300.

43. Vanggaard, T. (1972). *Phallos: A Symbol and Its History in the Male World*, Cape, London.

44. Virkkunen, M. (1974). Incest offenses and alcoholism. *Med. Sci. Law* 124–128.

45. Wilson, G., and Cox, D. (1983). Personality of pedophile club members. *Pers. Indiv. Diff.* 4: 323–329.

CULTURAL DIVERSITY AND SEXUAL ABUSE PREVENTION

Helen Noh Ahn and Neil Gilbert

In the public mind, child sexual abuse is associated with inexpressibly bad behavior. But when professionals try to mark the boundaries of this type of abuse, it is unclear where they should draw the line. The lack of agreement about the full range of behavior that constitutes child sexual abuse comes to light in the results of 15 surveys that attempt to estimate the prevalence of this problem. According to these surveys, the proportion of females sexually abused as children ranges from 6 percent to 62 percent of the population. The discrepancies among these findings are due in large measure to differences in the researchers' operational definitions of sexual abuse, which include sexual propositions, exposure to an exhibitionist, unwanted touches and kisses, fondling, sexual intercourse, and other physical contact.[1]

As these studies suggest, definitions of child sexual abuse include an array of behaviors that fall along a continuum ranging from serious offenses that almost everyone would agree constitute abuse to mild acts that many would find inappropriate, but few would label abusive. Between these ends of the continuum lies a gray area in which agreement about abusive behavior is difficult to establish.[2] This realm of ambiguity is no trivial matter since definitions of child abuse form the practical basis for identification, intervention, and prevention of the problem.

When considering definitions of child abuse, professionals continually caution about the need to recognize the implications of cultural diversity. As the Institute of Judicial Administration observes "Given the cultural pluralism and diversity of child rearing practices in our society, it is essential that any system authorizing coercive state involvement in child rearing fully take these differences into account."[3]

However, the official view of practices that are harmful to children is usually dictated by the conventional morality of the dominant culture. One can cite a number of incidents in which the official view of harmful practices censures adult behavior that may be deemed generally permissible in other cultures. For example, two Filipino nannies caring for children in the United States were accused of sexual abuse because they fondled and masturbated children in their care. The women claimed this to be an accepted practice in the Philippines.[4] A Korean man in Los Angeles was accused of sexual abuse for touching a young boy's genitals. In the context of the Korean culture, this behavior is considered an expression of adoration and pride for a male child who is to carry on the family name and tradition.[5] A Vietnamese father in northern California was charged with sexual abuse for playfully touching the genitals of his 6-year-old son. The charges were eventually dismissed. As explained to the authorities, in Vietnam such behavior is regarded as an expression of fondness, not a crime. Nevertheless, the father was ordered to undergo therapy to learn that he must respect his son's rights and privacy—an idea he found difficult to absorb because in Vietnam it is the children who are taught to respect the parents.[6]

These cases suggest that in some cultures it is not seen as necessarily unwholesome or detrimental for family members to touch, even fondle, the sexual organs of babies and young children. The reasons for this behavior vary. In some cases, such fondling represents an expression of family pride or the superstitious belief that it encourages the growth of the genitals; in other cases, it is done to keep children quiet or to help them fall asleep.[7] Among the cultures that accept them, these practices occur with no recognizable guilt in adults or psychological harm to children.

Almost one-third of the child-protective cases in the United States involve minority families.[8] While professionals readily acknowledge the need for "cultural sensitivity" in dealing with problems of child abuse, exactly what this sensitivity entails is unclear, nor is it apparent how it may be translated into policy and practice. The issue of culture, Ellen Gray and John Cosgrove explain, is frequently raised but almost never addressed. As they point out, "The only accepted statements on the subject are that cultural issues must be considered in examining child abuse and neglect; child abuse investigators, adjudicators and treatment professionals must take culture into account in performing their role and policies should not be made strictly from the perspective of dominant cultural values and practices. We do not know how to put these sentiments into practice, however."[9]

In a similar approach to the definition of the problem and its adjudication, professionals widely attest to the importance of cultural sensitivity in efforts to deter child abuse, particularly in sexual abuse prevention training programs. Although many studies have examined what children learn from these programs, there have been virtually no analyses of the cultural implications of prevention training.[10] To gain insight into the cultural sensitivity of these programs involves comparing what is being taught as appropriate attitudes and behavior for young children and how these attitudes and behaviors fit with the way families from different cultural groups normally interact.

WHAT PREVENTION PROGRAMS TEACH

Since the mid-1970s, sexual abuse prevention programs have been offered to millions of children in thousands of schools throughout the country. In 1984, for example, California initiated a $10-million-a-year program of classroom-based sexual abuse prevention training. Every child in the state was to receive training at four different times during his or her school career.[11] Currently, an estimated 60 percent of school districts in the United States conduct prevention training in their classrooms.[12] Although several models and various instructional techniques are employed by these programs, the most popular curricula are organized around a core of basic content, particularly for children in pre-school and the early elementary grades. Lessons focus on prevention concepts that involve teaching children about private parts of the body, children's rights, stranger avoidance, good and bad secrets, verbal assertiveness and, in some cases, physical self-defense, and inappropriate physical contact.[13]

A review of the core content reveals that lessons taught to both parents and children in sexual abuse prevention training courses convey prescriptive guidelines about acceptable expressions of intimacy and parent-child relations in family life.[14] For children as young as 3, for example, one of the key lessons entails teaching children how to interpret impermissible sexual behavior. The two basic approaches to this lesson rely on the use of intuition and learning social rules about being touched. Although lessons on the use of intuition are sometimes couched in different terms (e.g., good touch and bad touch, safe touch and unsafe touch, red light or green light), the essential message is that any physical contact that does not feel good is a bad touch, which the child should resist and report to other adults. Examples of "bad touches include scratchy kisses and tight hugs, as well as intimate contact with a child's private parts. Children are also told to remain alert to "confusing" touches, which the programs imply, are usually bad touches that children do not immediately recognize as such.

Some programs recognize that children's feelings are not always reliable in these matters and offer the simple rule that no one should touch his or her private parts except when being bathed or examined by a doctor. "It's against the law," some programs declare.[15] While definitions of private parts vary slightly among curricula, most programs define them as the parts of the body covered by a bathing suit.

In addition to classroom training for students, many programs offer instruction for parents. Parents are often informed that they should help their children at an early age to develop boundaries about touching and to encourage physical privacy. One of the most widely employed programs in the country offers parents the following advice:

> When bathing, you can teach a child to wash their own genitals, simply by telling them they are theirs to take care of. . . . At 6 or 7, children begin to be more private in various stages of undress, and ask for privacy when going to the bathroom, taking a bath, etc. RESPECT THEIR WISHES. Children begin to want their own room, closed doors, private time alone. It's important to foster that so that children learn that they have the right to control their own body and personal space. An analogy can be drawn between a bedroom door (closed) and sexual assault. If a door is closed, like your bedroom door, then another person should not enter without your permission.[16]

Devised with the objective of enabling children to protect themselves against sexual abuse, these lessons about touching and privacy embody a set of prescriptions for appropriate family interactions. This prescribed behavior is based on the views of a fairly small group of program specialists who design curricula for sexual abuse prevention training. With prevention programs subsidized by public authorities and presented in public schools, the state lends implicit sanction to these views. But to what extent do these views reflect what might be considered acceptable or unacceptable norms of intimacy in the family life of various ethnic and cultural groups?

PATTERNS OF FAMILY INTIMACY

How do prevention lessons about touching and privacy fit with the way families from different ethnic groups normally behave in regard to these matters? To explore this question, we examine data on patterns of family intimacy from a survey of 364 mothers representing six ethnic groups. The sample consists of 95 African Americans, 30 Cambodians, 56 Caucasians, 96 Hispanics, 57 Koreans, and 30 Vietnamese. The majority of the interviews were conducted by telephone, but in-person interviews were used when telephone interviews were not feasible. Nonprobabilistic purpose sampling was employed in the study. The majority of African-American, Caucasian, Hispanic, and Korean samples were drawn from the Bay Area and Sacramento, California, while Cambodian and Vietnamese mothers were sampled from Seattle, Washington. More African-American and Hispanic mothers, in particular, were sampled to allow for variability in socioeconomic status.

For the groups sampled in California, churches reflecting the major religion practiced by each of the four ethnic groups were selected as sampling sites. Protestant churches were selected for African Americans, Caucasians, and Koreans, and Catholic churches were selected for Hispanics. Churches were chosen as sampling sites mainly because they represent those rare organizations in the United States in which people of the same ethnic groups regularly congregate. For Cambodians, Vietnamese, and English-speaking Hispanics, and 35 African Americans, however, snowball sampling was used owing to the difficulty in locating appropriate religious organizations from which to sample.

Due to the purposive sampling procedure and self-selection bias of the sample, there is a limitation to the general applicability of the study results. To eliminate the potentially confounding factor of men and women's possibly different values, only mothers were included in the study. However, it should be recognized that this is another important limitation of the study. The field would benefit from other studies that include men to develop a broader picture of family norms, especially since men are most often identified as offenders of child abuse, in general, and sexual abuse in particular. As in all studies with a self-selected sample, one also has to be aware of the fact that the study excludes those unwilling to reveal their views about family intimacy and discipline.

The interview schedule developed for this survey was translated into Korean, Cambodian, Vietnamese, and Spanish. All interviews were conducted by interviewers of the same ethnicity and sex as the people they were questioning. Interviews with Cambodian, Vietnamese, Korean, and Spanish-speaking Hispanic respondents were administered in their native languages. A test-retest analysis of the instrument was performed with a sample of 41 individuals randomly selected from the total sample. Eleven questions that could be answered with a "yes" or "no" response were randomly selected from the instrument for retest. Retests were conducted within 2 months after the initial interviews. The test-retest reliability correlation coefficient of the instrument was .90.[17]

Among the areas of family intimacy examined in this survey, three realms of behavior are frequently related to sexual abuse prevention training: parent-child bathing practices, sleeping arrangements, and physical contact.

Familial Bathing Patterns

The mothers were asked to indicate the highest age at which they thought it would be appropriate for a parent to bathe with his or her child. As shown in table 1, except for the Vietnamese responses to the case of a mother bathing with her son, the Asian groups consistently favored parent-child cobathing for a longer period than other groups. In most cases, these differences were statistically significant.

The relatively strong disapproval of cobathing between mothers and sons (but not other pairs of parent-child cobathing) by the Vietnamese respondents is a striking exception that deserves some explanation. The aversion to this practice appears to stem from folk beliefs in Vietnam that women are impure and polluting.[18] A Vietnamese staff person working on this study reports that according to tradition, Vietnamese women are not supposed to walk in front of an altar when menstruating. They also do not bathe with children for fear that their impurity might contaminate them, causing them to become less intelligent. For similar reasons women's underwear are placed in separate buckets and washed separately from the clothes of the rest of the family. The idea that cobathing is unsanitary was reflected in the responses of many of the Vietnamese mothers who indicated that they were averse to this practice: "It is a custom. A woman never takes a bath or washes her underwear with her husband's or her children's clothes." "For sanitary reasons. People think that women should be taking baths alone." "People believe that it will dull the child's mind if he takes a bath with his mom."

It is interesting to note that while Vietnamese respondents were generally opposed to mothers taking baths with their sons, they were quite receptive to other pairs of parent-child cobathing. The reason for this unusual pattern of response is unclear. It may stem from the fact that of the three Southeast Asian countries in the study, only Vietnam was heavily influenced by Confucianism, mainly through its geographical connection to China and 1,000 years of Chinese domination between 111 B.C. and A.D. 939.[19] In Confucian tradition, sons are more valued than daughters because they carry on the family name and the duties of ancestor worship. Because Confucian tradition confers an inferior status on daughters (who are potentially also impure), there may be less concern about their being contaminated by bathing with mothers.

Overall, the Asian groups accepted parent-child cobathing to an older age than the other groups. Koreans tended to be the most liberal in this regard, with more than 20 percent of the sample expressing approval of same-sex bathing between parents and children forever. To some extent, these attitudes reflect the tradition of public baths in Korea and other Asian countries, where family members bathe together. As a whole, however liberal or conservative they were about cobathing, every group tended to be more tolerant of cobathing between parents and children of the same sex than cobathing between those of different sexes.

No one among the Asian respondents, even those who were least tolerant of parent-child cobathing, expressed explicit concerns that this behavior might be sexually stimulating. In several cases, however, they noted that nudity might cause some embarrassment. In response to a question

Table 1.

Ethnic Group Responses to Parent-Child Cobathing

	Age (in Years)		Ethnic Groups					
	Mean	SD	Vietnamese	African American	Hispanic	Caucasian	Cambodian	Korean
Highest age appropriate for a mother taking baths with her son:								
Vietnamese	.4	3.3						
African American	2.0	2.4						
Hispanic	2.8	2.8	*					
Caucasian	3.9	2.4	*	*				
Cambodian	4.4	2.9	*	*				
Korean	5.6	.8	*	*	*			
Total	3.1	3.0						

			Hispanic	African American	Caucasian	Cambodian	Korean	Vietnamese
Highest age appropriate for a mother taking baths with her daughter:								
Hispanic	3.4	3.6						
African American	3.4	3.6						
Caucasian	4.5	2.6						
Cambodian	6.1	2.2	*	*				
Korean	7.8[a]	3.0	*	*	*			
Vietnamese	8.4	2.9	*	*	*			
Total	4.7	3.7						

			African American	Hispanic	Caucasian	Cambodian	Vietnamese	Korean
Highest age appropriate for a father taking baths with his daughter:								
African American	.9	1.8						
Hispanic	1.4	2.4						
Caucasian	2.8	2.3	*	*				
Cambodian	3.9	1.6	*	*				
Vietnamese	4.2	1.9	*	*				
Korean	4.2	3.3	*	*				
Total	2.4	2.7						

			African American	Hispanic	Caucasian	Cambodian	Vietnamese	Korean
Highest age appropriate for a father taking baths with his son:								
African American	2.9	3.4						
Hispanic	3.5	3.6						
Caucasian	4.4	2.6						
Cambodian	6.0	2.3	*	*				
Korean	8.2[a]	3.1	*	*	*			
Vietnamese	8.7	2.5	*	*	*			
Total	4.6	3.8						

Note.—A one-way analysis of variance was used to test the differences between the means. When assumption of equal variance was not met, the Kruskal-Wallis one-way analysis of variance of ranks was computed to verify the validity of the results. SD = standard deviation.

[a]These mean ages were calculated based only on those who responded with actual ages. Including the total Korean sample, the figure would be considerably higher since 20%–40% of Korean mothers answered "forever" to the questions.

*Pairs of groups are significantly different at the .05 level (using the Sheffé test).

about whether it was acceptable for a mother to bathe with her 6-year-old son, for example, a Cambodian mother was concerned because "sometimes I drop my sarong, and the child might see my body."

While Asian mothers expressed few concerns about issues of sexuality in parents bathing with young children, Caucasian, African-American, and Hispanic respondents were more troubled by the sexual implications of this practice. When asked about the propriety of a mother bathing with her 6-year-old son, Caucasian respondents tended to disapprove on several accounts. For example, they claimed that "it's not healthy. It's pretty intimate behavior. Boys are pretty inquisitive." "They may think it's okay to do it with others. You need your privacy. That's when they should start learning that." "That's really wrong because of our sexual mores. It gives the impression that there are no boundaries. You need to establish personal space early on." "I'd wonder about the mother's motives. That's just a little strange." "You should get children independent as young as possible so that they don't regress."

Caucasian respondents objected to a mother's bathing with her 6-year-old son because they wanted to insure privacy, promote independence, and protect against sexual arousal. Similar themes were expressed by African Americans in explaining why they disapproved of this practice. In addition to these primary themes, a few African Americans also related the bases of their objections to religious doctrine. One respondent, for example, referred to a passage in the Bible that she interpreted as an admonishment against children seeing their parents nude. Another declared opposition to cobathing because "the devil works in mysterious ways." Such views lend support to the claim that biblical authority and religious premises guide child-rearing practices of many African Americans.[20]

Among the Hispanic respondents who disapproved of cobathing, in addition to emphasizing the importance of independence and privacy, the concern for the virtue of modesty was a predominant theme. These mothers tended to link nudity with "bad" or sexual thoughts.

Generally, Koreans were most accepting and African Americans and Hispanics least accepting of parents and children bathing together. In interpreting these findings, it is important to recognize that ethnic group differences can be confounded by other variables such as socioeconomic status and degree of acculturation. Although socioeconomic status is often defined as a composite measure of occupation, education, and income, education has been found to be among the strongest predictors of parental values.[21] It is also the best predictive measure of future socioeconomic status, particularly among students whose occupational status and income are temporarily diminished. Education was used as an indicator of socioeconomic status in this study because many of the subjects were graduate students or spouses of graduate students. Although controlling for the respondents' level of education did not alter the pattern of ethnic differences observed in Table 1, African Americans and Hispanics with 12 or fewer years of education were generally less tolerant of cobathing than those who had more than 12 years of schooling. Similarly, Hispanic subjects who had lived less than half of their lives in the United States were more restrictive of these practices than the American-born Hispanics.

Sleeping Arrangements

In response to the question, "Up to what age is it appropriate for a child to always sleep in the same bed with parents?" mothers from the Asian groups generally approved of cosleeping arrangements to a later age than Caucasian, African-American, and Hispanic mothers (see Table 2). Cambodian and Vietnamese respondents accepted cosleeping arrangements up to the latest ages (5.8 and 4.7 years, respectively), while Caucasians and African Americans indicated that such arrangements should stop before a child was 1 year old. A similar pattern emerges when respondents were asked the highest age to which it was appropriate for a child to sleep in the same room with parents. Although the mean age to which sleeping in the same room is accepted by each group is slightly higher than sleeping in the same bed with parents, the rank order among groups and the statistical significance of the observed differences remain almost the same.

Various reasons were given for the respondents' approval or disapproval of these parent-child sleeping arrangements. In explaining why they thought it appropriate for a 6-year-old girl to sleep in the same bed with her parents, Cambodians and Vietnamese (the groups most tolerant of this practice) tended to consider it a sign of parental care for children and family togetherness. They noted, for example, that "the child is small and needs care from her parents." "Children like to be with their parents when they are young, especially at night." "The child is afraid of ghosts." "The child feels close to her parents."

Among Caucasians, the group least tolerant of parent-child cosleeping arrangements, the reasons given for their disapproval most often reflected views that such behavior was an intrusion of privacy and slowed the development of independence in children. For example, respondents explained that "parents need to put their relationship first. A child can't always get what she wants and be the center." "Parents need time to themselves without the kid there. A child also needs time away from the parents." "That's not a place for the child—the marriage bed. A child has his own territory. At age six he should be able to stay by himself."

Some respondents observed that these sleeping arrangements might be acceptable in other cultures, but not in theirs, or that they were acceptable only as an occasional practice. Others indicated that sleeping in the parents' bed was sexually improper, unsanitary, or physically unhealthy for children.

Table 2.
Ethnic Group Responses to Parent-Child Cosleeping

	Age (in Years)		Ethnic Groups					
	Mean	SD	Caucasian	African American	Hispanic	Korean	Vietnamese	Cambodian
Highest age appropriate for a child always sleeping in same bed with parents:								
Caucasian	.4	1.0						
African American	.6	1.4						
Hispanic	.8[a]	2.1						
Korean	2.0	2.3	*	*				
Vietnamese	4.7	3.4	*	*	*	*		
Cambodian	5.8	4.9	*	*	*	*		
Total		1.7	2.9					
Highest age appropriate for a child sleeping in same room with parents:								
Caucasian	.7	1.1						
African American	1.2	1.4						
Hispanic	2.2	2.9						
Korean	3.2	2.8	*	*				
Vietnamese	5.2	2.6	*	*	*			
Cambodian	6.8	4.2	*	*	*	*		
Total		2.6	3.2					

Note.—A one-way analysis of variance was used to test the differences between the means. When assumption of equal variance was not met, the Kruskal-Wallis one-way analysis of variance of ranks was computed to verify the validity of the results. SD = standard deviation.

[a]This mean was calculated based only on mothers of Mexican descent ($N = 83$) in the Hispanic sample. The remaining Hispanics ($N = 13$) were excluded because they were found to be significantly different from the mothers of Mexican descent for this variable. (Mean for other Hispanics = .0, $p \leq .001$).

*Pairs of groups are significantly different at the .05 level (using the Sheffé test).

Table 3.

Percentage of Respondents Who Found Behavior Acceptable

	Ethnic Groups						
	Caucasian	African American	Hispanic	Korean	Vietnamese	Cambodian	Total
Mother who touches her 1-year-old son's genitals to calm him down	11.1	5.3	4.2	7.4	.0	13.3	6.4
Grandfather playfully touches his 3-year-old grandson's genitals with pride..	1.9	7.4	11.6	45.6	50.0	27.6	19.0*
Father and mother kiss in front of their 12-year-old son	100.0	96.8	91.4	68.4	26.7	10.0	77.6*
N	56	95	96	57	30	30	364

Note.—These sample sizes may vary slightly in different rows depending on the amount of missing data or responses other than "yes" or "no."

*$p \leq .001$ by chi-square.

Controlling for education and acculturation did little to modify the pattern of group differences observed in the initial analysis. However, compared to those who had lived most of their lives in the United States, the less acculturated Hispanic mothers were somewhat more tolerant of children sleeping in the same room, but not in the same bed as parents for a longer period of time.

Physical Contact

What are acceptable expressions of physical contact in families? Addressing this issue, mothers in the study sample were asked several questions concerning intimate behavior between family members. These questions were: (a) A grandfather touches his 3-year-old grandson's genitals with pride. Do you think this is okay? Could you explain why? (b)What if a mother touches her 1-year-old son's genitals to calm him down. Do you think this is okay? Could you explain why? (c) A father and a mother kiss in front of their 12-year-old son. Do you think this is okay? Could you explain why? As shown in Table 3, the patterns of response reveal some interesting similarities and differences among the ethnic groups. Controlling for education and acculturation revealed no significant changes in the overall pattern of ethnic differences and similarities.

The vast majority of respondents in every group thought it inappropriate for a mother to touch her 1-year-old son's genitals to calm him down. In contrast to this strong point of agreement, a considerable difference of opinion emerged in regard to the question of whether it was permissible for a grandfather to touch his 3-year-old grandson's genitals with pride. About half the Vietnamese and Koreans and 28 percent of the Cambodian mothers found the grandfather's behavior acceptable, while from 88 percent to 98 percent of the Caucasian, African-American, and Hispanic respondents found it unacceptable.

The high degree of tolerance for this behavior exhibited by Koreans and Vietnamese reflects what they consider a harmless custom of a grandfather expressing affection and pride for a male child. Respondents noted, for example, that "it's the Korean way of thinking. It's perfectly possible. Grandfathers and grandmothers feel very strongly about a grandson carrying on the family name. It's a way to express love." "It is an expression of pride that he has a grandson." "He did it out of love because he has someone to carry on the family name." "They do it in Korea, so you can't help it."

Among the Koreans who judged this behavior as inappropriate, about half the respondents noted that, although the grandfather's behavior would not be considered objectionable in Korea, customs in the United States were different. However, most of the Korean respondents, even those who objected to this behavior, did not interpret it as a sexually offensive act. Voicing a notably different opinion, the majority of Caucasian, African-American, and Hispanic mothers perceived this behavior as highly improper sexual activity, bordering on violation of the child's rights. These views were reflected in comments such as, "No reason for him to do that. It's violating the child." "We all have a right to privacy with our bodies. That's his. I would wonder about the grandfather's motivation." "With pride? It's nothing to be proud of." "I'm wondering what's going on in his (the grandfather's) head. I would want to talk to him about it."

On the question of whether it is appropriate for parents to kiss in front of their 12-year-old son, the data in table 3 reveal an interesting reversal from the previous question in the pattern of responses. While strongly opposed to the grandfather's behavior, the vast majority (over 90%) of Caucasians, African Americans, and Hispanics were quite comfortable with parents kissing in front of their child. More than simply an acceptable public expression of affection, most of these respondents perceived this behavior as a healthy demonstration of love that made children feel secure. In contrast, 90 percent of the Cambodian and 73 percent of the Vietnamese respondents disapproved of this behavior.

Koreans fell between the two extremes, with 32 percent expressing disapproval of parents kissing in front of a 12-year-old child. However, almost half the Koreans who found this behavior acceptable qualified their response, indicating that it was appropriate in the context of American life. While they themselves may not kiss in front of their children, this behavior seemed generally acceptable because children were frequently exposed to it through the mass media.

The negative response to parental kissing in front of children registered by the Asian groups, and Southeast Asians in particular, reflects conservative norms governing the public display of sexual behavior in many Asian cultures. In Korea, for example, kissing scenes are prohibited on television. Hugging and kissing between men and women in front of other people are regarded as an insult to women. In Vietnam and Cambodia, men and women holding hands in public is often considered undignified behavior. At the same time, walking hand-in-hand or arm-in-arm with a member of the same sex is deemed a normal expression of affection and closeness, in no way associated with homosexuality.[22]

IMPLICATIONS FOR PREVENTION TRAINING

The findings cited above reveal a number of significant variations among cultural groups in their views of acceptable family practices regarding parent-child bathing, sleeping arrangements, and touching. To observe that cultural differences exist is not necessarily a justification for accepting all sorts of behavior. One can imagine behaviors that different groups might practice that would be physically harmful to children and simply unacceptable in light of the prevailing standards of the majority community. Without making an extreme case for cultural relativism, however, there appears to be nothing physically harmful or inherently bad about parent-child bathing, sleeping arrangements, and a grandfather proudly touching his grandson's genitals. The different views of these practices reflect deeper, more basic, disagreements about the value of autonomy and privacy in parent-child relationships.

What are the implications of these differences for developing culturally sensitive sexual abuse prevention training programs? The most popular child sexual abuse prevention training curricula are based on the empowerment model. Starting at the preschool level, this model conveys a strong message about respecting children's privacy and encouraging their autonomy.[23] The programs recommend, for example, that as early as possible children should start to bathe themselves, be afforded privacy in their own rooms, develop a sense of physical boundaries and control of their own bodies, and learn to say "no" to the adults in their lives. Autonomy and privacy are more highly valued in parent-child relations by Caucasians, African Americans, and many Hispanics than by parents in the three Asian groups. Indeed, compared to the other groups, Asian children are more likely to be viewed as an extension of their parents, on whom they are dependent and to whom they owe strict obedience. Among most Asian groups, family unity and filial piety clearly take precedence over children's rights and independence.[24]

The lessons of child sexual abuse prevention training set boundaries that do not take into account the diverse patterns of acceptable behavior in American family life. When broad prescriptions for family relations recommended by these programs contradict values and traditions held by many parents in different cultural groups, how do we balance the collective obligation to protect children with the wish to respect diversity in family life? Three possible courses of action come to mind.

First, these programs might seek to change parental values and preferences. Working with Puerto Rican parents who were resistant to having their children taught assertiveness skills (i.e., saying "no"), for example, Geraldine Crisci and Maria Torres report that after considerable discussion they were able to convince the mothers to accept this practice.[25] This approach, of course, suggests that when group norms for family behavior differ from behaviors prescribed for sexual abuse prevention, the latter should prevail.

A reasonable case could be made for taking this approach if there were firm evidence that the behaviors prescribed in prevention training programs actually prevented the sexual abuse of young children (After all, diversity is not an ultimate value.) Such evidence, however, simply does not exist. As N. Dickon Repucci and Jeffrey Haugaard conclude: "There is no evidence, not even one single case example . . . that primary prevention has ever been achieved."[26] The lack of evidence on this point is not proof of ineffectiveness. However, serious questions about program effectiveness have been raised by evidence of the limited amount of classroom learning that takes place, the insufficient consideration given to developmental factors in curricula design, and unintended consequences of prevention training.[27] Under these circumstances, it is difficult to make a strong case for requiring families to conform to behavioral norms stipulated by prevention programs.

A second approach is to allow parents to exercise informed consent regarding their children's participation in these programs. Instead of imposing a set of standards for family behavior in the name of prevention, parents would be allowed to judge the extent to which they might change patterns of family interaction in light of the probable costs and benefits of prevention training. This would involve notifying parents about the program's philosophy, exactly what it intends to teach their children, and what is known about the effects of this training.

Many prevention programs have a parent component with which this information might be conveyed. However, the rate of parent participation in these programs appears rather low. Among 15 programs studied in California, for example, parent meetings were attended by only 13 percent of those with children in preschool programs.[28]

Many programs also require some form of parental permission before children are allowed to participate. This permission is usually requested through parental consent forms that convey little information about program content and present a highly skewed picture of potential risks and benefits. Often schools request only "passive" consent under which it is assumed that parents agree to their children's participation in the program unless forms are returned with an explicit refusal. A typical consent form concludes by telling parents, "We feel that this instruction is essential for the protection of all students. Should you prefer that your child *not* participate, please notify us. Your child will be provided this instruction unless you tell us you do not want your child to participate in this child abuse personal safety lesson."[29] In order for parents to exercise informed consent, they need to be made much more aware of what sexual abuse prevention programs are really about than is currently the practice.

Finally, efforts to achieve greater balance between respect for diverse patterns of family interaction and the community's obligation to protect children can be made by changing the basic orientation of prevention efforts. There are other ways to safeguard young children than providing assertiveness training that emphasizes autonomy and independence. Programs can be designed, for example, to sharpen the vigilance of parents, teachers, and other responsible caretakers and to emphasize adult responsibility for children.

This study suggests that in regard to cultural sensitivity, the prevailing model of child sexual abuse prevention training is deficient. Given the diverse norms regarding parent-child relationships among different groups and the fact that most school classes have students from several cultures, any classroom training of young children that is highly prescriptive about family behavior is likely to be found wanting.

NOTES

This study was supported by a grant from the Conrad Hilton Foundation.

1. David Finkelhor, Sharon Araji, Larry Baron, Angela Browne, Stefanie D. Peters, and Gail E. Wyatt, *A Sourcebook on Child Sexual Abuse* (Beverly Hills, Calif.: Sage, 1986).

2. Jeanne Giovannoni and Rosiana Becerra, *Defining Child Abuse* (New York: Free Press, 1979).

3. Juvenile Justice Standards Project, *Standards Relating to Abuse and Neglect* (Cambridge, Mass.: Ballinger, 1977).

4. Seth I. Goldstein, *The Sexual Exploitation of Children* (New York: Elsevier, 1987).

5. Kyung-Sook Song. *Defining Child Abuse: Korean Community Study* (doctoral diss., University of California, Los Angeles, 1986).

6. T. I. Nhu, "Fondling, or Just Fondness?" *San Jose Mercury News* (November 20, 1990). p. 7b.

7. Douglas G. Haring, "Aspects of Personal Character in Japan," in *Personal Character and Cultural Milieu*, ed. Douglas G. Haring (Syracuse, N.Y.: Syracuse University Press, 1956): and Alberto G. Serrano and David N. Gunzburger, "An Historical Perspective of Incest," *International Journal of Family Therapy* 5, no. 2 (1983): 70–80.

8. K. Burgdorf, *Recognition and Reporting of Child Maltreatment: Findings from the National Study of the Incidence and Severity of Child Abuse and Neglect* (Rockville, Md.: Westat, Inc., 1980), as cited in J. Alfaro, "Child Neglect and Cultural Condition," *Human Ecology Forum* 12 (1981): 26–30.

9. Ellen Gray and John Cosgrove. "Ethnocentric Perception of Childrearing Practices in Protective Services." *Child Abuse and Neglect* 9, no. 3 (1985): 389–96.

10. For a review of the research on what children learn from prevention training, see Jill Duerr Berrick and Neil Gilbert, *With the Best of Intentions: The Child Sexual Abuse Prevention Movement* (New York: Guilford, 1991).

11. Neil Gilbert, Jill Duerr Berrick, Nicole LeProhn, and Nina Nyman, *Protecting Young Children from Sexual Abuse* (Lexington, Mass.: Lexington Books, 1989).

12. National Committee for the Prevention of Child Abuse, *Teachers Confront Child Abuse: A National Survey of Teachers* (Chicago: National Committee for the Prevention of Child Abuse, 1989).

13. Berrick and Gilbert (n. 10 above).

14. Neil Gilbert, "Teaching Children to Prevent Sexual Abuse," *Public Interest*, no. 93 (Fall 1988), pp. 3–15.

15. See, e.g., Kathy Belland, *Talking about Touching* (Seattle: Committee for Children, 1986); and Children's Self-Help Project, *Preschool Curriculum* (San Francisco: Children's Self-Help Project, 1986).

16. Child Assault Prevention Training Center of Northern California, *Safe, Strong, and Free,* adult workshop information (Oakland, Calif.: Child Assault Prevention Training Center, 1986), p. 7.

17. For a more detailed explanation of the survey methods, see Helen Noh Ahn, "Intimacy and Discipline in Family Life: A Cross-cultural Analysis with Implications for Theory and Practice in Child Abuse Prevention" (doctoral diss. University of California, Berkeley, 1990).

18. Penny Van Esterik, "Cultural Factors Affecting the Adjustment of Southeast Asian Refugees," in *Southeast Asian Exodus: From Tradition to Resettlement: Understanding Refugees from Laos, Kampuchea, and Vietnam in Canada*, ed. Elliott Tepper (Ottawa: Canadian Asian Studies Association, 1980).

19. Ibid.

20. Paulette M. Hines and Nancy Boyd-Franklin, "Black Families," in *Ethnicity and Family Therapy,* ed. Monica McGoldrick, John K. Pearce, and Joseph Giordano (New York: Guilford, 1982).

21. James Wright and Sonia Wright, "Social Class and Parental Values for Children A Partial Replication and Extension of the Kohn Thesis," *American Sociological Review* 41 (June 1976): 527–37.

22. Pan Asian Parent Education Project, *Pan Asian Childrearing Practices: Filipino, Japanese, Korean, Samoan, and Vietnamese* (San Diego: Pan Asian Education Project, n.d.): and Van Esterik (n. 18 above).

23. Berrick and Gilbert (n. 10 above).

24. See, e.g., N.J. Han, *Study of Urban Families in Korea* (Seoul: Iljisa, 1984): H.C. Park, "The Urban Middle Class Family in Korea" (doctoral diss., Harvard University, 1973); William Caudill and David Plath, "Who Sleeps with Whom? Parent-Child Involvement in Urban Japanese Families," *Psychiatry* 29 (1966): 344–66; and D. Y. H. Wu, "Child Abuse in Tawian," in *Child Abuse and Neglect: Cross-cultural Perspectives*, ed. Jill Korbin (Berkeley and Los Angeles: University of California Press, 1981).

25. Geraldine A. Crisci and Maria I. Torres, "Prevention in a Hispanic Community," in *An Educator's Guide to Preventing Child Sexual Abuse*, ed. Mary Nelson and Kay Clark (Santa Cruz, Calif.: Network Publications, 1986), pp. 114–21.

26. N. Dickon Repucci and Jeffrey Haugaard, "Prevention of Child Sexual Abuse: Myth or Reality?" *American Psychologist* 44, no. 10 (October 1989): 1266–75.

27. For a review of this evidence, see Berrick and Gilbert (n. 10 above): and Deborah J. Tharinger, James J. Krivacska, Marsha Laye-Mcdonough, Linda Jaimson, Gayle G. Vincent, and Andrew D. Hedlund, "Prevention of Sexual Abuse: An Analysis of Issues, Educational Programs, and Research Findings," *School Psychology Review* 17, no. 4 (1988): 614–34.

28. Gilbert, Berrick, LeProhn, and Nyman (n. 11 above): Berrick and Gilbert (n. 10 above).

29. Berrick and Gilbert (n. 10 above).

Excerpts from the Sexual Exploitation of Children in Developing Countries

Ove Narvesen and Redd Barna

CHILD PROSTITUTION AND OTHER FORMS OF SEXUAL EXPLOITATION

The local investigations do not, to any degree, use historical data. It is therefore impossible to say anything definite about when exploitation of children first occurred in the various areas. There are, however, strong indications that the form of commercial sexual exploitation best known today, and which is usually referred to as child prostitution, is a relatively recent phenomenon.

The commercial sexual exploitation of children in **the Philippines** has to a large extent had its development in the 1970s and 1980s. The known cases of sexual assault on children from the 1960s and earlier are mainly cases of incest and rape.

The largest numbers of children in prostitution in the Philippines are to be found in Manila in the best known prostitution areas, Ermita and Malate. There are many children in Luneta Park in the city centre as well. This is an open air leisure area of about 32,000 hectares (12,800 acres). The roller skating rink is a particularly popular spot. The large shopping mall "The Harrison Plaza Complex" is another prostitution area. In Quezon City, which is part of Metro Manila, children are to be found particularly in the shopping mall, "Ali Mall". Cebu is another of the larger towns included in the Philippines investigation. It is a centre of commerce, and prostitution here is primarily directed towards businessmen.

Child prostitution is also particularly prevalent in the major tourist areas of the Philippines—primarily Puerto Galera, Boracay and Pagsanjan. Many of the children in prostitution in the tourist sites are from the same areas. However, it is not uncommon for children from other parts of the country to be taken to these areas by tourists or by people in the prostitution syndicates.

Large prostitution areas in which children are prevalent have also grown up around the American military bases near the towns Olongapo and Angeles.

The investigations in **Kenya** revealed that sexual exploitation of children occurs in all seven districts in the study. The dominant type of sexual exploitation varied from district to district.

Child prostitution was the dominant type in large towns like Nairobi and in tourist areas like Mobasa and Malindi and in some of the border towns, especially those on the border between Uganda and Tanzania. Small boys involved in prostitution are particularly numerous in and around Mombasa. They are called "beach-boys" or "guides". Some of them work in the hotels.

Child prostitution in Kenya tends to be both organised and unorganised. Some brothels operate under the guise of bar or restaurant. Reference is made to examples of children operating as messengers for the brothels. It may be a matter of running to give a message to a woman or man that she/he is wanted by a customer. These children can easily be inveigled into prostitution themselves.

Although the practice of marrying off young girls is accepted in some parts of Kenya, it was considered to be a form of sexual exploitation in the Kenyan investigation. The main reason for this was that these girls are under the age of 15 and therefore not in a position to express whether they want to enter into marriage or not. The practice can be regarded as a sort of trading in defenceless individuals.

Excerpts from *The Sexual Exploitation of Children in Developing Countries*, by Ove Narvesen and Redd Barna, 1989.

Kenyan law forbids the practice of marrying off young girls. It is not enforced very often though. Sexual exploitation in the form of child marriage is most prevalent in the areas where traditions have been most successfully preserved. Child marriage is common in Kilifi and Kajiado districts. There are only a few reported cases of childhood marriage in Kisumu and Busia districts. Among some of the Masai, tradition demands that girls are married off as soon as they have been circumcised i.e. when they are 11–12 years of age. Some girls in Kiliti are only about 6 years of age when they are married off.

In **Peru,** children and young people of both sexes trying to catch customers are to be found outside busy places such as cinemas, theatres, and restaurants. In the summer, they can be seen in numbers on the beaches. The port area of Callao, the beaches, Costa Verde and La Heradura are common haunts. The central park area in the Miraflores part of town and some of the big shopping malls are also popular. A few children are attached to more organised establishments such as massage-parlours, hotels etc. Organised child prostitution is a particular feature in the market place La Parada.

In **Thailand,** sexual exploitation of children occurs in many parts of the country. The problem is not just confined to the larger towns and tourist areas. It has been discovered that there are a number of small local brothels in Thai villages. These are particularly prevalent in Northern Thailand. On the whole, it appears that children are available in most areas where there is prostitution. In Thailand, prostitution is mainly the organised variety. There is very little unorganised street prostitution.

At the beginning of the 1970s **Sri Lanka** developed into an attractive country for tourists, especially from Central Europe and Scandinavia. Before the internal conflict began in 1983, and all tourist traffic gradually ceased, child prostitution, primarily the prostitution of boys was found to have developed quite extensively. The prostitution of boys was particularly prevalent in the south and west of the country mainly, especially Hikkaduwa and Negombo and the strip of coastline by Colombo.

In **India,** organised child prostitution is to be found concentrated in the prostitution districts of the towns. As in Kenya, it is common to marry off young girls for their bride price. This is regarded by many in India also as sexual exploitation. It is a characteristic peculiar to India that young girls are also recruited to prostitution through a religious ritual—the so-called Devadasi system (cf. also Chap. 7.7).

CHILD PORNOGRAPHY

Child pornography is another facet of the sexual exploitation of children. During the investigation it was revealed that child pornography exists in all the countries in the study. On the whole, it is very much the same children who are exploited in prostitution and child pornography. Most occurrences are cases of private production and usage. Customers are photographed together with the children and then keep the pictures as a memento. Privately produced pictures and videos are exchanged in paedophile circles. Examples of more professional makers of and traders in child pornography have also been discovered. However, it is claimed that there are probably relatively few who operate as professionals in this field. The risks are too great and prospects of profit too limited (Hebditch and Anning, 1988). One exemption is the Thai dealer in child pornography, Manit Thamaree who was arrested in Bangkok in August 1987. The arrest was the result of close cooperation between the American and Thai police. Thamaree had distributed large quantities of locally produced child pornography to customers in the USA and Europe. The USA and Europe are the prime markets for child pornography. It is claimed that there are about 500,000 paedophiles in the USA, and that they represent 85% of the consumers of all the child pornography produced (Op. cit. p. 313). It seems that the technical production is mainly carried out in certain European countries, much of the raw material—negatives etc—come from poorer countries, like Thailand and the Philippines.

WHAT DO WE KNOW ABOUT THE EXTENT OF THE PROBLEM?

As mentioned above, it was not one of the aims of this study to determine the extent of child sexual exploitation, either in developing countries in general or the countries in the study in particular. However, a number of figures have been gathered in the course of the study which give some indication as to the extent.

The investigators in the **Philippines** estimate that about 20,000 children are involved in sexual exploitation there. This estimate primarily takes into consideration the kind of child prostitution which is visible, particularly that in which street children are involved. There is also a hidden variety of child prostitution in the Philippines which takes place in bars, brothels etc. It is impossible though to estimate the numbers involved in this.

In **Thailand** there are quite considerable deviations in the estimates given by various organisations and government offices. One voluntary organisation, Foundation for Children, for example, claims that the number of children who are exploited sexually in Thailand is in the region of 800,000. The National Youth Bureau on the other hand, claims that the figure is no greater than 2,500 children. The majority of informed sources, examples of which are the Women's Information Center and the Ministry of Public Welfare, agree however that the correct figure is probably somewhere between 15,000–20,000 children.

Child prostitution in **Sri Lanka** in 1980, when tourism was at its height, was estimated to involve about 2,000 boys (Bond, 1980). This figure has since been strongly disputed by the authorities in Sri Lanka. Regardless of this, the figure seems now to be considerably smaller than it was in 1980. The reason for this, as mentioned before, is that the political and military conflict in the country has put considerable hindrances in the way of tourism. The number of boys in prostitution in 1987, estimated at the time of Red Barna's and the Ministry for Planning's investigation, was thought to be 100–200.

There is no reliable estimate of the total number of children involved in prostitution in **India**. The Indian women's organisation, Joint Women's Programme claims that there are probably 1.5–2 million persons involved in prostitution. It is also claimed that app. 20% of these may be considered to be minors. This would give a total of 300,000–400,000 children in prostitution. These figures must be viewed in the light of the fact that India has a population of about 700 million. The amount of child prostitution is comparable with that found in Thailand and the Philippines when considered in proportion with the population.

If the results of the investigations carried out in **Kenya** can be assumed to be representative of conditions in other African countries which have reached the same stage of economical development, then it can be concluded that the extent of child prostitution on this continent is considerably smaller than is seen to be the case in Asia. The investigation indicates that the number of children in prostitution in the whole of Kenya comprises a few thousand individuals. The investigators make the reservation however that probably only the tip of the iceberg has as yet become apparent. It is the first time an investigation of this kind has been carried out in Kenya, and it is desirable to investigate the problem further before saying anything definite.

There is only sketchy information available about the extent of sexual exploitation of children in Latin American countries. Prostitution is legal in many places, and fairly thorough checks of the registered women in prostitution (who are supposed to be over 18 years old) are carried out. There are said to be more than 5 million women in prostitution in Brazil alone. In **Peru** the estimated number could be around 100,000, according to sources within the Lima-based organisation "El Pozo". It is contended that a large proportion of the (legitimate) women in prostitution are minors who have acquired false identification papers. Moreover, it is contended that illegal prostitution is more prevalent than the legitimate kind, and the proportion of minors is probably very large in the former kind.

Promotion of child welfare is the special concern of the government institution, Instituto Nacional de Bienstar Familiar (INABIF) in Peru. In 1985 the INABIF carried out an investigation into the abuse of children. Data was gathered from hospitals and other institutions to which injured children were brought for treatment. 371 cases were investigated. In this sample 95 children, or 20% of the sample were victims of sexual abuse. 80% of these were girls. 25% of the 95 children were victims of commercial sexual exploitation (Mansilla, 1989).

It is not possible to draw any definite conclusions as to the extent of sexual exploitation of children in developing countries from this incomplete material and these rough estimates. However it can be maintained that all in all a considerable number of children must be involved.

It must be emphasized that the above-mentioned estimates refer only to the type of sexual exploitation which can be defined as child prostitution. In addition there are the varieties which are something between sexual exploitation and sexual abuse, of which the child bride who is married off for her bride price is one example. The investigators in Kenya have, as previously mentioned, defined this practice as sexual exploitation. In the Peru investigation, a more informal variety of this system was described: It is not uncommon for older men there to take very young girls (as sex partners) into their house, often by force. The girls may be as young as 12–14 years. This is certainly sexual exploitation. Exploiting children sexually in connection with other work—very often the case where young housemaids are concerned—is also sexual exploitation. The sexual abuse of children in institutions and schools is yet another variety, with particular references to cases where abuse is associated with the conferring of privileges such as being given lighter work or better marks. There is reason to assume that if all these varieties are included, the numbers of children being sexually exploited will reach tens of millions.

THE CUSTOMERS

The people who exploit children sexually are both local people from the child's own environment and strangers who come to the area. In tourist areas and near military bases the type of customer is, in the main, an outsider, though in some areas of this kind the proportion of local customers can be surprisingly high. Data from interviews in the Philippines indicates for instance that more than half the customers near the American military bases, Clark and Subic Bay, are local people.

The customers are predominantly men, irrespective of whether the exploited victims are girls or boys. In other words, there are both homosexual and heterosexual customers. Homosexual paedophile customers constitute a large proportion of the customers in Sri Lanka and parts of the Philippines. There were also indications of this in other countries investigated.

There is particular mention of female customers in the tourist areas along the coast of Kenya. These are claimed to be mainly middle-aged white European women. Some sources claim that female customers are also becoming more common in the tourist areas of Asia.

The children's relations with the customer are mainly influenced by the fact that it is a service which is paid for and provided on a single occasion. It entails no further obligations for either party. Many of the children reported that there were brutal and sadistic customers.

How many customers a child has to satisfy depends, to a large extent, on the environment in which they operate. Street children have, on average, only a few customers. As a rule they only use this way of making money when absolutely necessary. In the sample of 1,000 children in the Philippines only 17% had customers every day. Conditions are in general completely different for children controlled by the syndicates. These children may be forced to have sexual intercourse up to 20 times a day.

Some children have a permanent relationship with some of their customers. This is particularly the case in areas where paedophiles are prevalent. The relationship may last for several years, and is often referred to as though it were a close relationship. There are also cases where this "friend" is regarded by the child's whole family as a benefactor. He buys his way in with presents and money, and is often referred to as though he were a kind, rich uncle. It appears that in this kind of situation, some parents suppress the fact that the relationship between their child and the stranger is a sexual one. The child accompanying the stranger abroad also occurs.

The clear and unequivocal impression from this study is that the children most vulnerable to sexual exploitation in developing countries are those with particularly problematic backgrounds. These children come in the main from deprived families, i.e. those which belong to the lowest social and economic strata in their community. These are families which suffer from poverty, unemployment and lack of proper living accommodation. The families are often large ones—it is not unusual that there are 5–10 children in them. A picture is ascertained of children who are deprived in various ways because the structures around them are unable to provide adequate care and protection. A common feature is also that it is impossible for the parents to give the children an education—all the children at any rate.

ESPECIALLY VULNERABLE GROUPS

Poverty and lack of resources however, are not the only preconditions which propel children towards danger of sexual exploitation. It appears that some groups are more vulnerable than others. The so-called street children constitute an important group to be examined here. This group is very complex and not in any way homogeneous. Some of the street children are more prone to becoming victims of sexual exploitation than others. The investigations which have been made, particularly the one in the Philippines, have attempted to analyse what kind of street child becomes involved in prostitution.

It appears that children who, for various reasons, are forced to work, particularly within parts of the informal sector, are a category which is definitely at risk. Female domestic workers—the house-maids—are a prime example.

Children whose mothers make a living by prostitution is another category which have been described as especially vulnerable. The following is an analysis of the three risk-groups.

STREET CHILDREN

No-one has been able to say with any degree of certainty, how many street children there are in all, in the world today. Estimates vary from tens of millions to hundreds of millions. The deviation can be partly explained by the fact that it is impossible to make a general survey of street children and partly because there is no single definition of a street child. There are differences for example, among those who are considered "real" street children, those who live by making a living on the street, and those who try to find small jobs on the street in order to augment the family income but who generally stay at home at night.

The overriding majority of children who live and work on the streets in developing countries make a living in ways other than selling their bodies. They do small jobs such as cleaning shoes, selling newspapers, going on errands and guarding parked cars. Some of them sing on buses, others set up small "greengrocer" stalls on the pavement, provisioned with wares they have found or stolen from the market. Begging is also common for many of them. The inventiveness demonstrated by street children is practically limitless.

A number of street children may easily rub up against the law with their methods of survival. It is usually a question of petty theft or pick-pocketing. Some of them may also wander into hardened criminal circles though; they can for example, be recruited to run errands for drug dealers.

It is common for street children to band together in gangs which have a more or less strong inner cohesion. Gangs may control certain areas and show no mercy to intruders. There is usually a marked hierarchical system within the gang. The gangs may have their own special ways of survival. For example, gangs which guard parked cars are a familiar feature in many large towns. In Lima, people have given the gangs names which describe their activities: "Los Pirajas" specialise in assaulting people after they have been shopping in the market. "Los Culebritas" (little snakes) specialise in burgling private houses, while "Los Mandileros" are experts at stealing from street vendors.

There seems to be a definite tendency that the category of street children left completely to their own resources, or children who only have very sporadic contact with their families most easily get involved in prostitution. A large number of these children are from families which have disintegrated. They have fled from the quarrelling, the violence and abuse. Many of them have mothers who have been abandoned by their husbands. In cases where a mother has taken up with a new man, it is often reported that the "stepfather" is an additional burden on the children, particularly the girls. The stepfather often claims a right to have sexual relations with the daughters. In the sample of 1,000 children who were interviewed in the Philippines—and who were mainly street children—as large a proportion as 70% had had experiences which indicated sexual abuse. In most cases of abuse the child had been abused by a person it knew (IPC, 1988). Similar data is also to be found in the material from Peru: In 85% of the cases out of a group of 73 child victims of sexual abuse, the abuser was known to the child (Mansilla, 1989).

It is impossible to determine the proportion of street children that become involved in prostitution. In the Philippines the proportion is thought to be about 1% of the total number of street children. However this figure has been worked out by including all categories of street child. For the children discussed here, the "real" street children as it were, the proportion is probably considerably higher.

As the majority of street children who become involved in prostitution have prostitution as just one of their sources of income, it is incorrect to describe them as child prostitutes. It is not part of these children's identity. It is more accurate to say that some street children also have recourse to prostitution in order to earn a little money, a little food or shelter for the night. In this report the expression, children in prostitution is the phrase most often used, to emphasize the fact that children are inveigled into it through their sheer need, and they are inveigled into it by others. The children in prostitution are the victims of prostitution.

The most common way for street children to be inveigled into prostitution is through friends. More than half of the 1,000 children interviewed in the Philippines recounted that "friends" had "helped" them into it.

It appears that this was, for the children, the accepted way of doing things. In Peru it was reported that it was usual for one of the more "experienced" children to accompany a newcomer to the business when he or she went off with a customer for the first time.

For children to have their sexual début together with a customer appears to be rare. Many of them explained that they had had their first sexual experiences in the gang. However, as mentioned above, a large proportion of them had their sexual début in the form of sexual abuse, often at home.

As a rule children start with their first customers when they are 10–14 years of age. Among the 1,000 children in the Philippines investigation, 8 of them had had their first customer when they were around 6 years of age.

The way in which street children enter into prostitution indicates that it is a business which is not organised to any significant degree. Usually it is a question of direct contact between the children and their customers. Contact usually occurs when the customer visits the area where the children, known to be willing to sell sexual services, are to be found. These places may be particular streets, shopping precincts or parks. The customer may first have to approach one of the older children, most probably the gang leader who operates as a sort of pimp or "minder" for the children. This person is usually given a percentage of the child's earnings. Any greater degree of organisation in this sort of environment is rare. (The organised sector of child prostitution is described below cf. Chapter 6.)

Among the countries in this study, it seems that it is in the Philippines and the Latin American countries that the problem of street children being drawn into prostitution is greatest. The problem of street children is a relatively limited one in Thailand. According to the Foundation for Children, the number of street children in Thailand in 1987 was under 10,000 while the number for the Philippines was 1.5–2 million. The population of the two countries is comparable.

In the capital of Sri Lanka, Colombo, there are estimated to be about 2,000 street children. It is not thought that they are involved in prostitution to any great extent. It is not common for street children to be involved in prostitution in India either. It is an organised business there. Prostitution among street children occurs in Kenya, particularly in the capital, Nairobi.

HOUSEMAIDS

The sexual exploitation of children in connection with employment may occur in a number of ways. The most obvious is in connection with employment which borders on prostitution, such as work in bars, certain types of restaurant or hotel, massage parlours etc. In these places the work is deliberately combined with sexual exploitation. It is expected that the children make themselves available when sexual services are demanded, even though they may not actually be employed for such work. If they do not comply, they risk losing their jobs.

Sexual exploitation also occurs in connection with other types of employment. And the category of child worker which is particularly relevant is that of the young housemaid. This was pointed out in all the countries in the study. As mentioned above a separate study of this category alone was carried out in Kenya.

Housemaids may be extremely young when they start this type of work. A team from the University of Nairobi which carried out an investigation in 1985, documented that many housemaids were sent away from home when they were only 6–7 years old. As a rule they were sent to relatives in the first instance. This allowed the parents to circumvent the law concerning child labour. This law does not say anything which forbids setting children to work within the family, and in many developing countries the definition of the term "family" is usually quite broad (Bwibo/Onvago, 1985).

To begin with, the children were often left to look after smaller children while the mother and father are working. As a rule this duty rapidly expands into more comprehensive ones until the child is having to do all the housework. A working day can be anything up to 15–16 hours long.

The vast majority of young housemaids are girls from poor families in rural areas. Their parents can not afford to send them to school, and domestic service is considered appropriate experience for girls who are later to be "married off". On the whole boys are favoured when it comes to providing an education.

It is a known fact that many of the girls are in danger of being sexually abused while in their employer's house. The perpetrator may be the male head of the household, one of the sons in the house, a relative or a visiting male friend. The girl has to put up with the violation in silence or run away. If she tells anyone about it she will bring her employer, the employer's family, herself and her own family into disrepute.

In many cases of violation, pregnancy and dismissal result. Some girls are also dismissed because the wife in the house becomes aware of the sexual relationship. In practically all cases, going back to the family is not a feasible solution. The girls are in disgrace and are not wanted, they must try and fend for themselves. The majority end up in the slums, with their child (children). They have few prospects of making a living other than from prostitution.

There are no statistics available concerning the connection between employment as a housemaid and prostitution, but the above-mentioned investigation carried out by the University of Nairobi found a definite predominance of former housemaids among 12–15 year old girls who had been drawn into prostitution. In both Peru and Brazil it was stated by various sources that many families deliberately recruit young girls as housemaids for the purpose of letting their sons gain sexual experience with them.

THE CHILDREN OF WOMEN IN PROSTITUTION

As long as it is not possible to assess the extent of prostitution as such, it is equally impossible to say with any certainty how many children of women in prostitution there are, in all, in the world today. There is no doubt though, that there is a large number of such children. It is not customary for women in prostitution in developing countries to use contraception because it is either unavailable or the girls can not afford to buy contraceptives. Moreover the customers usually demand that contraceptives are not used. The Philippines investigators stated that as many as 70% of the girls interviewed had been pregnant, and 30% had one or more children. In India it is claimed that there are possibly 5 million children in all, belonging to women in prostitution. This has been calculated by presupposing that every woman has at least 2–3 children (Dr. Deepa Das, paper presented at the conference "Exploitation of women and children" New Delhi, Nov. 1988).

In many developing countries there is also a general increase in the number of very young, single mothers. Statistics from the Ministry of Health in Peru show, for example, that under age, single mothers constituted about 10% of those who gave birth in 1970; in 1986 the percentage had increased to 20% (Mansilla, 1986). A large number of these girls had become pregnant as a result of sexual abuse or sexual exploitation.

Children whose mothers are in prostitution are exposed to adverse influences. They can therefore naturally be considered as a group which is in danger of recruitment to prostitution.

The mothers themselves often belong to one of the groups mentioned above. They may have been street children or housemaids. In other words mothers bring their children into an environment where recruitment to prostitution is common.

A number of mothers manage to place their child outside this dangerous environment, usually with their families or good friends. The degree to which they practise this depends on how the particular cultures regard both prostitution and illegitimate children. It depends also generally, on how the family functions as a social system. In certain areas, it would be inconceivable to expect parents or relatives to bring up a child born out of wedlock; in other areas the family ties are such that the family would feel under an obligation to help. The study has not investigated this question sufficiently well to be able to say anything definite about which practices are most common in which areas.

It seems though that most mothers remain responsible for their children's upbringing. In the Philippines the following differentiation was found: It is more common to find a family looking after a "pure" Phillipino child than a child which is the result of a relationship between a Philippino girl and a "white" man. The socalled Amerasian children remained in larger numbers in the prostitution environment. In Thailand great differences were registered with regard to how prepared people were to welcome back to the village, daughters from Bangkok or other tourist areas with one or more children by unknown fathers. Generally more tolerance was shown in the northernmost provinces than in the rest of Thailand. As previously mentioned, it is from these provinces that most young girls are recruited to prostitution.

Children of mothers who earn their living through prostitution, are very much left to their own devices. This is not a problem which is peculiar to these children. Most children in slum areas are left on their own for long periods at a time. But the children of women in prostitution are left on their own for particularly long periods; the afternoons, evenings and nights. These children, left by themselves, are exposed to the dangers of a criminal environment, drugs and violence. They may easily become victims of sexual abuse.

In countries such as India where prostitution is highly organised and the victims of prostitution are kept under strict control, it is not uncommon for the brothel owner to consider the children of his prostitutes as his own property. He brings them into "the business" as soon as they are big enough. The girls are offered to customers as soon as they have matured sufficiently sexually, and the boys are made to run errands, solicit for customers etc.

The mothers often take their customers with them home—to where the children are. In India cases have been described of babies being given drops of opium to keep them quiet while their mothers are busy with customers. From a very early age children are witness to sexual exploitation, which is a particularly serious aspect of this activity. The sexual practices the children often are witness to, are combined with violence and sadism. Not infrequently the children are directly involved in the proceedings. It is claimed that this is the largest contributory factor to children being drawn into prostitution at a very early age. From Brazil it is reported that children as young as 3–4 years of age are sent out on to the streets to procure customers for their mothers. Many are starting to sell their own tiny bodies when they are only 9–10 years old.

It must be added though that women in prostitution, when asked about their children, nearly always say that they try to protect them from this sort of influence, if they can. They do not want their children to be drawn into prostitution. Their children are very important to most of them. They often provide the only chance these women get to give or receive human warmth. This is also one of the reasons why mothers shrink from sending their children away, even when they have the opportunity to do so.

CERTAIN CONSEQUENCES TO HEALTH

The national investigations were not intended to include detailed information about the physical and psychological state of the children who had been sexually exploited. More intensive research into fewer cases over a longer period would have had to have been carried out, in order to satisfy such a requirement. However, in the course of the investigation, certain general impressions have been gained.

The main impression is of children who experience a life full of disappointment, deprivation, poverty and violence. As mentioned earlier, about 70% of the children who had been drawn into prostitution on the streets in the Philippines had had experiences which indicated sexual abuse. In other words it appears that these children suffer badly even before they enter into prostitution.

In several of the countries investigated there are records from for example centres and hospitals, of children who have been subjected to great physical suffering in connection with sexual exploitation. Infections in and bleeding from the sexual organs and anus are common. The majority have or have had sexual diseases. It is impossible to tell how prevalent AIDS is among these children. No systematic investigation has been made. However, the number of cases may be considerable as contraception is seldom used and the customers have many partners. There is concern that the number of AIDS cases may be particularly high among boys who are exploited by homosexual paedophiles.

The children have often had their infections and injuries—for example injuries through violence or fights—for a long time before they seek help. The reason for this is partly that they can not afford to pay for treatment and partly because they are afraid of being "discovered". They can not imagine the authorities being on their side.

The state of the children's health is also affected by a deficient and inadequate diet, and the fact that they do not usually get more than 2–3 hours uninterrupted sleep a night.

Intoxicants are fairly prevalent, particularly among street children. In the main, they go in for sniffing. They can not afford the harder drugs. Some of the earnings from prostitution are used to buy intoxicants. It is not correct to say, though, that this abuse itself provides strong motivation for taking up prostitution. Intoxicants are used by the children primarily to help them to sleep and to help them to put up with their customers.

The investigators in the Philippines found that the children they interviewed were very fidgety and unable to concentrate. Evidence of emotional disturbance manifested itself in various ways. The children were almost always afraid, and they were afraid of the police most of all.

SEXUAL ASSAULT
OF ADULTS

THE SOCIO-CULTURAL CONTEXT OF RAPE:
A CROSS-CULTURAL STUDY

Peggy Reeves Sanday

In her comprehensive and important analysis of rape, Susan Brownmiller says that "when men discovered that they could rape, they proceeded to do it" and that "from prehistoric times to the present rape has played a critical function" (6, p. 14–15). The critical function to which Brownmiller refers has been "to keep all women in a constant state of intimidation, forever conscious of the knowledge that the biological tool must be held in awe for it may turn to weapon with sudden swiftness borne of harmful intent" (6, p. 209).

Brownmiller's attribution of violence to males and victimization to females strums a common theme in Western social commentary on the nature of human nature. Most of the popularizers of this theme present what amounts to a socio-biological view of human behavior which traces war, violence, and now rape to the violent landscape of our primitive ancestors, where, early on, the male tendency in these directions became genetically programmed in the fight for survival of the fittest. Human (viz. male) nature is conceived as an ever present struggle to overcome baser impulses bequeathed by "apish" ancestors. (For examples of this general theme, see 3, 17, 30.)

The research described in the present paper departs from the familiar assumption that male nature is programmed for rape, and begins with another familiar, albeit less popular, assumption that human sexual behavior, though based in a biological need "is rather a sociological and cultural force than a mere bodily relation of two individuals" (19). With this assumption in mind, what follows is an examination of the socio-cultural context of sexual assault and an attempt to interpret its meaning. By understanding the meaning of rape, we can then make conjectures as to its function. Is it, as Susan Brownmiller suggests, an act that keeps all women in a constant state of intimidation, or is it an act that illuminates a larger social scenario?

This paper examines the incidence, meaning, and function of rape in tribal societies. Two general hypotheses guided the research: first, the incidence of rape varies cross-culturally; second, a high incidence of rape is embedded in a distinguishably different cultural configuration than a low incidence of rape. Using a standard cross-cultural sample of 156 tribal societies, the general objectives of the paper are:

1. to provide a descriptive profile of "rape prone" and "rape free" societies;

2. to present an analysis of the attitudes, motivations, and socio-cultural factors related to the incidence of rape.

Profiles of 'Rape Prone' Societies

In this study a 'rape prone' society was defined as one in which the incidence of rape is high, rape is a ceremonial act, or rape is an act by which men punish or threaten women.

An example of a 'rape prone' society is offered by Robert LeVine's (16) description of sexual offenses among the Gusii of southwestern Kenya. In the European legal system which administers justice in the District where the Gusii live, a heterosexual assault is classified as rape when a medical examination indicates that the hymen of the alleged victim was recently penetrated by the use of

"The Socio-Cultural Context of Rape: A Cross-Cultural Study," by Peggy Reeves Sanday, reprinted from *Journal of Social Issues*, Vol. 34, No. 14, American Psychological Association, 1981.

painful force. When medical evidence is unobtainable, the case is classified as "indecent assault." Most cases are of the latter kind. The Gusii do not distinguish between rape and indecent assault. They use the following expressions to refer to heterosexual assault: "to fight" (a girl or woman); "to stamp on" (a girl or woman); "to spoil" (a girl or woman); "to engage in illicit intercourse." All of these acts are considered illicit by the Gusii. LeVine uses the term rape "to mean the culturally disvalued use of coercion by a male to achieve the submission of a female to sexual intercourse" (16).

Based on court records for 1955 and 1956 LeVine estimates that the annual rate of rape is 47.2 per 100,000 population. LeVine believes that this figure grossly underestimates the Gusii rape rate. During the same period the annual rape rate in urban areas in the United States was 13.85 per 100,000 (13.1 for rural areas). Thus, the rate of Gusii rape is extraordinarily high.

Normal heterosexual intercourse between Gusii males and females is conceived as an act in which a man overcomes the resistance of a woman and causes her pain. When a bride is unable to walk after her wedding night, the groom is considered by his friends "a real man" and he is able to boast of his exploits, particularly if he has been able to make her cry. Older women contribute to the groom's desire to hurt his new wife. These women insult the groom, saying:

> "You are not strong, you can't do anything to our daughter. When you slept with her you didn't do it like a man. You have a small penis which can do nothing. You should grab our daughter and she should be hurt and scream—then you're a man" (16).

The groom answers boastfully:

> "I am a man! If you were to see my penis you would run away. When I grabbed her she screamed. I am not a man to be joked with. Didn't she tell you? She cried—ask her!" (16).

Thus, as LeVine says, (16) "legitimate heterosexual encounters among the Gusii are aggressive contests, involving force and pain-inflicting behavior." Under circumstances that are not legitimate, heterosexual encounters are classified as rape when the girl chooses to report the act.

LeVine estimates that the typical Gusii rape is committed by an unmarried young man on an unmarried female of a different clan. He distinguishes between three types of rape: rape resulting from seduction, premeditated sexual assault, and abduction (16).

Given the hostile nature of Gusii sexuality, seduction classifies as rape when a Gusii female chooses to bring the act to the attention of the public. Premarital sex is forbidden, but this does not stop Gusii boys from trying to entice girls to intercourse. The standard pose of the Gusii girls is reluctance, which means that it is difficult for the boy to interpret her attitude as being either willing or unwilling. Misunderstandings between girl and boy can be due to the eagerness of the boy and his inability to perceive the girl's cues of genuine rejection, or to the girl's failure to make the signs of refusal in unequivocal fashion. The boy may discover the girl's unwillingness only after he has forced himself on her.

Fear of discovery may turn a willing girl into one who cries rape. If a couple engaging in intercourse out of doors is discovered, the girl may decide to save her reputation by crying out that she was being raped. Rape may also occur in cases when a girl has encouraged a young man to present her with gifts, but then denies him sexual intercourse. If the girl happens to be married, she rejects the boy's advances because she is afraid of supernatural sanctions against adultery. Out of frustration, the boy (who may not know that the girl is married) may resort to rape and she reports the deed.

In some cases one or more boys may attack a single girl in premeditated sexual assault. The boys may beat the girl badly and tear her clothing. Sometimes the girl is dragged off to the hut of one of them and forced into coitus. After being held for a couple of days the girl is freed. In these cases rupture of the hymen and other signs of the attack are usually present.

The third type of rape occurs in the context of wife abduction. When a Gusii man is unable to present the bridewealth necessary for a normal marriage and cannot persuade a girl to elope, he may abduct a girl from a different clan. The man's friends will be enlisted to carry out the abduction. The young men are frequently rough on the girl, beating her and tearing her clothes. When she arrives at the home of the would-be lover, he attempts to persuade her to remain with him until bridewealth can be raised. Her refusal is ignored and the wedding night sexual contest is performed with the clansmen helping in overcoming her resistance.

Of these three types of rape, the first and third are unlawful versions of legitimate patterns. Seduction is accepted when kept within the bounds of discretion. Abduction is an imitation of traditional wedding procedures. Abduction lacks only the legitimizing bridewealth and the consent of the bride and her parents. In both these cases LeVine says, "there is a close parallel between the criminal act and the law-abiding culture pattern to which it is related." Seduction and abduction classify as rape when the girl chooses to report the incident.

Data collected from the standard cross-cultural sample allows us to place the hostility characterizing Gusii heterosexual behavior in cross-cultural perspective. Broude and Greene (5), who published codes for twenty sexual practices, find that male sexual advances are occasionally or typically hostile in one-quarter (26%) of the societies for which information was available. They found that males were typically forward in verbal (not physical) sexual overtures in forty percent of the societies, that females solicited or desired physical aggression in male sexual overtures in eleven percent of the societies, and that males did not make sexual overtures or were different or shy in twenty-three percent of the societies.

Examination of a variety of 'rape prone' societies shows that the Gusii pattern of rape is found elsewhere but that it is by no means the only pattern which can be observed. For example, in several societies the act of rape occurs to signal readiness for marriage and is a ceremonial act. Since this act signifies male domination of female genitals, its occurance was treated as a diagnostic criterion for classification as 'rape prone.'

Among the Kikuyu of East Africa it is reported that in former times, as part of initiation, every boy was expected to perform the act of ceremonial rape called *Kuihaka muunya* (to smear oneself with salt earth) in order to prove his manhood. It was thought that until a boy had performed the act of rape he could not have lawful intercourse with a Kikuyu woman and hence could not marry. During the initiation period boys would wander the countryside in bands of up to 100 in number. The object of each band was to find a woman on whom to commit the rape. The ideal woman was one from an enemy tribe who was married. In practice it appears that the ceremonial rape consisted of nothing more than masturbatory ejaculation on the woman's body or in her presence. Immediately after the act the boy was able to throw away the paraphernalia which marked him with the status of neophite (15).

Rape marks a girl as marriageable among the Arunta of Australia. At age 14 or 15 the Arunta girl is taken out into the bush by a group of men for the vulva cutting ceremony. A designated man cuts the girl's vulva after which she is gang raped by a group of men which does not include her future husband. When the ceremony is concluded the girl is taken to her husband and from then on no one else has the right of access to her. (27).

In other rape prone societies, rape is explicitly linked to the control of women and to male dominance. Among the Northern Saulteaux the assumption of male dominance is clearly expressed in the expectation that a man's potential sexual rights over the woman he chooses must be respected. A woman who turns a man down too abruptly insults him and invites aggression. There is a Northern Saulteaux tale about a girl who was considered too proud because she refused to marry. Accordingly, a group of medicine men lured her out into the bush where she was raped by each in turn (11). Such tales provide women with a fairly good idea of how they should behave in relation to men.

The attitude that women are "open" for sexual assault is frequently found in the societies of the Insular Pacific. For example, in the Marshall Islands one finds the belief that "every women is like a passage." Just as every canoe is permitted to sail from the open sea into the lagoon through the passage, so every man is permitted to have intercourse with every woman (except those who are excluded on account of blood kinship). A trader, well acquainted with the language and customs of one group of Marshall Islanders, reported the following incident. One day while standing at the trading post he saw 20 young men enter the bushes, one after another. Following the same path, he discovered a young girl stretched out on the ground, rigid and unconscious. When he accused the young men of cruel treatment they replied: "It is customary here for every young man to have intercourse with every girl" (9).

In tropical forest societies of South America and in Highland New Guinea it is fairly frequent to find the threat of rape used to keep women from the men's houses or from viewing male sacred objects. For example, Shavante women were strictly forbidden to observe male sacred ceremonies. Women caught peeking are threatened with man handling, rape, and disfigurement (20).

Perhaps the best known example of rape used to keep women away from male ritual objects is found in the description of the Mundurucu, a society well known to anthropologists due to the work of Robert and Yolanda Murphy. The Mundurucu believe that there was a time when women ruled and sex roles were reversed with the exception that women could not hunt. During that time, it is said, women were the sexual aggressors and men were sexually submissive and did women's work. Women controlled the "sacred trumpets" (the symbols of power) and the men's houses. The trumpets are believed to contain the spirits of the ancestors who demand ritual offering of meat. Since women did not hunt and could not make these offerings, men were able to take the trumpets from them, thereby establishing male dominance. The trumpets are secured in special chambers within the men's houses and no woman can see them under penalty of gang rape. Such a threat is necessary because men believe that women will attempt to seize from the men the power they once had. Gang rape is also the means by which men punish sexually "wanton" women (23).

Another expression of male sexual aggressiveness, which is classified as rape in this study, is the practice of sexually assaulting enemy women during warfare. The Yanomamo, described by Napoleon Chagnon and Marvin Harris, are infamous for their brutality toward women. The Yanomamo, according to Harris (12), "practice an especially brutal form of male supremacy involving polygyny, frequent wife beating, and gang rape of captured enemy women." The Yanomamo, Harris says, "regard fights over women as the primary causes of their wars" (12). Groups raid each other for wives in an area where marriageable women are in short supply due to the practice of female infanticide. The number of marriageable women is also affected by the desire on the part of successful warriors to have several wives to mark their superior status as "fierce men." A shortage of women for wives also motivates Azande (Africa) warfare. Enemy women were taken by Azande soldiers as wives. Evans-Pritchard calls these women "slaves of war" and says that they were "not regarded very differently from ordinary wives, their main disability being that they had no family or close kin to turn to in times of trouble" (10). The absence of close kin, of course, made these women more subservient and dependent on their husbands.

Another source on the Azande discusses how the the act of rape when committed against an Azande woman is treated. If the women is not married, this source reports, the act is not treated as seriously. If the woman is married, the rapist can be put to death by the husband. If the rapist is allowed to live, he may be judged guilty of adultery and asked to pay the chief 20 knives (the commonly used currency in marriage exchanges) and deliver a wife to the wronged husband. This source indicates that the rape of a woman is not permitted but the punishments are established, suggesting that rape is a frequent occurrence (14).

Among some American Indian buffalo hunters, it is not uncommon to read that rape is used as a means to punish adultery. There is a practice among the Cheyenne of the Great Plains known as "to put a woman on the prairie." This means that the outraged husband of an adulterous woman invites all the unmarried members of his military society to feast on the prairie where they each rape the woman (13). Among the Omaha, a woman with no immediate kin who commits adultery may be gang raped and abandoned by her husband (7). Mead reports that the Omaha considered a "bad woman" fair game for any man. No discipline, no set of standards, other than to be cautious of an avenging father or brother and to observe the rule of exogamy, Mead says, kept young men from regarding rape as a great adventure. Young Omaha men, members of the Antler society, would prey upon divorced women or women considered loose (21).

Summarizing, a rape prone society, as defined here, is one in which sexual assault by men of women is either culturally allowable or, largely overlooked. Several themes interlink the above descriptions. In all, men are posed as a social group against women. Entry into the adult male or female group is marked in some cases by rituals that include rape. In other cases, rape preserves the ceremonial integrity of the male group and signifies its status vis-a-vis women. The theme of women as property is suggested when the aggrieved husband is compensated for the rape of his wife by another man, or when an adulterous woman is gang raped by her husband and his unmarried compatriots. In these latter cases, the theme of the dominant male group is joined with a system of economic exchange in which men act as exchange agents and women comprise the medium of exchange. This is not to say that rape exists in all societies in which there is ceremonial induction into manhood, male secret societies, or compensation for adultery. For further illumination of the socio-cultural context of rape we can turn to an examination of rape free societies.

Profiles of "Rape Free" Societies

Rape free societies are defined as those where the act of rape is either infrequent or does not occur. Forty-seven percent of the societies for which information on the incidence or presence of rape was available (see Table 2) were classified in the rape free category. Societies were classified in this category on the basis of the following kinds of statements found in the sources used for the sample societies.

Among the Taureg of the Sahara, for example, it is said that "rape does not exist, and when a woman refuses a man, he never insists nor will he show himself jealous of a more successful comrade" (4). Among the Pygmies of the Ituri forest in Africa, while a boy may rip off a girl's outer bark cloth, if he can catch her, he may never have intercourse with her without her permission. Turnbull (31), an anthropologist who lived for some time among the Pygmies and became closely identified with them, reports that he knew of no cases of rape. Among the Jivaro of South America rape is not recognized as such, and informants could recall no case of a woman violently resisting sexual intercourse. They say that a man would never commit such an act if the woman resisted, because she would tell her family and they would punish him. Among the Nkundo Mongo of Africa it is said that rape in the true sense of the word—that is, the abuse of a woman by the use of violence—is most unusual. If a woman does not consent, the angry seducer leaves her, often insulting her to the best of his ability. Rape is also unheard of among the Lakhers, and in several villages the anthropologist was told that there had never been a case of rape.

Other examples of statements leading to the classification of rape free are listed as follows:

Cuna (South America), "Homosexuality is rare, as is rape. Both . . . are regarded as sins, punishable by God" (29).

Khalka Mongols (Quter Mongolia), "I put this question to several well-informed Mongols: —what punishment is here imposed for rape? . . . one well-educated lama said frankly: "We have no crimes of this nature here. Our women never resist." (18).

Gond (India), "It is considered very wrong to force a girl to act against her will. Such cases of gho-tul-rape are not common . . . If then a boy forces a girl against her will, and the others hear of it, he is fined" (8).

The above quotes may obscure the actual incidence of rape. Such quotes, leading to the classi-fication of societies as 'rape free,' achieve greater validity when placed within the context of other information describing heterosexual interaction.

There is considerable difference in the character of heterosexual interaction in societies classi-fied as 'rape prone' when compared with those classified as 'rape free.' In 'rape free' societies women are treated with considerable respect, and prestige is attached to female reproductive and productive roles. Interpersonal violence is minimized, and a people's attitude regarding the natural environment is one of reverence rather than one of exploitation. Turnbull's description of the Mbuti Pygmies, of the Ituri forest in Africa, provides a prototypical profile of a 'rape free' society (31).

Violence between the sexes, or between anybody, is virtually absent among the net hunting Mbuti Pygmies when they are in their forest environment. The Mbuti attitude toward the forest is reflective of their attitude toward each other. The forest is addressed as "father," "mother," "lover," and "friend." The Mbuti say that forest is everything—the provider of food, shelter, warmth, clothing, and affection. Each person and animal is endowed with some spiritual power which "derives from a single source whose physical manifestation is the forest itself." The ease of the Mbuti relationship to their environment is reflected in the relationship between the sexes. There is little division of labor by sex. The hunt is frequently a joint effort. A man is not ashamed to pick mushrooms and nuts if he finds them, or to wash and clean a baby. In general, leadership is minimal and there is no attempt to control, or to dominate, either the geographical or human environment. Decision-making is by com-mon consent; men and women have equal say because hunting and gathering are both important to the economy. The forest is the only recognized authority of last resort. In decision making, diversity of opinion may be expressed, but prolonged disagreement is considered to be "noise" and offensive to the forest. If husband and wife disagree, the whole camp may act to mute their antagonism, lest the disagreement become too disruptive to the social unit (31).

The essential details of Turnbull's idyllic description of the Mbuti are repeated in other 'rape free' societies. The one outstanding feature of these societies is the ceremonial importance of women and the respect accorded the contribution women make to social continuity, a respect which places men and women in relatively balanced power spheres. This respect is clearly present among the Mbuti and in more complex 'rape free' societies.

In the West African kingdom of Ashanti, for example, it is believed that only women can con-tribute to future generations. Ashanti women say:

I am the mother of the man . . . I alone can transmit the blood to a king . . . If my sex die in the clan then that very clan becomes extinct, for be there one, or one thousand male members left, not one can transmit the blood, and the life of the clan becomes measured on this earth by the span of a man's life (24).

The importance of the feminine attributes of growth and reproduction are found in Ashanti reli-gion and ritual. Priestesses participate with priests in all major rituals. The Ashanti creation story emphasizes the complementarity and inseparability of male and female. The main female deity, the Earth Goddess, is believed to be the receptacle of past and future generations as well as the source of food and water (24, 25). The sacred linkage of earth-female-blood makes the act of rape incongruous in Ashanti culture. Only one incident of rape is reported by the main ethnographer of the Ashanti. In this case the man involved was condemned to death (25).

In sum, rape free societies are characterized by sexual equality and the notion that the sexes are complementary. Though the sexes may not perform the same duties or have the same rights or privileges, each is indispensable to the activities of the other (see 26 for examples of sexual equality). The key to understanding the relative absence of rape in rape free as opposed to rape prone societies is the importance, which in some cases is sacred, attached to the contribution women make to social continuity. As might be expected, and as will be demonstrated below, interpersonal violence is uncommon in rape free societies. It is not that men are necessarily prone to rape; rather, where interpersonal violence is a way of life, violence frequently achieves sexual expression.

Approaches to the Etiology of Rape

Three general approaches characterize studies of the etiology of rape. One approach focuses on the broader sociocultural milieu, another turns to individual characteristics. The first looks at how rapists act out the broader social script, the second emphasizes variables like the character of parental-child interaction. A third approach, which may focus on either individual or social factors, is distinguishable by the assumption that male sexual repression will inevitably erupt in the form of sexual violence. These approaches, reviewed briefly in this section, guided the empirical analysis of the socio-cultural context of rape in tribal societies.

Based on his study of the Gusii, LeVine (16) hypothesizes that four factors will be associated with the incidence of rape cross-culturally:

1. severe formal restrictions on the nonmarital sexual relations of females;
2. moderately strong sexual inhibitions on the part of females;
3. economic or other barriers to marriage that prolong the bachelorhood of some males into their late twenties;
4. the absence of physical segregation of the sexes.

The implicit assumption here is that males who are denied sexual access to women, will obtain access by force unless men are separated from women. Such an assumption depicts men as creatures who cannot control their sexual impulses, and women as the unfortunate victims.

LeVine's profile of the Gusii suggests that broader social characteristics are related to the incidence of rape. For example, there is the fact that marriage among the Gusii occurs almost always between feuding clans. The Gusii have a proverb which states "Those whom we marry are those whom we fight" (16). The close correspondence between the Gusii heterosexual relationship and intergroup hostilities suggests the hypothesis that the nature of intergroup relations is correlated with the nature of the heterosexual relationship and the incidence of rape.

The broader approach to the etiology of rape is contained in Susan Brownmiller's contention that rape is the means by which men keep women in a state of fear. This contention is certainly justified in societies where men use rape as a threat to keep women from viewing their sacred objects (the symbol of power) or rape is used to punish women. In societies like the Mundurucu, the ideology of male dominance is upheld by threatening women with rape. Just as the quality of intergroup relations among the Gusii is reflected in heterosexual relations, one could suggest that the quality of interpersonal relations is reflected in the incidence of rape. In societies where males are trained to be dominant and interpersonal relations are marked by outbreaks of violence, one can predict that females may become the victims in the playing out of the male ideology of power and control.

A broader socio-cultural approach is also found in the work of Wolfgang & Ferracuti (32) and Amir (2). Wolfgang & Ferracuti present the concept of the subculture of violence which is formed of those from the lower classes and the disenfranchised. The prime value is the use of physical aggression as a demonstration of masculinity and toughness. In his study of rape, Amir placed the rapist "squarely within the subculture of violence" (6). Rape statistics in Philadelphia showed that in 43% of the cases examined, rapists operated in pairs or groups. The rapists tended to be in the 15–19 age bracket, the majority were not married, and 90% belonged to the lower socioeconomic class and lived in inner city neighborhoods where there was also a high degree of crime against the person. In addition, 71% of the rapes were planned. In general, the profile presented by Amir is reminiscent of the pattern of rape found among the Kikuyu, where a band of boys belonging to a guild roamed the country side in search of a woman to gang rape as a means of proving their manhood and as a prelude to marriage. Brownmiller summarizes Amir's study with the following observations:

> Like assault, rape is an act of physical damage to another person, and like robbery it is also an act of acquiring property: the intent is to "have" the female body in the acquisitory meaning of the term. A woman is perceived by the rapist both as hated person and desired property. Hostility against her and possession of her may be simultaneous motivations, and the hatred for her is expressed in the same act that is the attempt to "take" her against her will. In one violent crime, rape is an act against person and property.

The importance of the work of Wolfgang and Ferracuti, Amir, and Brownmiller's observations lies in demonstrating that rape is linked with an overall pattern of violence and that part of this pattern includes the concept of woman as property. From the short descriptions of rape in some of the societies presented above, it is clear rape is likely to occur in what I would call, to borrow from Wolfgang, cultures of violence. Rape prone societies, as noted, are likely to include payment to the wronged husband, indicating that the concept of women as property also exists. This concept is not new to anthropology. It has been heavily stressed in the work of Levi-Strauss who perceives tribal women as objects in an elaborate exchange system between men.

The second type of approach to the understanding of rape focuses on the socialization process and psychoanalytic variables. This approach is reflected in the following quote from the conclusions of David Abrahamsen who conducted a Rorschach study on the wives of eight convicted rapists in 1954. Abrahamsen (1) says:

> The conclusions reached were that the wives of the sex offenders on the surface behaved toward men in a submissive and masochistic way but latently denied their femininity and showed an aggressive masculine orientation; they unconsciously invited sexual aggression, only to respond to it with coolness and rejection. They stimulated their husbands into attempts to prove themselves, attempts which necessarily ended in frustration and increased their husbands' own doubts about their masculinity. In doing so, the wives unknowingly continued the type of relationship the offender had had with his mother. There can be no doubt that the sexual frustration which the wives caused is one of the factors motivating rape, which might be tentatively described as a displaced attempt to force a seductive but rejecting mother into submission.

Brownmiller (6) includes this quote in her analysis of policeblotter rapists and her reaction to it is rather interesting. She rejects Abrahamsen's conclusions because they place the burden of guilt not on the rapist but on his mother and wife. The fact of the matter is that dominance cannot exist without passivity, as sadism cannot exist without masochism. What makes men sadistic and women masochistic, or men dominant and women passive, must be studied as part of an overall syndrome. Abrahamsen's conclusions certainly apply to Gusii males and females. With respect to the way in which Gusii wives invite sexual aggression from their husbands consider the following description of various aspects of Gusii nuptials:

> . . . the groom in his finery returns to the bride's family where he is stopped by a crowd of women who deprecate his physical appearance. Once he is in the house of the bride's mother and a sacrifice has been performed by the marriage priest, the woman begins again, accusing the groom of impotence on the wedding night and claiming that his penis is too small to be effective . . . When the reluctant bride arrives at the groom's house, the matter of first importance is the wedding night sexual performance. . . . The bride is determined to put her new husband's sexual competence to the most severe test possible. She may take magical measures which are believed to result in his failure in intercourse. . . . The bride usually refuses to get onto the bed; if she did not resist the groom's advances she would be thought sexually promiscuous. At this point some of the young men may

forcibly disrobe her and put her on the bed. . . . As he proceeds toward sexual intercourse she continues to resist and he must force her into position. Ordinarily she performs the practice known as *ogotega*, allowing him between her thighs but keeping the vaginal muscles so tense that penetration is impossible. . . . Brides are said to take pride in the length of time they can hold off their mates (16).

The relations between parents and children among the Gusii also fit Abrahamsen's conclusions concerning the etiology of rape. The son has a close and dependent relationship with his mother. The father is aloof from all his children, but especially his daughters. The father's main function is to punish which means that for the Gusii girl, her early connection with men is one of avoidance and fear. On the other hand, the relationship of the Gusii boy with his mother is characterized by dependence and seduction.

Studies of the etiology of rape suggest several hypotheses that can be tested cross-culturally. These hypotheses are not opposed; they are stated at different explanatory levels. One set phrases the explanation in socio-cultural terms, the other in psycho-cultural terms. Still another, only touched on above, suggests that male sexuality is inherently explosive unless it achieves heterosexual outlet. This latter assumption, implicit in LeVine's hypotheses mentioned above, also draws on the notion, most recently expressed in the work of Stoller (28), that sexual excitement is generated by the desire, overt or hidden, to harm another. If the latter were the case, we would be led to believe that rape would exist in all societies. The argument presented here, however, suggests that rape is an enactment not of human nature, but of socio-cultural forces. Thus, the prevalence of rape should be associated with the expressions of these forces. Some of these expressions and their correlation with the incidence of rape are examined in the next section.

Socio-Cultural Correlates of Rape

Four general hypotheses are suggested by the work of LeVine, Brownmiller, Abrahamsen, Wolfgang and Amir. These hypotheses are:

1. Sexual repression is related to the incidence of rape;
2. intergroup and interpersonal violence is enacted in male sexual violence;
3. the character of parent-child relations is enacted in male sexual violence;
4. rape is an expression of a social ideology of male dominance.

These hypotheses were tested by collecting data on: variables relating to childrearing; behavior indicating sexual repression; interpersonal and intergroup violence; sexual separation; glorification of the male role and an undervaluation of the female role.

The relevant variables are listed in Table 1 along with the correlation of each with the incidence of rape (see Table 2 for variable codes). The correlations presented in Table 1 supports all but the first of the general hypotheses listed above. There is no significant correlation between variables measuring sexual repression and the incidence of rape. Admittedly, however, sexual repression is very difficult to measure. The variables presented in Table 1 may not, in fact, be related to sexual abstinence. These variables are: length of the post-partum sex taboo (a variable which indicates how long the mother abstains from sexual intercourse after the birth of a child); attitude toward premarital sex (a variable which ranges between the disapproval and approval of premarital sex); age at marriage for males; and the number of taboos reflecting male avoidance of female sexuality.

The correlations presented in Table 1 support the hypothesis that intergroup and interpersonal violence is enacted in sexual violence against females. Raiding other groups for wives is significantly associated with the incidence of rape. The intensity of interpersonal violence in a society is also positively correlated with the incidence of rape, as is the presence of an ideology which encourages men to be tough and aggressive. Finally, when warfare is reported as being frequent or endemic (as opposed to absent or occasional) rape is more likely to be present.

Table 1.
Correlates of Rape

Variables Related to Sexual Repression[a]	Correlation with Incidence of Rape (RA4)[b]
1. Length of the post-partum sex taboo (Inf 10)	NS
2. Attitude toward pre-marital sex (Psex)	NS
3. Age at marriage for males (Agem)	NS
4. No. of taboos reflecting male avoidance of female sexuality (All)	NS
Variables Related to Intergroup and Interpersonal Violence	
5. Raiding other groups for wives (Wie)	$r = -.29$ (N = 83, p = .004)
6. Degree of Interpersonal violence (Viol)	$r = .47$ (N = 90, p = .000)
7. Ideology of Male Toughness (Macho)	$r = -.42$ (N = 73, p = .000)
8. War	$r = .21$ (N = 86, p = .03)
Variables Related to Childrearing	
9. Character of father-daughter relationships (Fada)	$r = -.20$ (N = 65, p = .06)
10. Proximity of father in care of infants (Inf 23)	$r = -.16$ (N = 83, p = .08)
11. Character of mother-son relationships (Moso)	NS
Variables Related to Ideology of Male Dominance	
12. Female power and authority (Stat)	$r = -.22$ (N = 83, p = .03)
13. Female political decision making (HO5)	$r = -.33$ (N = 88, p = .001)
14. Attitude toward women as citizens (HO8)	$r = -.28$ (N = 84, p = .005)
15. Presence of special places for men (Mho)	$r = -.26$ (N = 71, p = .01)
16. Presence of special places for women (Fho)	$r = -.17$ (N = 70, p = .08)

[a]Codes for variables are presented in Table 2.

[b]Correlation coefficient is Pearson r.

The character of relations between parents and children is not strongly associated with the incidence of rape. When the character of the father-daughter relationship is primarily indifferent, aloof, cold and stern, rape is more likely to be present. The same is true when fathers are distant from the care of infants. However, there is no relationship between the nature of the mother-son tie (as measured in this study) and the incidence of rape.

There is considerable evidence supporting the notion that rape is an expression of a social ideology of male dominance. Female power and authority is lower in rape prone societies. Women do not participate in public decision making in these societies and males express contempt for women as decision makers. In addition, there is greater sexual separation in rape prone societies as indicated by the presence of structures or places where the sexes congregate in single sex groups.

The correlates of rape presented in Table 1 strongly suggest that rape is the playing out of a socio-cultural script in which the expression of personhood for males is directed by, among other things, interpersonal violence and an ideology of toughness. If we see the sexual act as the ultimate emotional expression of the self, then it comes as no surprise that male sexuality is phrased in physically aggressive terms when other expressions of self are phrased in these terms. This explanation

Table 2.
Variable Codes for Correlations Listed in Table 1

1.	Info 10: 1 = intercourse after birth → 7 = intercourse after more than 2 yrs.
2.	Psex: 1 = premarital sex expected → 6 = strongly disapproved.
3.	Agem: 1 = men marry around puberty → 3 = 25 yrs. or older.
4.	All: 0 = no taboos reflecting male avoidance of intercourse → 3 = 3 taboos.
5.	Wie: 1 = Wives taken from hostile groups → 2 = practice absent.
6.	Viol: 1 = interpersonal violence mild or absent → 3 = strong.
7.	Macho: 1 = ideology of male toughness present → 2 = absent.
8.	War: 1 = war reported or absent or occasional → 2 = frequent or endemic.
9.	Fada: 1 = fathers affectionate with daughters → 2 = aloof, cold.
10.	Inf 23: 1 = no close proximity between fathers and infants → 5 = regular, close proximity.
11.	Moso: 1 = mothers affectionate with sons → 2 = aloof, cold.
12.	Stat: 1 = no female political or economic power → 6 = females have political and economic power.*
13.	HO5: 0 = females have no influence—public decision making → 1 = females have influence.
14.	HO18: 1 = males express contempt for women or citizens → 4 = women are respected as citizens.
15.	Mho: places where males congregate alone are present → 2 = absent.
16.	Fho: 1 = places where females congregate alone are present → 2 = absent.

*This variable forms a Guttman Scale. See Sanday, (26) for scale properties.

does not rule out the importance of the relationship between parents and children, husbands and wives. Raising a violent son requires certain behavior patterns in parents, behaviors that husbands may subsequently act out as adult males. Sexual repression does not explain the correlations presented in Table 1. Rape is not an instinct triggered by celibacy, enforced for whatever reason. Contrary to what some social scientists assume, men are not animals whose sexual behavior is programmed by instinct. Men are human beings whose sexuality is biologically based and culturally encoded.

Conclusion

Rape in tribal societies is part of a cultural configuration that includes interpersonal violence, male dominance, and sexual separation. In such societies, as the Murphys (23) say about the Mundurucu: "men . . . use the penis to dominate their women." The question remains as to what motivates the rape prone cultural configuration. Considerable evidence (see Sanday, 26) suggests that this configuration evolves in societies faced with depleting food resources, migration, or other factors contributing to a dependence on male destructive capacities as opposed to female fertility.

In tribal societies women are often equated with fertility and growth, men with aggression and destruction. More often than not, the characteristics associated with maleness and femaleness are equally valued. When people perceive an imbalance between the food supply and population needs, or when populations are in competition for diminishing resources, the male role is accorded greater prestige. Females are perceived as objects to be controlled as men struggle to retain or to gain control of their environment. Behaviors and attitudes prevail that separate the sexes and force men into a posture of proving their manhood. Sexual violence is one of the ways in which men remind themselves that they are superior. As such, rape is part of a broader struggle for control in the face of difficult circumstances. Where men are in harmony with their environment, rape is usually absent.

The insights garnered from the cross-cultural study of rape in tribal societies bear on the understanding and treatment of rape in our own. Ours is a heterogeneous society in which more men than we like to think feel that they do not have mastery over their destiny and who learn from the script provided by nightly television that violence is a way of achieving the material rewards that all Americans expect. It is important to understand that violence is socially and not biologically programmed. Rape is not an integral part of male nature, but the means by which men programmed for violence express their sexual selves. Men who are conditioned to respect the female virtues of growth and the sacredness of life, do not violate women. It is significant that in societies where nature is held sacred, rape occurs only rarely. The incidence of rape in our society will be reduced to the extent that boys grow to respect women and the qualities so often associated with femaleness in other societies—namely, nurturance, growth, and nature. Women can contribute to the socialization of boys by making these respected qualities in their struggle for equal rights.

REFERENCES

1. Abrahamsen, D. *The psychology of crime*. New York: Columbia University Press, 1960.

2. Amir, M. *Patterns in forcible rape*. Chicago, IL: University of Chicago Press, 1971.

3. Ardrey, R. *The territorial imperative*. New York: Dell, 1966.

4. Blanguernon, C. *Le hogger* (*The hogger*). Paris: B. Arthaud, 1955 (Translated form the French for the Human Relations Area Files by Thomas Turner).

5. Broude, G. J. & Greene, S.J. Cross-cultural codes on twenty sexual attitudes and practices. *Ethnology*, 1976, 15(4), 409–430.

6. Brownmiller, S. *Against our will*. New York: Simon & Schuster, 1975.

7. Dorsey, J. O. *Omaha sociology*. Smithsonian Institution, Bureau of Ethnology, Third Annual Report, 1881–82, pp. 205–370. Washington, D.C.: U.S. Government Printing Office, 1884.

8. Elwin, V. *The muria and their ghotul*. Bombay: Geoffrey Cumberlege, Oxford University Press, 1947.

9. Erdland, P. A. *Die Marshall-insulaner* (*The Marshall islanders*). Munster: Anthropos Bibliothek Ethnological Monographs 1914, 2(1). (Translated by Richard Neuse for Human Relations Area Files).

10. Evans-Pritchard, E. E. *The Azande*. London: Oxford University Press, 1971.

11. Hallowell, A.I. *Culture and experience*. Philadelphia, PA: University of Pennsylvania Press, 1955.

12. Harris, M. *Cannibals and kings*. New York: Vintage/Random House, 1977.

13. Hoebel, E. A. *The Cheyennes*. New York: Holt, Rinehart & Winston, 1960.

14. Lagae, C. R. Les Azande ou Niam-Niam. *Bibleotheque—Congo* (Vol. 18). Brussels: Vromant & Co., 1926. (Translated for Human Relations Area Files), New Haven, CT: HRAF.

15. Lambert, H. E. *Kikuyu social and political institutions*. London: Oxford University Press, 1956.

16. LeVine R. A. Gusii sex offenses: A study in social control. *American Anthropologist*, 1959, 61, 965–990.

17. Lorenz, K. *On aggression*. London: Methuen, 1966.

18. Maiskii, I. *Sovremennaia Mongolia* (*Contemporary Mongolia*). Irkutsk: Gosudarstvennoe Izdatel'stvo, Irkutskoe Otedelenie, 1921. (Translated from the Russian for *Human Relations Area Files* by Mrs. Dayton and J. Kunitz).

19. Malinowski, B. *The sexual life of savages in north-western Melanesia*. London: G. Routledge & Sons, 1929.

20. Maybury-Lewis, D. *Akwe—Shavante society*. Oxford: Claredon Press, 1967.

21. Mead, M. *The changing culture of an indian tribe*. New York: Columbia University Press, 1932.

22. Murdock, G. P. & White, D. R. Standard cross-cultural sample. *Ethnology*, 1969, 8, 329–369.

23. Murphy Y. & Murphy, R. *Women of the forest*. New York: Columbia University Press, 1974.

24. Rattray, R. S. *Ashanti*. Oxford: Clarendon Press, 1923.

25. Rattray, R. S. *Religion and art in Ashanti*. Oxford: Clarendon Press, 1927.

26. Sanday P. R. *Female power and male dominance: On the origins of sexual inequality*. New York: Cambridge University Press, 1981.

27. Spencer, Baldwin, & Gillen F. J. *The Arunta* (2 Vols.). London: Macmillan & Co., 1927.

28. Stoller, R. J. *Sexual excitement*. New York: Pantheon Books, 1979.

29. Stout, D. B. *San Blas Cura Acculturation*. New York: Viking Fund Publications in Anthropology, 1947, 9.

30. Tiger, L. *Men in groups*. New York: Random House, 1969.

31. Turnball, C. *Wayward servants*. New York: Natural History Press, 1965.

32. Wolfgang, M. E. & Ferracuti, F. *The subculture of violence*. London: Tavistock, 1967.

This research was supported by Grant No. RO1 MH 28978 awarded by the National Institute of Mental Health. I am grateful to Gloria Levin, former Deputy Chief of the National Center for the Prevention and Control of Rape, who administered this grant.

Correspondence regarding this article may be addressed to Dr. Peggy Reeves Sanday, Dept. of Anthropology, University of Pennsylvania, University Museum F-1, Philadelphia, PA 19104.

ADULT SEXUAL BONDING

HISTORICAL AND CROSS-CULTURAL PERSPECTIVES ON PASSIONATE LOVE AND SEXUAL DESIRE

Elaine Hatfield and Richard L. Rapson

In 1985, the International Academy of Sex Research sponsored a series of invited lectures and symposia on passionate love and sexual desire. The participants used the two terms almost interchangeably. This is probably not surprising. Passionate love has been defined as "a longing for union," and sexual desire has been defined as "a longing for *sexual* union" (65). In this paper, we will review what social psychologists, evolutionary theorists, anthropologists, historians, and cross-cultural researchers have discovered about the nature of passionate love, in general, and sexual desire, in particular.

Passionate love has been defined as "a state of intense longing for union with another. Passionate love is a complex functional whole including appraisals or appreciations, subjective feelings, expressions, patterned physiological processes, action tendencies, and instrumental behaviors. Reciprocated love (union with the other) is associated with fulfillment and ecstasy. Unrequited love (separation) with emptiness, anxiety, or despair" (67). The Passionate Love Scale (PLS) was designed to assess the cognitive, physiological, and behavioral indicants of such love (70). Approximately half of the items on the PLS measured a longing for *sexual* union. The Childhood Love Scale (CLS), which parallels the PLS, was developed to assess passionate love in children (64).

Most evolutionary and social psychologists have assumed that passionate love and sexual desire are cultural universals—existing at all times and in all places. Historians and cross-cultural researchers have explored how culture shapes the way that these universals are experienced and expressed at various times and in various places. In the following sections, we will review what theorists from these disciplines have learned about the nature of passionate love and sexual desire.

EVOLUTIONARY AND DEVELOPMENTAL PERSPECTIVES

Evolutionary Perspectives

Many have taken an evolutionary approach to explaining the origins of passionate love. Plutchik (110) argued that at every phylogenetic level (from the lowest single-celled organisms up to the highest primates), animals face many of the same problems. All must survive and reproduce. Thus, all have evolved a set of emotional "programs"—inherited, adaptive patterns of emotional experience, physiological reactions, and behavior—to deal with recurrent problems. Many evolutionary theorists believe that passionate love and sexual desire are built on the ancient circuitry that evolved to insure that mothers and infants remain closely attached and that adults mate and reproduce (3, 17, 19, 22, 67, 110).

Recently, Sommer (125) asked a challenging question: Did our ancient Homo sapien ancestors live in polygynous, monogamous, polygynandrous (promiscuous), or polyandrous communities? In other primates, four variables—sexual dimorphism (relative size of males and females), testes' weight, the existence of estrous swellings, and the duration of coitus seem to predict primates' sexu-

"Historical and Cross-Cultural Perspectives on Passionate Love and Sexual Desire," by Elaine Hatfield and Richard L. Rapson, reprinted from *Annual Review of Sex Research*, Volume IV, 1993.

al arrangements. (For example, in polygynous species, males are much bigger than females, whereas in monogamous species males and females are more similar in size. In both types of societies, females do not have estrous swelling and coitus lasts fairly long). When Sommer classified Homo sapiens on these characteristics, he was led to conclude that our human forbearers probably lived in polygynous communities; possibly in monogamous ones.

Fisher (51) provided conflicting data on the types of communities that are most common today. She pointed out that, throughout the world, the overwhelming majority of men and women are in monogamous marriages. When anthropologists examined the 853 societies tabulated in Murdock's *Ethnographic Atlas*, they found that, although 84% of societies permit polygyny, only about 10% of the men are actually involved in such arrangements. The remaining 16% of societies prescribe monogyny. Only 0.5% permit polyandry. In 99.5% of human cultures, women marry only one man at a time. (They are involved in either polygynous or monogamous marriages).

Recently, Jankowiak and Fischer (86) argued that romantic love is a panhuman characteristic stretching across cultures. They attempted to document the universality of passionate feelings. (They made a distinction between "romantic passion" and "simple lust"). They looked for evidence of romantic love in a sampling of tribal societies included in the *Standard Cross-Cultural Sample*. They determined whether romantic love was present or absent on the basis of five indicators: (a) accounts depicting personal anguish and longing, (b) the existence of love songs or folklore that highlight the motivations behind romantic involvement, (c) elopement due to mutual affection, (d) native accounts affirming the existence of passionate love, and (e) the ethnographer's affirmation that romantic love is present. They found clear evidence of passionate love in 147 of the 166 tribal cultures they studied. They could find no information as to whether or not passionate love existed in 18 societies. In only one society did the ethnographer state that romantic love did not exist. Jankowiak and Fischer pointed out that there was cultural variability in how *common* such passionate feelings were.

Some evolutionary psychologists have also contended that there are cultural universals in what men and women desire in a mate (28, 29, 31, 47, 127). Since Darwin's (36) classic treatise *The Descent of Man and Selection in Relation to Sex*, evolutionary biologists have been interested in mate preferences. Recently, in a landmark cross-cultural study, Buss (28, 29) asked over 10,000 men and women, from 37 countries located on six continents and five islands, to indicate what characteristics they valued in potential mates. (The countries involved in this study are listed in Table 1.) The 37 cultures represented a tremendous diversity of geographic, cultural, political, ethnic, religious, racial, and economic groups.

The authors asked men and women to consider 18 traits and to rate how desirable or important they thought each trait was in choosing a mate. Buss et al. (1990) found that, overall, the single trait that men and women in all the societies valued most in a mate was "mutual attraction-love." They cared next about finding a mate who possessed a dependable character, emotional stability and maturity, and a pleasing disposition.

Buss and Schmitt (31) also argued that there should be universal gender differences in what men and women desire in a mate. According to evolutionary biology, an animal's "fitness" depends on how successful it is in transmitting its genes to subsequent generations. It is to both men's and women's evolutionary advantage to produce as many progeny as possible. But men and women differ in one critical respect—how much they must invest in their offspring if they are to survive and reproduce: Men need invest little, whereas women must invest a great deal. On the basis of this logic, Buss and Schmitt proposed a "sexual strategies theory" of human mating. They argued that, in the course of evolution, men and women have come to be genetically programmed to desire different traits in a mate. They also argued that it is to men's and women's advantage to employ different strategies in short-term relationships (i.e., "one-night stands" or brief affairs) than in a long-term marital relationship. A sampling of the 22 hypotheses they derived from their model are:

Table 1.
Countries Participating in the Mate Selection Study

African	*European-Eastern*	*North American*
Nigeria	Bulgaria	Canada (English)
S. Africa (Whites)	Estonian S.S.R.	Canada (French)
S. Africa (Zulu)	Poland	USA (Mainland)
Zambia	Yugoslavia	USA (Hawaii)
Asian	*European-Western*	*Oceanian*
China	Belgium	Australia
India	France	New Zealand
Indonesia	Finland	*South American*
Iran	Germany-West	Brazil
Israel (Jewish)	Great Britain	Columbia
Israel (Palestinian)	Greece	Venezuela
Japan	Ireland	
Taiwan	Italy	
	Netherlands	
	Norway	
	Spain	
	Sweden	

1. In *short-term relationships*, it is to men's advantage to be attuned to signs which attest to women's reproductive fitness. They should care a great deal about physical appearance, health, and youth (preferring women with clear and lustrous hair, smooth skin, full lips, white teeth, a lively gait, and good health). Men should have evolved a powerful desire for multiple sexual encounters. They should be "turned off" by women who are prudish, sexually inexperienced, conservative, or who have a low sex drive and "turned on" by women who are easily available. In the absence of a desirable partner, however, men should be willing to engage in sexual relations with a wide array of partners in a wide array of circumstances. Men should be eager to avoid commitment or heavy investment in any one relationship.

Women in short-term relationships face a different set of adaptive problems. If women choose to pursue a short-term strategy, they can maximize their evolutionary outcomes by concentrating on immediate resource extraction (preferring men who are generous, give them focus on long-term goals, they must try to identify men who would be appropriate marital partners. Women must look for signs that men will be willing and able to protect them and their offspring. They should look for professional men with ambition, status, good earning capacity, and a strong career orientation. They should want mates who are kind and considerate, understanding, honest, dependable, easy-going and adaptable; they should seek out men who like children.) Women should insist on knowing men for a fairly long time before they become willing to risk a sexual encounter.

Men tend to be interested in "playing the field"; women in finding partners for a serious relationship (26, 27, 30).

2. In *long-term relationships*, men and women must confront a different set of problems. Men should still prefer women who are good looking, young, healthy, and of maximum reproductive value. But now they must also be concerned about finding a mate who is willing and able to commit herself to a long-term relationship, who will be faithful, and who possesses good parenting skills.

Women who are considering a long-term relationship tend to prefer a mate who seems able and willing to provide and protect them and their children. (Most women desire the same thing in short-term and long-term relationships.) They prefer men who will make a commitment, who are willing and able to invest resources in them and their children, who possess parenting skills, and who are willing and able to protect them from harm.

As men and women's investments become more similar (as they do in long-term relationships), both should become increasingly choosy about selecting a mate.

Buss and his colleagues collected considerable evidence in support of these hypotheses (31, 47). For example, in his study of 37 cultures, Buss (28) found that, as predicted, men and women did differ somewhat in how important the various traits were. Men seemed to care more about traits that signaled *reproductive capacity*. Men, worldwide, preferred marriage partners who were 2 to 3 years younger then they. They cared more about good looks than women did. In some cultures (but not all) men were more likely to insist on chastity than were women. Women worldwide seemed to care more about cues that signaled men's *resource capacity* (their ability to provide for her and her children) than did men. Women preferred men who were 3 to 4 years older than they. They, more than men, valued mates who possessed status, were good financial prospects, and who were ambitious and industrious. (For similar results in the modern, industrialized countries of the United States, Russia, and Japan, see 71)

The evolutionary approach has not been without its critics. Social learning theorists argue that it is not ancient wiring but sociocultural factors that can best explain existing gender difference in passionate and sexual choices and behavior (79, 112, 136). Culture has been found to have an important impact on social definitions of how men and women think, feel, and behave in the arena of love and sex (60, 68) Wallen (141), for example, conducted a reanalysis of Buss' data, in order to determine which was most important—culture or gender—in shaping people's preferences in mates. She found that for some traits—such as good looks and financial prospects—it was gender that had the biggest influence on preferences. (Gender accounted for 40%–45% of the variance; geographical origin accounted for only 8%–17% of the variance.) For other traits—such as chastity, ambition, and preferred age—on the other hand, it was culture that mattered most. (Gender accounted for only 5%–16% of the variance, whereas geographical origin accounted for 38%–59%, of the variance.) She concluded that, in general, a cultural perspective may be more powerful than an evolutionary perspective in understanding mate selection.

Researchers interested in individual differences have argued that men and women are more similar than different in their passionate sexual choices and behavior. Simpson and Gangestad (121), for example, found that men and women who possessed a *restricted* sociosexual orientation (as assessed by the Sociosexual Orientation Inventory) insisted on closeness and commitment before they were willing to engage in sexual relations. People with an *unrestricted* sociosexual orientation felt comfortable about engaging in sex without commitment or closeness. They tended to have more one-night stands and to have sex with several partners at the same time. They concluded that both men's and women's passionate sexual behavior was more dependent on their sociosexual orientation than on their gender.

Sociologists point out that political, economic, and social changes can produce marked changes in men's and women's sexual attitudes and behavior. In America, for example, the double standard (so popular 30 years ago), if not dead, is rapidly dying (38, 102, 126, 128, 129). There is some evidence that it may be on the wane in Russia and Japan as well (128).

Finally, Fisher (52) has argued that the fleeting nature of passionate love is a cultural universal. She contended that romantic and passionate love evolved for very practical genetic reasons. Presumably, adults are predisposed to remain passionately engaged with one another for about 4 years—just long enough for their first child to learn to survive on its own. (By 4 years of age, children in tribal societies have been weaned and have begun to spend most of their time in multi-age play groups.) Once it is no longer imperative for parents to remain together to insure the survival of their first child, Fisher argues, men and women generally fall out of love with their first partner and in love with someone new. Presumably, such serial monogamy (which she contends is the most common marital system) produces maximum genetic diversity, which provides an evolutionary advantage. To test her hypothesis, Fisher examined the divorce rates in collecting/hunting, agricultural, pastoral, fishing, and industrial societies, utilizing ethnographic records and the *Demographic Yearbooks* of the United Nations from 1947–1981. She found that, as predicted, throughout the world, couples are most likely to divorce in their 4th year of marriage (51). She concluded: "It is parsimonious to conclude that serial pairbonding evolved in hominid paleopopulations . . . as an adaptation to rear highly dependent young through infancy and this adaptation continues to contribute to the modern cross-cultural pattern of marriage/divorce/remarriage" (51).

Developmental Perspectives

Ainsworth (2) and Bowlby (17, 18, 19) studied the process of attachment, separation, and loss in infants and children. They found that normally, from about 9–18 months, infants become profoundly attached to their primary caregivers. (They prefer to remain in close proximity to them, become distressed when they are separated, avoid strangers, and immediately return to their caretakers when they are threatened.) Some social psychologists have argued that such early attachments are the forerunners of adults' passionate attachments—their "desire for union" (9, 67, 72). There is some evidence that children from a variety of ethnic backgrounds are capable of experiencing passionate love very early—as early as 3-1/2 to 4 years of age (11, 69, 64).

Shaver and Hazan (118) also proposed that children's early patterns of attachment should influence their adult attachments. For example, some children are *securely attached* to their mothers; they are both affectionate and reasonably independent. Such children are likely to mature into secure adults who are comfortable with intimacy and are able to trust and depend on those they care for. Some children are *anxious/ambivalent*. They may be clingy and dependent, terrified of being abandoned. They may get angry and upset at their caretakers when they leave and reject them when they return. Such children are likely to become anxious/ambivalent adults. Some may fall in love easily, seek extreme levels of closeness, and be terrified that they will be abandoned. In any case, such desperate love affairs are likely to be short-lived. *Avoidant*, rejecting children, may well become avoidant adults who are uncomfortable getting too close and have difficulty depending on others. The authors have amassed considerable support in favor of the contention that childhood patterns of attachment can be read in adult passionate attachments (9, 49, 74). Doherty and his colleagues (42) found that attachment style had the predicted relationship to people's passionate and companionate love experiences in Americans of European, Pacific Island, or Asian ethnic backgrounds.

Recently, researchers have found that the prevalence of children and adults who develop the various attachment styles is roughly the same in all cultures. Hazan and Shaver (72), for example, found that in the United States, approximately 56% of respondents classified themselves as securely attached, 19% as anxious/ambivalent, and 25% as avoidant. Wu and Shaver (144) found that in the United States, Australia, Israel, and China roughly the same percentage of adults placed themselves in these three categories.

If passionate love *is* rooted in childhood attachments, certain types of people caught up in certain types of situations should be especially vulnerable to passion. Anything that makes adults feel as helpless and dependent as they were as children, anything that makes them fear separation and loss, should increase their passionate craving to merge with others. There is some evidence to support these speculations. It has been found that individuals are especially vulnerable to passion when men's and women's self-esteem is threatened (9, 63, 84), when they are insecure and dependent or caught up in affairs that promote such feelings (15, 50), when people are unusually anxious (64, 108, 124), or when they are sexually needy and deprived (130).

There have therefore been social psychologists, evolutionary theorists, and developmentalists who have concluded that passionate love and sexual desire are human universals. Some social psychologists, historians, and cross-cultural researchers point out, however, that culture can have a great influence on how easily and how deeply people fall in love and how they try to deal with these tumultuous feelings.

HISTORICAL PERSPECTIVES

Literature tells us that passionate love and sexual desire have always existed—in all times and in all places. The earliest Western literature, bound up as it is between myth and reality, recounts thousands of stories of lovers caught up in a sea of passion and violence: Odysseus and Penelope, Orpheus and Eurydice, Daphnis and Chloe, Dido and Aeneas, Abelard and Eloise, Dante and Beatrice, and Romeo and Juliet. Such tales exist outside of Europe as well. For more than 4,000 years, China's history and art have been filled with stories of passionate love and sexual longing. In the Sung Dynasty (960–1279 A.D.) the *Jade Goddess* recounted the story of a passionate young couple, who defied their parents' wishes, challenged convention, and eloped, only to fall into desperate straits (115). (For an encyclopedic review of other Chinese love stories see 115, 85.) A similar record can be found in India, Persia, and practically all other ancient societies.

But the main message of historical research is not the universality of love, but its variability. In various eras and in varying societies, the very words *love, sex,* and *intimacy* have carried a huge array of differing and contradictory meanings (23, 37, 39, 56, 58, 99, 109, 132, 133). As D'Emilio and Freedman noted "sexuality has been associated with a range of human activities and values: the procreation of children, the attainment of physical pleasure (eroticism), recreation or sport, personal intimacy, spiritual transcendence, or power over others" (p. xv).

Although passionate love and sexual desire have always existed, they were rarely encouraged. Throughout history, until about 1500, most cultures (and the political and religious authorities who held power), viewed passionate lovers' primitive and powerful feelings as a threat to the social, political, and religious order. They tried to suppress such dangerous feelings. In the West, during the early Christian era, for instance, suppression was especially harsh. For 1,500 years—from the earliest days of the Roman Catholic Church in the 2nd century AD to the 16th century Protestant Reformation and Catholic Counter-Reformation—the Church proclaimed passionate love and sex (even marital sex) for any purpose other than procreation to be a mortal sin, punishable by eternal damnation (55). For most of Western history until the 18th century "Age of Reason," love was not expected to end well. Romeo and Juliet, Ophelia and Hamlet, Abelard and Eloise did not make love, get married, have two children, and live happily ever after. Juliet stabbed herself. Romeo swallowed poison. Ophelia went mad and died. Hamlet was felled by a poisoned sword point. Peter Abelard (a real person) was castrated and his beloved Eloise retired to a nunnery. The same miserable endings to love occurred elsewhere. In Japan, for example, love suicides have been an institution since the end of the 17th century (95).

Some traditional love stories sound strange to the modern reader. And so they should. In the realms of love and sex, a profound revolution has taken place in the last 3 centuries, and it is still happening (for better or worse, depending on one's own beliefs). It started in Europe, spread to the United States, and now appears to be reaching deep into the traditions of many non-Western societies. It is part of the dominant tendency of modern history in all phases of life, a tendency given the name of "Westernization." The historical model with which most scholars interested in world history operate (98, 113, 111) goes like this.

Throughout the centuries, four cultures possessed the most political and economic power and the most influential cultural traditions. The Big Four were the East Asia area (today's China, Japan, Korea, and southeast Asia); South Asia (India, Pakistan, Afghanistan, Sri Lanka); the Middle East or West Asia (Egypt, Persia [Iran], Mesopotamia [Iraq], Palestine, Syria, and other Arab countries); and Western civilization (Europe and, recently, the United States). There have been other strong, original cultures—in Africa, North and South America, the steppes of Asia, Polynesia, Oceania, and other places—but none of them could match the power and influence of those four. Until 1500, the four major groups were by-and-large separate and independent cultural units. They tended to move on parallel tracks, intersecting at times, but generally swerving away from one another. There barely existed even the concept of one world. In the realms of passionate love and sexual desire, different cultural groups possessed somewhat different ideas about the social rules governing them (20, 131).

All that changed after about 1500. Large transformations followed in the wake of the Renaissance, the Scientific Revolution, and the Industrial Revolution. By the late 18th century, the West began to alter its view of love and almost everything else. Western culture began to "invent" a number of unique and modern ideas. In the *material sphere*, it has meant the rapid expansion of urbanization, industrialization, and technology; in the *economic* and *political spheres*, it has meant a move toward democracy, capitalism, socialism, and/or totalitarianism systems; in the *philosophical sphere*, it has meant an increasing faith first in Christianity, and then humanism, secularism, and science; and (perhaps most importantly for our purposes) in the *psychological sphere*, it has meant an increasing insistence on individualism, the desirability of the goal of personal happiness and the reduction of pain, accompanied by personal and artistic freedom and more fluid class systems. Looming large in the psychological arena has been a metamorphosis in Euro-American approaches to love and sex, many of which are now occurring in corners of the non-Western world (98, 113, 131, 137).

The West initiated such ideas and practices (among many) as (a) a high value placed on romantic and passionate love; (b) marriage for love (as opposed to arranged marriage); (c) egalitarian families (as opposed to patriarchal, hierarchical arrangements); (d) sexual freedom for men and women; (e) the movement toward equality for women; and (f) childhood considered as a separate phase of the life cycle with children deserving special treatment (as opposed to treating very young children as miniature adults sent out to farm the fields as soon as they could walk) (6, 35, 91, 133). By 1800, the West had been transformed by these ideas. Have India, China, Japan, Egypt, Iran, the nations of Africa and Latin America escaped these revolutions? Not completely. Just how much such traditional societies have changed, and whether these changes are desirable, however, is debated.

There is one particularly intriguing and important phenomenon: It took the West over 500 years to embrace (or partially embrace) these "modern" ideas of love, sex, and intimacy. In some non-Western cultures, however, these same changes seem, at least superficially, to be repeating themselves in less than 50 years (13, 45, 143). It is as though history is hurtling through these societies at an ever-accelerating pace.

Recently, of course, there has begun to be a backlash against Western ideas and hegemony. Non-Western ethnic groups have begun to celebrate their own cultures; some resist wholesale Western cultural imperialism. Throughout the world, people have begun to speculate about the possibilities of taking only the best that the West has to offer and integrating it with the cultural traditions that are uniquely their own (8, 87, 122). Some feel it is best to try to turn back the clock and reject Westernization (which many associate with drugs, crime, licentiousness, and greed) entirely. The dialectic between Westernization and resistance to it defines much of international life today. Even in the United States and Western Europe, many citizens are repelled by sexual permissiveness, the ease of divorce, and the women's movement. Among historians, there is as yet no substantial disagreement with the contention that since 1800, the West has greatly expanded its influence upon the rest of the world (20, 98, 113, 131). There is serious debate, however, about how deep these influences go. Are they fundamental or cosmetic (8, 101, 122, 143)? And there is heated controversy about whether Western cultural expansion has been largely constructive or malignant (13, 45, 111, 137).

The current historical perspective suggests several questions for sex researchers: What aspects of love, sex, and intimacy are universal? Which are social constructions? Is the world in fact becoming one and homogeneous? Or are traditional cultural practices more tenacious and impervious to this sort of deep transformation than some have supposed 8, 87, 101)?

CROSS-CULTURAL PERSPECTIVES

Culture can, of course, have a profound impact on how people view love, how susceptible they are to falling in love, with whom they tend to fall in love, and how their passionate affairs work out. It can also effect the object of sexual desire as well as when, where, and why people feel sexual passion.

Culture has been defined as "the shared way of life of a group of people" (14). Cross-cultural psychologists have been interested in the similarities and differences between cultures, in cross-national comparisons, and in ethnic differences. They contribute to our understanding of passionate love and sexual desire in two different ways. First, they can give us some sense of what social structures and processes are found throughout the human family. Second, they give us some sense of how variable social arrangements can be. Let us review some of the major cross-cultural theorists' perspectives.

In 1830, DeTocqueville (40) observed that the United States was an individualist/materialist culture, compared to the Europe of his days. In *Democracy in America*, he detailed the consequences, positive and negative, of this type of individualist philosophy. Cross-cultural psychologists, too, have observed that the world's cultures differ profoundly in the extent to which they emphasize individualism or collectivism (although some would focus on related concepts: independence or interdependence; modernism or traditionalism; urbanism or ruralism; affluence or poverty). Individualistic cultures (such as the United States, Britain, Australia, Canada, and the countries of northern and western Europe) tend to focus on personal goals. Collectivist cultures (such as China, many African and Latin American nations, Greece, southern Italy, and the Pacific Islands), on the other hand, press their members to subordinate their personal interests to those of the group.

Triandis and his colleagues (138) identified several traits which seem to distinguish individualistic from collectivist cultures. In individualistic cultures, people are allowed to "do their own thing," to put their own needs first. In collectivist cultures, they are pressed to subordinate their needs to those of the group. Individualist cultures stress rights over duties; collectivists stress duties over rights. Individualists' behavior is shaped primarily by their own attitudes and preferences, by private cost-benefit analyses of what will work for them and what won't. Collectivists are expected to conform to social norms; deviant behavior is punished (p. 1007).

Triandis et al. (138) went on to note, "in collectivist cultures there is much emphasis on hierarchy. Usually, the father is the boss and men superordinate women. This is not nearly as much the case in individualistic cultures" (p. 1007).

Triandis et al. (138) also developed a scale to classify cultures as individualist or collectivist. Within a given culture, of course, people can vary in their philosophies. Their scale also indicates how idiocentric (individualistic) or allocentric (collectivist) individuals are.

Markus and Kitayama (97) argued that culture has a critically important impact on people's self-construals (on the way they see themselves and others). Culture, they contended, affects cognitions, emotions, and motivations. In many Western, *independent* cultures there is a faith in the inherent separateness of distinct persons. These cultures value individuality, uniqueness, and independence. Many non-Western, *interdependent* cultures, on the other hand, insist on the fundamental connectedness of human beings. The self is defined in relation to ancestors, family, and those around them. These cultures emphasize attending to and fitting in with others and the importance of conformity and harmonious interdependence.

Asian scholars have also theorized about cultural differences in people's views of passionate love and sexual desire (or at least about their sexual attitudes, feelings, and behavior). Chu (33) contrasted the traditional American and Chinese views of self.

> The American self seems to be characterized by individualism. It tends to assert one's self rather than accommodate others and to strive for a high degree of self-reliance and independence. . . . The traditional Chinese self exists primarily in relation to significant others. Thus, a male Chinese would consider himself a son, a brother, a husband, a father, but hardly *himself*. It seems as if . . . there was very little independent self left for the Chinese. This point can be further illustrated by the position of women in traditional China. Before marriage, a woman followed her father. After marriage, she followed her husband. After the death of her husband, she followed her son. The self had little meaning outside these rigidly defined social contexts. The idea that a woman could stand on her own, and be herself, simply did not seem possible. A person, in this case a woman, measured the

worth of herself not by what she had personally achieved, but by the extent to which she had lived up to the behavioral expectations of the significant others as defined by the predominant cultural ideas. (pp. 257–258)

As a consequence, Chu observed, American and traditional Chinese men and women desired very different qualities in a mate. "In traditional China the selection of a marital partner was made by parents, who relied on go-betweens. The main criteria were known as *men tang hu tui*, that is, the doors of the two families should be of similar texture and the houses must face each other. In other words, comparability of family social status was of paramount importance. Whether the young couple were compatible and could get along with each other was of little consequence" (p. 264).

For Americans, love and compatibility are the first priority. Chu expressed considerable alarm that in the wake of the Cultural revolution, modern Chinese men and women have become increasingly self-centered and materialistic; they have, he fears, lost their traditional anchorage. Today the young seem to care nothing about scholarly achievements and knowledge. Family and relatives are totally rejected. Young women seem to be totally self-centered and materialistic. He asked, "How can one explain this change from the past?" Chu postulated that the Cultural Revolution probably caused this "decline." The new Chinese self was no longer so strongly anchored in traditional values. Families lost power and influence. Parents were so busy striving for material goods that no one stayed home to care for the "latchkey" children. Young people learned that moral principles did not pay. They saw opportunists gain power. Violence was encouraged. The result was that young people became less submissive to authority figures, more assertive, and less accommodating. Chu held on to the hope, however, that this trend would be reversed. (We would, of course, see such changes more neutrally, as evidence of embryonic Westernization of China and its adoption of more individualistic values.)

Hsu (82) also contrasted Western and Chinese values concerning passionate love and intimacy. American culture, he argued, is interested in personality; it is individual-centered. It attaches great importance to emotional expression. Chinese culture is situation-centered. Individuals are caught up in "a web of interpersonal relationships" (82). Group members are required to conform to "the interpersonal standards of the society" (80). Chinese men and women tend to "underplay all matters of the heart" (80). Hsu (81) argued that such differences have a critical impact on how romantic love is viewed in each society. The concept of romantic love fits in well with a North American cultural perspective but *not* with a Chinese cultural orientation, where one is expected to consider not just one's own personal feelings, but obligations to others, especially one's parents. Hsu wrote, "an American asks, 'How does my heart feel?' A Chinese asks, 'What will other people say?'" (p. 50). He claims that the Western idea of romantic love has not had much of an impact on young adults in China. Hsu pointed out that the Chinese generally used to term love to describe not a respectable, socially sanctioned relationship, but an *illicit* liaison between a man and a woman.

Hsu (80, 82) also noted that culture has a profound impact on where people seek intimacy and how likely they are to find it. In the West, people focus on romantic love; it is in passionate affairs that they expect to find intimacy. It is considered immature to remain dependent on one's parents. In Chinese society, men and women expect less from marriage. Parents and kin are the source of intimacy. Men and women assume they will be tied to their families throughout life. Love may fail, but families do not. Hsu (82) remarked "most parents are like dogs; one can kick them in the teeth and they will still come back for more. No one can take his peers for granted to that extent. He and they are likely to compete for the same things. His desire for mastery over them is matched by theirs over him. He has to satisfy his peers as much as they have to satisfy him" (p. 38).

Ho (75) also distinguished Western from Eastern ideas about love, sex, and marriage. In Ho's analysis, Western psychologists tend to think in individualistic terms; they talk about the self and personality. Asian psychologists' concepts are relational. Ho argued that behavioral scientists should expand their focus:

My intention is not to derogate individualistic concepts; much has been achieved through their use, and their respectability is well-deserved. Nevertheless, so long as they remain the primary constructs to be relied upon, behavioral science will continue to be individual-centered, wedded to the ideology of individualism. And dissatisfaction with this ideological bias has been voiced. . . . The point I wish to emphasize is that social behavior is inherently relational in nature: Individual behavior assumes social meaning only in the context of human relations. . . . The basic unit of analysis is therefore not individual behavior, but behavior-in-a-relational-context. (p. 233)

Doi (44) contended that a key to understanding the Japanese cultural perspective is to understand the concept of *amae*. The verb *amaeru* can be translated as "to depend and presume upon another's love" or "to indulge in another's kindness." (43). This word describes what infants and small children feel for their mothers: a desire for infantile dependency—a wish to cling to her, to have someone attend to one's every need, to resist being cast into the cold world of objective reality. In adulthood, Doi (44) argued "*amae*, generally speaking, is an inseparable concomitant of love (*koi*)" (p. 118).

Doi (44) elaborated on the vocabulary of *amae*:

The word *amae* itself is far from being an isolated expression of the *amae* psychology in the Japanese language. A large number of other words give expression to the same psychology. The adjective *amai*, for example, is . . . a description of a man's character: thus if A is said to be *amai* to B, it means that he allows B to *amaeru*, i.e. to behave self-indulgently, presuming on some special relationship that exists between the two. . . . Next, there is a group of words such as *suneru*, *higamu*, *hinekureau*, and *uramu* that relate to various states of mind brought about by the inability to *amareru*. *Suneru* (to be sulky) occurs when one is not allowed to be straightforwardly self-indulgent yet the attitude comprises in itself a certain degree of that same self-indulgence. *Futekusareru* and *jakekuso ni naru* (indicating, respectively, the attitudes of defiance and irresponsibility in speech or behavior associated with a "fit of the sulks"), are two phenomena that arise as a result of *suneru*. *Higamu* (to be suspicious or jaundiced in one's attitude), which involves laboring under the delusion that one is being treated unjustly, has its origins in the failure of one's desire for indulgence to find the expected response. *Hinekureru* (to behave in a distorted, perverse way) involves feigning indifference to the other instead of showing *amae*. Under the surface one is, in fact, concerned with the other's reaction; although there appears to be no *amae*, it is there, basically all the time. *Uramu* (to show resentment toward or hatred of) means that rejection of one's *amae* has aroused feelings of hostility; this hostility has a complexity not present in simple hatred, that shows how closely it is linked with the *amae* psychology. (pp. 29–30)

According to Doi (44), the Japanese assume that amae will continue to cement their most intimate of relationships throughout their lives.

The Japanese have a second term, *enryo*, which may be roughly translated as "restraint" or "holding back." In one sense, people do not hold back with their intimates as they do with outsiders. In another sense, they are more likely to show restraint and consideration for those they care for. Doi (44) continued: "In Japan, little value is attributed to the individual's private realm as distinct from the group" (p. 42).

The presence or absence of *enryo* is used by the Japanese as a gauge in distinguishing between the types of human relationships that they refer to as "outer" and "inner." One's relatives, with whom no *enryo* is necessary, are in one's "inner" circle—literally, since the term *miuchi*, "relatives," means something like "one's inner circle"—but *giri*-type relationships where *enryo* is present are the "outer" circle . . . in contrast to the world of *tanin*, with whom one is quite unconnected, and where there is no need, even, to bring *enryo* into play. (p. 40)

Doi (44), too, seems to share Western theorists' observation that the Japanese are much more concerned with in-group and out-group differences than are Westerners. Theorists, then, make it clear that we might expect to find both cultural similarities and differences in the way that men and women view love, and that culture plays a significant part when it comes to love and sex.

Let us now turn to recent research into the impact of culture on passionate love and sexual desire.

THE CROSS-CULTURAL DATA

Culture and the Definition of Passionate Love

Are there cultural differences in how men and women view passionate love? Wu and Shaver (144, 119) interviewed young people in America, Italy, and the People's Republic of China about their emotional experiences. In all cultures, men and women identified the same emotions as basic, prototypic, emotions. These were joy/happiness, love/attraction, fear, anger/hate, and sadness/depression. They also agreed completely as to whether the various emotions should be labeled as positive experiences (such as joy) or negative ones (such as fear, anger, or sadness). They agreed completely except, that is, about one emotion—love. American and Italian subjects tended to equate love with happiness; both passionate and companionate love were assumed to be intensely positive experiences. Chinese students, however, had a darker view of love. In Chinese there are few "happy-love" ideographs. Love tends to be associated with sadness, pain, and heartache. Chinese men and women generally associated passionate love with such ideographs as infatuation, unrequited love, nostalgia, and sorrow-love.

Students from the East and West never did come to an agreement as to the nature of love. Each cultural group continued to regard one another's visions of love as "unrealistic."

Culture and Susceptibility to Love

It has been claimed that Americans are preoccupied with love (103). When Hendrick and Hendrick (73) asked University of Miami students "Are you in love now?" 46% of them said they were. Eighty-nine percent of them said they had been in love at least once in their lives. Only 11% had never been in love. Men and women seem to differ in their vulnerability to passionate love. In the Hendrick and Hendrick study, 46% of men and 66% of women admitted they were in love at the present time.

How about men and women in the rest of the industrialized world? Some early researchers (59, 114) assumed that romantic love would be most prevalent in modern, industrialized, countries. The emerging evidence, however, suggests that men and women in a variety of cultures (industrializing as well as industrial) are every bit as romantic as Americans. Sprecher et al. (127), for example, interviewed 1,667 men and women, all college students, in the United States, Russia, and Japan. Similar percentages of men and women in the various cultures said they were currently in love (see Table 2). Passion was more common worldwide than the researchers expected. They had expected American men and women to be most vulnerable to love; the Japanese the least. In fact, they found that it was the Russians who reported being currently in love the most often. American men and women were intermediate and the Japanese were least likely to be in love. (The percentage of those currently in love was "surprisingly" high in all three societies, however.) In all three cultures, men were slightly less likely than were women to be in love at the present time.

Surveys of Mexican-American, Chinese-American, and Euro-American students have also found that in a variety of cross-national groups, young men and women show high rates of reporting being in love at the present time (7).

Culture and Intensity of Passionate Love

What impact does culture have on how passionately men and women fall in love? In one study, Hatfield and Rapson (65) asked American men and women of European, Filipino, and Japanese ancestry to complete the Passionate Love Scale (PLS). Men and women from the various ethnic groups seemed to love with equal passion (see Table 3).

Culture and the Willingness to Marry Someone You Do Not Love

In the West, people generally assume that couples should be romantically in love with who ever they choose to marry. In the mid-1960s, Kephart (88) asked more than 1,000 American college students: "If a boy (girl) had all the other qualities you desired, would you marry this person if you were not in love with him (her)?" He found that in the 1960s, men and women had different ideas as to how important romantic love was in a marriage. Men thought passion was essential. Women said that the absence of love would not necessarily deter them from considering marriage. Kephart suggested that whereas men might have the luxury of marrying for love, women did not. Women's status was dependent on their husbands'; thus, they had to be practical and take a potential husband's family background, professional status, and income into account. Since the 1960s, sociologists have continued to ask young American men and women this question. They have found that, year by year, young American men and women have come to demand more and more of love. Simpson and his colleagues (120), for example, found that in the 1980s, 85% of American men and women would not even consider marrying someone they did not love. In the most recent research, 86% of men and 91% women answered the same question "No!" (4).

Today, American men and women assume that romantic love is so important that they insist that if they fell out of love, they would not even consider *staying* married! (120). Of course, with more experience they might find that they are willing to "settle" for less than they think they would.

How do young men and women in other countries feel about this issue? Sprecher et al. (128) asked American, Russian, and Japanese students, "If a person had all the other qualities you desired, would you marry him/her if you were not in love?" (Students could only answer *yes* or *no*.) The authors, of course, had expected that only the individualistic Americans would demand love *and* marriage; they predicted that both the Russians and the Japanese would be more practical. They found that they were wrong. Both the Americans and the Japanese were romantics (see Table 4). Few of them would consider marrying someone they did not love. (Only 11% of Americans and 18% of the Japanese said yes.) The Russians, especially the women, were more practical; 30% of the Russian men and 41% of the Russian women said they would accept such a proposal.

The preceding studies, then, suggest that the large differences that once existed between Westernized, urban, modern, industrial societies and Eastern, modern, urban industrial societies are fast disappearing. Those interested in cross-cultural differences may only find them if they begin to explore some of the most underdeveloped, developing, and collectivist of societies—such as in Africa or Latin America, in China or the Arab countries (Egypt, Kuwait, Lebanon, Libya, Saudia-Arabia, Iraq, or the U.A.E.). Not surprisingly, data on passionate love and sexual desire are collected primarily in the West, where such feelings are valued. Collectivist societies, which denigrate such feelings, forbid such data collection. Thus, the very societies in which we would be most interested are also the most inaccessible. There are some data, however, which suggest that, even there, the winds of Westernization and change are blowing.

Table 2.

Percentage of Men and Women in Various Countries Who Are Currently in Love

Cultural Group	Percentage in Love	
	Men	*Women*
American	53	63
Russian	61	73
Japanese	41	63

Note. Source: Sprecher et al. (1992)

Table 3.

Intensity of Passionate Love in Various Ethnic Groups

Ethnic Group	Average PLS[a] Score	
	Men	*Women*
Euro-Americans (Mainland USA)	97.50	110.25
Euro-Americans (Hawaii)	100.50	105.00
Filipino-Americans (Hawaii)	106.50	102.90
Japanese-Americans (Hawaii)	99.00	103.95

Note. Source: Hatfield & Rapson (1987a)

[a]PLS = Passionate Love Scale.

Culture and Sexual Desire

China is often cited as the prototype of a sexually repressive culture (115). Yet, Deng Xiaoping's far reaching reforms have begun to change (for better or worse, depending on your point of view) even Chinese attitudes toward passionate love and sexual desire. Recently, *Time* magazine, in a report entitled "The sexual revolution hits China," observed "millions of Chinese, newly exposed to Western ideas, have fallen prey to notions of romantic love and sexual fulfillment" (24). Their conclusion was based on interviews with China's new sexologists. One was Liu, a Chinese sexologist, who added, "the Chinese are like people who have been in the dark a long time. . . . Suddenly, when the windows are opened, they feel dizzy." (24).

Change is sweeping China. . . . and the rest of the world. Liu lectures on sex and has written 30 best-selling books on love, sex, and marriage. He is not alone. In 1993, China founded the Chinese Society for the Scientific Study of Sex and held their first meetings. In 1993, the first Sino-North American Symposium on Sexuality, sponsored by the Chinese Medical Association, will be held in Beijing, in the People's Republic of China.

As yet, cross-cultural researchers have collected little data on sexual desire. They have devoted their first efforts to studying sexual attitudes and values and sexual behavior. We can get some sense, however, of how quickly things are changing in these ways. For the first time, such data are being collected in the most remote corners of the world. In a culture that does not value or is attempting to suppress sexual passion, such data would not be collected. Second, an overview of the following data on sexual attitudes and behavior suggest that although cultural differences still exist in sexual attitudes and behaviors, some profound changes do seem to be occurring: The double standard, for example, seems to be steadily eroding, even in some of the most traditional societies of the world. Also, in most societies, young people are beginning to have more favorable views of passionate love and sexuality.

Table 4.

Percentage of American, Russian, and Japanese Men and Women Willing to Marry Someone They Did Not Love

Cultural Group	Percentage Willing To Marry Someone Not Loved	
	Men	*Women*
American	13	9
Russian	30	41
Japanese	20	19

Note. Source: Sprecher et al. (1992).

They are beginning to marry for love in increasing numbers. People are beginning to engage in more sexual activity and experimentation.

Liu (93) and 500 volunteer social workers, for example, interviewed 23,000 men and women in 15 Chinese provinces using a 240-question survey. Liu found that 86% of the respondents approved of premarital sex. A surprising 69% of them said they saw nothing wrong with extramarital affairs. Liu (cited in 24) estimated that up to 30% of Chinese youth have engaged in premarital sexual activity.

Men, especially those living in rural areas, reported they got more satisfaction from sex than did women. Liu found that only 17% of couples living in the city, but a full 34% of the couples living in the countryside, said they engaged in either no foreplay at all or in less than a minute of foreplay. Partly as a result of this, 37% of the rural wives reported having pain during intercourse. Pan (cited in 25) found that whereas men reached orgasm about 70% of the time, women did so only 40% of the time.

We therefore must not exaggerate the changes in China. Women who are "promiscuous" are still sentenced to prison for prostitution or adultery. Homosexuals are still condemned as hooligans. (Some gay clubs have begun to open in the largest cities, however.)

Surveys conducted in America (with a variety of ethnic groups) and in a number of other cultures also testify to the changes sweeping the world. Obviously, there is neither time nor space to review all these articles. We can, however, alert readers to a sampling of the articles that have been published since 1980. In the following studies, men and women from various cultures and ethnic groups were interviewed about their sexual *attitudes* and *values*. In America, researchers have interviewed African-American (46), Chinese-American (134), Japanese-American (1), and Mexican-American (105) respondents. Throughout the world, they have interviewed men and women in Australia (78), China (32, 104, 107), Columbia (5), France (142), Holland (116), Hungary (140), India (16), Iran (61, 76, 117), Israel (92), Japan (128), Mexico (90), Sweden (54), and Zimbabwe (96).

In some studies the emphasis has been on *sexual behavior*. In America, researchers have interviewed African-American (10, 12, 53, 89, 145, 146), Chinese-American (83, 134), ethnic groups in Hawaii (100), and Mexican-American (105) respondents. Throughout the world, they have studied cultural groups in China (32, 94, 106, 147), Colombia (5), Hong Kong (32), India (16), Japan (41, 62), Northern Ireland (123), Norway (135), Peru (77), Samoa, (100), Sri Lanka (41), United Kingdom (21, 139), and West Germany (34).

CONCLUSIONS

From our own work as psychotherapists in Hawaii (with clients from a variety of cultures), from our work as professors at the University of Hawaii (with students from a variety of cultures), and in an attempt to summarize the existing historical and cross-cultural research, we would like to offer some observations that temper the cross-cultural theoretical statements with which we began this paper. We would argue:

1. *The major cultural groups are more similar in their views of love, sex, and intimacy than the stereotypes would suggest.* In making theoretical distinctions, it sometimes helps to sketch extreme distinctions between "ideal" types. In today's reality, however, none of the major industrial and industrializing cultures—China, Japan, India, Africa, North America, Europe, or South America—can accurately be portrayed as purely individualistic or purely collectivist. In *all* cultures, people must often put themselves first. In *all* cultures, people must sometimes sacrifice themselves for others if the marriage, family, or community is to survive. Real people in all cultures are always engaged in a balancing act. They must balance their own self-oriented concerns against the desires of the group. In fact, it is almost certainly true that people from modern industrialized countries, East and West, have a good deal more in common than not. Differences exist, but we must be careful not to exaggerate them.

2. *Cultural and gender differences may often be less powerful than individual personality differences in shaping attitudes and behavior.* Culture has a powerful impact on romantic and sexual attitudes and behavior. Nonetheless, the sparse research that exists—comparing cultural, gender, and individual differences—seems to suggest that within a given culture or gender, sizable individual differences exist in romantic and sexual attitudes and behavior.

3. *"Westernization" may very likely prevail in the arenas of love, sex, and intimacy.* Among historians, there is as yet no substantial disagreement with the contention that since 1800, the West has greatly expanded its influence upon the rest of the world. There *is* serious debate, however, about how deep these influences go. Some argue that these transformations are deep and long lasting; others that they represent merely temporary accommodations. And there is heated controversy about whether Western cultural expansion has been constructive or destructive. The dialectic between Westernization and resistance to it defines much of international life today.

From our survey of the existing literature on passionate love and sexual desire (especially, when we focus on social changes in sexual attitudes and behavior from, say, 1930 to the present) we would risk some conclusions. Throughout the developed world, two changes have occurred that seem likely to continue: (a) There has been a movement in the direction of equality for men and women (although actual equality remains far off); (b) Societies have increasingly come to accept the notion that the pursuit of pleasure and the avoidance of pain are desirable goals. The growing acceptance in these arenas of what were once considered "Western" values, and now, slowly beginning to be thought of as part of a universal bill of human rights, has produced a variety of changes in people's views of love and sex. It has produced an increasing acceptance of passionate love and sexual desire as legitimate, expressible feelings. It has produced an increasing trend toward marriage for love. It has led to more sexual permissiveness. In these areas, we might expect that personal freedom, once experienced, would be difficult to surrender. But no one can foretell the future, and the tempestuous story of passionate love and sexual desire remains to be written.

ACKNOWLEDGEMENTS

Our thanks to Dr. Susan Sprecher and Rachita Shri Chandak (Illinois State University) and Kari Thompson (University of Hawaii) for their help in tracking down recent articles concerning sexual attitudes and behavior in a variety of societies.

REFERENCES

1. Abramson, P. R., & Imai-Marquez, J. (1982). The Japanese-American: A cross-cultural, cross-sectional study of sex guilt. *Journal Of Research In Personality*, 16, 227–237.

2. Ainsworth, M. D. S. (1989). Attachments beyond infancy. *American Psychologist,* 44, 709–716.

3. Ainsworth, M. D. S., Blehar, M.C., Waters, E., & Wall, S. (1978). *Patterns of attachment: A psychological study of the strange situation.* Hillsdale, NJ: Lawrence Erlbaum.

4. Allgeier, E. R., & Allgeier, A.R. (1991). *Sexual interactions* (3rd. ed.). Lexington, MA: D.C. Heath.

5. Alzate, H. (1989). Sexual behavior of unmarried Colombian university students: A follow up. *Archives Of Sexual Behavior,* 18, 239–250.

6. Aries, P. (1962). *Centuries of childhood.* New York: Random House.

7. Aron, A., & Rodriguez, G. (1992, July 25). Scenarios of falling in love among Mexican-, Chinese-, and Anglo-Americans. Paper presented at the Sixth International Conference on Personal Relationships. Orono, ME.

8. Axtell, J. L. (1981). *The European and the Indian: Essays in ethnohistory of colonial North America.* New York: Oxford University Press.

9. Bartholomew, K., & Horowitz, L. M. (1991). Attachment styles among young adults: A test of a four-category model. *Journal of Personality and Social Psychology,* 61, 226–245.

10. Belcastro, P. A. (1985). Sexual behavior differences between black and white students. *The Journal Of Sex Research,* 21, 56–67.

11. Bell, S. (1902). A preliminary study of the emotion of love between the sexes. *The American Journal of Psychology,* 13 325–354.

12. Bell, A. P., Weinberg, M. S., & Hammersmith, S. (1981). *Sexual preference: Statistical appendix.* Bloomington, IN: Indiana University Press.

13. Bendix, R. (1964). *Nation-building and citizenship; studies of our changing social order.* New York: Wiley.

14. Berry, J. W., Poortinga, Y. H., Segall, M. H., & Dasen, P. R. (1992). *Cross-cultural psychology: Research and applications.* Cambridge, England: Cambridge University Press.

15. Berscheid, E., Graziano, W., Monson, T., & Dermer, M. (1976). Outcome dependency: attention, attribution, and attraction. *Journal of Personality and Social Psychology,* 34, 978–989.

16. Bhatia, J. (1986). Lifting India's fig-leaf prudery. *Far Eastern Economic Review,* 131, 37–38.

17. Bowlby, J. (1969). *Attachment and loss: Vol. 1. Attachment.* New York: Basic Books.

18. Bowlby, J. (1973). Affectional bonds: Their nature and origin. In R. Weiss (Ed.), *Loneliness: The experience of emotional and social isolation* (pp. 38–52). Cambridge, MA: MIT Press.

19. Bowlby, J. (1980). *Attachment and loss: Vol. 3. Sadness and depression.* New York: Basic Books.

20. Braudel, F. (1984). *The perspective of the world.* (S. Reynolds, Trans.). New York: Harper & Row.

21. Breakwell, G. M., & Fife-Schaw, C. (1992). Sexual activities and preferences in a United Kingdom sample of 16–20 Year Olds. *Archives of Sexual Behavior,* 21, 271–293.

22. Brown, D. E. (1991). *Human universals.* Philadelphia, PA: Temple University Press.

23. Bullough, V. L. (1990). History and the understanding of human sexuality. *Annual Review of Sex Research,* 1, 75–92.

24. Burton, S. (1988, September 12) The sexual revolution hits China. *Time,* p. 65.

25. Burton, S. (1990, May 14). Straight talk on sex in China. *Time,* p. 82.

26. Buss, D. M. (1988a). Love Acts: The evolutionary biology of love. In R. J. Sternberg & M. L. Barnes (Eds.), *The psychology of love* (pp. 100–118). New Haven: Yale University Press.

27. Buss, D. M. (1988b). The evolution of human intrasexual competition: Tactics of mate attraction. *Journal of Personality and Social Psychology,* 54, 616–628.

28. Buss, D. M. (1989). Sex differences in human mate preferences: Evolutionary hypotheses tested in 37 Cultures. *Behavioral And Brain Sciences,* 12, 1–49.

29. Buss, D. M. and 49 others. (1990). International preferences in selecting mates: A study of 37 cultures. *Journal Of Cross-Cultural Psychology,* 21, 5–47.

30. Buss, D. M. & Barnes, M. (1986). Preferences in human mate selection. *Journal Of Personality And Social Psychology,* 50, 559–570.

31. Buss, D. M. & Schmitt, D.P. (1993). Sexual strategies theory: An evolutionary perspective on human mating. *Psychological Review,* 100, 204–232.

32. Chan, D. W. (1990). Sex knowledge, attitudes, and experience of Chinese medical students in Hong Kong. *Archives Of Sexual Behavior,* 19, 73–93.

33. Chu, G. C. (1985). The changing concept of self in contemporary China. In A.J. Marsella, G. DeVos, & F. L. K. Hus (Eds.) *Culture and self: Asian and Western perspectives* (pp. 252–277). London, England: Tavistock.

34. Clement, U., Schmidt, G., & Kruse, M. (1984). Changes in sex differences in sexual behavior: A replication of a study on West German students (1966–1981). *Archives Of Sexual Behavior,* 13, 99–120.

35. Coontz, S. (1988). *The social origins of private life: A history of American families, 1600–1900.* London, England: Verso.

36. Darwin, C. (1871). *The descent of man and selection in relation to sex.* London: Murray.

37. Degler, C. N. (1980). *At odds: Women and the family in America from the revolution to the present.* New York: Oxford University Press.

38. Delameter, J., & MacCorquodale, P. (1979). *Premarital sexuality: Attitudes, relationships, behavior.* Madison, WI: University of Wisconsin Press.

39. D'Emilio, J., & Freedman, E. (1988). *Intimate matters: A history of sexuality in America.* New York: Harper & Row.

40. DeToqueville, A. (1830/1981). *Democracy in America.* New York: Vintage Press.

41. Dewaraja, R., & Sasaki, Y. (1991). Semen-loss syndrome: A comparison between Sri Lanka and Japan. *American Journal Of Psychotherapy,* 45, 14–20.

42. Doherty, R. W., Hatfield, E., Thompson, K., & Choo, P. (1993). Cultural and ethnic influences on love and attachment. Unpublished manuscript.

43. Doi, L. T. (1963). Some Thoughts on Helplessness And The Desire To Be Loved. *Psychiatry,* 26, 266–272.

44. Doi, L. T. (1973). *The anatomy of dependence* (J. Bester, Trans.). Tokyo: Kodansha International.

45. Dunn, J. (1989). *Modern revolutions: An introduction to the analysis of a political phenomenon.* Cambridge, England: Cambridge University Press.

46. Dunn, K. M., & Wyatt, G. E. (1991). Examining predictors of sex guilt in multiethnic samples of women. *Archives Of Sexual Behavior,* 20, 471–485.

47. Ellis, B. J., & Symons, D. (1990). Sex differences in sexual fantasy: An evolutionary psychological approach. *The Journal Of Sex Research,* 27, 527–555.

48. Family Planning Association of Hong Kong. (1987). *The adolescent sexuality study 1986. Household survey: Summary of findings.* Family Planning Association, Hong Kong.

49. Feeney, J. A., & Noller, P. (1990). Attachment style as a predictor of adult romantic relationships. *Journal of Personality and Social Psychology,* 58, 281–291.

50. Fei, J., & Berscheid, E. (1977). *Perceived dependency, insecurity, and love in heterosexual relationships: The Eternal Triangle.* Unpublished manuscript, Minneapolis: University of Minnesota.

51. Fisher, H. E. (1989). Evolution of human serial pairbonding. *American Journal Of Physical Anthropology,* 78, 331–354.

52. Fisher, H. E. (1993). *Anatomy of love: The natural history of monogamy, adultery, and divorce.* New York: W. W. Norton.

53. Fisher, S. (1980). Personality correlates of sexual behavior in black women. *Archives of Sexual Behavior,* 9, 27–35.

54. Foa, U. G., Anderson, B., Converse, J. Jr., Urbansky, W. A., & Cawley, M. J. III. (1987). Gender-related sexual attitudes: Some crosscultural similarities and differences. *Sex Roles,* 16, 511–519.

55. Gay, P. (1984). *The Bourgeois experience: Victoria to Freud. Education of the senses* (Vol. 1). New York: Oxford University Press.

56. Gay, P. (1986). *The Bourgeois Experience: Victoria to Freud. The Tender Passion* (Vol. 2). New York: Oxford University Press.

57. Gill, V. E. (1991). An ethnography of HIV/Aids and sexuality in The People's Republic Of China. *The Journal of Sex Research,* 28, 521–537.

58. Gillis, J. R. (1985). *For better, for worse: British marriages, 1600 to the present.* New York: Oxford University Press.

59. Goode, W. J. (1959). The theoretical importance of love. *American Sociological Review,* 24, 38–47.

60. Griffitt, W., & Hatfield, E. (1985). *Human sexual behavior.* Glenview, IL: Scott, Foresman.

61. Hanassab, S., & Tidwell, R. (1989). Cross-cultural perspective on dating relationships of young Iranian women: A pilot study. *Counselling Psychology Quarterly,* 2, 113–121.

62. Hatano, Y. (1991). Changes in the sexual activities of Japanese youth. *Journal of Sex Education & Therapy,* 17, 1–14.

63. Hatfield, E. (1965). The effect of self-esteem on romantic liking. *Journal of Experimental Social Psychology, 1,* 184–197.

64. Hatfield, E., Brinton, C., & Cornelius, J. (1989). Passionate love and anxiety in young adolescents. *Motivation and Emotion, 13,* 271–289.

65. Hatfield, E., & Rapson, R. L. (1987a). Passionate love: New directions in research. *Advances in Personal Relationships, 1,* 109–139.

66. Hatfield, E., & Rapson, R. L. (1987b). Passionate love/sexual desire: Can the same paradigm explain both? *Archives of Sexual Behavior, 16,* 259–278.

67. Hatfield, E., & Rapson, R. L. (1993). *Love, sex, and intimacy: Their psychology, biology, and history.* New York: Harper Collins.

68. Hatfield, E., & Rapson, R. L. (in press). *Passion and its enemies: A cross-cultural look at love and sex.* Needham Heights, MA: Allyn & Bacon.

69. Hatfield, E., Schmitz, E., Cornelius, J., & Rapson, R. (1988). Passionate love: How early does it begin? *Journal of Psychology and Human Sexuality, 1,* 35–52.

70. Hatfield, E., & Sprecher, S. (1986a). Measuring passionate love in intimate relations. *Journal of Adolescence, 9,* 383–410.

71. Hatfield, E., & Sprecher, S. (1993). Men's and women's mate preferences in the United States, Russia, and Japan. Unpublished manuscript.

72. Hazan, C., & Shaver, P. (1987). Romantic love conceptualized as an attachment process. *Journal of Personality and Social Psychology, 52,* 511–524.

73. Hendrick, C., & Hendrick, S. S. (1986). A theory and method of love. *Journal of Personality and Social Psychology, 50,* 392–402.

74. Hindy, C. G., Schwarz, J. C., & Brodsky, A. (1989). *If this is love, why do I feel so insecure?* New York: The Atlantic Monthly Press.

75. Ho, D. Y. F. (1982). Asian concepts in behavioral science. *Psychologia, 25,* 228–235.

76. Hojat, M., & Shapurian, R. (1985). Sexual and premarital attitudes of Iranian college students. *Psychological Reports, 57,* 67–74.

77. Holmes, K. K. (1993, July 1). Sexually transmitted disease seroprevalence related to general knowledge, attitudes, beliefs, and practices among the general population in Lima, Peru. Paper presented at the International Academy of Sex Research, 19th Annual Meeting. Pacific Grove, CA.

78. Hong, S-M. (1991). Gender differences in Australian attitudes toward premarital sex: A reexamination. *Psychological Reports, 68,* 418.

79. Howard, J. A., Blumstein, P., & Schwartz, P. (1987). Social or evolutionary theories? Some observations on preferences in human mate selection. *Journal of Personality and Social Psychology, 53,* 194–200.

80. Hsu, F. L. K. (1971). Psychosocial homeostasis and jen: Conceptual tools for advancing psychological anthropology. *American Anthropologist, 73,* 23–44.

81. Hsu, F. L. K. (1981). *Americans and Chinese: Passage to difference* (3rd. ed.). Honolulu: University Press of Hawaii.

82. Hsu, F. L. K. (1985). The self in cross-cultural perspective. In A.J. Marsella, G. DeVos, & F.L.K. Hsu (Eds.), *Culture and self: Asian and western perspectives* (pp. 24–55). London, England: Tavistock.

83. Huang, K., & Uba, L. (1992). Premarital sexual behavior among Chinese college students in the United States. *Archives of Sexual Behavior, 21,* 227–240.

84. Jacobs, L., Berscheid, E., & Hatfield, E. (1971). Self-esteem and attraction. *Journal of Personality and Social Psychology, 17,* 84–91.

85. Jankowiak, W. R. (1993). Sex, death, and hierarchy in a Chinese city: An anthropological account. New York: Columbia University Press.

86. Jankowiak, W. R., & Fischer, E. F. (1992). A cross-cultural perspective on romantic love. *Ethnology, 31,* 149–155.

87. Kagiçibasi, C. (1990). Family and socialization in cross-cultural perspective: A model of change. In R.A. Diensbier (Ed.), *Nebraska Symposium on Motivation: 1989: Cross-cultural perspectives,* 37, 136–200.

88. Kephart, W. M. (1967). Some correlates of romantic love. *Journal of Marriage and the Family,* 29, 470–479.

89. Klassen, A. D., Williams, C. J., & Levitt, E. (1981). American Sexual Standards. Unpublished manuscript. Alfred C. Kinsey Institute For The Study Of Sex, Gender And Reproduction, Bloomington, IN.

90. LaBeff, E. E., & Dodder, R. A. (1982). Attitudes toward sexual permissiveness in Mexico and the United States. *The Journal of Social Psychology,* 116, 285–286.

91. Ladurie, E. L. R. (1979). *Montaillou: The promised land of error* (B. Bray, Trans.). New York: Vintage Books.

92. Linn, R. (1991). Sexual and moral development of Israeli female adolescents from city and Kibbutz: Perspectives of Kohlberg and Gilligan . *Adolescence,* 26, 69–71.

93. Liu, D. (1991). National sex civilization survey. Shanghai, China. Sex Sociological Research Center.

94. Liu, D. (1992). Sexual behavior in modern China. A report of the nation-wide sex civilization survey on 20,000 subjects in China. Shanghai: SJPC Publishing Co. (In Mandarin).

95. Mace, D., & Mace, V. (1980). *Marriage: East and West.* New York: Dolphin Books.

96. Marindo, R., & Wilson, D. (1989). Erotophobia and contraception among Zimbabwean students. *The Journal of Social Psychology,* 129, 721–723.

97. Markus, H. R., & Kitayama, S. (1991). Culture and self: Implications for cognition, emotion, and motivation. *Psychological Review,* 98, 224–253.

98. McNeill, W. H. (1963). *The rise of the west: A history of human community.* Chicago: University of Chicago Press.

99. Mintz, S., & Kellogg, S. (1988). *Domestic revolutions: A social history of American life.* New York: Free Press.

100. Mokuau, N. (1986). Human sexuality of native Hawaiians and Samoans. Special issue: Human sexuality, ethnoculture, and social work. *Journal of Social Work and Human Sexuality,* 4, 67–80.

101. Moore, B., Jr. (1966). *Social origins of dictatorship and democracy: Lord and peasant in the making of the modern world.* Boston: Beacon Press.

102. Muehlenhard, C. L., & Quackenbush, D. M. (1988, November). *Can the sexual double standard put women at risk for sexually transmitted diseases? The role of the double standard in condom use among women.* Paper presented at the Annual Meeting of the Society for the Scientific Study of Sex, San Francisco, CA.

103. Murstein, B. I. (1986). *Paths to marriage.* Beverly Hills, CA: Sage.

104. Ng, M. L., & Lau, M. P. (1990). Sexual attitudes in the Chinese. *Archives of Sexual Behavior,* 19, 373–388.

105. Padilla, E. R., & O'Grady, K. E. (1987). Sexuality among Mexican Americans: A case of sexual stereotyping. *Journal of Personality and Social Psychology,* 52, 5–10.

106. Pan, S. (1990, November 7–8). *Manual, oral, anal, and homosexual behavior today in Chinese civil peoples.* Paper presented at the First Sino-American Management of HIV Disease Symposium. Beijing, China.

107. Pan, S. M. (1993). *China: Acceptability and effect of three kinds of sexual publication archives of sexual behavior,* 22, 59–71.

108. Peele, S. (1975). *Love and Addiction.* New York: Taplinger Publishing.

109. Phillips, R. (1988). *Putting asunder: A history of divorce in western society,* New York: Cambridge University Press.

110. Plutchik, R. (1980). *Emotion: A psychoevolutionary synthesis.* New York: Harper and Row.

111. Rapson, R. L. (1988). *American yearnings: Love, money, and endless possibility.* Lanham, MD: University Press of America.

112. Reiss, I. L., & Lee, G.R. (1988). *Family systems in America* (4th ed.). New York: Holt, Rinehart and Winston.

113. Roberts, J. M. (1976). *History of the world.* New York: Knopf.

114. Rosenblatt, P. C. (1967). Marital residence and the function of romantic love. *Ethnology,* 6, 471–480.

115. Ruan, F. F. (1991). *Sex in China.* New York: Plenum.

116. Schuijer, J. (1990). Tolerance at arm's length: The Dutch experience. *Journal Of Homosexuality,* 20, 199–229.

117. Shapurian, R., & Hojat, M. (1985). Sexual and premarital attitudes of Iranian college students. *Psychological Reports,* 57, 67–74.

118. Shaver, P., & Hazan, C. (1988). A biased overview of the study of love. *Journal of Social and Personal Relationships,* 5, 474–501.

119. Shaver, P. R., Wu, S., & Schwartz, J. C. (1991). Cross-cultural similarities and differences in emotion and its representation: A prototype approach. In M.S. Clark (Ed.), *Review of Personality and Social Psychology,* (Vol. 13, pp. 175–212). Beverly Hills, CA: Sage Publications.

120. Simpson, J. A., Campbell, B., & Berscheid, E. (1986). The association between romantic love and marriage: Kephart (1967) twice revisited. *Personality and Social Psychology Bulletin,* 12, 363–372.

121. Simpson, J. A., & Gangestad, S. W. (1991). Individual differences in sociosexuality: Evidence for convergent and discriminant validity. *Journal of Personality and Social Psychology,* 60, 870–883.

122. Skocpol, T. (1979). *States and social revolutions: A comparative analysis of France, Russia, and China.* New York: Cambridge University Press.

123. Sneddon, I., & Kremer, J. (1992). Sexual behavior and attitudes of university students in Northern Ireland. *Archives of Sexual Behavior,* 21, 295–312.

124. Solomon, R. L., & Corbit, J. D. (1974). An opponent process theory of motivation. I. The temporal dynamics of affect. *Psychological Review,* 81, 119–145.

125. Sommer, V. (1993, November 13). Primate origins: The hardware of human sexuality. Paper presented at the meeting of The Society for the Scientific Study of Sex. San Diego, CA.

126. Sprecher, S. (1989). Premarital sexual standards for different categories of individuals. *The Journal of Sex Research,* 26, 232–248.

127. Sprecher, S., Aron, A, Hatfield, E., Cortese, A., Potapova, E., & Levitskaya. (1992). *Love: American style, Russian style, and Japanese style.* Paper presented at the Sixth International Conference on Personal Relationships, Orono, ME.

128. Sprecher, S., & Hatfield, E. (1993). *Premarital sexual permissiveness and the double standard: Cultural and gender comparisons.* Unpublished manuscript. University of Illinois. Normal, IL.

129. Sprecher, S., McKinney, K., Walsh, R., & Anderson, C. (1988). A revision of the Reiss Premarital Sexual Permissiveness Scale. *Journal of Marriage and the Family,* 50, 821–828.

130. Stephan, W., Berscheid, E., & Hatfield, E. (1971). Sexual arousal and heterosexual perception. *Journal of Personality and Social Psychology,* 20, 93–101.

131. Stavrianos, L. S. (1981). *Global rift: The third world comes of age.* New York: Morrow.

132. Stone, L. (1977). *The family, sex, and marriage: In England 1500–1800.* New York: Harper & Row.

133. Stone, L. (1990). *Road to divorce: England 1530–1987.* New York: Oxford University Press.

134. Sue, D. (1982). Sexual experience and attitudes of Asian-American students. *Psychological Reports,* 51, 401–402.

135. Sundet, J. M., Magnus, P., Kvalem, I. L., Samulsen, S. O., & Bakketeig, L. S. (1992). Secular trends and sociodemographic regularities of coital debut age in Norway. *Archives Of Sexual Behavior,* 21, 241–252.

136. Tavris, C., & Offir, C. (1984). *The longest war: Sex differences in perspective* (2nd ed.). New York: Harcourt, Brace, Jovanovich.

137. Toynbee, A. J. (1962). *A study of history.* New York: Oxford University Press.

138. Triandis, H. C., McCusker, C., & Hui, C. H. (1990). Multimethod probes of individualism and collectivism. *Journal of Personality and Social Psychology, 59,* 1006–1020.

139. Turner, C., Anderson, P., Fitzpatrick, R., Fowler, G., & Mayon-White, R. (1988). Sexual behavior, contraceptive practice and knowledge of AIDS of Oxford University students. *Journal of Biosocial Science, 20,* 445–451.

140. Vincze, L. (1985). Hungarian peasant obscenity: Sociolinguistic implications. *Ethnology,* 24, 33–42.

141. Wallen, K. (1989). Mate selection: Economics and affection. *Behavioral and Brain* 12: 37–38.

142. Werebe, M. J. G., & Reinert, M. (1983). Attitudes of French adolescents toward sexuality. *Journal of Adolescence, 6,* 145–159.

143. Wittfogel, K. A. (1957). *Oriental despotism: A comparative study of total power.* New York: Yale University Press.

144. Wu, S., & Shaver, P. R. (1992, July 23–28). *Conceptions of love in the United States and the People's Republic of China.* Paper presented at the Sixth Conference of the International Society for the Study of Personal Relationships. Orono, ME.

145. Wyatt, G. E. (1989). Reexamining factors predicting Afro-American and white American women's age at first coitus. *Archives of Sexual Behavior,* 18, 271–298.

146. Zelnik, M., & Kantner, J. (1980). Sexual activity, contraceptive use and pregnancy among metropolitan-area teenagers: 1971–1979. *Family Planning Perspectives,* 12, 230–237.

147. Zessen, G. Van, & Sanfort, T. (1991). *Seksualiteit in Nederland.* Amsterdam: Swets & Zeitlinger.

MARRIAGE AND INCEST

Edgar Gregersen

Several kinds of marriage may be recognized within a single society. An extremely complex situation occurs among the Dahomey of Benin in West Africa. They permit 13 different kinds of marriage each depending on a different economic arrangement. In ancient Rome, at least two types of marriage were distinguished: free marriage, in which the wife and her property did not come under the power of her husband; and marriage with *manus* (literally "hand," referring to the hand of the husband), in which the woman's status was changed so that she was legally the equivalent of her husband's child and was adopted into his family.

But there is no need to go so far afield. In the contemporary western world, there is traditional monogamous marriage defined either by a religious or civil ceremony (or both) as well as common-law cohabitation. Although the living arrangements may be identical, money interests and the legitimacy of children are different in the two situations. The much publicized legal battle in 1979 between the American movie star Lee Marvin and a woman he had lived with for several years but never married, illustrates the difference well. In spite of the social acceptability of their relationship (at least in the circles they moved in), legally she was not entitled to alimony (the money settlement she did get was facetiously termed "palimony"). In some circles even homosexual unions are sometimes referred to as marriages. This is not legally the case, though various proposals have been made for the legal recognition of such unions.

In some societies it is the custom to arrange marriages between living people and the dead. The best known example of this is contemporary American Mormons, who believe that being married is a necessary condition for being saved and going to heaven, and that dead unbelievers can be saved by posthumous marriages with Mormons. Among traditional Chinese groups, if a couple betrothed as children both die, they are married anyway in a kind of heavenly marriage, in part to placate their ghosts.

All of these ritual joinings and others like them have been called pseudomarriages. But even if we do not consider them in defining marriage cross-culturally there are other problems. The definition given by a basic reference book *Notes and queries in anthropology* (1951), put out by the Royal Anthropological Institute, is useful in a rough and ready way, but even the following definition is too specific to apply in all societies:

> Marriage is a union between a man and a woman such that the children born to the woman are recognized as legitimate offspring of both partners.

If we are concerned that marriage (and with it its minimal domestic realization—the nuclear family) should be a universal category, then this definition will not do.

The classic counterexample dealing with the first part of the definition ("a union between a man and a woman") is found among the Naayar of India. Before she began to menstruate, a Naayar girl is supposed to go through a four-day ceremony that links her to a man who has been described as a ritual husband. A special pendant is tied around her neck indicating that, in a sense, she is married. But this does not mean that she is going to settle down and form a family with her "husband." On the contrary, it means that she is now free to have as many lovers or "visiting husbands" as she likes. These

---

"Marriage and Incest," by Edgar Gregersen, reprinted from *Sexual Practices: The Story of Human Sexuality,* Franklin-Watts, 1983.

men come to her room in the great house where she lives with her mother's family. Her lovers do not live with her, they merely spend the night. Any children born after the marriage ceremony are legitimate, but if the woman has a baby before the marriage she is punished. In short, the ritual husband is totally peripheral to her family unit, though essential for legitimizing children.

An interesting relationship exists between the Naayar and the Nambuutiri Braahmans, who belong to a higher caste. Among the Nambuutiri Braahmans, only the eldest son is allowed to marry and raise a family. His younger brothers instead arrange alliances with Naayar women. For the Braahmans such alliances do not count as legal marriages and the resulting children are not considered legitimate. For the Naayars, however, they are a source of prestige and the offspring are legitimate.

Because of the Naayar, Kathleen Gough has proposed a definition of marriage that is considerably more general than the one quoted earlier from *Notes and queries*. But her definition also emphasizes the notion of legitimacy, the second part of the *Notes and queries* definition. However, a rule of legitimacy is also not a cultural universal.

The Caribbean is a case in point. This is an area of the world where the rule of legitimacy is lacking. An unusually high percentage of children are here born to unmarried women: between 53 and 56 percent of the births are "illegitimate" in Guatemala, Jamaica and Trinidad; 67 percent in Martinique. Leyburn maintains that "there is less marriage in Haiti than anywhere else in the world." It is true that upper-class groups in these areas follow the western rule of legitimacy, but the other groups do not. There is no stigma in being illegitimate. The people who are not upper class and who do marry—they sometimes do this when their children are grown up—do not do so to legitimize their children, but to hold a large party (*fête*), thereby meeting their social obligations and expressing group solidarity. To hold such a *fête* even after one's children have grown up is prestigious among these groups. To get married in a church at any time without a *fête* is deviant and despised. Nevertheless, people may get married for different reasons; certain jobs such as school teacher, for example, are open only to married parents.

Clearly there are many problems in getting a cross-cultural definition of marriage. I shall not belabor the point further but use the term "marry" in the following pages in an informal and practical way.

In western society, the only form of marriage legally recognized is that between one man and one woman at a time: monogamy. The great majority of people in the history of mankind have lived in monogamous marriages and the great majority of people in the world today are monogamous. The preferred form of marriage, however, in most societies is, and has been, a kind of polygamy in which a man is married to several women at one time, technically known as polygyny. Nearly half (44 percent) of all the societies in Murdock's *Ethnographic atlas*—a compilation of information on 862 cultures throughout the world—regard polygamy as the norm, and 39 percent permit it along with monogamy. Only 16 percent insist on monogamy. (The remainder have other arrangements.)

Furthermore, even though monogamy is the reality (but not the ideal) for most people, an enormous number of them have more than one spouse in a lifetime. Liberalization of divorce in the West has resulted in multiple marriages, often called serial monogamy. According to the *Guinness book of records* (1979), the greatest number of such serially monogamous marriages is 20, entered into by Mr Glynn de Moss Wolfe, an American. Serial monogamy is also reported for other monogamous groups such as the Hopi Indians and the Siwans of Egypt.

Having more than one wife at a time is generally considered shocking and immoral in the West. In most parts of the world, however, it is a sign of being successful, rich, even powerful; such a man might well be considered a good match and accumulate still more wives. Usually there is a ranking system among the co-wives so that their status is reasonably defined. To offset favoritism, traditional polygamists normally institutionalize some form of rotation system so that a man must spend an equal amount of time with each wife. In spite of these safeguards and considerations, much ill will may exist between co-wives. In Hausa, the very term for co-wife is *kíishiyáa*, which means "partner in jealousy." Nevertheless, Christian missionaries who try to break up polygamous families have reported that the women object most to the imposition of monogamy.

All the men in a society cannot have many wives only because the sex ratios are fairly equal: one does not find normal populations with two or three times as many women as men. The number of women available depends in part on the absolute number of wives permitted. In some the number is enormous—at least for kings and noblemen. King Solomon is described in the Bible as having 700 wives and 300 concubines. A chief of the Bakuba and Bakete tribes in Zaire, called Lukengu, had 800 wives according to the *Guinness book of records* (1964). But the all-time record seems to be the 3,000 wives of one of the Monomotapa kings in what is now Zimbabwe.

In some societies, such as that of the Tiwi of Australia or the Zande of central Africa, the older, richer men take up all the marriageable women of whatever age and younger men must delay marriage until their 30s and 40s or until they "inherit" their fathers' wives (all except their own biological mother). A kind of widow inheritance is known from the Bible: a widow was supposed to marry one of her dead husband's brothers. This custom is found in a number of societies throughout the world.

For a woman to marry a number of men at the same time—a form of polygamy known as polyandry—is very rare: only four societies in the *Ethnographic atlas* permit polyandry. Societies permitting polygyny are roughly 100 times that number. This makes sense in light of an interpretation of marriage offered by Claude Lévi-Strauss, that it is the "gift" of women exchanged between men. He formulates the reality of the situation thus: "Men exchange women; women never exchange men." Marvin Harris adds that sex (through such marital gifts) is used in most societies as a reward for male bravery: "No battle-hardened headhunter or scalptaker is going to settle down to connubial bliss in the company of four or five of his boon companions under the tutelage of a single woman . . . "

True polyandry involving a stable household where a woman's husbands all share the same residence is unusual and found mainly in the Himalayas. Such households almost always involve a number of brothers who share a wife. One of the major advantages of such a system is that it prevents the breaking up of family wealth or property.

All forms of polyandry are exceedingly rare at present and it seems likely that it was always so. Consequently nearly all anthropologists reject a suggestion by J. F. McLennan, a nineteenth-century ethnologist, that polyandry was the normal form of marriage at one stage in the development of human social organization.

In the African forms of polyandry (found in a limited number of groups in Nigeria), the husbands do not live together. They are not brothers and the wife circulates from one household to another. Furthermore, both polyandry and polygyny occur, so that some men have several wives living with them in the same household—unlike the women, who never have several husbands living with them.

Another variety of polyandry characterizes the preferred and most common form of marriage among the Pahaarii of northern India. Their custom requires a very high bride-price, a gift given by the groom's family to the bride's family. Because of this great expense, brothers normally pool resources and acquire a wife in common. Later, when they can afford other wives, they will again acquire them in common. This is not really polyandry but what is called group marriage (less commonly, polygynandry). The Pahaarii are apparently the only society in the world in which group marriage is the cultural norm.

An even more extreme form of group marriage, known as complex marriage, was practiced for a short time by the Oneida community, a utopian Christian religious group founded by John Humphrey Noyes in Putnam, Vermont, in 1841. The group moved to Oneida, New York, in 1847. In this society every man was the husband of every woman and every woman the wife of every man. This aspect of the society evoked considerable hostility from the surrounding communities. In 1879, Noyes recommended that the complex marriage system should be abandoned.

In almost all societies—whatever form of marriage is permitted—a marriage can be ended by divorce. The traditional western Christian view that marriage is indissoluble is practically unique, Hinduism being the only other important tradition to take the same position. Hindus have even frowned on the remarriage of widows. Until the practice was outlawed by the British in 1829, the prestigious way for a widow to mourn for her husband was to burn herself to death on his funeral pyre, a custom called *satii*.

In some groups, such as the ancient Scythians (as reported by Herodotus) or the Zande of modern times, some of the wives or concubines of a king are killed at his death and buried with him. This custom is rare cross-culturally. In 1971, a mass grave was found in Yugoslavia dating about 1800 BC. In it, the body of a man (presumably a chief) was surrounded by the bodies of 15 women who were believed to be his harem.

The Kubeo of South America require a boy to copulate with his mother to mark the beginning of his official sex life. This is the only instance in the world that I have heard of compulsory mother-son incest. Marriage between them is forbidden, however.

Among the Tutsi (or Watusi) or East Africa, a cure for the impotence that a bridegroom may experience on his wedding night requires that he copulates with his mother.

These are the only well-attested rules for all the cultures of the world promoting mother-son matings. A number of dubious or unreliable reports suggest that even mother-son marriages are possible in some societies, but they cannot be taken seriously.

A tabu on mother-son marriage can safely be cited as a cultural universal. Moreover, any form of approved, institutionalized incest is decidedly rare, and more commonly incest tabus are extended beyond the nuclear family to larger kinship groups.

The great social and cultural importance of incest regulations has not escaped anthropologists and other social scientists. The pioneer thinkers Sigmund Freud, Lewis Henry Morgan and Claude Lévi-Strauss, approaching the subjects from totally different perspectives, suggest that human social organization as we know it today began with the conscious institution of incest tabus. In the Freudian model, one of the prices one has to pay for being civilized, one of the prime discontents of civilization, is the suppression of the satisfaction of incestuous urges. But Freud was partially wrong: this is not restricted to civilized man. Even the otherwise promiscuous chimpanzee would be given a good slap by his mother if he attempted to copulate with her. Mother-son matings have rarely, if ever, been reported by field observers of any of the primates. Nature has its discontents, too.

Any examples of institutionalized incest have occasioned great interest. The most common exceptions to universal tabus on incest involve brother-sister marriage practiced by the royal families of ancient Egypt, Hawaii and the Inca, among others. Cleopatra is the classic example: she was simultaneously her husband's sister as well as his wife. Unfortunately for her young husband-brother, Cleopatra had him murdered when he was 15 in order to pursue some nonincestuous unions with Julius Caesar and Mark Antony: politics rather than a horror of incest seems to have been her primary motivation.

Half-sibling, occasionally also full-sibling, marriage was legal and fairly common in the ancient Near East and was found among the ancient Persians (at least among the upper classes) and probably the ancient Hebrews at one point. The ancient Greeks also permitted it, though Roman law forbade it altogether. The Lakher of southeast Asia permit the son and daughter of one mother but two different fathers to marry. Elsewhere, when half-sibling marriages are permitted, this would most likely be forbidden.

In Bali, both full-and half-sibling incest is forbidden with one interesting exception. It is assumed that the twin brother and sister have already been intimate in the womb. With an appropriate ceremony of purification, they are allowed to marry each other when they grow up. The Aymará of South America also permit twins to marry. The Marshallese of the Pacific believe that twins have indeed committed incest in their mother's womb, but unlike the Balinese, feel they must therefore kill at least the boy.

The Lamet of southeast Asia permit brother-sister marriage if the couple has been brought up in different households: they are then not viewed as members of the same sociological family. Similarly, the Nuer of East Africa feel that incest has not occurred if the relationship is not known (unlike the ancient Greeks, as seen in *Oedipus rex*). Interestingly, the same argument applies in a recent and as yet unresolved legal proceeding in Sweden. A government official discovered by accident that a man and woman who were married were brother and sister, and therefore under Swedish law the marriage was null and void. When the couple was confronted with the matter, it turned out that they did not know they were related because they had been separated as children and had lost contact with one another. The couple decided to challenge the law. Their argument is that even though they are biologically brother and sister, sociologically they are not, and therefore they should not be forced to separate.

Father-daughter incest is occasionally tolerated or institutionalized but doing so is very rare, much more so than brother-sister unions. (As a matter of fact, however, father-daughter incest is the most common form of incest in the modern western world.) The Persian emperor Artaxerxes was said by Plutarch to have married his own daughter, and the Egyptian pharaoh Amenhotep III is known to have married at least one daughter: his son Akhenaten several. The Roman situation is unambiguous. Here nuclear family incest was totally forbidden, but a few royal instances that went unpunished existed; Caligula committed incest with his three sisters, and even married one, Drusilla. Another sister, Agrippina, was rumored to have sex with her son also, the emperor Nero. This was not something traditionally permitted to the royal family in Roman eyes.

More widespread and of great importance in anthropological theorizing are restrictions on cousin marriages. The majority of societies in the world today prohibit marriage to any kind of cousin. In Murdock's *Ethnographic atlas* a wide-ranging sample of 762 cultures throughout the world, about two-thirds forbid cousin marriage.

In the Judaeo-Christian tradition, considerable variation has occurred with regard to the question of cousin marriage. The Bible does not prohibit cousin marriage of any kind, and Jews have allowed it throughout their history. But under Pope Gregory "the Great" (AD 590–604) marriage between third cousins was forbidden. A little more than a century later, Pope Gregory III (AD 731) forbade marriage even between sixth cousins.

These fairly extreme rules were changed by Innocent III in the fourth Lateran Council in 1215, when marriage beyond third cousins was permitted. Modern Roman Catholic marriage laws date from the Council of Trent (1563): second cousin marriage is permitted, and sometimes even first cousin marriage (but special permission is required).

The living law can change. Two interesting examples are known from outside Christendom. The emperor Claudius petitioned the Roman senate to change the incest laws so that he might marry his niece, Agrippina, who has been mentioned before as being involved in other incestuous unions. The senate made the required change, but according to Suetonius, a contemporary of Claudius', there was no great rush by uncles and nieces to get married.

The second historically attested change occurred because the prophet Muhammad received a special revelation permitting him to marry Zaynab, the wife of his adopted son, counted as a blood son. From then on inheritance laws were to differentiate between adoptive and blood relatives.

To return to the question of cousin marriage. The marriage laws of the western world take into account only such distinctions as first and second cousin; but other societies observe different ones. For example, 20 percent of the *Ethnographic atlas* sample prohibit marriage between a man and his father's brother's daughter and his mother's sister's daughter but permit it between a man and his mother's brother's daughter. A few societies are even more selective and insist on only one kind of cousin as a possible spouse. Less than four percent (32 out of 762) of the *Ethnographic atlas* samples permit and encourage marriage between a man and his mother's brother's daughter. Less than one percent (4 out of this 762) require marriage between a man and his father's brother's daughter.

But the question remains: why should any rules about incest exist at all? This is a perennial topic among anthropologists and a variety of answers have been proposed. For the most part, anthropologists (but not sociobiologists) reject the idea that incestuous matings have been tabued because the children of such matings may be deformed, insane, sterile or markedly unhealthy in other ways. Such results are not inevitable; primitive peoples have no knowledge of genetics and explain misfortunes in terms of witchcraft or similar supernatural events; and the marriage laws of a society may exclude some close relatives but permit others equally close (as we have just seen with cousins).

Theories more popular with anthropologists to account for incest rules have played up a number of different, quite diverse considerations. For example, incest rules force people to get ties with other families that are important socially, economically and politically (a view championed by Edward Burnett Tylor, the first professor of anthropology at Oxford and in the world, whose position can be summed up in his motto "marry out or be killed off"). Or, tolerating incest would create jealousy in the family and disastrous role confusion (associated with Bronislaw Malinowski; summed up in the words of an American song from the 1940s, "I'm my own grandpa"). Or, early childhood association kills off sexual interest (the "familiarity breeds contempt" theory, associated with Edward Westermarck and directly at variance with Freudian notions). Or, modern incest tabus simply spell out what in prehistoric times was improbable for a number of factors including longevity, e.g. people then seldom lived beyond 30, making parent-child marriage unlikely (a theory proposed by Mariam K. Slater, partially summed up by the sentiment "the old ways are best").

Traditional approaches to incest are at least equally varied in non-western societies. The !Kung of southern Africa give no explanation for such tabus at all: it is simply so horrible they refuse to theorize about it: "Only dogs do that—not men," they say. And, "it would be dangerous, like going up to a lion." The Yapese of Oceania also think incest is something animals do, not human beings. But they regard it as impractical rather than horrible, and betray no sense of deep revulsion. However, they believe that a woman who has committed incest can never bear children.

The Kágaba of South America think incest has no biological effects whatever, and will certainly not produce deformed or retarded children. The Comanche Indians seem to lack an idea of incest altogether: they consider incest neither a crime nor a sin, but impossible. The Tallensi of West Africa condemn brother-sister incest intensely but find the idea of mother-son incest incredible and ridiculous because a grown man's mother is inevitably thought of as an unattractive old woman.

A cross-culturally common explanation for tabuing incest assumed that kinsmen share the same blood, and that mixing this blood together is harmful. Though scientifically untrue (blood is not even involved in fertilization), this belief is still held by many Westerners—including, to my surprise, many of my own students. In some societies, other shared substances are believed to render individuals inappropriate as mates, so that in addition to what we can call "blood" incest (the usual kind), at least two other kinds exist.

(1) Milk incest: people who have drunk milk from the same wet nurse may not marry. This tabu is found in the Koran and is absolutely binding on all Muslims. (Malayan Muslims get round the rule by a ritual pardoning.) Milk incest may have been an ancient Mediterranean custom and is still found among Eastern Orthodox Christians, southern Italians and various Spanish groups. It may also have been more general in all of Christendom. We still find expressions like "milk brother" in French and German, although milk incest is not recognized among them at present.

Another kind of milk incest occurs among certain groups in the Transkei of South Africa: if a man drinks milk from the cattle of another family line, he may not marry a woman of that family.

(2) Name incest: a person may not marry someone who has the same personal name as one of his parents or siblings (a common surname is not in question here). This rule is found to my knowledge only among the Bushmen of southern Africa and Orthodox Jews.

Other kinds of incest exist that are symbolic extensions of parent-child relations:

(3) Spiritual incest: among Roman Catholics and Eastern Orthodox Christians, godparents are thought of as spiritual parents. Consequently, it is tabu to marry one's godparent and in some groups even the children of godparents. In Latin America, the *compadrazgo* (godparenthood relationship) has been elaborated to an extent rare in Europe.

(4) Teacher-student incest: among the Balinese it is forbidden to marry the daughter of one's teacher; among the Vietnamese it is forbidden to marry his widow.

(5) Master-servant incest: among Albanians of Martanesh, a servant could be condemned to death for seducing the daughter of his master because in a sense his master was his "father" and he had committed incest.

(6) Midwife incest: among the Semang of southwest Asia, a man may not marry the midwife who assisted at his birth, nor may his father marry her. The Zande of Central Africa have a similar rule, but it apparently does not apply to the man's father.

The extension of incest tabus in these ways readily fits in with Tylor's model that it is impractical to marry into groups one already has ties with. But even so, I do not think this proves that incest tabus necessarily began because people realized the practical consequences of setting them up.

According to Marco Polo, "no man [in Tibet] would ever on any account take a virgin to wife. For they say that a woman is worthless unless she has had the knowledge of men." He maintains that foreigners were besieged to sleep with unmarried girls and to give them some trinket as a sign that they had a lover. Although this description may be inaccurate or exaggerated, reports from contemporary societies suggest it could be true. Clearly, premarital virginity is not a universal value.

On the other hand, in many other societies there is a mania for virgins, and premarital virginity is highly prized, but almost always in the female only. Many societies have devised various tests for determining whether a bride is a virgin at her first wedding. In a sample of 141 societies, Broude and Greene found that 36 required brides to be virgins, and meted out severe punishments for those who failed virginity tests. On the other hand, an almost equal number of societies, 34, were found to approve of girls having premarital sex. An additional 29 societies tolerated premarital sexual behavior in girls if they were discreet. Broude and Greene offer no information about attitudes toward premarital sex on the part of males. The general impression one gets from the ethnographic literature is that males are usually expected to have had some sexual experience before marriage.

In the western world, controversies exist as to the value of virginity. Of course, some positions are merely repetitions of the traditional Judaeo-Christian moral code. But there are various arguments that have a more general significance. Some theorists have argued that cultural evolution is largely an outcome of diverting sexual energy into socially desirable goals. Havelock Ellis, for one, suggested that "it is impossible to say what finest elements in art, in morals, in civilization generally may not be rooted in an autocratic impulse . . . arising from the impeded spontaneous sexual energy of the organism and extending from simple physical processes to the highest psychic manifestations."

The Freudian theory of sublimation, which is perhaps the most important nonreligious argument for sexual abstentions of any kind, was first written in 1905 in *Three essays on the theory of sexuality*. Briefly, sublimation is the doctrine that psychosexual energy (libido) can be directed away from sexual gratification to nonsexual ends. Freud viewed the diversion and desexualization of such energy as one of the most important ways that civilization was achieved, the prime example mentioned as an instance of sublimation being artistic activity.

The authors of *Sexual behavior in the human male* considered the question in some detail. Kinsey, Pomeroy and Martin assumed that "if sublimation is a reality, it should be possible to find individuals whose erotic responses have been reduced or eliminated, *without nervous disturbance*, as a result of an expenditure of energy in utterly nonsexual activities."

Two groups were considered by them, together totaling over 4,200 males who had either unusually low rates of sexual activity or were consciously trying to sublimate. Kinsey and his co-workers were unable to find any clear-cut cases of successful sublimation.

There is another line of argument. Since sublimation has been regarded as one of the great civilizing factors, if the theory makes any sense there should be some sort of cross-cultural confirmation of this.

The most ambitious attempt to get cross-cultural support for such a theory—not couched entirely in Freudian terms, however—is that by J. D. Unwin in his book *Sex and culture* (1943). This is a serious contribution to the subject, and one of the first cross-cultural anthropological studies on a truly massive scale designed to test any hypothesis.

What Unwin specifically tries to establish is that the mental level of a culture is directly correlated with the number and severity of impediments that the society places in the way of sexual contacts.

An impartial examination of Unwin's data shows that a correlation of some sort exists between the classes of culture he sets up and the impediments to sexual contact. Unwin's study is based on an analysis of some 80 non-European societies, ranged on a cultural scale whereby the mental level of a society can be deduced.

Unwin believes that his data show that sexual restrictions produced a higher level of culture. He argues that a cultural advance must depend upon a factor that produces thought, reflection and social energy. The compulsory check of sexual impulses is that factor. He grants that continence may produce morbid symptoms in some individuals, but he insists that when sexual opportunity of a society is reduced almost to a minimum (particularly for women before marriage) the resulting social energy produces "great accomplishments in human endeavor" and "civilization." When the compulsory continence is of a less rigorous character, lesser energy is displayed, and lower level cultures result.

A later study by a professional anthropologist, G. P. Murdock, corroborates a good deal of what Unwin discovered. Murdock's study of 400 societies generally goes along with Unwin's finding that the stricter the rules for premarital sex behavior, the greater the degree of cultural complexity of a society. But Murdock gives a different explanation for this finding. For example, [he says that in advanced societies practicing intensive agriculture, a high level of self-discipline and industriousness is expected: the young must spend a considerable amount of time acquiring needed skills and discipline and cannot be allowed to indulge themselves in unrestricted sexual freedom. In simpler hunting and gathering societies, the same rules do not apply. The fewer the skills demanded, the fewer the sexual restrictions. But if this is so, how can we account for the spread of permissive standards in contemporary American society?

The answer Murdock suggests is not altogether compelling. He finds a relationship between permissiveness and the fact that a newly married couple establish their own place to live without reference to the families of either the bride or groom. In cultures where a bride must live with her husband's family, on the other hand, there is also a demand for virginity in the bride. When people know they can eventually escape from the control of their parents and kinsmen, they are more apt to establish permissive rules. This is precisely the case in contemporary America.

Murdock concludes his article with the observation that if a fully permissive code of premarital sexuality is achieved in the United States and elsewhere in the civilized world it would mean that there would be "a reversal of the long-term direction of cultural evolution, at least with respect to premarital sexual morality."

One of the problems in Unwin's and Murdock's discussion is that they talk about morality and codes of permissiveness as opposed to what people really do. But the theory of sublimation deals not with moral codes but behavior. There is no necessary correlation between the two. Murdock suggests—quite accurately, it seems to me—that American society in the 1940s and before would have to be characterized as having restrictive premarital sex norms, in contrast to the 1960s, when there was a tendency toward permissiveness. Nevertheless, some scholars maintain that behavior has remained relatively constant, although a greater freedom to talk openly about sex may generate a belief to the contrary. John L. Gagnon and William Simon, former senior research sociologists at the Kinsey Institute, state that "the evidence is that very little has changed in American sexual patterns over the past four decades." Whatever the truth of this assertion, we must emphasize again that what people say sexual behavior should be need not necessarily have anything to do with what the people themselves actually do. The Kinsey report was not controversial for nothing.

How then can we explain Unwin's and Murdock's findings? Perhaps there are factors that neither has considered.

Consider simply the factor of age of marriage. It is surely one thing to tabu premarital promiscuity if the average age of marriage is 15, quite another if it is 25. Westerners tend to forget that Biblical standards of premarital virginity presuppose very early marriage: about 13 for girls (as practiced among Orthodox Jews until quite recently). Christian tradition has the Virgin Mary becoming the Mother of God at 14—and age was not the miraculous part of this event.

From a survey by Ludwik Krzywicki, it would seem that members of hunting and gathering societies tend to marry soon after puberty, at about 15. Note that it is these societies that are always listed as being among the most permissive, although the marriages are overwhelmingly monogamous. Moni Nag's latest cross-cultural survey of societies with relatively recent data tends to confirm a tendency toward early marriage for women (at 18 or younger) in most societies; of 48 societies in his sample, 37 had early marriage.

Why then strict rules about sex before marriage? Murdock's suggestion of the need for a greater concentration on acquisition of skills in more complex societies has a certain plausibility. Surely someone in constant pursuit of sex partners simply has not adequate time to learn many other things. This does not confirm the theory of sublimation, however, only the very obvious fact that one seldom can do two things at one time. It would be equally reprehensible, by the same token, for a youth to spend all his time reading and rereading *Bambi*.

What is more important with these tabus is their economic implications. They may simply boil down to attempts to ensure legitimate inheritance and succession. Because inheritable property and high social status are negligible in hunting and gathering groups, there would be little motivation at that level to develop elaborate rules for establishing such legitimacy, but there would be a great deal of interest at higher levels. Contemporary American society does not go against these economic interests: because of effective contraception, legitimate heirs can be guaranteed in spite of actual promiscuity.

The cultural differences in permissiveness and restrictiveness do not, as we have seen, provide a convincing case for sublimation. The question, however, is more profound than a cross-cultural test might suggest. What is needed is detailed information about the energy levels and cultural accomplishments of individuals. It is quite plausible to assume that high levels of cultural productivity could go along with comparably high levels of sexual performance, which the careers of artists such as Boccaccio and Fragonard might suggest. Certainly, the prodigious Bach, with his incredible musical output as well as 20 children, was not sublimating all the time. These are admittedly isolated examples. However, of the six most active males in the Kinsey sample—men with maximum orgasm frequencies during 30 continuous years, ranging from 10.6 to 33.1 weekly orgasms—two were physicians, one an educator, one a lawyer and one a scientific worker.

Societies vary to a certain extent with regard to which sexual behaviors are prohibited as well as in the severity of the punishments handed out. A striking example of this is rape. In western society at present even the most ardent liberalizers of the sex laws are opposed to rape and want it punished as a serious crime. The Model penal code sponsored by the American Law Institute proposes that all sexual acts performed in private by consenting adults be decriminalized, but retains rape as an offense—presumably not because of its sexual nature but because it involves violence and is nonconsensual. However, the Judaeo-Christian tradition nowhere singles out rape as a sin. It is forbidden in the Bible when committed against a betrothed or married woman. Even then the victim may have a hard time proving her case because if she was raped in a city she was expected to call for help and prevent it. This sort of reasoning was incorporated into the laws of Rome under the Christian emperor Constantine.

In two societies—the Marshallese and the Baiga—rape is reportedly the preferred form of sexual activity and goes totally unpunished. A number of societies similarly ignore rape altogether; these societies are fairly numerous and include the Copper Eskimo, Kaska, Mundurucú, Trumai, Navaho, Hadza, Lepcha, and Trobiand islanders.

In most societies, however, rape (particularly of a married woman) is one of the most serious sexual offenses. Death is regarded as the appropriate penalty for rape among some societies, severe punishment among others, and still others ridicule the rapist or impose a token punishment. The spectrum is fairly wide.

Again, the same sort of variation is found with regard to male homosexual acts. In some societies they are universal and compulsory, as among the Étoro. Among the ancient Hebrews and Aztecs they were punishable by death.

The most frequently tabued and most severely punished sexual acts are incest, abduction and rape. The least frequently mentioned and most lightly punished infractions include premarital promiscuity and intercourse with the person one is betrothed to. Adultery (particularly by a woman) is generally a serious offense but seldom considered as serious as rape or incest. Punishment may typically include public ridicule, disgrace and divorce. However, in some societies people guilty of adultery may be killed along with their lovers. The Jívaro of South America permit a betrayed husband to kill or mutilate the genitals of his adulterous wife and to slash her lover's scalp. A woman found guilty of adultery among the Vietnamese might formerly be thrown to a specially trained elephant, who in turn threw her into the air with his trunk and when she had landed, trampled her to death.

The more people a sexual infraction involves, the more severely it is punished. Solitary masturbation, for example, may be considered reprehensible but is seldom punished in any way but through ridicule. The suggestion in the Jewish tradition that death is appropriate for masturbation (being a total "waste of nature" and hence the most reprehensible of sexual crimes) is decidedly at variance with cross-cultural judgments. Generally, sexual acts involving a married person are more serious than other acts, perhaps because marriage in most societies is not only a union of two people but also of two kin groups. Thus, adultery is more serious than premarital promiscuity; rape of a married woman is more serious than rape of an unmarried girl.

The actual punishments used for a particular sexual offense may vary considerably from society to society. The Ganda of East Africa, for example, traditionally punish incest by drowning the offenders; the Vietnamese and Aztecs by strangulation. Among the Cayapa of Ecuador, anyone guilty of incest was formerly punished, say informants, by being suspended over a table covered with lighted candles and slowly roasted to death.

Rape occurs as a form of punishment in a number of societies for a woman's adultery. Among the Cheyenne, a man who discovered that his wife had committed adultery invited all the unmarried men in his military society (except his wife's relatives) to a feast on the prairie. This means that the woman is raped by each of these men in turn. A woman who survived being raped by 30 to 40 men had the unending burden of the disgrace. Gang rape as a means of social control is reported from several other societies.

Mutilation of one sort or another is used by a number of groups as punishment for adultery. Fairly common throughout the world has been cutting off the nose of an adulterous wife. A Freudian explanation for this is tempting; since adultery in men is seldom punished and often expected, cutting off a woman's nose (a phallic symbol) can be seen as equivalent to castration. Nose-cutting was practiced by Plains Indians such as the Comanche and Blackfoot. Similar punishment was meted out in England in the time of King Canute, who ruled from 1017 to 1035: a woman caught in adultery was to have her nose cut off as well as both her ears. In twelfth-century Naples, adulterous women and procuresses had their noses slit (elsewhere in the Holy Roman Empire under Emperor Frederik Barbarossa, cutting off the nose was a punishment for whores). The cutting off of an adulteress's nose was recommended in ancient Mesopotamian legal codes; her lover could either be castrated or put to death. This same custom of nose amputation in ancient India prompted what may be the first known attempt at plastic surgery.

The Zande punish the wife's lover by very severe mutilations; the ears, upper lip, hands and penis—but not nose, interestingly—might all be cut off the man unlucky enough to be found out. If caught in the act both he and the woman could be killed. Among the Ashanti, adultery in a wife required compensation to the husband by the lover; but adultery involving the wife of a paramount chief required that she should undergo an excruciating, long-drawn-out surgical death.

Among some Zulu groups, adultery could be punished with death, but flogging the offenders with thorny bushes also occurred, and the adulterous wife was sometimes punished by having cacti thrust into her vagina. The Igbo punished adultery by a chief's wife by forcing her to copulate publicly with her lover and hammering a stake some five feet long through his back until it came out through her body.

Burning an adulterous wife to death seems to have occurred at some time among the ancient Egyptians. Both the Hebrews and Aztecs killed such a woman by stoning. According to the Koran, a woman convicted of adultery or fornication should be killed by being locked inside a room until she dies (the severity of this sentence mitigated by the necessity of four witnesses to an adulterous act before a verdict is reached). In point of fact, stoning has been the traditional punishment in Muslim countries.

Among the ancient Romans, seducers of married women were occasionally castrated. Other more unusual punishments have also been recorded. According to Juvenal and Catullus, the lover of a married woman who was caught could get the hair on his buttocks burnt off with red-hot ashes, or the head of a certain fish covered with spines shoved up his anus. The Emperor Aurelian punished one of his soldiers for having seduced his innkeeper's wife with a punishment considered so terrible and unprecedented that the whole Roman army was said to be seized with fear; the guilty soldier was tied by his feet to the tops of two trees that had been bent over; suddenly, the trees were let go so that he was literally snapped apart.

Punishments for sexual crimes have grown increasingly less severe in the West. Nevertheless there are certain broad categories of acts that are universally tabu and generally punished with severe penalties: incest and acts involving violence and a lack of consent among the parties concerned.

AGING AND DYSFUNCTION

SEXUALITY IN AGING:
A STUDY OF 106 CULTURES

Rhonda L. Winn, Ph.D. and Niles Newton, Ph.D.

INTRODUCTION

The extent to which sexual activity assumes an adaptive role in the lives of older individuals is a question that has yet to be adequately answered. While various researchers (1, 2, 4, 9) have found that many individuals in the United States continue sexual activity until the eighth and ninth decades of life, negative attitudes toward sexual activity in the aged are widespread (8), and cultural censure may be expected to affect, in complex ways, the level of sexual activity and the degree of sexual adjustment of individuals in this age group.

The scholarly literature on humans reared in societies other than our own may be seen to provide important clues to both the regularities in sexual behavior and the differing patterns that may occur with aging. The mediating effects imposed by culture on this biological base can thus be examined.

The ethnographic literature contains little quantitative data relating to the sexual behavior of older individuals, however. Merriam (5), writing about the Bala, and Marshall (3), about the Mangaians of Polynesia, both report data indicating varying levels of sexual activity in older males.

Merriam, in attempting to ascertain the frequency of intercourse among his informants, on 10 consecutive days asked 11 men, ranging in approximate age from 23 to 66, how many times they had had intercourse in the preceding 24 hours. Responses raged from a high of 1.9 times per day for the 23-year-old to a low of 1.2 times per day for three individuals, aged 39, 63, and one of unknown age. The average frequency reported by the oldest informant, aged 66, was 1.5 times per day.

Marshall reported figures obtained from a group of Mangaian informants that indicate a moderate decrease in the frequency of sexual intercourse with increasing age as well as a decrease with age in the average number of orgasms per night. These informants estimated 7 to be the "average" number of nights per week during which sexual activity occurred in males of approximately 18 years; this decreased to a frequency of 2-3 nights per week in males of approximately 48 years. The "average" number of orgasms per night decreased from three in males of approximately 18 years to one in males of approximately 48 years.

These findings raise a number of questions about the regularity with which changes in sexual behavior occur with age, the magnitude of changes found in differing cultures, and societal factors that can be seen to relate to changes that can be identified in both males and females.

The purpose of the present study will be to review Human Relations Area Files cross-cultural materials relating to the issue of sexuality in older individuals, noting how a diversity of societies have patterned the sexual behavior of their older members.

. . .

"Sexuality in Aging: A Study of 106 Cultures," by Rhonda L. Winn, Ph.D., and Niles Newton, Ph.D., reprinted from *Archives of Sexual Behavior,* Vol. 11, No. 4, Plenum Publishing, 1982.

CONTINUED SEXUAL ACTIVITY IN OLDER MALES

Regarding the age at which sexual activity ceases or declines in older males, wide variation exists in observers' reports concerning the 28 cultures on which data were available.

In 20 of these cultures (70%), observers cited evidence to demonstrate continued sexual activity in males of very old age. DeGroot, for example, reporting on the Taoist sects of China, cited examples of men retaining their procreative powers and sexual desires until "beyond the age of 100."

Other Asiatic societies in which sexual activity in aged males was cited include the Tsarang of Tibet, the Kerema of Okinawa, the Lepcha of Himalaya, and the Kota of India. Although many of these reports are general in nature, and specific ages and frequencies of sexual contacts are not given, observers make clear that sexual activity remains an important part of the lives of males in these societies until an advanced age.

Specific frequencies for coitus in various age groups are cited only in the case of the Mayurbhanj Santal of India. Numerous informants stated that the average frequency of coitus for a male, aged 60, remained approximately once per day and that males aged 70 often maintained this level of sexual activity. These figures were reported as a continuation of data on sexual frequency in younger males, which is reported to be two to four times per day before the birth of children, lending support to findings by Newman and Nichols (7) in the United States that individuals with higher rates of sexual frequency in younger years maintain a higher level of sexual activity in old age.

Similar patterns are cited in Africa. Among the Nupe, "old men" are described as taking young women as brides and maintaining sexual vigor through the use of aphrodisiacs. The Tiv believe that reductions in sexual capacity are the result of witchcraft and fetishes, not merely old age, and that many older men remain active and "hot" for many years after they become gray-haired.

Middle Eastern societies reported to have males who continue active sexual contact in old age include the Bedouins of Kuwait and the Kanuri of Bornu. Dickson, writing of the Kuwait Bedouins, cites large numbers of men "of 80 years" and over who still continued to marry and produce children, and Cohen states that sexual potency may remain in Kanuri males after old age. Even in the case of old men who could not have intercourse, he reports, frequent marriages still took place and romantic interest continued.

Among North American societies, the Ojibwa of Ontario and the Navajo of southwestern United States are both cited as cultures in which men retain sexual potency until late in life. Kluckhohn notes that information on frequency of sexual intercourse for Navajo males over age 50 was extremely scanty but cites an impression from the available data that a markedly bimodal distribution existed, with one group of men sharply slackening sexual activity after age 50 and the other showing only a gradual diminution after age 60.

A number of observers writing about the sexual activity of older males in the Oceanic societies cite frequent sexual relationships between "old men" and much younger girls. These relationships range in intensity from casual sexual contact with promiscuous girls or prostitutes to more permanent liaisons. Suggs, reporting on the sexual activity of older male inhabitants of the Marquesas Islands of French Polynesia, states that males in their 60's and 70's are, in general, capable of sexual intercourse as in their youth, but with reduced frequency, which he terms "reasonably frequent." He notes, however, that fellatio and cunnilingus are practiced, as well as homosexual relations with age-mates. Suggs notes that fellatio was often practiced in cases of impotence in older men, the young prostitutes bringing these men to orgasm in this manner. Among the Truk Islanders of Micronesia, reports of frequent sexual liaisons between young girls and "old men" with no other sexual outlets were also characterized by the use of alternative sexual techniques, the old men performing cunnilingus on the girls.

In contrast to the 20 reports of continued sexual activity in aged males, some observers cited evidence of an absence of or decline in sexual contact associated with aging. In eight (30%) of the 28 societies on which information was available, observers noted examples of older males who were sexually inactive, impotent, or disinterested in sexual activity. Illustrative of this type of report, Barnett notes that a decline in sexual intercourse occurs with age among males in the Hokkien Sanlei Ts'un peoples of Taiwan. Among the Lapps of Norway, older males tend to become strict and puritanical irrespective of past activities, according to Pehrson; and the old men of Yap Island in Micronesia, who are reported to be "too old to be chasing after women," spend their time sitting in clusters talking.

Despite the widespread custom of old men marrying young wives, observers in two cultural settings have noted that these marriages are frequently characterized by a lack of interest in sexual contact on the part of the aged husbands and/or the loss of ability to impregnate or satisfy their wives. Such examples were cited among the Murngin of Australia and the Tiwi of Melville and Bathurst Islands.

A variety of attitudes are recorded concerning the loss of sexual virility on aged men in the cultures studied. The Ila of Northern Zimbabwe, for example, see the decline of potency that comes with age as a severe loss, accompanied by despair, and spend considerable time in "vain attempts" to continue the active sexual life of youth.

Loss of sexual interest is viewed as an inevitable accompaniment of aging by the Woleaians of Micronesia, and the object of humor by younger males, while the Cagaba of Columbia see the decline of virility as merely a release from physical effort, a return to serenity and reflection.

Thus, although some decline in the sexual activity of aged males is recorded in a significant proportion of the societies studied, many cultural groups have expectations for continued sexual activity for older men that imply little, if any, loss of their sexual powers until very late in life. In those societies where observers noted a decline in sexual activity, potency, or sexual interest in aged males, a variety of attitudes toward this loss were found, ranging from despair to a sense of relief at the release from physical effort.

CONTINUED SEXUAL ACTIVITY IN OLDER FEMALES

Of the 26 societies for which information was available relating to the sexual activity of older women, 22 (84%) were found to contain reports of continued sexual contacts during aging (see Table 1).

A number of these reports included comments by observers comparing the degree of sexual activity found in aged men and aged women. In each instance where a difference was noted in regard to level of sexual interest or activity, this difference was found to lie in the direction of greater sexual involvement in women.

Among the Lepcha of Himalaya, for example, Gorer reported that his native informants agreed that women enjoy sexual activity later in life more than men do. He noted that older women were more likely to express sexual interest and that women "as old as 80" were even eager to interpret questions from him and his colleagues relating to sex as attempts at seduction. Morris, also writing of the Lepchas, quoted informants as saying that while old men did eventually lose interest in the sexual act beginning at approximately age 65, old women continued to "take pleasure in the operation up to the time they die." He noted that menopause was hardly recognized by the women of this society and that certainly no reduction in sexual behavior or psychological disturbances were associated with menopause. Among the Tiv of Nigeria, Bohannan and Bohannan likewise reported that aged women do not recognize menopause as a sign of physical or sexual decline, but as just a "point in a woman's life." They emphasized that women might not cease sexual activity for many years afterward.

A number of observers have made note of the practice of older women seeking sexual partners outside of their age cohort. In fact, of the 22 reports of sexual activity in aged women, 18 (82%) were characterized by a sexual coupling of an older woman with a partner other than an older man. These sexual partners were, in all but two instances, much younger men.

Table 1.

Continued Sexual Activity in Aged Females

	Cultural group	Type of sexual activity reported	Age if specified	Partner if specified
AK 5	Lepcha	Intercourse "enjoyed later in life than men," promiscuous intercourse with younger men	To age 80 "harridans," aged 60 and over	Males, especially young men of the village
AW 42	Mayurbhanj Santal	Intercourse "once per day," stroking, body massage after intercourse	At least until age 60	Husbands
FF 57	Tiv	Intercourse, "sexual activity"	Many years after menopause	—
FX 14	Lovedu	Intercourse	Mothers, grandmothers	"Frequently" with younger man
NV 9	Tzeltal	"Keen interest in sex," intercourse	After menopause	Young, unmarried men in some cases
MS 14	Kanuri	Sexual activity, potency	"Old" age	—
OJ 27	Wogeo	Intercourse	—	—
OL 6	Trobriands	Intercourse	"Very old, decrepit"	Young boys, in some cases
OM 10	Lesu, New Ireland	"Sexual activity"	"Old women"	Young boy in one example cited
OR 19	Truk	Oral stimulation, bestiality in old women with no other outlets	"Old women"	Dogs
OU 8	Samoa	Intercourse	"Old women"	Young boys
OX 6	Marquesas	Intercourse, "reasonably frequent" brief liaisons with much younger males	Aged 60's and 70's	Younger men those with no other outlets
OY 2	Easter Islanders	Intercourse	"Old women" no longer attractive	Young boys, sometimes young girls
SC 7	Cagaba, Kogi	Intercourse, instruction of young boys in intercourse	"Old women," "old widows"	Youth
O1 8	Aranda	Intercourse, old women "more interested" in sex	"Old women"	Males of village
OI 17	Murngin	Intercourse, seduction of young men	"Old women"	Young men
SE 13	Inca	Intercourse	"Old women"	Young boys
SM 3	Caingang	Intercourse, including adultery	"Old age"	—
SO 9	Tupinamba	Intercourse, instruction of boys in sex	"Old women discarded by husbands"	Young boys
SP 7	Bacairi	Intercourse	"Old women"	Young men
SP 17	Nambicuara	Intercourse, marriage to young men who cannot get young women	"Old women"	Young men
SP 23	Trumai	Intercourse	"Very old women," "too old and ugly for marriage"	Promiscuous males of village, young men

Among the Lovedu of South Africa, for example, older women described as "old enough to be their mothers or grandmothers" had "frequent" sexual liaisons with young married men. Nash, reporting that many older women begin to take a keen interest in sex, also found frequent instances of widows and other "old women" engaging in sexual relations with young married men.

Despite references by the observer to a decrease in those qualities usually assumed to contribute to sexual allure, older women were noted to achieve considerable success in attracting youthful sexual partners. Hogbin, writing of the Wogeo of New Guinea, described one old woman as "a toothless old crone" who, when questioned about her success with many of the youths of the island, said, "Desire doesn't disappear with the teeth, and so long as a woman can still dig she wants to do a little something now and then."

Malinowski, in the same vein, reports an example of a Trobriand woman "so old, decrepit, and ugly" that no one suspected her of being the source of a venereal disease that infected all of the young boys of the island. He found instances in most of the villages where he worked of "old and thoroughly repulsive" women who were able to obtain young and attractive boys as lovers.

Several authors noted, in this regard, that older women were resorted to as sexual partners only by young men who were able to find no other outlets, as in the case of the Marquesas Islanders of French Polynesia, the aboriginal Easter Islanders, the Inca of Peru, the Nambicuara of Brazil, and the Trumai of Mato Grosso. Older women were also utilized by young boys as sexual initiators and sexual instructors in several of the societies reported, as in the Tupinamba of northeast Brazil, the Easter Islanders, and the Cagaba of Columbia.

The difficulty of older women finding sexual partners is thus underscored by the underlying motivation of the young men described in these reports. If, in fact, sexual interest remains stronger in aged women than in aged men, and if the increased longevity of women in most societies produces a larger population of aged widows seeking sexual partners, then the further reduction of the number of available aged men as a result of marriage to younger women, as previously cited, may be seen to result in a set of circumstances that leaves few alternatives for the older woman seeking gratification of sexual needs.

In most of the instances of sexual coupling of older women and younger men cited in the literature, no discussion was made of the opinions of the society in general regarding these behaviors. In one report, however, it was noted in regard to the sexual involvement of a woman of 65 with a man of 35 in the Marquesas Islands of French Polynesia that no societal censure whatsoever was directed at either of the persons involved. Except for expressions of repulsion on the part of some of the observers toward the physical characteristics of the aged about whom they wrote, little indication of strong societal feelings about the sexual behavior of older women can be gleaned from the data available.

Half of the reports of a decline in sexual activity in older women were found in the context of discussion of a change in aged females' role as procreants. Of the four references in the literature relating to a reduction in older women's sexual behavior, two concerned the loss of her reproductive powers and the concomitant lessening of her value as a wife. Among the Tallensi of Ghana, an "old woman" frequently left her husband altogether and went to live with her oldest son. Since her procreative function had ceased, her sexual value was no longer sufficient to make her desirable as a wife. Fortes quotes Tallensi informants as equating reproductive power with sexuality and stresses the native point of view that, once the childbearing years are over, a woman ceases to have sexual value.

Aged women of the Kanuri tribe of northeastern Nigeria are cited as finding it difficult to remarry for the same reason and also live with adult sons. Thus, these references to the decline of sexuality in aged women concern reproductive rather than strictly sexual behavior, although a reduction in sexual contacts appears to result from these societal views.

Other references to declining sexual activity in older women were found concerning the Tiv of Nigeria and the Lesu of New Ireland Island in Oceania. Aged Tiv women were reported to decide to give up sexual activity in some cases, but this was by no means the rule. Older women who did cease sexual intercourse wore an ornamental stone necklace that signified continence. Powdermaker cites the case of an "elderly" Lesu woman who revealed a loss of sexual interest in her old age. She stated that "in the past she enjoyed copulating very much, but that now she is old and does not care for it." In both of these reports, a loss of sexual interest was cited independently of any cultural prescription regarding the proper sexual role of aged women vis-á-vis their reproductive function.

In general, then, the data indicate that older women frequently express strong sexual desires and interests, that they engage in sexual activity in many instances until an extreme old age, and that possibly because of the smaller number of older men available as sexual partners, older women may form sexual liaisons with much younger men. The number of reports of continued sexual activity in aged females was greater than the number found for aged males. In addition, observers' remarks tended to be more detailed and explicit in regard to descriptions of behavior and to be accompanied by generalizations intended to apply to most or all aged women of the society studied.

REDUCTION OF INHIBITORY MECHANISMS IN OLDER INDIVIDUALS

Associated with continued sexual activity in aged persons was a finding that older individuals, especially older women, tended to become less inhibited in regard to conversation related to sexuality, sexual humor, and indecorous or sexually tinged gestures.

In 23 (22%) of the 106 files containing information concerning the sexual behavior of old men and women, reference was made by observers to instances of ribald or salacious remarks or sexually suggestive behavior by aged persons. Of these 23 instances, 17 (74%) involved older women and six (26%) involved older men.

In the case of older women, the most frequently reported manifestation of this lessening of inhibition concerned observations of immodest behavior and sexual aggressiveness that were recorded in many areas of the world, including the Hokkien Sanlei Ts'un of Taiwan, the Trumai of Brazil, the Tiwi of Australia, the Wogeo of northwestern New Guinea, the Tzeltal of Yucatan, the Balinese of Oceania, the Tepoztlan of Mexico, the Navajo of the southwestern United States, the Cubeo of South America, the Muria of India, the Okinawans of Asia, the Lepcha of Himalaya, and the Kwoma of northeastern New Guinea. These behaviors included exposure of the genitals, suggestive dancing, imitation of copulatory movements in public, clutching the genitals of men in public, and requesting sexual intercourse from strangers. Barnett, writing of the Hokkien Sanlei Ts'un of Taiwan, noted that it was the "old women of the village" who talked "dirty" and acted as the village clowns and teasers. He found that, in contrast to the younger women who, up to age 35, were extremely shy in public, women past 60 years of age became very aggressive. Instances of changes in mode of dress in older women were also recorded, the women becoming riggish, wearing more colorful ornamentation or appearing bare-breasted in public.

A second frequently noted manifestation of this decrease in inhibitions in older women was found in association with numerous instances of sexual humor or joking on the part of aged females. A number of observers reported anecdotes concerning the tendency for older women to delight in off-color jokes or sexual stories. Such accounts were recorded among the Lepcha of Himalaya, the Okinawans of Asia, the Muria of India, the Cubeo of South America, the Gros Ventre Indians of west central United States, the Pawnee Indians of western United States, the Navajo Indians of southwestern United States, the Bali Islanders of Oceania, the Tepoztlan of Mexico, the Wogeo of northwestern New Guinea, and the Trumai of Brazil.

In addition, systematically gathered test data relating to sexual inhibitions were reported in the case of one cultural group. Gladwin and Sarason, on the basis of Rorschach protocols of a 1951 sample of Trukese natives of various ages, concluded that a weakening of inhibitory tendencies occurred with aging, older subjects becoming more likely to freely discuss sexual matters or to express their sexuality verbally. These findings were true for both female and male subjects.

Although most of the observers who allude to the more open sexual expression of older women suggest no explanations for these behaviors, several of the authors offer comments that may shed light on possible reasons for a lessening of sexual inhibitions in this age group. One such factor relates to the changing role of older women in the sexual practices of the society. Belo, in his discussion of the aged Balinese female, posits that the image of the "old woman" as being sexually insatiable, rapacious, and more dangerous than either younger women or old men may be expressive of a phase of development in this particular culture. He notes that the aged play a dominant role in the affairs of Balinese society and that sexual aggressiveness might be one aspect of the psychological characteristics of this age group.

Nash suggests that freedom from the restrictions imposed on women of childbearing age may be associated with a concomitant liberalization of sexual behavior in aged women. He notes that among the Tzeltal of Yucatan a noticeable personality change may be observed as women move out of the "chrysalis of their reproductive cycle," many older women beginning to take a keen interest in sex and becoming more immodest in their public behavior. Because of the abrupt change in their sexual role after menopause, the de-emphasis of their reproductive responsibilities and their duties as mothers, and the end of the necessity for societal regulation of their sexual behavior, Nash maintains that older women for the first time may feel free to fully express their sexual natures. Goldman, referring to the unrestricted sexual behavior of older Cubeo women during festivals and at other times, suggests more direct biological factors as causes of the increase in "licentious" actions with aging. He quotes a number of Cubeo women past menopause as attributing their unrestrained sexuality to increase in sexual appetite.

The number of observations of a diminution of restraint in regard to sex-related conversation or behavior in aged males was smaller than the number recorded for aged females, and the content of these observations was less anomalous than those described above for older women.

While aged males were seen to become less concerned with societal prescriptions regarding decorous behavior, to engage more frequently in salacious or lewd conversation with their peers or with younger persons, and to be more likely than younger men to tell obscene jokes and stories, no instances of extreme immodesty or sexual aggressiveness were recorded for older males. Of the six observations of sex-related conversation or behavior in aged men, five were related to an increase in spoken references to sexuality, and one concerned the more immodest sitting position and nudity of an aged subject. These observations were recorded for the Bambara of West Africa, the Bushmen of South Africa, the Alor Islanders of Oceania, the Chiriguano of Bolivia, the Yahgan of South America, and the Tucana of Amazonia.

In their discussion of Rorschach data for a 1951 sample of Trukese natives, Gladwin and Sarason speculate on the possible reasons for the lessening of inhibitions relating to sexual conversation found in their male subjects. They suggest that since much emphasis is placed on sexual prowess and performance in youthful males, a release from the stress of high expectations for performance that occurs with aging encourages more open conversation among individuals in this age group.

FACTORS INHIBITING SEXUAL ACTIVITY IN THE AGED

Identifiable within these data also are certain factors that may be seen to inhibit sexual activity in the aged in some of the cultures reported. Among these factors are cultural censure of sexual activity in this age group and tendencies by young individuals to view the old as sexually undesirable.

In relatively few reports were there indications of cultural censure or negative opinion regarding the sexual behavior of the old. Of the 106 cultures to which references were made of any type of sexual activity in aged men or women, only three—the Hokkien Sanlei Ts'un of Taiwan, the Sarakatsani of northern Greece, and the Bontok Islanders of the Philippines—were accompanied by statements of disapproval of reports that such behavior violated the mores of the society. For instance, Barnett notes that, among the Hokkien Sanlei Ts'un of Taiwan, a couple continuing to have children after they became grandparents experienced much ridicule.

More common were observations relating to expressions of distaste by younger individuals regarding the sexual desirability of the old. A total of 15 reports were recorded that reflected some degree of repulsion toward the aged as sexual objects. Of these 15 reports 5 (33%) concerned older males and 10 (67%) concerned older females.

The most frequent observation relating to the sexual desirability of older males involved the reluctance of younger women to marry old men. Such reports were recorded for the Lovedu of South Africa, the Kapauka of western New Guinea, the Trobriand Islanders of Oceania, and the Buka of the Solomon Islands. Malinowski, for example, identified old age, with its accompanying "lessening of physical attractiveness," as one of the most important factors in the failure of "old men" to acquire wives among the Trobriand Islanders. The wrinkled skin, white hair, and toothless jaws of old age are enumerated as characteristics considered repulsive by younger women. In addition, aged men among the Trumai Indians of central Brazil were designated by the society in general, not only by prospective wives, in uncomplimentary terms and were considered to be of the lowest status, repugnant, unclean, and unkempt.

Of the 10 references within the literature expressing distaste regarding the sexual desirability of older women, 6 (60%) concerned the marriageability of this age group. Among the Kanuri of northeastern Nigeria, the Isneg of the Philippines, and the Murngin of northern Australia, it was noted that older women had very little chance for marriage and that such women were considered to be of no value as procreants or as sexual objects. Warner, for example, quotes native Murngin informants as stating that "old wives" were "all the same as rubbish," since they could not have children, and lost their physical attractiveness, looking "all the same as a man."

In those societies where younger males had no choice but to marry old women, whether because of the unavailability of younger women as wives or because of inheritance practices that left older women to them, reference was frequently made to the sexual undesirability of these women. Among the Ngonde of Tanganyika, men who inherited wives were required by ritual laws to have intercourse with all of them, but if the wife were "old," the husband would never lie with her again, being repulsed by her age and "ugliness." In the case of the Nambicuara and Trumai cultures of South America, young men who married older women because of the unavailability of younger women were reported to decline sexual activity with their wives, expressing lack of interest in these women.

It might be noted that, despite these expressions of distaste for the physical attributes of older women, the reports emphasize that many of these aged women, notably among the Wogeo and Lesu tribes, do remain sexually active, frequently with much younger men, reflecting the difficulty of young men in obtaining young sexual partners as well as the strength of sexual drives in the older women described.

Thus, of the cultures of which reference was made of the sexual activity of older individuals, relatively few reports of direct cultural censure of sexuality were found. Full sexual expression among aged men and women, however, may be seen to be affected by negative valuations of the sexual desirability of older persons.

REFERENCES

1. Kinsey, A. C., Pomeroy, W. B., and Martin, C. E. (1948). *Sexual Behavior in the Human Male*. Saunders, Philadelphia.

2. Kinsey, A. C., Pomeroy, W. B., Martin, C. E., and Gebhard, P. H. (1953). *Sexual Behavior in the Human Female*. Saunders, Philadelphia.

3. Marshall, D. S. (1971). Sexual behavior on Mangaia. In Marshall, D. S., and Suggs, R. C. (eds.), *Human Sexual Behavior: Variations in the Ethnographic Spectrum*. Basic Books, New York.

4. Masters, W. H., and Johnson, V. E. (1966). *Human Sexual Response*. Little, Brown, Boston.

5. Merriam, A. P. (1971). Aspects of sexual behavior among the Bala. In Marshall, D. S., and Suggs, R. C. (eds.), *Human Sexual Behavior: Variations in the Ethnographic Spectrum*. Basic Books, New York.

6. Murdock, G. P. (1975). *Outline of Cultural Materials*. Human Relations Area Files, New Haven.

7. Newman, G., and Nichols, C. R. (1968). In Shiloh, A. (ed.), *Studies in Human Sexual Behavior: The American Scene*. Thomas, Springfield, Illinois.

8. Pfeffer, E. (1976). Sexual behavior in old age. In Bell, B. (ed.), *Contemporary Social Gerontology*. Thomas, Springfield, Illinois.

9. Pfeiffer, E., Verwoerdt, A., and Wang, H. (1968). Sexual behavior in aged men and women. *Arch. Gen. Psychiat.* 19: 753.

MAGICAL PENIS LOSS IN NIGERIA: REPORT OF A RECENT EPIDEMIC OF A KORO-LIKE SYNDROME

Sunny T. C. Ilechukwu

In this paper I will describe an epidemic of a koro-like syndrome that occurred in Nigeria between the last week of October and the first week of November 1990. This epidemic occurred in a setting of severe economic depression amidst speculation about currency change and elections. In contrast to classical descriptions of koro, however, in the Nigerian epidemic, afflicted men claimed that their external genitalia had simply vanished. The onset involved a characteristic march of features: cue, flash, check and alarm. The cue was usually a touch, a verbal or written inquiry, or a handshake from a stranger. The flash was a fearful realization (often described as a shock, jolt, sinking feeling in the abdomen or scrotal spasm) that a sinister cue had been received. The individual then involuntarily reached for his genitals to check for their intactness. With the conviction that the genitals had vanished, he sounded a loud alarm. The victims were mostly men although women were also said to be afflicted.

This syndrome was commonly understood as a supernatural occurance in which the afflicted were robbed of their genitalia in order to magically benefit other people. People identified as benefitting from the 'genital theft'—who were often prosperous looking strangers or women— received very rough treatment at the hands of the alarmed crowd. Among the many emergent themes that may have contributed to the epidemic are male resentment of women's success during a period of social strain and the symbolic equation of masculine sexuality with economic, social and creative prowess in many cultural myths.

KORO-LIKE SYNDROMES

Koro, a syndrome consisting of genital retraction accompanied by the fear that death would occur following complete retraction into the abdomen, has been associated with the geographical regions of Southeast Asia (25, 30, 33, 34, 38). While both indigenes and Chinese migrants are affected, Yap (38) described it as a culture-bound syndrome restricted to this cultural/geographical area. Since the initial reports of Rin (33) and Yap (38), however, a number of interesting developments have occurred: (1) cases have been reported outside South East Asia; (2) epidemics of koro or koro-like syndromes have been reported in both South East Asia and beyond; (3) a variety of sociopolitical situations have been associated with epidemic outbreaks.

One of the earliest indicators that koro might occur outside Southeast Asia was the report by Rin (33) of two patients of central Chinese origin living in Taiwan. Carstairs (5) reported koro-like symptoms in Indian males but did not link them with koro. He described chronic anxiety, exhaustion, inertia, inanition and a belief that leakage of semen, which was regarded as the reservoir of health and

"Magical Penis Loss in Nigeria: Report of a Recent Epidemic of a Koro-Like Syndrome," by Sunny T. C. Illechukwu, reprinted by permission of the author from *Transcultural Psychiatric Research Review,* Volume 29, Number 2. Sunny T. C. Ilechukwu, M.D., formerly Senior Lecturer and Head of the Department of Psychiatry, College of Medicine, University of Lagos, Lagos, Nigeria. Now Assistant Professor and Medical Director, Consulting Liaison Unit, Department of Psychiatry and Behavioral Neuroscience, Wayne State University, Detroit, Michigan.

strength, was responsible for the symptoms. Kiev (23) suggested that there was a connection between this symptom complex and koro. [See the discussion of that syndrome by Paris in this issue.] There have been sporadic reports from all over the world associated with various psychiatric disorders. In Canada, Lapierre (24) reported a case in a patient with a fronto-temporal tumour. Psychotic patients manifesting koro have been reported in the United Kingdom (1, 4, 7, 8) and the United States (9, 12) as well as in Jewish immigrants from Yemen and Georgia (18). In Africa, Baasher (3) described koro-like symptoms in young, immature Sudanese males who feared that their penchant for masturbation might "maim the penis, paralyse the [masturbating] hand and rot the brain." These patients, however, reported sensations of genital shrinkage but no fear of retraction into the abdomen and subsequent death. Ifabumuyi and Rwegellera (20) reported a Nigerian case associated with panic attacks. Obviously, sporadic cases of koro-like syndromes can no longer be said to be confined to any geographical area or to be uniquely determined by any regionally restricted cultural notions.

Koro was thought by Rin (33) and Yap (38) to be a sporadic and infrequent affliction. It took Yap fifteen years to collect 19 cases for his 1963 report, but perhaps it was his hospital vantage point that made the disorder seem infrequent. We now know that epidemics of koro have been noted in Hainan for more than one hundred years (37). While the most exhaustively studied epidemic of koro occurred in Singapore in 1967 (16, 17, 27, 29), there have been reports from Thailand (22, 36), India (6, 10, 35), China (22, 37) and Nigeria (21).

Epidemic cases in Asia were characterized by acute anxiety, with fears of collapse and death, related to the morbid belief that the sufferer's penis was shrinking into his abdomen. Rin (33) attributed the symptomatology to indigenous theories relating koro to an imbalance between the vital principles of yang and yin. *Suo-yang* (defect of male principle), *shin kuei* (vital defect) or *shern-kuei* (spiritual defect) were thought to arise from nocturnal emissions and habitual masturbation since semen represented the vital essence and bodily energy. This deficiency was often combated by oral ingestion of herbs, human placenta, boy's urine, large meals or heavily spiced foods (33, 37).

Yap (38) argued that these cultural beliefs were not just pathoplastic but actually pathogenic. In other words, he thought the symptoms of koro could not exist without the specific Chinese beliefs of suo-yang. However, in the Singaporean epidemic only a quarter of over 500 persons affected had ever heard about suo-yang. Instead, the epidemic seemed related to newly introduced estrogen pellets for chickens and a misapprehension that similar female hormones were being used in injections for swine during an epidemic of swine fever. It was feared that consumption of pork from such swine would lead to feminization (emasculation) (17, 29).

The Thai epidemic seemed to have been triggered by sociopolitical stresses and xenophobia (22). Thailand faced the threat of invasion by Vietnam and the internal challenge of a commercially aggressive Vietnamese refugee population. In addition, the Vietnamese refugees brought stories hinting at the possibility of control of male potency and fertility through the use of native herbs by the communist government. It did not take too much imagination to fabricate the story of a planned sabotage of Thai sex life by refugee Vietnamese and this rumor quickly spread (28, 36). Common to both the Singapore and Thailand epidemics were the themes of threat of physical or psychological emasculation or feminization. The fear of economic domination by undeserving persons was also evident in the later case. The Indian epidemic on the other hand seemed to have started in a setting of civil strife (6). At the time of the koro epidemic, the settled tribal population of Santals, with well known martial traditions, had planned some violence against immigrant Bengalis. The government suppressed this uprising with the military but passions still ran high. Young men, women and even children were affected with genital retraction in an epidemic that was sometimes portrayed with comical aspects in urban Calcutta, where it was referred to as 'disco' (10).

THE NIGERIAN EPIDEMICS

In an earlier publication, I have presented a general profile of previous epidemics in Nigeria (21). Briefly, they were associated with crowded markets and bus stops, a common perception of strangers as the repository of evil or target for exploitation, and cultural myths about the magical potency of external genitalia. The relative lack of medicalization of these symptoms in Nigeria has made case collection very difficult, so that I can provide only three first hand accounts—one of which occurred during the epidemic and two before the epidemic. This contrasts sharply with the situation in Singapore, referred to above, where hundreds of people sought help in hospitals. I will, however, present information collected from other sources including interviews with general practitioners and traditional healers and culled from the print and electronic media.

In the Nigerian epidemics, the penis (and sometimes the breasts) were more often said to vanish than to shrink. When they 'vanished' they did not lodge inside the body but were supposed to have been 'taken' by magically powerful persons or their agents. A four stage sequence in the Nigerian pattern of genital loss could be identified: cue, flash, check, and alarm.

The *cue* took the form of a stranger asking for the time of day or for help in following directions often written down on a piece of paper. It could also take the form of ordinary body contact—a handshake or an accidental bump of body or shoulder on the street—which was thought to be deliberately contrived. Even customary exchanges of greetings or hand waving were sometimes interpreted as cues for the 'taking' of genitalia. A cue might, however, be retrospectively recognized following secondary cuing by oneself or bystanders (see Case 2 below), such that symptoms appeared some variable time after the contact cue.

Following a cue, most victims reported a *flash*, like an electric shock, a "sickening and sinking feeling" or a chill or movement within the scrotum. One doctor reported complaints of persistent 'shock-like feelings,' including sizzling sensations like the flow of a current that went right through the groin, trunk and head, accompanied by agitation and profuse sweating.

The *check* was a very brief phase in which the afflicted person reached out for his external genitalia, to confirm his feeling that the genitalia had indeed been 'taken.'

In Lagos the typical *alarm* was "Ole! Oko mi ti loo!" ("Thief! my genitals are gone!": Evening Times, October 30, 1990). This followed the check response as the individual was convinced that his genitals were gone. The person would often strip publicly to convince sympathizers that his penis had indeed been 'taken'. A crowd would immediately get involved and the person responsible for the 'theft' was identified and either implored to return the penis or roughly threatened.

Thereafter, either spontaneously or following the response of others, some 'victims' realized that their genitals were intact. However, many then claimed that they were 'returned,' at the time they raised the alarm or that, although the penis had been 'returned,' it was shrunken and so probably a 'wrong' one or just the ghost of a penis. The mob usually continued to beat or lynch the 'genital thief.' A few persons whose attacks started spontaneously in a private setting, or who did not wish to attract attention sought treatment with doctors or herbalists.

THE ROLE OF PUBLIC RESPONSES

Any alarm in a Nigerian urban centre is likely to attract a crowd. If the alarm includes the word "thief" or any vernacular equivalent, it is often a lynch minded mob which may inflict serious bodily injury before the police arrive. During the 'missing genitals' saga in Nigeria, the crowd's responses (in order of descending frequency) were as follows: (1) With or without ascertaining the nature of the complaints, the crowd would immediately take steps to punish the 'genital thief' by beating, clubbing, or even burning. It was held that the rougher the treatment, the more likely it was that the 'thief' would relent and "return the seized genital" (*Spear* Magazine, February, 1980). In some cases when the 'taker' was known or influential, there was a preliminary effort to plead with him to return the genitals. A fatal outcome was usually avoided if the 'accused' was a well known person in the neighbourhood or if the police intervened early. (2) The aggrieved person and the accused genital thief were at times taken to the police (citizen's arrest). (3) The person who suspected that his genital had been 'taken' simply reported this to the police without inciting a crowd. (4) A report was made to an influential person in the neighbourhood by either the victim or the accused.

Incidents quickly spread throughout the country, leapfrogging from Lagos to Ibadan, but skipping the rural areas. This caused much fear in the populace and some defensive personal manoeuvres were reporterd (Daily Times, October 30, 1990). Men could be seen in the streets of Lagos holding on to their genitalia either openly or discretely with their hands in their pockets. Women were also seen holding on to their breasts directly or discretely by crossing the hands across the chest. It was thought that inattention and a weak will facilitated the 'taking' of the penis or breasts. Vigilance and anticipatory aggression were thought to be good prophylaxis. This led to further breakdown of law and order.

Police made efforts to contain the epidemic. People participating in lynching or similar acts were arrested and charged with attempted murder, assault, or other crimes depending on the circumstances. As well, people who publicly claimed genital loss were arrested and charged with spreading false rumours or conduct likely to cause breach of peace. Many influential citizens, including a lower court judge (Evening Times, October 3, 1990), were enraged when the police released "genital thieves" from police custody. During a previous epidemic, one traditional court judge was reported to have sentenced a 'genital thief' to twelve strokes of the cane and ordered him to return the stolen genitals or face further sanctions. These legal responses tended to establish 'genital theft' as fact. Finally, the police high command put out announcements denouncing the incidents as the result of a hoax masterminded by criminal elements who wanted to create the type of chaotic situation that would enable them to destroy and loot other people's property or cause bodily harm to targeted individuals in settlement of old personal scores (Evening Times, October 31, 1990). The police also often arranged to conduct physical examinations designed to prove the falsity of the claims and if necessary take victims to doctors for examination, reassurance and treatment.

THE ROLE OF CULTURAL AND POLITICAL EVENTS

Many knowledgeable people claimed that there was a real—even if magical—basis for the incidents. The media assembled panels of influential people to explain the events. One panel consisted of a traditional healer, an astrologer and a journalist well known for his reports of unusual events. Expectedly, they pronounced that it was impossible to remove anyone's penis except by conventional surgery. However, the traditional healer insisted that it was possible to render the male genitals 'weak' by magical means. One council of traditional healers issued a similar statement (Daily Times, November 7, 1990).

Plans to install a new non-military ruling class by electoral process and to introduce new currency denominations were cited as underlying causes of anxiety. It was claimed that some people were accustomed to achieving political leadership not by consensus but by magical methods that compelled choice or benumbed the senses of the electorate. The genitalia 'taken' in the streets were used to reinforce such magical power. There had long been stories of 'occult' methods used to enslave other human beings and, in some magical way, make them produce new paper money. Newspaper reports hinted that male genitalia were needed to "stoke up the private mints" in the event of currency changes (Daily Times, October 30, 1990). It was thought that rich and powerful men hired thieves who magically 'took' genitalia in the streets. Such genitalia were said to be instantaneously transported to the shrines of their sorcerers or juju men.

A few rational persons, however, blamed the epidemics on the persisting economic downturn and the uncertainty that often accompanied changes of political leadership. Some claimed a politically powerful social class that had been banned from contesting for legislative positions had invented the hoax in order to sabotage the election process (Tribune, November 12, 1990).

CASE REPORTS

Case 1 (Culled form the news magazine, 'Spear,' February 1980)

A police constable had just bought some meat from a butcher in the Benin market. As he was about to leave, the butcher asked him "*Oga,* please what says the time". The policeman told him and almost immediately started shouting "My prick, my prick . . .my prick has disappeared" [Prick = penis in pigeon English]. The butcher was taken aback but the policeman was not kidding. He pulled down his pants to convince the crowd that had gathered. He knelt down and begged the butcher for mercy. The embarrassed butcher denied possession of any magical power or of knowing what to "do with another man's penis". The crowd booed and mobbed him, and were relentlessly tearing away at him until a passing police patrol intervened.

Case 2

Anselm, a 17 year old male Igbo trader's apprentice with only six years of primary school education, was accompanied to the clinic by his 'master' (or *oga*) who was also a relative. It was their second visit to the general practitioner, the first being one week previously, at the peak of the 1990 epidemic. The history was that Anselm had reported one evening after normal work that his penis had been 'taken.' His oga conducted a physical examination and pointed out to him that his penis was there and seemed normal. Anselm insisted that his penis and scrotum were shrunken and that he had felt no erection throughout that day. His oga then took him to see the doctor.

At psychiatric interview, the boy claimed that he had become aware of the genital loss earlier on the day in question when he was taking a ride at the back of their business van. As the van was in motion, a man, with no particularly distinctive features, touched him. A few seconds later it occurred to Anselm that the touch was rather suspicious. Immediately, he reached for his penis and scrotum and felt neither of them. He raised no alarm at this time but later mentioned the events to his peers, who advised him to report to his oga.

Anselm was a rather shy boy. His mother supplemented the meager income from his father's stone cracking trade by some petty trading and farming. Anselm and his family were devout Catholics. When his peers made typically uncouth sexual jokes, he neither contributed nor shared in their amusement. He denied masturbation, sexual fantasies or any previous sexual experience. He seemed rather passive except in his quiet conviction that something had gone wrong with his sexual function. He said he would know when his penis returned to normal.

There was only a single one hour interview and further follow up plans failed. He was taken to his home village for treatment by a herbalist. At the time of consultation, Anselm was not sure that he wanted to see a herbalist but was convinced that his parents would know what to do. In the process, he did have a holiday that boys in his position usually have only once every one or two years.

Case 3

Mr. Charles, a 23 year old single Igbo businessman, was seen in consultation in Lagos in June 1979. At the time he had mild complaints of palpitations and vague head discomfort. However, he claimed that the main reason he sought consultation was to clarify certain issues raised when he had read a popular publication regarding masturbation which claimed that it could lead to impotence and mental disturbances. He could not be sent off with hurried reassurances and during the discussion became quite weepy and agitated about a supposedly inevitable impending sad fate. He reported that he masturbated quite often, 2-3 times a week, to the point of orgasm. He vividly recalled one of his neighbours about whom others made sneering remarks since he would noisily celebrate the birth of each of his children whereas everyone knew, in fact, that he was not the father of his wife's children. They pitied him—he was just the husk of a man, "big for nothing". "When I look at this man, I see myself . . . so this is what they will be saying about me . . . and all my efforts." The interview lasted over one hour at the end of which I determined he was depressed and prescribed antidepressant medication. Mr. Charles claimed to have felt better with my "advice" and never returned for follow up.

During the 1990 epidemic, I met Mr. Charles socially and found that he had fallen victim to the 'penis snatchers'. Mr. Charles declined my invitation to discuss the experience. Evidently, this is one case of a preexisting sexual anxiety reactivated by the epidemic. I suspect that many others might belong to this category.

Case 4

Mr. Bozimo, aged 24 years, was seen about six months before the 1990 epidemic. He was an engineering student in a university outside Lagos and was accompanied by his elder brother. He complained that one afternoon when he was passing by a well known market place, he encountered an elderly woman who seemed to say some words of greeting. On passing her, he had a brief, sharp sensation in his groin, lower abdomen and head. He knew immediately that his penis had vanished. He returned home in a daze and complained to his elder brother. He had difficulty concentrating and could not sleep that night. The next day he was passing by the same marketplace at about the same time and saw the old woman again. She was dressed like an *alhaja* (a prosperous Moslem women). But he could not make up his mind whether she was a real *alhaja* or a ghost. This time he had palpitations and uncomfortable head sensations for which he insisted on seeing a doctor. His brother had done a physical examination on the first day and found no abnormality. When the patient's brother gave this information to me, the patient was visibly upset. He said it showed a basic lack of understanding of the principle involved. What his brother saw and what I later found on physical examination was, he insisted, just the husk of his genitalia—the inner or vital component was gone and without it life did not hold much meaning. He could not satisfactorily explain why he was in Lagos when he was supposed to be attending lectures at school. Preexisting psychopathology was suspected. He was moderately depressed and irritated at everyone's seeming lack of understanding. He accepted my antidepressant prescription with little enthusiasm. He promised to return for the next appointment but never did.

DISCUSSION

In the above accounts, as well as those previously reported (21), there appear to be both genuine and factitious cases. The factitious cases are those who loudly proclaim that they have lost their genitals in crowded places in order to rob someone. After 'casing' a conspicuously affluent person, a well organized gang would set in motion a well choreographed sequence in which one of its members played the role of a member of the public whose genitals were taken by the 'genital thief.' Evidently, it was implied that the thief must have become affluent by 'taking' penises! While an unsuspecting crowd dealt out instant 'jungle justice' to the genital thief, the members of the gang relieved him of his valuables and disappeared. Perhaps related to this is the observation that persons whose affluence ran against the grain of societal norms (eg., by virtue of sex or occupational status) often fell victim to accusers. An alternative pattern proposed that the criminals colluded with unscrupulous traditional healers who made brisk business from restoring lost genitalia for a fee forcibly extracted from the alleged genital thief (Daily Times, November 17, 1990).

The index case that Murphy (28) suggests usually sets the pattern in any epidemic hysteria, may on occasion have been factitious, while subsequent cases were *bona fide*. The core symptom complex in the authentic cases seems to be a sudden feeling of emptiness in the groin area which is not abolished by self-palpation. There are also associated sinking feelings in the pit of the stomach, tingling sensations in the lower abdomen and groin areas, palpitations and uncomfortable feelings in the crown of the head. Tingling and shock-like sensations may persist for some time throughout the body or in the groin area. The disappearance of the genitals is entirely subjective. Even the claims of genital shrinkage have been refuted in those cases where doctors made single or serial examinations.

There are a variety of beliefs relating to loss of genital function which may be perhaps concretely described as genital loss in the various Nigerian cultures (21). One Igbo traditional healer insisted that it was possible to render a man impotent if he persisted in meddling sexually with another man's wife despite repeated warnings. He doubted whether this could be done by a casual touch by a stranger. But, as already noted, several traditional healers around Lagos were quoted in the past as saying that it was quite possible. The Igbo healer in question regarded impotence as the equivalent of not having a penis.

The case of the traditional court judge (i.e., a judge who dispenses justice according to religious and native law) and the lady magistrate who thought genital thieves should be prosecuted, have already been mentioned. Even some of the Christian sects endorsed the validity of fears of 'genital theft'. Citing the biblical episode where Jesus asked "Who touched me?" because the "power had gone out of him," a priest insisted that agents of Satan were at work, and were responsible for 'taking' people's genitals.

It seems quite clear, therefore, that there are strong beliefs within many Nigerian cultural traditions, as well as in recent Islamic and Christian religious experience, that tend to treat "genital theft" as factual rather than symbolic. But could the myths be the underlying basis for symptom construction in these epidemics? Before attempting an answer I will further explore the myths of the acquisition of personal power, fortune or other personal advantage by appropriation and control of sexual energies.

Anthropologists are frequently confronted with the prepotency of sexuality in traditional societies but the attempts of Sigmund Freud to introduce such notions into mainline western thinking have probably only met with qualified success. The brazenness and starkness of much 'primitive' art and myth leave us in no doubt about the primacy of sex in unconscious mentation. The facts of death and the consequent logic of discarnate existence; the relationship of the sexual act to the creation of new life; and the social exchanges and rituals that surround marriage, which provides the setting for bringing forth new members into human societies, must be responsible for many extravagant beliefs relating to sex, life and creativity (32). According to Mead (26), the Arapesh believed not only that the child was the product of the father's semen and the mother's blood but that the father must sustain sexual intercourse to make the child grow in the early phases of pregnancy. Postnatally, he had to refrain from sexual intercourse until the child reached toddler stage, in order to maintain the strength and well being of the child. Here we see a powerful demonstration, not just of the links between the male 'seed,' the fetus and child, but also of the role sexual intercourse as a means of converting the energy latent in semen into health and vitality.

Many fertility rituals also implicate virility in agricultural productivity. Irrigation and rainfall are viewed as a form of divine ejaculation (32). Possession of a penis is associated with power in the Brazilian Urubu mythology of Mair. In this myth, Mair, by sheer enterprise, tracks down the clan's primordial penis (previously available only to women), cuts off its head and passes out small pieces to men who, in this manner, receive penises for the first time. Mair keeps the head (glans) for himself. Subsequent cannibal execution of Mair, turns him into thunder while his executioner becomes a man of power (19). We also recall that in Egyptian mythology, the very stars of heaven were the result of the god Geb (earth) impregnating Nut (the sky). Again the Greek goddess of beauty, Aphrodite was created literally from the womb of the ocean when Cronos castrated his father, Uranus, and threw the phallus into the Sea.

Hence by a series of metaphors and analogies the phallus has come to represent life, fertility, creativity and power. (There are, of course, equally rich antecedents referring to symbolism of female fertility and creativity). By conserving the sexual energy, the Arapesh believe they achieve results outside the individual including the well being of a child. By spending sexual energy, they ensure growth of a fetus; by redirecting it (sublimation), highly desirable social ends may be achieved (14).

In a similar way, by the logic of sympathetic magic, the Nigerian juju man or sorcerer believes he can accumulate personal power or help his clients achieve social or economic success by "taking penises". Fortunately for the sorcerer, no one seriously accuses him of committing any crimes in the statute books. As Prince (31) has pointed out, sorcery was still an offense in Nigeria under some traditional or native laws that were operative during the colonial era.

CONCLUSION

Among the 'genuine' cases of magical penis loss are persons who probably had preexisting psychopathology predisposing them to the occurrence of koro-like symptoms during or before the epidemic. Most of Yap's (38) patients were characterized as "quiet, slow, nervous, shy, worrying, unaggressive, and immature" and showed evidence of sexual maladjustment. The absence of an appropriate father figure for early childhood identification was also frequently noted.

In our study, the profile of most of the cases was not available because the subjects did not present clinically. However, the characteristics of our clinical cases (especially Anselm and Charles) seem similar to those reported by Yap (38). The epidemic may have created the right atmosphere to offer secondary gains to various persons including those with sexual dysfunctions who could thus, receive social justification and sympathy for their distress as well as seek scapegoats to assuage their personal suffering.

Some doubt may be entertained whether this Nigerian phenomenon fits into the generic syndrome of koro. The conviction of sudden loss or impending loss appears crucial and similar in both syndromes. Many differences seem to be cultural overlay. Many authors (13) regard koro as an underlying physiologic dartos or cremasteric reflex to fear or cold which culture and personal psychopathology then shape. Yap's (38) characterisation of these syndromes as "genital depersonalization" can hardly be improved upon. Murphy (28) has pointed out that the epidemic forms of koro have a hysteria-like quality. He has suggested either a strong belief connecting genital vulnerability with a supposedly noxious agent or a strong but unconscious genitally-focused anxiety as etiological factors. He also suggests that the genitalia comprise the most suitable symbol onto which prevailing anxieties might be focused by facilitators of an epidemic. Perhaps, we have identified such a facilitator in the Nigerian political and economic climate which serves to recruit some primordial anxieties. Some authorities have suggested a ten year cycle (Murphy, (28); Ugochukwu, *personal communication*, 1991). The first major epidemic in Nigeria was in 1980 and the last was in 1990—the possibility of cyclicity should be observed further.

The Nigerian experience outlined above enables us to break the koro syndrome into component parts in a way that has not previously been possible. This should facilitate further theoretical analysis. The scheme in Figure 1 is presented as a tentative one that is consistent with the observations. It is in substantial agreement with mechanisms summarised in Edwards (13) and goes beyond them in the sense that these are observable events. I suggest that a scheme of this nature remains valuable in understanding the experiences elsewhere even where centuries or decades of familiarity have blurred the sequence or where the manifest expression of koro shows marked variation. It may be possible to retrospectively analyze the experiences elsewhere and see whether they tend to fractionate in any particular pattern.

In offering this model, I am emphasizing the continuity or similarities between koro and the Nigerian cases of 'magical penis loss.' Although the initial claim of loss of genitals is a striking feature of the Nigerian epidemic, these claims usually metamorphosed into fears of loss of potency, virility and vitality. For this reason, I think these cases are closely allied to koro and it would be unjustified to create a new syndrome.

Indeed, I found that the groups of educated Nigerians, including doctors, whom I talked to during the epidemic, were quite surprised but relieved that similar syndromes occurred in other parts of

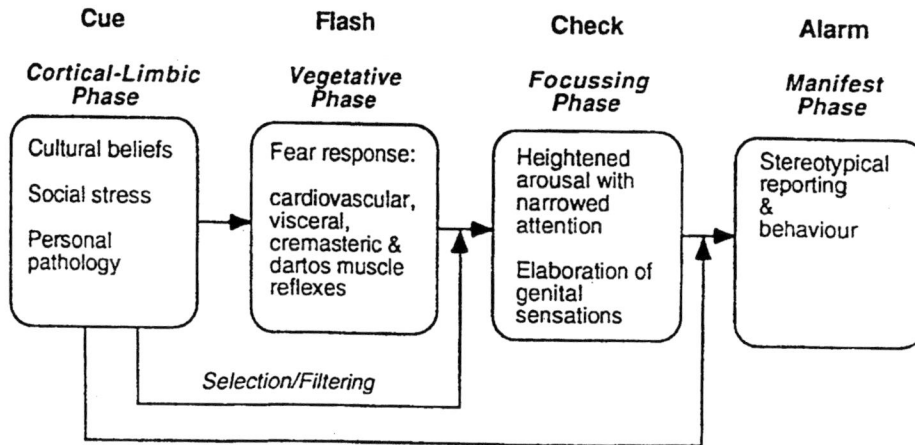

Cue	Flash	Check	Alarm
Cortical-Limbic Phase	**Vegetative Phase**	**Focussing Phase**	**Manifest Phase**

Figure 1. Possible mechanisms of koro-like syndromes derived from the Nigerian experience.

the world. The fact that there was a widely accepted name for the syndrome (koro) was additionally reassuring. With some local variation, clinical experiences from diverse places have been integrated into the wider body of medical knowledge in our setting. This approach may better serve the needs of medical science in our part of the world.

ACKNOWLEDGMENT

To Mr. Onyema Ugochukwu, Editor, Daily Times of Nigeria who supported this presentation by providing material from the Daily Times of Nigeria Library.

REFERENCES

1. Ang, P. C. & Weller, M. P. (1984). Koro and psychosis. *British Journal of Psychiatry*, 145: 335.

2. Anonymous Abstracter (1964) below. *Transcultural Psychiatric Research Review*, 1(1964), 37.

3. Baasher, T. A. (1963). The influence of culture on psychiatric manisfestation. *Transcultural Psychiatric Research Review*, 15, 51–52.

4. Barret, K. (1978). Koro in a Londoner. *Lancet, 2. no.* 8103, 1319.

5. Carstairs, G. M. (1956). Hinjra and Jiruan, *British Journal of Medical Psychology*, 29, 128.

6. Chakraborty, A., Das, S. & Mukerjee, A. (1983). Koro epidemic in India. *Transcultural Psychiatric Research Review*, 20, 150–151.

7. Constable, P. J. (1979). Koro in Hertfordshire. *Lancet, 1,* no. 8108, 163.

8. Cremona, A. (1981). Another case of koro in a Britain. *British Journal of Psychiatry*, 138, 180–181.

9. Dow, T. & Silver, D. (1973). A drug induced koro syndrome. *Journal of Florida Medical Association*, 60, 32–33.

10. Dutta, D., Phookan, R. & Das, P. D. (1982). The koro epidemic in Lower Assam. *Indian Journal of Psychiatry*, 24, 370–374.

11. Ede, A. (1976). Koro in an Anglo-saxon Canadian. *Canadian Psychiatric Association Journal.* 21, 389–392.

12. Edwards, J. W. (1970). The koro pattern of depersonalization in an American schizophrenic patient. *American Journal of Psychiatry*, 126, 1171–1173.

13. Edwards, J. G. (1984). Indigenous koro, a genital retraction syndrome of Insular South East Asia—A critical review. *Culture, Medicine and Psychiatry*, 8, 1–24.

14. Freud, S. (1949). An Outline of Psychoanalysis. New York: Morton and Company.

15. Gwee, A. L. (1963). Koro—A cultural disease. *Singapore Medical Journal*, 4, 119–122.

16. Gwee, A. L. (1968). Koro—Its origin and nature as a disease entity. *Singapore Medical Journal*, 9, 3–6.

17. Gwee, A. L. (1971). Koro. *Transcultural Psychiatric Research Review*, 8, 32–34.

18. Hes, J. & Massi, G. (1977). Koro in a Yemenite and Georgian Jewish immigrant. *Confinia Psychiatrica*, 20, 180–184.

19. Huxley, F. (1974). The Way of the Sacred. London: Aldus Books Ltd.

20. Ifabumuyi, O. I. & Rwegellera, G. G. C. (1979). Koro in a Nigerian male patient: A case report. *African Journal of Psychiatry*, 5, 103–105.

21. Ilechukwu, S. T. C. (1988). Koro-like syndromes in Nigeria. *Transcultural Psychiatry Research Review*, 25, 310–314.

22. Jilek, W. & Jilek-Aall, L. (1977). A koro epidemic in Thailand. *Transcultural Psychiatric Research Review*, 15, 57–59.

23. Kiev, A. (1972). Transcultural Psychiatry. Harmondsworth, England: Penguin.

24. LaPierre, Y. D. (1972). Koro in a French Canadian. *Canadian Psychiatric Association Journal*, 17, 333–334.

25. Linton, R. (1956). Culture and mental disorders. G. Devereaux (Ed.), Springfield, Illinois: Charles C. Thomas.

26. Mead, M. (1935). Sex and Temperament in Three Primitive Societies. London: Routeledge and Kegan Paul.

27. Mun, C. T. (1968). Epidemic koro in Singapore. *British Medical Journal*, 1, 640–641.

28. Murphy, H. B. M. (1982). Comparative Psychiatry. New York: Springer-Verlag.

29. Ngui, P. W. (1969). The koro epidemic in Singapore. *Australia and New Zealand Journal of Psychiatry*, 133, 263–266.

30. Palthe, V. W. P. (1936). Psychiatry and Neurology in the Tropics. In *A Clinical Textbook of Tropical Medicine*, C. D. de Langen and A. Lichtenstein (Eds.), Batvia: G. Kolff and Co.

31. Prince, R. H. (1975). Some Yoruba views of the causes and modes of treatment of antisocial behaviour. *African Journal of Psychiatry*, 2, 133–137.

32. Rawson, P. (Ed.) (1973). Primitive Erotic Art. New York: G. P. Putnam's Sons.

33. Rin, H. (1963). Koro: A consideration of Chinese concepts of illness and case illustrations. *Transcultural Psychiatric Research Review*, 15, 23–30.

34. Rin, H. (1965). A study of the aetiology of koro in respect to the Chinese concept of illness. *International Journal of Social Psychiatry*, 11, 7–13.

35. Shukla, G. D. & Mishra, D. M. (1981). Koro-like syndrome: A case report. *Indian Journal of Psychiatry*, 23, 96–97.

36. Suwanlert, S. & Coates, D. (1979). Epidemic koro in Thailand: Clinical and social aspects. *Transcultural Psychiatric Research Review*, 16, 64–66.

37. Tseng, W-S., Mo, G-M., Jing, H., Li, L-S., Ou, L-W., Chen, G-Q., & Jiang, D-W. (1988). A socio-cultural and clinical study of a koro (genital retraction panic disorder) epidemic in Guangdong, China. *American Journal of Psychiatry*, 145, 1538–1543.

38. Yap, P. M. (1963). Koro or Suk-Yeong—An atypical culture-bound psychogenic disorder found in Southern Chinese. *Transcultural Psychiatric Research Review*, 1(1964), 36–38.

Enriching the Sexual Experience of Couples: The Asian Traditions and Sexual Counseling

Harrison Voight

In ancient India, a ceremonial sex ritual evolved from the philosophies and spiritual practices described in Hindu and Buddhist Tantric scriptures. Contemporary references to this sex ritual as "Tantric sex," while technically inaccurate, nonetheless have come to connote the mystical and the esoteric aspects of sexuality toward which many are drawn. The term Tantra, from the Sanskrit, means integration, urging full involvement with all natural human drives and experiences while on the path to fully awakened and realized existence. Departing from the asceticism characteristic of classical yogic practices, which emphasized extinguishing sensuous experience and sexual expression, Tantrism holds that the realm of sexual expression may serve as a vehicle for spiritual development and personal transformation. The expression "One must rise by that by which one falls" reflects the Tantric approach to sexuality. It signals the diverse potentials of expressing sexual energy: from productive use as a means toward spiritual growth, or becoming consumed by its appetites and lost in the realm of the senses.

The Tantric sexual ritual, as it will be called for convenience, utilizes the expression of sexual energy to promote dramatic change in consciousness and in experience when practiced regularly over time. These rituals exist in a variety of forms, and all are very complex and intricate. It is important to note that, traditionally, practicing the ritual itself is a culmination of a lengthy sequence of philosophic/religious studies and spiritual practices under the guidance of a recognized teacher or master, and that the history of transmission of such knowledge has been primarily through oral tradition. The essence of the ritual involves sequences of visualizations, breathing practices, chanting, bathing, joint meditations, shared consumption of ceremonial food and drink, and sexual intercourse in a prescribed fashion. Differing versions of the ritual abound, but Garrison and Douglas and Slinger provide the interested reader with both essential background and effective description.

Tantrism is a path of action, which has as its goal the experience of transcendent unity and harmony. In the Hindu Tantric tradition, the exalted state involves the ultimate union within of male and female principles—the two polar extremes of the universal life force. In the Buddhist Tantric tradition, practices lead to the attainment of a state of egolessness, in which the distinction between self and object is lost and enlightenment is attained. The omnipresent image of the yogically seated couple in the Tantric Buddhist art of Tibet has emerged as a universal symbol of enlightenment.

EXPANDING THE CONTEXT FOR SEXUAL COUNSELING

Examination of the Tantric sexual ritual reveals some important dimensions in approaching sexual experience, which crystalize differences between Western and Asian values and approaches. When Tantra is defined as integration, the application of Tantric principles to today's sexual counseling can be used to attempt to unify some apparent opposites, which represent ways of understanding

"Enriching the Sexual Experience of Couples: The Asian Traditions and Sexual Counseling," by Harrison Voight, reprinted from *Journal of Sex and Marital Therapy*, Vol. 17, No. 3, Brunner/Mazel, Inc., 1991.

contrasting domains of experience from Western and Asian perspectives. Such perceived polarities are: doing vs. being, stimulation vs. stillness, activation vs. meditation, and outcome-focus vs. process-immersion.

When we, as therapists, grasp the meaning of the collective essence of these experiential parameters, a new context for our work with couples can emerge. It becomes possible to make a deliberate choice between working to promote symptom remission, as with conventional approaches to sexual problems, and a commitment to transformation of a couple's sexual experience. Similarly, we can contrast the usual emphasis on progress or movement with that of purposeful shifting or expansion of the meaning of sexual experience for clientele. We can, on the one hand, view orgasm as resulting from proper stimulation and effective technique and, on the other hand, understand orgasm as a product of deep relaxation and a profound level of contact between partners. Overall, then, rather than focus on one partner or the other, we can, through deploying techniques such as those outlined below, approach what existentialists and phenomenologists call the *between*: the self of a couple that manifests in subtle realms.

The specific techniques presented below differ substantially from most conventional behavioral assignments used in sexual counseling and therapy, though there are some parallels. The techniques basically involve simple ways of being with each other and focusing on something other than problem solving, sexual performance, sexual satisfaction, or the pursuit of orgasm or pleasure. These are methods of approaching change through indirect rather than direct means. Taken together, the exercises facilitate a restructuring of sexual experience by promoting breakdown of the usual conditioned and culturally reinforced parameters of sexual practices.

FIVE TANTRIC EXPLORATIONS FOR COUPLES

Ritual

Jointly creating a ritual can simultaneously celebrate and sanctify the sexual exchange. It puts partners in touch with their abilities to create together something unique and private, which may for some feel decidedly sacred. A simple ceremony provides a formal transition to intimate contact, highlighting the special attention and intention partners bring to each other. In creating a ritual, a couple decides what for them would constitute a meaningful sequence of preparatory exchanges and environmental trappings to set the tone for shared sexual expression.

Rituals take on as many forms as there are couples, drawing upon various preferences and experiences for what would constitute for each a unique interpersonal and external climate within which to carry out a sexual exchange. Contributing elements to the climate for intimacy can be candles, colored lighting, flowers, perfumes, lotions, background music, or a special room or bed. Personalized expressions of affection, including creative self-expression, may be sequenced in some meaningful way—sensual massage, reciting poetry, chanting together, joint meditation, playing musical instruments or singing, or anything that has some personal meaning to partners as they approach a special experience.

Synchronized Breathing

Lying together and tuning into breathing involves both proximal and distal aspects. Proximal attunement is being able to coordinate breathing while embracing or touching. Distal attunement takes considerably more practice and occurs when partners are able to engage in synchronized breathing without direct body contact when there is physical distance between them.

Bringing the focus of attention to coordinating the breathing process between partners is both a test and a task. As a task, successfully synchronizing the breathing as partners lie together in any position may touch the limits of the abilities of partners to set aside thoughts and preoccupations, in much the same way as with yogic or other breathing practices. Devoting complete attention to the breathing process tests the control of the attention. Paradoxically, however, too much effort may be counter-productive and lead to a sense of struggle. Best is a "soft focus" wherein, through a combination of intention, attention, and relaxed physical contact, the breathing patterns of partners are simply allowed to come together.

Sustained Eye Contact

Sustained, steady eye contact is an exceptionally powerful and deeply intimate method through which union can be experienced, with almost unlimited potentional for generating profound change in sexual experiencing. Fixing one's gaze into a partner's eyes throughout all phases of the sexual exchange can lead to experiencing a merging of oceanic dimension. Clients often feel awkward during initial practice with this, but typically come to a more relaxed place later on with patience and dedication. Because steady eye contact runs so strongly counter to culturally learned and reinforced eyes-closed intimacies, it is useful for therapists to suggest that initial efforts be for brief periods and extended gradually as comfort increases. It is especially important to anticipate discomfort and to emphasize the importance of maintaining over time these explorations into the unfamiliar. On the other hand, it is also helpful to suggest avoiding undue struggle should efforts prove consistently problematic.

Motionless Intercourse

To broaden the applicability of this exercise to both heterosexual and homosexual couples, I wish to expand the usual frame of reference for the concept of intercourse. It might be more useful to conceive of this in terms of making motionless the peak sensual or sexual experience in the couple's lovemaking repertoire. For a typical heterosexual couple, this might mean that the couple becomes motionless after intromission or at some natural point following penetration. For homosexual—or other heterosexual—couples, it may mean maintaining relative stillness after that peak point of sensual or sexual contact is initiated, bringing a still point to sexual connection, contrasting with the perpetual motion characteristic of conventional lovemaking. Duration of the period of stillness can be varied—a few minutes at first, longer periods later on. The activity that becomes the still point may be a deep kiss, the mouth on the genitals, a hand cupping the testes or a breast, or the penis moving in the vagina.

Intercourse/Sexual Exchange Without Orgasm

An expansion of the customary admonition to refrain from orgasm during a portion of the treatment period in typical sex therapy, this exercise involves experimenting with all the dimensions of sexual contact that are possible without orgasm. What becomes available to experience is the different nature of sex and of our partner when we release ourselves from the programming that is involved in seeking out and moving toward orgasm. In Tantric practice, the purpose of avoiding or refraining from orgasm is to intensify the sexual-spiritual energy. When this exercise is used in work with couples, it can be used to facilitate a breakdown of the usual conditioned sequences of sex practices and responses so as to enable a more complete restructuring of sexual experience together.

Harrison Voigt, Ph.D., is Director of Professional Training, Psychology Doctoral Program, California Institute of Integral Studies, 765 Ashbury Street, San Francisco, CA 94117.